**Thought, Fact,
and Reference**
The Origins and Ontology
of Logical Atomism

Thought, Fact, and Reference
The Origins and Ontology of Logical Atomism

by
Herbert Hochberg
Professor of Philosophy
University of Minnesota

UNIVERSITY OF MINNESOTA PRESS □ MINNEAPOLIS

Published by the University of Minnesota Press,
2037 University Avenue Southeast, Minneapolis, Minnesota 55455,
and published in Canada by Burns & MacEachern Limited,
Don Mills, Ontario

The University of Minnesota
is an equal opportunity
educator and employer.

Library of Congress Cataloging in Publication Data

Hochberg, Herbert Irving, 1929-
    Thought, fact, and reference.

    Includes bibliographical references and indexes.
    1. Logical atomism. 2. Thought and thinking.
3. Facts (Philosophy) 4. Reference (Philosophy)
I. Title.
BC199.L6H62   146'.5   78-12616
ISBN 0-8166-0867-9

For Susanne

Preface

Chapters I, III, X, XII, and XIII are based on a series of five lectures in the philosophy of mind given at the University of Gothenburg in the fall of 1970. Discussions with Ivar Segelberg and Per Lindström of that university were helpful. Richard Adler, Stephanie Eller, and Jeffrey Wilkin raised helpful questions about parts of the manuscript. I am grateful to the John Simon Guggenheim Memorial Foundation for a fellowship to work on the philosophy of Moore and to the University of Minnesota for both a summer and a single-quarter leave to work on the book.

For simplicity and clarity (and from ingrained habit), I have not used parentheses and quoting conventions uniformly. Thus, although 'Fa' is used, so is 'F(A)', and double quotes are sometimes used in place of single quotes.

St. Paul   H. H.
July 1978

Introduction

Moore and Russell turned a significant segment of contemporary philosophy onto an analytic and linguistic course with their early attack on idealism. Together with Wittgenstein's early contributions, doctrines of the Cambridge philosophers formed what Russell called "Logical Atomism." From that period to the present, philosophers have constantly heard of and read about "analysis," "what can be shown and not said," "logical and grammatical form," "ordinary meaning," "simple and unanalyzable," "knowledge by description and knowledge by acquaintance," "atomic sentence," "denoting expression," and "the present King of France." In spite of the varied criticism and controversy spawned by the doctrines of the logical atomists, little has been done to place those doctrines in the perspective provided by the critique of idealism and to connect that attack with the construal of logical concepts, such as *negation* and *existence*, with views about analysis and reduction, with proposed solutions to the problems of intentionality, with Russell's theory of descriptions, and with other views Moore and Russell held in the years before the epoch-making papers and books of 1903 and 1905. Linking the philosophies of F. H. Bradley, the early Moore, and Frege helps to place Russell's work in perspective and to clarify Moore's philosophical method as well as aspects of Wittgenstein's philosophy.

Logical Atomism was one of the increasingly dwindling number of attempts to formulate a comprehensive philosophical "system" within the restraints imposed by "empiricism" and a "vivid sense of reality." Moore's early work was crucial to its development. Yet, paradoxically, the analytic techniques he employed, altered by his desire to *prove* realism and refute ethical naturalism, led the foremost critic of idealism to propound the ordinary word as the final truth. Common sense and common usage, reflecting modes of thought, came to determine the way things are. The irony was historical as well as logical. The patterns of ontological analysis Moore early invoked were transformed by himself, Wittgenstein, and later English-speaking philosophers into a method of transforming ontological analysis into linguistic analysis via the bridge of "conceptual analysis." Russell, the early Wittgenstein, and Moore himself, along with the philosophy of Logical Atomism, became prime targets of criticism as examples of the mistakes fostered by ignoring the ordinary uses of words. As Heidegger's pronouncements became whipping phrases for Carnap and the Viennese positivists, so the claims of Russell and Moore about perception, belief, and sense data provoked numerous illustrations of how we do and should use words like "see" and "know." Attention was shifted to the analysis of how words and "concepts" *do their jobs* and away from the analysis of facts, perception, and belief.

The problems of intentionality provided a consistent set of issues that dramatized weaknesses in the systematic views of the Cambridge philosophers. Moore and Russell, although agreeing on much in their joint attack on Bradley's idealism, eventually formulated distinct approaches to such problems. Perhaps influenced by his reading of German philosophy, Moore took seriously and sympathetically the need to invoke a basic intentional relation and spoke freely of mental acts. But, ultimately unprepared to pay the ontological price, he found a convenient escape route provided by "Common Sense" and ordinary *meaning*. Russell, influenced by Moore, was also early attracted to the apparatus of propositions, mental acts, and intentional connections. Later, along with Wittgenstein, he struggled to arrive at a satisfactory analysis of thought and belief without recognizing such entities and such a relation. In more recent times, Gustav Bergmann and Wilfrid Sellars, two of the few systematic philosophers who write in the analytic vein of

Moore and Russell, represent the two different approaches, while a number of philosophers, notably W. V. Quine, have attempted to revive Russell's relational analysis of judgment. Since this book is an attempt to resolve some problems about thought, truth, and reference within the tradition of Logical Atomism, readers of Bergmann and Sellars will find, not surprisingly, familiar themes.

As with the idealists Moore and Russell opposed, facts have once again become unpopular. In defending the atomist's correspondence theory of truth, I shall consider Frege's early attack on that theory as well as recent criticisms that reproduce, wittingly or unwittingly, the familiar idealistic patterns. In returning to the idealist's arguments, some "analytic" philosophers echo themes revived by Sartre, without providing the detailed argument of the latter. By contrast, Sellars attacks atomism at a seemingly vulnerable point. He argues that the atomists did not and cannot resolve Bradley's puzzles about predication. This is a dominant theme behind his attempt to defend the current revival of nominalism—a gambit he shares with Quine. It also reveals a link between the new nominalism and the revival of idealism. Bradley's views thus affect a number of issues discussed, including the connection of Russell's theory of descriptions with questions about concepts, particulars, predication, and judgment. This theory, in turn, provides an obvious link with Russell's critique of Frege, which is explicated and defended. One of the surprising features of recent philosophy has been the unfair, unfounded, and often abusive commentary on Russell's early work and, in particular, his criticism of Frege. Unfortunately, the prevalent assumption that Russell both misunderstood Frege and was guilty of elementary errors has prevented an adequate understanding of the origin of his theory of descriptions and his analysis of judgment. The early critique of Frege helps to clarify basic features of Russell's philosophy and reveals further connections with the views of Bradley and Moore. It is also crucial for the comprehension of Russell's views about names, reference, existence, and truth. These are important for the analysis of intentional contexts presented in this book. The examination of such fundamental aspects of Russell's philosophy naturally involves a consideration of recent criticisms of Russellian themes by Strawson, Sellars, Carnap, Quine, and others.

What is attempted is the resolution of some issues that preoccupied Russell, Wittgenstein, Moore, and their successors, as well as an explication of some links between Logical Atomism and Moore's early assault on idealism. The book is thus a partial study of the ontology and the history of Logical Atomism.

Table of Contents

**Thought, Fact,
and Reference**
The Origins and Ontology
of Logical Atomism

I

The Analysis
of Perception

Moore's most systematic attempt to handle the problems of intentionality occurs in connection with his analysis of perception in *Some Main Problems of Philosophy*. He begins the book with the following account of belief.[1] Suppose one believes that an object is white. Then, there is a belief which is a particular *act* occurring at a specific time. In one sense, the phrase "a belief" stands for a particular occurrence of what we might call a generic kind, *believing*, just as the page upon which these words appear is a specific individual of the generic kind *page*. As philosophers traditionally speak we are dealing with a particular instance of a general kind or universal. This means that, in another sense, the phrase "a belief" also refers to the kind or universal that is involved. To fix the distinction, let the term 'm_1' stand for a particular instance of believing, a particular act of belief that occurs at a more or less specific time, and let 'B' stand for the general kind of which m_1 is a particular instance. Being a particular, m_1 is, in that sense, of the same logical kind as the white object, and B is of the same logical kind as the color white, since both the latter may be construed as properties of particulars. If one is bothered by speaking of a belief as a particular occurring at a specific time, because it may appear more natural to consider a belief as a disposition of a person, I would ask the reader to bear with me. We shall eventually discuss "dispositions." One might also recall the common distinction between episodic occurrences and dispositions, and take me to speak

3

of "thoughts," since the *having of a thought* is more readily taken as an episode occurring at a specific time. Thus, we can consider *the thought that* the object is white rather than *the belief that* it is so. Since Moore speaks of belief, I shall continue to do so, as well as to use 'thought' and 'belief' relatively interchangeably. This will not prejudge any issues or affect the problems discussed.

The content of our belief, or thought, is determined by the proposition indicated by the sentence 'a_1 is white', where 'a_1' names the object. At the beginning of Moore's book, it is clear that he holds there are such things as propositions. Moreover, such "things" are said to be *directly apprehended*. For the time, I shall take that to mean that a particular act, such as m_1, stands in a unique relation to a proposition. This relation we shall indicate by 'DA' and simply transcribe that term by the phrase 'directly apprehends'. With 'Wa_1' transcribing 'a_1 is white', we may represent the statement that m_1 directly apprehends the proposition expressed by the sentence 'Wa_1' by

(1)   DA $(m_1, [Wa_1])$,

with a sentence within brackets being taken to refer to a proposition. Moore also holds that the proposition $[Wa_1]$ is *about* the object a_1. This is in keeping with the apparently straightforward claim that the proposition $[2 + 2 = 4]$ is in some sense about the number 2 and the proposition that this is a piece of paper is about the object I am thinking of or pointing to. We thus have, on his account, a second relation, *aboutness*, which holds between propositions and the things referred to by the signs used in a sentence expressing the proposition. This relation we may indicate by 'AB'. We then have a second claim:

(2)   AB $([Wa_1], a_1)$.

Moore goes on to hold that the belief, which is a direct apprehension of the proposition $[Wa_1]$, is an *indirect apprehension* of the object a_1. We, thus, have a further relation of *indirect apprehension*, which we may indicate by 'IA' and the further claim:

(3)   IA(m_1, a_1).

Taken together, (1), (2), and (3), along with 'Bm_1', sum up what he starts out with, in his attempt to analyze what takes place when there is a belief (thought) that a_1 is W. We even have a simple diagram:

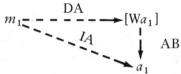

Moore is interested in the analysis of belief or thought for its own sake, and, in particular, the analysis of false belief. But, he has another motive. He thinks that the pattern we just considered will apply to the case of perception in such a way as to enable him to do justice to the classical problems of perception, while avoiding phenomenalism. That is, he sees in such a pattern the basis for a successful defense of realism, in the sense that he will be able to maintain that we perceive physical objects like chairs and tables and are not limited to the perception of sense data and other phenomenal entities.

Moore will attempt to argue that all that phenomenalists can establish is that we do not directly apprehend physical objects, but what *they must* establish to reject realism is that we do not apprehend physical objects in any way and, hence, that we do not *indirectly apprehend* them. Thus, he will hold that we are conscious of or "know" physical objects by indirect apprehension.

Moore begins his analysis of perception by accepting the standard phenomenalistic arguments that when we ordinarily say we perceive a material object we really are *directly apprehending* sense data and are not directly apprehending the material object itself. He accepts such a conclusion on the basis of the well-known examples involving the perception of different shapes, shades of color, etc., depending on angle of vision, lighting, condition of the eye, and so forth. Hence, to use Moore's example, when there is, as we ordinarily would say, a perception of an envelope, there is an act of direct apprehension, let it be m_2, which directly apprehends a sense datum, say a_1, and perhaps others as well. Hence, just as in (1) we have a case of direct apprehension, but now the object is a sensum rather than a proposition. Mental acts can thus directly apprehend both propositions and sensa. But, we must not limit our analysis of perception to the direct apprehension of sensa.

When we perceive a material object, we are directly apprehending a sense datum, but we are doing other things as well. For, there is also the indirect apprehension of the material object. But, then, what is the connection between the sensum and the physical object, and how is it that we know of such a relation as indirect apprehension? Moreover, how do we know that such a relation holds between mental acts and material objects? To make the connection Moore appeals to his analysis of belief. When we perceive a material object, we are in fact believing that there is a material object related to a (or several) sense datum (sensa) that we are directly apprehending. Thus, in the perception of a material object, two things (at least) are being directly apprehended, a sense datum and a proposition. In fact, two distinct acts of direct apprehension appear to be involved on Moore's account. One act takes the sense datum as an object; the other apprehends the proposition that there is a material object related to the sensum. Thus, we have the following situation when someone perceives an envelope. There is, to begin with, an act of direct apprehension of, say, a white sensum. Here, it is not clear if the act, m_2, is a direct apprehension of the sensum a_1, or of the fact that a_1 is white, or of the white color of a_1, and so on. There is a reason for this lack of clarity which will be relevant to our discussion, so I shall interject a different theme at this point. Consider the white sense datum a_1. We can distinguish the particular or individual datum from its color: a_1 from the color white. But we may also use the term 'a_1' to refer to *the colored datum*, the white patch as it were. One may, then, think of the sense datum in two ways: as a particular which, although distinct from a color, exemplifies the color or as the colored object, where one does not distinguish the object from the fact that it is of a certain color. In the former case, one construes the datum as a constituent of a fact; in the latter case one in effect identifies the datum with a fact. Some philosophers think of properties in terms of quality instances rather than in terms of universals. They hold that the white color of two white patches is not one and the same "in" both, but, rather, that the two patches have (or "contain") exactly similar but numerically distinct *instances* of white. Suppose such a philosopher further thinks of the patch as somehow composed of a set of such quality instances "tied" together: an instance of color, a shape, etc. He may then think of a sense datum as either the quality instance or the composite of several such; i.e., as *this white* or as *this white square patch*. Moore tends to think of color properties in terms of quality instances.[2] Hence, he thinks of such properties as particulars or individuals. Thus, he can come to think of a property like white as *a sense datum* rather than as a property of sense data. In short, he sometimes mixes all the various senses of the phrase "sense datum" that we have just distinguished. Consequently, sometimes when he speaks of a "sense datum" he means one thing and sometimes quite another thing. That is why it is not exactly clear what it is that stands in the relation of direct apprehension to a mental act, when the latter directly apprehends a sense datum. For our present purposes, I shall ignore this complication and simply represent the state of affairs that holds when m_2 directly apprehends a sense datum by

(4) $DA(m_2, a_1)$.

(4) merely asserts that some act directly apprehends some sensum. For there to be a *perception* of a *material object*, there must also be another mental act, say m_3, which is a *belief* that there is a material object in some relation to a_1. We must, then, consider the structure of the sentence that expresses the proposition directly apprehended by m_3 or, as we might say, which m_3 intends. Let 'MO' transcribe 'material object', and let 'R' stand for an unspecified relation. Then our sentence might be

(5) $(\exists x)[MO(x) \ \& \ R(a_1, x)]$.

Of course, one must say some further things about the property MO and the relation R. We shall shortly. For the moment, let us note that with (5) we can now specify a further state of affairs involved in the analysis of the perception of the envelope:

(6) $DA(m_3, p)$,

where 'p' stands for the existential proposition expressed by (5). To complete the analysis of the perceptual situation based on the earlier analysis of the belief context, let 'O' stand for the material object whose existence would make (5) a true statement. Then,

(7)   AB(p,O)

is the correlate of (2), and

(8)   IA(m_3,O)

is the correlate of (3). (4), (6), (7), and (8), together with 'Bm_3', constitute the specification of what takes place when there is a perception of a material object O. To say that the material object O is seen or perceived is construed, upon Moore's analysis, in terms of (4), (6), (7), (8), and 'Bm_3'. We can now turn to the problems raised by Moore's account of perception.

Foremost among such problems is the claim that there is a relation of indirect apprehension. What is it? How do we know that there is such a relation? We should first note that if one raises similar questions about the relation of direct apprehension, Moore would reply that one directly apprehends the relation of direct apprehension as one directly apprehends sensa, qualities, and spatial relations. No argument is required to establish the existence of such a relation, merely phenomenological introspection. One knows that such a relation exists and what it is directly, as one knows what white is and that such a color is presented on some occasion. Moreover, one could claim that since we directly apprehend sensa on occasions, there must be such a relation. To say that sensa are apprehended or presented is to report a simple fact. The analysis of such a fact involves holding that a relation obtains between a sensum and what it is that does the apprehending. Assume this is unproblematic. Can similar claims be made for indirect apprehension? To get at the question we must first consider a point regarding the apprehension of properties and relations. To apprehend a property or relation is to apprehend an exemplification of it. One is not presented with the color white without something being white, and one is not presented with the spatial relation *being to the left of* without being presented with something being to the left of something else. Such a claim has been called a "principle of exemplification"[3] for properties and relations. If we hold to it, then to directly apprehend a relation would always involve directly apprehending terms in a specific exemplification of it.[4] Hence, to say one directly apprehends the relation of direct apprehension is to say that what is apprehended is such a relation, a mental act, and the object apprehended by the act. '*Object*' is here taken in a broad sense that includes facts and propositions. If Moore were to say that the relation of indirect apprehension is directly apprehended, he would be forced to say that an act and an object are also directly apprehended. But, this clearly violates his gambit. For, the whole point of introducing indirect apprehension is to hold that certain objects can be apprehended which cannot be directly apprehended. To suggest that the relation of indirect apprehension is itself indirectly apprehended or that, although the relation is directly apprehended, one of its terms is indirectly apprehended by a further act obviously will not do. The first reply is, thus, not open in the case of indirect apprehension. Two gambits remain. First, one can argue, following the second line of reply in the case of direct apprehension, that there must be such a relation since some objects are indirectly apprehended. But, what force is there to the claim that some objects are indirectly apprehended? Clearly, one cannot rest the appeal on phenomenological grounds, as one perhaps can in the case of direct apprehension. To do so would return us to the claim that the relation of indirect apprehension and its terms are directly apprehended. Or, to put it another way, one cannot question the existence of objects of direct apprehension in the way in which one can question supposed objects of indirect apprehension. Moore must argue that there are objects of indirect apprehension in a way that he need not argue for the objects of direct apprehension. To the latter one need, so to speak, only point, even if merely metaphorically. In a sense, that is what the problem of realism is all about. Perhaps, this is why Moore proceeds in the style he does. He starts with the question of belief contexts. Assuming we are convinced that there obviously is a relation of indirect apprehension, on the basis of his consideration of belief contexts, he transfers the pattern of such contexts to the consideration of perception. He takes it to be obvious that such a relation holds in belief contexts since, at times, we clearly think of and believe things about objects we are not directly apprehending. We shall shortly consider the question of the relation of aboutness that supposedly holds between a proposition like [Wa] and the object a, but for the time we are only concerned with the claims expressed by (5) and (8).

One strange feature of Moore's use of the pattern of belief contexts and his talk of indirect apprehension in the case of perception is that a perceptual situation involves a belief in an existential proposition. Seeing, in short, is a form of believing. Aside from this peculiarity and the obvious phenomenologically based objections that could be raised, an internal problem remains. What is it to indirectly apprehend the object of the belief when one believes something about it? The way we have put the question suggests the answer of the last gambit. The relation of indirect apprehension is a product of two relations, DA and AB. For a mental act to be an indirect apprehension of an object is for that act to directly apprehend a proposition about the object. Thus, we could define 'IA' by:

$$IA(x,y) = df. \quad (\exists p)(DA(x,p) \ \& \ AB(p,y)).$$

But, now, an act will be an indirect apprehension of a material object, O, only if some proposition is about O. And, surely, we can only know that a proposition is *about* O if we know that O exists. We can no longer argue that O exists because there is an indirect apprehension of it. It is possible that Moore implicitly makes use of a very bad argument, in spite of the obvious point just made. There is a philosophically problematic sense in which statements expressing thoughts and beliefs may be said to be *about* nonexistent objects. The judgment that Pegasus is white is in some sense about Pegasus, as we ordinarily speak. In the same sense, a judgment that there is a material object associated with a presented sense datum may be said to be about such a material object. Let us assume we make such judgments. Nevertheless, it would no more do to use this as evidence for the existence of material objects than it would do to use the previous judgment as evidence for the existence of Pegasus. Yet, commonsensically, we are aware that we make judgments about objects that we know exist but that are not perceived at the time of the judgment. The act of judgment has some connection with such objects. Call the connection *'indirect apprehension'*. There is then a sense in which we may be said to experience or be aware of such a connection. All this is well enough insofar as common sense is good enough for philosophical perplexities. But, as soon as we start probing, it becomes clear that we cannot mean that we experience such a connection in that we have a direct apprehension of such a relation. Yet, some of the things Moore writes suggest that he makes such a transfer from the informal way we may speak of being aware of such a connection to the suggestion that we directly apprehend a relation of indirect apprehension. As this will clearly not do, he is left with the problem of establishing the existence of material objects in order to hold that there is a relation of indirect apprehension and, hence, to substantiate his account of perception. This he proceeds to attempt to do. In fact, we can now see a possible motive behind his well-known argument that material objects exist, since it is more probable that they exist than that any argument to the contrary is cogent. Since he must establish the truth of (5) as a basis for his account of perception, including the introduction of the relation IA, he must argue for (5) independently of that account and independently of any use of IA. This leads to his argument from common sense, which supposedly provides a basis for (5). For the present, I am not concerned to take up the question of the cogency of that aspect of Moore's philosophy. Rather, I wish to separate some distinct claims that are involved. The distinctions will help us to see a crucial feature in Moore's celebrated refutation of idealism as well as reveal why the argument in the paper of that title is incomplete as it was presented there. This will help us to see, in turn, how and why Moore attempted to revise his arguments for realism and against idealism in *Some Main Problems of Philosophy*.

There are three ways in which we can take the idealist position, given the terms of our discussion. First, we can take the idealist to hold that (5) is not a meaningful proposition since neither 'MO' nor 'R' is a meaningful predicate. This is, perhaps, the strongest form of idealism since, according to it, Moore's realism involves a meaningless claim. Here, we might recall that one aspect of Berkeley's view was the claim that "matter" was a meaningless notion and that Bradley repeated the line with respect to the notion of a "bare particular" or "substratum." Second, one could hold that (5) was meaningful but false. Like the first gambit, this would deny that one can reasonably adhere to the claim that there are material objects associated with objects of direct apprehension. But, on this gambit, it is at least sensible to claim that there are such objects. Third, one need not hold that (5) is either meaningless or false but merely that we do not know, or cannot know, that it is true or, perhaps, cannot know that it is meaningful. Moore simultaneously argues against all three gambits. It is worth noticing how his classical argument in "The Refutation of Idealism" fits with these alternatives. In that paper, Moore takes the idealist to claim that when there is an existent object, it must be the object of an act of direct apprehension. From such a claim, it obviously follows that (5), if meaningful, is false, since one of the things Moore means by an object being a material object is that it need not be an object of direct apprehension (in fact he also means that no material object ever is directly apprehended and even that none can be).[5] If one is not too careful about the use of the term 'meaningful', one might think that it further follows that (5) is meaningless. (5)'s being false is a consequence of the meaning of certain terms, *'material object'* for example. Hence to hold that (5) is true is to ignore the meaning of such terms and, in some sense, to make a meaningless claim. This would be to use 'meaningless' as some do when they hold contradictory claims to be senseless, absurd, or meaningless. Moore's classical line of argument in "The Refutation of Idealism" is to hold that the idealist fails to establish the claim that an existent must be an object of direct apprehension. Moreover, even the idealist must deny the claim, since an act of direct apprehension, which is an existent, need not itself be the object of a further act of direct apprehension, nor is any such act its own object.

While scoring such a simple point, Moore's main line is that 'O exists' does not imply 'O is an object of an act of direct apprehension'. To put the matter this way involves making a sharp distinction between an object of an act and the act itself, a distinction that Moore finds the idealist failing to make. Moore finds himself forced by the logic of his argument to hold that no object of an act of direct apprehension is such that its existence implies that such an act exists. This leads him to hold that sensa are also independent of such acts and, hence, we are led to the possibility of unsensed sensa. This he later rejected. The point is that Moore's argument is not simply an argument for the existence of material objects, but an insistence on the logical independence of objects and acts. Nevertheless, he nowhere in that early paper argues against the strongest claim that the idealist can make: that (5) is a meaningless proposition. We already noted how one could think he has done so, since if 'O exists' implies 'O is an object of an act of direct apprehension' then there is a sense in which it is meaningless to assert (5). But, the claim that (5) is meaningless, since terms like 'MO' and 'R' will not be legitimate on a certain meaning criterion, is quite a different claim from that regarding the supposed implication. Moore does attempt to meet the claim that (5) is meaningless in *Some Main Problems of Philosophy*. To see how his implicit argument goes, let us first try to state the idealist's claim a bit more precisely.

Assume we are considering a subject-predicate language schema much on the order of *Principia Mathematica* with the requirement that all primitive predicate terms refer to properties and relations presented in acts of direct apprehension and that all proper names refer to objects also so presented. We may call such a requirement a *principle of acquaintance*. One may now put the idealist's claim as follows: The terms 'MO', 'R', and 'O' cannot be introduced into such a language and still retain the role or use that we have put them to. Moore is arguing that this is not the case. Consider the term 'MO' and the following definition:

$$(D_1) \quad MO(x) = df. \sim (\exists y) \, DA(y,x)$$

According to D_1 something is a material object if and only if it is not directly apprehended. For the moment I do not want to consider the obvious point that this will not do since other sorts of things might also not be objects of direct apprehension.[6] Rather, let us simply consider whether one can sensibly speak of objects that are not directly apprehended, for one may take the idealist to claim that we cannot do so. One point implicit in Moore's argument is that we can do so since the right-hand side of D_1 is meaningful. In short, since we know what it is to be directly apprehended or an object of experience, we know what it is for something not to be such an object. The idealist's mistake is to think that to claim to know on the basis of experience what it is to be an object that is not experienced is to claim to experience an object that is not experienced. Of course the latter claim is absurd. But all that one need assert is that the right side of D_1 does not violate the principle of acquaintance, and it does not since no primitive predicate occurring in it violates that principle. Two counterarguments are still open to the idealist. It may be argued that the relational predicate 'DA' violates the principle of acquaintance, since no such relation is given in experience. That is, the notion of an *object of experience* is not itself something presented in experience. But this is weak since the dispute between Moore and the idealist then reduces to a question about the phenomenological data. And, by so reducing the dispute the idealist no longer offers an argument, merely a claim that contradicts Moore's. Moreover, Moore can argue that if his opponent questions the legitimacy of the predicate 'DA', then the idealist's case cannot be stated, because the idealist holds that for every object x there is an act y that stands in DA to x. All this is not surprising since, in one obvious sense, the realist's claim must be meaningful if it is a denial of the idealist's, and the latter is meaningful. If the relation of direct apprehension is essential to the assertion of the idealist, then Moore's point is made. However, the idealist can still raise a question about the use of the logical signs in D_1—the quantifer, the variables, and the negation sign. The idealist may hold that the logical apparatus is applicable only to the sorts of things referred to by the primitive signs of the language: to objects, properties, and relations that are or that can be directly apprehended. Perhaps one might put it in terms of objects that are apprehended or that are acts of apprehension. In a way it makes no difference, since, on Moore's view, acts of direct apprehension *can be* objects of direct apprehension even if they *are not*, but a material object *cannot be* an object of an act of direct apprehension. Either way the point would be that the existential quantifier ranges only over objects of direct apprehension and mental acts. (Here we are speaking of the quantifier at the lowest level in a *Principia* type of language schema. Quantifiers at the first predicate level would then range over properties and relations of such objects.) Put in such a way, the idealist's position has nothing to do with the meaningfulness of '$\sim(\exists y)DA(y,x)$'. For, his claim relates to the values of the

variables, so to speak, in that expression. Thus, the idealist-phenomenalist could accept '$\sim(\exists y)\,DA(y,x)$' as a meaningful context
but still hold that the claim that there are material objects, in
Moore's sense, is meaningless. This contention would be based on
the further claim that the term 'MO', as introduced in D_1, could
apply only to phenomena (or complexes of phenomena) or mental acts, since those are the only values of the zero-level variables.
Further, it could be held that the assertion '$(\exists x)\sim(\exists y)\,DA(y,x)$'
would be taken as true or as false, depending on, first, whether
one insisted that all mental acts must themselves be objects of direct apprehension and, second, whether the idealist-phenomenalist
would allow for the possibility of unsensed sensa. Here, we could
distinguish different senses of idealism in terms of whether one
treated such a statement as true or as false and in terms of what
sort of truth or falsehood one took it to be: synthetic, analytic,
synthetic a priori, etc.

We can see the point in another way. Consider the expression
'$\sim(\exists y)\,DA(y,O)$', where we use 'O', as we did earlier, to refer to
a specific material object in Moore's sense. To the idealist-phenomenalist both the sentence and the term 'O' are illegitimate or
meaningless. Thus, there can be no question of an inference to an
existential generalization or to the assertion that there is a material
object from such a statement. Since 'O' does not refer to a phenomenal object or mental act, it must be introduced by terms that
do so refer and by the logical apparatus. One possibility would be
to introduce material object terms by complex expressions whose
constituent terms refer only to phenomenal entities, properties
of such, etc. In effect, this would mean that material objects were
construed as complexes of phenomena, relations among them,
facts about them, and so on. Moore wishes to avoid such an analysis of a material object. It would be inadequate in that it does not
enable us to capture what is involved in the claim that there are
material objects. An analysis that would be adequate brings us
back to the relation R. One could suggest that a term like 'O' refers to an object that stands in R to some particular sensum. But,
either 'R' violates the principle of acquaintance or, by the principle of exemplification, we must be directly presented with O if we
are presented with R. Hence, one must make use of the logical ap-

paratus by holding that there is some relation that some material object stands in to a specific sensum. Once again, the problem of the legitimacy of the application of the logical apparatus arises. The idealist is claiming that we only sensibly apply expressions like 'there is an object such that . . .' and 'there is a relation such that . . .' in the context of a schema in which such quantifiers range over objects and properties of a certain kind. Moore is implicitly arguing that we can sensibly use such expressions with other values for the variables—values that are not and cannot be objects and properties that we directly apprehend. To put it another way, the idealist is claiming that our concepts of *object*, *property*, and *existence* originate in and are bound to the existents, objects, and properties we directly apprehend. We cannot extend those concepts to objects and properties that are not the kinds of things we do or can directly apprehend. Moore is arguing that our concepts of *existence*, *property*, *object*, etc., are not so bound. This I take to be one thing that is involved in the claim that '*Esse* is *percipi*' and lies behind Berkeley's apparently absurd claim that to attempt to imagine an object that is not experienced is impossible since we then, by imagining it, make it an object of experience. In a way, Moore is claiming that we can have a thought whose text would be expressed by '$(\exists y)(\exists R_1) R_1(a_1,y)$' and that the variables are not determined to range over phenomenal entities. The idealist is claiming, at least, that such variables must be limited in range. Moreover, if we take certain things Berkeley says into account, he may also claim that we cannot even have such a thought, since it would be "abstract" and without content. There could only be a thought expressed by something like '$R(a_1,O)$', where 'R' and 'O' must, like 'a_1', stand for objects of experience. The issue comes down to a question about the logical apparatus. It is, then, natural to raise a question about the connection of the logical signs and the principle of acquaintance.

We have been assuming that the logical signs are exempt from the requirements of a principle of acquaintance in that we have not spoken of them as referring to "elements" of experience. In one sense, the idealist has applied the principle to them by insisting that they may be sensibly used only with a restricted range of application. One might seek to strengthen such a claim by insisting that logical notions like existence, generality, negation, etc., must themselves have an empirical basis, i.e., stand for aspects that are directly apprehended. In fact, I think one theme implicit in Moore's argument is that since the logical notions do not stand for aspects of experience, there is no force to the idealist's claim that they must be restricted to objects, etc., of direct apprehension. We know the meaning of 'there is . . .', 'not . . .', etc., without directly experiencing anything they stand for. Hence, there is no point to the claim that we can use such signs only in the restricted way we have been considering. Of course, even if one held that a logical sign stood for something directly apprehended, it would not follow that its use was restricted in the way the idealist claims. The old question of abstraction would obviously arise. Recall, here, Berkeley on *extension* and *color*. In fact, we shall see that Moore obviously would hold that even if the concept of *existence* did, in some sense, originate in our apprehension of phenomenal objects and properties, it would be legitimate to abstract it from such contexts. As we shall see, he says as much about *extension*.

In a way, then, Moore and the idealist are at a standoff regarding the application of the logical apparatus. But, insofar as Moore is attempting to show that the idealist has not presented a conclusive argument and merely made a claim, he has a point. At least, he has made his point until we probe further into the questions surrounding the use of the quantifiers and variables. It is interesting to note that Russell explicitly employed the pattern Moore uses. In *An Introduction to Mathematical Philosophy* and even earlier in *The Problems of Philosophy*, he held that since we know what a correlating relation is, as a purely logical notion, we can speak of there being objects standing in one-one or one-many relations with objects of experience.[7] Moreover, since we know what it is to be an object of experience and we know what 'not' means, we know what it is not to be an object of experience. This does not mean that we "know" such objects in that we have *experienced* unexperienced objects. It merely means that certain sentences are meaningful. Thus, Russell, like Moore, rejects the extreme form of idealism, the claim that the realist position is meaningless, on the basis of the independence of logical notions from phenomenalistic contexts.

There is a rather obvious connection between the dispute about the application of the logical apparatus—in effect the use of the existential quantifier in the claim that there are material objects—and Russell's theory of descriptions. The latter theory supposedly supplies us with a way of "referring" to or "talking about" things that are not objects of acquaintance, while allowing us to remain within the constraints of a Russellian *principle of acquaintance*. Thus, we might think of the theory as providing a basis for referring to material objects, along the lines Moore seeks to establish. In fact, Moore sometimes writes as if he is using Russellian definite descriptions:

> many of them seem to think that this part of the surface of this inkstand could be correctly described as *the* cause of this presented object. They suggest, therefore, the view that what I am judging in this case might be: "This presented object has one and only one cause, and that cause is part of the surface of an inkstand." It seems to me quite obvious that *this* view, at all events, is utterly untenable. I do not believe for a moment, nor does any one, and certainly do not judge, that this presented object has *only* one cause . . . hence my judgment certainly cannot be "*The* cause of this part of the surface of an inkstand." . . . It seems to me it would be highly improbable we could truly say that what we are judging in these cases is: "This presented object has one and only one cause, of this special kind."
>
> The only other suggestion I can make is that there may be some ultimate, not further definable relation, which we might for instance, call the relation of "being a manifestation of," such that we might conceivably be judging: "There is one and only one thing of which this presented object is a manifestation, and *that* thing is part of the surface of an inkstand."[8]

Thus, we could "refer" to a material object by using something like '$(\iota x)(R(a_1,x))$' and claim that '$E! (\iota x)(R(a_1,x))$' is true or known to be true, or, at least, meaningful. But, clearly the basic issue is about the existential quantifier. Definite descriptions, after all, merely provide a concise notation for the writing of quantified statements. Yet, Russell's distinction between knowledge by acquaintance and knowledge by description does reflect the issue at stake. However, Moore's pattern of argument was articulated some years before Russell's *On Denoting* of 1905. One early attack on idealism occurs in "The Nature of Judgment" of 1898. There Moore attempted to use an analysis of *propositions*, *objects*, and the concept of *truth* to rebut Bradley's absolute idealism. In 1901, he used a related line of attack centering on the concept of *numerical difference*, and its connection with the notion of a "particular," in his paper "Identity." We shall consider such themes in detail in Chapter IV. In 1903, the distinction between an act and an object and the recognition of the relation DA became central to his critique of idealism. But, he also employs, in "The Refutation," a pattern of argument that he had used in his critique of naturalistic analyses of the concept *goodness*, in *Principia Ethica*, also published in 1903. The influence of this pattern on his rejection of idealism, his notion of "analysis," and his appeal to Common Sense shall occupy us in subsequent chapters. Here we need only note that the argument pattern he used against naturalism in ethics was the basis of his insistence that the concept *exists* does not *contain* the concept *perceived*. In this simple theme, we can find the fundamental issue regarding the question of the range of application of the concept *exists*. In fact it is quite explicit. Moore treats *exists* as a simple, unanalyzable concept. By so doing, he holds that one can "separate" it from the concept of *being perceived* and, hence, one must allow for the logical possibility of something existing unperceived. We shall return to Moore's crucial claim that some concepts are simple and unanalyzable as well as to the idea of "analysis" that he periodically invokes.

The appeal to the relation IA is also involved in the claim that existential statements *about* material objects may be meaningfully made. To judge that a thing exists is construed, by some, to be a judgment *about* what is claimed to exist. The idealist may, then, be interpreted as holding that in order to make a judgment about something one must "know" it or have one's "mind" in some relation to it or, in short, "apprehend" it. Supposedly one cannot, as Moore admits, directly apprehend material objects. Not being able to apprehend them one cannot judge about them. Thus, one cannot judge that they exist. Hence, the claim that material objects exist is meaningless. It is clear how Moore's notion of indirect apprehension is thought to counter such a pattern. In judging that a material object, which is related in some way to a directly apprehended sense datum, exists, one is indirectly apprehending it. In that sense, there is an act that is in a relation to such an object and, hence, may be said to "know" it. Putting matters in this way should serve to reveal yet another link with the ideas involved in Russell's theory of descriptions and the distinction between knowledge by description and knowledge by acquaintance. It is almost as if Moore were to speak of knowing an object indirectly as opposed to knowing it directly. After all, what he holds to be an object of direct apprehension, a sense datum, for example, would be the kind of thing that Russell took one to be directly acquainted with. Moore, however, does not speak of knowledge in such cases. In fact, he is concerned to distinguish *direct apprehension* from *knowing*, and, in particular, to distinguish direct apprehension from what he calls *immediate knowledge*. But, this has to do with his holding that knowledge involves our direct apprehension of *propositions*, not objects. Thus, the term 'know' aside, his view is similar to Russell's in some fundamental respects.

Moore is not content to let matters rest with the claim that it is meaningful to assert that material objects exist. He also wishes to argue that the assertion that there are material objects is true. Moreover, he will attempt to say something further about the relation between sensa and material objects. Before proceeding to such questions, it will help to return briefly to the issue of unsensed sensa.

I mentioned earlier that Moore's argument in "The Refutation of Idealism" is an argument for the existence of objects of direct apprehension independently of any act of apprehension. Hence, one further version of idealism could be the claim that it is meaningless to assert that there are unsensed sensa. In the terms of our discussion, the claim that there are unsensed sensa could be put as '$(\exists x)[(y){\sim}DA(y,x) \ \& \ (z){\sim}DA(x,z)]$'. *There is something that is neither directly apprehended by, nor is a direct apprehension of, anything.* Here, unlike our earlier case, the variables range over the sorts of things that are *capable* of being directly apprehended. Hence, the idealist, who raises a parallel argument, must hold that the variables can range only over objects that in fact *are* directly apprehended or that *are* mental acts. Every individual object would then be either an apprehension of something else (not necessarily an object) or directly apprehended itself. The statement that there are unsensed sensa *could not* then be true within a language schema with such a restriction and, in that sense, would be meaningless. But, once again, we are dealing with a prescription rather than an argument. Yet, it is worth noting that Moore later came to feel that the notion of an unsensed sensum was paradoxical and rejected his earlier view and, hence, his earlier refutation of idealism.

Suppose we now assume that Moore's line is cogent and that we do not restrict the application of the logical apparatus along the idealist's lines. What more can Moore say regarding the truth of the critical statement about material objects and the relation between such objects and phenomena? An interesting point comes out if we consider a view that Moore does not hold but that, as I see it, he comes close to adopting. Usually, he suggests that when there is an indirect apprehension of an object, there is always a proposition that is directly apprehended. But, at places he considers the possibility that something else may be directly apprehended instead of a proposition. "The only connection between the two is this, that whenever you indirectly apprehend any one thing, you must be *directly* apprehending *something else—either* some proposition about it, or perhaps sometimes something other than a proposition."[9] What could the other thing be? An obvious line would be to hold that one can directly apprehend a sense datum and that such a direct apprehension is also an indirect apprehension of the material object that is somehow related to the sensum. This would have the advantage of eliminating the need for a belief whenever there is a perception of a material object. It would have another consequence as well. So long as one directly apprehends a proposition when one indirectly apprehends a material object, the relation between what is directly apprehended and what is indirectly apprehended may be construed as the intentional relation AB. But, a sense datum cannot be *about* a material object as a proposition may be said to be. Hence, to explain what we mean by saying that a direct apprehension of a sensum is also an indirect apprehension of a material object, we would have to offer a new explanation of indirect apprehension. We cannot, in short, still consider it to be a relational product of DA and AB, since the latter would not enter into the present situation. To clarify the status of IA we should then obviously have to clarify what R is, for R is the relation between the sensum and the physical object. To continue to talk in terms of *some* relation rather than to specify R would be totally inadequate, since, among other things, a sensum could stand in some relation to one material object and in some other relation to another material object. To know what it is to indirectly apprehend a material object when we directly apprehend a sensum is to know what the connection between the two is. Clearly, we informally make use of such a connection in our discussion, for we are thinking of the sensum as somehow belonging to or being caused by the material object. Now, Moore does, at times, come close to specifying the relation R, and in a way that fits with the problem about specifying what IA is.[10]

As I indicated earlier, Moore uses the phrase 'sense datum' ambiguously. He also uses the notion of a property ambiguously. He sometimes thinks of a color property as a particular quality instance belonging to one and only one object and sometimes as a common universal. Consider a sense datum that is both white and square and, for simplicity, has no further nonrelational qualities. Moore tends to think of such a sensum as a complex of two particular quality instances, say $white_1$ and $square_1$. He also thinks of the two quality instances as sense data. But, he further tends to think of the qualities as being qualities of something that is not a quality. Fusing all these lines, it would be easy to come to think of a sense datum as a quality of a material object. R would then be the relation between a subject and its properties. The material object would be the underlying substratum of properties—the bare particular Bradley scorned and the matter of Berkeley's Hylas. The properties would be the sensa of the phenomenalist tradition, which are characteristically fusions of universals like white, quality instances like $white_1$, and objects like the white square patch that is directly apprehended. It is precisely such a fusion that would lend itself to one's taking sensa as properties of material objects. A further line aids the gambit. Moore sometimes thinks of some properties, shapes, as properties of material objects while also being sense data![11] This, of course, fits with the classical notion that material objects are essentially extended or spatial objects and the old distinction between primary and secondary qualities. In fact, Moore is tempted by the view that sensa occupy the space of material objects. Thus, both sensa and material objects would be in the same *area*.[12] He may even be thought to identify the material object with "its" area or, at least, say some things that suggest such an identification. But, for a number of reasons, he finally does not construe sensa as properties of material objects.[13] First, he comes to distinguish the shape of the sensum and the shape of any physical object on the basis of his distinction between quality instances and common qualities. The shape of a sensum is a quality instance and, hence, numerically distinct from the shape of any material object or any other object. But, the shape of a sensum and the shape of a material object, as particular instances, can be qualitatively the same in that they are both shapes of the same kind. Thus, we do not directly perceive *the* shape of a material object, though we can perceive the shape of a sensum. Here, it is interesting to note how he makes use of the idea that we can sensibly attribute properties of directly apprehended quality instances to material objects. This is similar to the case of the logical concepts we discussed earlier. It is also worth noting that in Moore's early writings the universals, exemplified by the quality instances, are not themselves directly apprehended when a sense datum is an object of direct apprehension. They are more on the order of abstract Platonic universals. Thus, material objects and sensa share properties in a two-fold sense. They both contain quality instances and those instances are of the same sort, which is to say that the quality instances exemplify one and the same universal. Moore thus ends up with material objects and quality instances contained in them, neither of which are directly apprehended. Perhaps, material objects are then implicitly taken to be complexes of such quality instances, for he sometimes thinks of objects being complexes of qualities. If this is so, then Moore's realism does not involve a substratum that is never apprehended, but it does involve quality instances that we do not apprehend and combinations of such. One difference between material objects and sensa would then be that the latter are composed of *directly apprehended* qualities and, among such, would be qualities of a kind that were not involved in the constitution of material objects—color, for example. If he takes material objects to involve a substratum, as well as quality instances, while sensa are simply combinations of quali-

ty instances, then there would be a further radical difference between the two kinds of objects. But, if he takes sensa to also involve a substratum, he would face a problem regarding the direct
apprehension of such an entity. He would have to hold either that
such an entity is directly apprehended, as are the qualities, or that
there is a constituent of a sensum that is never so apprehended.
The former seems absurd; the latter goes against Moore's line of
thought. The simplest gambit would be to hold the material object
to be an unapprehended substratum, area, or part of space of
which sensa are properties. However, Moore, as I noted, believes
that we never directly apprehend the real shape of a material object. To hold that we do so apprehend the shape would apparently force one to hold that a material object had several shapes,
colors, etc. There is a further reason for Moore's not holding that
we indirectly apprehend a material object when we directly apprehend its sensory qualities. It may seem to some to be a disadvan-
tage of Moore's analysis that he holds perception to involve a belief. To Moore there is a distinct advantage to his view. He wants
to conclude that when we perceive a material object we can be
said to *know* that there is a material object. He feels that if we
merely directly apprehend sensa, which were in fact connected to
material objects, we could not be said to know that there is a material object. We can be said to know such a thing *if* we are directly apprehending an existential proposition (as well as a sense datum), *if* that proposition is *about* a material object, and *if* we
know that proposition to be true. Thus, he requires the perception
of material objects to involve the direct apprehension of propositions and not merely of phenomena. To show that we know that
there are material objects then amounts to showing that we know
such a proposition is true. Along with this pattern, there is a third
reason for Moore's appeal to propositions in his analysis of perception. Moore holds that we are conscious of material objects in
some way when we perceive them. This cannot reduce to direct
apprehension of sensa which are in some relation to material objects, for that would not reflect our awareness of the material objects. But, in view of propositions *being about* material objects,
the use of such a relation will reflect the fact that we are conscious

of material objects in some sense. Hence, IA can be analyzed in terms of DA and AB.

Moore, consequently, does not take the relation between sensa and material objects to be that of property instances being constituents of or belonging to a substratum. The relation between the two sorts of things is never clearly specified except as *the relation* between a sense datum and *the material object* it stands in *that* relation to. In a similar vein, *the material object* is merely specified as the object which the directly apprehended sense datum stands in *that relation* to. At one place, Moore directly appeals to Russell's distinction between knowledge by description and knowledge by acquaintance to defend such characterizations.

... if there is anything which is this inkstand, then, in perceiving that thing, I am knowing it *only* as *the* thing which stands in a certain relation to this sense-datum. ... If there be such a thing at all, it is quite certainly only known to me by description, in the sense in which Mr. Russell uses that phrase; and the description by which it is known is that of being *the* thing which stands to this sense-datum in a certain relation.[14]

Hence, ignoring the additional claim of *uniqueness*, the critical statement (5) becomes

(5') $(\exists x)(\exists R)[MO(x) \ \& \ R(a_1,x)]$.

The confrontation between realist and idealist-phenomenalist now concerns the truth of (5'). Moore's attack takes three routes. First, he analyzes and seeks to refute some ways of construing the idealist's arguments by employing the distinction between an act, an object, and the relation DA that obtains between the act and its object. We have touched upon this theme and shall return to it in the next chapter. Second, he appeals to Common-Sense truths and our common and "popular" understanding of such truths to argue that no phenomenalistic analysis of the perceptual situation can do justice to the facts to be analyzed. For, no such analysis will fit with obvious features that we take to be involved in perceptual situations as we ordinarily consider them. Such a line raises questions about the notions of "analysis" and "Common Sense" as well as questions about their connection. Such issues will also concern us in the next chapter. A third line of argument that Moore employs makes use of a simpler appeal to "common sense." This is Moore's notorious argument that we have more reason to believe (5') than any set of premises that would establish the negation of (5'). In advocating this latter line, Moore does not merely assert that the proposition,

(K)   I do know that this pencil (or envelope) exists,

is more likely to be true than the premises from which a sceptic or phenomenalist concludes that (K) is false. He does set the argument up so that, with 'P' for such a set of premises, both Moore and the phenomenalist agree that

P ⊢ ∼(K)

holds. The question, then, is whether one knows *that* P or *that* (K). If the latter, then one can conclude that P contains a false statement. Moore claims this to be the case since he claims to know (K) to be true. One cannot reject his claim, as some phenomenalists would, by arguing that the phrase 'this pencil' in (K) must refer to *a* or *a set* of sensa. Moore has carefully set the stage to block this line by his analysis of perception in terms of DA and IA. Thus, (K) is elliptical for 'I do know that (5')'. Part of Moore's argument is that if one construes (K) as he does, it is not subject to standard criticisms associated with Hume. This involves him in critically scrutinizing assumptions he believes that Hume makes. But, Moore's basic argument for the claim that we do know that (K) is true depends on his distinguishing "mediate" from "immediate" knowledge. We have immediate knowledge when we directly apprehend a proposition and know it to be true "without knowing any other proposition from which it follows." One can be said to know a proposition when one directly apprehends it, when one believes it, when the proposition is true, and when a fourth unspecified condition is also fulfilled. This latter unspecified condition supposedly takes care of cases where we "accidently" believe correctly or believe correctly, but for the wrong reasons, and so forth. Moore argues that the phenomenalist presupposes that to know (K) is to know it *mediately*, as *inferred* from propositions about sensa. Moore denies such a move by holding that we must distinguish between knowing something only upon certain conditions, such as the direct apprehension of sensa, and knowing a proposition because one knows other propositions describing those conditions.

It might be said: I certainly do not know immediately that the pencil exists; for I should not know it at all, unless I were directly apprehending certain sense-data, and knew that they were signs of its existence. And of course I admit, that I should not know it, unless I were directly apprehending certain sense-data. But this is again a different thing from admitting that I do not know it immediately. For the mere fact that I should not know it, unless certain other things were happening, is quite a different thing from knowing it *only* because I know *some other proposition*. The mere direct apprehension of certain sense-data is quite a different thing from the knowledge of any proposition; and yet I am not sure that it is not by itself quite sufficient to enable me to know that the pencil exists.[15]

He then proceeds to conclude:

But whether the exact proposition which formed my premiss, namely: I do know that this pencil exists; or only the proposition: This pencil exists; or only the proposition: The sense-data which I directly apprehend are a sign that it exists; is known by me immediately, one or other of them, I think, certainly is so. And all three of them are much more certain than any premiss which could be used to prove that they are false; and also much more certain than any other premiss which could be used to prove that they are true.[16]

Moore does not, and apparently cannot, explicate any further the basis of his "certainty." He would think that he need not. By distinguishing between mediate and immediate knowledge as he does, he prepares his reader for the *implicit* claim that (K) is self-evident. What he does can be understood in terms of his views about "analysis" and the "knowing of concepts." Such themes shall be considered shortly. Let it suffice here to suggest that Moore is maintaining that by understanding concepts such as *exists*, *material object*, and *sense-datum* the way we do, we immediately understand that (K) is true. Ironically, in his way, Moore does exactly what the idealist does, as Moore saw it, with respect to the concepts *exists* and *being perceived*: claiming that one directly (or intuitively) apprehends a certain connection between them. Realism is "established," in short, by the same kind of "insight" about concepts that reveals that *goodness* is not to be identified with, or analyzed in terms of, *pleasure*. Thus, this argument from "Common Sense" links up, through the implicit appeal to *concepts* and *analyses*, with the other appeal to Common Sense that explicitly involves those notions.

There is, however, an unresolved problem in Moore's pattern that forces him to make yet another appeal to Common Sense. We noted that it is problematic to specify *both* the material object *and* the relation it stands in to the datum a_1 by means of definite descriptions as he does. In an obvious sense, this will not do as a reply to the phenomenalist, for the latter may be taken to see the problem in terms of the need to specify just what the relation R is. To say that the relation is the relation that holds between the material object and the datum or that it is the relation of "being a sign of" or of "manifesting" is of no help. As the idealist-phenomenalist sees it, the need to specify the relation leads directly to his own view, since the only cogent way of taking the relation is to hold that physical objects are collections of sensa. Moore must hold that we understand what he means when he speaks of such a relation in terms of our ordinary way of thinking about physical objects and experiences "associated with" them. This means that the predicate 'R' is to be understood in terms of our ordinary talk about such objects and such experiences. We can neither define 'R' nor take it to stand for a relation we are acquainted with in the sense in which he can hold we are acquainted with DA. As we noted, he faces the same problem with both IA and R, a problem he will try to resolve by shifting the discussion to the question of the *intentional* connection between beliefs and facts. This effort of his we shall return to in Chapter III. The other attempt to "solve" the problem simply amounts to using the common-sense context to provide a more or less definite description of *the* relation. Yet, this is hardly an argument against the idealist's attack on Common Sense, since Moore was supposedly *defending* the belief that there is such a relation and not merely *appealing to* such a belief.

The crucial point is that even if we take (5′) to involve legitimate uses of the quantifiers, the proposition (K), expanded in terms of definite descriptions or, ultimately, existential statements, does not provide a suitable basis for Moore's argument. It does not in that such a statement is too "weak" without specification of R. To put it another way, (K), upon expansion, may turn out to be true under conditions that do not supply grounds for Moore's realism. It will not suffice to hold that:

There is an x such that x is a material object and there is a relation such that x and only x has that relation to the datum a_1.

This is clearly not what we believe when (and if) we believe that "this pencil exists," though it may *follow* from what is believed when we believe the latter. What is wanted is something on the order of:

There is an x such that x is a material object and there is a relation such that x and only x has that relation to the datum a_1 *and that relation is such that . . .*

But all Moore offers us for the '. . .' is that the relation is such that the material object x stands in it to the datum a_1. More is required for the explication of "this pencil exists" and hence of (K). As I noted above, this leads Moore to appeal to the common-sense context, on the one hand, and to turn to the analysis of intentional contexts, on the other.

Idealism, Realism, and Common Sense

The relatively simple and classic argument that Moore offers against the phenomenalist in "The Refutation of Idealism" goes something like the following.[1] We distinguish the act, m_a, from its object, say s_1, in a case of an awareness of the datum. As in the later pattern of *Some Main Problems of Philosophy*, we have an act, an object, and a relation between them. The idealist claims that "To be is to be perceived." Therefore, he claims that from

(a) s_1 exists

it follows that

(b) s_1 is perceived.

(b) may be construed as,

(c) $(\exists x)\, DA(x, s_1)$,

where 'DA' indicates the relation of "awareness of." Consequently, the idealist claims that (c) follows from (a). But, (c) does not follow from (a), as those propositions are presently expressed. Hence, the idealist must construe 'exists' in (a) in such a way that the implication holds and may, then, offer a "definition" so that

(d) y exists = df. $(\exists x)\, DA(x, y)$.

Yet, using (d) trivializes the claim that to be is to be perceived. To avoid such a trivial position, the idealist may hold that 'exists' is to be "analyzed" in terms of other concepts, say $\emptyset$ and ψ, such that

(c) will follow from the statement that s_1 is an instance of one of them, say $\emptyset$. But, we have the same problem regarding the inference from '$\emptyset s_1$' to (c). For, either we take '$\emptyset$' to be defined in terms of 'DA', as 'exists' is in (d), or we do not obtain the inference we require. Once again, we appear to trivialize the claim, unless we hold that $\emptyset$ and $\emptyset$ are such that

(e) $(x)(\emptyset x \supset \emptyset x)$

necessarily holds *and* that (e) is *not* analytic or tautological. Then, from '$\emptyset s_1$' it "follows" that '$\emptyset s_1$' holds and, hence, that s_1 is an object of acquaintance. However, this gets us nowhere, since the problem is now moved to the claim about (e) being "necessary." The idealist, in short, is forced to appeal to an "intuition" about (e) or about "esse est percipi" as a *synthetic* a priori truth. With such a claim, Moore feels he cannot and need not argue, since the idealist no longer offers an argument. Moreover, we can understand how an idealist like Berkeley comes to think he has done more than appeal to a stipulative definition or an intuition. The idealist mistakenly analyzes the perceptual situation. When we perceive *blue*, there is an awareness or consciousness of blue, which the idealist construes to be a "whole" of which blue and consciousness are constituents, just as a blue square may be taken to be a whole of which blue and square are constituents. Moore, thus, seems to assume that the idealist takes objects as "bundles" of properties or concepts. (We shall see why he does this in a later chapter, as well as note the connection of this question about the construal of particular objects to the idealist's position and to issues involved in the analysis of thought and belief.) Taking an object to be a bundle of properties, one then takes the predicative relation in language to reflect a connection between such a bundle or collection and a constituent concept or property. The idealist, as Moore sees it, then makes the mistake of treating *the sensation of blue* as an object, just as *the blue square* is an object. The sensation, as an object, is composed of the concept or property blue and another concept or property—*being a sensation*, or *awareness*, or, as Moore sometimes puts it, *consciousness*. Thus, a sensation of blue is composed of *blue* plus *consciousness*, as a blue square might be thought to be composed of *blue* plus *square* (or squareness). Consequently, given that there is a sensation of blue, it follows that there is consciousness, and one is led to hold that given that there is such a sensation, there must be an awareness or conciouness of it. As Moore sees it, there are two simple and fundamental mistakes in all this. One mistake is to take the relation between a sense datum or *object of* sensation and an *awareness* of it to be the same relation that holds between an *object* and a *concept* that is a constituent of it; to take the relation between blue and the blue square to be the same relation that holds between blue and an awareness or experience of blue. Instead of noting that there is a basic and unique relation between acts and objects, DA of Chapter I, the idealist takes both consciousness and a property like blue to be constituents of blue sensa or sensations of blue, and mistakenly concludes that blue, as a constituent property of a sensation, is attributed to something mental, the sensation. This is aided by a second mistake; an ambiguous use of the term 'sensation'. In the above pattern, one mixes three uses of that term. First, there is the sense in which something is a sensation in that it is *the object* of an *act* of awareness or consciousness. Second, there is the sense in which *the act*, being an act of awareness or of sensing, *is a sensation*. Third, there is the construal of the "whole," which is *the act in relation to the object*, as a sensation. In this latter sense, the "sensation" is identified neither with the act nor with the object but with *the fact that* the object is related to the act in a definite way. Putting matters as Moore does, in terms of the act m_a, the sense datum s_1, and the relation of direct awareness DA, enables us to clearly distinguish the act, the object, the relation, *and the fact* that m_a stands in DA to s_1. The idealist's talk of "consciousness" and "sensation" fuses these distinct "things." Once we separate them, we recognize that s_1 does not relate to m_a as it does to blue, i.e., that DA is not exemplification. (This can be insisted upon irrespective of the way one analyzes an object and of what one takes to be the relation between an object and a property of it.) Moreover, we shall no longer be tempted to hold that from the *existence* of *the sensation* it follows that "it" is sensed. For, such a claim would return us to asserting either that (c) follows from (a) or that (e) is a necessary truth but not a logical truth, in a standard sense of 'logical'. Thus, if we distinguish

m_a, s_1, DA, and the fact *that* m_a stands in DA to s_1, and if we accept Moore's analysis of the perceptual situation, we purportedly refute the idealist's gambit, on one way of construing it. It does not, however, refute that gambit as we construed it in the last chapter. Nor does it establish realism in Moore's sense, for he has not established the truth of (5′). Yet, in "The Refutation of Idealism" Moore thinks he can immediately conclude that realism has been established.

If, on the other hand, we clearly recognize the nature of that peculiar relation which I have called "awareness of anything"; if we see that *this* is involved equally in the analysis of *every* experience—from the merest sensation to the most developed perception or reflexion, and that *this* is in fact the only essential element in an experience—the only thing that is both common and peculiar to all experiences—the only thing which gives us reason to call any fact mental; if, further, we recognize that this awareness is and must be in all cases of such a nature that its object, when we are aware of it, is precisely what it would be, if we were not aware: then it becomes plain that the existence of a table in space is related to my experience of *it* in precisely the same way as the existence of my own experience is related to my experience of *that*. Of both we are merely aware: if we are aware that the one exists, we are aware in precisely the same sense that the other exists; and if it is true that my experience can exist, even when I do not happen to be aware of its existence, we have exactly the same reason for supposing that the table can do so also.[2]

Here, Moore argues in two steps. First, he reiterates a claim he made earlier in the paper: the idealist's pattern cannot be applied to mental acts like m_a. That is, the idealist cannot hold that "to be is to be perceived" leads us to conclude that acts like m_a exist only if perceived or experienced. The point is a familiar one and a theme that concerns philosophers as diverse as Moore and Sartre. As Moore sees it, to apply the idealist's formula to such acts would force one to hold that when m_a exists, there is a further act, say m_{a_1}, which stands in the relation of "being an awareness of" to the act m_a. But, then, for m_{a_1} to exist there must be a further act, m_{a_2}, which is an awareness of m_{a_1}, and so on ad infinitum. To avoid the infinite regress, Moore holds that the idealist must acknowledge that some things, mental acts at least, exist "unperceived." But, if this is so, then as the relation "being an awareness of" is the same in the case of an awareness of an act, a sensum, or a physical object such as a table, one acknowledges that the object which is an *object of such an act need not be*. Hence, the fact that something *is* an object of such an act does not imply that it *must be* the object of an act. Consequently, physical objects can exist without being the objects of acts of awareness.

In setting up his argument as he does, Moore ignores two crucial themes of Berkelian idealism. First, Berkeley does not claim that the formula "to be is to be perceived" universally holds, for he asserts that "to be is to be perceived or to be a perceiver." But, since developing this point would lead us too far afield into a consideration of the concept of *self*, and the question of the connection of Moore's acts to a self, I merely mention the point.[3] Second, and more germane for our concerns, Berkeley does not hold that what is aware, be it act or self, is aware of "itself" in the same way that it is aware of "objects" such as sensa. Admittedly, the questions I just mentioned, which I do not want to pursue, arise here as well. But, there is one point we should note. Berkeley was forced to acknowledge a second relation that held when a mental substance was aware of itself. Transposed into Moore's talk about acts, this would mean that Berkeley's claim that a self had a *notion* of itself would amount to the introduction of a second relation whereby acts, by standing in that relation to themselves, could be said to be self-awarenesses. The pattern is actually adopted by Sartre in *The Transcendence of the Ego*. Sartre, while proclaiming himself an opponent of idealism and purporting to offer a refutation of it, accepts what Moore takes to be the heart of a consistent idealist's position: the acceptance of the claim that acts, to exist, must be experienced. He denies that this means that such an act must be an *object* of awareness in the sense that there is some *other* act which is an awareness of it. Taking a cue from Berkeley, Sartre holds that the act in question stands to itself in the second relation when it stands in the relation "is an awareness of" to some *object*.[4] Thus, on Sartre's pattern we would have

    (1) $DA(m_a, s_1)$

and

    (2) $SA(m_a, m_a)$

with 'SA' standing for the second relation. Putting it this way does not capture the flavor of Sartre's theme, since much is said to argue that SA is *not a relation, as DA is*, and, hence, in (2), m_a is not a "term," as s_1 is in (1). Such details aside, and ignoring the incredible terminological morass that results from Sartre's way of putting his view, the point is that he presents a position that *denies, first*, that DA suffices to analyze our awareness of acts, *second*, that to hold that each act is "grasped" by an awareness is to invite an infinite regress, and hence, *third*, that one is forced to acknowledge that acts like m_a exist without, *in any sense*, having something be "aware of" them.

All this is not merely to make "historical" connections. Such points illustrate the oversimplified pattern of Moore's argument and point to a fundamental flaw in it. Moore simply proceeds to assume that acts like m_a stand in the same relation of awareness to physical objects that they do to sensa or to other acts. That is, he simply asserts that we are, in his latter phrase, "directly aware" of physical objects. But, one rather straightforward way of understanding the idealist's position is that the latter claims that we are *not* directly aware of physical objects but only of sensa or "sensations." Hence, Moore merely begs the question.[5] Obviously, he later realized this, and that was *one* of the reasons he came to express dissatisfaction with "The Refutation of Idealism."[6] The structural evidence for this is that he later distinguished IA from DA and sought to refute idealism by establishing (5′) with radically different arguments.

I have not claimed that Moore's "first stage" of the argument is question-begging. The distinction between act and object and the analysis of the perceptual situation when one has, as he puts it, "an awareness of blue" can be taken to establish the logical independence of the object from the act. What this leads one to conclude is that a sense datum can exist without being an object of awareness. Hence, if Moore establishes anything, by the argument of "The Refutation," he establishes that there can be unsensed sensa. By the time of "The Status of Sense Data," of 1913-14, he was quite clear that the pattern of argument of "The Refutation" established the *possibility* of the existence of unsensed sensa, now called 'sensibles', and he cited a "strong propensity to believe" that such sensibles did in fact exist even though they were not experienced. "We must, for instance, suppose that the sensibles which I should see now, if I were at the other end of the room, or if I were looking under the table, exist at this moment, though they are not being experienced."[7] The problem with the argument of "The Refutation" is the assumption that physical objects are the objects of acts of direct awareness, or direct apprehension, which leads Moore to conclude that physical objects, which *we know* to exist as experienced, have been shown to be capable of existence unexperienced. Once he distinguishes IA from DA, and, in effect, adopts the pattern of representative realism, the illicit argument for realism that ends "The Refutation" no longer jibes with his analysis.

From what he later wrote, it appears that Moore had believed that by establishing the existence of unsensed sensa, such as colored patches, he had shown them to be parts of the surface of a physical object. Later, holding that sense data such as toothaches and after-images could not exist unperceived,[8] he concluded that no sense data could.[9] This led him to hold that one did not directly apprehend such "parts" of physical objects, though he also was inclined, on other grounds, to think that one did so apprehend such surfaces.[10] Moore's later rejection of the claim that an object that was in fact directly apprehended could exist unperceived reflected a drastic shift in his thought, as well as a sharp break with Russell. Moreover, he was not forced to so totally reject his earlier pattern. It would be consistent with themes of his later discussion to hold that *some* data of direct apprehension could exist unperceived, but other sense data could not. For, his earlier pattern would allow him to hold that there is a necessary "synthetic" connection between the property of *being a toothache* and that of *being perceived*, but no such connection holds between *being blue* and *being perceived*. Moore seemed to move from denying his earlier claim in the case of data like toothaches to denying that it held for any object of direct apprehension. I suspect that the transition is aided by his concern with the fact that a property like *blue* applies to sense data that are after-images as well as to data we directly apprehend when we "see" physical objects. Be that as it may, it should be emphasized that what Moore rejected was that he had proved the idealist wrong. For, he no longer believed that he had shown that sense data *can* exist unperceived. He did not reject the claim that the idealist had not shown that *to be is to be perceived*. The idealist must still merely intuit the connection between *existence* and *being perceived*, as Moore apparently intuits the connection between *being a sense datum* and *existing only if perceived*. Although he did feel that one should offer an argument to show that such was the case, he could not think of one.[11] We can then see what led Moore to the pattern on which he argues for (5′). As we noted, one attempt to do so involved the claim that any argument that establishes that (5′) is false is more likely to have a false premise or be logically inept than to have a true conclusion. The other line of argument is more complex, far less clear, and far more consequential for the subsequent history of philosophy. It is that argument or, rather, pattern of argument that defends the truths of Common Sense.

Moore's other argument against the idealist takes the form of an attack on the attempt to construe physical objects as, in some sense, bundles of phenomena on the basis of the claim that phenomenal objects are the only objects we are directly acquainted with. We have already examined that part of his argument which culminates in the claim that (5′) is true. What he must do is establish the truth of (5′) to complete the critique of the phenomenalist's position. He begins by speaking of "Common Sense" in the following way:

> There are, it seems to me, certain views about the nature of the Universe, which . . . are so universally held that they may, I think, fairly be called the views of Common Sense. . . . Common Sense . . . has, I think, very definite views to the effect that certain kinds of things certainly are in the Universe, and as to some of the ways in which these kinds of things are related to one another. . . .
>
> To begin with, then, it seems to me we certainly believe that there are in the Universe enormous numbers of material objects.[12]

He further characterizes the Common Sense view of "material objects" by holding that it is a belief that men have held as long as they have believed anything at all. It is not only a belief that men have always held but a belief that has always remained the same. In addition to such a belief, there are other beliefs of Common Sense to the effect that there are a great number of "mental acts" or "acts of Consciousness." Moreover, there are Common Sense beliefs about the relation between the two kinds of things that Common Sense believes to exist: material objects and acts of consciousness. Among such relations are those that consist of experiences or perceptions of material objects and of awarenesses of facts about such objects "which I was not at the time observing, such as, for instance, the fact, of which I am now aware, that my body existed yesterday." It is a feature of our Common Sense beliefs that we further believe that we "really know" such things. And we further know that many "material objects exist when we are not conscious of them."

In saying all this, Moore claims that he has assumed that he has been using terms and phrases in their "ordinary" or "popular" meaning:

> In what I have just said, I have assumed that there is some meaning which is *the* ordinary or popular meaning of such expressions as 'The earth has existed for many years past'. And this, I am afraid, is an assumption which some philosophers are capable of disputing. They seem to think that the question 'Do you believe that the earth has existed for many years past?' is not a plain question, such as should be met either by a plain 'Yes' or 'No', or by a plain 'I can't make up my mind', but is the sort of question which can be properly met by: 'It all depends on what you mean by "the earth" and "exists" and "years": if you mean so and so, and so and so, and so and so, then I do; but if you mean so and so, and so and so, and so and so, or so and so, and so and so, and so and so, then I don't, or at least I think it is extremely doubtful.' It seems to me that such a view is as profoundly mistaken as any view can be.[13]

The mistaken view is due to a confusion between *understanding the meaning* of a statement like "There are material objects that exist unperceived" or "The earth has existed for many years past" with *knowing what it means* in the sense of being "able to *give a correct analysis* of its meaning."

In a well-known paper, Malcolm has challenged Moore's claim to be using words in their ordinary sense.[14] Malcolm speaks of ordinary and "correct" usage. But, his use of "correct" seems redundant, for the correct is no more than the prosaic. What he has in mind is that Moore is not using words in their ordinary sense since the *situation in which he uses them*, namely to respond to the philosophical sceptic or phenomenalist, is not an ordinary situation. What is an ordinary situation is specified by example. If we ask what determines an example to be an ordinary example, Malcolm, of course, can have no real answer; he can only isolate the philosophical uses from the "correct" uses. He would let matters rest there when, as I see it, what has been achieved is merely a prologue to considering the problems the philosopher's uses reveal. Yet, there is a point to this objection that focuses our attention on an ambiguity in Moore's use of "ordinary." The point, however, is far different from the one Malcolm intends. The point he wishes to make is that the phenomenalist's or sceptic's use is not an everyday use of words in the sense in which one speaks in shops and courtrooms. One raises philosophical questions only in philosophical contexts, which is to say, nonordinary contexts. This being so, the philosopher's use is nonordinary and, hence, by stipulation "incorrect." With such a line of "argument" we need not bother, since it has been exhausted in recent years. The real point involved is that in one sense Moore's talk about physical objects being known to exist and being perceived is taken as a response to a philosophical question and, hence, states a philosophical position. Insofar as stating a philosophical position involves the "extra-ordinary" use of language, Moore is not using terms in their "ordinary" and "popular" context and, hence, "sense." Insofar as he does use them in an ordinary and popular sense, he does not appear to respond to the sceptic or phenomenalist. For the latter may also acknowledge knowing, as we ordinarily speak, that there are physical objects and perceiving them. It is, then, no wonder that all Moore can say when philosophers refuse to answer with a "plain 'Yes' or 'No' " is that they are "profoundly mistaken." Wherein lies the mistake? All Moore's hypothetical opponent does is suggest that there is *a* sense in which all parties to the dispute can agree that there are physical objects that are seen, felt, etc., and that do exist when they are not being perceived. In this sense, he distinguishes the chair he sits upon from *the* winged horse of Greek mythology. But, he suggests that there is a *further* sense in which there is a dispute between phenomenalists and sceptics, on the one hand, and "realists" on the other. Consider Moore's rejection of a typical phenomenalistic pattern.

But now, I ask, is this, in fact, what you believe, when you believe you are travelling in a train? Do you not, in fact, believe that there really are wheels on which your carriage is running at the moment, and couplings between the carriages? That these things really exist, at the moment, even though nobody is seeing either them themselves, nor any appearances of them? . . . This first theory, as to our knowledge of material objects, does, I think, plainly give an utterly false account of what we do believe in ordinary life . . . so soon as you realise what it means in particular instances like that of the train . . . it seems to me to lose all its plausibility.[15]

What Moore appears to do is to claim that there is an ordinary sense of "material object" and that the phenomenalist's position, which "construes" a material object as a collection or bundle of sensa, does not "fit" with that ordinary sense. Thus, a purported philosophical *analysis* must "fit" or jibe with our ordinary common-sense beliefs. But, what does it mean for an "analysis" to *fit* with or to *contradict* such beliefs? And, for that matter, just what is an analysis as Moore understands it? If one means by giving an *analysis* doing the sort of thing some philosophers go through

consider the sentence "It's perfectly certain that that is a tree." If we are walking on a meadow in a heavy fog and a tall, indistinct object looms ahead, and one of us wonders whether it is a tree or a telephone pole, it would be a natural thing for one of us to say, "It's perfectly certain that that is a tree, because if you look carefully you will see the faint outline of the branches on either side." That is one example of circumstances in which the sentence "It's perfectly certain that that is a tree" would be correctly used, although it might not be *true* that that object was a tree. Whether or not it was a tree could be determined by walking closer to it. Consider another example . . . [16]

then clearly the philosopher who is a phenomenalist does not offer an "analysis." Although Moore sometimes seems to lapse into the elaboration of the tedious, he often does not. Perhaps this latter fact is the basis for Malcolm's criticism that Moore "misuses" the term 'know' in his reply to the phenomenalist. There are clearly two distinct tendencies in Moore's writings. One leads him to do something similar to the kind of thing Malcolm does as providing an analysis. The other leads him to undertake the *kind* of analysis we witnessed in Chapter I and shall shortly consider in taking up his arguments about particulars and identity. When he does the former, Moore writes as if he is teaching a foreigner or a child how to use English expressions in everyday mundane contexts. But, even then, he is not really lapsing into the kind of thing Malcolm does. For, what he has in mind, I believe, is that our interconnected Common Sense beliefs about material objects, consciousness, experience, space, time, etc., are related in ways that we must make explicit. Undertaking to exhibit such connections is to offer, in one sense, an "analysis" of such beliefs and the concepts they involve.

> For by knowing what they mean is often meant not merely understanding sentences in which they occur, but being able to analyze them, or knowing certain truths about them—knowing, for instance, exactly how the notions which they convey are related to or distinguished from other notions. We may, therefore, know quite well, in one sense, what a word means, while at the same time, in another sense, we may not know what it means. We may be quite familiar with the notion it conveys . . . although . . . we are quite unable to *define* it.[17]

This is one sense of engaging in "philosophical analysis." Yet, Moore also seeks a philosophical position, which involves a coherent "fitting" together of *philosophical claims*, in the traditional sense, and, finally, a *fitting* of such a position *with* the former elaboration of our ordinary "conceptual scheme" or framework of Common Sense beliefs and concepts. Thus, although Moore sometimes construes "analysis" in a way that will eventually give rise to the ordinary language tradition, he obviously takes *analysis* in other ways as well. In his well-known rejection of purported analyses of the concept *good*, along hedonistic as well as other lines, Moore held that *good* was an unanalyzable concept. What his argument amounted to was the claim that no analysis of the concept in *terms* of other concepts, i.e., taking it to be a complex concept in the sense in which *white horse* may be taken to be a complex concept with respect to the *simpler* concepts *white* and *horse*, or identifying it with a concept such as *pleasure*, would fit with certain ordinary features of our concept of goodness. That, for example, one could always conceive of the possibility that something was an instance of the concepts employed in the purported analysis and yet was not good, or vice versa, would be one such feature. Given this feature, no analysis is feasible, and, hence, we may conclude that goodness is unanalyzable. This conclusion is the result of a philosophical analysis that was not simply confined to describing features of our ordinary concept of goodness, though it involved doing that. For, it is in terms of a descriptive account that one attempts to rebut any purported analysis of goodness. Yet, one does more than describe relationships among ordinary concepts when coming to such conclusions.

Moore's point was that, given an action A,

(G)   A is good $\equiv$ A is pleasurable

is neither "analytic" nor tautological. It is, if significant, a factual claim. Hence, the hedonist cannot hold that the concept pleasure is involved in an analysis of the concept *good*. The pattern is the same one he uses in an argument against

(x) [x exists $\supset$ x is perceived]

as the rendition of "*esse est percipi*." He supports his claim by appealing to the "meaning" of the concepts. Moore held, as we shall discuss in Chapter IV, that one directly grasped both the meaning of simple concepts *and* that such concepts were simple. He was naturally led to appeal to the ordinary usage of words to support such a claim about a specific concept—*good* in this case. The point was that since (G) was not analytic, any viable philosophical position would have to understand the terms '*good*' and '*pleasure*', as used in the "theory," so that (G) did not get transformed into an analytic truth. Any theory that so transforms (G) is inadequate. Thus, the pattern of Moore's argument implicitly acknowledges the three aspects of "analysis" we noted above: (1) The elaboration of the structure of our ordinary "conceptual scheme" whereby we note that (G) is not tautological or analytic or "true by meaning." (2) A proposed philosophical position about judgments like 'x is good' that relates them, among other things, to claims like 'x is pleasant'. (3) Noting the "fit" between the statements of (2) and those of (1) in the sense, at least, that we just considered. That is, do nonanalytic sentences of (1), like (G), get "transformed" into analytic ones in (2)? Are truth values preserved? The underlying theme is no different from that whereby we expect a system of formal logic to preserve validity of "obviously valid" ordinary language arguments, as well as elucidate the "reasons" why they are valid and "resolve" uncertain cases.

Moore, as we noted in Chapter I and shall clearly see in Chapter III, held, at times, that propositions and facts exist.[18] One may reasonably suggest that he held that certain features of our ordinary beliefs were such that to accept such beliefs *implied* acknowledging propositions, facts, universals, etc. In reaching such a conclusion, one does not merely elaborate features of our ordinary conceptual scheme but argues that certain claims are *implied* by it or are *implicit* in it. Just what it means for such claims to be implied by ordinary beliefs, or implicit in their acceptance, is problematic. To spell it out involves, in effect, spelling out a further sense of "philosophical analysis." In so doing, one is not merely pointing out that we use concepts like "there are" and "proposition" in such a way that we commonly hold that there are propositions, since people believe certain propositions and, hence, it trivially follows that *there are* propositions that are believed. Furthermore, in holding that there were such things as facts, Moore was concerned with their "analysis" in the sense of asking what the *constituents* of facts were and what the *structure* or *logical form* of a fact was. He was especially concerned with such a question with regard to the facts that provided the basis for the truth of claims like "Jones believes that p"; and his concern about the existence of propositions had to do with whether or not one could analyze such facts without holding that propositions were to be included in one's ontological inventory.[19] Moore was also concerned with the classical problem of universals, and, as we shall soon see in detail, at one time he held that a particular object could be *analyzed* as a *complex of universal concepts*. In so doing, he offered an analysis of our *concept of an object* in terms of notions, such as *universal concept* and *complex of concepts*, that do not appear to be part of our ordinary conceptual apparatus or scheme. Moreover, it is not at all clear how *Common Sense* can arbitrate in such matters, unless one holds that since we do not ordinarily say such things, or, for that matter, even understand, in

an ordinary context, what they mean, it follows that such statements are pointless or meaningless. What Moore seemed to have in
mind was the idea, once again, that certain of our ordinary beliefs,
such as that different objects have the same property, must be
taken to *imply* such a *view* and that alternative *views*, such as that
universal concepts do not exist, are not compatible or do not *fit*
with our ordinary beliefs. It seems that when a philosopher holds
that material objects are really constructs from sensations, he runs
directly afoul of our beliefs regarding material objects. But, when
a philosopher holds that objects are complexes of universals, he
does not do so in that *Common Sense* neither affirms nor denies
such a claim. Yet, though our ordinary beliefs neither *directly* affirm nor deny such a claim, one may hold that a number of our
common beliefs can be affirmed and held to cohere only on the
condition that we accept such a claim. But, again, what is it to
speak of 'implication', or to hold that common beliefs "can be
affirmed" on "condition," in such matters? Moreover, a further
problem arises. Does not the phenomenalist also claim that certain
beliefs or knowledge about experience, and the process of having
experiences, *imply* that we cannot know things about material objects that we claim to know or that we commonly believe we do
know? That is, is the phenomenalist not pointing out that there
are inconsistencies implied by or involved in our ordinary conceptual scheme? And, if so, how can we dismiss such objections by
pointing out that a philosopher who raises them rejects certain beliefs of *Common Sense* or specific criteria for the application of
ordinary concepts? To think of philosophical analysis in terms of
uncovering implications of our ordinary conceptual scheme appears to provide an opening for the kind of philosophical position
that Moore seeks to reject. Moore's rejection of such philosophical
gambits thus seems to involve an arbitrary appeal to *Common
Sense* or ordinary belief. The situation can be clarified, even resolved, by making some appropriate distinctions.

Clearly, there are the common-sense beliefs and concepts of
which Moore speaks and whose structure he seeks to elaborate.
This is not to claim that the notion of a commonsensical belief, or
a belief belonging to our ordinary conceptual scheme, is unproblematic. Specifying such beliefs is not a matter of simple reporting

of usage. Be that as it may, consider a number of alternative philo-sophical positions that seek to *analyze* such beliefs, and the con-cepts they employ, without, for the moment, specifying the sense of 'analysis' involved. Let us assume that such analyses must, in some sense, *fit with* such beliefs: with the elaboration of structure that the philosopher seeks to provide. How are we to specify the sense in which the ordinary beliefs may be said to *imply* or to *fit with* or contradict philosophical claims?

One may take the phenomenalist to deny that *physical objects*, as we ordinarily understand that notion, are *literally* perceived and that we literally perceive the same "things" at different times or in different perceptual situations. The phenomenalist, then, literally denies that one "sees" the *same* chair at breakfast and dinner, the *same* house in the morning and evening, and the *same* car day after day. So interpreted, phenomenalism is open to the kind of refuta-tion by example that Moore excelled in and others have copied. One *can* so interpret the phenomenalist, but we need not do so, irrespective of how some traditional "empiricists" may have un-derstood, or thought they understood, what they were claiming. One gets a far more interesting and illuminating sense of the phe-homenalist's view if we interpret it in a different way. Let the phe-nomenalist acknowledge, along with Moore, that we may correctly say that the chair is now perceived and, moreover, is the same as the chair previously perceived. But, let such a philosopher be un-derstood to claim that this is so insofar as we speak in the contexts we are ordinarily accustomed to, and not in the context of a *philo-sophical* dispute about *perception, substance*, etc. The defender of *Common Sense* is quite right in holding that there are conditions governing our use of terms like 'same' and 'identical' in *such every-day* contexts. But, the phenomenalist raises a question about how to treat the notion of a material object so that one can respond cogently to certain dialectical puzzles that are raised about knowl-edge, experience, existence, etc. Such puzzles, and responses to them, provide another context for concepts like *material object* and *perception*. Thus, the concept of a *material object* belonging to the one context is not the same as the concept employed in the other. In holding that a material object is *really* a class of phe-nomenal entities, the phenomenalist is not denying that we literally see the same object from time to time or that we may retain the things we purchase; just as the phenomenalist is not claiming that it is appropriate to shop for a class of sensations rather than a chair. Instead, claims made in and concepts belonging to the ordinary context are *mapped against* claims and concepts of a quite extraordinary context wherein one proposes and defends philosophical *analyses*. To propose a philosophical analysis is to offer a set of interrelated concepts and claims that may be coordinated to the concepts and claims of our ordinary conceptual scheme. Hence, the ordinary claim that we see the same material object from time to time is coordinated to the claim that two phenomenal entities are members of a class which is, in turn, the *representative* of the ordinary physical object in the philosopher's scheme. So taken, the ordinary true claim is coordinated to one taken to be true in the extraordinary context. Alternatively, one may seek to map such ordinary claims and concepts onto claims involving the concept of a *material substance* or *continuant*, rather than a class of phenomenal entities. On such an alternative view or "analysis," one not only acknowledges that the chair is literally the same, as spoken about in the ordinary context, but is represented in such a way in the extraordinary context that *the* object of perception is held to be numerically identical, as spoken about in the latter context, when *it* is perceived at different times. The crucial point, though, is that the ordinary concept of a material object is no more to be identified with the materialist's concept of a continuous physical object, as used in the extraordinary context, than it is to be identified with the phenomenalist's concept of a material object as a certain kind of class of phenomenal objects. Both views employ concepts and claims that belong to a rather special context from which they partially derive their "meaning." The philosophical disagreement between them is confined to such an extraordinary context, and it is no more appropriate for a representative of the one view to applaud my claim that the chair I now sit on was the one I saw last year than it is for the other to challenge it. Both, as a minimal requirement, must fit their respective views to the elaborated detail of the ordinary context. As we noted, both do in that, on the basis of the sketch mentioned above, both views would map an ordinary statement onto a claim of the metaphysical context. It does *appear*, however, that one philosopher *seems* to reproduce the ordinary context more literally by holding that what is seen, as reconstrued in the philosophical context, is literally one and the same from time to time. Yet, that philospher does not literally reproduce the ordinary claim not only in that the notion of a material substance is not the same as our ordinary concept of a physical object but also in that the use of 'same', as it belongs to the extraordinary context, is not, if I may so put it, the *same* as our ordinary use of the term. Yet, there is a point to the claim that one philosophical position is closer to the ordinary context, even if it does not literally reproduce that context.

We can see this point by making use of Moore's distinction between DA and IA that we discussed in Chapter I. In the ordinary context, we say, or as Malcolm might put it, we "correctly" say

   (S$_1$)   I see a chair.

We do not say

   I see a chair-percept

or

   I see a chair-shaped patch of color

or

   I now perceive a sense datum caused by a chair.

In such a context, we clearly distinguish things like chairs and tables from sensations, feelings, states of mind, and so forth. Moreover, we do not take chairs to be made of sense data as they are made of wood, leather, etc., or "consist" of legs, seats, backs, and so forth. And, like Malcolm, the ordinary person does not understand what the phenomenalist is driving at when the latter holds a chair to be a "bundle" of sensa. "Bundle, like a bundle of laundry?" Thus, the phenomenalist correlates "things" in ways we do not and asserts things that one would either not "understand" or think "mad" in an ordinary context. Forget that, for the moment, and consider:

   (a)   The chair is red
   (b)   The chair is on the rug.

The phenomenalist produces correlates of (a) and (b): call them (a_p) and (b_p). They are such that

$$(a) \equiv (a_p)$$
$$(b) \equiv (b_p).$$

A correlate of (S_1) is constructed in the same way. After all, much of the development of this view is devoted to such schematic constructions. Suppose a phenomenalist follows Moore's analysis of perception, except for taking material objects to be classes of sensa, and speaks of indirectly apprehending such a class when one directly apprehends a sense datum belonging to it. Thus, we may indirectly apprehend the same object from time to time but never directly apprehend the same sense datum more than once. The phenomenalist, then, has a way of acknowledging that we "see" the same material object on different occasions.[20] The direct "realist" does not distinguish DA from IA and holds that we *perceive* the *same* chair from time to time. Both views, in a sense, fit *their* analyses to (S_1), as they do to (a) and (b). But the direct realist, not distinguishing DA from IA, develops a view that is "closer" to the ordinary view reflected in ordinary usage. For, we ordinarily do not make a distinction corresponding to the phenomenalist's distinction. The philosophical realist and the nonphilosophical "ordinary man" share a theme that is rejected by the phenomenalist. To put it another way, there is a feature of the direct realist's view that corresponds to our ordinary way of talking about perception. To take such a fit with the ordinary scheme as a merit is to do something different from taking the fit with (a), (b), and (S_1) as a requirement. To do so is to return to the sort of thing Malcolm does and that Moore sometimes seems to lapse into. The dialectics of such moves are not my concern in this book, though from time to time we shall come across similar themes. All I wish to note here is that one line of argument Moore employs in his defense of (5') may involve him in such a move. Malcolm's complaint that Moore misuses ordinary language can now be more fully understood. Moore's mistake is to take the phenomenalist's talk seriously and to deny that the phenomenalist is correct. The latter's *view* does not "fit" with our ordinary beliefs. Hence, by responding to a philosophical question, Moore misuses language.

One should not *respond* to such questions; one should *recite* tales illustrating ordinary uses. This approach obviously ignores one causal feature of the development of phenomenalism. In addition to the kinds of cases Malcolm cites, there are many and well-known features of our "common-sense" beliefs and scientific findings about perception. Some of these do not seem to fit very comfortably with the unreflective way we ordinarily consider perceptual situations. The phenomenalist is attempting to reconcile the resulting tensions, just as the *philosophical* realist advocates an alternative way of achieving the same result. After all, that is what philosophers attempt when, like Moore, they seek to analyze the perceptual situation. One may ignore such problems or even not understand them. This is one thing. Offering an argument is another thing. Malcolm does not offer an argument, merely a stipulation. At a crucial point, Moore *seems* to do the same.

Yet, although Moore may have argued weakly for direct realism in "The Refutation," he has adopted the pattern of an indirect realist, through the introduction of IA, in *Some Main Problems*. Both Moore and the phenomenalist, then, develop views that do not jibe with the common-sense "failure" to make the distinction. Moreover, Moore develops the distinction to deal with the same familiar puzzles that the phenomenalist seeks to resolve. Thus, Moore certainly cannot take the failure to make such a distinction as a mark of an analysis that fits with Common Sense, in the way he is denying that the phenomenalist's analysis fits. Moore seeks to refute the phenomenalist and defend his own indirect realism by holding that the former's view does not jibe with

(S$_2$)   The chair is not *composed of* phenomena,

taken as a statement of, or implicit in, Common Sense, and that Moore's own view *does fit* with (S$_2$).[21] Defending a phenomenalistic analysis along the lines I have been using, one could reply that if the phrase 'composed of', in (S$_2$), is taken as we ordinarily use such a phrase, (S$_2$) is acceptable. The phenomenalist is not claiming that the chair is "composed of" sensa as it is composed of wood or a seat, etc. The phenomenalist need only deny (S$_2$) *if it is understood* to be elliptical for a denial of the phenomenalistic analysis of concepts of the ordinary context. To say the chair is

composed of sensa merely means, in short, that the chair is correlated to a class of phenomena, on the phenomenalist's analysis, in
order to deal with the classical puzzles of perception, knowledge,
etc. Thus, the phenomenalist denies that (S_2) can be effectively
employed by Moore to rebut phenomenalism and insists that to
so use (S_2) amounts to packing a realistic philosophical position
into "Common Sense." It would require that a philosophical
analysis jibe with Common Sense, already understood in terms of
one philosophical analysis: realism. In terms of (S_2), the phenomenalist has a point, but has been forced to argue in such a way that
Moore's point can now be simply and cogently made.

The phenomenalist has implicitly acknowledged that the class
of phenomena associated with the chair (call the class '$\{C\}$') can be
talked about in the ordinary context. Phenomena and collections
of them are quite commonsensical *things*, though perhaps not
everyday topics of conversation. We can, then, consider two statements of the ordinary context:

(S_3) $\{C\}$ = the chair on the rug

and

(S_4) $\{C\}$ is "associated with" the chair on the rug.

Speaking commonsensically, we can make quite clear what "associated with" means, in an ordinary sense of 'means'. In the terms
of the ordinary context, (S_3) is false. On the phenomenalist's account, $\{C\}$ is coordinated with the chair. Such a coordination is
what the *nonordinary* use of the notions of 'the chair' and of '$\{C\}$'
amount to. Thus, the phenomenalist arrives at a purported identity which, of course, does not jibe with (S_3) being false. Moore, by
contrast, attempts to deal with the same puzzles that perplex the
phenomenalist, but Moore deals with them in such a manner that
his treatment of the notions of 'the chair' and '$\{C\}$' involves a denial of a corresponding identity statement. Hence, Moore's handling
of such concepts, in an admittedly philosophical or nonordinary
context, does jibe with the falsity of (S_3) *of the ordinary context*.
The phenomenalist's insistence on the separation of the ordinary
and the special or philosophical context does not suffice to blunt
Moore's point. The latter can be reinforced by considering (S_4).

Since one would naturally specify the phenomena "in" {C} by reference to the particular physical object, there is a sense in which (S_4) may be taken to be tautological or analytic or *redundant*.[22] In short, we "mean" by 'the class {C}', 'the class of phenomena *associated with* the chair on the rug'. Hence, if we replace the expression '{C}' by the descriptive phrase, we get something on the order of 'The woman with Jones is with Jones'. This could explain why the phenomenalist might fail to see that his view does not jibe with the denial of (S_3). For, thinking in terms of (S_4), the phenomenalist notes that the statement of the ordinary context is, in a way, "analytic"; and the correlation of {C} to the chair makes the claim that the chair is a class of sensa "analytic". It does so in that it (a) reflects a phenomenalistic analysis of material objects and (b) will be a formal truth in such a schema since 'the chair' and '{C}' of ordinary language are coordinated to the *same* linguistic pattern of the schema. The phenomenalist, therefore, may think that by holding that (S_4) is "analytic" in the ordinary context, as well as in the proposed schema, (S_4) has been adequately reflected and (S_3) shown to be true, properly understood, in the ordinary context. The point about (S_3) is mistaken, possibly owing to the mixing of questions we just separated, and, moreover, so is the claim about (S_4).

{C} will contain phenomena. We assume, recall, that the recognition of phenomenal entities, sense data, mental states, etc., is part of the ordinary context. That is what both Moore and the phenomenalist, as I have portrayed the latter, accept. Consider, then, a particular phenomenal entity, a sense datum, "caused" by or "associated with" the chair. It is a *fact* that the particular datum was caused by or associated with the chair. Insofar as *we distinguish* the chair from the set {C}, we hold *the connection* between them to consist of a number of such facts, as well as some general statements of lawful correlations between data of certain kinds and the presence of physical objects. But, such a factual connection is lost upon the phenomenalist's reconstruction, which can reflect it only in terms of factual connections with other members of {C}. Insofar as we acknowledge the chair and {C} as separate "things," in the ordinary context, we recognize that (S_4) is not an analytic statement, properly understood. Actually, a simple feaure of Russell's theory of descriptions reveals the point. (S₄), in explicit form, contains two descriptive clauses:

> *the class* of phenomena associated with *the chair*. . . .

Thus (S₄) states that *there is a class*, obviously taken as nonempty, and, hence, *there are elements*, and that *there is a chair and* that the elements of the class are *in fact* "associated with" (causally connected with, etc.) the chair.

The point here is not the same as the one Strawson seeks to establish, by using a similar argument, when he rejects "bundle" theories of the self. In that case, there is a question of whether or not *there is an entity*—the self. Here, *both* the phenomenalist and Moore have *accepted* physical objects and phenomena. This is not a purported *proof* that physical objects cannot be shown to be phenomena. It is an argument that if one starts with the recognition of two sorts of *objects* of "experience," physical objects and phenomena, as recognized in the ordinary context, the present attempt to defend phenomenalism, from Moore's defense of Common Sense, does not succeed. The phenomenalist must, then, challenge the Common Sense claim that physical objects are *not* identical with "collections" of sensa. This would return us to Moore's assertion that he "knows that the pencil exists" *immediately*. I am not here arguing that the phenomenalist fails, merely that the attempt to construe phenomenalism as not being a challenge to Common Sense fails. As some would put it, I am not arguing against classical phenomenalism, which challenges Moore's purported Common Sense "knowledge," but against the "reconstructed" version of phenomenalism which seeks to reconcile the classical view, as "reconstructed," with Common Sense. Moore, I think, was right on two counts: phenomenalism does challenge Common Sense and, consequently, if certain Common Sense beliefs are correct the phenomenalist is mistaken. There still remains the problem, for Moore, of cogently arguing *for* realism by providing an adequate philosophical analysis of his own.[23] This returns us to the problematic relation IA.

III

Thought and Belief

Moore's account of perception depends on the discussion of belief and the introduction of propositional entities. A thought, say m_1, that occurs at a particular time has the content it does because of the proposition it directly apprehends. Propositions give content to thoughts. Such thoughts would also have certain generic properties. For example, a thought that a_1 is W is different from a doubt. We can consider a set of predicates, 'T', 'D', etc., to stand for generic properties that we would ordinarily indicate by 'thinking', 'doubting', etc. (or 'is a thought', 'is a doubt', etc.). Thus, when there is a thought that a_1 is W, we have a situation expressed by the following:

$$T(m_1) \ \& \ DA(m_1, [Wa_1]).$$

The first conjunct tells us what sort of mental act m_1 is and the second tells us what its content is. Moore comes to be suspicious of propositional entities as his lectures progress. He comes to hold that propositional entities are not acceptable, since they are introduced to account for false belief and he cannot accept the introduction of an entity to ground a falsehood. What he has in mind is this. If we confine ourselves to true statements, sentences like 'Wa_1' can be taken to stand for facts. When we deal with false sentences, we do not have such facts, since it is the very absence of a fact that makes the sentence false. Hence, m_1 could not stand in a relation to a fact when it is a false thought or belief. Thus, one introduces propositions to give content to false beliefs. Treating thought and belief uniformly in the case of true and false beliefs, one then holds that in the case of a true belief what is directly apprehended is also a proposition and not a fact. This also fits with the idea that we can truly think that a_1 is W without apprehending the fact that it is. Moore, bothered by propositional entities, overlooks this latter small point and seeks to revise his analysis to rid it of the ontological commitment to propositions. The alternative he develops is that a belief has the content it does by standing in relation to a fact. If the fact exists, the belief is true; if the fact does not exist, the belief is false. Facts become both the ground of truth and falsity for beliefs and the basis for their having the content they do have. Between beliefs and facts there is then a fundamental relation Moore calls 'referring', which supposedly replaces the relation between a belief and a proposition and that of the latter to a fact. Let me spell this out a bit.

The view appealing to propositions and facts is more complicated than some realize. Not only must one speak of a connection between the thought m_1 and the proposition $[Wa_1]$, but one must also recognize a connection between the proposition and the fact whose existence makes it true and whose nonexistence makes it false. Thus, there are two crucial features. One is expressed by

$$DA(m_1, [Wa_1]).$$

The other could be expressed by

$$AB([Wa_1], Wa_1)$$

where the sign '$[Wa_1]$' stands for the proposition that a_1 is W and the sign 'Wa_1' stands for the fact whose existence would make that proposition true. But, just as propositions were introduced to supply another term for the relation DA when thoughts were false, we now face the quandry of introducing another term for the relation AB in such cases. For, the proposition is *about* a certain fact whether that fact exists or not! Hence, one who introduces propositions to analyze the case of false belief is forced to speak of such things standing in a relation to facts, whether the latter exist or not. We, thus, come to speak of existent and nonexistent facts, or, more traditionally, we can speak of possible facts that may or may not exist. In either case, we introduce an ontological category in addition to propositions and "ordinary" existent facts. This suggests that it is a mistake to introduce propositions in the first place. Why not simply speak of possible facts? The thought m_1 would then have the content it does because it stands in a relation to a possible fact. One could speak of the thought intending such a possibility and the relation being an intentional one. I suspect one reason Moore rejects propositional entities is an implicit recognition of the need to speak of nonexistent facts with or without propositions. In fact, it may even be quite explicitly recognized at some places in *Some Main Problems*.[1] Be that as it may, Moore introduces a variant of the appeal to possible facts. He speaks of facts and of nonexistent facts. One could construe his talk of nonexistent facts as simply another way of speaking about possible facts, since particular thoughts would intend and, hence, be related to nonexistent facts. This would be to recognize nonexistent facts as entities introduced into the analysis of intentional contexts. But, another way of taking what Moore says is to hold that the intentional relation is unique in that it does not require relata. Thus, an act can intend a nonexistent fact, but that does not mean that one gives any ontological status to the nonexistent fact. Rather, it is a unique feature of intentionality that we point to when we speak of nonexistent facts. As far as I can see, there is no difference that makes a difference in the two alternatives. To avoid possible facts by citing the uniqueness of a relation that is sometimes not a relation is to avoid an ontological commitment by a feat of verbal gymnastics, rather than by a succinct philosophical analysis. Unfortunately, this is what Moore appears to do. In any case, he must take one of the "two" alternatives when he abandons propositions. That he does, and must, is obscured by the way he speaks of belief and a complication that results. Moore appears to abandon propositions by speaking of *a belief* standing in a relation to a fact. But what Moore means by "a belief" is a kind of belief and not a particular act of thought or belief. Thus, the belief that a_1 is W can be instanced or held on various occasions. So we must distinguish a belief, or thought, in the sense of a particular act that occurs at a particular time, from a belief in the sense of something common to several acts: *the particular act* of thought, which is my belief or thought at a certain time, that a_1 is W from *the belief* that a_1 is W. The latter is like a common characteristic that particular acts exemplify. What makes m_1 a belief that a_1 is W is that it is an instance of the property which all thoughts that a_1 is W, and only those, exemplify. Such characteristics replace the propositional entities of Moore's earlier discussion. These characteristics may be suggestively called propositional characters. They, in turn, must play the role propositions were required to play. They must be held to stand in some relation to the fact whose existence makes *a belief* true and whose nonexistence makes it false. We are, then, back to possible facts or the unique intentional relation that is not always a relation. In a way, then, Moore retains propositions under the name of beliefs, owing to his not clearly separating a particular act of thought from the kind of thought that it is. Only, propositional entities are now properties of particular acts, and the relation of an act to a proposition is the relation of exemplifying rather than of directly apprehending.

Let the predicate 'B' stand for the generic property all acts of belief exemplify, the predicate 'F_1' stand for the property all acts that are beliefs that a_1 is W share, and '*Ref.*' for the relation between a *kind* of belief and the fact whose existence makes the belief true. We, then, have the following analysis of an intentional situation:

$$B(m_1) \ \& \ F_1(m_1) \ \& \ Ref. \ (F_1, Wa_1).$$

The first conjunct expresses a fact that a particular has a certain property and the second that the same particular has another property as well. The third conjunct is quite different. Before considering it, we may note that for such belief contexts Moore's relation AB may now be analyzed in terms of the relation *Ref.* Let us call the sentence 'p' *the sentence expressing* the kind of belief or propositional character referred to by a predicate 'F_1' when '*Ref.* (F_1, p)' is true. Assume 'p' is a subject predicate sentence or a conjunction, disjunction, etc., of such. A kind of belief or, better yet, a propositional or intentional character is *about* an object a if that character stands in the relation *Ref.* to a fact of which a is a constituent. One can put it linguistically as follows: a propositional character is about something if the sentence expressing it contains a term standing for the thing in question. The qualification about subject-predicate sentences occurs since it is problematic to speak of universal or existential facts, as well as of quantified sentences being about something. For that matter, corresponding questions may be raised about conjunctions, etc. We shall ignore such issues for the time being. Since Moore's concern is really with an existential sentence and, moreover, one that is implicitly understood to claim that one and only one material object exists related to a specific sensum, we shall take him to hold that an existential sentence asserting that something unique exists is about the object whose existence makes the sentence true. Thus, in such cases a propositional character is about an object if the sentence expressing the character is "made true" by the existence of the object.

In a derivative sense, one may also speak of particular acts of thought being about objects if the former exemplify a propositional character that is about the object. To say a mental act indirectly apprehends an object is to say that act is about the object. The key relation, however, is *Ref.*, and a fundamental question remains about the nature of sentences like '$Ref.(F_1,Wa_1)$'. What sort of truths and falsehoods are such sentences? Or, what is the connection between a propositional character and a fact? Moore's solution is simple. We use one and the same sentence to indicate a belief and a fact:

> It is, therefore, I think, true that *the* fact to which a belief refers is always the fact which *has the very same name* which we have to use in naming the belief. But obviously the fact that this is the case won't do as a *definition* of what we mean by the fact to which a belief refers. It cannot possibly be the case that what we mean by saying that a belief is true, is merely that there is in the Universe the fact which *has the same name*. If this were so, no belief could possibly be true, until it had a name. It must be the case therefore that there is always some *other* relation between a true belief and the fact to which it refers—some *other* relation which is *expressed* by this identity of name.[2]

Since the use of the same verbal expression to stand for two things, the belief and fact, indicates a relation between them, Moore proceeds to specify what the relation is. Note that the belief spoken of is a *kind* of belief or propositional character, as we have construed it. Thus, when we inquire into what the relational predicate

'*Ref.*' stands for, we are raising the same problem Moore deals with. However, Moore's way of putting the matter suggests a modification in the schema we have been using. A sentence like '*Ref.*(F_1,Wa_1)' does not reflect his point that we use the same sentence to stand for the two things that stand in the relation we are concerned about. Yet, if we use '*Ref.*(Wa_1,Wa_1)', with the first occurrence of 'Wa_1' standing for the propositional character and the second for the fact, we invite ambiguity. We can capture what he is after by a simple device. Let us return to the way we indicated propositions by putting brackets around the sentence when we refer to the propositional character and simply use the sentence without brackets to stand for the fact. So our sentence now becomes '*Ref.*$([Wa_1],Wa_1)$'. We may, then, be said to use the same sentence to stand for both the fact and the propositional character, but we do not quite use the same expression and hence avoid an obvious ambiguity. The use of such a sign for the propositional character reflects something else. As Moore sees it, there is a necessary connection between the propositional character $[Wa_1]$ and the fact indicated by 'Wa_1'. Assuming uniqueness, it is the character that stands in *Ref.* to the fact, and the same sort of thing may be said for the fact. Thus, if we treat the sign '$[Wa_1]$' as a predicate of the same logical kind as predicates like 'W', since it stands for a property of particulars, we may construe such a predicate in terms of

(I) $(\iota f)Ref.(f,Wa_1)$

just as we may construe an expression standing for the fact in terms of

(II) $(\iota p)Ref.([Wa_1],p)$

with 'p' as a variable ranging over facts. Whether (I) and (II) are as symmetrical as would appear, we shall consider later. Let us continue to use the sentence to stand for the fact (existent or nonexistent, recall) and note that we then have two ways to indicate the propositional character: by '$[Wa_1]$' or by '$(\iota f)Ref.(f,Wa_1)$'. The necessary connection between such a character and its corresponding fact would be reflected, in the first case, by a rule permitting the formation of predicates for propositional characters by putting sentences in brackets and, in the second case, by an appropriate existential assumption. To ask for the basis for either such a rule or such assumptions is to return to the question about the relation *Ref.* I said earlier that Moore's solution is simple. He holds that we know what such a relation is by "acquaintance" and, moreover, that we know which fact is related to a propositional character if we know the propositional character. To know what is believed, i.e., to apprehend a proposition or, as we may now put it, to have an act exemplifying a propositional character, is to know what fact it refers to. Such claims, of course, raise further issues. Moore says:

Obviously this expression 'referring to' stands for some relation which each true belief has to one fact and to one only; and which each false belief has to no fact at all; and the difficulty was to define this relation. Well, I admit I can't define it, in the sense of analysing it completely: I don't think this can be done, without analysing belief. But obviously from the fact that we can't analyse it, it doesn't follow that we may not know perfectly well *what* the relation is; we may be perfectly well *acquainted* with it; it may be perfectly familiar to us; and we may know both that there is such a relation, and that this relation is essential to the definition of truth. And what I want to point out is that we do in this sense *know* this relation. . . . Take any belief you like; it is, I think, quite plain that there is just one fact, and only one, which would have being—would be in the Universe, if the belief were true; and which would have no being—would simply *not be,* if the belief were false. And as soon as we know what the belief is, we know just as well and as certainly what the fact is which in this sense corresponds with it.[3]

and later,

We know that this is so; and of course we could not know it, unless we are *acquainted* with the relation between the fact and the belief, in virtue of which just the one fact and one fact only corresponds to each different belief. I admit that the analysis of this relation is difficult. But any attempt to analyse it, of course, presupposes that there is such a relation and that we are acquainted with it. If we weren't acquainted with it, we couldn't even try to analyse it. . . .
. . . in merely attempting to answer these questions, we do, I think, presuppose that we are already acquainted with it—that we have it before our minds.[4]

We, then, know three things by "acquaintance": that there is the relation *Ref.*, *what* its role is in connecting beliefs and facts, and given any belief we know which fact it *refers* to. It is interesting that Moore speaks of our being acquainted with the relation rather than saying that we directly apprehend it. On the way he uses 'direct apprehension', he speaks of our directly apprehending sensa, in that they are objects of sensation, and propositions, in that we grasp the meaning of sentences. He apparently did not hold, *then*, that when we directly apprehend a sense datum, say a white patch, that we directly apprehend a universal property—the shade of color that the patch *has*. The color that we sense or perceive is apparently, for Moore at this time, a particular quality instance. He wonders, in *Some Main Problems*, whether there is also a universal which such quality instances exemplify, as in his article "Identity," or if the universal property can be construed in terms of membership in a resemblance class. Such universals, or relational universals like *resemblance*, would apparently be apprehended as propositions are. They would be "present to the mind" or conceived and, hence, objects of acquaintance, but they would not be apprehended in sensation. To have such a pattern jibe with a principle of acquaintance would seem to require that one hold that we can conceptually apprehend such (simple) universals only if we *experience* instances of them. This raises a question about the need to experience the terms of a relation if one experiences an instance of the relation. We shall return to this question shortly in connection with the relation *Ref.* There is a further question about the connection between the universal concept, which is "held before the mind," and the universal property that a quality instance exemplifies. (An object, such as a colored sense datum, will *have* such a property since it *contains* an appropriate quality instance.) The concept *in* the *thought* would appear to be the same as the universal that is exemplified. To have an idea or concept of white is thus to be *in a relation* to that universal; to be white is to be *in a different relation* to it. The proposition (belief) that an act (self) directly apprehends could be taken to contain the universal (concept, property). This pattern requires a number of "predication" relations: that in the proposition, that between a quality instance and the universal, that between a particular and a quality instance. Such a pattern is in a familiar tradition that takes a "form" to *inform* both a mind and an object. In the one case, this results in knowledge; in the other case, the result is an object of a *kind*. Whatever problems reside in the claim that there are different ways in which a form *informs*, the gambit avoids *the* problem faced by those who take the concept to be *of*, rather than identical with, the universal property. This problem concerns the connection of the concept and the property, and, hence, it is also a problem about the connection of propositions with facts. Some seek to avoid the problem by denying facts as grounds of truth. Others, such as Russell in 1905-7 and Moore in "The Nature of Judgment," identify facts with true propositions. Russell also recognized "fictions" or nonexistent facts, and Moore, then, acknowledged false propositions as entities. In *Some Main Problems*, Moore, like Russell in 1910, holds to a correspondence theory of truth. Hence, he separates beliefs (propositions) from facts. Thus, he faces the problem of their connection. This question arises in his discussion of the relation *Ref.* But, it is not clear whether concepts are constituents of beliefs (as propositions or propositional characters) *and* of facts. In any case, *Ref.* is a universal and we are supposedly "acquainted" with it in the sense that it can be "held before the mind." But, a fundamental problem remains. If we apprehend it in *that* sense, did we at least once apprehend it, or an instance of it, as relating a proposition (belief, propositional character) and what the proposition *refers to*? The question is awkward on two counts. First, as we are apprehending *a fact*, that a proposition stands in *Ref.* to some fact (existent or nonexistent), we are using 'apprehend' in the sense in which one apprehends that a patch is white or that a patch is to the left of another. Yet, one *constituent* of the fact is a proposition. Second, on Moore's pattern one knows what fact a proposition (belief) refers to without apprehending the fact. It suffices to *grasp* the belief, to know what the belief is, in order to know what fact it refers to. Of course, Moore's view is not unique in this respect. Anyone who deals with the question will have to hold that we do know what fact a belief refers to without directly apprehending the fact. However, to hold that on *some* occasion one directly apprehends a proposition in the relation *Ref.* (or an instance of it) to the corresponding fact and, hence, knows the relation by direct apprehension goes against both the way Moore treats concepts (and our grasp of them) and the way he argues for our knowing what the relation *Ref.* is.

He appears to hold that whenever *we have a concept* "before our minds," there exists such a concept. It is enough to know, in an informal sense, that we have the idea of a relation between facts and beliefs to know that the relation labeled '*Ref.*' exists. Similarly, one might hold that the concept of a unicorn exists since we have the idea of one or can imagine one. One consequence of identifying *concepts* with universal *properties*, while retaining the ordinary force of the former term, is that a relation like *Ref.* exists not only as an object of conception but as a relation between a belief and a fact. In this respect, *Ref.* is quite different from the concept of a unicorn, which does not exist as a property of anything on the ground that we can conceive of such a property (or thing). All this raises further problems about concepts and properties that we shall return to later. Knowing that there is the concept *Ref.* and knowing its role does not guarantee that we know its "analysis." To know its analysis would be to hold the relation before our minds and to see that some set of terms other than '*Ref.*' refers to the same relation. There is also a weaker sense of "analysis." We could give a definition that would pick out some relation that would be equivalent to *Ref.* in the sense that a fact and belief stood in *Ref.* if and only if they stood in this other relation. Moore's notion of analysis stems from his early views about concepts. Some concepts are complex, some simple; but all concepts are objective existents independent of the minds which grasp them or are "acquainted with" them. To see that a concept is simple or complex and, if the latter, what its constituents are is a matter of direct inspection. Hence, it is difficult, if not impossible, to give criteria for analysis. One need only recall the notorious discussions about the concept of goodness and the "naturalistic fallacy." Moore's earlier views still appear to hold in *Some Main Problems of Philosophy*.

The only point as to which I can see any room for doubt whether these definitions do fulfill all the requirements of a definition of the words 'true' and 'false' as we should apply them to this particular belief, is that it may be doubted whether when we say that the belief is 'true' or 'false', these properties of 'correspondence to a fact' and 'not corresponding to a fact' are the properties which we actually *have before our minds* and express by those words. This is a question which can only be settled by actual inspection; and I admit that it is difficult to be quite sure what result inspection yields.[5]

But, it also appears that *Ref.* may be incapable of analysis and that no analysis is really necessary. We can indicate the relation we mean by the definite description we have used: the relation that holds (necessarily) between any belief and one and only one fact if the belief is true. We could do the same for the color vermilion by identifying it as the color of such and such an object or the *n*th color on some color chart, etc., without being able to give constituent concepts or a definition of the term 'vermilion', in the sense in which we can give a definition of 'unicorn' and perhaps hold that the concept of a unicorn is complex. Vermilion would, then, be incapable of analysis. We could "see" by direct inspection that it is a simple concept. Sometimes *Ref.* appears to Moore to be like vermilion.

The essential point is to concentrate attention upon the relation *itself*: to hold it before your mind, in the sense in which when I name the color 'vermilion', you can hold before your mind the colour that I mean. If you are not acquainted with this relation in the same sort of way as you are acquainted with the colour vermilion, no amount of words will serve to explain what it is, any more than they could explain what vermilion is like to a man born blind.[6]

Note that we are to hold vermilion "before our minds" and not that we are to directly apprehend a patch of that color. Of course, there is a play on the term 'acquaintance' here. We can hold vermilion before our minds now, since we have been acquainted with it in the sense of directly apprehending a patch of that color—otherwise the point about the blind man is irrelevant. We can be acquainted with *Ref.*, not because we have directly apprehended an instance of that relation, but because we have the idea of a relation between a fact and a belief. In the one case, we may be said to experience the color; in the other case, we experience thinking about a relation, not the relation itself. Yet, somehow doing the latter involves the existence of the relation as more than an object of thought or as more than a partial content of a thought, for it holds as a relation between a belief and a fact.

What is involved in Moore's claim of acquaintance with *Ref.* can be seen in terms of our sketch of his analysis of intentional contexts. Consider a thought that there is a griffin with 'G' standing for the property, or concept, *being a griffin*. Then we have

$$(A) \quad Tm_i \ \& \ [(\exists x)Gx]\,m_i \ \& \ (\exists R_1)R_1\{[(\exists x)Gx]\,,(\exists x)Gx\}$$

where, recall, the sign '$[(\exists x)Gx]$' stands for the propositional *character* that thoughts have when they are thoughts that there exists a griffin. Given that (A) is true, it does not follow that '$(\exists x)GX$' is also true.[7] But, consider a thought that there is a relation, *Ref.*, between a particular thought that a_1 is W and a purported fact. We would, then, have

$$(B) \quad Tm_n \ \& \ [(\exists R_1)R_1\{[Wa_1]\,,Wa_1\}]\,m_n \ \& \ (\exists R_2)R_2$$
$$\{[(\exists R_1)\,R_1\,\{[Wa_1]\,,Wa_1\}]\,,(\exists R_1)R_1\{[Wa_1]\,,Wa_1\}\}$$

In effect, Moore is arguing that since we have such thoughts, there is a relation R_1, which we have called '*Ref.*'. Thus, since (B) is true, so is

$$(C) \quad (\exists R_1)R_1\,([Wa_1]\,,Wa_1),$$

assuming that 'Wa_1' stands for a fact. Since there is, first, a propositional character, whose existence we know of because we have certain thoughts, and, second, a fact the sentence states, there is, then, *a further fact*, namely that the relation *Ref.* holds between the character and the first fact. The question then arises of how the truth of (B) grounds the truth of (C). Moore holds that since there are thoughts like m_n, the relation *Ref.* must exist; but, since this involves the inference from (B) to (C), his argument appears to be without any force. One cannot hold that we admit of such a relation by the use of the above statements, for we were merely making use of Moore's analysis to present his claim in its terms. Since what is at issue is a question about the relation between propositonal characters and facts, that analysis is also in question. In presenting (A), (B), and (C) as we have, we were not presupposing that Moore is correct. What Moore must apparently do is claim that he directly apprehends the relation *Ref.* or argue for its exis-

tence as he argues for the existence of material objects and of a relation between such entities and sensa. He cannot merely claim
that (C) follows from (B). But, he offers no further arguments; he
merely appeals to acquaintance with the thought that there is
such a relation, which, in this case, is the appeal to (B) as the basis
for (C) being true.

Perhaps, Moore would appeal to common sense—to the purported fact that we commonly believe that there is a relation between beliefs and facts and that any adequate philosophical analysis must then recognize such a relation. But, this is another matter.
One may well argue that a relation like *Ref.* must be involved in
any cogent philosophical position, but this is not to appeal to acquaintance to establish both its existence and our knowledge of
what it is. However, if one operates under the guidance of a principle of acquaintance, what can be said about the relation in question? One can *say* one directly apprehends it, just as some say they
directly apprehend substrata or bare particulars; but then the appeal rests on weak phenomenological grounds and seems more in
the nature of a desperate move to save a gambit rather than of a
suggestive insight. Moreover, the claim would be empty unless
one held that one apprehended a case where the relation obtained
between terms. And this reveals that there is a further difficulty
with such an appeal to direct apprehension. If we appeal to the
direct apprehension of *Ref.*, we must also hold that we directly apprehend the terms of the relation: facts (as possibilities) and propositional characters. Hence, if I am right in claiming that the kind
of analysis we have considered must recognize that propositions
refer to possible facts, we would then have to hold that we directly apprehend such possibilities. To get at this strange question of
possible facts and to clarify some suggestive features of Moore's
talk of aquaintance, it will help if we first consider the question of
reference as it comes up between a sign and an object or property.
We shall then return to the connection between a propositional
character and a fact.

Let us say that a sign 'a_1' is used to refer to the object a_1 and
the predicate 'W' to the property W. Moreover, let us consider the
sign in quotes to stand for the class or property or type rather

than the specific token within the instances of quotation marks. The name and the predicate are then like propositional characters in being properties or common characters, rather than particular physical objects, such as blobs of ink. We then have

(S_1) $Ref.('a_1',a_1)$

(S_2) $Ref.('W',W)$

expressing the connections between the signs and the object and property, respectively. We establish the connection between signs and things by what some would call a semantic rule. It is surely not a question of factual truth when we make such a connection, though it is, of course, a factual truth that we have made it after we have done so. But, that it is a fact that someone employs or obeys a rule does not make the rule a factual claim. The question for us is what is the meaning and the role of *'Ref.'* when we treat (S_1) and (S_2) as rules or stipulations or, even, axioms in some linguistic schema? In saying that (S_1) and (S_2) reflect stipulations rather than factual claims, we are recognizing that to establish a relation between signs and things is not to apprehend that a relation holds, as we do apprehend that a relation holds when we see that a_1 is to the left of a_2 or even, perhaps, when we apprehend that a_1 is W. In Moore's terms, the relation of direct apprehension is thus irrelevant to the holding of *Ref.* between 'a_1' and a_1. We can only *establish* the relation if there are two things to be related, but we could only *apprehend* it obtaining between two things if we apprehended the two things as standing in it. Thus, the relations expressed in (S_1) and (S_2) may be established if the relevant entities exist; we need not require that we directly apprehend them in establishing the connections. This is not to say that we can establish such a connection without using a token of a type that has already been connected or a definite description. Such questions are not my concern here. We may then say that we know what the relation *Ref.* is, as it occurs in such contexts, because we are familiar with mental acts that establish such connections. Such acts are neither direct apprehensions that a relation does hold nor are they thoughts that such a relation does hold. Since they are not the former, we can then know that *'Ref.'* *refers* to a relation in (S_1) and (S_2) *without apprehending* it to hold between two things, and we can then know what it is for it to hold without, in some cases, knowing that it does hold. Whether we can legitimately establish such a relation only between signs and objects, *which we directly apprehend on some occasion*, is a further issue and one that is relevant to a principle of acquaintance. We are concerned with a more basic issue involved in the analysis of intentional contexts: that we can know what *Ref.* is without apprehending it to hold between two things, since the mental acts relevant to the establishment of such a connection between signs and things are unique. They are neither beliefs nor direct apprehensions of objects, facts, etc. In a sense, we can say with Moore that we are acquainted with *Ref.*, for we are acquainted with acts that assign a term to an entity. We know what we do when we label an object or a property. This is not to say, with Moore, that *Ref.* exists as a relation between a fact and a belief since we have a thought that a belief refers to one and only one fact.

To get to the connection of a belief and a fact, consider next the sign sequence 'Wa_1'. We stipulate or let the sign sequence refer to the exemplification of W by a_1. Simply put, this is why one must recognize possible facts, since the sign sequence is taken to refer to the exemplification of W by a_1 irrespective of whether a_1 *actually* or *in fact* exemplifies W, and, hence, irrespective of whether the sentence 'Wa_1' is true. Note that we have talked of possible facts without speaking of propositional characters or intentional contexts. To assign the sentence to the fact is to recognize

(S₃) $Ref.('Wa_1', Wa_1)$

as a further case of a connection involving the relation *Ref.* Insofar as *Ref.* is a relation, we must then recognize that it connects terms. To say, at this point, that in (S₃) '*Ref.*' plays a logically different role than it does in (S₁) and (S₂) and does not, in (S₃), stand for a relation that connects terms is to do one of two things. On the one hand, such a claim merely reflects a verbally more acceptable way of acknowledging possible facts without appearing to accept such repugnant entities. In short, the gambit is a mere euphuism. If taken seriously, on the other hand, such a claim means that '*Ref.*', as it occurs in (S₃), is not to be construed as standing for the same relation that the term stands for in (S₁) and (S₂).

This is to replace the introduction of possible facts with a mystery. We need neither retreat behind verbal gymnastics nor take refuge in a mysterious relation. (S_3) reflects the same sort of stipulation that is involved in (S_1) and (S_2). However, since we now deal with combinations of signs, sentences, which *refer* but need not be true or stand for facts, we are forced to speak of *possibilities*. We do not establish or "bring about" such possibilities by mental acts, just as we do not bring about the objects or properties mentioned in statements like (S_1) and (S_2). All we bring about is that the sign sequence stands for such a possibility. Similarly, when we now introduce

> (S_4) $Ref.$ ('$[Wa_1]$', $[Wa_1]$),

we state that a sign refers to a propositional character; we do not establish the existence of properties of thoughts by such stipulations. Thoughts that exemplify the property $[Wa_1]$ exist, just as objects exemplifying W exist. We "create" neither the facts expressed by sentences like 'Wa_1' nor those expressed by sentences like '$[Wa_1]m_1$' as we do bring it about that (S_1), (S_2), (S_3), and (S_4) hold. This difference may lead us to say that (S_1), (S_2), (S_3), and (S_4), considered as true statements, are linguistic truths, or logical truths, or rules, or stipulations.

We may now turn to the question of the connection between propositional characters and facts, to the statement:

> (S_5) $Ref.$ ($[Wa_1]$, Wa_1).

Let us begin with a simple observation. A thought that a_1 is W can occur in many ways. One would involve the occurrence of a complex visual image involving an image of the sign 'a_1' to the right of an image of the sign 'W'. The particular thought may be considered either as the complex image consisting of the one image occurring to the right of the other (or the fact that the one occurs to the right of the other) or as a particular that in some sense contains (or is related to) the two images so related. That such an object will also have or exemplify a further property that makes it a belief, or a doubt, or a thought I ignore for the moment, since we are concerned with the question of the content of thoughts, beliefs, etc., and not with their generic qualities. The particular thought is then a particular in the sense in which any m_i is a particular as opposed to a kind, but it is *of* a kind. In this respect, the particular thought and its kind may be considered analogously to the way in which we speak of signs as tokens of a kind or type. In fact, we may consider such visual images as further tokens of linguistic types. That is, we may consider both a visual image and a blob of ink of similar shape, the shape of the sign 'a_1' for example, to be tokens of the type or property or class which is the name of the object a_1. In a similar way, we could consider extending the type or property to include auditory tokens, both in the sense of ordinary sounds and products of the so-called "inner voice." When we have a thought, we then have an arrangement of tokens. Whether we construe the thought as something related to the tokens or as being the tokens in the relations they stand in, as a fact whose constituents are the tokens, is irrelevant for the time. In either case, the particular thought is about the fact it refers to since the tokens and their arrangement have been connected to the constituents of the fact and the fact itself, just as a written sentence and its constituent signs have been so connected. There is no difference in the way a sentence refers to a fact and the way a thought refers to a fact. The difference lies in the kind of thing a written token is and the kind of thing a particular thought is and, naturally, in the different properties they have. But, insofar as both refer to a fact, they are merely different tokens of the same type. There is no mystery about the occurrence of the relational predicate '*Ref.*' in (S_5). The propositional character is about the fact since it characterizes a thought consisting of a linguistic pattern that has been stipulated, through (S_1), (S_2), and (S_3), to refer to the fact. A thought is then a kind of sentence. The type common to all tokens of the sentence 'Wa_1' is also the type of all instances of the propositional character [Wa_1]. To put it another way, consider the class of all tokens of the sentence and the class of all instances of the propositional character, as a character of the visual images we have taken thoughts to be. The latter class is included in the former. We need appeal to no new or unique relation in (S_5). The only mystery about '*Ref.*' is that it is a primitive predicate in all the (S_i) we have considered, and it is de-

pendent upon a unique kind of act, which we might well call an
intentional or *stipulational* one.

Several objections arise. Some we shall take up now; some we
shall consider later in connection with the views of other philosophers. One is that thoughts may, on some occasions, occur as visual images of signs, but they also occur in other forms. The thought
that a_1 is W may occur as a series of auditory images or in the
form of a colored patch. Note, however, that the sentence 'Wa_1'
may be considered in the narrow sense of the set of all written
tokens or in an enlarged sense to include spoken as well as written
tokens. Moreover, suppose we introduce further labels for the object a_1 and the property W, say 'b_1' and 'V'. The sentences 'Wa_1'
and 'Vb_1' are tokens of different geometrical patterns, and this
leads us not to take them as tokens of the same type. But, just as
we may hold that two tokens of the type 'Wa_1' are not tokens of
the same sentence if they are not used with a constant reference,
so we may hold that two tokens of different geometrical patterns are tokens of the same sentence if they employ different
constituent signs referring to the same objects and properties or relations. What is crucial about two tokens being tokens of the same
sentence is that they are used to say the same thing: that their
referential role is the same. Such duplication in language is logically unnecessary. Hence, one often considers philosophical problems
about reference in terms of an idealized schema of a language
where such ambiguities are ruled out. Thoughts as a matter of fact
do occur in different ways. But, the crucial point is the same.
Where one and the same (kind of) thought occurs in different
forms there are duplications of referential roles. The case of a
thought in the form of an auditory series is an obvious one, but
the case of a representational image is only slightly less so. There
the particular image and color stand for a particular object and
a similar or identical color property, respectively. In view of the
similarities, the establishment of the referential connection is
deemed unnecessary or overlooked. Nevertheless, it is implicitly
involved, for it is established by the similarity and habitual uses we
make of such similarities. Adopting and accepting a stipulation are
one and the same—logically. This kind of point is behind Wittgenstein's identification of thought and language in the *Tractatus*. In

their descriptive roles, whereby we think or state how the world is, language and thought are logically one in the sense in which two interpretations of an abstract axiom schema may be said to be logically the same.

A second question may arise in connection with how one treats the difference between contexts, in which we are aware of something like a_1 being W, and those seemingly self-referential contexts, in which we are aware that we are aware of something having a property. To get at this we shall have to consider cases of direct apprehension of phenomena. Recall that there are two forms the present view may take regarding thoughts. On the one alternative, we would have a thought being a complex or fact, made up of certain data in some one or more relations. The generic properties, *being a thought*, *being a belief*, etc., would then be properties of such complexes. We used brackets around sentences to form signs standing for propositional characters; let us continue to do so. Such characters are common properties of all mental acts with a certain content. But, the mental act itself is now a fact consisting of certain related images. The propositional characters are then properties of such facts. In the case of the thought that a_1 is W which we considered above, we would have two images, one of the shape 'a_1' to the right of one of the shape 'W'. Call the first 'I_1' and the second 'I_2' and let 'L' stand for *left of*. The fact is referred to by the sentence '$L(I_2, I_1)$'. Let us put a pair of '$<>$' around a sentence, when it is to be used as a subject term, so that we may say which propositional character a fact, which is a mental act, exemplifies. We may then write

$$[Wa_1] < L(I_2, I_1) > \ \& \ T < L(I_2, I_1) >,$$

or, if we recognize that mental acts are such facts, we may still refer to them by using the signs 'm_1', 'm_2', etc., for simplicity. The second alternative would have signs like 'm_1' stand for mental acts. However, such acts are not to be construed as facts, but as particulars logically like a_1, in the sense in which a color spot, a sound, and a pain are logically alike. Such particulars would then stand in some special relation to the constituents of facts like $< L(I_2, I_1) >$, and to the facts as well. But, unlike facts, they would be simple particulars. If we, then, wrote

$[Wa_1] m_1$ & Tm_1

to reflect what is the case when there is a thought that a_1 is W, the sign 'm_1' would stand for a different sort of thing than it does if we take it as a simplified way of representing the fact $< L(I_2, I_1) >$. These two alternatives suggest different ways of construing the case of the direct apprehension of a_1 being W, as opposed to a thought or belief that a_1 is W. Since the gambit suggested by the second alternative is both simpler and likely to be more familiar to readers of Moore, I shall begin with it.[8]

A direct apprehension of a_1 being W would be an act, say m_a, which, like a thought that a_1 is W, exemplifies the propositional character $[Wa_1]$. It also exemplifies the property of *being a direct apprehension*, rather than the property T. Let us use 'DA' for such a simple, nonrelational property in this context. We would, then, have

(M₁) $[Wa_1] m_a$ & DAm_a

expressing that there is a direct apprehension that a_1 is W. If one is also aware that there is such a direct apprehension, the state of affairs would be expressed by

(M₂) $[[Wa_1] m_a] m_b$ & DAm_b

or, perhaps, by

(M₃) $[[Wa_1] m_a$ & $DAm_a] m_b$ & DAm_b.

The propositional character exemplified by m_a is not referred to by a predicate that contains a sign referring to a mental act. This shows that (M₁) does not indicate a case where there is a self-awareness or an awareness of an act of awareness. What (M₁) expresses is that there is an awareness that a_1 is W; (M₂), or (M₃), expresses the fact that there is an awareness of an awareness that a_1 is W.[9]

In keeping with the first alternative, the direct apprehension of a_1 being W *would be* the fact that a_1 is W. The mental act would be distinct from the particular a_1 but would be identified with the complex particular or fact that a_1 is W. Such a fact would then exemplify the character DA. Thus, we would have

$DA < Wa_1 >$

instead of (M_1). In the case of an awareness of the awareness of a_1 being W, the fact that $<Wa_1>$ exemplifies DA would itself exemplify DA. We would then have

$$DA<DA<Wa_1>>$$

expressing that state of affairs. Just as on the alternative gambit, we have a further mental act in the latter case, for $<DA<Wa_1>>$ is a different fact, and hence different act, than $<Wa_1>$. When there is not an awareness that the fact $<Wa_1>$ is directly apprehended, there is not a direct apprehension that the fact $<Wa_1>$ exemplifies the property DA, even though it does do so. This corresponds to (M_1) showing, on the second alternative, that the propositional character exemplified by m_a does not involve a reference to an act of awareness. (M_1) expresses the fact that there is a direct apprehension of the fact that a_1 is W, but *that* apprehension is not itself apprehended.

It is worth contrasting the treatment of the direct apprehension of a_1 being W with a thought that a_1 is W on the first view. The difference between the two cases is more marked than on the alternative view, where the difference lies in the generic properties T and DA that are exemplified by the different acts. On the present view, which I have called the first alternative, there is one fact, $<Wa_1>$, which is both *what* is apprehended and *the act* of apprehension. This is not to identify the datum, a_1, with the mental act. In turn, this reflects a fundamental difference between particulars which are mental acts and particulars like a_1. The former, being facts, must be complex; the latter *may be* construed as simple substrata related to a variety of properties by the tie of exemplification. Irrespective of how such sensa are construed, they are fundamentally different from acts of direct apprehension, being constituents of the latter. On the second alternative, things like a_1 and m_a are logically of the same kind. Thoughts, on the first alternative, are facts, like acts of direct apprehension. But, thoughts are connected with, or intend, other facts, and direct apprehensions, as facts, are acts of apprehension and apprehended facts. Acts of direct apprehension need not *refer to* other facts; thoughts as mental acts do refer to other facts. Thus, though thoughts may be said to be *about* something, acts of apprehension are *of* something.

Notice how all this fits with two fundamental features of thought and direct apprehension. Thoughts can be true or false and, hence, there must be some feature or characteristic of thoughts that accounts for this. Referring to or being about facts, which may or may not exist, is such a feature. We can think about what is not the case, but we cannot directly apprehend what is not the case. Acts of direct apprehension must be radically different from thoughts in this respect. They are on the present account, since a direct apprehension of a fact is identical with the fact apprehended. Given a direct apprehension of the fact $<Wa_1>$, it follows from the very way we are construing mental acts that there is such a fact. Thus, 'Wa_1' is a consequence of '$DA<Wa_1>$'. On the other pattern, 'Wa_1' is not a consequence of '$[Wa_1]m_a$ & DAm_a' merely on the basis of the pattern of the analysis. One must add that it is so as an ad hoc stipulation or insist that it is a matter of a synthetic a priori truth or addition to the rules of logic. This is a consequence of that alternative's use of a propositional character referring to a fact, rather than the fact itself, in the analysis of direct apprehension. Such a difference is a strong point in favor of the first alternative.[10]

There are other interesting consequences of the first alternative, which construes mental acts as facts rather than simple particulars. As we saw, on this alternative there is no mystery about the reference of thoughts to facts. Nor, as we just noted, is there a problem about connecting an act of direct apprehension to a fact. On the alternative view, there is a problem in both cases, since both cases rely on the connection of a propositional character to a fact. How is the connection to be understood on the alternative view? One must hold that the propositional character is about a fact since the constituent sentence in the sign for the character also stands for the fact. But, this illustrates, rather than solves, the problem of the intentional connection; for, the propositional character is not composed of the referents of the signs in the sentence. It is a simple character represented by a peculiar type of sign — a sentence, which is a complex sign, formed into a primitive predicate to show what fact the character refers to. Such a referential tie does not reduce to the simple uses of *Ref.* as we considered it in (S_1) through (S_5). We considered the relation *Ref.* in terms of the first alternative we developed, where a propositional character is analogous to the type common to a variety of tokens, which are the particular mental acts construed as facts. On the problematic alternative a mental act, say m_a, is not a fact connected to further fact (if it is a thought) as a sentence is. Rather, such an act is connected to a fact since it exemplifies a primitive character that is connected to the fact. But, there is no answer to the question about this connection, as there is on the alternative view suggested here. On the view I have advocated, the connection is the same as the stipulated connection between a sign and its referent. We have seen why there is no problem regarding the connection of a propositional character and a fact in a case of direct apprehension, on the first alternative, since no propositional character is involved. In the case of a thought, the difference comes out in the nature of the propositional character on the different views. On the first alternative, the propositional character is analogous to a property shared by all written tokens of certain kind. Thus, one could specify it in terms of the kinds of constituents of the mental act and their connection to their referents and to each other. The predicate referring to such a propositional character is a defined predicate, just as one could define a predicate specifying tokens of a written or spoken sentence in terms of the kinds of constituent tokens, their arrangement, and the objects and properties they refer to. On the second alternative, one may take the predicate to be primitive, even though it is a complex sign, in that it contains other signs. Or, one construes it in terms of a definite description, as '$(\iota f)\ Ref.(f, Wa_1)$' for example. Either way, the relation *Ref.* does not function in the straightforward way in which it does on the first alternative. That the propositional characters are different sorts of things on the two views is just a reflection of the fact that the alternatives treat the relation *Ref.* and mental acts differently. These differences culminate in (S_5) being no different from (S_1), (S_2), or (S_3) on the first alternative, and, on the second, it expresses a unique kind of truth. Moore, recall, suggests that we just know that there is one and only one fact that makes a belief true and that we indicate both by the same sentence. Gustav Bergmann who, as we shall see, adopted a variant of Moore's pattern, speaks of his version of (S_5) as a "logical truth."[11] In short, on the second alternative, (S_5) reflects two problems: the problematic status of the unique relation *Ref.* and the problematic nature of the truth expressed by (S_5). On the first alternative, the relation and the statement are no more problematic than the relation mentioned in (S_1), (S_2), and (S_3) and the statements themselves.

The differences between the two alternatives also bear on one of Moore's early arguments to refute idealism. One argument, recall, is that since we distinguish an act like m_a from an object like a_1 (or from the fact that a_1 is W), which is apprehended by the act, it is logically possible for the object a_1 (or the fact that a_1 is W) to exist without there being any mental act that directly apprehends the object (or fact). Hence, such objects and facts can exist without being experienced, and, consequently, *to exist* does not involve *being experienced*. This pattern fits neatly with the second alternative, though, as we noted earlier, it has a consequence that Moore later found unacceptable, since any sensum is then capable of existing without being sensed. On the first alternative, the apprehended fact is a mental act, and hence exemplifies DA. It would, then, appear that one cannot distinguish a mental act from the fact that a_1 is W. One could, however, phrase Moore's argument in terms of a fact like $<Wa_1>$ not necessarily exemplifying DA, and hence not necessarily being a mental act, even though it does exemplify DA and is such an act. The difference between the two alternatives would not then affect the use of either analysis to state Moore's argument. But, we should recall that the point the idealist is trying to make is more cogently put in terms of the kinds of things the primitive terms of the schema stand for, phenomenal objects and their properties. Moreover, Moore insisted that we must distinguish the object of an act from the act itself. In holding a fact like $<Wa_1>$ to be an act of direct apprehension, we do not do this. Yet, interestingly, we can still make his claim: that $<Wa_1>$ is not *necessarily* a mental act, for it need not exemplify DA. This can be taken to show one of two things. Moore was mistaken about the identification of act and object being essential to idealism, or the pattern advocated here has aspects that are idealistic. But, I see no reason to make the latter claim.

To speak of mental acts as facts obviously involves a number of issues and problems. I am concerned, in this book, with those centering around belief and intentionality, rather than the problems of perception. Before expanding and exploring the gambit suggested, I would like to consider how such a view can be seen to evolve from the writings of Russell and Wittgenstein, and in response to some contemporary puzzles associated with Quine and Russell's theory of descriptions. Moreover, we can see more of the strength of such a view by contrasting it with the approach to intentionality taken by Bergmann's variant of Moore's analysis. For the time then, we need merely keep the view in mind as a point of return and, hence, postpone consideration of objections to it and further arguments for it.

It has been suggested, by Moore and others, that thoughts are propositional in content. We do not think of a_1, we think that a_1 is W, or that a_1 is C, and so on. This goes along with the claims about direct apprehension that are expressed in a principle of exemplification: we directly apprehend properties as exemplified and objects having properties, we apprehend neither properties without such objects nor objects without properties. Such a claim about direct apprehension is a simple consequence of the structure of the first alternative, since acts of direct apprehension are facts. It goes along with the second alternative, if one stipulates that mental acts must exemplify propositional characters, and does not introduce further properties, like being a thought of a_1 or a direct apprehension of a_1, which mental acts could exemplify. That apprehension is propositional thus naturally fits with the first alternative in a way that it does not with the second. The question of whether there are thoughts that are not propositional in content is a further point to take up. Raising this latter question serves as an introduction to a further theme of Moore's discussion: the consideration of imagination and memory.

Moore's analysis of perception depends on his discussion of belief contexts and the existence of the relation of indirect apprehension as a way of being conscious of objects without directly apprehending them. We noted that there was a crucial problem surrounding our knowledge that there is such a relation and what it is. Moore seeks to convince us of his account by considering memory. Consider a case where we remember the datum a_1. Suppose that in so doing we directly apprehend an image very like a_1, which we shall label 'a_2'. As Moore sees it, for us to have a memory of a_1 we must recognize that there is more involved than the direct apprehension of a_2 and the similarity of a_2 to a_1. We must also be conscious that a_2 is not identical with a_1, and that the present act is a memory of a_1, not a direct apprehension of that datum. But, if this is so, then we must recognize that we are conscious, in some sense, of the object a_1. In short, a present mental act stands in the relation of indirect apprehension to that datum. We must, then, recognize that such a form of consciousness exists, and this is to recognize both that there is a relation of indirect apprehension and that we know what it is. For the moment, I do not want to consider the cogency of Moore's claim, as based on the case of memory. Instead, I want to consider a consequence of it that bears on the recognition of possible facts and propositions. Moore seeks to reject such entities. We have already seen that he does not really avoid propositions, since they become propositional characters or kinds of belief, which are exemplified by particular acts of belief, on his account. In view of all that has been said so far, I shall then consider his discussion as if it is an argument for the rejection of possible facts rather than a rejection of propositions. The consequence Moore faces is that the pattern he applies to memory seems to lead him to an unpalatable admission with regard to imagination. Consider a case where we imagine a griffin. Just as with memory, there will be a direct apprehension of some data. There will no more be a direct apprehension of a griffin than there is a direct apprehension of the remembered object. We also seem to recognize that the present act is an indirect apprehension of an imaginary object, a griffin, just as a memory is an indirect apprehension of the remembered object. Surely, there is something wrong with introducing imaginary objects and, hence, with any account of imagination that forces us to do this. Moore suggests that the problem about the imaginary griffin is exactly the same as the problem about false belief and the introduction of possible facts or nonexistent facts. He does not, however, proceed to offer an argument, merely the assertion that in the case of false belief, the belief refers to a nonexistent fact. This I have suggested is totally inadequate, since it amounts either to the recognition of nonexistent facts, in the ontology embraced by Moore's analysis, or to a problematic use of the reference relation. What I wish to consider here is the reversal of Moore's line of argument. If he is correct in holding that the cases of imagination and false belief go together, and if we recognize possible facts to account for sentences and beliefs being false, must we not then recognize imaginary objects? If this is so, have we not arrived at a *reductio*? For, although possible facts may be tolerated by one who is not inclined to totally dismiss such issues, surely imaginary objects suffice for the dismissal of any philosophical position that is forced to recognize them. We seem obliged, then, to consider Moore's case of imagining a griffin, but, for simplicity, let us begin by considering an object that consists of a white square resting on a green rectangle.

What occurs when we imagine such an object? Consider that one of two things takes place. Either a propositional content, in the form of either visual or auditory linguistic patterns, or an image "of" the imagined object is presented. In both cases there would also occur some feature that leads one to speak of an act of imagination rather than an act of belief. That is, each type of mental act exemplifies a generic characteristic over and above the data that give it the specific content it has. In the case of the data being in the form of a linguistic pattern, which might be expressed by '$(\exists x)(\exists y)[Wx \& Sx \& Gy \& Ry \& Oxy]$', with the interpretation of the predicates being obvious, there is no difference in content between such an act and an act of belief. The same is true in the case of the occurrence of an image. Yet, what is meant by holding that it is an act of imagination insofar as the image *represents* or *refers* to or *stands for* or is "of" an object? Cases of imagination are apparently thought, by Moore, to involve intentional reference just as cases of belief do. That is obviously why the puzzle about imaginary objects arises and poses one problem. But, we might hold that even in the case of the visual image we deal with a propositional content, for the visual image operates as a fact standing for another fact, just as we noted such images may function in belief contexts. The visual image is a sort of "linguistic" pattern. What such contents of acts of imagination stand for, if they stand for anything, are facts. Since we deal with propositional contents, we deal with possible facts. To speak of imaginary objects may then be taken to be a way of speaking of possible facts, and we need not recognize further unusual entities: a category of imaginary objects. To put it concisely, we can imagine that something is composed of a white square over a green triangle, or that something green is at some place, or that something is a griffin, or that there is a griffin in the house next door, or that some object, say a_1, has a property that it does not in fact have. In all these cases, we imagine certain facts to hold and, hence, the mental act intends or refers to a possible state of affairs or fact, not to an object other than a fact. Perhaps it helps to recall that something being green is a fact even though we tend to think and speak of "the green object." One might have to introduce imaginary objects if one held that mental acts of imagination and belief could intend nonexistent objects without any reference to characteristics of such objects. Insofar as intentional contexts are held to be propositional in content, this cannot happen. In fact, this would be a reason for holding that every intentional context is propositional. It also fits with another basic theme of Wittgenstein's logical atomism: that complex "objects" are facts, and not really objects. In effect, what I am saying here is that to imagine an object is to imagine a fact to hold. Simple objects cannot furnish the sole content for acts of imagination. This, of course, also fits with themes of classical empiricism. One might think of an exception: the stipulational context where one assigns a sign to an object. In those contexts, we have acts represented by expressions like (S_1). If we assign a name to an object we are directly apprehending, it is clear that we shall apprehend it as exemplifying some properties. If we are not apprehending it, then we shall either refer to it by a description and, hence, deal with a propositional context involving properties, or we shall refer to it by a previously assigned name. But, in this latter case, even if we do not consider the assignment of a name through the relation *Ref.* to be a genuine propositional context, we cannot be dealing with an "imaginary" object if we are using a legitimate name. For we must have had a previous assignment of a name to the object, and this could have been done only if the object were directly apprehended or the name assigned through a description. In either case, we would have a propositional context.

This brings us to a connection with Russell's theory of descriptions. One motive for the theory of descriptions was to have a way of speaking about nonexistent objects, or imaginary objects, without making ontological commitments to such peculiar entities. If, however, we are forced to recognize possible facts in order to account for how language and thought are about the world, then irrespective of the use of Russell's analysis of definite descriptions, we admit such facts into an adequate ontology. Moreover, if, as suggested here, to speak of imaginary objects is just another way of speaking of possible facts, then irrespective of the theory of descriptions, we have recognized such objects. Russell showed that we need not recognize objects as referents of certain expressions; he did not show that we need not recognize entities corresponding to certain sentences. What Russell may be taken as having shown, by means of the theory of descriptions, is that we need not recognize, among *the simples* or *basic objects* of an ontology, such peculiar *entities* as imaginary objects. Definite descriptions, recall, are contextually meaningful signs and are not given a referential function by being correlated with objects, as names are correlated. In our terms, a definite description is not put into the relation *Ref.* with any object by a stipulation or rule. Being meaningful in *the context* of a sentence, such signs can be taken to express possible facts in such contexts.

Yet, several distinctions must be made. Consider an object, a_1, that exemplifies the properties F_1 and F_2, but not F_3. Suppose, further, that no object exemplifies all three properties, but that

$$(\exists x)(F_1 x \ \& \ F_2 x \ \& \ F_3 x)$$

is not contradictory or does not express an "impossibility." We might hold that three distinct possible facts were expressed by the three sentences:

   (a) $F_3 a_1$

   (β) $F_3 a_1 \ \& \ F_2 a_1 \ \& \ F_1 a_1$

   (γ) $(\exists x)[F_3 x \ \& \ F_2 x \ \& \ F_1 x]$.

We might, but we need not. For, whatever lack of clarity there is in the notion of a possible fact, it should be clear that we can talk sensibly of possible facts only when we are prepared to acknowledge existent facts. To speak of (β) expressing a possible fact thus involves the commitment to hold that (β) would stand for an *existent fact* if a_1 *actually* exemplified all three properties. This means that we would recognize *complex* facts—in this case a conjunctive fact. I shall argue later that we need not recognize such facts. However, for the present, that theme will be ignored in order to consider some related points. We shall tentatively acknowledge atomic, complex, and quantificational facts. It may be recalled that Russell recognized such facts and, therefore, could not reject existential possibilities on the ground that he did not recognize existential facts.

(a), (β), and (γ) express possible facts or possibilities. In the case of (a), it is clear that we do not have, in any reasonable sense, a "possible object," since a_1 is an existent object. In what sense can one hold that (β) may be taken to indicate a "possible object"? Assume, for simplicity, that a_1 has only the properties F_1 and F_2. We may consider the object a_1 in two ways. One may hold that given any ordinary object, we must distinguish the name 'a_1', as it stands for the object *with* properties, from its use as an indicator of the object as *distinguished from* all properties. In the latter sense, we may take the name to stand for the object as a *simple* or as a *bare* or *pure* subject of attributes. Taking the name 'a_1' in this latter sense, to represent the object, so to speak, *without* or *distinct from* its properties, we can consider the sign pattern

(O_1) $Ex(a_1, F_1, F_2)$

to represent the object *with* properties. Here, 'Ex' stands for the connection between the object, taken as a mere subject or as "bare," and the properties it exemplifies. 'Ex' stands for the connection that is normally expressed by the predicative copula. We may look upon

(O_2) F_1a_1 & F_2a_1

as a consequence of our so understanding (O_1). We can then take "the object," in one sense, to be *a complex*, as indicated by (O_1), or as a conjunction of atomic facts and, hence, *a complex fact*, as indicated by (O_2). In the sense in which the object is represented by (O_1) or (O_2), we may speak of (β) representing a possible object. For, it represents a possible fact and correlates with a sign complex,

(O$_3$)   Ex(a_1,F$_1$,F$_2$,F$_3$),

just as (O$_1$) correlates with (O$_2$). There is no corresponding sense in which 'a_1' stands for a *simple* possible object or in which anything said so far indicates a category of such objects. Moreover, (γ) does not force us to talk of such a category. If we take (γ) to indicate a possible fact, we do not have a corresponding object. We have no composite expression corresponding to (γ), as (O$_3$) corresponds to (β). Yet, if one *imagines* that there is something having all three properties, one may be said, in a philosophically harmless or ontologically neutral manner, to be *imagining* an object. What is more interesting is that it makes no sense, as we noted earlier, to speak of imagining or thinking of a specific nonexistent object in the sense of a pure or simple object. In the sense in which 'a_1' stands for the object *simpliciter*, we may be said to think of that object in such a way by thinking *that there is such an object*. If we express this symbolically by

(δ)   ($\exists$x)(x = a_1)

we can take (δ) to express the content of a thought, since 'a_1' is a name of an object. Where 'a_1' is not a legitimate name, such linguistic patterns are not sentences.

Even if we recognize that (β) and (a) stand for possible facts, we do not then recognize that there are, in addition, possible objects. In the sense in which we recognize the object *simpliciter*, represented by the name 'a_1', as a constituent of and thus distinct from facts, and distinguish it from the complex object, represented by (O$_2$), we do not recognize a category of possible, imaginary objects. The *reductio* argument against possible facts is thus misleading and faulty. One does not establish the absurdity of recognizing possibilities in that one does not force the recognition of imaginary objects on the same pattern. Rather, sensible talk of imaginary objects (complex objects) reduces to talk of possible facts.

There is a further fundamental flaw in Moore's analogy between false belief and imagination. Consider the imagining of a griffin in terms of an image one has. In virtue of what is such an activity an imagining and, specifically, the imagining of a griffin? Moore is clearly right in thinking that the image, call it a griffin-image, is not so classified because it is related in some way (stands for, is of, represents, etc.) to an imaginary object. It is classified as it is because characteristics of the image represent properties, and the image, as an *object with properties*, represents *something having such properties*. The latter aspect becomes clear when we realize that we may be said to imagine a griffin when we have an appropriate image and *believe that* there is a similar or corresponding object. We then believe that or imagine that there is a griffin, i.e., something with certain properties. Clearly, what is involved is a possible fact, as we have spoken about such "things." Is there not then a difference between imagining a griffin and imagining *that there is* a griffin? Just as we distinguish the fact that a_1 exists from the object, must we not distinguish the imagined fact that there are griffins from an imaginary object? There is no need to. To imagine a griffin without believing that there are griffins would simply be to have an appropriate image (or other mental content) involving characteristics that are involved in the content of the belief (or doubt, etc.) *that* such things exist (or do not exist). In short, the image *represents* a possible fact: something having the properties represented by the characteristics of the image.

The basic point involved is how and when complexes represent. The image in question may be construed as a complex: a particular, g_1, exemplifying a number of properties, F_1, F_2, etc. Contrast such an image with the sentence 'Wa_1'. Since the signs 'a_1' and 'W' stand for an object and a property respectively, the complex sign stands for the possibility that the object has the property. In the case of the griffin-image, the particular g_1 does not stand for anything, since it has not been coordinated to any object as the name 'a_1' has been coordinated. Thus, even though properties of g_1 may be taken to represent properties of physical objects (color, etc.), the complex—the griffin-image—does not represent anything in the way that the sentence 'Wa_1' does. Of course, one might coordinate either the complex griffin-image to some object or the particular, g_1, to an object. Doing the former would be no more relevant to the issues at hand than our taking the sign pattern 'Wa_1' to be the name of a new family pet. Doing the latter could lead one to say that the object to which g_1 is coordinated is then *imagined* to be a griffin. One may say so, but all that would be meant by such a claim is (1) that such a coordination has been made and (2) that the properties of g_1 represent properties, by definition, of a griffin. It is clear that what the object g_1 stands for is not *an* imaginary object; rather, what might be called an imaginary object is the complex consisting of the represented object and the griffin properties. This returns us to a case we have already considered. Moore's argument against possible facts thus collapses, since the analogy with "imaginary objects" is ill-founded.

Let us now return to the case of memory. When we remember a_1, there is, according to Moore, something, a_2, that we directly apprehend, which is different from a_1 and which bears a relation to a_1 that enables us to hold that we indirectly apprehend a_1 and that we remember it. If a_2 is a proposition, whether a Platonic entity or simply a token of an interpreted pattern, then the relation to a_1 is AB. The proposition would be *about* a_1 in that an element of it would refer to a_1. If a_2 is an image, then the relation to a_1 could be taken in one of two ways. Either *the image* as a complex *whole* will *refer to* a_1 or *an element* of the complex, perhaps the particular, as distinguished from the particular *with* the properties (which is the complex), will refer to a_1. This reraises a fundamental problem faced by any purported analysis of intentional contexts: the specification of the relation of "aboutness' that holds between "thoughts" and objects and the specification of the conditions under which it obtains.

If a_2 is a proposition, we obviously deal with a propositional content. But, suppose a_2 is an image which we take, as a whole, to refer to a_1. It is not *about* a_1 in the sense that a proposition is, since no element of the image, in this case, *refers* to a_1. If this is overlooked, one might think that the image functions as a proposition since, first, it is "about" a_1 and, second, it is a complex. But, the image is not about a_1 in the sense in which a proposition may be about a_1. How, then, does it "refer" to a_1? Clearly, it has not been coordinated with a_1 as a sign is coordinated with its referent. Moreover, if a simple element of such an image refers, say the particular taken as a simple subject, in virtue of what does it do so?

Once we raise such questions, we recognize that there is a corresponding question in the case of a propositional content. Given
that a token of a name occurs "in thought," in virtue of what does
it function on that occasion as a *token of the name* and not *merely as an instance* of a *kind of inner sound*, visual pattern, etc.? In
that Moore's analysis does not probe into these questions, it is
not satisfactory. And to present a more viable account we shall
have to return to them. Moreover, recall that Moore's strategy involved convincing us of our recognition of the relation IA in the
case of memory, in order to have such a relation for the analysis
of belief and perception. What I have argued is that Moore fails in
that we are led back to the relations of *reference* and *aboutness*,
without any clear sense of their use or cogency for resolving the
issues. Since we would, quite commonsensically, hold that a
memory content is "about" the remembered object, Moore proceeds to use such a notion of "aboutness" unproblematically in his
analysis. If such a notion is unproblematic, then so is IA, in the
case of memory, since the latter can be defined in terms of DA
and "about." Yet, to call attention to Moore's problematic use of
reference is not to suggest that an *analysis* of such a notion or an
explication of the intentional role of images will be presented. As
Moore implies, and as we shall see, *basic* concepts are involved.

IV

Moore and Bradley on Particulars, Predicates, and Predication

Bergmann's notion of a bare particular is at the heart of both his version of realism and his analysis of mind. Moore's concept of a particular was similarly crucial, not only in the formulation of his views regarding belief and perception, but for Russell's analyses of thought and reference. Moreover, understanding Moore's early analyses will help us to understand both Russell's very early views, which provided a foil for the emergence of his theory of descriptions, and Frege, whom Russell explicitly attacked. As we shall see, Frege and Moore developed quite similar themes. Finally, Moore's views on particulars provide supporting arguments for the more obvious attacks against idealism that we have considered. They serve to "round out," as it were, Moore's purported "refutation" of idealism.

Moore's early analysis encompasses two distinct stages. In the early paper "The Nature of Judgment," he developed a view influenced by F. H. Bradley. Bradley had held that the notion of a "bare particular" was absurd. He argued that an "ordinary" particular must be understood to be a combination or bundle of properties affirmed as existing. What he was claiming was that to think of an object was to think of it in terms of properties of it. One could not conceive of or have an idea of or consider a thought of a bare or simple or pure particular. When we judged of an object, say a_1, that it had a property, say F_1, this meant that we judged F_1 to *cohere with* or *combine with* other properties—those in

terms of which we thought of a_1 in that particular judgment. Let
'ϕ' stand for such properties. This meant that what corresponded
in thought to the subject term 'a_1' was *the concept* ϕ. We then
judged that ϕ and F_1 existed together, in the judgment expressed
by 'a_1 is F_1'. Bradley's way of putting this was both dramatic and
confused. Since both ϕ and F_1 were properties, or concepts, or
"predicates," he held that the content of judgment was a property which, in judging, we ascribed to *reality* as the subject. Reality,
or the absolute, thus became the *real* subject of subject-predicate
judgments. In judgment, we then attributed what was in thought,
the concept (property) ϕ *and* F_1, to what was not conceived or
thought, *reality*. Part of what Bradley was saying can be put in less
dramatic terms. He is suggesting that we are to construe judgments
expressed by sentences like 'a_1 is F_1' as existential judgments and,
hence, more perspicuously expressed by sentences like '$(\exists x)(\phi x$ &
$F_1 x)$'. Another related theme is that objects are to be "analyzed"
or understood *to be* collections of properties. In combining these
themes, Bradley does not clearly distinguish a *particular* object *as
a complex of* properties from a particular object *as a complex*
property. This easily leads to the doctrine that there is only *one
particular*—the absolute—since existent objects are, as complex
concepts, attributes of it. Moreover, such a pattern provides a basis
for distinguishing between *objects* (*of* thought) and *the reality* to
which they are *attributed* and, hence, contributing to the idealistic
pattern. For, as distinguished from, but attributed to, reality, such
objects are *ideal* rather than *real*. The details and defects of Bradley's view are not my present concern. Enough has been suggested
to see the influences on Moore's early view.

Moore held that universal concepts (properties, sometimes
called "predicates") were the ultimate constituents of the universe.[1] Among simple concepts, Moore included such properties as
red, *now*, *this*, and *existence*. *Propositions*, as distinguished from
sentences, were held to be composed of such concepts. In fact, all
existents were held to be composed of concepts. In Moore's view,
the object a_1 was a *composite* of concepts, including *existence*.
Thus, we might represent the object by a functional expression

(1) $\phi_1(F_1, F_2, \ldots, \text{existence})$

where 'ϕ_1' stands for a relation obtaining among the constituent concepts to *form* the object. There is also, on Moore's analysis, a *concept of* a_1. This is a complex concept composed of the concepts *in* the object *except* for *existence*. Thus, we would have

(2) $\phi_2(F_1, F_2, \ldots)$

representing *the concept of* a_1. The concept of a_1 differs from the object in that ϕ_1 differs from ϕ_2 and in that existence is a constituent of the object but not of the concept. A concept like *the concept* of a_1 is not a concept in the sense in which, say, *red* or F_1 or *existence* is: it is not a universal property. It is a concept, in the sense in which universal properties are, in that it is present to the mind in thought. Moreover, it is a universal in a way: for it can be *common* to many minds (or mental acts) and it is what makes such acts thoughts of the object a_1, just as red is what is common to and that in virtue of which objects are correctly classified as red.

The proposition expressed by 'a_1 exists' is, on the pattern, a combination of concepts. What concepts? Obviously those *in the concept* of a_1 as well as the concept existence. It may then be represented by

(3) $\phi_3(F_1, F_2, \ldots, \text{existence})$

But, (3) looks strangely like (1). All that distinguishes them is the use of 'ϕ_1' in the one and 'ϕ_3' in the other. What is the difference between ϕ_1 and ϕ_3? For Moore there is none, and he identifies existent objects with existential propositions:

> The opposition of concepts to existents disappears, since an existent is seen to be nothing but a concept or complex of concepts standing in a unique relation to the concept of existence. Even the description of an existent as a proposition (a true existential proposition) seems to lose its strangeness, when it is remembered that a proposition is here to be understood, not as anything subjective—an assertion or affirmation of something—but as the combination of concepts which is affirmed.
>
> If now we take the existential proposition "Red exists," . . . my meaning is that the concept "red" and the concept "existence" stand in a specific relation both to one another and to the concept of time.[2]

The proposition expressed by 'a_1 is F_1' is not identified with the object a_1. It is a complex of concepts, but it is not clear whether it would be more perspicuously represented by

(4) $\phi_3(F_1, F_2, \ldots)$

or by

(5) $\phi_3[\phi_2(F_1, F_2, \ldots), F_1]$.

That is, by (4) a complex concept would not be a constituent of the proposition, whereas by (5) there is such a constituent. Moreover, it is also not clear whether all the constituent concepts that are in (2), what may be called *the* complete concept of the object, go into (5). Thus, when one believes that a_1 is F_1, is the concept *one has*, expressed by 'a_1', the complete concept or a partial one composed of some constituents of (2)? Bradley had held the latter, and it seems likely that Moore, in some manner, does also. Besides *the* concept of a_1, there would then be a number of other *partial* concepts of a_1.

A thought or belief has the content it does owing to its being related (the DA of Chapters I and III) to a proposition. The latter is *about* the relevant object, since the proposition *contains* a concept that is a concept *of* the object. But, what is it for a concept to be a concept *of* a particular object? It is easy to see how a complete concept picks out its object, since the set of constituents of the latter *is* the set of constituents of the former plus the concept of existence. If thoughts are held to involve the complete concept, the problem of specification does not arise, but a problem of plausibility obviously does. What is required is a means of having a partial concept pick out, or uniquely specify, an object. We shall return to this question when we take up Russell's early views.

Another theme involved in Moore's view concerns the truth of propositions. One aspect of Bradley's idealistic philosophy involved the distinction between thought and reality—between the proposition (or propositional content) and what Bradley called "reality." This led Bradley to advocate a coherence theory of truth. The line of argument is quite simple. Given a proposition, we cannot know any correspondent that can "make" it true or ground its truth, since what can be known is what can be a content for thought. But, only propositions, or ideational contents—complex properties or concepts, can be contents of thought. Hence, the mind cannot *compare* a proposition to, say, a fact and determine the former to be true in that it "corresponds" to some fact. All one can do is compare propositions. Hence, truth must be understood in terms of a content (proposition) fitting with other contents. Not only *the criterion* for ascribing a content to reality is thus coherence, but the very meaning of "is true" is to be understood in terms of "coherence." Moore seeks to reject Bradley's idealism by rejecting a coherence theory of truth. One way he does so, in this early paper, while avoiding the classical idealist objection centering on the purported correspondence between propositions (thoughts) and facts (external reality), is to *identify* the true proposition with the fact. We have already seen how he does that in the case of true existential propositions, where such propositions are identified with the existent objects. In such cases, we have a three-fold identification of

(a) The true existential proposition that a_1 exists
(b) The fact that a_1 exists
(c) a_1.

In the case of a proposition expressed by 'a_1 is F_1', what grounds the truth of the proposition is *the* relation between the constituent concepts:

It is of such entities as these that a proposition is composed. In it certain concepts stand in specific relations with one another. And our question now is, wherein a proposition differs from a concept, that it may be either true or false.

It is at first sight tempting to say that the truth of a proposition depends on its relation to reality; that any proposition is true which consists of a combination of concepts that is actually to be found among existents. . . .

It would seem, in fact, from this example, that a proposition is nothing other than a complex concept. The difference between a concept and a proposition, in virtue of which the latter alone can be called true or false, would seem to lie merely in the simplicity of the former. . . . A proposition is constituted by any number of concepts, together with a specific relation between them; and according to the nature of this relation the proposition may be either true or false. What kind of relation . . . cannot be further defined, but must be immediately recognized.[3]

This means that the difference between true and false propositions is an internal one in the sense that the combining relation differs in the two cases. But, this, clearly, is a way of treating propositions as facts and recognizing two kinds: existent facts and mere possibilities. Thus, we have a basic connection with the view of *Some Main Problems of Philosophy* rooted in another line of argument against idealism: the attack on the coherence theory of truth.

In 1901 Moore introduced a further argument against idealism.[4] An idealistic theme common to Bradley and Berkeley is the construal of an object as a complex of qualities (properties, attributes). Berkeley's attack on the notion of a material substratum and Bradley's similar criticism of the idea of a bare particular are first steps in the "analysis" of an ordinary object, say a_1, as a composite of qualities. The second step is the identification of qualities with concepts, ideational contents, or sensations. Berkeley, in nominalistic fashion, had problems with qualities *as* universals. Bradley's qualities are clearly universal concepts or, as Moore said, "universal meanings." Moore seeks to refute the idealist line by challenging the first move: the construal of the object as a complex of qualities. He seeks to do this by holding that such a view denies the existence of "numerical difference" and of "particulars." Such denials, he argues, are mistaken. To deny numerical difference is to assert that for two objects, say two white squares, to differ they must differ conceptually, i.e., in a property or "predicate." He thus implicitly equates three claims:

(A)   There are no particulars.

(B)   There is only conceptual difference.

(C)   Objects are composed of universal properties
          (concepts, qualities).

One can understand why he equates (A), (B), and (C). Suppose one holds (D) *that two complex entities to be two must differ in a constituent.* If one also held that objects were composites of their universal properties, he would hold that two such composites must differ in at least one constituent property. Thus, if there are two, they differ conceptually. Likewise, if one object had a property that "another" did not, there would clearly be two objects and not one. For, if there were not, one and the same object both would and would not have a certain property. Hence, there will be two objects if and only if they differ conceptually. On the other hand, if two objects can only differ conceptually, then one is led to take them as composites of qualities. For, if they were not, they would contain something other than a quality to ground their difference. But, this would give rise to the possibility of the objects differing without differing in a quality. Implicitly assuming (*D*) can thus lead one to equate (*B*) and (*C*). To hold that objects are composed only of universal properties and hence (assuming (*D*)) that if objects differ they differ in a concept, or conceptually, is to deny that there are constituents of the different objects which are *not* universals and which *just differ*, from each other and from every other similar sort of thing *in* any other object. Such things, if there are any, would be *particular* to each object, as opposed to universals which are *common* to different objects, and, hence, they would be, simply, *particulars*. They are particulars not only in that they are particular to different objects, but in that they *just differ* from each other. They are *just* particular, or different, as opposed to *differing in a way*, or property. Different concepts or universals, like whiteness and squareness, may be held to just differ also, but they are different concepts and may be held to differ conceptually or "in a way." (This makes use of an ambiguity in the notion of *conceptual difference*, which is another factor in Moore's argument that we shall have to consider later.) In this way, the proponent of (*C*) denies particulars and asserts (*A*). Since (*C*) is equated with (*B*), to assert (*B*) is also to assert (*A*). But, (*B*) also *directly* fits with (*A*), since, if there were particulars, two objects could, by (*D*), differ in that their constituent particulars differed, and, hence, the objects need not differ in a universal property or "conceptually." Likewise, two particulars, being such things, would *just differ* and not differ *in a property*. The phrase "in a property" requires comment that will recall our discussion in Chapter I. Holding that particulars are constituents of ordinary objects, one holds that they are related to the other constituents, the properties, of the objects. In a sense, then, one speaks of both the object and the special constituent of the object, the particular, as "having" properties. Just as, in one sense, for Aristotle, the combination of form and matter *has* the form and, in another sense, the matter *has* it, or is related to it. Thus, two objects, having different particulars, could differ in a constituent, but not in a property; and their particulars would also not differ *in a property* in that they would be related to exactly the same properties. The existence of particulars is thus equated with the recognition of numerical difference, as opposed to conceptual difference. Two objects, differing only in constituent particulars, would differ numerically, and the two particulars would also differ numerically. Hence to deny (*A*) is equivalent to denying (*B*). With such points in mind we may turn to Moore's argument.

Let us suppose that there is no such thing as numerical difference. In that case, when two things have the same predicate, the only difference between them consists in the difference between two different predicates, one of which belongs to one and the other to the other. But what are the things to which these different predicates belong? We predicate of the things both a common predicate, and a different predicate of each. Either then we must say that the things are the different predicates, and that it is to those that the common predicate belongs; or else we must say that the things are another pair of different predicates, to each of which one of the first pair and to both of which the common predicate belongs. But in either case the common predicate belongs to or is predicated of that which is different in each of the things.[5]

As Moore sees it, to hold that there is no such thing as numerical difference is to hold that two things with the same *predicate* must differ in another *predicate*. Moreover, the difference of predicate or property will be the only difference between the objects. If one then asks, what are the things of which we predicate both the common and the different predicates, we must conclude that we predicate the common predicate of the different predicate. For, since the two things are analyzed into (1) a point of difference, (2) a relation of predication, and (3) a common point, and, since the latter two are identical in each of the two things, he concludes

that the things "turn out to *be* merely their points of difference."
One cannot even say that the "groups" consisting of the common
predicate, the differentiating predicate, and the relation of predication are different; since only the different predicates in each are
different, and nothing can be true of the groups except that "they
are three."

Accordingly our two must be analyzed into: (1) point of difference; (2) relation of predication; (3) common point; of which (2) and (3) are absolutely
identical in each. But, if this is so, the things turn out to *be* merely their
points of difference. Of the group (1) (2) (3), which is what we originally
supposed to constitute a thing, nothing can be true except that they are
three. We cannot say of (a) (2) (3), which is what we originally called the one
thing, that *it* is different from the other (b) (2) (3). It is only (a) and (b)
which differ from one another and are two. In fact our original supposition
was that (3) could only be predicated of (a) and (b), not of anything else.
And if this supposition holds it is plain that anything else which we might
try to predicate of the group, as such, would turn out to be predicated only
of (a) and (b). We can never by any possibility get a number of predicates to
combine in forming a new thing, of which, as a whole, anything can be predicated. We must start, on this theory, with two points of difference — two simple predicates having conceptual difference from one another; this is essential
to there being two things at all. And then we may try to form new things,
also differing from one another, by finding predicates of these points of difference. But whatever we find and however we may add, we still leave the
points of difference as they were — the only things of which duality can really
be predicated. For anything we predicate of them, and the relation of predication itself, may always both belong to some other point of difference, so
that every property by which we may try to distinguish our new thing from
the old, will merely identify part of the new thing with something else, without producing any whole, which, as a whole, differs from everything else in
the world, in the way in which our original points of difference differ from
one another.[6]

Moore concludes that the view that there is only conceptual difference, and, hence, that things may be analyzed solely into predicates and the relation of predication, is false. His argument may be
put in the following way. Consider four things: a white square, a
white circle, a black square, a black circle. Assume, for simplicity,
they have no other nonrelational properties. Call them Peter, Paul,
Mary, and Joan. To say that Peter is white, on the view Moore

wishes to refute, is to say that the predicate white is related by
predication to the predicate square, the latter being the point of
difference with the white circle, Paul. Moreover, Peter is identified
with the predicate square. But, to say that Mary is black is to say
that black is related to square, by predication, and to identify
Mary with the predicate square, since that is the point of difference with the black circle, Joan. We, thus, identify Peter with
Mary. Moreover, they cannot be differentiated, even by introducing relations, since it will always be the same *universal* square that
is involved in any relation to anything else.

We can never say, "This red differs from that red, in virtue of having a different position"; or "in virtue of having a different spatial relation to this other
thing"; or "as being the one I think of now, whereas that was the one I
thought of then." The positions differ, the spatial relations differ, my thinking now differs from my thinking then; but it is always the same red which is
at both positions, and is thought of at both times.[7]

Thus, Moore feels that he has reduced the opposing view, the view
expressed by (*A*), (*B*), and (*C*), to an absurdity.

Moore's argument depends on his holding that the view he is refuting implies that

(i)   predicates cannot combine in forming a new thing, of
       which, as a whole, anything can be predicated.

(ii)   the different predicates "in" things are the only things
       that really differ.

(iii) the things are identified with such distinguishing
       predicates—with their points of difference.

(iv)   predication is then a relation between predicates.

To examine his argument, we must consider why he attributes
these four propositions to his opponent.

We may start by noting an inherent ambiguity in the dichotomy of conceptual and numerical difference. Conceptual difference
has to do with concepts or universals (properties, predicates, qualities). But, then, when Moore holds that two things differ conceptually, is he holding that they differ in a property but that they
need not be properties, or is he asserting that only properties (concepts) differ conceptually? Even if he does not insist that only

concepts differ conceptually, we have two senses of conceptual difference. The two senses may then be confused. If he thinks of conceptual difference in the sense in which concepts are said to differ conceptually, he could come to hold that a philosopher who asserts that there is only conceptual difference also asserts that only concepts (predicates) may differ. This would immediately explain why Moore would attribute (i), (ii), (iii), and (iv) to a philosopher who claims that there is no such thing as numerical difference. For, if only universals can differ, then universals cannot combine into things other than universals which, in turn, would differ. Since predication is a relation between two different things, it then must hold between universals or concepts as the only things capable of differing. One could not then predicate of something which was a combination of concepts but not itself a concept. This could lead one to hold that the properties combined into something, the colored patch, which was itself a property. This would be grotesque since, first, we would confuse the property *white-square* with *a* white square; second, one would not predicate white of the property *white-square*; third, the properties *white* and *square* do not combine into the complex property *white-square* by means of the predication or exemplification relation.

That the sense of conceptual difference whereby concepts differ conceptually is involved in Moore's argument seems to be indicated by his saying: "We must start, on this theory, with two points of difference—two simple predicates having conceptual difference from one another; this is essential to there being two things at all." Properties, or "predicates" as Moore says, thus conceptually differ from each other, and this does not seem to have anything to do with their differing in that one *has* a second-level property that the other does not have. They just differ; but that is considered, in the beginning of the paper, to be conceptual difference. Later, after numerical difference has been introduced, Moore will hold that two concepts differ both numerically and conceptually. But, the distinction between the two senses of difference, as applied to properties, will not be explained. Perhaps, what is involved is this. When two properties are said to differ conceptually, *we mean* they are *different* properties; but when they are said to differ numerically, *we mean only* that they are *different things*. There is, thus, a difference between the idea of two predicates differing conceptually and the idea of their just differing. When we think about it, we just "see" the difference between what is meant by "conceptual difference" and "numerical difference" as applied to predicates. Moore's use of this sort of appeal to our just seeing or realizing that concepts or ideas are different (that the concept of *conceptual difference* is different from the concept of *numerical difference*, for example) is crucial, as we have noted, to his notion of philosophical analysis. It is one of the key themes in his rejection of the "naturalistic fallacy," and it stems, ultimately, from his early view that the world is composed of concepts (Platonic universals) which the mind grasps in some way. Thus, one just sees that two concepts are different as one ordinarily sees that a table is not a chair—simply and directly. All this aside, the point is that stressing the sense of conceptual difference, whereby two simple concepts are said to differ conceptually, may lead him to think that the opponent of numerical difference really holds that only concepts differ conceptually. This suggestion may be made more plausible by putting it a bit differently. Moore thinks that according to the opponent of numerical difference two things, like Peter and Paul, differ *only* in a concept or predicate. Differing only in a concept, they differ in *no other way*. Hence, their difference *reduces* to the difference of different concepts. The assertion that things differ *only in* a concept may then be taken to mean that *only concepts really differ*. This clearly fuses the two senses of conceptual difference.

The reduction of the assertion that Peter and Paul differ conceptually to the assertion that a constituent concept of the one differs from a constituent concept of the other could thus lead one to hold that predication, on the view Moore wishes to refute, relates concepts and not a "thing" and a concept. Moore could also be led to this conclusion by another sense of "reduction." He could hold that to analyze a thing into other things forces one to acknowledge that what is really there are the elements which, on the analysis, make up the object. Hence, to predicate something of the original object is really to predicate of a constituent of it, for only the constituents are really "there." In short, the object is reduced to its constituent elements. To hold that the original object is analyzable into its predicates, in the special relation of predication, is then to hold that to predicate one of the properties of the "thing" is to predicate it of some other quality of the thing. One could not predicate a property of itself or of the relation of predication. To predicate white of Peter is then to predicate the property white of the property square. In this connection, it is highly relevant to note that, after Moore introduces his special kind of particulars, instances of universals (this whiteness, this redness), which are constituents of ordinary objects like Peter, the exemplification relation is taken to hold between such particular quality instances and universal properties or concepts. The relation between ordinary objects and *particular* quality instances becomes that of whole to part.

Just as the notion of reduction may provide one key to Moore's argument, his concept of "group" may provide another. He holds that "nothing can be true of the group (a), (2), (3) except that they are three." Thus, the group cannot be construed as a particular to which properties may be ascribed, especially not the properties that are constituents of it. Moore may be thinking of a group as a class. This would explain his insistence that one cannot attribute properties like white, square, etc., to the group. For, one does not attribute a member of a class to the class. Even if one included a combinatorial relation, like ϕ_1, in the class, this would not help. Moore might also not consider the possibility of construing 'Peter is white' as a statement of class membership since he appears to take a class to be a universal, as opposed to a particular.[8] Hence, a class of qualities could not be a particular having those qualities.

Taking a particular to be a class contrasts sharply with taking the "group" to be a complex *composed* of the members of the class in a special relation, as represented by (1) above. On this latter alternative, such a composite individual would then be the subject of predicative ascription. Since this is really the most cogent version of Bradley's pattern, one may wonder why Moore does not explicitly consider it. This is especially puzzling as he himself had advanced a similar view only a short time earlier. The reason may lie in his concern with fitting an analysis to ordinary usage.

We start from the statement 'Peter is white', where 'Peter' refers to an individual and 'white' to a quality or universal. Thus, the sentence is taken by Moore to assert a relation between the individual and the quality. This relation is indicated by the predicative 'is'. If one then analyzes the individual into a set of qualities in a relation, this linguistic "picture" of things will no longer do. For, whether Peter is taken to be a complex of qualities in a special relation or a set whose members are the qualities and a combining relation, what was a relation between an individual and a quality is transformed into a relation among the collection of qualities. Thus, a critic of such a view might hold that since what corresponds to predication in language is a relation among a group of qualities, to predicate in a statement is to assert a relation among such qualities. Predication is thus fundamentally altered from what it appears to be in the original expression. One might suggest that upon such an analysis ascriptions of predicates are replaced by ascriptions of the relation of part to whole. Thus, if Peter is taken as a complex of qualities (but not a class) in some structural relation, the sentence is transcribed as 'White is a part of Peter' or 'Peter contains white'. Yet, on either alternative, the linguistic expression ('contains', 'part of') does not stand for a relation between the referents of the signs the expression connects. The basic relation, recall, connects the qualities that constitute Peter. Taking the original sentence to assert a relation between an individual and a quality can then lead one to hold, first, that only an analysis which leads to the assertion of a relation between an individual and a quality will capture the sense of the original expression; and, second, that if it is claimed on the analysis in question that a relation holds between qualities, then one must assert just that. Hence, if the relation holding among the qualities is the "predication" relation, one is forced to attribute white to another quality. Thus, Moore may come to believe that on the view he is attacking, one is forced to claim that 'white' is predicated of another quality, and not of the individual that is white. Moore may be implicitly requiring that one's metaphysical analysis correlate entities to the elements of the "ordinary" sentence we start with, while correlating a relation among such entities to sentential predication. Starting from a sentence with a subject, predicate, and predication relation, we must end up with an individual connected by a relation, that is the referent of the predicative 'is', to the referent of the predicate. The alternative he is attacking does not provide an analysis of the object that mirrors the original sentence in this way. Forcing the proponent of this view to identify the relation that connects the qualities with exemplification, Moore reduces the view to absurdity, since the various qualities of an object must then exemplify each other.

That one must ultimately predicate qualities of qualities on the view he wishes to refute is integral to the way Moore states his argument. As he states it, it is also a variant of the argument that qualities cannot differentiate objects since we could have two different things alike in all qualities. But, Moore also has another argument, which does not rely on the absurdity of attributing different qualities of objects to each other. He is arguing that a quality cannot distinguish an object since it *may* belong to any other object and, hence, will be a common rather than a distinguishing feature. This being so for all qualities, it follows that it holds for any set of predicates, since one may consider a set of properties as a complex property, and, hence, something which could belong to two things. Likewise, it holds for the property taken as the point of difference. Three arguments are operating here. First, assuming predication is of some predicate, the point of difference is a universal. As no universal, by itself, necessarily distinguishes an object, the universal taken as a point of difference need not. Second, if we take a complex of predicates as individuating ones, we may ask "What is the object of the predication?" If we say, "a predicate," the first argument reappears. If we say something else, then we abandon the view Moore is purporting to refute. As Moore sees it, no other alternative is open, since he refuses, as we saw, to take a complex of qualities as an object of predication. Third, no complex predicate need individuate since it may belong to more than one object. This third argument can be stated independently of Moore's forcing his opponent to predicate of a quality, as the subject and point of difference. What Moore is insisting upon is that a set of qualities, to individuate, must necessarily do so but cannot, by the very fact that qualities are universals. What he has in mind is, I take it, something like the following. Take two white, bright, squares. Assume they have no more properties. From a list of the properties involved, it would not follow how many things there were. Even if one included spatial coordinates, it would still be possible for there to be one thing at two places or two things at one place. But, suppose, instead of listing universal properties, one considers particularized properties; this white, that white, etc. Particular properties being individuals, this white is just numerically different from that white. They are not sharable, not being universals. Nor would it make sense to hold that one ordinary object that is white contains two particular whitenesses. Thus, given that two whitenesses are involved, it follows that we are dealing with two white objects and not one. Moore, thus, implicitly requires that from a metaphysical analysis, we must be able to derive ordinary facts. It does not suffice to say properties (universals) may individuate, since no two objects have all in common. What individuates must be such that it is not possible for two objects to have "it" in common. This requires something introduced for that purpose and, hence, which necessarily individuates, particular properties. We shall return to the details of this argument. For the present, we may note that Moore argues in this way against conceptual individuation to suggest that the concepts we have of *differing* and *differing in a quality* are just not the same. The purpose of his arguments is to get us to see this conceptual difference.

Can *two objects* have all properties in common? The answer one gives may be taken to reflect one's notions of "object" and of "difference." Moore is arguing that from the notion of a *universal* property and of the analysis of an object, as a group of such properties, it follows that it is not possible. To claim it is possible is to claim there is another notion of difference besides conceptual difference. We saw earlier that the claim that there is only conceptual difference is taken to be equivalent to the claim that an object is a group of qualities. Hence, to show that this latter is mistaken is to argue for the *possibility* of *two objects* having all properties in common and, consequently, for the *existence* of *numerical difference* as distinct from conceptual difference. Thus, Moore takes the argument we considered to establish the possibility that two objects have all properties in common. One aspect of his argument seems to rely on this being assumed to be the case. For, universals may not individuate since, being universal, they *may* be common to more than one object. However, Moore is not begging the question. He is arguing that no listing of universals can guarantee or necessitate individuation. As noted earlier, if we list the nonrelational universals of our two white squares (white, square), it will not follow from the list of properties that there are two individuals, i.e., that some object is different from some other object. If we add the relational universal *left-of*, this will not help, since it is logically possible for a thing to be to the left of itself. Hence, it does not follow that there are two objects from the list of universals: white, square, left-of. This part of Moore's argument is obscured by holding that relations cannot individuate, since the relation would have to be "predicated of" a universal, say white, which would be the *same universal* in both objects. Thus, he makes use of his contention that one must predicate *of* universals (on the view he is criticizing) to argue that relations do not help. But that aspect can be left aside in order to see that he is also claiming that if universals are to individuate they must necessarily do so. Yet, being universals, they cannot. Even if one were to contend that it is logically impossible for two objects to share all properties (including relations), by the very notion of object, this would not touch Moore's argument. For, this latter claim would hold that from the fact that there are two objects, it follows that they differ in a relation. Moore is implicitly arguing that from no list of universals would it follow that there were two objects rather than one. But, he goes further and takes this to show that it is possible that two objects can have all properties in common. Holding, (I) that a set of properties does not necessarily determine whether one or two objects exemplifies members of the set, one holds it is possible to have one set of properties and two objects. This is then easily confused with (II) the possibility of there being two objects, *each* of which exemplifies *all* the properties in the set. Thus, Moore, in "establishing" (I), takes it that (II) is established. This being so, the view he is arguing against is refuted, for that view is equated with the denial of (II). One must, then, distinguish three main aspects of Moore's argument. First, there is the argument that relies on the absurdity of predicating of predicates. This is weak, for his opponent need not hold, as Moore does, that one is forbidden to predicate of "groups." Yet Moore has shown something. His opponent cannot take the 'is' of predication in 'Peter is white' to reflect the tie of exemplification between the referents of the subject and predicate terms. Thus, one who analyzes objects as complexes of universals does not have a neat picturing of "facts" by sentences. Second, there is the argument that confuses (I) with (II), and is thus mistaken. Third, there is an argument that is based on (I) alone. For, one may argue that the view Moore wishes to refute is refuted in that it does not guarantee individuation in view of (I). These latter aspects call for further comment.

Since (I) is fused with (II), Moore does not seem to have established, by arguing for (I), that it is possible for two objects to share all properties. It may be that it is just obvious to Moore that it is possible—that there is just a *conceptual difference* between the concept of numerical difference and that of conceptual difference. At various points in his writings, Moore makes use of the notion that one notes, on examination, that two concepts just differ. In this vein, he would not be offering an argument, but either proposing an explication of his notions of "thing" and "difference" or simply reporting a sort of intuitive insight about the "concepts" of difference. This latter would somehow be based on not "seeing" any contradiction in there being two objects that share all properties. In the former case, one may look upon Moore's analysis as clarifying his notion of "thing." For example, adhering to the possibility of two things sharing all nonrelational properties, one would deny that a thing could be taken as a class of properties, since, as the term "class" is commonly understood, we could not have two classes with all members in common. Likewise, in view of such a possibility, one could not hold a thing to be a complex of properties and also hold that the only sense of difference was "conceptual difference." Moore's analysis can thus be taken to point to internal inconsistencies in certain conceptions of "thing" and "difference." But, there is a clear sense in which Moore can be said to provide an argument for the distinction between conceptual and numerical difference. Even though (I) and (II) are not identical claims, one may argue that (I) implies (II). For, given that universals cannot provide a ground for individuation or difference, one may be led to hold that something other than a property must provide such a ground. Two different objects will then differ in virtue of their containing (or being connected with) such "individuators." But, then we have a further sense of difference: differing with respect to such individuators as distinct from differing in a property. Thus, we have a concept of difference distinct from conceptual difference. Or, to put it another way, given that something other than a universal property is the ground of individuation, it becomes a logical possibility for two objects to share all properties but differ only in respect of their individuators. Arguing for numerical difference in such a way, one argues that two things need not differ in a property. As we noted earlier, this can be taken as equivalent to arguing against things being complexes of universal properties. As we also noted, another crucial assumption in all this is that complexes must differ in a part or constituent. This assumption leads one to hold that something other than a property must be a part of two complex things that are "conceptually identical." But, one could deny the assumption that to differ, complexes must differ in a part. This shows that holding things to be composites of properties is not equivalent to holding that there is only conceptual difference. Alternatively, if one equates these two claims, as we saw Moore does, then if he also holds that there is numerical difference as distinct from conceptual difference, he will naturally come to equate numerical difference holding between two objects with there being a special kind of entity—particulars. Thus, he introduces numerical difference together with his particulars, particular properties or property instances. Before discussing his appeal to such things, we shall take up the crucial question of relational properties and individuation. For, although it may well seem unproblematic to hold, through the notion of numerical difference, that it is logically possible for two objects to have all nonrelational properties in common, it seems quite problematic to hold that they also may have all relational properties in common. That is, a consequence of distinguishing between conceptual and numerical difference is recognizing that it is logically possible for *two* objects to share all relational properties.

Moore's argument against individuation by relations is the last step in his refutation of the claim that things are complexes of qualities that differ only conceptually. As he states the argument, it depends on his holding that predication, on the view he seeks to refute, reduces to predication of one quality of another. Hence, since qualities are the only subjects, any relations between the complexes of qualities (objects) would really have to hold between (constituent) qualities of the objects. Thus he argues:

> We can never say, "This red differs from that red, in virtue of having a different position," or "in virtue of having a different spatial relation to this other thing" or "as being the one I think of now, whereas that was the one I thought of then." The positions differ, the spatial relations differ, my thinking now differs from my thinking then; but it is always the same red which is at both positions, and is thought of at both times. And whenever we attempt to say anything of the red at this position, as, for instance, that it was surrounded by yellow, or that it led me to think of a soldier's coat, exactly the same must be true of the red at that position, which was surrounded by blue or led me to think of a house on fire. We are unable to distinguish the two except by their relation to other things, and by whatever relations we attempt so to distinguish them we always find we have not succeeded. We can never say, "The red I mean is the one surrounded by yellow, and not the one surrounded by blue." For the one surrounded by yellow is also surrounded by blue: they are not two but one, and whatever is true of that which is surrounded by yellow is also true of that which is surrounded by blue.
>
> All this I regard as a *reductio ad absurdum* of the theory that there is no difference but conceptual difference. If any one can avoid assuming that something may be true of a quality at one position, which is not true of the same quality at another position, then he will be entitled to assert that all difference is conceptual difference. But this will at all events not be possible for those who hold that things conceptually the same may be distinguished by their relations to other things.[9]

As Moore states it, the argument is cogent. If one holds that when two red spots are such that one is to the left of the other he must express this by holding that the quality red is to the left of the quality red, then the spatial relation cannot serve to enable us to describe the one spot in a way which will not also describe the other. But, the cogency of the argument is based on the insistence that a universal is the term of the relation. Let us consider a more general version of the argument that relations cannot be used to differentiate objects. The spatial relation cannot be what serves to differentiate the objects since we must presuppose them to be different to start with. Otherwise, it *could be* one and the same object which stands in the spatial relation "being to the left of" to itself. Thus, one assumes that there are two objects or, what comes to the same thing, that the spatial relation is asymmetrical. Since it is logically possible for an object to be to the left of itself, we must hold that the two are different independently of their standing in the relation. In short, a spatial relation cannot differentiate since it is not logically necessary that it hold between *two different* things when it does hold. So stated, the argument explicitly incorporates the demand that the existence of the purported basis of individuation, or difference, logically imply that there are two things rather than one. This is the requirement Moore implicitly uses against qualitative individuation.

Just as it is held to be possible for two objects to have all non-relational properties in common, this argument holds that the relational property need not distinguish, since it could be a further common quality. Thus, the exemplification of the relation would not provide a ground for their being two objects, i.e., from the fact that the relation was exemplified, it would not follow that there were two objects rather than one.

To get at the argument, let us ignore relations for the moment. Suppose one were to argue as follows. Consider two colored patches, one black, one white. On the view that there is only conceptual difference, such a difference in color could serve to differentiate the objects. But, this will not do. For, it could be one and the same object that is both black and white. Hence, we must assume that there are two different objects. Thus, the difference in quality will not serve to ground the difference between the objects, i.e., that there are two rather than one. The one object possibly being both black and white would contain both qualities. There would not be two sets of qualities, one containing black and one containing white, which would correspond to two distinct objects.

This argument reveals that one supposed argument against relations individuating has nothing *essentially* to do with relations. It is an implicit argument against qualitative individuation. Hence, the supposition or, if you will, fact that two objects have all non-relational qualities in common is irrelevant. More important, however, is the fact that the opponent of individuation by qualitative

difference does not really grant that qualities would serve to individuate if it were impossible to have two things that shared all
qualities. For, the same argument he uses against relational individuation could still be raised against individuation by nonrelational qualities. But, this fact, in turn, reveals the weakness of this
argument against relational individuation. Consider the case of the
black and the white patch in a more extreme way. Suppose one
holds that we may observe that the black spot is not white and
that the white one is white. Hence, to say that there is only one
spot is to say that it is both white and not white. Here, one cannot play on it not being a matter of pure logic that something cannot be both black and white. Recognizing that such a theme is involved, we might well feel justified in rejecting the claim that one
spot could be both black and white. This, in turn, could lead us to
reject the implicit criterion that we must logically derive that there
are two objects from the fact that something is to the left of something else, in order to hold that qualities and relations are sufficient to individuate. But, that aside for the moment, we have a
way of putting the case so that to say there is only one object is
to say it is both white and not white. Clearly, something has gone
wrong. Given that something is white and something is not white,
we must, to avoid contradiction, conclude that there are two objects. But, exactly the same point can be made in the case of relations. We observe a white spot to the right of a white spot. We,
then, may be said to observe of *a spot* that *it has* a white spot to
its right, and observe of *a spot* that it *does not have* a white spot
to its right. Consider the property indicated by the predicate 'WR'
defined as

WRx = df. ($\exists$y)(Wy & Ryx),

where 'W' stands for 'white' and 'R' for 'right of'. To say there is
only one spot is, then, to say that '($\exists$x)(WRx & ~WRx)'. Thus,
just as in the nonrelational case, one contradicts oneself.

The point is that the argument against using relational properties to individuate is also an argument against using nonrelational
properties for that purpose. Moreover, the argument can be put in
a quite simple form. The (universal) quality white cannot be what
distinguishes Peter from Paul, since there must be something that

has the quality and something that does not. Those "things" or "subjects" must already differ, and, hence, the quality does not distinguish them. This holds for any quality or set of such; hence, the difference between Peter and Paul must be accounted for by something other than qualities. Being other than qualities, or concepts, such individuators need not differ conceptually but only "numerically." Their numerical difference will, in turn, account for the difference between Peter and Paul, i.e., that there are two, rather than one. Putting the matter as I just did leads to another variant of the argument against relations individuating. For, one may argue that a relation cannot distinguish relata, since the exemplification of the relation presupposes distinct relata. Hence, to attempt to ground the difference between Peter and Paul in a relation they stand in would involve us in a vicious circle. To get at what is involved, let us consider the case of a nonrelational quality and a claim that predicating such a quality presupposes a subject distinct from it. There is one obvious sense in which we may take this claim. To predicate is to attribute a quality to something other than the quality. Or, perhaps better, to hold that a quality is exemplified is to presuppose that there is something other than the quality. Hence, the act of predicating and the relation of exemplification presuppose two things: a quality and a subject. Thus, if we predicate white of Peter, and thereby assert that Peter exemplifies the color, we presuppose that Peter is not identical with the color white. This seems an obvious enough consequence of what is involved in the notions of predicating and exemplifying. But, one may also hold that if Peter is considered to be a composite or collection of qualities including white then, first, the patch is not really distinct from the quality and, second, predicating one term of another would not then reflect, in language, a relation between two things. One may believe so, since one may think that if white is part of Peter, then a sentence like 'Peter is white' becomes tautological, in that the predicate is contained in the subject. For, as these phrases are used, since the predicate is contained in the subject, the subject is not distinct from it in that the subject cannot be conceived of apart from the predicate. Thus, the belief that sentences like 'Peter is white' become tautologically empty on the view that the patch is a composite of qualities can lead to the further belief that, on such a view, the subject-predicate distinction, in language, no longer reflects a relation between two "distinct" things. What is required, in part, is an analysis of what does happen to statements like 'Peter is white' if the patch is held to be a composite of qualities. Nevertheless, the position cannot be ruled out by simply insisting that something completely distinct or independent must be related to the quality by exemplification. This would, in effect, be to require, as we have seen that Moore implicitly does, that since the subject and predicate terms are distinct, in that one is not defined in terms of the other, they must refer to objects that are not "parts" of each other. To require this is to use the subject-predicate distinction, and the demonstrative function of names, to derive ontological consequences in an overly simplistic manner.

We start from an object and a quality that we can distinguish. This does not determine a metaphysical position, except insofar as any position will have to reflect this distinction. But, that does not preclude the view that the relation between the object and quality is a whole-part relation. A similar point holds in the case of relational properties. We start from two things in a relation. That there are two objects is a fact from which we begin. But, it is argued that a relational property cannot distinguish two things alike in all nonrelational properties, in that the exemplification of the relation presupposes that there are two. This suggests that just as the subject is held to be necessarily independent of its quality in the nonrelational case, the two objects must be independent of the relation they exemplify. Thus, one comes to hold that *they must be two* irrespective of whether or not they exemplify any relation. But, it is not clear what "presuppose" means in such a line of thought. It is clear that a two-term relation being instanced or exemplified presupposes two things simply in that what one means by a two-term relation being exemplified is that two subjects stand in the relation. (Forget, for the moment, the ambiguity of the word "term," whereby a reflexive relation is a two-term relation.) The exemplification of a relation requires subjects, just as the exemplification of a nonrelational quality requires a subject. But, the fact that a quality is exemplified by a subject, and hence presupposes such a subject, need not be taken to establish that such a quality cannot be held to distinguish the subject. For there is an ambiguity in the notion of a quality being exemplified by a subject. On the one hand, we can take that in a neutral sense as another way of expressing that an object has a quality. This would, then, be susceptible to alternative analyses. On one such, the object is construed as a composite of qualities containing the particular quality in question. On the other, one could have a particular analysis in mind, to the effect that an exemplification relation holds between a quality and a subject that is "independent" of qualities. This would mean that such a subject neither contains a quality as a constituent nor depends on any quality to ground its difference from other subjects. We have seen how one can be led to believe that a quality cannot individuate by implicitly holding that the subject and quality must be independent for the meaningful ascription of a predicate to a subject.

We also saw that, for Moore, another aspect of the issue was the contention that a universal quality could not individuate an object, since it could belong to more than one object. Supposedly, what individuates *must necessarily* individuate. Something "necessarily individuates" when it is logically impossible for two objects to "have it." In this vein, the possibility of two things sharing all qualities is equivalent to the impossibility of qualities being the basis of individuation. Recalling these points helps clarify the problem of relational individuation in that they bring us to some further fundamental and distinct senses of "presuppose." To take a relation as the ground of individuation might be held to imply that the exemplification of the relation must necessarily individuate. Thus, if *a* has R to *b* and the two objects are held to be distinguished by the relation, then it is held that '*a* ≠ *b*' must follow from 'R*ab*'. But, '*a* ≠ *b*' only follows from 'R*ab*' *and* the assertion that R is either irreflexive or asymmetrical, given the standard definition of '='. However, to assume that R is irreflexive or asymmetrical is held to beg the question. On this line of thought, what is assumed is that one must prove '*a* ≠ *b*', i.e., that there are two things, on the ground that the relation R is exemplified. Nonrelational qualities are held not to be a ground of individuation, since it is logically possible for two things to have any set of these. Relational qualities, like R, are held not to individuate, since it is not logically necessary for two things, rather than one, to exemplify the relation. If one, then, means by the claim that "relations cannot distinguish or individuate objects, since they presuppose distinct terms," that from 'Rxy' we cannot infer 'x ≠ y', then what one says is trivially true.

But, suppose one holds, in connection with an earlier point, that one sees that a is to the right of b and that b is not to the right of b. The opponent of relational difference might balk at the latter claim, since the denial that relations individuate stems, in part, from the argument that we cannot hold that b is not to the right of b unless we presuppose b is different from a. That is, we must assign the names 'a' and 'b' to different objects to start with. Yet, everyone would acknowledge that there are two objects from the outset. This cannot be the point of the argument against relational individuation. One may argue that holding '∼Rbb', with 'R' for 'right of', is to presuppose that $b \neq a$, since one holds 'Rab' to be true. But, "presuppose" is a problematic term here. Assume the Russell-Leibniz definition of '=', 'Rab', and '∼Rbb'. It follows that $a \neq b$. This gives one sense of presuppose: one proposition, Q_1, presupposes another, Q_2, if Q_1 implies Q_2. Here, it is paradoxical. For, on the one hand, the argument against using relations to individuate insists that from a relation holding of a and b it must follow that $a \neq b$ and, on the other hand, if '$a \neq b$' follows from a set of statements, it is held that the assertion of such statements presupposes that $a \neq b$. In part, the paradox stems from the acknowledgment that there are two objects to start with, together with the implicit demand that one prove that there are two. In part, it stems from another sense of "presuppose" that is involved. The former point we shall take up later. The latter we can get at by starting, once again, with nonrelational qualities.

Consider our two objects, a and b. Let two sets, A_1 and B_1, of nonrelational properties be coordinated to them, A_1 to a, B_1 to b. It is understood that each member of the set associated with an object is ascribable to that object. We can uniquely indicate the objects by reference to the sets so long as the latter differ in one member. Having the representative sets differ can then be taken as the basis for asserting that the objects differ. We may even identify the objects with the sets. To have a member of A_1 not be a member of B_1 is to logically imply '$A_1 \neq B_1$'. By the very "notion" of set, if one has a member the second does not, they are two and not one. We may then feel we have not "presupposed" that there are two objects by identifying a with A_1 and b with B_1, and proving '$A_1 \neq B_1$'. Suppose that the same set is coordinated with both objects, since they have all nonrelational properties in common. Is it in principle possible to alter the picture by the use of relational properties so that two distinct sets are coordinatd to the two objects? Let it be the case that the object a is to the right of the object b. Let $\{F_1, \ldots, F_n\}$ be the set of nonrelational properties both share. Can we then form two sets, $\{F_1, \ldots, F_n\}$ and $\{F_1, \ldots, F_n, R\}$, to coordinate to the two objects? One may say "no" for two reasons. First, R is not a quality of either object; it is a quality holding *of* or *between both*. One notion in the original program was that every member of the set could be ascribed to the associated object. R cannot be so ascribed. This brings us to another fundamental sense in which relations are held to "presuppose" objects and hence cannot differentiate them. If we identified the members of the associated set as the parts of the object, we would be led to hold that a relation cannot be a part of an object. Not being a part, as each nonrelational quality is, the relation must be exemplified by the object as a whole (together with another object). Thus, since it is not capable of being a part, the relation's being exemplified presupposes the differentiated object in a way a nonrelational property's being exemplified does not. In short, a constituent does not presuppose the object of which it is a part as a property of the whole presupposes a subject to exemplify it. This is one way of asserting that if objects are held to be composites of qualities, then they must *exemplify* relations, whereas they *contain* nonrelational properties. The point involved also ties in with Moore's forcing his opponent to predicate one quality of another. For the object, considered as a composite of qualities, could not be said to exemplify one of its parts. Thus, one either abandons the exemplification relation or takes something other than the composite object as the subject of it. To speak of a nonrelational property's being exemplified by the object, on such a view, is thus to speak elliptically. A second objection to the use of the set $\{F_1, \ldots, F_n, R\}$ would be that we could not determine which object to coordinate it with, except by fiat.

Suppose we alter the picture by bringing in relational properties as opposed to relations. Let 'R^b' be defined by '$R^b x$ = df. Rxb' and the set $\{F_1, \ldots, F_n, R^b\}$ be associated with a. The new set removes both prima facie objections, since every member of it can be ascribed to a and it is clear which of the two objects the set is to be associated with.

But, one can raise some new objections, as well as reraise the point about presupposing the existence of the differentiated object, rather than "accounting" for it. With respect to this latter point, a critic may point out that a's exemplifying R^b "presupposes," by the definition of 'R^b', that a has R to b, which, in turn, presupposes the existence of a and b to exemplify the relation. Here, we must separate *three* senses of "presuppose." We have already distinguished the sense of 'presuppose', where Q_1 is said to presuppose Q_2 if Q_1 implies Q_2, from the sense where a relation or quality which is exemplified by, but not a part of, an object is said to presuppose the object. A third sense would be that in which R^b, or '$R^b a$', is said to presuppose R or 'Rab', respectively. This is not the same as the notion of presuppose based on logical implication. For, given the definition of 'R^b', '$R^b a$' and 'Rab' imply each other, but only one is said to presuppose the other. Hence, a defined predicate's being ascribed to something may be said to presuppose that the predicates defining it are ascribed, or a property indicated by the defined predicate may be said to presuppose the properties indicated by the defining predicates. One may also point out there is a sense in which R^b presupposes R that is not symmetrical. Given that R^b is exemplified, it follows that R is; but, given that R is exemplified, it does not follow that R^b is. In spite of this, the crucial sense in which R^b is said to presuppose R reduces to the fact that 'R^b' is a defined predicate. The issue is, then, whether the property indicated by such a defined predicate may be said to be part of the object a. There are three questions here. First, are the properties indicated by defined predicates to be taken as existents in one's ontology? Second, may such properties, if acknowledged as existents, be taken as parts of objects? Third, may properties indicated by predicates like 'R^b', in whose definition relational predicates occur, be taken as parts of objects, since the relations themselves are not such parts? Assume that a philosopher who seeks to account for individuation by relational properties acknowledges (1) that one must account for difference in terms of an entity in one's ontology and (2) that such an entity must be a part of the object. Such a philosopher will have to hold that defined predicates indicate entities that may be parts of objects.

In thus answering the first two questions, a philosopher can meet the objection posed by the third by arguing that the sense of presupposition involved in one predicate's being defined in terms of another is not crucial for this issue. It only appears so if we take it to reflect some sort of ontological or temporal ordering, so that it appears as if a's having R^b requires a having R to b as a condition, but not vice versa. But, given the definition, this is misleading, or, at least, it says no more than that 'R^b' is defined by means of 'R' and 'b'. Some may be bothered by the fact that '$R^b a$' and 'Rab' say the same thing, by definition. For if one statement involves exemplification of a relation by two composites, how can the other involve a property's being a part of an object? With this question, we arrive at the issue of internal relations. On the one side, we have the insistence that since 'R^b' is defined by reference to a relation, which admittedly is not part of an object, it cannot refer to a property that is such a part. On the other side, some may insist that the exemplification of R by a and b if and only if a has R^b reflects the fact that when a relation is exemplified objects have correlated relational properties as parts. One may then suggest that the definitions of relational predicates like 'R^b', in terms of corresponding relations, differ from definitions like that of 'WS' as 'being white and square'. First, only one predicate, a relational one, is involved in the definition of 'R^b' and, second, what is achieved is not an abbreviation but a means of expressing something we could not express before: that an object has a relational property. Thus, in the context of the philosophical issues and positions involved, '$R^b a$' does not "say" exactly the same thing as 'Rab' does, though '$R^b a \equiv R ab$' is analytic. The claim can be strengthened by noting that a philosopher who recognizes a property corresponding to 'R^b' need not think in terms of defined predicates. In fact, it is misleading to do so.[10] One forms a predicate, following Russell's early notation, R$\hat{x}b$' by the use of an *abstraction* operator. Given that we have the propositional function 'Rxb' and the abstraction operator, we can *construct*, rather than define, such a predicate. It is true that to ascribe 'R$\hat{x}b$' to an object, a, is to hold 'Rab', but it is also true that

$$(\exists f)(f = R\hat{x}b)$$

holds. The question of the existence of properties indicated by constructed predicates, such as 'R$\hat{x}b$', is thus crucial, and, recall, we assumed that properties indicated by what we earlier called "defined predicates" exist. Moreover, one who holds that predicates stand for properties, rather than classes, may well deny that predicates stand for the same property, even if it is a logical truth that they have the same extension. Thus, owing to different ways of dealing with the problem of negation, and similar questions, one might hold that 'W' and '$\sim\sim$W' (or '$\sim\sim$W$\hat{x}$') do not stand for the same property even though

$$(x)(Wx \equiv \sim\sim Wx)$$

is a logical truth. One might hold that

$$W \neq \sim\sim W\hat{x}$$

holds, given that he explicitly *denies* an extensionality axiom, such as

$$(f)(g)\{(x)(fx \equiv gx) \supset f = g\}$$

to hold. He thus refuses to ignore $\sim\sim$W$\hat{x}$ as a property. In a similar manner, one can argue against the elimination of R$\hat{x}b$ as a property. All this relates our problem to a number of other issues we shall consider in later chapters. I merely note their relevance here and that, consequently, we cannot take certain features of the "problem of individuation" to be as simple and clear-cut as some would have it. Here, in a way, we have come to a dead end. To insist that 'R^b' cannot be cogently employed in the issues we are discussing is to insist that it cannot be treated like other one-term predicates applicable to a, because 'R$^b a$' is equivalent to 'Rab'. To insist that 'R^b' can be employed is to hold that the "definitional" equivalence between the statements does not force us to treat the property R^b as an external property. In a way, one philosopher holds that as relations are external, in that they are exemplified by composite objects, so are relational properties. The other holds that, since relational properties may be taken as internal, there is a sense in which relations are internal to objects.

Other objections arise to the use of 'R^b'. The definition is peculiar in that the property indicated is not, as WS might be taken to be, a complex of other properties. The name 'b' occurs in the definition and, hence, the use of such a predicate may be said to "presuppose" differentiated objects in yet another sense. Also, one might object that since the name 'b' occurs in the definition of 'R^b', the property, in some sense, contains the object b as a part just as WS might be said to contain white and square as parts. Thus, a, containing R^b, is no longer a complex of properties only. Finally, one may object that to use 'R^b' in the list of members of the set associated with a is to abandon the use of it as a defined predicate, for, it cannot be replaced, on the list, by its definition. In part, one here plays with the phrase "defined predicate." 'R^b' functions like any other contextually defined predicate in that it is replaceable in statements in which it occurs as a predicate. To use it on the list is not to use it in a statement as a primitive predicate, it is merely to *make use of it* as a one-term predicate. If, instead of defined predicates, we use propositional functions or abstracts on the list, we could use 'Rxb' or '$R\hat{x}b$' in place of 'R^b'. As for the object b being a part of the property R^b, we clearly have a different sense of the term "part." If one considers the referents of terms occuring in a definition to be "parts" of the referent of the defined predicate, then, in this sense, b is part of R^b. But R^b is held to be a part of a in a different sense. One who is more impressed by the similarity of term and by the transivity of "part of" (as a spatial relation for example) may come to insist that on such a view, b is part of a and all things are parts of all other things. But, as long as we are clear how such slogans arise, no harm is done. It is only when one begins to conclude, on the basis of an ambiguous use of expressions like "part of" or "internal to", that "a is part of b" or "everything is part of everything else" or "all is one" that problems arise.

The claim that the use of the name 'b', in the definition of 'R^b', presupposes the differences of *a* and *b* raises more interesting aspects of the issue. What one, apparently, has in mind here is that the terms '*a*' and '*b*' must be coordinated to the two objects by reference to the sets A_1 and B_1. In short, to individuate by properties and/or relations is taken to involve providing definite descriptions for the two objects. Thus, we cannot employ purely indicative terms, like names, for the objects, in order to construct predicates to use in such definite descriptions. Assume one agrees to this condition. In our case, one might then suggest the use of 'R^1' defined as

$$R^1x = df. (\exists y)(Wy \ \& \ Sy \ \& \ Rxy)$$

and reminiscent of 'WR' used earlier. With 'W', and 'S' for "white" and "square," 'R^1' expresses "having a white square to the left." A question arises about a description using 'R^1', instead of 'R^b', to refer, uniquely, to *a*. One might claim to see that *b* is not to the right of itself and also admit the possibility that *a* has another white square to its right. Hence, 'R^1' would, or could, apply to both *a* and *b*, whereas 'R^b' would apply to *a*. Thus, 'R^1' need not denote a property that serves to distinguish *a* from *b*. Here, we return again to the idea that to hold a property individuates, one must hold it necessarily does so. An ambiguity arises owing to the fact that if a property set does individuate, it is necessarily the case that two things cannot have all the members of the set. This is not to say that a property set that in fact is an individuating set is necessarily one. That a set of properties like $\{F_1 \ldots F_n, R^1\}$ can serve to individuate, i.e., uniquely describe *a*, is a matter of fact, not logic. The point is that its being a matter of fact does not weigh against relations being used to individuate. It will only appear to do so if one holds that for a set of properties to individuate, it must logically follow that only one thing has the properties belonging to the set. But, this is an extreme requirement. In a way, we have a corollary of the requirement we discussed earlier: a relation can be the ground of difference of two objects only if it logically follows from the fact that the relation is exemplified that there are two objects. Here, it is suggested that a set of properties, including relational ones, *can individuate* if and only if it logically follows that only one object can have them all. In fact, this does seem to be involved in Moore's argument that universal properties cannot individuate since, being universals, it is possible for any one or any set to be had by two objects. But, to employ this notion as a criterion would require that it be a logical truth that if something has all the properties in the set, *only one* thing has them. This is far too strong. All that can reasonably be required is that given a situation, like our domain of two white squares, we can construct descriptions that are in fact individuating ones, or, better yet, that there are no reasons which, in principle, prevent us from doing so.[11] But, raising the question of the necessity of a set of properties individuating enables us to see a difference between a property like R^1 and a property like W. If we have two squares where one is white and the other black, then holding that something cannot be both white and black, one must hold that there are two objects. Moreover, we can immediately construct descriptions based on the one being white and the other black or not white. But, if I see, in the case of two white squares, that one has R^1, I *might hold* it to be possible that the other does also, even though I do not see that it does. In this sense, I can see, in the former case, that the objects differ in a color quality in a way that I cannot see, in the latter case, that the objects differ with respect to R^1. What is involved here is not really a difference between nonrelational and relational properties, but one between the use of existential clauses and the use of names. We can see that this is the relevant factor when we note that 'R^b', unlike 'R^1', does not involve a similar problem. R^b cannot be a property of both a and b, just as white cannot be a property of the black square. The use of the demonstrative term 'b' in the definition of 'R^b' is thus the basis of the difference between 'R^b' and 'R^1'. But, this difference is not crucial, if we do not require that purported descriptions necessarily individuate. Another factor involved is the contrast between definite descriptions and names. Descriptions contain universally quantified clauses. Hence, to ascribe a property through a definite description is to make an implicit claim about everything. In this way, an element of corrigibility is involved in the use of definite descriptions that is apparently not involved in the use of names. This feature of descriptions reveals another facet of the issue. As we have considered matters thus far, the proponent of relational individuation accepts the condition that objects must be referred to by definite descriptions employing relational predicates. A critic may now argue that by so doing a simple fact of experience is distorted. In seeing and asserting that there are two squares, there is, in the first place, no doubt that there are two, and, in the second place, no implicit claim about anything else, let alone about everything else. To use descriptions to assert that there are two or that one is to the right of the other is to lose these two features of the situation. Hence, the proponent of relational individuation must distort what is involved in seeing, and asserting, that one square is to the right of the other. By contrast, the use of proper names, under the rule of one name for one thing, preserves these features. The first is preserved in that to use two names reflects that there are two objects; the second is preserved in that statements such as 'Rab' are atomic sentences. To use only descriptions to refer to individuals precludes there being atomic sentences about individuals. We thus come to another implicit criterion imposed by the opponent of individuation by relations. But, it really amounts to a restatement of the idea that when we say that *a differs from b*, we may mean that they simply or numerically differ and not that they differ in a property. What is captured by the use of names, as opposed to descriptions, is that *a* and *b* "just differ." What is relevant here, however, is not that we might mean that two things just differ, without intending to claim that they differ in a property. Rather, the question is whether two things may be two without differing in any way whatsoever. It is one thing to assert that when I say 'p v q' I don't *intend* or *mean* to say '~(~p & ~q)'. It is another thing to claim that 'v' cannot be defined in terms of '~' and '&' because of this. Similarly, that one can think or notice that *a* differs from *b*, without thinking or noting that they differ in a property, does not mean that the claim that two things to differ must differ in a property is mistaken. What the critic of relational individuation seems to be suggesting here is that we simply have the idea or experience of two things just differing. And this is distinct from, and irreducible to, the notion of things differing in a property. But, there is an ambiguity in this. It is one thing to suggest that one has a thought involving the notion of disjunction without considering a definition of it; it is another to insist that one has a thought of disjunction as distinct in meaning from any purported definition in terms of negation and conjunction. The former is irrelevant. The latter begs the question. For, in effect, in the latter case what is being claimed that is relevant to the issue under discussion is not merely that we notice two things without noting how they differ, but that two things can differ without differing in a quality. The proponent of relational difference is, then, being asked how that possibility can be accounted for. Of course, it cannot, but the question is whether that is a possibility. We might recall here Wittgenstein's cryptic "refutation" of the claim that to differ was to differ in a quality. The claim is false, he contended, since it was logically possible for two things to share all properties. To settle the issue by having an idea of "numerical difference" applying, while not thinking that the objects in question differ in a property, is not adequate. However, to hold that *numerical difference* is not analyzable along the lines associated with Russell and Leibniz does provide a basis for claiming that it is *logically possible* for two objects to differ numerically without differing in a property (other than numerical difference itself and "compounds" of that "relation"). We shall return to this question. For the moment, I am merely noting that the fact that one can have a mental state, either a perception or a belief, which would be expressed in terms of '$\neq$' rather than in terms of a purported definition of '$\neq$' as '$(\exists f)(fx \,\&\, \sim fy)$', does not establish that the concept of numerical difference is basic and unanalyzable.

V

Names, Individual Concepts, and Ontological Reduction

Throughout the discussion of relations and individuation, two issues have been left unresolved. One concerns the assumption that properties or relations, to individuate, must be "parts" or "constituents" of objects. The second concerns the assumption that the proponent of relational individuation may not use proper names of objects in a perspicuous schema, but must construct definite descriptions for them.

The use of the phrase 'part of' lends a specious plausibility to the argument against relational individuation in that one implicitly uses the idea that colors and shapes, being located in space "where" the object is, may be spoken of as parts, but a relation, and hence a relational property, cannot be said to be "where" any one object is. This makes use of an analogy between "part" in a spatial sense and "part" in an ontological or metaphysical sense. But, once we forget such misleading analogies, we recognize that to say that white is a part of *a* is to speak in a special or esoteric sense. It has been tied up with the theme that to think or conceive of the object is to think in terms of qualities of it. Thinking in terms of qualities of the object, we "reduce," in thought, the object to such qualities. This raises the question of "individual concepts" and their role in judgment. We shall return to that issue shortly. For the present question of "individuation," we can avoid the phrase 'part of' and take the object to be coordinated to a set of properties or the name to a list of predicates. Such coordinations can be taken to express the idea that what is really involved is having, in principle, unique descriptions. What is then wrong with including 'R^1' on such a list? Supposedly, its use "presupposes" the existence of two distinct objects. But, there is a completely innocent sense of "presuppose" involved in that we start out, without dispute, with two objects. However, the opponent of relational individuation falls back on another, and not so innocent, sense of "presuppose" that we have considered. As we have seen, what the critic insists on is not that we start from two objects and coordinate two sets of qualities to them, but that from inspection of the members of the sets alone we demonstrate that there are two objects. And this can only be achieved if, on the list of all elements of both sets, there occur two unique elements so that it logically follows from the existence of such elements that there are two objects. Such a logical guarantee is furnished by such elements being just the kinds of entities they are, i.e., particulars or individuators. To be a particular is to be particular to, or capable of belonging to, one and only one object. In short, the requirements of individuation are so set up that only special things called individuators can individuate. We can see how empty the line is, if we consider a defect of Moore's view. For Moore, our two white squares would each be composed of a set of particularized properties, say W_1, S_1 for one, and W_2, S_2 for the other. From a list of the constituents 'W_1, W_2, S_2, S_2', it would follow that there was more than one thing, since we build into the idea of, or role of, a particularized property that two of the same kind cannot belong to one object. After all, it would be absurdly redundant to hold that an object has two colors that are exactly alike. But, suppose we consider a case where we have a white square and a black circle with no other properties. For Moore, one is composed of W_1, S_1 and the other of B_1, C_1. But, from the list 'W_1, B_1, C_1, S_1', we cannot conclude that there are two objects, *without the assumption that one object cannot have two colors and shapes*. Yet, this is exactly the same assumption required of the proponent of differentiation by universal properties; only the type of case is different. *Paradoxically, by his own implicit criterion, Moore cannot ground the difference of two objects which differ in all properties for the same reason that his opponent, supposedly, cannot differ-*

entiate two objects that share all nonrelational properties! But, we can avoid this problem. All we need do is introduce into each set a unique element, say X_1 and X_2. These elements are such that each can belong to one and only one object. Now, from a list of the members of the sets, we can determine exactly how many objects there are. But, such individuating entities perform their task only if we implicitly rule that to each object we coordinate one individuator. That this is the very idea of an individuator is just another, more innocent-sounding way of putting the matter. But, once the coordination feature enters the picture, the proponent of individuators presupposes as much as the proponent of qualitative individuation. Both make use of the fact that there are two objects to start with; and both coordinate sets of elements to them. In one sense, then, all alternatives presuppose that there are two objects. This is crucial, since the opponent of relational individuation argues, in effect, that one cannot hold that two things differ relationally without mentioning or referring to, and hence presupposing, the existence of the two things. But, this involves a shift in the sense of "presuppose." Supposedly, the proponent of pure individuators can hold that there are two things, ordinary objects, without covertly referring to them, since one need refer only to the individuators. But, the individuators do the job they do only under the implicit rule that no two are to be coordinated to one object. What the issue comes down to, then, is this. Assume one coordination of the two sets $\{F_1, \ldots, F_n, R^1\}$ and $\{F_1, \ldots, F_n\}$ to the two objects a and b and another of the two sets $\{F_1, \ldots, F_n, X_1\}$ and $\{F_1, \ldots, F_n, X_2\}$ to the same two objects. Consider only the first pair of sets and not the objects. It is *not* logically necessary, by our coordinating procedure, that one must coordinate the sets to two objects, since it is logically possible that all members of the set $\{F_1, \ldots, F_n, R^1\}$ are predicable of both objects. This is obviously another way of saying that from the assertion that all the members of $\{F_1, \ldots, F_n, R^1\}$ are exemplified, it does not follow that there are two objects. By contrast, the sets $\{F_1, \ldots, F_n, X_1\}$ and $\{F_1, \ldots, F_n, X_2\}$ *must be* coordinated to two objects, since we have a rule that no two X_i can be coordinated to the same object, and each X_i must be coordinated to a different object. Or, to put it another way, from the list '$F_1, \ldots, F_n$,

X_1,X_2', it follows that we must coordinate the members to two objects. Thus, we are back to the basic implicit criterion that from a list of the members of the coordinate sets, and the coordination procedure, it must logically follow that there are two objects. This points up why the opponent of relational individuation feels that to individuate by relational properties "presupposes" that there are two objects in a way that individuating by special "individuators" does not. To hold that relational properties suffice, one *must* speak of coordinating the sets, and, hence, group their members, according to which object, *a* or *b*, has which properties. We, then, have two sets, by virtue of our forming or grouping them, which we coordinate to the two objects. The proponent of pure individuators reflects how many objects there are *without* forming the sets, since for each X_i there is one object. Once again we reach a dead end. For, clearly, all that is reflected is the *logical possibility*, in the same sense of that phrase which allows one square to be "possibly" black and white all over, of R^1 being exemplified in a domain of one object. By contrast, each X_i is just that sort of entity that is not possibly "in" or "associated with" two objects. The argument that qualitative individuation "presupposes" what individuation by particulars does not thus amounts to the requirement that a ground of individuation must be such that it is logically impossible for two objects to share "it." Pure individuators, or "bare particulars," are precisely those entities invented to fill this requirement.

There is a specious argument which might tempt one to accept the requirement of a logical guarantee that the pure individuators satisfy. Consider the case of universals. Briefly, one holds that a universal "in," or connected with, each object is the ground of a true predicative ascription in the case of a predicate like 'white'. But, then, given that the ground exists, it logically follows that the object is white. Is it not, then, reasonable to have a similar requirement for the solution of the problem of individuation? This argument derives its plausibility from an ambiguity. What provides the ground for the truth of the predicative ascription is the *universal's being a part of (or connected with) the particular object*. It is not the presence of the predicate on a list of entities or the fact that the universal is exemplified by *something*. In a similar way, *the presence of a relational property in or exemplified by one object, and not another, does logically guarantee that they are different.* This must not be confused with the fact that a relational property's being exemplified does not logically guarantee that there are two objects. If one confuses these two very different conditions, one might be led to require entities from whose existence alone we can logically derive that there are two objects rather than one: to pure individuators or particulars.

To use a property like R^1 instead of R^b to differentiate a and b is to acknowledge that one may not use proper names, but must construct descriptions, if one holds that relational properties may individuate objects. One motive for acknowledging such a restriction may be thought to be involved in the very idea of an ontological analysis. To give such an analysis may be taken to be tantamount to providing a list of entities one takes to be constituents of the objects being analyzed. In effect, one maps such a list onto an object. But, we could not then include the name of the object on such a list. Here, we are in danger of being entranced by the notion of mapping such a list. It is one thing to agree that the name of the object cannot occur on a list of constituents of the object; it is another to hold that, in a perspicuous language, the name of the object must not occur. One thing involved we have already discussed: the apprehension that if the name of an object occurs in a definition of a predicate like 'R^b', then to hold R^b is "part" of a is to hold b is "part" of a. But, as we saw, one need not hold b is a part of a if one holds R^b is a part of a. There is another point involved. We need not think in terms of mapping lists of constituents, but rather in terms of true statements of a perspicuous or ideal language. Why could one not then use the names 'a' and 'b' to assert 'Rab' instead of constructing descriptions? It would appear that the only reason would be a principle to the effect that the use of such names, as primitive terms, commits one to simple entities corresponding to them. The view that the objects a and b are complexes of qualities acknowledges that the objects have constituents and, hence, are not simple. Thus, in a perspicuous language, names must not occur for them. But this "picturing" principle is not sacrosanct. We may look at the issue in the following way. We start out with two objects and coordinate to them the names '*a*' and '*b*'. This, indeed presupposes that there are two objects, but only in that innocent sense in which any account of individuation presupposes that there are two: as a fact from which we start. Having the names '*a*' and '*b*', we can then say, in a perspicuous language, 'R*ab*' and introduce 'R^b' or 'R$\hat{x}b$'. This is irrelevant for the *analysis* of either *a* or *b*. One need not require that a perspicuous language *show* or *picture* an ontological analysis of the objects, in that the signs which refer to them reveal that they are complexes and of what they are composed. Such an analysis is stated explicitly by one's comments about both the perspicuous language and the object. To use the signs '*a*' and '*b*' is not to presuppose that there are particulars, in the sense of either Moore's particulars or pure individuators, unless one adopts a picturing principle as a necessary requirement for a language's being used as a tool in ontological analysis. Perhaps, one adopts such a principle in the belief that one then avoids making metaphysical statements, which reflect one's ontological analysis. For, with such a principle, one may believe one's metaphysical analysis "shows itself." Such a Wittgensteinian motive is understandable, if one fears metaphysical assertions cannot be meaningfully made and believes that we need not make them by employing such a principle. But, both these latter claims are certainly arguable. If we separate the question of the ontological analysis of an object from the use of a purely demonstrative or indicating sign to refer to it, we avoid another motive for the introduction of pure individuators. Such entities may be taken as hypostatizations of the simple indicating function of proper names.

One last point emerges in connection with the previous discussion of R^b, or R^1, being a "part" of the object *a*. One could hold that only nonrelational properties were parts of objects, but that objects exemplified relational properties as well as relations. That is, one would not include in the ontological analysis of the object any relational properties. Thus, two objects could have the same ontological analysis in the sense of the same constituents, i.e., the same nonrelational simple properties. They would be two in virtue of *exemplifying* different relational properties. The immediate objection to this would be the old one that we already presuppose that they are two. But, again, it is the innocent sense of "presuppose." Coordinating two names to the two objects clearly presupposes that there are two, but no more than coordinating two pure individuators to the two objects "presupposes" that there are two. If one then asks what accounts for there being two, since every part of one is now held to be a part of the other, the reply would be that the fact that one exemplifies R^b, and the other does not, accounts for there being two. In this sense, the property R^b can be held to be a ground, but need not be held to be a part or constituent. In short, to say that there are two objects is equivalent to saying that one has a property the other does not have. But, "having a property" covers the two cases of constituent nonrelational properties and nonconstituent relational properties. Or, to put it another way, the problem of individuation need not be thought of as a quest for unique constituents of objects. Rather, we can consider it in terms of specifying conditions that will hold if and only if there are two objects. One proposal is that one object have a property that the other does not have. It is clear that if *a* has W and *b* does not, *a* must differ from *b*. They differ in a property and hence are different. That is, for any x and y, *if* $(\exists x)(\exists y)(Wx \ \& \sim Wy)$, *then* x is not identical with y, on any reasonable use of 'identical'. Hence, given that some object has F and some object does not, we may conclude there are two objects. The critical question is whether the implication holds in reverse, for there is the idea that to give an analysis of "difference" or a solution to the problem of individuation, the equivalence between "there are two objects, *a* and *b*" and "*a* has a property *b* does not have" must be "analytic." But, whether it is will clearly depend on how one takes the notions of *object* and *difference*. If one claims that an object contains a pure individuator, which is the ground of difference, the implication does not hold. If one takes the "identity of indiscernibles" to be involved in the notion of object, then the implication trivially holds. It is pointless to argue whether the claim that indiscernibles are identical, as such, is an analytic truth. Russell recognized this when he "proved" the identity of indiscernibles to be analytic by taking objects to be classes of properties. To hold to this equivalence is, then, to state, in part, what one takes an object to be, i.e., what one means by 'object'. In a way, one then *makes* the identity of indiscernibles analytic, *given this notion of object.* Considering the matter this way, however, precludes attempting to "prove" that the identity of indiscernibles holds for objects.

Having argued that particulars exist, Moore proceeds to characterize them. As we noted, his particulars are neither objects like colored squares nor substrata. Thus, he speaks of a particular being related to *its* universal and also "when it is asserted of one of them that it is black and woolen, this is not to be understood as an assertion that one individual has two predicates, but that two individuals have a certain relation."[1] Particulars are thus particularized properties or quality instances. *The whiteness* of a white square object *a* is a particular that is a constituent of *a* and numerically different from *the whiteness* of another object *b*, though both whitenesses are related to one and only one *universal whiteness.* Both the whiteness of *a* and that of *b* are conceptually identical with all other particular whitenesses, and with each other, but all are numerically different. All such conceptually identical particulars stand in a fundamental asymmetrical relation to *the* universal whiteness, which is also conceptually identical with, but numerically distinct from, each such particular. An ordinary object like *a* is then taken as a composite of such quality instances, a color, a shape, etc. In this way, Moore has two kinds of individuals, as opposed to universals. One kind, the quality instances, is simple, and the other, ordinary objects, is complex.

In a classic paper, Russell also argued for particulars. His arguments essentially reproduce those in Moore's virtually ignored paper. It is clear from the way Russell characterizes the view he is refuting—the view that denies there are particulars—that he insists the proponent of such a view must hold universals to be the terms of spatial relations. "The theory of sensible qualities which dispenses with particulars will say, if the same shade of colour is found in two different places, that what exists is the shade of colour itself, and that what exists in the one place is identical with what exists in the other."[2] Since the universal whiteness would be one and the same in both patches, nothing can distinguish the two patches:

It will become impossible to distinguish the two patches as two, unless each, instead of being the universal whiteness, is an *instance*. It might be thought

that the two might be distinguished by means of other qualities in the same
place as the one but not in the same place as the other. This, however, presupposes that the two patches are already distinguished as numerically diverse, since otherwise what is in the same place as the one must be in the
same place as the other.[3]

In short, the term of the spatial relation cannot be the universal
whiteness, since we would have only one object when white is to
the left of white. Consequently, we could not account for the difference of the two objects. Moreover, the patches cannot be collections of universals, since it is logically possible for the two objects not to differ in nonrelational properties:

They may or may not have intrinsic differences—of shape, or size, or brightness, or any other quality—but whether they have or not they are two, and it
is obviously logically possible that they should have no intrinsic differences
whatever. It follows from this that the terms of spatial relations cannot be
universals or collections of universals. . . . Moreover, however many qualities
we add, it remains possible that the other subject may also have them; hence
qualities cannot be what constitutes the diversity of the subjects.[4]

This tendency to treat a collection or bundle of universal qualities
as a complex universal quality is revealed again when Russell
claims:

But these subjects cannot be mere bundles of general qualities. Suppose one
of our men is characterized by benevolence, stupidity, and love of puns. It
would not be correct to say: 'Benevolence, stupidity, and love of puns believe
that two and two are four'. Nor would this become correct by the addition of
a larger number of general qualities.[5]

It also seems that Russell, like Moore, is insisting that the predication relation between a subject term and a predicate must be preserved from common usage. For, he seems to be suggesting that a
quality of an individual cannot be used to characterize a collection
of qualities, and, hence, the individual cannot be construed as such
a collection. If he is not suggesting this, it would appear that he is
rejecting a metaphysical view on the ground that it involves odd or
"incorrect" locutions.

In addition to the above arguments, Russell also contends that
the logical possibility of one thing having the two relational properties of being surrounded by red and being surrounded by black

(simultaneously) shows, first, that such relational difference cannot ground the diversity of the two patches and, second, that we presuppose the numerical diversity of two patches if we hold that nothing can have both relational properties.[6] All the above arguments we have considered earlier. But, Russell's central argument appears to be a new argument. He takes his main argument to be based on the two-fold claim that spatial relations like "right of" *imply* the diversity of their relata and that it is an evident fact of experience that spatial relations are exemplified. In short, from "*a* is to the right of *b*" it follows, owing to synthetic but self-evident characteristics of "right of," that *a* is different from *b*. Hence, *a* and *b* are neither universals nor collections of such. If they are universals, they need not be diverse, since whiteness could be to the right of whiteness; and if they are collections of universals, the same possibility arises, since the collection of whiteness, a shape, a size, etc., could be to the left of such a collection. This latter claim obviously depends on taking a collection of universals to be a complex universal. Ironically, the pattern of argument that Moore and Russell use depends on a confusion that we saw to be an essential part of Bradley's pattern: the taking of *a complex of properties* to be *a complex property*. It should, then, be apparent that Russell's argument that particulars exist since spatial relations imply diversity is new only in that he explicitly insists that a bundle of universals is a universal. For, the argument involves the claims: (1) two collections of nonrelational universals could not be two if they had all constituents in common; (2) relational properties cannot differentiate objects since, first, relations are not intrinsic constituents and, second, an irreflexive relation holding between *a* and *b* implies that *a* is different from *b*, and, hence, presupposes their difference rather than grounding it; (3) a collection of universal qualities is itself a universal rather than a particular, since the collection at two places would be one and the same collection. Perhaps, (1) and (3) can be taken as different ways of putting the same claim. That aside, Russell's argument for particulars from the assumption that *a* is to the right of *b* is really a compact way of putting together the various other arguments we have considered.

It is clear that Russell is right when he holds that if "*a* is to the right of *b*" implies "*a* is different from *b*," then *a* and *b* cannot be universals if a universal, simple or complex, is taken to be something that can be at two places at the same time.[7] Thus, whether one considers the universal whiteness or the complex universal white-square, neither could be the term of a spatial relation. But, it is not at all clear that a particular cannot be a complex of universals. That is, it is not clear that complex of universals need itself be a universal. One may claim that a complex of universals, a, is one particular and that there may be a different particular, b, which is a complex of exactly the same universals. In short, one may deny both that a complex of universals is itself a universal and that two complex objects to be two must differ in a constituent. Even if one rejects only the former, the claim that a complex of universals is itself a universal, one may still maintain that Russell has not shown that one needs particulars other than as complexes of universal properties. For one may still hold that a relational property like R^b or R^1 could be a constituent of a. This returns us to our earlier discussion of relational individuation. But, we might note that to reject R^b as a ground of individuation, on the basis of it being a universal and hence possibly holding of both a and b, would be awkward for Russell. On the one hand, he would hold that it is self-evident that a is not b if a is to the right of b; on the other, he would admit that b could be to the right of itself.

Even if Russell and Moore have successfully argued that there are particulars, they have not shown that a particular cannot be a complex of universals. At most, they have shown that a view which holds that there are only universals cannot account for two objects, alike in all nonrelational qualities, exemplifying spatial relations and, hence, admittedly being different. Simply put, Russell's argument for particulars amounts to the claim that an object cannot be a universal, since if it were, it could be here and there. Although this is true of universals, it is not true of either ordinary spatial objects or particulars. Hence, such objects *must be*, or contain, *particulars* and not be complexes of universals that are, in turn, universals. But, this does not involve their being, or containing, particulars in the sense of either quality instances or substrata. For, they may be complexes of universals, which are not universals. Moore's particulars are quality instances. Russell's particulars may also be quality instances. But, there are things Russell says that indicate he is arguing for substrata or bare particulars. Although he does speak of instances of whiteness, he also holds that such an instance has other qualities, i.e., shape and brightness:

What exists here is something of which whiteness is a predicate — not, as for common sense, the thing with many other qualities, but an instance of whiteness, a particular of which whiteness is the only predicate except shape and brightness and whatever else is necessarily connected with whiteness.[8]

Perhaps *instance* is to be thought of as a composite of the particular and the qualities whiteness, the shape, and brightness. In any case, Russell does distinguish the particular from the several qualities it has. We can then distinguish this kind of view from one which would hold that a quality instance has only one quality. On this latter view, the characterized object, the white patch, would be construed to consist of an instance of whiteness, an instance of a shape, and an instance of a degree of brightness. These three quality instances would be different particulars and not qualities of a bare particular or substratum. The former view would seem to involve a substratum exemplifying various universals, whereas the latter avoids a substratum by holding *each* quality of the patch to be a *particular* constituent of it. I am suggesting that Russell's view is the former and Moore's is the latter. If this is so, then even though both have argued for particulars, they have not argued for the same kind of entity. Moreover, if the argument I have presented is correct, neither established what he purported to prove, though they did establish that particulars exist in that objects cannot be taken *to be* universals. But, this latter claim suffices to refute the idealist's line of argument that depends on assimilating the notion of a complex property with that of a complex of properties.

We have considered alternative "solutions" to the problem of individuation and the analysis of the notion of an "object." I have also suggested that the problem itself is a pseudo-problem. I would like to develop that hint and connect it to themes directly involved in questions about the structure of thought and belief: those themes have to do with *reference* to objects, in thought, and with *individual concepts*.

Given an object, we can simply indicate it by a label or name. Once we so indicate it, no characterizing description of the object is such that where '*a*' is the label and '$(\iota x)(\emptyset x)$' the definite description,

$$\ldots a \ldots \equiv \ldots (\iota x)(\emptyset x) \ldots$$

is a logical truth. (A description like '$(\iota x)(x = a)$' is not a characterizing description through its use of the label '*a*'.) This can lead one to hold that the object is indicated irrespective of any property it has and, hence, purely as an object. In turn, this can lead one to hold that one indicates a bare particular, which exemplifies the properties. Alternatively, we need not take any*thing* so postulated to be indicated. The use of such labels, to repeat, simply reflects our referring to an object as an object irrespective of any properties it has. Taking such a line, we dismiss the problem of individuation as a pseudo-problem. This does not mean that we cannot retrieve several issues that were meshed together into the so-called problem of "individuation." Can one construe '$x = y$' in terms of '$(f)(fx \equiv fy)$'? Need one have labels for individuals, or can one replace such labels by definite descriptions? Must one replace labels by definite descriptions? Must one replace labels by descriptions in a perspicuous schema? If one uses labels, or names, do we then recognize that all sentences of the form '$a = (\iota x)(\emptyset x)$', where '*a*' is a name and '$E!(\iota x)(\emptyset x)$' is not a theorem or logical truth, are not theorems or logical truths? Is the linguistic relation of predication to be understood as reflecting a part-whole or set-membership relation between a property and an object, or is the predication relation to reflect something like exemplification, where one may speak of the relation as "external" in specified senses? Are subject-predicate sentences analytic in a perspicuous schema? Do relational predicates hold of objects in the way monadic predicates do in the sense that the terms of the relation are literally the subjects of nonrelational properties? In short, there is no one problem of individuation. There is a cluster of questions, not all genuine, about the use of and the understanding of names and descriptions in a perspicuous schema. That feature of the use of names as mere labels, which gives rise to the ontological illusion of bare particulars, may be retained without postulating such suspect entities.

Recognizing such a role for mere labels, that they stand for objects qua objects, has consequences for problems in intentionality and concerns about ontological reduction. I shall take up the latter first. Consider a simple kind of checkerboard pattern where we have a square composed of four smaller squares, two black and two white.

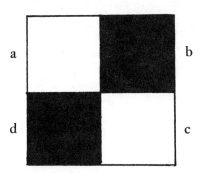

Call the large square 'A', and let the lower-case letters name the smaller squares. Do we have five objects, or can one be "reduced" to the other four? Here, we have, in simple terms, the kind of question philosophers tackle when they worry about existence and reduction. Clearly, A cannot be reduced to a, b, c, and d in the sense that it can be identified with the class whose members are a, b, c, and d. On the other hand, the area A occupies is exhausted by the areas of the smaller squares. Moreover, consider the statements:

(1) $S(A)$ & $A \neq a$ & $A \neq b$ & $A \neq c$ & $A \neq d$.

(2) $(\exists x)(Sx$ & $x \neq a$ & $x \neq b$ & $x \neq c$ & $x \neq d)$.

(3) $C(A)$.

(4) $(\exists x)Cx$.

where 'C' is a predicate standing for the pattern of A and 'S' is read 'is square'. Clearly, (1)-(4) are true. Consider next:

(1$'$) Sa & Sb & Sc & Sd & $R(a, b, c, d)$.

(2$'$) Sa & Sb & Sc & Sd & $R(a, b, c, d)$.

(3$'$) Sa & Sb & Sc & Sd & $R(a,b,c,d)$ & Wa & Wc & Bb & Bd.

(4$'$) $(\exists x)(\exists y)(\exists z)(\exists w)$ [Sx & Sy & Sz & Sw & Wx & Wz & By & Bw & $R(x,y,z,w)$] .

with 'R' for the spatial relation holding among the "constituents" of A, and 'W' and 'B' continuing to stand for the colors white and black. Suppose we now ask if $(1')$-$(4')$ can be taken to replace (1)-(4) in that the former reflect "analyses" of the latter. One line of argument would be that we cannot since something is left out. We do not reflect the fact that we are dealing with the object A rather than any complex square of the pattern C. This objection would be expressed in that we do not catch the difference between (1) and (2) without bringing in a reference to A. So, for example, if we introduced a relational predicate 'Con', for 'contains', we might use:

$(1'')$ $Con(A,(a,b,c,d))$ & $(1')$

$(2'')$ $(\exists x)(\exists y)(\exists z)(\exists w)(\exists v)\,[Con(x,(y,z,w,v))$ & Sx & $x \neq y$ & $x \neq z$ & $x \neq w$ & $x \neq v]$

$(3'')$ $Con(A,(a,b,c,d))$ & $(3')$

$(4'')$ $(\exists x)(\exists y)(\exists z)(\exists w)(\exists v)\,[Con(x,(y,z,w,v))$ & Sx & Sy & Sz & Sw & Sv & Wy & Ww & Bz & Bv & $R(y,z,w,v)]$

to analyze (1)-(4). The use of the name 'A' in (1) and (3) and of 'Con' in $(1'')$-$(4'')$ can be taken to show that A is not reduced to a, b, c, and d or eliminated in terms of such objects. But, is there an object A, in addition to a, b, c, d and the fact that obtains among the latter? Does the fact that we can attach, or do attach, a label to A, without using a description to do so, suffice as a ground for holding that A exists in addition to a, b, c, and d and the facts obtaining among the latter? To resolve such a question, we must clarify our notion of "reduction." To do so, let us shift our attention to the predicate 'C', and aside from any question about A, consider whether we can *define* 'C' by using $(4'')$ without '$(\exists x)$', hence with 'x' free. The question is ambiguous, for a problem arises that corresponds to the question about A. Of course, we can define a term 'C' as earlier. But, given that we *assign* a predicate 'C' to the pattern property of A, can we then consider that predicate to be defined? If one is asked to specify just what property is being coordinated to 'C' in such an assignment, the response might well be in terms of such a definiens. This does not mean that 'C' is "now" defined. Yet, we "know" that something will exemplify C only if it satisfies a predicate so defined, since we "know" that

(5) $(x)[C(x) \equiv 4''(x)]$

holds, with '$4''(x)$' for the relevant expression. 'C' is coordinated to a "complex" property. Yet, it need not be, for we can take the expression to the right either to define 'C' or to coordinate it to such a property. This corresponds to a question one may raise about coordinating names to objects by means of definite descriptions. One may introduce a zero-level sign as an abbreviation of a definite description, as opposed to using such a description to coordinate a constant to an object. In the first case, we may clearly hold that the constant is not a name but a "disguised description." What about the second case? The key to an adequate answer is the treatment of the sentence '$a = (\iota x)(\emptyset x)$', where '$a$' is the constant and '$(\iota x)(\emptyset x)$' is the descriptive phrase. Insofar as the descriptive phrase is in the schema, such a sentence is significantly different from any other sentence of the same form with a *different* description. For, the sentence '$a = (\iota x)(\emptyset x)$' functions like an interpretation rule.[9] The point is no different if one employs a description of the background language that one uses in interpreting the schema. Such identities cannot be treated as ordinary factual claims about objects having certain properties. The same type of query may be raised about the status of statement (5). Is it an empirical generalization? An analytic proposition? A stipulation? Perhaps a simpler case will help. Let 'WS' stand for the color-shape of a, so that we may take

(6) $(x)[WS(x) \equiv W(x) \& S(x)]$

to be a simpler version of the case that (5) involves. Is 'WS' defined by '$W(x) \& S(x)$'? Suppose we do not offer (6) as a purported definition but use '$W(x) \& S(x)$' to coordinate the predicate 'WS' to the property in question. Two questions may be confused. One is the question of whether there is an additional property or whether the property WS is "reduced" to W and S. The other question is a question about the truth of (6), given that 'WS' is not defined by '$W(x) \& S(x)$' but *coordinated*, by use of that latter expression, or simply by our taking that predicate to stand for *the color-shape* of *a*. The first question we shall return to in a later chapter. So long as we keep the questions distinct, it suffices for my present purposes to concentrate on the second.

In Chapter II we noted that Moore once held that those who sought to analyze the concept *good* committed a fallacy. He seems to have believed that one can simply *see* that *good* is unanalyzable, since we recognize that for any proposed analysis of *goodness* it would still be possible to have an object either be good and not fulfill the condition of the analysis or vice versa. He did not further explain how one knows that that is possible. Supposedly, we merely note what we *mean* by '*good*' and by the terms of the proposed analysis, and then we contemplate the concepts involved. The "fallacy" he rejected was simply making a mistake about such an "inspection" of concepts. The same point seems to be involved here with 'WS', 'W', and 'S', where we do not use the above stipulative definition. What we recognize is that we could just as well introduce 'WS' as such a defined expression *and not change the meaning* or the *concept* we take 'WS' to express. We, thus, recognize it to be a different case from that of 'good' and 'pleasure.' The use of the signs 'WS', 'W', and 'S' is irrelevant. We could have used 'Ø' instead of 'WS'. Moore is right, I think, in that there is no further justification to warrant the analysis expressed in (6). What we can do is note how *problematic cases* differ from cases like that of (6). For example, one readily uses the expression 'the color-shape' in the case of WS, as well as a conjunction formed from 'W' and 'S' to indicate what 'WS' *refers to*. What would one use in a *corresponding* way in the case of 'good'? Given that one recognizes such a point in the case of 'WS', let us return to the more complex case of 'C'. There is one difference at the outset. In the case of 'C', we must have a relation like Con in order to have the expressions on the left and right side of the biconditional apply to the same thing, A. What this shows is that one may argue that we cannot take 'C' to stand for a property that *reduces* as 'WS' does, since without 'Con' we get one statement, (1') or (3'), simply replacing another, (1) or (3). And, moreover, if we employ 'A', as in 'C(A)', that statement cannot be replaced. Alternatively, we may use 'A' and 'Con' and recognize that A is not reduced in that the sign 'A' occurs in (1''). Yet, we also recognize that

$3 \equiv 3''$

has to hold, by the very way we take 'C'. Again, no further basis for such a claim can be found. One may say it is by the *meaning* of 'C', but this is merely a summary, not a reason. If Moore is right, and I think he is, the point is that no further reasons are to be found. But, now, is A reduced to the *facts* about *a*, *b*, *c*, *d*? Are we using 'A' as a label, just as we used 'WS' and 'C' as labels? In those cases, we recognized the reduction of properties in that we recognized (5) and (6) to be truths expressing "analyses." What about the name 'A'? If you treat 'A' as a label and take 'Con(A,*a*)' to be a statement relating two individuals, then one can say that A is not reduced for the following reason. From '$(\exists x)(x = A)$', it does not follow that 'Con (A,*a*)' holds, whereas if we use some description for A, such as '$(\iota x)(\ldots x \ldots \& \text{Con}(x,(a,b,c,d)))$' abbreviated as '$(\iota x)(\not\!\emptyset x)$', then from '$E!(\iota x)(\not\!\emptyset x)$' it will follow that 'Con $((\iota x)$ $(\not\!\emptyset x),a)$' holds. But, then, may one use such a label in *any* case where we can specify a description? This seems to bring us back to the issue about bare particulars. For, is not the notion of a bare particular merely an ontological phrase for pointing to a feature of signs that are labels? If we can label the large square by 'A', then we can hold it is not reduced along the lines indicated by applying Moore's criterion for rescuing "good" from analysis. So long as we use a label, we can hold, for example, that the object labeled need not have contained the objects *a*, *b*, *c*, and *d* and yet *be* the same. But, doesn't this show that something is wrong with the pattern? Moreover, when can we really label "something"? Consider a pattern like that of A with the squares at some distance. Do we have an object B, in addition to the small squares? Of course, one can say we "make" objects by our way of construing things—as some maintain we do for macro-physical objects composed of micro-objects and relatively large "spaces." That is not a point I am concerned with, though it raises the issue of idealism. We may note that such a claim makes sense only if we recognize *a*, *b*, *c*, and *d* as *elements*, *relative* to the purported or rejected *complex* objects A and B. What arrangements of elements one may take to be further objects is another question, as is the question of whether there are ultimate elements in some reasonable sense of 'ultimate'.

This latter question is also not my concern, while the former is of only passing concern for my purposes in this book. Hence, I shall only sketch an answer to it. The problem arises from our acknowledging that we can coordinate a label, like 'A' or 'B', and then holding that the "objects" labeled are reduced or eliminated. For, we clearly presuppose that an object exists if we hold that we label "it." Yet, just as clearly, we do not *establish* that an object, such as B, exists by holding that we may "attach" labels with an expression of the form "let 'B' name the x such that . . ." We *cannot hold* that there is an object where we attach a label by *referring* to *that* which *contains* a set of objects in relations. *Such a pattern leads to absurdity.* The alternative pattern holds that we *need not* accept a *complex* object, where we can specify *it* in some such way (in terms of *simpler* objects). This does not lead to absurdity. Nor should it lead one to deny what we noted about sentences employing 'A', as opposed to descriptions. Having a description specifying A *in terms of constituents* gives us a basis for rejecting 'A' as a (logically) proper name in a perspicuous schema. We may also avoid the question of whether we have *really* reduced or eliminated such an "object," just as a logicist need not bother with a question of whether numbers are *really* classes or properties. We, thus, have a situation analogous to that involving WS. Just as in that case, there is no conclusive argument. We simply note two things. First, the reductive pattern, when systematically employed, does not lead to absurdity. By contrast, the systematic application of the contrary pattern does reduce that pattern to absurdity. Second, there are numerous cases where we must explain (even to ourselves) what we intend to name in terms of specifying constituent entities and relations among them. Once we do that, we may recognize that there is no ground for not extending the pattern to those cases where we *might directly* attach a name to a complex object, but where we *need not do so*.

Nothing I have said suggests that A, or B, is a *mere* class of elements *a*, *b*, *c*, and *d*. There are facts of the kind indicated by the constituent sentences of (3′). This provides another sense in which both A *and* B are not reduced or eliminated. We may, then, take such "things" to be *compounds* of facts or ˋclasses of facts. This would not really add anything. The points to note are that A and

B are not to be taken as objects, but, rather, are to be thought of in terms of facts. And, given the appeal to facts like those indicated in (3′), it makes no sense to say that A, or B, has been *reduced to* (or eliminated in terms of) the *elements a*, *b*, *c*, and *d*. What is reduced or eliminated or analyzed is a purported fact expressed by a sentence like 'S(A)'. All this, of course, reflects the theme of the *Tractatus* that *complex objects* like A are not objects and that all complexes, having a structure, are facts.

One way of calling attention to the connection between our talk of labels and traditional talk of bare particulars is to note that a bare particular analyst would likely point out that, in the case of A, the relation Con indicates a spatial connection between particulars and not an ontological relation. Thus, the object A is recognized in that the label 'A' stands for a particular that has its area including the area of the object *a*. In that sense, A may be said to "contain" *a*, but one would not, then, be tempted to think of "analyzing" A in terms of *a*. In a similar vein, one could reject the ontological analysis of a macro-physical object in terms of micro-objects. What such "reductions" amount to is merely a reflection of more complicated physical relations between macro-objects and particles than the relatively simple spatial relation between A and *a*. We may, then, note that talk of the reduction of mental states or phenomenal entities like sensa to brain states or more complex physiological states, or even particle states of the "body," is quite absurd in that in no sense of "part" could one take mental states or sensa to have brain states or physiological states or particles as "parts."[10] Such points aside, we may note that the idea of a bare particular is of something that cannot be *reduced*, in that it is not complex and it has no parts. The use of a simple label, a name, reflects that way of construing an object. In any case, the use of a label precludes taking a sentence without the name as elliptical for a subject-predicate sentence with the name, unless, of course, one uses another mere label for the same object. Labels cannot be eliminated by employing sentences that state the "same thing" and yet do not use labels. Thus, *if we recognize* A and B *as objects* and use labels for them, sentences like 'C(A)' cannot be transcribed without using the sign 'A' in the new sentence, and, hence, in that sense, we still acknowledge the object A. All one can do is advocate the replacement of such sentences by others, say (3′) or, perhaps, (4′). But, one no longer offers an argument or an analysis by merely employing a replacement. Yet, in much talk of ontological reduction, that is all one seems to be offered.

The question of labels bears on our concern with belief contexts. Suppose one believes that A is C. How do 'A' and 'C' function in such thought patterns? That is, does 'A' function as a mere indicating label, and does 'C' function as elliptical for a "definition"? The question of definition and belief contexts will be postponed for later chapters. Here we shall stay with the question of names or labels in such contexts, and its connection with the dispute about bare particulars.[11]

There are two aspects to the issue of bare particulars. One concerns Bradley's claim that the notion of a bare particular is unintelligible. Alternatively, some philosophers, like Bergmann, find such entities indispensable to account for "individuation," and to refute idealism. Such concern with unintelligibility led Bradley to adopt a particular analysis of judgment. To judge that A is C is to think that an object has a property. For Bradley, this meant that one thinks that an object having certain properties also has C, since one could not think *of* an object except in terms of properties. Without such properties "in mind," one would have no "concept" of the object and, hence, one would take *it* as an unintelligible bare subject of a property. This claim asserts, in effect, that in thought we employ descriptions and not mere labels. Bradley thought that the two claims—that in thought we employ labels rather than descriptions and that we recognize bare particulars— were either the same or, at least, logically connected. Rejecting bare particulars would then provide a reason for advancing his other claim. There is another reason for believing that descriptions must be employed in belief contexts. Compare two thoughts with the texts:

A is C

and

$(\iota x)(\emptyset x)$ is C.

Let us assume that we construe such thoughts along the lines

sketched in previous chapters, so that we have occurrences of two
"verbal facts." One may now ask how it is that the thoughts are
about the object A, assuming *that* A = (ιx)($\emptyset$x). In the case of the
second text, *given that predicates stand for properties* or concepts,
a philosopher may hold that the judgment is about whatever fulfills the property $\emptyset$. (Recall Moore's way of connecting a concept
with "its" object.) What the subject *has in mind* is precisely *that*
property or concept, and one judges that *what* has it also has C.
This line would be supported by the belief that thought is always
in terms of concepts or properties. A thought or a self is, in judgment, always related to one or several properties or concepts, as
Moore seems to have held at one time. Such a pattern would, of
course, deny the way I am construing thoughts. For, on the pattern we are developing, what occurs in the thought is a token of a
predicate and not the concept or property. That aside, one who
thinks along the lines of Bradley's pattern would then hold that
the use of the label 'A' covers up the need for a concept, *"in" the
thought*, which indicates the object A. One concludes that in
thought we cannot use mere labels of objects, since we, then, have
no concept of the object. *Being identical with* A is not a legitimate
concept, since it removes the problem only one step in that we still
use a label. The idea is that the verbal pattern of the description is
associated with or expresses a concept or property, and the label
'A' does not.[12] Hence, with the former there is a "content" for
thought, which the latter does not provide. Thus, the verbal pattern 'A is C' must either be taken to express a thought like
'(ιx)($\emptyset$x) is C' does, only in condensed form, or not to express a
thought at all. Such a pattern appeals to thoughts as separate from
verbal facts. It is the pattern implicit in Frege's analysis of thought
and meaning and the pattern Russell rejected in developing a view
that is a kind of prototype for the one we are developing. We shall
proceed to the controversy in subsequent chapters of the book. Before doing so, I want to consider another way of looking at the supposed problem. Given the occurrence of a particular token fact of
the form 'A is C', how is it that that occurrence of the token of
'A' intends or stands for the object A and is known to do so by
the person making the judgment? One aspect of the appeal of
propositions, concepts, and senses along Fregean lines is often

overlooked. A Fregean view supposedly enables us to answer this question in that, on such a pattern, a person, or a mental state of a person, is in relation to a concept or sense that stands for or indicates the object. A thought is about an object in virtue of some relation between the concept and the object. If we reject entities like concepts, senses, and propositions, we must return to the problem. We shall do both. For the moment, we may merely note that the use of mere labels in belief contexts, without taking them to be elliptical for definite descriptions in such contexts, is one aspect of the set of issues associated with the puzzling notion of a "bare particular."

Recognizing the problem of individuation to be a pseudo-problem or, at least, not *a* single problem, has another important consequence. We can acknowledge a primitive concept of *numerical difference*, along with Moore and Russell, without accepting special entities to "ground" the *fact* that such a relation holds between two objects. Attempts to analyze such a notion and define an appropriate predicate stem, in large part, from a desire to avoid "pure" individuators or "bare" particulars. One may recognize that *difference* is not to be understood in the Russell-Leibniz fashion. It is simply a basic notion that holds between any two entities, be they simple or complex. In a perspicuous schema that allowed only one "label" for each basic entity, such a relation would be "shown" by the occurrence of different signs for different entities, be they particulars or properties. If one now insists that all that is meant by holding that bare particulars exist is that we accept such a concept of *numerical difference*, we have reached a good point to proceed to another issue. What he can *reasonably* have in mind is that treating *numerical difference* as a basic notion acknowledges the logical possibility of having *two* objects that do not differ in a property, just as treating 'A' as a logically proper name can lead one to hold that that object could be *the same* and not have *a*, *b*, *c*, and *d* as constituents. Here, we are, clearly, at the limits of discussion. I have suggested that we deal with a feature of labels as simple designating signs. Others seek an ontological ground for such a feature. Perhaps, it is worth noting that the logical possibility depends upon (1) the use of labels for the objects, (2) the representation of numerical difference either by a primitive relational predicate, say 'D', or by having only one label for an object, and (3) a standard "formal" explication of "logical possibility." If one introduced a primitive predicate 'D' for numerical difference, then it would be the case that where two objects differed numerically, they would also differ in a "property." In that sense, the proponent of numerical difference must acknowledge that two objects cannot differ numerically and share all "properties."[13] Of course, that relational property (and compounds of it) can be precluded as not being a property among properties. Let us grant that. Can one still hold that it is not possible, in some reasonable sense, to have *two* objects differ numerically and yet agree in all properties? I do not wish to appeal to the time-honored claim that it simply makes no *sense* to say two different objects can agree in all properties (except, again, for contexts involving difference and identity). Yet, an opponent who would not take that for an answer *must make exactly the same kind of reply if we reverse the situation.* For, if there is a basic relation of numerical difference, it is logically possible for *an* object to differ from *some* object in a property and yet *not be numerically different from it.* But, this is clearly absurd. The problems are covered up by having numerical difference represented by different names for different objects. It is permissible to do so if we do not thereby overlook such puzzles. A perspicuous schema is not to be employed to help us "skirt by" or overlook difficulties. One can avoid such problems by recognizing that numerical difference itself is to count among the relational properties in the range of the quantifier in a Russell-Leibniz definition of '≠', or of '='. This is not to say that '≠' is to transcribe numerical difference. We distinguish between '≠', as defined, and 'D', as primitive. One absurdity is then precluded, since we *assume* '(x)~Dxx' holds and, hence, '(x)(y)[Dxy ⊃ x ≠ y]' will follow. The other absurdity would be precluded by assuming that '(x)(y)[x ≠ y ⊃ Dxy]' holds. Yet, neither assumption is a standard logical truth. In the same vein, cannot one merely assume that numerical difference is represented by different labels for different objects *and* that it is not *possible* to have two objects agree in all properties, with numerical difference no longer taken as a relational property? This would remove the last vestige of Bradley's "abominable" bare particular.

A simple argument for taking numerical difference to be un-analyzable is based on the difference of properties from each other and from particulars. It would be philosophically grotesque to hold that basic properties were really complexes that included an individuating constituent. It would also be problematic to hold that properties differed in that one exemplified a higher-level property that the other did not. For, one thereby recognizes an infinite hierarchy of types of properties. It is far simpler, and more cogent, to acknowledge that basic properties *just differ*. Numerical difference applies uniformly to simples and complexes without requiring a ground, in either the case of simple properties or the case of particulars. That there are two entities, in a given situation, *and* that they are presented as two, whether they be particulars, properties, facts, or, for that matter, a particular and a property, are situations that neither require nor are capable of further analysis.

VI

Frege's Account of
Reference and Thought

Frege resolved the problem about the content of thoughts, expressed by sentences employing names or labels, by holding that names, like definite descriptions, *expressed senses* that were constituents of propositions expressed by sentences. Thus, names and descriptions stood in two relations to entities: they *referred* to objects and *expressed* senses. Sentences, likewise, referred to truth values and expressed propositions or thoughts. Predicates, logical connectives, and quantifiers were "function signs" that *stood for* "functions" or "concepts." There has long been a controversy over the interpretation of his claims regarding predicates and function signs, and their connection with his views about meanings (senses, thoughts) and referents (objects). I have argued elsewhere that we must understand his views to involve the recognition of three distinct entities connected to predicates, connectives, and quantifiers.[1] Here, I shall briefly state, without defense, the interpretation. Consider the predicate 'is green' transcribed as 'F_1x'. Associated with it is, first, *a function*, say f_1, that correlates objects to the truth values: *The True* and *The False*; second, *a function*, f_2, that correlates the *senses* of objects to some propositions that contain such senses; third, *a concept* that combines with senses of names (and of descriptions of objects) to constitute propositions or thoughts that are *about* such objects. This gives rise to two basic ways in which Frege employs his notions of "incomplete" and "unsaturated" in connection with predicates.

Functions are incomplete as correlators of *objects* (including senses, truth values, and propositions along with "ordinary" objects). *Concepts* are incomplete as furnishing the needed link to bind the constituents of a proposition into a compound entity. This latter role of concepts provides Frege with a way of avoiding Bradley's purported regress. Frege solves the problem of connecting the constituents of the proposition, without introducing an *additional* constituent to play such a connecting role and, hence, inviting a question about what, in turn, connects the new constituent to the other parts of the proposition, by having the connection supplied by the unsaturated concept. Frege's belief that the elements of a proposition cannot be linked, if they are all saturated, corresponds to Bradley's claim that if the relation of exemplification is a distinct entity from the terms it relates, it must, in turn, be related to them by a further relation. It is, thus, the solution to the problem of predication which forces Frege to take concepts as constituents of propositions and, hence, not as functions. He also requires propositions, and hence constituent senses, as terms for relations like *believes*, *thinks that*, etc. Perhaps, the dual use of the notion of a concept by Frege, as a constituent of a proposition and as a function mapping senses onto propositions, may help to explain why the earlier noted double role of predicate signs, as signs for two functions (like f_1 and f_2), is not explicit in his discussion. Thinking of the predicate as a sign for an incomplete constituent of a proposition, one would naturally not take it as a sign for two distinct functions. As an incomplete constituent of a proposition, the concept a predicate sign stands for is unique. In fact, when he considers the concept as such an incomplete constituent of propositions, Frege does not seem to think of it as a function at all. The idea of a function comes in when he speaks of the domain of objects and of "truth." Part of the problem of interpreting Frege stems from the fact that he sometimes speaks as if the concept, which is a constituent of the propositions, is one and the same thing as the function which correlates an object to a truth value. Some other things he says would lead one to hold that he recognizes two entities and takes one to be the sense and the other the referent of a predicate like '$F_1 x$'. The constituent of the proposition would then be the sense, and the function f_1

would be the referent of the predicate 'F_1x'. This would require that such senses be incomplete, since they are functions, and yet *denote* other functions. This means that Frege not only recognizes two kinds of senses, incomplete functions and complete "objects," but has functions as *terms* of a denoting relation. All this is highly problematic on his pattern and introduces problems we shall take up shortly. Frege does not seem to explicitly recognize the function f_2.[2] It is obvious why he would not. Since a proposition is a complex of constituents, one of which is a concept, he thinks of predicates as standing for or expressing such entities when he discusses propositions. Since a truth value does not have constituents, as a proposition does, there is not, in Frege's pattern, any complex in which f_1 may be a constituent. Hence, when he talks of objects and truth values, Frege thinks of the predicate 'F_1x' as standing for the function f_1, since there is no incomplete *constituent* to confuse with the function. Thus, talk of functions goes naturally with discussions of the realm of objects, and talk of incomplete concepts goes just as naturally with the discussions of senses and propositions. But, the two distinct senses of 'unsaturated' which result—the sense in which functions are unsaturated (as requiring completion by arguments to determine values) and the sense in which concepts are incomplete constituents of propositions—are consequently never clearly distinguished by Frege. To clearly distinguish them would involve the explicit recognition of f_1, f_2, *and* the incomplete constituent of propositions which 'F_1x' also "denotes." All this shows why the problem is more transparent in the case of a concept like negation than in the case of a concept like *is green*. For, in the case of negation, one just as readily speaks, in Frege's terms, of a truth function *and* of a propositional function. Yet Frege also speaks of negation as an incomplete constituent of propositions.

Consequently the thought that contradicts another thought appears as made up of that thought and negation. (I do not mean by this, the act of denial.) But the words 'made up of', 'consist of', 'component', 'part' may lead to our looking at it the wrong way. If we choose to speak of parts in this connexion, all the same these parts are not mutually independent in the way that we are elsewhere used to find when we have parts of a whole. . . . The two components, if we choose to employ this expression, are quite different in kind and contribute quite differently towards the formation of the whole. One completes, the other is completed.[3]

Thus, we clearly have the three-fold *use* of negation as a function *or* concept.

Frege's view is problematic in another way. A proposition is held to be true when it refers to *the* truth value *The True* and false when it refers to *The False*. Aside from the problem introduced by recognizing such entities, there is an ambiguity in the view. By talking of *The True* and *The False*, Frege avoids, as we noted, recognizing facts (and negative facts). But, either he takes a proposition, say that expressed by the sentence '$F_1 a_1$', *standing in* a relation (referring) to the entity *The True*, as constituting the ground of truth for the proposition; or he merely takes the claim that the proposition stands for *The True* to be a way of saying that it is true without recognizing any such fact as its ground.[4] The latter alternative amounts to a way of illicitly avoiding the issue that we shall discuss in a later chapter in connection with Tarski's Convention T. The former alternative can be taken to be a fanciful way of recognizing facts and negative facts. On it, one faces a problem about the structure of facts. Alternatively, one can recognize a fact such as that referred to by

(A) $R (F_1 a_1, T)$,

where R is a relation between propositions and truth values, and 'T' stands for *The True*. But, in such a case, what does the sentence '$F_1 a_1$' stand for? Frege, as far as I know, does not include the sign 'T' in the schema in such a way to allow for (A), but (A) is in keeping with his taking *The True* as an object that *falls under* some concepts. Moreover, he explicitly repudiates facts. This suggests that either he ignores the philosophical problems surrounding the notion of "truth," especially the question of what *condition* corresponds to the truth of a proposition, or he implicitly takes the proposition to be its own truth ground, somewhat in the fashion of Moore. If we raise the question about a truth condition in terms of Frege's schema, problems arise.

One could take *the sentence* '$F_1 a_1$' in (A) to stand for the truth value *True*, but this would mean that (A) would state that the truth value refers to itself. For (A) to express what it should, we must take the sentence *to stand for* the proposition that it normally, on Frege's view, would be taken *to express*. This means that when the sentence '$F_1 a_1$' occurs as a term in the sentence (A), it does not refer to what it "normally" refers to. This feature fits with other aspects of Frege's view. One role his propositional entities play is to enable him to analyze intentional contexts involving mental "verbs." On Frege's view, "I believe that a_1 is F_1" is to be construed as

(B)   Bel $(I, F_1 a_1)$

where 'Bel' stands for a belief relation holding between a person and a proposition. Thus, in (B) the sentence '$F_1 a_1$' stands for the proposition it normally expresses, and not a truth value. Frege can, then, account for the rejection of an argument like

George IV believes that Scott is an author, therefore
George IV believes that Scott is Scott

without abandoning the idea that one can replace one name of *The True* by another name of the same "thing," since in belief contexts sentences do not name truth values but propositions. Similarly, Frege introduced *senses* or *meanings* expressed by names, such as 'a_1', so that in a sentence like

(C) $a_1 = a_2$

where 'a_2' is another name referring to the same object (or a definite description applying to it), the identity could be taken to be significant. It could be so taken, by contrast with

(D) $a_1 = a_1$

since in (C), although both terms "refer" to the same object, they *express* different senses. Here, instead of having the terms denote their senses, as the sentence '$F_1 a_1$' denotes its "sense" in (B), Frege merely takes the "fact" that the terms express different senses to account for the significance of (C) as opposed to (D). In both cases, it is the appeal to meanings as entities that is crucial.

The feature of the Fregean view whereby names and sentences shift reference in intentional contexts has led to a widely accepted interpretation of the pattern of analysis that recognizes senses and propositions. On the pattern, in

(S$_1$)   I believe that a_1 is F$_1$,

the sentence 'a_1 is F$_1$' is taken to *denote* the proposition it "normally" *expresses* or *means*. Since the referent of a complex sign, such as a sentence, is, on the pattern, "determined" by the referents of its constituent signs, one is led to hold that the name refers to its sense, a constituent of the proposition. Those who think along such lines generally do not bother to think about the predicate in such cases. Given the ambiguities about Fregean concepts that we noted earlier, that is understandable. That aside, some then proceed to hold that in

(S$_2$)   I believe that I believe that a_1 is F$_1$,

the sentence 'a_1 is F$_1$' refers to the sense or proposition *it* expresses when it occurs in (S$_1$), and the name 'a_1' refers to the *sense of the sense* of 'a_1', if I may so put it. That is, in 'a_1 is F$_1$', the name 'a_1' expresses a sense, call it 'SA'. In (S$_1$), the name 'a_1' supposedly refers to SA and expresses a further sense, call it 'SSA'. In (S$_2$), the name 'a_1' supposedly refers to SSA, while expressing yet a further sense, and so on. We shall shortly discuss one basic problem with expressions like 'the sense of "a_1"' and 'the sense of the sense of "a_1"' when we consider Russell's critique of Frege's appeal to senses. For the present, we need only note that one may also attempt to interpret Frege to take a sentence to both express and denote the proposition it normally only expresses. Then, the proposition expressed by (S$_1$) has as saturated constituents *the sense of* 'I' and *the proposition* that a_1 is F$_1$. These are combined by the unsaturated concept or "function" *believe* to constitute the proposition, which we may represent by

(P$_1$)   [Bel (sense of 'I', [a_1 is F$_1$])] .

I shall use the sign '(P$_1$)' to stand for the proposition *depicted* by the above sign pattern. (P$_1$) is what the sentence 'I believe that a_1 is F$_1$' refers to, as that sentence occurs in (S$_2$). The sentence (S$_2$) expresses the proposition that may be represented by

(P$_2$)   [Bel (sense of 'I', [Bel (sense of 'I', [a_1 is F$_1$])])] ,

with the brackets indicating that we have a propositional entity.

But, since the constituents of the proposition (P_2) are *the sense of* 'I' and the proposition (P_1), combined by the concept *believe*, the sentence 'a_1 is F_1' denotes exactly the same proposition in (S_2) that it does in (S_1), and the name 'a_1' denotes exactly the same sense in its occurrences in (S_1) and (S_2).

While one may hold Frege to need a *new* entity as the sense of 'a_1 is F_1' in (S_1), Frege's account becomes problematic if such an "entity" is introduced. The new entity would be either a *thought* (proposition) or a sense that is not a proposition. In the latter case, we might think of it as the sense of an expression like 'the proposition that a_1 is F_1', where such an expression denotes [a_1 is F_1]. If the new sense is a proposition, it *cannot* denote a truth value. For, it is introduced to denote the original proposition that the sentence 'a_1 is F_1' expresses. One must recall that meanings (senses or propositions) are said to *denote*, as well as the phrases that express such meanings. Paradoxically, the new propositional entities could not denote truth values, which is what propositions supposedly do. Such new entities, by the very manner of their introduction, must always denote a proposition. Of course, one can *give* such an entity the same truth value as the proposition it denotes. But, then, we might as well identify "it" with the original proposition and avoid introducing *two ways* of connecting propositions to truth values as well as such useless entities.

If the new entity is taken to be a nonpropositional sense, then in (S_2), the sentence 'a_1 is F_1' will supposedly denote that new sense. This means that 'a_1 is F_1' no longer denotes a proposition. Such a move clearly violates the original intent of Frege's gambit, by having a sentence, in some contexts, not express a proposition, as in (S_1), and neither express nor denote a proposition, as in (S_2). Yet, taking propositions (or senses) to denote themselves introduces a *referential shift* into the *domain of entities*. Not only is reference no longer determined by sense, but the connection between sense and reference becomes unintelligible. Either way, then, Frege's treatment of oblique contexts is problematic. If we use denoting phrases, so that (S_1) and (S_2) become, respectively,

($S_1{}'$)   I believe the proposition that a_1 is F_1,

and

(S$_2'$)   I believe the proposition that I believe the
proposition that a_1 is F$_1$,

a feature of Frege's gambit is made explicit, though an obvious
question arises about the referent of the embedded sentence 'a_1
is F$_1$'. That aside, the denoting phrase would take a nonpropositional sense as its sense or meaning. But, our problem would recur
as a question about the constituent of the sense of the denoting
phrase, say 'the proposition that a_1 is F$_1$', that would be expressed by the sentence 'a_1 is F$_1$'. Is *it* a proposition, and, if so,
what proposition? Of course, one can propose a metalinguistic
replacement of such sentences by using

(S$_1''$)   I believe the proposition expressed by the sentence
'a_1 is F$_1$'.

and

(S$_2''$)   I believe the proposition expressed by the sentence
"I believe the proposition expressed by the sentence
'a_1 is F$_1$'."

Such a move treats the expression " 'a_1 is F$_1$' " as having the same
referent in (S$_1''$) and (S$_2''$) and achieves the *shift* in reference
by the explicit use of different names of sentences. This move
introduces a series of issues that we shall deal with in subsequent
chapters, though not in the context of a further exposition of
Frege's pattern. In fact, we shall see that the use of such metalinguistic expressions as occur in (S$_1''$) and (S$_2''$) lies behind Russell's
puzzling attack on Frege in "On Denoting." We shall turn to that
attack shortly. For the present, we may note that the introduction
of (A), earlier in the discussion, fits with yet another aspect of
Frege's view.

A puzzle long associated with that view has stemmed from
Frege's insistence that predicate terms, or function signs, cannot
occupy the subject place of sentences, and, correspondingly, functions cannot play the role of saturated senses in propositions.
Thus, if one speaks of *the* function or concept F$_1$ and asserts that
the concept F$_1$ is a concept, Frege holds that the assertion is false,
since the phrase 'the concept F$_1$' cannot be used to refer to a con-

cept or function in that it is not a predicate or function sign. He, therefore, introduces *concept correlates* and holds that, corresponding to *the* function[5] referred to by the predicate 'F_1', there is a concept correlate referred to by the phrase 'the concept F_1'. There is a puzzle about such entities. Resolving the puzzle points to a basic problem of the view. When 'a_1 is F_1' is true, Frege sometimes says that a_1 *falls under* the concept F_1. Thus, he has a relational concept denoted by the phrase 'falls under'. With 'U_2' for 'falls under' and 'the concept F_1' denoting the concept correlate F_1, such a "situation" is expressed by

(E) U_2 (a_1, the concept F_1).

Frege, thus, *implicitly* recognizes a correspondent of *the fact* that a_1 is F_1.[6] Only, the constituents of "the Fregean fact" are the object a_1, the relation U_2, and *the concept correlate of* F_1, rather than the concept or function denoted by 'F_1'. Frege acknowledges a proposition expressed by 'a_1 is F_1' and composed of

the sense of 'a_1' and F_1

and he *implicitly* recognizes *a fact* composed of

a_1, the concept correlate of F_1, and U_2.

The proposition is true or refers to *The True*, since the fact corresponding to (E) *exists*. (A) and (E) can be looked upon as different ways of acknowledging the role of facts in Frege's schema. Frege, thus, returns to the problem of predication in connection with facts, but only in the case of the special function U_2 or the object *The True*. The use of U_2 does not really differ from the insistence by others that *exemplification* is a *tie* or *nexus*, rather than a relation, and both properties and objects are *terms* for such a tie or nexus. But, Frege's pattern does not really rule out Bradley's puzzle, anymore than such gambits do, without further argument. Moreover, Frege's pattern is problematic in view of the ambiguities we noted earlier, the appeal to senses and propositions, the introduction of *The True* and *The False* as objects, the role of concept correlates, and the connections between the various entities.

I have not been claiming that Frege explicitly took concept correlates along the above lines, anymore than I claimed that he explicitly recognized the three functions associated with a predicate term. Rather, it is a question of recognizing what is logically involved in his pattern. Michael Dummett seeks to resolve the problem by taking '∅ is a concept' to be expressed by '(x)(∅x v~∅x)', with the latter expression being an incomplete, hence "functional," expression of the "second-level." This, supposedly, fits with Frege's desire to have an expression that would correspond to 'x is an object', where the latter expression is a function expression of the first level that "becomes" a sentence when the free variable is replaced by a sign for an object.[7] In the case of '(x)(∅x v~∅x)', we would obtain a sentence by replacing '∅' with a first-level function sign. Dummett's solution is hardly surprising, given Wittgenstein's remarks in the *Tractatus*:

> 4.1272   Thus the variable name 'x' is the proper sign for the pseudo-concept *object*.
>
> Wherever the word 'object' ('thing', etc.) is correctly used, it is expressed in conceptual notation by a variable name.
>
> For example, in the proposition, 'There are 2 objects which . . .', it is expressed by '(∃x,y) . . .'.
>
> Wherever it is used in a different way, that is as a proper concept-word, nonsensical pseudo-propositions are the result.
>
> So one cannot say, for example, 'There are objects', as one might say, 'There are books'. . . .
>
> The same applies to the words 'complex', 'fact', 'function', 'number', etc.
>
> They all signify formal concepts, and are represented in conceptual notation by variables, not by functions or classes (as Frege and Russell believed).

In this connection, Russell's suggested transformation of sentences having predicates as subject terms, such as 'Red is a color', into sentences employing predicates only as predicate terms, '(x)(if x is red then x is colored)', is also relevant, as is Frege's use of a similar pattern in defining 'the concept F is equal to the concept G' in terms of: "There exists a relation ∅ which correlates one to one the objects falling under the concept F with the objects falling under the concept G."[8] One may take Wittgenstein to have seen that even though 'x is an object' did not pose the same *formal* puzzle as 'x is a concept', it was a statement of the same categorial type and, hence, did pose the same *basic* problem. In any case, Dummett's solution is no solution. All he does is repeat, in different words, Wittgenstein's claim *that* " '∅' is a concept-word" and "∅ is a concept" should be *shown* and not said. Dummett merely takes *a use* of the concept sign, as such, to do this, rather than have the syntactical features of the sign *show* it. Thus, he could also take '(∃x)(∅x v~∅x)' or '(x)(∅x ⊃ ∅x)' to *state that* ∅ is a concept. But, making such Wittgensteinian moves on Frege's behalf merely covers problems inherent in Frege's pattern by transforming the latter. The problem is that Frege acknowledges concepts as entities and, yet, does not comfortably fit them into his ontology. His not allowing predicate signs to occupy subject places in sentences is a symptom of this. Thus, he cannot say that ∅ is a different concept from 𝜓, nor does he hold that such a difference "shows" itself by the occurrence of different signs standing for the different concepts in a perspicuous schema, as Wittgenstein might do.[9] Rather, what Frege does is hold that, *corresponding to* the relations of *identity* and *difference* for objects, we can consider functions to *have* identical or different *extensions*.[10] This is not satisfactory for one who recognizes concepts as entities. Thus, what Dummett does merely highlights the problem; he does not offer a solution to it. This becomes quite clear when we consider (E) and note that such a claim, as an alternative to (A), is a way of stating a Fregean truth condition. The use of (E) amounts to a way of abandoning a fundamental idea of Frege's pattern, in that it may be seen to be a complicated way of talking about exemplification. Thus, it returns us to the problems surrounding the use of a "tie" of exemplification and the supposed treatment of concepts or properties as terms of a relation. This, of course, is to treat them as "objects" in Frege's sense. These problems we shall take up in Chapters X, XI, and XIV. The use of (A) is also problematic, as I suggested above; such problems, too, will occupy us in Chapters X and XIV.

Aside from any question about facts and truth conditions, the basic problem for Frege is that he, like others, rules out the use of predicates as subject signs. But, whereas someone like Quine will proceed to hold that he does not, then, acknowledge concepts or functions or properties as entities, Frege does recognize such "abstract" entities. Moreover, their being taken as the "incomplete" entities they are is essential to his handling of the problem of predication and his use of propositions. Of course, he could have held, or one could hold for him, that in a perspicuous schema it would be shown that concepts are concepts *and* that objects are objects *and* that different concepts are different. But this does not jibe with the way he did treat questions of identity and difference for concepts. Frege, after all, did not write the *Tractatus*. Thus, like Russell in the period of logical atomism, he faces the forced transformation of every *purported* statement *about* concepts into a statement where the concept word is used as a predicate.

Some aspects of the above issues were considered when it was earlier suggested that propositions and propositional characters (as in Chapter III) can be dispensed with for purposes of providing content to thoughts. We shall return to such themes in chapters XII and XIII. Other aspects of the issues will be considered in the next chapter when we take up Russell's attack on Frege's appeal to meanings and senses. For the present, we may note that propositions are not only not needed for purposes of handling intentional contexts but are pointless for other purposes they purportedly serve. Propositions are sometimes introduced for the same reasons we have sometimes talked about possible facts or "possibilities." Given that an atomic sentence, 'F_1a_1', is false, how do we acknowledge the fact that we nevertheless take it to *stand for* a *situation* which does not obtain? Propositions, taken either as the *meanings* of sentences or as what sentences *express*, supposedly account for the basic fact that sentences, or beliefs, may be false as well as true. Existent facts cannot be taken as the meaning, or the ground of meaning, for sentences, since such entities would not exist when the sentences in question were false. *Indicating or referring to a fact* would thus be inadequate as a criterion for a sentence being meaningful in a way that *referring to an object* is not inadequate as a criterion for a sign's being meaningful or acceptable as a proper name. Propositions provide an entity for a sentence to be connected with irrespective of whether it is true or false, and they thus supply *the* meaning for a sentence even when the sentence is false and the fact in question does not exist. There is an obvious alternative criterion of meaning for a sentence. An atomic "sentence" is meaningful if all its constituent terms are meaningful—have referents—and if it is grammatically well formed. Such a simple proposal appears to do the job that propositions are introduced to do. And, it does not appeal to problematic entities. However, the problem remains, for we appeal to the grammatical arrangement of the terms. The real question is not whether a sentence is meaningful or not. It is a question of *what* a sentence means in the sense of *what truth condition* it indicates. This is not to insist that there must be "something" which a sentence means. It is to insist that a sentence like '$F_1 a_1$' indicates or is associated with a definite truth condition. The truth condition, on a correspondence theory, is taken to be a fact. If all atomic sentences were true, one might hold that the grammatical arrangement of the terms of the sentence indicated the structure of the corresponding fact. In this sense, the fact, with a certain structure, would ground the correlation of the sentence with what it is "about." But, as sentences may be false without differing in what they (are used to) assert, one cannot appeal to facts as being what sentences "stand for." The point is that the sentence does indicate or pick out one definite condition. Yet, the fact, as Moore put it, may be nonexistent. Hence, one may say that what it indicates is a possibility, or that the sentence expresses a certain proposition or, perhaps, a thought. The introduction of such terms in this context marks the recognition of two things. A sentence's connection to its truth condition is not reducible to the connection that its constituent terms have to what they denote, or indicate, or stand for or, even, "are true of." And, the connection its constituent terms have to each other, in the sentence, marks a further tie between language and the world. In the case of definite descriptions and defined predicates, one may hold that sentences containing such terms may be about the world without the respective terms being tied to objects and properties. The sentences in question are elliptical for other sentences that do not contain the terms at issue. But, it is clear that a sentence is not reducible to its terms in the way in which a defined sign is reducible to other signs. For defined signs are reducible in that they are eliminable, but sentence structure is not eliminable. A sentence, like a defined sign, may be called a "complex sign," but it is a vastly different kind of complex sign. It is this feature of a sentence that we are asked to attend to by those who speak of propositions or possibilities.

The question, "How is it that a name or a predicate can be used to speak about the world?" requires the partial reply that they stand for objects and properties, respectively. Similarly, the question "How is it that we can use atomic sentences to assert something about the world?" seems to require the reply that they stand for, indicate, or express possibilities or propositions. (Another way of putting the last question would be "Why is it that a sentence is more than a set of terms?") Nevertheless, although some such entity appears to be required, propositions or Fregean thoughts are problematic. The problem arose in an earlier discussion of Moore. Sentences may be about facts, or at least purport to indicate facts. If we introduce propositions to solve the problem about sentences indicating nonexistent facts when they are false, such sentences are not about nor do they indicate such propositions. Rather, they are said to *express* or *mean* the relevant propositions. The propositions, themselves, are said to *indicate* or *stand for* the facts in question. A sentence is then taken to indicate a fact derivatively. But, what is the connection between a proposition and the fact that "makes" it true? And, when the fact does not exist, how is it that the proposition indicates or singles out *that* definite fact? We, thus, face the same questions that led to the introduction of propositions. We have additional entities but neither an answer nor a solution. Recognizing this, we may reject propositions as Wittgenstein and Russell did. Rejecting Fregean propositions, Wittgenstein spoke of possibilities or situations, while treating propositions only as interpreted sign sequences that obey grammatical rules. He had a variety of terms for such "entities." One almost suspects he is seeking to avoid recognizing them by constantly shifting the terms he uses. Thus, he speaks of 'possibilities', 'possible facts', 'possible situations', 'situations', 'possible states of affairs', 'possibility of structure', 'pictorial form', and 'possibility of existence'. Yet, one may question whether the introduction of possibilities is more viable than the appeal to propositions. The problem is to state why the structure of a sentence enables a sentence to be linked to a fact. By introducing propositions, we link the structure of the sentence with that of the proposition. But, that does not link either of these with the structure of the fact. Acknowledging possibilities grounds the link between the sentence and its truth condition, irrespective of the truth value of the former. By tying a sentence to a proposition, one fails to link the sentence to its truth condition, unless one ties the proposition, in turn, to that condition. But, one can only do the latter by having the structure of the proposition stand for the structure of the fact, irrespective of whether the proposition (and hence the sentence) is true or false. One, thereby, introduces possibilities in addition to propositions. By contrast, if one introduces possibilities, one need not acknowledge propositions in order to ground the connection between a sentence and what it is about.

It is worth recalling how Moore avoided the problem of connecting a proposition to a fact in his early view. On his alternative, the proposition was identified with the existent fact when true. A proposition had the same constituents, whether true or false, but these constituents were "combined" in one relation when the proposition was true and in another relation when it was false. There is, then, no problem of introducing a fact for the proposition to stand for. The proposition, as it were, becomes the fact when it is true. Propositions are their own grounds of truth. But, whether one speaks as Moore does, or whether one speaks about propositions that can be facts, or about existent facts and possibilities, or about possibilities that can be actualized, or, as we shall see, in certain ways about positive and negative facts, one adopts a gambit that recognizes a basic feature of atomic sentences. An atomic sentence, irrespective of its truth value, is coordinated to *something* and that "something" is of one of two *kinds*. Its being of one kind, rather than the other, accounts for the difference in the truth value of the sentence or belief. But, there are crucial differences between the variations on that theme. These will be considered later.

One motive for Frege's holding that propositions denoted the objects *The True* and *The False* was his belief that the correspondence theory of truth, whereby a sentence is held to be true if it corresponds to a fact, was paradoxical.

Can it not be laid down that truth exists when there is correspondence in a certain respect? But in which? For what would we then have to do to decide whether something were true? We should have to inquire whether it were true that an idea and a reality, perhaps, corresponded in the laid-down respect. And then we should be confronted by a question of the same kind and the game could begin again. So the attempt to explain truth as correspondence collapses. And every other attempt to define truth collapses too. For in a definition certain characteristics would have to be stated. And in application to any particular case the question would always arise whether it were true that the characteristics were present. So one goes round in a circle. Consequently, it is probable that the content of the word 'true' is unique and indefinable.[11]

There are two basic arguments in the passage. The second, and simpler, is that no definition of 'is true' is feasible since such a definition will be of the form:

$$\ldots \text{is true} \equiv \ldots \text{is } \emptyset,$$

for some condition $\emptyset$. But, if this is so, then to hold that something is true is to hold that it is true that that something has $\emptyset$. Hence, in any given case, we would be involved in a vicious circle. Even the kind of pattern associated with Tarski's Convention T will not help. For, take the case,

$$\text{T`W}a_1\text{'} \equiv \text{W}a_1.$$

There is no characteristic $\emptyset$, as above. But, on Frege's line, we would have to know what 'truth' means, in order to know that the sentence "T`Wa_1' $\equiv$ Wa_1" is true. Hence, there is still a circle; it just closes very quickly. Or, to put it another way, such a definition of *truth* would, for Frege, say no more than that a sentence is true if and only if it is true. The occurrence of the predicate 'T', on the left side of the biconditional, adds no content to that sentence. Frege does have a point, but it is a familiar one and not really paradoxical. If you are going to give a definition of 'truth', or a theory of truth, you have to know what it is to be true in order to know whether the theory *is true* and whether the *definiens* applies in a given case. It does not follow from this that we cannot give such theories or "definitions." What follows is that we must make certain distinctions. We all know, in an ordinary context, what it is for an object to be white rather than red. This is not, as Moore might have put it, to know what it is in the sense of knowing an adequate (philosophical) analysis. The same sort of distinction is relevant here. We have ways of evaluating philosophical theories and arguments for such theories. In that sense, we do not have to have a theory of truth in order to discuss and argue about a proposed theory. That is one matter involved in Frege's argument. Another is that we can propose either

$$T'. . .' \equiv_{df.} . . .$$

or

$$T'. . .' \equiv_{df.} '. . .' Ref. . . . \& . . .$$

as a pattern for a definition of a truth predicate, without the use of 'T' on the right side. There is a difference between assigning a truth value and stating that something is true. This is a trivial second aspect that is relevant to Frege's argument. There is also a play on the notion of 'inquire' and, implicitly, on the term 'know' in Frege's argument that makes it similar to one version of the Bradley paradox. The latter we shall consider later. The idea is that to *know* that the left side of the defining biconditional is true we must know that the right side is true. But, to know that the right side is true we must know, by the definition itself, that the sentence *stating that it is true* is true. This requires us to know that another sentence is true, and so on. Hence, we cannot be said to know that the first sentence of the chain is true, for any definition of 'T'. Like the Bradleyian argument, this particular argument assumes that if the first member of the chain *entails* the second, and so on, the truth of the first *presupposes* the truth of the second, and so on. Hence, to "know" the truth of the first, we must know the truth of the second, and so on. The implicit presupposition is that we cannot know the first to be true without knowing what it *presupposes* to be true. But, as 'presuppose', in this sense, is mingled with *entails*, once we separate the themes the argument disappears. All that is being pointed out is that, if we allow for embedded uses of the predicate 'T', we have an unending series of true sentences, given the introduction of the predicate 'T' and the correspondence pattern.

There is a second, and more interesting, argument. As Frege sees it, the correspondence theory holds that

(C) $T'Wa' \equiv_{df.} (\exists f_1) ['Wa'$ corresponds to $f_1]$,

with the quantifier ranging over "facts." But, then, (C), itself, will be true if and only if:

(C₁) $(\exists f_2) ["T'Wa' \equiv (\exists f_1)('Wa'$ correspond to $f_1)"$ corresponds to $f_2]$

is true. Hence, by continuing the process, (C) will be true only if there are an infinite number of facts. Thus, we cannot set down the conditions for the truth of (C) and, similarly, for 'Wa'. There is an implicit assumption. Different sentences are taken to have different truth conditions. For, if the fact that is the truth condition for (C₁) is also the condition for the right side of (C), as well as for 'Wa', then we have not set down a characterization of a *new* truth condition in (C₁). There is not an unending series of facts in such a case. There is an unending series of sentences, allowing for embedded uses of 'T' and 'corresponds to'. But, there need be only one fact, that to which 'Wa' corresponds. In short, the fact that a is W grounds the truth of 'Wa' and each member of the series

T'Wa',T'''T'Wa'''',T'T'''T'Wa'''''', ...

Moreover, one who holds that there is an infinite series of facts, corresponding to the series of sentences, need not hold that the sentence 'Wa' (or "T'Wa'") *corresponds* to the series. Given such an assumption, and the use of 'T', one knows that if there is a fact corresponding to 'Wa', there are an infinite number of facts. This is not any more paradoxical than holding that the series

Wa, Wa v Wa, (Wa v Wa) v Wa, . . .

generates an infinite number of facts, but 'Wa' *corresponds* only to one (with parallel assumptions about disjunction). Such points indicate an ambiguity in Frege's use of 'corresponds to'. On a correspondence theory, we must distinguish between the possibility an atomic sentence *corresponds to* and the fact that *makes* a sentence true. Thus, one can hold, as I shall later, that the fact that a is W grounds the truth of 'Wa v Wa'. Yet, the disjunction does not correspond to the atomic fact, in the sense that 'Wa' corresponds to it. The sense of 'corresponds to' must be specified. This we can do, in the case of an atomic sentence, along the lines suggested in Chapter III. Taking '*Ref.*', as specified in that discussion, we can consider the specific case of 'Wa' in terms of

(C′)   'Wa' *Ref.* Wa & Wa.

The first conjunct reflects one notion involved in the ambiguous term 'corresponds', the linking of an atomic sentence with a possibility. The second conjunct reflects the other notion, the existence of the fact as a ground of truth. In effect, Frege argues that (C′) involves an endless regress. This, too, is reminiscent of Bradley. As we shall see, it correlates with a more profound version of the Bradleyan regress. In Frege's version, the advocate of the correspondence theory must purportedly admit that (C′) is true only if it corresponds to a further fact, and so on. But, it does not. The first conjunct is true by the rules of the schema and the interpretation of the sentence 'Wa'. It does not, however, either state those rules or state, about itself, that it is interpreted the way it is. This would indeed generate a paradox and a regress. Moreover, it does not state that a is W. The second conjunct does state that a is W. Together, they state what condition must obtain for the sentence 'Wa' to be true. Given the context of the correspondence theory, we know it is the existence of a fact that is taken to be a truth condition of 'Wa'. This is not to say that (C) or (C′) *states* the correspondence theory of truth as applied to a specific case. They are understood in the context of such a theory and our discussion of '*Ref.*' in Chapter III. There is no regress, though there are serious problems about the notion of a *possibility* and talk of *existent facts*. They contain the seeds of the Bradleyan regress, and we shall return to such questions. They are not Frege's questions. His question has been answered. In that connection, we should note that there is no need to hold that (C′), in turn, stands in the relation *Ref.* to some possibility and, if true, is made true by a "conjunctive" fact. We have talked about possibilities only in connection with atomic sentences. We shall have no need to talk of "them" in connection with conjunctions. Similarly, we shall have no need to talk of conjunctive facts. Finally, neither "'Wa' *Ref.* Wa" nor "'a' *Ref.* a" *states* either that we have interpreted certain signs in certain ways or that certain signs stand for certain "things." That we have interpreted the signs is a fact, and such sentences are, in a sense, true *in virtue of* such facts. But, they do not *state* such facts. The phrase 'in virtue of', as I just used it, is not to be confused with the use of 'grounds', when one says that the fact that *a* is W grounds the truth of 'W*a*'. If we had not interpreted the sign '*a*', then " '*a*' *Ref. a*" would be gibberish. And, if we had named a different object by using the sign '*a*', then the second occurrence of '*a*', in " '*a*' *Ref. a*", would name a different individual. Thus, " '*a*' *Ref. a*" *reflects* factual circumstances. Yet, given that '*a*' has been interpreted, we may infer " '*a*' *Ref. a*". Furthermore, if we confine ourselves to signs of a perspicuous schema, instances of the pattern " '. . .' *Ref.* . . .", for primitive constants, are consequences of our interpretation rules. Thus, it obviously will not do to hold that " '*a*' *Ref. a*" *states* that the sign '*a*' has been coordinated to the individual *a*. For, had we interpreted the sign differently, we would still have an instance of the general pattern " '. . .' *Ref.* . . .', and, hence, a true statement. One cannot argue that the original statement is no longer true, since the "new" true statement is a different statement. It is true that, given a different interpretation, we have a different statement. But, we do not have an "old" statement that is now false. The *sign pattern* " '*a*' *Ref. a*" will be a *true sentence or statement* under any interpretation of the sign '*a*'. Hence, if it is a statement at all, i.e., an interpreted sign pattern, it is true. In that sense, it cannot be taken to *state* a fact. The same holds in the case of 'W*a*'. As some see it, the problem Frege's argument establishes is that on the correspondence theory we cannot go from (C'), as stating the truth condition for "T'W*a*' ", to

$$T'Wa' \equiv Wa.^{12}$$

For, although we can get

$$T'Wa' \supset Wa,$$

we cannot get

(a) $Wa \supset T'Wa'$,

since that involves deriving

(β) $Wa \supset 'Wa' \ Ref. \ Wa.$

But, this latter is supposedly not derivable from a definition of 'T', employing '*Ref.*', and the interpretation rules for the schema. However, that depends on how one takes (C′) and the rules. We deal with interpreted signs. The sign pattern 'W*a*', as such, is not the sort of thing that is true or false. What is true or false is an interpreted pattern. Given the schema, the context of interpretation, and the way we construe '*Ref.*', " '*Wa*' *Ref.* Wa" is a consequence of the rules for the schema. Hence, it trivially holds. Consequently, so does (β), and, hence, (α). There are other aspects to the use of " '*Wa*' *Ref.* Wa." In the context of the issues we are dealing with, it is understood that an atomic sentence stands for a possibility. This sort of claim is hardly a matter of syntax and interpretation rules. What this shows is that a philosophical position is not reflected by sentences of the schema, but in terms of a discussion of the interpretation of the schema. In that sense, we must understand the statement of the correspondence theory in terms of a general statement about atomic sentences of schemata, and not in terms of sentences in such schemata. We shall return to the question of such a statement in Chapter X. Perhaps Frege's objection reduces to the point that *in one sense* to state that 'W*a*' is true is to do *no more* than assert that *a* is W. If one then offers a theory of truth, he purports, in another sense, to say something more. He does not simply reiterate that *a* is W. To think that the two observations show that such theories are hopeless is to mistake a definition of 'T', in a schema, for a theory of truth. Such a definition is no more a theory than the statment " '*a*' names *a*" is an interpretation rule for the sign '*a*'.

We can now return to the sentence (A). If it states a truth condition, then Frege has recognized facts of a peculiar sort. If it does not state such a condition, his notion of *denotation*, as holding between a proposition and a truth value, is empty. For, if denotation is not a relation between the two entities, what are we stating when we say that the one denotes the other? It does not help to say that, on Frege's view, we must understand the claim in terms of there being a function that *maps* the *pair* of objects, the proposition and the truth value, onto the truth value. For, on Frege's pattern, to say the latter is just to say that the pair of objects *falls under* the concept (correlate) *denotation*. But, the same question arises about *falls under* as about *denotation*. It appeared as if Frege, by introducing the apparatus of senses, functions, falling under, propositions, *The True*, *The False*, and denotation, was going to provide an ontological assay to resolve the puzzles about truth, meaning, and falsity. But, in the end, he has no theory at all; just a complicated apparatus for restating that a sentence is true.[13] Such complications are dramatically exposed when we note that there will be a concept correlate, an object, corresponding to *is true* (*a* function), if he acknowledges such a *truth function*. (He sometimes does recognize such a function, though he also doubts if it adds, as a concept, to the content of a proposition). One may now ask if *the concept truth* is identical to *The True*. If one says yes, then we have the following peculiar situation. Consider

U₂ (W*a*, the concept truth).

If the concept truth is identical with *The True*, then a proposition will both denote and fall under one and the same thing. If the "two truths" are not identical, the compounding of entities becomes pointless. For, we have two objects — the concept truth and *The True* — without having a theory of truth.

One may deny that 'W*a*' denotes a thought in expressions like (A). The point would be that it should be taken to stand for a truth value, and, hence, we should use the expression 'the thought that *a* is W' in place of 'W*a*'. But, note that we have the function expression

(A′)   the thought that . . .

and the sentence, as a linguistic argument, to form

(B′)   the thought that *a* is W.

What does the sentence stand for here? If it stands for the truth value, then, to have (B′) denote the proposition we intend it to denote, we shall have to take the proposition to be the value of the function (*the thought that* . . .) for the truth value as argument. The proposition will be, as one says, a function of the truth value. This will not do, as Russell argued. Thus, we take the sentence to stand for the proposition in (B′). Dummett speaks of the sentence *expressing* the thought in an expression like (B′).[14] That will not do either, *unless* it both denotes and expresses it (and, hence, the thought *denotes* itself). The sense of (B′), recall, determines its denotation. Hence, if (B′) expresses a *complex* sense, containing the sense of 'W*a*' and a function *associated with* (A′), the sense of 'W*a*' (as well as the sentence in (B′)) must denote *the proposition* that *a* is W and not a truth value. This is required if the denotation of (B′) is to be a function of the denotation of 'W*a*'. This leads us directly to Russell's critique of Frege.

Russell's Critique
of Frege and the Origin
of the Theory
of Descriptions

One of the most abused and misunderstood arguments in the most
celebrated philosophical paper of the twentieth century opens
with the phrase "The relation of the meaning to the denotation involves certain rather curious difficulties" and ends with the claim
"Thus the point of view in question must be abandoned."[1] Here,
I am not primarily concerned with a line by line exposition of the
discussion that the passage requires and deserves. That task has
been performed elsewhere.[2] Rather, I am concerned with the merit
of the argument, actually several arguments, as directed against a
Fregean type of analysis. Therefore, I shall proceed by specifying
and defending the lines of argument, while only briefly indicating
how the arguments, so understood, fit with and make sense of the
text.

Consider a *denoting phrase*, in the sense in which Russell used
the phrase in "On Denoting."

> By a 'denoting phrase' I mean a phrase such as any one of the following: a
> man, some man, any man, every man, all men, the present King of England,
> the present King of France, the centre of mass of the solar system at the first
> instant of the twentieth century. . . . Thus a phrase is denoting solely in virtue
> of its *form*. We may distinguish three cases: (1) A phrase may be denoting,
> and yet not denote anything; e.g., 'the present King of France'. (2) A phrase
> may denote one definite object; e.g., 'the present King of England' denotes a
> certain man. (3) A phrase may denote ambiguously; e.g., 'a man' denotes not
> many men, but an ambiguous man.[3]

We are concerned with a *definite denoting* phrase, such as '*the author of Waverley*'. On Frege's view about such denoting phrases, there are three "things"; the phrase, the denotation or referent, and the sense or meaning of the phrase. The phrase denotes the denotation and expresses (or means) the sense (or meaning). We thus have

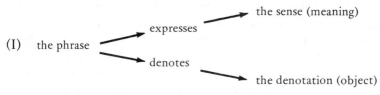

as a simple diagram of Frege's view. On Russell's view, in *The Principles of Mathematics*, such a denoting phrase is held to express a denoting concept which, in turn, denotes what is *not* a concept. He does not put it quite that way, but the sense is clear:

> There is a sense in which *we* denote, when we point or describe, or employ words as symbols for concepts; this, however, is not the sense that I wish to discuss. But the fact that description is possible—that we are able, by the employment of concepts, to designate a thing which is not a concept—is due to a logical relation between some concepts and some terms, in virtue of which such concepts inherently and logically *denote* such terms. . . . a concept *denotes* when, if it occurs in a proposition, the proposition is not *about* the concept, but about a term connected in a certain peculiar way with the concept.[4]

In the above passage, the term "proposition" is not used in the sense of "sentence." As I see it, Russell's view is parallel to Frege's. And, since he speaks of propositions as *expressed* by words, "There are two allied propositions expressed by the same words, namely 'Socrates is a-man' and 'Socrates is-a man',"[5] we may illustrate that view by the following diagram

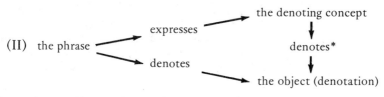

In view of Russell's speaking of employing "symbols *for* concepts," one is naturally led to speak of a sense in which the phrase *denotes*

the concept, which in turn denotes* the object or denotation. Such a way of speaking (or thinking) further complicates matters, if we do not clearly separate that use of '*denotes*' from denotes* *and* from the connection between the phrase and the object.

In the case of a proper name, rather than a denoting phrase, the situation depicted in (I) does not change on Frege's view. We simply have a name that expresses a sense, or has a meaning. On Russell's view, there is a radical difference. A name does not express a denoting concept. A name *directly* denotes or *refers* to the object it names. It does not refer to that object through an intermediary, a denoting concept.[6] This involves a complication in Russell's notion of a proposition. In the case of a subject-predicate sentence (verbal proposition) with a denoting phrase as subject, such as 'The author of *Waverley* is tall', the proposition expressed contains the denoting concept *joined to* the concept tall. This is similar to Frege's thought (expressed by a sentence) which contains a saturated sense (of the denoting phrase) and an unsaturated "concept" (expressed by the words 'is tall'). This is not to say that either the "predicate concept" or the predicative *connection* are thought of in the same way by Frege and Russell.[7]

For Russell, the sentence 'Scott is tall' is connected with a proposition of a radically different kind. He holds that such a proposition contains the object, Scott, and not a concept which denotes* that object.

Whatever may be an object of thought, or may occur in any true or false proposition, or can be counted as *one*, I call a *term*. This, then, is the widest word in the philosophical vocabulary. I shall use as synonymous with it the words unit, individual, and entity. . . . A term is, in fact, possessed of all the properties commonly assigned to substances or substantives. . . . I shall speak of the *terms* of a proposition as those terms, however numerous, which occur in a proposition and may be regarded as subjects about which the proposition is. . . . Socrates is a thing, because Socrates can never occur otherwise than as term in a proposition: Socrates is not capable of that curious twofold use which is involved in *human* and *humanity*. Points, instants, bits of matter, particular states of mind, and particular existents generally, are things in the above sense. . . .

Predicates are distinguished from other terms by a number of very interesting properties, chief among which is their connection with what I shall call *denoting.* . . . *Words* all have meaning, in the simple sense that they are symbols which stand for something other than themselves. But a proposition, unless it happens to be linguistic, does not itself contain words: it contains the entities indicated by words. . . . But such concepts as *a man* have meaning in another sense: they are, so to speak, symbolic in their own logical nature, because they have a property which I call *denoting.* That is to say, when *a man* occurs in a proposition (*e.g.* "I met a man in the street"), the proposition is not about the concept *a man*, but about something quite different, some actual biped denoted by the concept. Thus concepts of this kind have meaning in a non-psychological sense. And in this sense, when we say "this is a man," we are making a proposition in which a concept is in some sense attached to what is not a concept. But when meaning is thus understood, the entity indicated by *John* does not have meaning, as Mr. Bradley contends; and even among concepts, it is only those that denote that have meaning. The confusion is largely due, I believe, to the notion that *words* occur in propositions, which in turn is due to the notion that propositions are essentially mental and are to be identified with cognitions.[8]

Russell thus uses the term 'proposition' in two distinct senses, in addition to the sense in which a sentence may be said to be a verbal proposition. One kind of proposition is very like a Fregean thought; the other kind of proposition is closer to Russell's notion of an atomic fact, in the period in which he developed the philosophy of logical atomism. For Frege, the sentence 'Scott is tall' would express a proposition or thought that contained the (or *a*) sense of the name 'Scott'. Thus, his view does not involve the two senses of proposition that are implicit in Russell's discussion. Let us, for future reference, refer to Russell's Fregean-style propositions as "propositions$_F$," and propositions with objects as constituents as "propositions$_R$." We may then refer to verbal propositions or sentences as "propositions$_V$." Russell was clearly aware of the difference between his use of 'proposition' and Frege's use. This is the point of a footnote in "On Denoting":

Frege distinguishes the two elements of meaning and denoting everywhere, and not only in complex denoting phrases. Thus it is the *meanings* of the constituents of a denoting complex that enter into its *meaning*, not their *denotation.* In the propositon 'Mont Blanc is over 1,000 metres high', it is, according to him, the *meaning* of 'Mont Blanc', not the actual mountain, that is a constituent of the *meaning* of the proposition.[9]

If one was not familiar with Russell's earlier view, such a statement would be puzzling or odd, as some critics of Russell's critique of Frege do find it. Knowing the earlier view, we understand that the last sentence of the passage contrasts that view with Frege's. Moreover, there is nothing puzzling about his speaking of a denoting complex *having* a meaning. Russell uses 'denoting complex', by contrast with 'denoting concept', in two ways. Sometimes, he speaks of the denoting phrase as such a complex, and sometimes he speaks of the denoting concept in that way. Thus, he proceeds to say: "In this theory, we shall say that the denoting phrase *expresses* a meaning; and we shall say both of the phrase and of the meaning that they *denote* a denotation. In the other theory, which I advocate, there is no *meaning*, and only sometimes a *denotation*."[10] Those who dismiss his discussion with the easy accusation of confusion over "use" and "mention" should take the time to read the passage.

In "On Denoting," Russell argues that both Frege's view and his own earlier view are mistaken. Moreover, they are mistaken for precisely the same reasons, since their basic defects are shared. "I have discussed this subject in *Principles of Mathematics*, Chap. V, and §476. The theory there advocated is very nearly the same as Frege's, and is quite different from the theory to be advocated in what follows."[11] The controversial passage I cited at the opening of the chapter contains the arguments. To understand the first argument, we must complete the diagram of Frege's view in one crucial respect. The sense and the denotation of the denoting phrase are both entities, on the Fregean view, just as the denoting concept (or complex) and the object (or denotation) are on Russell's pattern. Since they are entities, the type of theory that recognizes such "things" must acknowledge a relation between them. Russell, recall, acknowledged a "logical" relation to obtain between a denoting concept and what it denotes. He does not confuse his own view with Frege's, when he insists that Frege must acknowledge such a relation as well. He is insisting that a Fregean style view is compelled to hold that there is such a relation. And, as that relation obtains between *entities*, as opposed to *words*, it must *not* be of a *certain kind*. It must *not be merely linguistic*. Frege does recognize *a* relation to obtain between the sense and the denotation or, at least, that appears to be the import of his statement: "The regular connection between a sign, its sense, and its reference is of such a kind that to the sign there corresponds a definite sense and to that in turn a definite reference, while to a given reference (an object) there does not belong only a single sign."[12] But, what kind of a relation holds between the sense and the referent of a denoting phrase? Russell's argument is that the question cannot be unproblematically answered.

One answer is to hold that the relation, call it 'D*', holds between a sense and a denotation when a phrase *means* the first and *denotes* the second. This, Russell argues, will not do, for we specify the relation "through the phrase." To do so is to take the relation to be "merely linguistic." That is, we define 'D*' by:

$$xD^*y =_{df.} (\exists z)\,[z \text{ means } x \,\&\, z \text{ denotes } y]\,,$$

where the only relations mentioned in the definiens are relations between a word or phrase and an entity. Thus, D* is *merely linguistic*, though it supposedly obtains between entities. Russell is clearly correct in believing that a merely linguistic relation will not do, and he is right in two ways. First, by the very notion of a philosophical, or metaphysical, or ontological analysis, one purports to specify what entities, and relations among them, are needed to account for the fact being analyzed. In the present case, what is being *explained* is how a phrase in a sentence, or a particular act of thought, in the sense of Chapter I, is *about* an object. On the account being criticized, the explanation is in terms of a relation between a sense (or denoting concept) and the object. Hence, it is clearly circular to explain the latter relation in terms of what it purports to explain. Second, even if one quarrels with my comment about the nature of an ontological analysis, it is clear that Frege accepts the condition involved with respect to the present issue. That is evident from the quotation cited just above. It is also obvious from his taking his analysis to solve the problem of how a true identity sentence can be significant. Such sentences are significant when *the senses* of the denoting phrases (or names) involved are different, but where such senses *denote* the same object. If he explains the latter situation in terms of the definition of 'D*' above, he has said nothing. And, if he merely states that the phrases denote the same object while expressing different senses, without appealing to the connection between the senses and the denotation, he also says nothing. For, he will not have explained why the expressing of different senses makes the identity sentence significant, if those senses do not *connect with* the denotation.

A second answer is to hold that both *means* and D* are basic relations and that we may define 'denotes' in terms of them as:

$$x \: denotes \: y = \text{}_{df.} \: (\exists z) \: [x \: means \: z \: \& \: z \: D^* \: y] \: .$$

This is in keeping with the passage quoted from Frege, as well as with Russell's earlier view. The problem with this alternative is three-fold. D* is a basic relation, but we have no idea what it is. That is, we use 'D*' as a primitive relational predicate without really knowing what it means. The term and the relation it purportedly stands for are "mysterious." Moreover, so is the entity, the *meaning* or *sense* or *denoting complex* that stands in D* to the object denoted. Finally, the relation *means* (or *expresses*), which purportedly obtains between a phrase and an entity, is also mysterious. We no more know what it is than we know what D* is. This is obvious from our having to speak of the meaning of a phrase in a merely linguistic manner. Suppose one asks *what kind* of entity, and *which* entity of that kind, is *expressed by* a particular denoting phrase. The response is that it is *the meaning* of the phrase. What is D*? It is *the relation* that holds between *the meaning* and the denotation of the phrase. What is the meaning or expressing relation? It is *the relation* that holds between the phrase and *the meaning*. Such are the answers on the view in question. They are clearly circular and empty.

Frege apparently thought such answers to be adequate. "In order to speak of the sense of an expression 'A' one may simply use the phrase 'the sense of the expression "A"'."[13] One may not cogently object to the criticism by claiming that we know perfectly well how to use the terms 'means' and 'denotes' in ordinary contexts. Supposedly, Frege is offering an ontological analysis which *jibes with* or *explains* such facts regarding thought, speech, meaning, and reference. Thus, it will hardly do to explain the explanation in terms of what we purportedly are explaining. One may, however, ask for further elucidation of Russell's use of 'mysterious'. We may get to that matter by considering a third attempt to answer the question about D*.

The third answer is to take D* and *denotes* as basic and attempt to explicate 'means' in terms of them. But, this cannot be done, since the relation D* is many-one. In short, we cannot take

x means y = $_{df.}$ ($\exists$z) [x denotes z & y D* z]

to explicate 'means', since many meanings stand in D* to a denotation. This being so, we cannot specify the meaning of 'the author of *Waverley*' as *the* meaning that stands in D* to the object denoted by the phrase. (Since some phrases will not have a denotation, there is another reason why that move will not do.) If one could use the relations D* and *denotes* to specify the relation *means* and what a meaning is, some of the "mystery" would be removed. For, *denotes* is not a mysterious relation, in one sense. It is clear, given the circularity involved in the uses of the expressions 'the meaning of the phrase . . .', 'the relation between the phrase . . . and the meaning of the phrase', and 'the relation between the meaning and the denotation of the phrase . . .', what Russell's complaint is based upon. Contrast this situation with the case of *denotes*. We can denote the denotation by the use of 'the denotation of the phrase . . .'. But, this is neither the only nor the fundamental way of denoting the object. In fact, it is parasitic on our having other ways of connecting such a phrase to the object and other ways of denoting the object. Consider the name 'Scott'. It is absurd to take 'the denotation of "Scott"' to specify the denotation of the name, though such a denoting phrase does, trivially, denote what the name refers to. We would not be able to coordinate the name to the object by the use of the phrase 'the coordinate (denotation) of the name "Scott"' (without a supplementary coordination procedure). We must have other ways of connecting a sign to a denotation. The same applies to a denoting phrase like 'the author of *Waverley*'. The phrase 'the denotation of "the author of *Waverley*"' cannot furnish the connection between the phrase 'the author of *Waverley*' and the latter's denotation. The former depends, for its having a denoting role, on the latter's having such a role. One of Russell's points is that in the case of the phrase 'the meaning of . . .' there are no alternative denoting phrases. We must specify the meaning of a phrase as 'the meaning of the phrase . . .'. Hence, we specify it through the sign. If we could denote the meaning by using D* and the denoting relation, this problem would not arise, since we can specify the denotation of a sign in ways that are not merely linguistic. But this alternative is not viable. As Russell put it, we cannot go backward from denotation to meaning.[14] Even if this were not a problem, a problem about the relation D* would remain. It is mysterious in yet another sense, besides its being parasitically specified as a basic relation holding between meanings of phrases and denotations of phrases. What is this other sense? In setting that out, I can no longer claim to be presenting an argument on Russell's behalf, but what I shall say is, I believe, in keeping with both his "vivid sense of reality" and his developing distinction between knowledge by description and knowledge by acquaintance.

Let us get at what is involved by reversing matters and starting with a case where D* would not be "mysterious." Taking the meaning to be a property which only the denotation has would be such a case. D* would then become the exemplification relation between a property and an object. This would require that Fregean senses be attributes or, in Frege's terms, *functions* or *concepts*, rather than *particulars* or *objects*. Once again, we encounter the difference between construing a complex of properties as a property or as a particular. To take the sense or meaning of a "singular term," say 'a_1', as a property or function would mean that the proposition expressed by 'Fa_1' would have as constituents the function which was the *sense* of 'a_1' and the function F. We would then be very close to Bradley's view that such a "judgment" is properly construed as an existential claim: the claim that the relevant properties *exist together*.[15] Frege's move is reminiscent of Bradley's but profoundly different. Bradley was led to turn subject-predicate judgments (propositions) into existential ones and to abandon the exemplification relation. Frege accepts the distinction between *subject and predicate elements* in a proposition and seeks to resolve the question of their connection by his notions of *function* and *concept*. Thus, senses, like the sense of 'a_1', become special constituents of propositions, similar to Moore's complex concepts *of* objects. All this leads to the problems we discussed earlier. Now, we are considering further problems Russell finds in the view. Since the sense of 'a_1' is not a property that a_1 uniquely exemplifies, a question arises about its connection with the object a_1. Attacking the connection as problematic leads Russell to reject senses in the case of names and to think in terms of a unique property in the case of descriptive phrases, such as 'the author of *Waverley*'. This, we shall soon see, leads directly to his theory of descriptions. That aside, the point here is that *exemplification* is not *mysterious*, since it is a basic relation we are acquainted with, in that we are acquainted with particulars, properties, and facts— i.e., a particular's exemplifying a property. But, neither Fregean senses nor denoting concepts (expressed by definite denoting phrases) are properties. Hence, D* is not exemplification.

To hold, as Russell does, that D* is mysterious, if it is taken as primitive or basic or, perhaps more accurately, if it is taken to be indicated by a primitive term, does not mean that Russell holds that all relations indicated by primitive terms are mysterious. Consider a referring relation as holding between a name and an object, when I stipulate that the name is to refer to that object. Assume that we accept a Russellian type principle of acquaintance to the effect that primitive predicates must stand for (1) a property or relation that is instantiated and (2) a property or relation that is experienced in at least one instantiation by the user of the predicate. A primitive predicate is mysteious if it does not fulfill condition (2) while it is assumed that it fulfills condition (1). D* is, purportedly, mysterious in this sense. *Reference*, as I used it in the case of the naming of an object just above, and *exemplification* are not mysterious. We may hold that we *experience* the relation of *referring to*, just as we *perceive* the relation of *left of* when we see one object to the left of another. Moreover, such an "experience" is two-fold. We know what we do when stipulating such a connection to hold, and we know what we do when using a name to refer. As some would put it, we know, *by acquaintance*, what it is *to intend*. Recall Moore's relation of direct acquaintance in his analysis of perception. He held that he knew what such a relation was, since there were experiences (acts) of the relation of direct acquaintance holding between an act and an object. We earlier considered such a pattern in connection with the relation *Ref.*

Thus, we may claim to know what we mean when we say "let 'a_1' refer to that" on a given occasion. We know that without necessarily being able to give an explication of the term 'refer' and without needing to give such an explication. We do not know, in that sense, what we mean when we say 'the meaning stands in D* to the denotation'. Taken one way, D* is parasitic on *reference*, as holding between a name and what it refers to. As such, it is not what it ought to be in the Fregean-style scheme. Taken another way, it is unintelligible.

Again, I do not believe that one can cogently object that I presuppose too much, or beg the question, by appealing to acquaintance and experience. One must accept the implications of one's ontology. A philosopher defending Frege either reverts to our "ordinary context" talk of meaning and reference or presents a philosophical analysis appealing to Fregean senses and D*. To do the former, as I indicated earlier, is to beg the question. To do the latter is to accept such entities, as postulated "things," with which one cannot claim *acquaintance*. Of course, one may use that expression in the sense in which Platonists and neo-Platonists may be said to "grasp" the *forms* and the *One*. That, indeed, would illustrate the sense of 'mysterious'.

Such is the line of argument in Russell's paper. It is clear, from the opening sentence of the passage cited at the beginning of the chapter, that he is concerned with the relation between the meaning and the denotation, on a Fregean-style view. What has prevented the understanding of the passage is the key sentence: "Thus taking any denoting phrase, say C, we wish to consider the relation between C and 'C', where the difference of the two is of the kind exemplified in the above two instances." The sentence occurs after Russell has introduced the convention whereby he will refer to the meaning of a phrase by putting the phrase in inverted commas. It should then be clear that in the sentence just above he is talking about the relation D*. The occurrence of the letter "C" in inverted commas stands for the meaning of the phrase in question. The immediately prior occurrence of that letter, in the phrase "C and 'C'," stands for the denotation of the phrase in question. What has caused all the fuss and abuse regarding Russell's purported confusion between words and things is the occurrence of the letter

"C", without inverted commas in the first part of the sentence. Since Russell talks about the phrase, one might expect him to put the letter in inverted commas or double quotes. It is obvious why he would not put it in inverted commas. He has *just* introduced the convention whereby he refers to a meaning by doing so. There is an equally good reason for not putting it in double quotes. Russell is *using* the letter C (was I just clear enough without using quotation marks?) *as a variable. He does not want to talk about the letter* "C". He wants to talk about *any* denoting phrase. He is faced with the same sort of problem associated with Quine's use of corner quotes and Tarski's results in connection with the definition of a truth predicate. If he had written

Thus taking any denoting phrase, say "C", we . . . ,

he would have written nonsense, for the letter "C" is not a denoting phrase. Understanding this simple point, we can see that the next sentence merely says that when a denoting phrase is used, we speak about the denotation, and when the phrase in inverted commas is used, we speak about the meaning of the phrase. He then proceeds to make the claim about the need for the "logical relation" D*, as opposed to a merely linguistic relation. I have unpacked what I take to be involved in that line of argument. What is confusing is that the details of Russell's following discussion take the argument, as I have presented it, for granted. What Russell argues in detail is that we are forced to use a merely linguistic denoting phrase, such as 'the meaning of "C"', to denote a meaning, because we cannot use a denoting phrase like 'the meaning of C'. Of course, here, putting a phrase in inverted commas is merely elliptical for the expression 'the meaning of . . .', where the phrase in double quotes would replace the dots. This follows Russell's understandable practice of using the inverted commas when he speaks about an expression as well as according to his special convention for speaking about meanings. We must not confuse his doing this with his being confused. Of course, if we do that, we are saved the labor of trying to understand him. The argument against using phrases like 'the denotation of Scott' and 'the meaning of Scott' is obvious and correct. In the first case, we denote what *the person*, Scott, *denotes*, if *he* denotes anything at all; in the second

case, we denote what *the person*, Scott, *means*, if he means anything at all. Far from referring to what we want to refer to, we end
up with nonsense in both cases. In the example of Gray's *Elegy* we
do not end up with nonsense. We simply denote the wrong sentence, in the one case, and the meaning of the wrong sentence, in
the other. The fact that we do end with the wrong meaning, rather
than gibberish, as in the case of the name 'Scott', is probably why
Russell chose to illustrate the point in terms of a phrase like 'the
first line of Gray's *Elegy*'. Unfortunately, such an example unnec-
essarily complicated and confused the making of a simple point.
The complication is further compounded by Russell's use of inverted commas in two ways: to speak of a phrase and to speak of
the meaning of a phrase. Once we note that, we can see that what
Russell is saying in the discussion of the meaning of the phrase
'the first line of Gray's *Elegy*' is quite simple. Consider the *phrase*:

(1)   The meaning of *the phrase* 'the first line of Gray's *Elegy*'.

That phrase, the whole of (1), does not denote the same "thing"
as the phrase:

(2)   The meaning of the first line of Gray's *Elegy*.

The latter phrase, the whole of (2), does denote the same thing as
the phrase:

(3)   The meaning of the sentence 'The curfew tolls the knell
        of parting day'.

This means that if we want to denote the meaning of the phrase:

(4)   the first line of Gray's *Elegy*,

we must use either (1) or the *expression*:

(5)   'the first line of Gray's *Elegy*'.

The inverted commas in (5) are employed, of course, in accordance with the special convention about their use to denote the
meaning of a phrase. Thus, the inverted commas in (1) and (3) are
used in a different way from the use of such commas in (5). In (1)
and (3) they are put around a linguistic expression to indicate
which expression we are talking about. In (5) they are used in accordance with the special convention introduced to talk about

meanings of expressions—denoting concepts and propositions$_F$. Once *we understand that*, there is no problem. The double use of inverted commas comes out clearly in the next passage. There Russell makes exactly the same point about the expression 'the denotation of . . .' that he has just made about the expression 'the meaning of . . .'. We must keep in mind that the sign "C" is not a phrase but a variable that may be taken to be a different denoting phrase at different places in the discussion. Thus, he wishes us to consider the *denoting complex*, in the sense of *denoting phrase*,

the denotation of C

where the letter "C" is replaced by the phrase

the denoting complex occurring in the second
of the above instances.

Making such a replacement, we arrive at the denoting phrase,

(G)   the denotation of the denoting complex occurring in the second of the above instances.

But, this complicated denoting phrase does not denote what we want to denote. We want to denote the denoting phrase (complex)

the first line of Gray's *Elegy*.

Earlier, recall, we wanted to denote the meaning of that phrase and failed. We now fail because the phrase,

the denoting complex occurring in the second of the above instances

denotes the phrase,

the first line of Gray's *Elegy*.

Therefore, the complicated denoting phrase, (G), denotes *the denotation* of the denoting phrase,

the first line of Gray's *Elegy*,

and not that denoting phrase. Thus, we end up denoting the sentence

The curfew tolls the knell of parting day.

And that is not what we wanted to denote. So, just as in the case of *meaning*, where we ended up denoting the meaning of the sentence

    The curfew tolls the knell of parting day

and not the meaning of the phrase

    the first line of Gray's *Elegy*,

we once again denote the wrong "thing."

    Russell sums the point up, immediately following his discussion of *the line* from Gray's *Elegy*, in the lengthy sentence that begins with "The difficulty . . ." and ends "which was not intended." If we understand that he is (a) talking about a verbal proposition (a proposition$_V$ rather than a proposition$_F$ or a proposition$_R$), (b) using 'denoting complex' in the sense of 'denoting phrase', and (c) employing single quotes to speak about the phrase, there is no problem of understanding what he says. It is a simple and straightforward summary of the preceding discussion. Moreover, given his concern with the phrase, in the preceding discussion, there is no question that that is what he is doing.[16]

    The argument has been that we must refer to a Fregean sense or a Russellian denoting concept either by a merely linguistic denoting expression or by an expression of the form 'the meaning of . . .', where a denoting expression that does not mention a phrase replaces the dots. He has argued that the latter will not do, in that we do not get to denote the meaning we intend to denote. We must use an expression that is of the form 'the meaning of the phrase . . .', where an expression that denotes another expression replaces the dots. This does not do, since we then denote meanings "through the phrase" or "merely linguistically." Thus ends one line of argument. Russell then proceeds to reiterate that if one makes a distinction between the meaning and the denotation one, in effect, stipulates that we talk about the meaning by the use of such a merely linguistic phrase or by the use of inverted commas. Moreover, such a philosopher takes the meaning to be a denoting complex, since it stands in D* (or purports to so stand) to a denotation. This, of course, is not to confuse such a denoting complex with a denoting phrase. And, he points out that the meaning, as a denoting complex, differs from the denoting phrase, as a denoting complex, in that the meaning does not express a meaning. It *is* a meaning. Meanings, or Fregean senses, do not express other meanings. They only denote (or purport to). Thus, a meaning as a denoting complex does not have both a meaning and a denotation. Rather, to repeat, "some meanings have denotations." Russell also, I believe, emphasizes, by his choice of phrasing, that a denoting phrase denotes an object by expressing a meaning. Given a phrase, "we must be dealing with the meaning." It is the meaning which denotes, in the basic sense, and, consequently, is the fundamental kind of denoting complex. In a way, the phrase should not be taken to be a denoting complex that has both meaning and denotation. To say that a phrase has a denotation is to say that it expresses a meaning which denotes*. Putting it this way calls attention to the fact that, as Russell sees it, Frege explicates the denotation relation, as holding between a phrase and a denotation, in terms of the mysterious relation D*.

Russell then proceeds to a second argument against the Fregean view. It is this argument that has confused and confounded some critics and, by frustrating attempts at interpretation, set off much pointless and scandalous abuse. The argument begins with the opening of the next paragraph, "But this only makes. . . ." What he is claiming is, again, quite simple. Since a Fregean view introduces meanings, we should be able to talk about them and, hence, denote them. But, there is a problem in attempting to do so. To see what that is, we must recall that the letter "C" is a variable. We must not automatically take Russell to be using it, as he used it earlier in the discussion, to speak about a denoting phrase that *denotes some object as contrasted with a meaning or sense.* The letter "C", as a variable denoting phrase, if I may so put it, is specified differently at different points in his paper. Earlier, we took it as "representing" a denoting phrase that denoted some *object*, the center of mass of the solar system, the first line of Gray's *Elegy*, etc. Now, it is clear, if one reads the passage with care, that Russell is taking the denoting phrase to denote a *meaning* or *sense* (of some other denoting phrase, naturally). This should be obvious, since he wants to point to a problem that arises when we speak about, hence denote, meanings or senses. Once we understand that, we can proceed to understand the argument.

The argument is this. Given a denoting phrase that denotes a *sense* (or meaning or denoting complex), there will be a meaning or sense of that denoting phrase. Consequently, there will be, on the Fregean view, a further meaning that *denotes** the meaning we started talking about. Given a sentence that contains the denoting phrase, the sentence will express a proposition$_F$, which *contains* the further meaning. Thus, let the letter "C" *be* the denoting phrase that denotes the meaning we wish to speak about. Let m* be that meaning. There is a further meaning, m**, which stands in D* to m*. Carnap and others have pointed to an infinite chain of entities which Frege's view promulgates. Russell had pointed that out in *The Principles of Mathematics*: "If one allows, as I do, that concepts can be objects and have proper names, it seems fairly evident that their proper names, as a rule, will indicate them without having any distinct meaning; but the opposite view, though it leads to an endless regress, does not appear to be logically impossible."[17] Here he is concerned to press the point about the *mysterious* relation D* and the multiplication of *mysterious* entities by the use of *merely linguistic* denoting phrases. Thus, he asks whether m* can be identified with m**. He argues that it cannot; that m* must differ from m**. His argument is based on the point he had just established. Given any denoting phrase, say the letter "C", the denoting phrase 'the denotation of C' cannot be taken to denote what the original phrase denotes. Recall the point in terms of the name 'Scott' and the denoting phrase 'the denotation of Scott'. Only now, he is putting the point in terms of *meanings* and the relation D*. Suppose m* is identical with m**. Then, since m* denotes* an object, say Scott, m** *will not denote** m* but the object Scott. Hence, a nonverbal proposition, a proposition$_F$, which is supposed to be about m* will not be about m* but about Scott. If we identify m* and m**, we shall not succeed in denoting what we want to denote, m*. This is exactly what he showed to happen in the case of Gray's poem. And, now, we see the point of his spending so much time with that example. He wanted to prove that m* *cannot be identified with* m**, on a Fregean view. Consequently, we must acknowledge an unending sequence of *meanings that denote* meanings*. And this dramatizes the mysterious nature of the relation D*. For, we have now compounded the mystery by holding that D* obtains between two meanings. *Both the relation* and *the two terms* of it are *mysterious*, to Russell. This differs from the original case where we at least had one term, an ordinary object, say Scott, which was denoted* by *a* mysterious entity, m*. Now, we have *two* mysterious entities, m* and m**, standing in a mysterious relation, D*. Moreover, not only do we have an unending sequence of such mysterious entities, but the series is built on the merely linguistic denoting phrase 'the meaning of the phrase "C" '. This is Russell's second argument.

The argument is complicated by Russell's subsidiary claim that m** cannot contain m* as a constituent. Keep in mind that we are talking about denoting complexes as entities, Fregean senses, and not as phrases. What he means is this. Consider m** to be the meaning of the denoting phrase 'the father of the author of *Waverley*'. Take m* to be the meaning of the denoting phrase 'the author of *Waverley*'. Then, on a Fregean style view, m** is *made up of* m* and the function *expressed by* 'the father of x'. We may then think of m** as a function of m* in that with m* as argument for the function *the father of*, the sense m** is determined as value. One should not be bothered by my speaking of the function *the father of* as a *correlator* of senses or meanings. Recall, from our earlier discussion of Frege, the two functions, f_1 and f_2, associated with a function expression. In short, just as we have a function connected with the phrase 'the father of x', which correlates Scott to his father, so we have a second function that correlates the sense of the denoting expression we put for the 'x' with the sense of the resulting denoting expression. In this case, the two senses are m* and m**. Moreover, no problem results, since the resulting sense, m**, denotes* what we want it to, the father of Scott. But, now, revert to the case where m** is supposed to denote* m*. We cannot take m* to be a constituent of m** in such a case, as we can take the sense of the phrase 'the author of *Waverley*' to be a constituent of the sense of the phrase 'the father of the author of *Waverley*'. (In this latter case, it would be a constituent along with the (sense) function expressed by the phrase 'the father of x'.) We cannot do so, since m** cannot denote* what we want it to *as a function of what* m* denotes*. The reason is that m* denotes* an object, and, hence, what m** denotes* will be a function of that object, i.e., will be determined by the object. But, the object cannot determine m*, for the relation between sense and denotation is many-one. Russell, once again, applies the earlier point about Gray's poem. Here, he draws the general conclusion that on a Fregean view a meaning, like m**, which supposedly denotes* another meaning, m*, cannot contain the latter as a constituent. Thus, the newly introduced mysterious entities are not "functions" of those we have already introduced. This is why he speaks of there being no backward road from denotation to meaning. This is not to say that if we have an expression denoting a meaning, say the sign 'm*', we cannot use the denoting phrase 'the meaning m*' to denote what we want to denote. For, the sense of that denoting phrase will not contain m* but the sense of the sign 'm*'. Consequently, the sense of the whole denoting phrase 'the meaning m*' can denote precisely what the sign 'm*' denotes, namely m*. This is no different from the case where 'Scott' and 'the person identical with Scott' denote the same object, Scott.

Such is Russell's second line of argument. There is a third, which connects with our earlier discussion of Frege and truth conditions. The final argument is stated in the remainder of the long passage I quoted at the opening of the chapter. It begins with the words, "Moreover, when C occurs in a proposition. . . ." As I see it, there are two arguments here. The first is this. Consider two Fregean propositions. Let one be expressed by the sentence

(S_1) Scott = the author of *Waverley*,

and the other by

(S_2) Scott = Scott.

The first proposition$_F$ will contain the senses of 'Scott' and 'the author of *Waverley*' *tied* together by the function expressed by '='. The second will contain only the sense of the name 'Scott' (once or twice?) and the function expressed by '='. Suppose one now asks about the difference between the two propositions. As Russell sees it, the answer that one proposition$_F$ contains the sense of 'the author of *Waverley*', and the other does not, *is not* an answer. It is not because if one is then asked why the sense of 'Scott' is different from the sense of 'the author of *Waverley*', the reply must be that they just differ. One cannot reply that the senses differ since their denotations differ, for the denotations are the same. And, one cannot reply that the senses differ, since they, in turn, express different senses (i.e., the meanings, in turn, have different meanings). For, he has already argued that meanings do not *have* meanings. But, if the senses just differ, we have not given an account. We have merely reproduced what we can say about the words or phrases themselves. Why not just say that the verbal propositions (S_1) and (S_2) differ in that they contain different words? Nothing is added by the appeal to senses. Nor would one blunt the argument by citing a case where we have different denoting phrases that purportedly have the same meaning. For, there is no way, on the Fregean account, to provide a ground for the claim that the meanings are the same. All one does is hold that the claim that there is one meaning fits a situation where we would ordinarily say that two expressions have the same meaning. The basis for the claim, in short, is the ordinary use of 'meaning' in the ordinary context. Frege's analysis provides no guide. It will also not help to argue that an analysis of the senses reveals different constituents in the case of 'Scott' and 'the author of *Waverley*'. For, this too will depend on the use of different words. Moreover, one cannot then hold that two different phrases have the same meaning. To escape the problem, one can only have recourse to talk about ordinary uses and ordinary senses of 'meaning'. Frege's postulated senses are, thus, not only not forced upon us, but are clearly *mere* reflections of common uses of 'meaning'. Rather than provide an ontological assay for such uses, we simply mirror them. Later, Strawson does exactly the same thing when he revives Frege's *thoughts* in the guise of *assertions*. There *are* assertions, since we may be truly said to assert things on certain occasions.

Russell's second argument is more interesting. It focuses on a basic weakness in the Fregean pattern. The problem is one of specifying truth conditions on the Fregean analysis. As I construe the argument, Russell is raising a question about what a sentence *states*, on the Fregean view. He holds that the denotation is not the only thing that is relevant (occurs) for determining what a sentence states. Yet, on the Fregean view only the denotation is relevant, as Russell sees it. So put, his claim seems to ignore an ob-

vious feature of the Fregean analysis. On that analysis, *senses* are
relevant to what sentences *mean*. Thus, the denotation of a denoting phrase is not the only thing relevant to the meaning of a sentence in which the phrase occurs. Noting this obvious point, critics
leap to accuse Russell of misunderstanding Frege. Russell does not
misunderstand Frege. His critics misunderstand what is at issue. He
is talking about what a sentence *states*, *not what it means*, in
Frege's sense of 'meaning'. That is, he is concerned with the *stating* of a *truth condition* by a sentence. To see what is involved,
consider, again, (S_1). Suppose we raise a question about the truth
condition for the corresponding proposition$_F$. What must obtain
for the proposition to be true? On the Fregean pattern, there are
only two feasible answers. One answer is that the denoted object is
self-identical. This is the same condition that obtains for the proposition expressed by (S_2). A second reply is that the meaning of the
denoting phrase 'the author of *Waverley*' denotes* what the name
'Scott' denotes (or the meaning of the name denotes*). Thus,
meanings enter into truth conditions. If the appeal to Fregean
propositions is not to be pointless, such propositions must indicate what truth conditions obtain if they are to be true. Russell is
claiming that the conditions for (S_1) and (S_2), and, hence, for the
propositions they express, must be different.[18] The first reply, on
the Fregean view, does not allow for that. But, on the second reply, the proposition is taken to *state* that a constituent of it, a
sense, denotes an object. Such a proposition is then *about* a sense
that is a constituent of it. But, it cannot be. This Russell has argued in the preceding paragraphs. Thus, the Fregean view fails.

By talking of *The True* and *The False*, Frege avoids the question
of the connection of a proposition with a truth condition. This,
undoubtedly, stems from his belief that correspondence theories
and attempts to define 'true' are paradoxical. Yet, once we recognize the need to indicate such truth conditions, we see why Russell's criticism of Frege is cogent.[19] (S_1) will be true if Scott has
the property of being the only author of *Waverley*, and (S_2) will
be true if Scott is self-identical. Thus, an adequate analysis must
construe (S_1) and (S_2) so that this difference is reflected. The
theory of descriptions he proceeds to offer does just that. On Russell's theory, verbal propositions like (S_1) differ *logically* from ver-

bal propositions like (S$_2$), since they state different truth conditions. These different conditions, the propositions$_R$ of the *Principles*, will become the *facts* of the logical atomists. Frege's theory does not capture the difference. For Frege, both names and definite descriptions express senses and denote objects. Thus, the Fregean propositions expressed by (S$_1$) and (S$_2$) are of the same *logical kind* or *structure*, though they supposedly differ in constituent senses. Frege's theory does not, for Russell, capture the purely referential or indicating function of names. This is a theme that not only lies behind his criticism of Frege, but links the earlier theory of 1903 with the new theory of 1905. For, in *The Principles*, names were not terms that *indicated* denoting concepts, which, in turn, denoted objects. When Russell holds that the meaning must be relevant, what he means is that the denotation of 'the author of *Waverley*' is not *all* that is relevant to the truth of (S$_1$). On the Fregean view, one must hold that it is or that the sense of the denoting phrase enters into the truth condition. Either alternative is problematic. Of course, on Frege's view, (S$_1$) and (S$_2$) express different propositions. That is not the point. The question is how, on Frege's view, one *shows* that the truth conditions are different, assuming that they must be. One interpretation of Frege acknowledges that they are not different. The other interpretation makes the correspondence between senses and objects the truth condition. This leads Russell to hold that a Fregean proposition, in stating what must obtain for the proposition to be true, is *about* its constituent senses or meanings and not just about the denotations of the phrases (or the senses, for that matter). It may help to think of Russell's argument as somewhat analogous to the claim that identity statements like 'Scott = Sir Walter' cannot be treated metalinguistically, as the claim that the two names name one thing, since then the sentence would be *about* words that refer and not just *about* the referent of the words. In Russell's critique of Frege, the claim is stronger, since Russell finds the Fregean view paradoxical in that the nonverbal proposition *cannot* be about its constituent senses. By contrast, on the metalinguistic treatment of identity statements, one advocates the *replacement* of one sentence by another. Such a move is not open to Frege without basically changing his analysis.

We are now in a position to partially resolve the problem about thoughts, as facts, being about objects. When there is a thought expressed by

(S₃)   The author of *Waverley* is tall,

there is the fact, which is a mental state, consisting of the occurrence of such a token pattern. Given that predicate expressions and their tokens are constant in that each occurring token stands for the property coordinated to the type, (S₃) can be taken to be about Scott in that Scott is the individual that has the property indicated by

x wrote *Waverley* and (y)(y wrote *Waverley* if and only if y = x).

Definite descriptions thus provide a means for linking thought patterns employing them to denoted objects. In that they do so, they function like Fregean senses. Yet, such descriptions do not involve an appeal to such Fregean entities nor to the mysterious relation D*. Associated with a definite description is a *property*, not a sense, which is exemplified by an object that the thought is then *about*.

This still leaves the problem of using labels or names, which do not then have an associated property. As I noted earlier 'x = a', where 'a' is a name, does not indicate a legitimate property in that the name occurs in the expression. Moreover, the question persists in the case of tokens of predicates being taken to refer to a given property, which has been coordinated with the type, on every occasion of their occurrence. We did, after all, assume that in the above paragraph; but such an assumption merely covers over the same problem that arises in the case of the use of a name as a mere label. There is, however, one difference. Part of the traditional problem about names and "particulars" is that one does not have, in thought, a property or concept associated with a proper name. In the case of a predicate, one may be said to always have a relevant "concept" furnished by the property that is indicated by the predicate type. This reflects the traditional notion that prime matter or "bare" particulars are "unintelligible." We must then distinguish two aspects of the problem. One is the idea that tokens of labels require corresponding properties (definite descriptions), since only then will there be a thought with content. A second theme is the idea that there is a problem regarding the connection of an occurring token of a name with an object. The two themes blend in that the property supplied in response to the first query is taken to answer the second question as well. But there are two distinct issues. Moreover, the problem raised in the second query arises in connection with the occurrence of predicate tokens. Hence, the response to the first question does not suffice as an answer to the second, since the latter question may be raised about the predicate involved. Thus, one may be led to give up the attempt to specify thoughts in terms of token-facts and hold that thoughts are *particulars* related to propositional entities. This returns us to a problematic gambit along the lines of Moore or Frege.

Since Russell first propounded the theory of descriptions, there has been a continuous dispute: (1) whether *names* can be *attached* by means of descriptions or whether the *terms* so attached to objects are really truncated descriptions *of* the objects; (2) whether names can be attached to future and past (but presently nonexistent) objects and fictional (or, simply, nonexistent) objects; (3) whether one could use a sign *as* a name of an object with which one was not acquainted; (4) whether one *can refer to* such future, past, and fictional objects as well as to objects that are not objects of acquaintance. Much of the discussion has amounted to stipulations about the use of 'name' and 'refer' which, then, purportedly fit, more or less, with common usage of 'names' and 'refers to'. But, the real problem is a problem about what one can *intend*.

We know what it is to intend or refer to an object or property (in the sense of *Ref.*), since we are acquainted with such intentional acts in cases where we directly apprehend such objects and properties. The paradigmatic case of intentional reference is a case of demonstrative reference to an object or property that is directly apprehended. The questions that arise are questions about the extension of the notion of intentional reference to other cases. It is the question that arose in connection with Moore's use of 'about' and 'indirect apprehension'.

Consider the claim that I can now use 'Bismarck' and 'Aristotle' as *names* or *attach* such *names* to "those" individuals by means of definite descriptions. How are 'name' and 'attach' used in such claims? The first thing to note is that we deal with a *token*, whether I stipulate that 'Aristotle' names the so and so or whether I hear such a statement as a "link" in a causal chain. Thus, the question is whether such a token, or subsequent tokens, are used to intend or refer to an object, in the sense in which I intend or refer to an object when I say "This is Ø" or "Let 'a' Ref. to this." Of course, we do not intend objects only by means of such tokens. Consider an image. Images are sometimes images *of* objects. The use of 'of' locates the intentional role of images. You see an object and, shortly after, "have" an image of it. You know *that* the image is *of* something and *what* it is an image of. This is not to say that the occurrence of an image is equated with an occurrence of an intentional event. But, it is also not to say that there must be something further, which connects an image to what it intends, when it does occur *intentionally*. There is nothing further. This is a simple fact about thought. The same is true of the demonstrative use of 'this' in the presence of an object or property. We *intend* presented objects by the use of "demonstrative" tokens. We also intend objects, once presented but no longer so, by the use of images, and we intend or refer to properties that are not presently apprehended. To deny these claims is not only to deny apparent facts of experience but to limit the activity of thinking. This is what leads some to say that we *recognize* properties, in subsequent instantiations, and that memory is involved in the attribution of a property to an object.

There is a further point about properties that bears on the issue. Consider an object *a* that has a color, and only one color, Ø. Thus, we assume the truth of 'Ø = the color of *a*'. But, clearly, if I do not *know what* color Ø is, I do not know what 'Ø' *means* in a very basic sense of 'means'. I can neither recognize the color nor recall it. If I have a thought *about* Ø, it will be in terms of the occurrence of a token of 'Ø', or a token of a description, or something similar. But, what can 'about' mean here? I do not think *of* Ø as I think *of* red when I assert that red is a color or wonder if Ø is *the* color red. The question is not just about the term 'Ø'; it is also a question about the phrase 'the color of *a*'. I do not intend or think of a color by using a token of that phrase. Insofar as the sign '*a*' is meaningful, the descriptive phrase is a meaningful phrase. But, I do not know, in *a* clear and simple sense, *what* it *means* or *refers to*. And, in that sense, I cannot think *of* the color. There is a further crucial sense in which one does not know *what* is *meant* by a description.

Consider "Let 'Aristotle' name the G" (or, a history teacher's assertion *about* Bismarck). The descriptive token is not one that intends (is used to intend) an object, as a demonstrative token or a token of a noncontroversial name may do. This we may assume, for otherwise there is no issue, since the descriptive token then functions as a name and one merely *attaches* one name by means of another. Moreover, it must be the case simply because the token is a token of a description. This means that a *property* is *intended*, i.e., *being uniquely* G.[20] This property, in turn, we assume to be exemplified. Thus, we have a token intending a property and a property being exemplified by an object. We have, in effect, defined the use of 'name' as it occurs in " 'Aristotle' names Aristotle." We need not complicate matters by putting the point in terms of thoughts and tokens. To say that 'Aristotle' names Aristotle is to say that there is:

  (1)   a stipulation of the form "Let 'Aristotle' *Ref. d*,"
        where '*d*' is a description,

and

  (2)   '*d*' *denotes* Aristotle.

But, 'names', in " 'Aristotle' names Aristotle," is not to be confused with '*Ref.*'. When one uses a token as a description, one intends a property which, if exemplified, means that the descriptive token *denotes*, not *refers to*, the object. This does not mean that the token of a purported name, linked by means of a description, is used to intend the object. One can only declare that this is so. The issue is about what is meant by "Let 'Aristotle' name the G." If 'name' is taken as '*Ref.*', which we understand in terms of our use of demonstratives and our familiarity with images *of* things, there is no ground for claiming that tokens of such terms function like demonstratives, images, or labels of experienced objects. The point is that "names" do not *attach* to objects. We can pronounce "Let 'Aristotle' name *the* G," but that merely produces a *token* of 'Aristotle'. There are no objects of apprehension, in the occurrence of the thought that such a stipulation expresses, other than the tokens themselves. Thus, one cannot speak of a *stipulative act connecting* a demonstrative token with an object. Even where we have such an act, a *type* is not linked with an object. A person can become "conditioned" to *intend* certain objects by the use of tokens of a particular type. (This is not to say that one instance does not suffice in some cases.) One can also indicate an object by a token, without having used a token of that type to indicate that object on previous occasions. Look at an object. Refer to it by any term that "comes into your head." You know what you referred to and that you referred to it. But none of these things can be done with 'Aristotle' to *link* it to *the* G. What one can do is build up associations with tokens of descriptions. This is no better than *linking* the "name" with an image *of* a bust *of* Aristotle.[21]

The pattern suggesting that we use 'Bismarck' and 'Aristotle' as names is aided by the fact that one cannot say what is meant by the claim that a memory image is *of* an object or a token is used intentionally. Likewise, one cannot say *what* it is *that* one knows when one knows an object by acquaintance. One knows or is acquainted with the object and, hence, can remember, recognize, and *intend* it. We know, by acquaintance, what it is to intend and to be acquainted with objects. And, we also know that we cannot claim acquaintance with Bismarck or that we *intend him* by any token or image. It is worth noting that the claim that the type 'Bismarck' is attached to Bismarck amounts to the acceptance of Fregean senses under the guise of types. Only, we apparently create such entities by stipulational ceremonies. To stipulate that my use of a specific token of the pattern 'Bismarck' is used to refer to Bismarck is to hold that there is some connection between a type, as a Fregean entity, and Bismarck. The token I use names Bismarck, since the type does so. Naming thus becomes a form of voodoo. If one tries to avoid this by holding that a particular token is used to refer to Bismarck, not merely because it is of a certain pattern, but because I intend Bismarck by the use of that to-ken, the gambit is abandoned. For, one has not connected that token to Bismarck by the previous stipulation that employed a description. The most one could do is state a law connecting such stipulations with such a subsequent use of tokens. But, even then, one cannot give the law as a reason for saying that a particular token is used to refer without presupposing what is at issue, i.e., that tokens of that pattern *are used to refer* to Bismarck on other problematic occasions.

If one accepts the pattern that allows for the connection of a name, by means of a description, to an object that is not an object of experience, we can solve Moore's problem about the indirect apprehension of material objects. We simply hold that sense data may intend material objects.[22] Whatever other relations there are between sensa and material objects can be ignored. We can speak of intending a material object when sensing a datum. The object O, of Chapter I, is *the* object intended when the sensum is directly apprehended. We can, then, even attach a name to O, for we can use the description in the previous sentence to do so. In a way, we did that by using 'O'. But, this is not surprising, for in ordinary usage we do *know* what material object we "see" and we do use 'Aristotle' and 'Bismarck' as names. We even use 'Pegasus' as one.[23]

VIII

Descriptions, Substitution, and Intentional Contexts

Russell made use of a nonextensional context in his presentation and defense of the theory of descriptions in "On Denoting." There, he claimed that his theory enabled us to solve the puzzle of why the argument

(A_1) 1. George IV wished to know whether Scott was the author of *Waverley*.

2. Scott is the author of *Waverley*. Therefore,

---

3. George IV wished to know whether Scott was Scott.[1]

is not valid, while retaining the rule that two names for the same thing can be interchanged in any context where they are *used*, as opposed to mentioned. Thus, his theory of descriptions constitutes, in part, an alternative to Frege's way of handling the same problem. In a detailed discussion of Russell's theory, Linsky claims that the use-mention confusion and "a fallacy in reasoning that since p and q are logically equivalent so are $f(p)$ and $f(q)$ for *any* function of propositions f" are involved in Russell's discussion.[2] What Linsky refers to as a "fallacy in reasoning," and what others call a criterion of extensionality, is one *principle* Davidson appeals to in an argument we shall take up later. Let us refer to such a principle or claim as (P_1), and let it be understood that, for purposes of this chapter, a nonextensional or intentional context is one that contains a verb like "to know" or "to believe." Thus, a question that arises is whether we may employ (P_1) in nonextensional contexts or whether doing so constitutes a fallacy. We shall return to this shortly. For the moment, we may note that Russell's discussion in "On Denoting" may lead one to dismiss some of what he says on the basis of the use-mention confusion, if one is predisposed to look for it. But Russell returned to the discussion in the essays on Logical Atomism, and it is quite clear what he is holding.

> If you were to try to substitue for 'the author of *Waverley*' in that proposition any name whatever, say '*c*' so that the proposition becomes 'Scott is *c*', then if '*c*' is a name for anybody who is not Scott, that proposition would become false, while if, on the other hand, '*c*' is a name for Scott, then the proposition will become simply a tautology. It is at once obvious that if '*c*' were 'Scott' itself, 'Scott is Scott' is just a tautology. But if you take any other name which is just a name for Scott, then if the name is being used *as* a name and not as a description, that proposition will still be a tautology. For the name itself is merely a means of pointing to the thing, and does not occur in what you are asserting, so that if one thing has two names you make exactly the same assertion whichever of the two names you use, provided they are really names and not truncated descriptions.[3]

Russell is claiming that *a* difference between a name and a description is that (A_1) is invalid, whereas a corresponding argument using the two names 'Scott' and 'Sir Walter'

(A_2) 1. George IV wished to know whether Scott is Sir Walter.
2. Scott is Sir Walter. Therefore,

_____

3. George IV wished to know whether Scott is Scott.

is valid. It is valid, as Russell sees it, because both 'Scott' and 'Sir Walter' are used as names, and names of the same thing, by whoever states the argument. The idea can be put without use of a context involving a verb like 'to know'. Where 'Scott' and 'Sir Walter' are two names for the same thing the identity 'Scott = Sir Walter' is a tautology. But, where '$(\iota x)(Wx)$' is any nontrivial description of Scott, i.e., not something like '$(\iota x)(x = \text{Scott})$' or, in general, not any description where the statement that it is fulfilled is a logical truth or a consequence of the interpretation rules of the schema, the identity 'Scott = $(\iota x)(Wx)$' is not a logical truth or such a consequence. In the case of (A_2), if George IV had asked "Is Scott Sir Walter?", while using both as names and hence *knowing* what they named, he could as well have asked "Is Scott Scott?", as Russell views names. Alternatively, if someone was reporting something about what George IV wished to know, and not about what he literally asked or said, and used both terms as names or mere demonstrative indicators, then the argument is also valid. For, George IV, as the argument is stated, does not want to know if a certain object is called 'Scott' or is called 'Sir Walter'. He wishes to know if a certain object, Scott, is identical with a certain object that we may refer to by either of the two names. Since Scott is the thing referred to, whether one uses the name 'Scott' or 'Sir Walter', (1) and (3) of (A_2) make the same assertion for Russell. In effect, (2) is unnecessary, since it merely reflects that both names name the same thing, and this is already presupposed by their use as names. Put in terms of a schematic formalism or ideal language, the point would be that (2) of (A_2) would be a consequence of the interpretation of the schema or of the "semantical rules," while (2) of (A_1) would not so follow.

Russell's way of considering things overlooks a complication involved in such contexts. Although names are demonstratives, there is a difference between George IV asking "Is that Scott?" and "Is that that?" In the latter case, we would be quite sure that the first gentleman of Europe was interested in the law of identity, but it is difficult to take the former question as indicating such an interest. What is involved can be brought out by considering two modifications of (A_2).

(A_2') 1. George IV wished to know whether Scott is called 'Sir Walter'.

2. Scott is Sir Walter. Therefore,

---

3. George IV wished to know whether Scott is called 'Scott'.

(A_2'') 1. George IV wished to know whether Scott is called 'Sir Walter'.

2. Scott is Sir Walter. Therefore,

---

3. George IV wished to know whether Sir Walter is called 'Sir Walter'.

The first, (A_2'), is obviously invalid, since premise (2) is irrelevant, and (1) and (3) do depend on George IV using or asking about specific names. But, (A_2''), as Russell considers names, is valid. For, George IV asked about the object, which both names name, if that object was called 'Sir Walter'. The first premise of (A_2'') and the conclusion thus state or report the same situation.[4] Taken together, (A_2') and (A_2''), point to a peculiarity of (A_2). The names in (A_2), given the ordinary context of such statements, function as more than mere demonstratives, such as 'this' and 'that'. It is obvious that where we use names like 'Scott', there is the implicit presupposition of constancy of use carried over from other contexts. This is made explicit in (A_2') and (A_2'') by using the phrase "is called." It was implicit in (A_2) in the order in which the names occurred. Our ordinary language reflects this in that "George IV wishes to know if that is Scott" is acceptable, but "George IV wishes to know if Scott is that" is not. The use of a pure demonstrative in such cases indicates an object about which we then ask or state something: "Is that Scott?", "Is that person called 'Scott'?", but hardly ever "Is that that?" or "Is this that?". Thus (1) and (3) of (A_2) would generally indicate that you are doing more than just *pointing* to a presented object. A token is being used to refer in a way that involves memory. This we shall take up later.

Russell's way of handling the puzzle about (A_1) was to hold that the premise (2) of (A_1) was not really a sentence of the form '$x = y$', and the same applied to the identity clause of (1). Consequently, there is not *really* any constituent term 'the author of *Waverley*' in the clause 'Scott is the author of *Waverley*' in premise (1). In short, there is no term in premise (1) that may be replaced by the term 'Scott' in order to obtain the conclusion from (1) and (2). As Russell put it in "On Denoting":

The puzzle about George IV's curiosity is now seen to have a very simple solution. The proposition 'Scott was the author of *Waverley*', which was written out in its unabbreviated form in the preceeding paragraph, does not contain any constituent 'the author of *Waverley*' for which we could substitute 'Scott'.[5]

By contrast, in (A_2) premise (2) is of the form '$x = y$', and, hence, there is a term to replace in premise (1) to obtain the conclusion. By holding (A_2) to be valid, Russell adhered to the principle of the substitution of *names* in *all* contexts where they were *used*. As I mentioned above, this is because the identity premises, with names, are really unnecessary, since they merely reflect the interpretation of the names. This is summed up in Russell's statement that true identity statements using only names are tautological. Putting it this way, however, brings out the fact that Russell is not holding that (A_2) is valid since 'Scott = Sir Walter' is logically equivalent to 'Scott = Scott', as both sentences are tautological. Nor need Russell hold that one can replace logically equivalent sentences in nonextensional contexts. Such an issue is not involved in his claim that (A_2) is valid but (A_1) is not. The issue is relevant, however, to any consideration of the theory of descriptions.

Linsky, and others, have raised questions about the replacement of a description by its contextual definition in nonextensional contexts. Thus, the argument:

(A_3) 1. Strawson believes that George IV wished to know whether Scott was the author of *Waverley*. Therefore,

---

2. Strawson believes that George IV wished to know whether one and only one individual both wrote *Waverley* and was identical with Scott.

is thought to show that one cannot make such a replacement.[6] For, assuming Strawson does not agree to Russell's contextual replacement, the premise of (A_3) may be true with the conclusion being false. It is clear, I believe, that Russell thought that replacements of descriptions by contextual definitions were permitted in nonextensional contexts, since by replacing a defined expression, one merely specified what was meant.

To return to George IV and *Waverley*, when we say, 'George IV wished to know whether Scott was the author of *Waverley*', we normally mean 'George IV wished to know whether one and only one man wrote *Waverley* and Scott was that man'; but we *may* also mean: 'One and only one man wrote *Waverley*, and George IV wished to know whether Scott was that man'.[7]

One might hold, with Linsky, that in view of (A_3) and similar contexts, Russell was wrong in holding that one could replace descriptions in nonextensional contexts. This would not affect the point Russell tried to make regarding a difference between descriptions and names, since, as we saw, he could simply have contrasted the statements 'Scott = Sir Walter' and 'Scott = $(\iota x)(Wx)$' as being, in his terms, respectively tautologically and factually true. Nor would he have had to abandon his solution to the puzzle posed by the argument (A_1). For, as Russell saw the puzzle, it was based on a substitution of singular terms supposedly warranted by the second premise. But, if that premise is expanded by replacement of the description, there is no longer any basis for making a substitution in premise (1) to obtain (3). However, to hold that (A_3) shows that descriptions may not be replaced in intentional contexts is to consider such contexts in an oversimplified manner. It is not obvious that (A_3) is invalid. Rather, what is obvious is that we ought to raise some questions about the use of 'believes' in (A_3). Consider the following five senses of 'believes'.

(I)   x believes$_1$ that p if and only if x has a belief state (whether one takes this to be a mental state, a behavioral disposition, or a physiological state is irrelevant here) which is uniquely related to or expressed by the sentence 'p'. If one thought in terms of a disposition to behave, one might include the disposition to utter a token of 'p' under certain circumstances, for example.[8]

(II) x believes$_2$ that p if and only if x has a belief$_1$ expressed by some sentence 'q', and 'p' differs from 'q' only in the replacement of a name for another name of the same object or of a defined expression by its definition (or vice versa).

(III) x believes$_3$ that p if and only if x has a belief$_2$ that p and x has a belief$_1$ expressed by the appropriate identity statement or definitional statement. As we might ordinarily put it, in this case, x believes the relevant identity or definition (or is aware of or "knows," but I wish to avoid the maze surrounding "to know" and, for our purposes, we may do so).

(IV)   x believes$_4$ that p if and only if x has a belief$_1$ related to some sentence 'q' and 'p' is a logical consequence of 'q'.

(V)   x believes$_5$ that p if and only if x has a belief$_4$ that p and x also has a belief$_1$ that 'q' implies 'p'.

If we now return to the argument (A$_3$), it should be obvious that we shall answer the question about its validity in terms of which sense (or senses) of 'belief' we take to be involved. For example, if we treat the occurrence of 'believes' in both the premise and the conclusion as 'believes$_1$', then it is clear that the premise may be true and the conclusion false, irrespective of whether we accept Russell's transcription of descriptive phrases. If, however, we construe the sense of 'believes' in premise (1) to be 'believes$_1$' *and we assume* Russell's theory of descriptions, then if we take the occurrence of 'believes' in the conclusion to be 'believes$_2$', we may conclude that the argument is valid. Since Strawson presumably does not or need not have a belief$_1$ that would be expressed by a Russellian definitional equivalence, then if the use of 'believes' in the conclusion is taken in the sense of 'believes$_3$', and the use in the premise is taken in the sense of 'believes$_1$', the argument is invalid.

The argument (A$_3$) does not pose a puzzle for Russell's theory of descriptions with respect to nonextensional contexts. It merely forces us to be clearer about such contexts. The distinctions we have made with respect to (A$_3$) may also be applied in the case of (A$_1$) and, in effect, allow us to retain the point Russell was making in that case without falling prey to the puzzle posed by (A$_3$). What we have done is acknowledge that there is a sense of *belief*, whereby one may not replace defined expressions by defining expressions and still retain the truth of certain sentences containing intentional verbs. This sense is essentially that of 'believes$_1$'. Unfortunately, in talking of what we "normally mean" (and, in other contexts, of what we "really mean") Russell glossed over corresponding different senses of 'means'. In one sense, what I mean when I say that the present king of France is bald is *that* the present king of France is bald. In another sense, what I mean can only be talked about in terms of the context of utterance, etc. In yet another sense, what is meant can be spoken of only by talking about a mental state that I am "in." In a further interesting sense, what I mean is what is proposed as an adequate philosophical analysis designed to dissolve certain puzzles about denoting phrases and nonexistent objects. The relevance of all this for the so-called paradox of analysis should also be obvious. In short, nonextensional contexts no more invalidate Russell's views on definite descriptions than they invalidate his proposed analysis of arithmetical concepts. With the proper distinctions, we may recognize which intentional contexts are susceptible to the relevant replacements and which are not.

Russell's analysis of (A_1) is more complicated than some realize. Russell held that if the scope of the description was primary in premise (1) of (A_1), then one could take the argument to be valid. Where the premise is so taken, he held we could "verbally" make the substitution of 'Scott' for 'the author of *Waverley*' to arrive at the conclusion: ". . . does not interfere with the truth of inferences resulting from making what is *verbally* the substitution of 'Scott' for 'the author of *Waverley*', so long as 'the author of *Waverley*' has what I call a *primary* occurrence in the proposition considered."[9] What Russell may have had in mind can be shown by considering the following version of (A_1). We construe the argument as:

(PA_1) 1. $(\exists x)(x$ is the one and only author of *Waverley* and George IV wishes to know whether x is Scott).

2. Scott is the author of *Waverley*. Therefore,

---

3. George IV wishes to know whether Scott is Scott.

In (PA_1), premise (1) states that there is an individual that is the author of *Waverley* and George IV wishes to know about *that* individual if it is Scott. Although the individual is, in fact, the author of *Waverley*, that feature does not enter into George IV's query.

That is, if George IV articulated what he wished to know it would not be expressed by "Is Scott the author of *Waverley*?" but by "Is that Scott?." In the conclusion of (PA$_1$), the same situation is described. For, we could say that he asked about Scott "Is that Scott?" That is, he is not asking "Is Scott Scott?", but he is asking *about* Scott if that individual is Scott. Hence, as Russell sees it, (PA$_1$) is essentially the same as (A$_2$). But, note, in spite of what Russell apparently says, (PA$_1$) is not valid because of a substitution based on premise (2), since there is no more a term 'the author of *Waverley*' in premises (1) and (2) of (PA$_1$) than there is in the corresponding premises of (A$_1$). To see whether (PA$_1$) is valid, we must consider it in expanded or unabbreviated form.

(PA$_{1'}$)   1. ($\exists$x)(x is the one and only author of *Waverley* and George IV wishes to know whether x is Scott)

2. ($\exists$x)(x is the one and only author of *Waverley* and x is Scott)

---

3. George IV wishes to know whether Scott is Scott.

The argument is valid since the conclusion can be derived from the premises in a standard system of logic without any question of substitution involving a definite description, since none occurs in (PA$_{1'}$).[10] One may, thus, speak of a "verbal" substitution, since wherever we have a valid argument making use of an apparent substitution or an identity involving a definite description there will be a valid argument in expanded form that does not employ such a replacement. But, I do not know if this is just what Russell had in mind. For, the difference between (PA$_1$) and (A$_1$) is not that one has a term, the definite description, that the other lacks, but that one cannot get from the premises of

(A$_{1'}$)   1. George IV wished to know whether ($\exists$x)(x is the one and only one author of *Waverley* and x is Scott)

2. ($\exists$x)(x is the one and only one author of *Waverley* and x is Scott)

---

3. George IV wished to know whether Scott is Scott.

to its conclusion by employing a standard system of logic. In a sense, the first premise of ($A_{1'}$) could not even be stated without significant additions to such a system. Actually, it is not that clear that ($PA_{1'}$) is valid. Holding it to be so presupposes that

George IV wishes to know whether Sir Walter is Scott

is a sentence in which we can replace names by other names of the same individual. Russell is assuming, wrongly I believe, that it is such a context. I say "wrongly" in view of the ambiguities noted in our earlier discussion of the various senses of 'believe' relevant to such issues. The distinctions made then reflect current discussions of the use of names in argument patterns containing *epistemic* terms. Consider (A_2) altered to fit with out distinctions concerning the senses of 'believes', so that we have:

(B)   1. George IV believes that Scott is Scott.

       2. Scott is Sir Walter. Therefore,

---

       3. George IV believes that Scott is Sir Walter.

In the sense of 'believes$_1$', this is not a valid argument. As some would put it, we have an "opaque" context with 'believes$_1$'. With other senses of 'believe', (B) can be taken as valid. Thus, we face a general problem concerning the replacement of different signs for the "same things" and not merely a problem for Russell's theory of definite descriptions.

Such contexts have led to a good bit of discussion of names and *opaque* and *transparent epistemic* contexts.[11] Two prevalent themes in such discussions are (a) the search for an "analysis" of *belief* that will allow for replacements of "names" that "fulfill" certain conditions (standard names, vivid names, *known* names, etc.) and where relevant identity sentences are true; and (b) the *reduction* of some sense of 'belief' to others. Thus, Sellars seeks to define the "fully transparent" sense of 'belief' in terms of the "opaque" sense. Earlier, in Chapter III, we were concerned with different basic senses of 'belief', given the distinction between *particular* (*episodic*, some might say) *states of belief* and the propositional characters that indicate *kinds of belief states*. Later, we shall work out the details of such a view and the results it imposes on questions of inference with respect to *epistemic* contexts. In the present chapter, I am merely concerned with the relevance of such contexts for some restricted questions about Russell's theory of descriptions. Nevertheless, we may note a point relevant to the general question of the "logic of belief." No *analysis* of a concept of *belief* that allows for substitutions of different names of the same thing can provide an analysis of that basic sense of 'belief' involved in 'believes$_1$'. (I preclude stipulations or fiats whereby one may say that if there is a mental episode containing a token of the name 'Scott', then *there is* an episode containing the name 'Sir Walter' provided both name-types fulfill certain conditions.) This is so for two reasons, one obvious, one not so obvious. The obvious point is that in the sense of 'belief' whereby we speak of particular episodes (or "facts" as in Chapter III) we cannot infer from the occurrence of one such episode to the occurrence of another. We enter an area where we deal with empirical generalizations, if we deal with anything at all. Epistemic logics, as some conceive of them, are irrelevant for such matters. There is a second reason why this is so. Assume there are two "standard" names for the same object. Assume, also, that one does not trivially mean by 'standard' that we may interchange them in epistemic contexts, thereby ruling out negative cases as irrelevant to the sense of 'belief' the "logic" applies to. Let there be a belief state that uses a token of one of them. There will still be the added *intentional* feature that such a token is used on that occasion *as a token of the name* of the object. This point, as we shall later see, is crucial in the analysis of "intentionality." For the present, we need only note that just as the token's being of a certain "pattern" does not mean that it is a token of a type that has been interpreted in a certain way, so its being a token of a type that has been interpreted does not mean that *its* occurrence "in" an episode of thought is *as* a token that refers to or *intends* the named object. But, then, we obviously cannot have a condition that will allow for replacement. For, even if the occurrence of an episode of one "type" was *connected* with the occurrence of an episode of a *related* type, this would not guarantee that the "replacement" token of a different type would be *used* with the same *intention*. Nor would it help to

add that the belief state incorporates a token of an identity state-
ment (or of an "interpretation rule"). An obvious regress begins.
We shall return to such questions later. Now we may return to
Russell.

To help clarify what Russell is getting at, suppose George IV to
ask, on some occasion, "Is that Scott?" Knowing it to be true that
the person indicated by the demonstrative 'that' is the author of
Waverley, let us consider the following three propositions:

(R$_1$)   George IV wishes to know if that is Scott.

(R$_2$)   George IV wishes to know if the author of *Waverley*
        is Scott.

(R$_3$)   George IV wishes to know if Scott is Scott.

(R$_1$) we may take to be an unproblematic report. But, recall, that
on Russell's view of names the first occurrence of 'Scott' in (R$_3$) is
a mere indicator, a sign that plays the role of 'this' or 'that'. (R$_3$)
is, thus, no different from (R$_1$). Nor is it any different from (R$_1$)
when we take the occurrence of 'Scott' in (R$_1$) and the second occurrence of 'Scott' in (R$_3$) to be mere indicators. We must inhibit
the temptation to use either (R$_1$) or (R$_3$) to reflect what George
IV asks. We are reporting what he wishes to know, not what he is
asking or "uttering." He wishes to know if a certain specified individual is identical with Scott, whom he knows. We can indicate
that individual either as *that*, on a certain occasion, or by the
name 'Scott'. We can also specify which individual by using the
descriptive phrase 'the author of *Waverley*', so long as we give it
primary scope. That is, where a description has primary scope,
Russell takes it to function as a mere indicator of an object. The
descriptive phrase as a whole does not function like a name, but
the bound variable 'x' or the expression 'that individual', in an ordinary rendition of the last clause 'x = Scott' of premise (1) in
(PA$_1$), functions as a mere indicator or demonstrative. Hence,
(R$_2$), (R$_1$), and (R$_3$), so understood, are all true reports. Thus, as
Russell puts it, the use of primary scope is called for on some occasions: "This would be true, for example, if George IV had seen
Scott at a distance, and had asked 'Is that Scott?' "[12] In his discussion Linsky misses the point. He takes Russell to hold that interpreting premise (1) of (A$_1$) as containing a description with pri-

mary scope is wrong. But Russell does not hold this. Russell holds that what we "normally mean," when using such a sentence, is reflected by taking the description to have secondary scope. Linsky proceeds to argue that Russell failed to show that it was wrong to take (1) of (A_1) with primary scope.[13] Linsky then argues that *it is wrong* to take (1) as having primary scope. "If *Waverley* had been co-authored it would not, on the primary interpretation, be logically possible that George IV wished to know whether Scott was the author of *Waverley*."[14] It is true that if *Waverley* had been co-authored one could not ask, on Russell's theory, about *the* author of *Waverley* "Is that Scott?" But, according to Linsky, premise (1) of (A_1) is true if George IV "should have asked in all seriousness, 'Is Scott the author of *Waverley*?'" Linsky concludes: "Now surely he could have seriously asked this question though *Waverley* had been co-authored." Therefore, according to Linsky, we must conclude that interpreting the first premise of (A_1) as containing a description with primary scope is mistaken.[15] There is a mistake, but it is in Linsky's argument. If George IV asked, whether in all seriousness or in complete frivolity, "Is Scott the author of *Waverley*?", Russell would take the first premise of (A_1) to contain a description with secondary scope. If the report that George IV wished to know whether Scott was the author of *Waverley* is based on George IV's asking that question, then the statement of the report about George IV should be construed along the lines of what we "normally mean." That George IV could ask such a question in all seriousness does not show that we cannot take such a statement, (1) of (A_1), to contain a description with primary scope. It shows that on some occasions we should not take it to do so. A statement like (1) of (A_1), or any statement with a definite description of ordinary language, and, hence, without a scope operator, that allows for a difference of scope *when the statement is transcribed* by means of Russell's theory, does not unambiguously reveal the scope of the description. According to Russell, such statements are ambiguous as they stand. Recall the sentence "The present king of France is not bald." On Russell's theory, such a sentence presents us with an ambiguity. Many things may reveal which way we ought to transcribe it to reflect what was intended, as in the case of George IV and what he literally asked. All Linsky shows is that in certain contexts we ought to take a scope in a secondary way. He does not show, as Russell's example reveals, that it is wrong to take the scope in a primary way in all contexts. Linsky's argument involves a mistake that is similar to one in a recent article by C. E. Cassin on Russell's distinction between primary and secondary scope. She criticizes Russell as follows: "It is important that there should be a clear criterion for deciding whether a descriptive phrase has primary or secondary occurrence. Unfortunately, Russell's various definitions of his distinction do not provide such a criterion."[16] One indicates, unambiguously in *Principia*, the scope of a description by a scope operator.[17] What is asked for is a way of telling the scope of a description in an ordinary language sentence, say (1) of (A_1), *just by considering the sentence.* Such a criticism is based on a simple misunderstanding, which I shall point to by an example. Assume we use our standard way of reporting time without the suffixes P.M. and A.M. A statement like "It is seven o'clock" is thus ambiguous. Suppose further that a Russell among us seeks to remove the ambiguity by suggesting the use of the suffixes. Finally, imagine that someone reports that a train will arrive at seven o'clock the next day. Would we now criticize our new convention as inadequate since the report was ambiguous, or would we point out the ambiguity and ask whether he meant seven A.M. or seven P.M.? The point, of course, is that a convention that enables one to avoid an ambiguous use does not guarantee that it will be used on all occasions.

Linsky has not shown what he claims to have shown, that (A_1) cannot be construed as (PA_1). Consequently, he has not shown that "we escape the conclusion" that (A_1), so construed, is a valid argument. Since this is so, we face a slight complication regarding (A_3), for we can consider the conclusion of (A_3) to be rewritten to reflect a primary scope for the description. We need not consider cases where the argument would have a premise expanded with one scope and the conclusion expanded with the other, for we are concerned with the replacement of a description, according to Russell's theory, in nonextensional contexts. We are not concerned with the relationships between various existential statements in such contexts. Altering the conclusion of (A_3) to reflect the employment of a description with primary scope, we arrive at the following:

(A$_{3'}$)   1. Strawson believes that George IV wished to know whether Scott was the author of *Waverley*. Hence,

---

2. One and only one individual both wrote *Waverley* and is such that Strawson believes that George IV wished to know whether that individual was identical with Scott.

Let us again assume we are employing Russell's theory but overlook for a moment the various senses of 'belief' we discussed in connection with (A$_3$). There will be some, but to be sure rare, cases where the report expressed in (1) of (A$_{3'}$) will lend itself to transcription into (2) of (A$_{3'}$). Other contexts will indicate that (1) cannot be so transcribed. The basic point is that all the arguments (A$_1$), (A$_3$), and (A$_{3'}$), are ambiguous because premise (1) in each is context relevant. Moreover, all the arguments we have considered involving intentional verbs are ambiguous in the sense brought out in our discussion of 'believes' and (A$_3$).

The points we have been concerned with lie behind a fashionable but fallacious argument that purports to reduce the way we have considered facts to an absurdity. Davidson has claimed that if there are facts, there is exactly one fact: the Great Fact. The argument purporting to establish this conclusion goes as follows:

Indeed, employing principles implicit in our examples, it is easy to confirm the suspicion. The principles are that if a statement corresponds to the fact described by an expression of the form 'the fact that p', then it corresponds to the fact described by 'the fact that q' provided 'p' and 'q' are logically equivalent sentences, or one differs from the other in that a singular term has been replaced by a coextensive singular term. The confirming argument is this. Let 's' abbreviate some true sentence. Then surely the statement that s corresponds to the fact that s. But we may substitute for the second 's' the logically equivalent '(the x such that x is identical with Diogenes and s) is identical with (the x such that x is identical with Diogenes)'. Applying the principle that we may substitute coextensive singular terms, we can substitute 't' for 's' in the last quoted sentence, provided 't' is true. Finally, reversing the first step we conclude that the statement that s corresponds to the fact that t, where 's' and 't' are any true sentences.[18]

To see why the argument is fallacious, let us consider it in a slightly more explicit form. Let (P_1) and (P_2) be the principles Davidson employs: the first dealing with the replacement of logically equivalent sentences, the second concerning the replacement of a sentence by another that differs only in containing a different, but coextensive, singular term. Let us use the expression " 's' Den. s" to state that the sentence 's' corresponds to or stands for *the fact that* s. The argument may then be put as follows:

1. s
2. t
3. 's' Den. s
4. $(\iota x)(x = \text{Diogenes} \ \& \ s) = (\iota x)(x = \text{Diogenes})$
5. $(\iota x)(x = \text{Diogenes} \ \& \ t) = (\iota x)(x = \text{Diogenes})$
6. $(\iota x)(x = \text{Diogenes} \ \& \ s) = (\iota x)(x = \text{Diogenes} \ \& \ t)$
7. 's' is logically equivalent to '$(\iota x)(x = \text{Diogenes} \ \& \ s) = (\iota x)(x = \text{Diogenes})$'
8. 's' Den. $(\iota x)(x = \text{Diogenes} \ \& \ s) = (\iota x)(x = \text{Diogenes})$
9. 's' Den. $(\iota x)(x = \text{Diogenes} \ \& \ t) = (\iota x)(x = \text{Diogenes})$
10. 't' is logically equivalent to '$(\iota x)(x = \text{Diogenes} \ \& \ t) = (\iota x)(x = \text{Diogenes})$'
11. 's' Den. t.

Hence, where 's' and 't' are any true sentences, either one stands for the fact we might think to be expressed by the other. Consequently, there is no point distinguishing, or trying to distinguish, among so-called *facts*.

Steps (1), (2), and (3) may be taken as premises of the argument. Steps (4) and (5) follow from the premises, by standard logical procedures, with two implicit assumptions. We assume, first, that we are employing Russell's theory of descriptions, with respect to the understood expansions of the definite descriptions, in context, and, second, that the sentence '$E!(\iota x)(x = \text{Diogenes})$' is true. Step (6) is a consequence of steps (4) and (5) by the standard rules for identity. Step (7) also involves standard logical procedures together with two implicit assumptions. Again, we assume we are employing Russell's theory of descriptions and, moreover, we assume that the sentence '$E!(\iota x)(x = \text{Diogenes})$' is not only true but *logically* true. Step (8) is justified by (P_1) and steps (3) and (7). Step (9) follows from steps (6) and (8) by use of (P_2). Step (10) follows for the same reasons as step (7). Step (11) follows from steps (9) and (10) by the application of (P_1).

Since the argument makes implicit use of Russell's theory of descriptions, it is necessary to examine it in a form where such contextually defined signs are replaced by their definitions. But, if one expands the descriptions in (4)-(8), it immediately becomes obvious that the argument is invalid. There is no way to get from the sentences, so expanded, to (9). In fact, (P_2) becomes totally irrelevant. This situation contrasts sharply with the case of (PA_1) and (PA_1'). There, recall, the legitimacy of the substitution, based on an identity statement containing a definite description, re-flected the validity of an argument pattern in unabbreviated form. It is easy to see why the problem arises here. The sentence (4) is merely a rewriting of the conjunction 's & $(\iota x)(x = \text{Diogenes}) = (\iota x)(x = \text{Diogenes})$'. The same holds for the corresponding sen-tences involving 't' and both 's' and 't'.[19] If one, then, considers an argument expressed in terms of such conjunctions, it becomes clear that one could get to the purported conclusion if one em-ployed a totally specious principle. That principle, call it (P_3), would be something on the order of: any true sentence may re-place any other true sentence to the right of 'Den.' in contexts of the form " '. . .' Den. . . .". We may thus go directly to (11) from (1), (2), and (3). But, then, the "problem," along with Davidson's "argument," has disappeared. The apparent plausibility of the ar-gument, as originally formulated, depends on the use of a descrip-tive phrase, containing a conjunction sign, as an apparent subject term. Definite descriptions allow for a typographically condensed way of expressing a conjunction in an *apparent* subject-predicate form. Thus, one can apparently apply the principle (P_2). But, that principle may be used only if it reflects a valid argument in unab-breviated form. In this case it does not, and the form of notation disguises the fallacy, since it appears to permit the use of (P_2). Since such an application is blocked, in the expanded form of ex-pression, we need not feel arbitrary in rejecting apparent descrip-tions like '$(\iota x)(x = \text{Diogenes} \& s)$' for replacements in identity contexts by using (P_2). The validity of an argument can not be made to depend on its occurring in typographically abbreviated form. Recall, again, that the validity of (PA_1), forgetting the ambiguities we have considered in such contexts, does not depend on the abbreviated form but is valid only because $(PA_{1'})$ is. Davidson's argument, by contrast, is invalid for precisely the reasons (A_1) is invalid when the description in premise (1) is taken to have secondary scope. Just as we cannot get to the conclusion of (A_1), in such a case, we cannot get to Davidson's conclusion. We, thus, see that 'Den.' contexts are *demonstrated* to be like "belief" contexts in a crucial way.

It is interesting to note that what blocks Davidson's argument is precisely what Russell took to block the validity of (A_1), with the descriptions taken as having secondary scope. But, even more interesting is the fact that we can reject Davidson's argument *without* having to claim that (P_1) or (P_2) must be abandoned since the argument involves nonextensional contexts, i.e., the statements containing 'Den.'.

One may suggest taking the descriptions to have primary scope in (8) and (9). It would be illicit to do this in step (8), since we are using (4)-(7) in the argument. Expanding the descriptions in (4)-(7) prohibits the use of primary scope in (8). This would involve an additional assumption that one may do so in such contexts, whatever that would mean. This suffices to reject Davidson's argument irrespective of questions of scope. But, to see another point, let us assume such manipulations of scope are permitted. If we *adopt* primary scope in (8), we can get (9). This is easy to see. We have s, t, and

$$(\exists x)(y)\,[\,((x = \text{Diogenes \& } s) \equiv x = y)\, \&\, \text{'s' Den. } x = x]$$

as an expansion of (8), with primary scope. All we need do is extract 's' from (8), so expanded, and *replace* it by 't'. This can be done by moves of standard logic. But, we still have no way to get to (11). Hence, the argument still fails, even with the assumption about scope. What we can do, however, is get a "peculiar" result from (8), expanded as above, or (9), expanded as

$$(\exists x)(y)\,[\,((x = \text{Diogenes \& } t) \equiv x = y)\, \&\, \text{'s' Den. } x = x]\,.$$

This, given the standard uses of '=', permits us to get to " 's' Den.

Diogenes = Diogenes". We, thus, have 's' standing for the *fact* that Diogenes is Diogenes. Hence, the illicit move to primary scope does "cover" something. We can see what by considering the following pattern:

1. s
2. 's' Den. s
3. s ⊃ [p v ~p) ≡ s]
4. (p v ~p) ≡ s
5. 's' Den. p v ~p.

With (1) and (2) as premises and (3) and (4) obtained by propositional logic, we get (5) by employing a replacement based on *material* equivalence. Doing so, we end with 's' *standing in* Den. to a logical truth, as above. This is what the shift to primary scope amounts to in the above pattern. Once again, we have an illicit use of material equivalence as the basis of a replacement. That is what the use of descriptions covers up in the argument. Hence, we see what is peculiar about the *use* of true sentences, 's' and 't', in such arguments. Given the truth of a sentence, it is materially equivalent to a logical truth, which then replaces it. We might just as well adopt (P_3) or a general rule for replacing true sentences with true sentences.

The use of primary scope brings all this out when we recall that on Russell's theory there is supposedly no difference between the use of primary and secondary scope *when the descriptions are fulfilled, except for nonextensional contexts.* Recall the difference between (A_1) construed in terms of secondary scope and (PA_1). To take the contexts involving 'Den.' to be extensional in that there is no difference regarding scope is to explicitly acknowledge the use of (P_3), since it is covertly employed where we expand the descriptions with secondary scope. To seek to establish Davidson's conclusion by the use of an explicit primary expansion of the description is to assume, by such an expansion, that we may replace 's' by a tautology in contexts involving 'Den.', and hence make use of (P_3) in the assumption of primary scope. What we learn from Davidson's argument is that some singular terms, in the form of definite descriptions, can only be unproblematically "replaced" in some argument patterns if we accept (P$_3$). All this is not surprising when we recall other uses of Davidson's borrowed argument. As Quine put it: "Anything x, even an intension, is specifiable in contingently coincident ways if specifiable at all. For suppose x is determined uniquely by the condition 'ϕx'. Then it is also determined uniquely by the conjunctive condition 'p · ϕx' where 'p' is any truth, however irrelevant."[20] The use of 'specifiable' covers a gap which some seek to turn into a mine of philosophical problems. As many put it, the contexts 'ϕx & p' and 'ϕx', given that 'p' is a true sentence, have the same extension or are satisfied by the same "objects." Suppose that such contexts uniquely determine an object, *a*. The interesting questions are: (A) Does the description '(ιx)(ϕx & p)' *specify a* as the description '(ιx) (ϕx)' does, so that we may say that the sentences 'W(ιx)(ϕx & p)' and 'W(ιx)(ϕx)' both state, *about a*, that it has W? (B) Can 'ϕx & p' and 'ϕx' be taken to *specify* properties of *a* and, if so, different properties? The answer to both questions can be given without going into details about the notions of "property" and "specify." For, we need only recall that 'W(ιx)(ϕx & p)' is logically equivalent to 'p & W(ιx)(ϕx)'. Thus, one who holds that the answer to (B) is yes also holds that the sentence 'p & W(ιx)(ϕx)' is used to ascribe to *a* something more than we assert about *a* when we use 'W(ιx)(ϕx)'. He might, then, just as well claim the same about the sentences 'p & W*a*' and 'W*a*'. This, I submit, is grotesque. The same point is involved in (A). To hold that 'W(ιx)(ϕx & p)' or 'p & W*a*' are used to ascribe W to *a* is to say no more than that W is ascribed to *a* in one conjunct of a conjunction. The argument:

(Q$_1$)　1. W(ιx)(ϕx).

　　　　2. (ιx)(ϕx) = (ιx)(ϕx & p). Therefore,

---

　　　　3. W(ιx)(ϕx & p).

appears to be like

(Q$_2$)　1. W(ιx)(ϕx).

　　　　2. (ιx)(ϕx) = (ιx)(ψx). Therefore,

---

　　　　3. W(ιx)(ψx),

but it is merely a rewritten version of

(Q_3) 1. $W(\iota x)(\phi x)$

   2. p. Therefore,

---

   3. $W(\iota x)(\phi x)$ & p.

As (Q_3), it is uninteresting. Rewritten as (Q_1), it leads some to draw philosophical conclusions about facts and reference. Notational conveniences ought not to have ontological consequences. Rather, what we may conclude is a point modeled on Russell's early discussion of (A_1). Russell avoided a puzzle in that case by insisting that we consider statements containing descriptions in expanded form. So, we may avoid puzzles generated by the use of expressions like '$(\iota x)(\phi x$ & p)', as so-called singular terms, by noting what *their* use amounts to in unabbreviated statements without such *terms*.[21] Such definitional replacements enable us to make transparent what some would leave philosophically opaque.

A consideration of open sentences like 'ϕx & s' may suggest that Davidson's argument can be saved, without appealing to (P_3), by using a modified version of (P_2) as follows:

$(P_{2'})$ Any open sentence may replace any other open sentence in any context where both are satisfied by only one object and by the same object.

The replacement of the defined expressions will no longer block the argument. For, we shall be able to replace 'x = Diogenes & s' by 'x = Diogenes & t' in either (8) or its expansion:

(8')   's' Den. $(\exists x)\,[(x = $ Diogenes & s) & (y) $\{(y = $ Diogenes & s) $\supset y = x\}$ & x = x]

But $(P_{2'})$ is of no help, for, together with (P_1), we may trivially derive (P_3). Hence, using $(P_{2'})$ with (P_1) amounts to the use of (P_3) with (P_1). In fact, $(P_{2'})$ involves the use of an even more general "principle": one may replace a true sentence by any other true sentence in any context. We can easily see that this is the case. Assume, again, that 's' and 't' are true and that 'E! $(\iota x)(x = $ Diogenes)' or, more simply, '$(\exists x)(x = $ Diogenes)' is a logical truth. Let 'f(s)' stand for any context containing 's' and 'f(t)' stand for the same context where some occurrence of 's' has been replaced by some occurrence of 't'. Take as premises:

1. s

2. t

3. f(s)

4. E!$(\iota x)(x = \text{Diogenes})$

We may then derive f(t) by moves parodying Davidson's. Since 'f(s)' is any context containing 's', we have established the "general" principle.

This does not mean I am offering an argument against the use of (P_1) and $(P_{2'})$, as I *did* offer an argument against the use of (P_1) and (P_2). Rather, the point is that one does not need to offer an argument. To suggest the use of $(P_{2'})$ would be as pointless and irrelevant as proposing the general replacement of any true sentence by any other true sentence. The paradoxical force of the "great fact argument" derives from its *apparent* use of (P_1) and (P_2). I suspect that the underlying psychological element is that (P_3) seems to follow from (P_1) and (P_2), although we do not suspect that it does. If it did, the problem would seem to lie with contexts containing 'Den' and talk of "facts." For, surely, we ought to allow for the replacement of one expression by another in such contexts where they both *refer to* the same *constituent* of a fact. We ought to and we can without being forced to *the Great Fact.* There is no suggestion of paradox once $(P_{2'})$ replaces (P_2). When we talk of exchanging "open sentences" with the same extension, we no longer deal with cases of *reference* to a constituent of a fact—with the replacement of *singular terms* by others having the *same extension*—i.e., *denotation* or *referent.* In short, the original force behind accepting (P_2) is that for singular expressions there is a bridge between the notions of *extension, denotation,* and *referent.* There is no such link in the case of open sentences. The problematic nature of open sentences emerges strongly when we ask what an open sentence could be taken to "stand for." One would seem to have a choice among an individual, a class, or a property. But, just as the *Great Fact argument* is invalid with definite descriptions of individuals, it is invalid with definite descriptions of classes or properties. To hold that 'ϕx & t' may replace 'ϕx & s' because both stand for the same property or class will not do. This would attempt to employ the identity

$$(\iota f)(x)[fx \equiv (\phi x \& s)] = (\iota f)(x)[fx \equiv (\phi x \& t)]$$

as the basis for a substitution. But when the property or class abstract is expanded, one runs into exactly the same difficulty that we noted with definite descriptions applicable to individuals like Diogenes. The expansion blocks the replacement. Hence, one must appeal to open sentences. But, this is superficial and trivial, since the above argument deriving (P_3) from (P_1) and ($P_{2'}$) is utterly trivial in that there is neither paradox nor point to such a "derivation." Moreover, a philosopher who appeals to facts as truth condition has no need to take ($P_{2'}$) seriously.

Quine has used the illicit pattern we have been discussing to formulate a purported counterexample to a proposal of Sellars.[22] Construing such purported "singular terms" as we have disposes of his argument as it disposes of Davidson's. But, Sellars's view involves problems that are significant and instructive. He proposes to analyze *the* transparent sense of *belief* in terms of *the* opaque sense in such a way as to make the former *safe* for substitution. To do so he introduces a "fragment of a neo-Fregean semantical theory." Thus, his definition is:

$$^{\mathrm{t}}Bfa =_{df.} (\exists i) \, i \, ME \, a \, \& \, {}^o Bfi.$$

The definiens tells us that "some individual concept is such that *it* is materially equivalent to **a** and Jones believes (in the opaque sense) that f *it*."[23] The sign 'a' is a sign for an individual concept, as is 'b', and we have been previously told that

$$\mathbf{a} \, ME \, \mathbf{b} \equiv a = b.$$

With '$^{\mathrm{t}}B$' transcribing the transparent sense of 'believes' and with the reference to Jones "incorporated" into the predicate, the definition presents Sellars's analysis.

The problem is indicated by (1) the awkward ordinary language transcription Sellars gives to the conjunct '$^o Bfi$'; (2) the use of the variable 'i' in that conjunct; and (3) the use of constructions like

$$(S_1) \qquad B((\exists x) \, wise \, x)^{24}$$

and

(S_2) $(\exists i)\,^{\circ}B(\text{wise } i)$.

The problem itself is two-fold. First, such "neo-Fregean" patterns must recognize propositional entities, constituents of such propositions that are individual senses and other constituents that are predicative concepts, and either connections of such different constituents or "forms" of the propositions so that the proposition is understood to consist of the sense (or senses) attached to the concept. Second, one takes belief to be a two-term relation connecting a person and a proposition, no matter how one writes the appropriate belief sentence. This is clear from (S_1) and the implicit appeal to propositions in (S_2). Consequently, one faces the problems imposed by the use of a sentence as a linguistic term of a relation. If one does not so use a sentence, but uses, instead, a sign pattern that contains a sentence, 'that-p' or '[p]', for example, one faces corresponding problems. These have to do with the role of sentences so used, or that-clauses so introduced, in inference patterns. The obvious and perennial case has to do with existential generalization and (S_1) and (S_2). What this shows is that a neo-Fregean view, as in Sellars and a similar analysis of Kaplan's,[25] is a hybrid of a propositional analysis and a relational analysis of belief. Sentences, or that-clauses, operate as terms in other sentences, and these latter sentences thus express a relation between an individual and proposition. Yet, one seeks to quantify over terms in such embedded sentences. Hence, one also treats, or attempts to treat, a belief context along the lines of a relational analysis. To do so, Sellars must treat the defining clause

$(\exists i)\, i \text{ ME } a \,\&\,^{\circ}Bfi$

as reading something like:

(F)   There is a sense and it denotes the same object that the sense of 'a' denotes and Jones believes the proposition which contains that sense and the *concept* f (appropriately connected).

This, as we shall see later, not only connects Sellars's analysis with Kaplan's but shows both to be closely related to Bergmann's analysis. It also shows that the form of expression Sellars uses as a defining clause is misleading in that he does not perspicuously reveal the structure of such belief sentences. Were he to do so, his symbolism would be more on the order of:

> (∃i)(i ME the sense of '*a*' & (∃p)(Bp & p contains i &
> p contains f & p is in subject-predicate form));
> with 'p' as a propositional variable.

Actually Sellars does something like this when he makes the expected move and transposes his "neo-Fregean" view into a more familiar gambit by speaking of dispositions to utter *sentences*. If, for the moment, we think of Jones having a belief in terms of Jones having some relation to a sentence, then we can see that (F) becomes something like:

> (S)   There is a term that denotes the same object as '*a*' and
> Jones believes (is in the appropriate relation to) some
> sentence which contains that term and the predicate 'f'
> in the subject-predicate juxtaposition.

Both (F) and (S) provide the obvious difference between (S₁) and (S₂), as well as immunity from Quine's use of descriptions. We shall return to Sellars's shift to talk of sentences and dispositions in a later context. For the present, we may note an interesting feature of a Fregean-style gambit that is brought out by one line of reply that Sellars makes to Quine.[26]

Assume that the sign 'a' names the sense of '*a*', and, hence, that

> (S₃)   a = the sense of '*a*'

is true. Can one then replace the 'a' in

> (S₄)   ᵗBfa

by "the sense of '*a*'"? Recall that we so read 'ᵗBfa' that we do not hold that Jones believes that f applies to a, but to *a*. With this reading understood, there is a justification for the replacement, since (S₄) is read, in effect, as

> (S₅)   Jones believes that the object, signified by the sense
> a, is f;

and this unproblematically goes to

(S₆)   Jones believes that the object, signified by the sense of '*a*', is f.

Where a problem arises is in the use of a name, '**a**', being replaced by a description. Thus, if we ignore (S₅) and (S₆) and go from (S₃) and (S₄) to

(S₇)   ᵗBf(ιi)(i is the sense of '*a*')

a question arises about the expansion of the description into '(∃i) (. . . i . . . & ᵗBfi)' or "ᵗB(∃x)(. . . x . . . & fx)' or "ᵗB(∃i)(. . . i . . . & fi)'. Clearly, the latter two versions will not do: the one because Jones does not believe that *there is a sense*; the other because Jones does not believe *the proposition* that there is an object. . . . The first alternative will not do either, since there is no provision for contexts like "ᵗBfi'. But, that is easily repaired by taking "ᵗBfi' in terms of '(∃j)(j ME i & °Bfj)'. The transcription then becomes '(∃i)(. . . i . . . & (∃j)(j ME i & °Bfj))'. So, taking (S₇) allows it to follow from (S₃) and (S₄), just as (S₆) follows from (S₅) and (S₃). This focuses attention on the awkward formulation that Sellars must use to guarantee that Jones does not attribute f to the *sense* but, rather, attributes f to some*thing* by means of some *sense*. The awkward formulation shows that Sellars must bring in the reference to the connection between the sense and its denotation as in (F), (S₅), and (S₆).

Sellars could suggest that on his gambit, one may refuse to expand the description in (S₇) until that sentence is transposed into

(∃j)(j ME (ιi)(i is the sense of '*a*') & °Bfj).

He would, thus, *insist on an order for replacing defined signs*. This is a move that is inadequate, since his gambit is, in part, designed to avoid appealing to moves characteristic of nonextensional contexts. There are further problems. Sellars recognizes that he must accommodate the difference between:

There is a unique Ø and Jones believes of that Ø that it is f.

and

Jones believes that there is a unique Ø which is f.

The first he cannot transcribe as

$$(\exists x)(y)[(\emptyset y \equiv y = x) \& Bfx],$$

whether the 'B' is '^{o}B' or '^{t}B', since that poses a problem by the use of an "object" variable. This we shall return to. The second sentence he has to transcribe as

$$B(\exists x)(y)[(\emptyset y \equiv y = x) \& fx].$$

If the 'B', here, is '^{t}B', we should transcribe it into a form with '^{o}B'. Doing so should yield something like

$$(\exists p)[p \text{ ME } (\exists x)(y)((\emptyset y \equiv y = x) \& fx) \& {}^{o}Bp],$$

with 'p' as a variable over neo-Fregean propositions. This not only brings us back to (F), but raises questions about the use of ME as a relation between propositions and between *concepts*. These, we shall see, are detrimental to Sellars's analysis. If the 'B' is taken as '^{o}B', the same questions directly arise, since one takes the existential sentence to *shift reference* in the context 'B . . .' and refer to a Fregean proposition. If we put the Fregean view perspicuously, along the lines of (F), (S$_5$), and (S$_6$), no problem of substitution arises, since we understand that the description in (S$_7$) is taken as having primary scope. But, this means that Sellars has not succeeded in making '^{t}B . . .' a *transparent* context. What is more important is seeing that the Fregean analysis involves making several existential claims, as in (F), including one about senses and one about objects, and, consequently, also making a claim about the connection of such "things" in that one *refers to the other*. This can be emphasized by returning to the analysis of a sentence like

Jones believes of something that it is f,

as a simpler case of the problem posed by the use of an "object" variable. Sellars renders such statements as:

$$(\exists i)[(\exists j) i \text{ ME } j \& {}^{o}Bfi].^{27}$$

Thus, the claim that there is some*thing*, which Jones believes to be f, is expressed by the assertion that a sense is materially equivalent to some sense and Jones believes . . . . The connection of the belief to the object *and* the existential claim about the object are thus carried by the equivalence condition for 'ME':

a ME B ≡ $a = b$.

This is how Sellars avoids making explicit claims about the existence of senses, or roles, and of objects and of their *connection*. He seeks to avoid appealing to an *intentional* relation of *standing for* or *referring to* by speaking of natural connections and semantical uniformities involving roles (senses), tokens, and objects. This goes along with his attempt to avoid abstract entities, such as properties, connectives, and propositions as well as facts. I shall argue, in later chapters, that he does not succeed in his general pattern. We shall soon see that his rejection of abstract entities leads to a serious problem with the notion of transparent belief contexts. For the present, we may note how all the issues are connected. (F) reveals that just as the neo-Fregean speaks of senses he will speak of propositions and concepts (including negation). Hence, Sellars will have to argue that his analysis of belief does not involve correlating such "senses" to corresponding objects in the way that a corresponds to a. He will also seek to avoid a "pseudo" relation of reference, between a and a, by construing senses as linguistic roles ($^{\bullet}a^{\bullet}$ replacing a) and thoughts in terms of dispositions to utter tokens characterized by such "metalinguistic sortals." We then realize that the analysis of (S_4) is far from perspicuous, since the appropriate complications are, as it were, packed into the equivalence condition for 'ME'. Moreover, the use of 'ME' in Sellars's analysis involves him in a problem that is easily seen. Consider two predicates, say 'rational animal' and 'featherless biped', and the proposition:

ᵗB that—rational animal (a).

This is transcribed, for our purposes, into:

($\exists$i)($\exists$f)[i ME $^{\bullet}a^{\bullet}$ & f ME $^{\bullet}$rational animal$^{\bullet}$ & °Bfi] .

But, Sellars must, and does,[28] treat ME between concepts quite differently from its use between senses. Thus, whereas we have

$$\dot{a}\dot{}\ \text{ME}\ \dot{}b\dot{}\ \equiv a = b,$$

we also have

$$\dot{}\emptyset\dot{}\ \text{ME}\ \dot{}\not\emptyset\dot{}\ \equiv (x)(\emptyset x \equiv \not\emptyset x).$$

This is done to avoid the use of '$\emptyset = \not\emptyset$' and the implied recognition of abstract entities. Consequently, Jones believes, in the transparent sense, that a is a rational animal if he believes, in the opaque sense, that a is a featherless biped. With the obvious extension to propositions, Jones will believe any true proposition, in the transparent sense, if he believes one true proposition in the opaque sense. If Jones, like most of us, also believes (opaquely) some false proposition, then he transparently believes every proposition (with a truth value). This, of course, is an awkward sense of 'belief'. What is interesting is that the pattern is not an unreasonable one, *if it is confined to individuals*, owing to the "identity condition." It becomes unreasonable when it gets wedded to Sellars's views about abstract entities. Were he to allow his concepts (like ˙rational animal˙) to correlate with properties, as concepts *of* individuals, namely senses, correlate with individuals, Jones could *sensibly* be said to have a belief that a is a *rational animal*, if he believed a proposition employing a *concept standing for that property*. This suggests that a cogent analysis of belief that allows for "substitutions" will acknowledge *properties* and *references* to them.[29] It is also interesting to compare this feature of Sellars's analysis with Davidson's introduction of *The Great Fact*. There, too, we saw that no problem arose by allowing the substitution of signs that *referred* to the same constituent of a fact. Here, we may also note that all this tacitly acknowledges that descriptions do not function in transparent belief contexts as they do in contexts where scope is irrelevant when the descriptions are fulfilled. Thus, Sellars has not given an analysis that *preserves* such features of so-called extensional contexts. He recognizes this and attempts to justify his analysis by holding that he does not "reject the principle that expressions which have the same reference may be substituted for one another *salva veritate*."[30] He does not do that because, on his view, the singular terms in (S_3) do not have the same reference in belief contexts even though (S_3) is true. Although Sellars appears to hold that 'a' may be introduced as a name for the sense of 'a', he also holds that in 'Bfa' the use of boldface type indicates that the context 'Bf . . .' shifts the referent of whatever expression replaces the dots *from* the normal referent *to* the normal sense of that expression. With that reading understood, we can use 'Bfa' or 'Bf*a*'. Hence, (S_3) does not provide a basis for replacement. One can only replace 'a', in 'Bfa', by a sign that would shift to the same referent '*a*' shifts to in the context. One can see an aspect of the problem by realizing that it makes a difference when the "shift" occurs in the case of a description—before or after the description is expanded. If it shifts after, the pattern makes no sense, since there is only a bound variable within the context 'Bf . . .': if before, we implicitly treat the description as having secondary scope, if *it* can be said to be a description in such a context of shifting reference. This aside, it is misleading to suggest that one has preserved substitution *salva veritate*. Such a claim implies that for any context '$\emptyset a$' if 'a' and 'β' have the same referent, i.e., if '$a = \beta$', then '$\emptyset a \equiv \emptyset \beta$'. Sellars, following Frege, replaces the substitution rule by: for any context '$\emptyset a$', one can replace 'a' by 'β' if *in* '$\emptyset a$' and '$\emptyset \beta$' the terms have the same referent. This is a different rule which brings out the fact that Frege's view involves the distinction between the reference of a term and the reference of a term in a context. Or, as one might put it, the context determines the sense and the referent. Hence, only in the context of a sentence does a word have the sense and referent it does have. Given the two-fold use of 'reference', Sellars can hardly claim that he does not reject the principle in question.

There is a further peculiarity about the shift in reference. In 'Jones believes that *a* is f' we can replace 'that *a* is f' by 'the proposition that *a* is f', on a normal reading as well as on a Fregean analysis. This means that contexts like 'Jones believes . . .' are not such that what replaces the dots shifts reference. Instead, in contexts like 'Jones believes that . . .', the *sentences* that replace the dots shift reference. Thus, 'that *a* is f' can be taken to refer uniformly to a proposition. And, one can take 'that . . .' to be a function that determines a proposition to be the referent of the expression obtained by replacing the dots with a sentence. The proposition will be the one normally expressed by the sentence replacing the dots. This means that the function indicated by 'that . . .' is abnormal in that it determines a referent or denotation or value on the basis of the sense of the argument expression and not the denotation of the latter. And that, in turn, reveals that there is an ambiguity in the notion that belief contexts involve referential shifts. For, one may suggest that the shift is not brought about by the context containing 'believes' but by the occurrence of 'that'. Yet, the peculiarity of the function signified by 'that . . .' leads to an obvious point. Employing such a function presupposes a shift in reference of the sentence, used as an argument expression, if we are to treat the function as coordinating a proposition to itself. This is another way of expressing what I called the "abnormal" feature of the function. Thus, we must acknowledge that in some contexts sentences have to function as *names* of propositions. We cannot achieve the "shift" by introducing a *standard* function. (This recalls Russell's point that one cannot go backward from the denotation to the meaning.) Yet, the introduction of a device such as 'that . . .' or some other device, such as square brackets used in earlier chapters, aids in the perspicuous representation of belief sentences. Let us replace 'Bfa' with 'B that $-fa$' understood in the above terms. We may now unproblematically replace 'that $-fa$' with any other name of the same proposition. Moreover, the problem of existential generalization *into* belief contexts is seen as a problem of quantification into a complex name, on a neo-Fregean view. We no longer quantify into "sentences." Consider

(P)   B that $-fa$

(C) $(\exists i)$ B that $-fi$.

The expression 'that $-fi$' is not a name of a proposition. Hence, if we wish to incorporate such "generalization" into our inference patterns, we must construe (C) along the lines of asserting that "there is a proposition and a sense such that . . ." That is, we must construe (C) in terms of (F). Even if we do not state it so explicitly, we pack such an interpretation into our construal of such contexts. The implicit use of (F) becomes quite clear when we consider the question of replacing 'a' or 'a' in Bfa' or 'Bfa' by a description like '$(\iota x)\emptyset x$', where, '$(\iota x)\emptyset x = a$', or by '$(\iota i)(i = a)$', where obviously '$(\iota i)(i = a) = a$'. One cannot allow for such replacements where one takes the scope of the descriptions to be secondary, since we obtain different propositional signs—'that $-(\iota x)\emptyset x$ is f' and 'that $-(\iota i)(i = a)$ is f'. One could accommodate the first case by a shift in the sense of 'believes', along the lines we discussed earlier in the chapter. But that is not really to the point. If we take primary scope to be involved, we require an adjustment in the reading of the belief context. In the case of '$(\iota i)(i = a)$' the adjustment would be along the lines of the reading of (C) in terms of (F) and, hence, could be allowed. In the case of '$(\iota x)\emptyset x$' the adjustment would be in terms of something like:

(F′)   There is one and only one $\emptyset$ and there is a proposition and there is a sense and that sense *refers to* the $\emptyset$ and is a constituent of the proposition and . . .

The point is that in both cases one must explicitly quantify over propositions *and* senses as well as specify that a sense and a concept are constituents of some proposition and, finally, state that a sense *refers to* or *denotes* an object. One does not do that in (P), since 'that $-fa$' functions as the name of a proposition *and* specifies the structure of the proposition. This not only suggests, again, the closeness of Sellars's neo-Fregean view to Bergmann's analysis, but invites a closer look at devices for "naming" propositions. Those familiar with Bergmann's analysis will recognize a problem long associated with his view: the claim that propositional "characters" are simple and yet are signified by predicates formed from sentences by the device of corner quotes. Thus, one may begin to suspect that if Sellars's neo-Fregean view (or David Kaplan's similar sketch) is put in an explicit and perspicuous form, it becomes very like Bergmann's pattern. We shall return to such matters in Chapters XII and XIII.

Sellars's analysis highlights the fundamental defect that any Fregean or neo-Fregean view faces. If we take the shift of reference to involve the acknowledgment of a new entity, a further sense that the expression then means, we face two problems. One is the well-known awkwardness of acknowledging an infinite number of entities for each expression. The other is the paradoxical result we noted in Chapter VI. Such new propositional entities cannot denote truth values. If one holds, as suggested in Chapter VI, that an expression may both denote and express the same entity, a problem remains. For, if one then holds that a propositional entity is like a sentential expression in that what it denotes is determined by a context, one holds that such entities also shift denotation. This is clearly awkward. It is one thing to hold that an expression is used one way in one context and another way in another context: it is quite another thing to hold that such shifting usage corresponds to shifting relationships among entities. Alternatively, to hold that such propositional entities denote (stand in D* to) two things—themselves and truth values—and that the *linguistic* context indicates which connection is *selected* for a given expression on an occasion of its use is to abandon the idea that sense determines reference. This is also awkward on a Fregean analysis.

IX

Existence, Predicates, and Properties

Russell declared existence not to be a property. The claim, subject to some doubts of Moore's, was fairly common doctrine until concerns about non-naming names, so-called free logics, and "possible worlds" surfaced to reraise Moore's classical concerns about assertions of existence and nonexistence. Just as Russell's claim that existence was not a property was reflected by the lack of a predicate for such a property, in a standard *Principia*-type schema, and the consequent use of the existential quantifier to make existential claims, current claims have to do with the reintroduction of a predicate, say 'E', into such schemata. The claim that existence is a property is, then, taken to be substantiated by the claim that such a sign is a predicate among predicates.[1]

Two ways of introducing such a predicate seem obvious: as a primitive predicate or as defined by something like

$$(D_1) \quad Ex =_{df.} (\exists y)(y = x)$$

If one introduces 'E' by (D_1) and includes open sentences among predicates, a trivial answer is forthcoming: 'E' is a predicate. But, then, we did not really introduce a predicate of existence; we had one all along. Moreover, insofar as the relevant open sentence involves the use of the existential quantifier, there is a clear sense in which one may hold that existence is basically expressed by quantification, not by a predicate, and, hence, we point to a logical difference between 'E', defined by (D_1), and basic predicates. There is a similarity in that, where 'F_1' is a primitive predicate, both 'F_1x' and '$(\exists y)(y = x)$' yield sentences when we replace the free variable by a constant or bind the variable. Yet, there is a simple difference. We have the predicate 'F_1' corresponding to the open sentence 'F_1x'; we have no predicate sign corresponding to the open sentence '$(\exists y)(y = x)$' unless we introduce one by definition. A basic asymmetry unfolds. Whereas 'F_1x' is an open sentence *since* 'F_1' is a predicate, 'E' would be a predicate *since* '$(\exists y)(y = x)$' is an open sentence. Talk of *predicates* as *open sentences* blurs the difference. Of course, if one insisted, in the manner of Frege, that 'F_1x' was the appropriate predicate expression, in place of 'F_1', this difference might seem to disappear. I say "seem to disappear," since one can still distinguish the constituent signs in a sentence form like 'F_1x' (i.e., the variable 'x' and the sign 'F_1'), whereas one cannot so distinguish such constituents in the case of '$(\exists y)$ $(y = x)$'. Be that as it may, it is worth noting that the Fregean treatment of predicates lies behind the contemporary nominalistic gambit which seeks to deny that predicates are "names" of properties by distinguishing between singular and general terms. The latter are open sentences that are "true of" objects but do not refer to *one* entity, whereas singular signs "purport to refer to one and only one" thing. It is, thus, ironic to defend the construal of existence *as a property* by obliterating the difference between 'F_1' and 'E', defined by (D_1), by speaking of open sentences. This difference between 'F_1' and 'E' is avoided if one construes 'E' as a primitive predicate. But, before considering 'E' as a primitive predicate, we may note a more significant difference between 'E' and predicates like 'F_1' which obtains whether 'E' is taken as primitive or as defined by (D_1). To get at it, I shall take up a seemingly unrelated matter.

One may consider definite descriptions, treated in Russell's fashion, to be grammatically classed as names, along with individual constants, in that signs of both kinds can replace the free variable in 'F_1x' and the result is a sentence of the schema. However, a description, say '$(\iota x)(\emptyset x)$', is not logically of the same kind as a name, say 'a_1', in that '$(x)\emptyset x \supset \emptyset a_1$' is, but '$(x)\emptyset x \supset \emptyset(\iota x)(\emptyset x)$' is not, an inferential consequence of '$(x)\emptyset x \supset \emptyset y$', in a *Principia*-type system, even though both "instantiations" are well-formed formulae or sentences. Hence, 'a_1' and '$(\iota x)(\emptyset x)$' function differently in inference patterns. This is a major difference; a logical difference, in a straightforward sense of 'logical', between them. It justifies, insofar as anything justifies conclusions in such matters, our taking 'a_1' and '$(\iota x)(\emptyset x)$' to be logically different kinds of signs, even though they are grammatically the same, in the sense we considered above. The point bears on our concern with 'E'. One attempt to claim that 'E', whether taken as primitive or as defined by (D_1), is a legitimate predicate is to point to a role it has in inference patterns. In fact, the main point of introducing such a predicate has to do, first, with a concern to assert, nontautologically and hence nontrivially, sentences like 'Ea_1' and, second, in allowing for such statements, to hold that

(I) $\dfrac{(x)\emptyset\!\!\!/x \ \& \ Ea}{\emptyset\!\!\!/a}$

should replace

(II) $\dfrac{(x)\emptyset\!\!\!/x}{\emptyset\!\!\!/a}$

as our pattern for universal instantiation. Then, even if 'E' is defined by (D_1), the use of such a predicate in the *rule* (I) and in nontautological existential claims like 'Ea_1' blunts the charge that the use of (D_1) reveals the triviality of the claim that 'E' is a predicate and, hence, of the notion that existence is a property. The replacement of (II) by (I) allows for the use of names that do not name in inference patterns, without leading to perplexities such as

(P) $\dfrac{(x)(\emptyset x \ v \sim \emptyset x)}{}$
(C) $\overline{\emptyset b_1 \ v \sim \emptyset b_1}$

where (C), following from the logical truth (P), is itself a logical truth and hence requires us to hold that one of the disjuncts of (C) is true, where 'b_1' is a name that does not name, i.e., where '$\sim Eb_1$' is true. Put more emphatically, since '$(x)(\exists y)(y = x)$' is a standard logical truth, (II) would allow us, with *names* like 'b_1', to infer '$(\exists y)(y = b_1)$', where b_1 does not exist. Hence, if we render 'b_1 does not exist' by '$\sim(\exists y)(y = b_1)$', we have a formal contradiction. Even if we construe 'b_1 does not exist' in terms of '$\sim Eb_1$', with 'E' as a primitive predicate, we then have '$(\exists y)(y = b_1)$ & $\sim Eb_1$'. The latter is, at best, an uncomfortable truth to acknowledge. (I) rescues us from such ontological discomforts. It *appears* to do so without our having to talk about truth value gaps or limiting inferences governed by (II) to cases where the names actually designate, and, hence, explicitly bringing a semantical condition into the characterization of universal instantiation. In short, (I) preserves the syntactical characterization of the instantiation rule while accomplishing the same thing as a limitation on (II) would. Replacing (II) by (I), we have

$$\frac{(x)(\exists y)(y = x) \ \& \ Eb_1}{(\exists y)(y = b_1).}$$

If 'Eb_1' is false, we are not forced to accept '$(\exists y)(y = b_1)$', even if we acknowledge '$(x)(\exists y)(y = x)$' as a logical truth. Such a use of 'E', even if defined by (D_1), thus points to the significance of 'E' as a predicate.

There is, however, a somewhat paradoxical consequence. Implicit in the idea of replacing (II) by (I) is the notion that we deal with *all predicate contexts*, so that '$\emptyset$' can be replaced by such a context. Moreover, implicit in the introduction of 'E' is the idea that the context 'Ex v $\sim$Ex' will yield a true sentence for any individual constant replacing the 'x', whether that constant actually names something or not. Hence,

(III) $$\frac{(x)(Ex \ v \sim Ex)}{Eb_1 \ v \sim Eb_1}$$

holds, as a pattern of (II), whereas predicates like 'F_1' are not such that

(IV) $$\frac{(x)(F_1x \ v \sim F_1x)}{F_1b_1 \ v \sim F_1b_1}$$

is a valid pattern. That was the point of replacing (II) by (I). Even if one insists that we must apply the pattern (I) in the case of '$(x)(Ex \ v \sim Ex)$', it reduces to the pattern (II), since

(V) $$\frac{(x)(Ex \ v \sim Ex) \ \& \ Eb_1}{Eb_1 \ v \sim Eb_1}$$

holds if and only if (III) holds. Thus, the use of (I) in place of (II) singles out 'E', whether defined by (D_1) or taken as primitive, from "normal" predicates like 'F_1'. This can be taken to illustrate the point that 'E' is not a predicate among predicates, just as definite descriptions are not names among names with respect to the inference patterns in *Principia*-type systems.

One may object that on some accounts, which acknowledge non-naming names like 'b_1', sentence patterns like '$F_1 b_1$ v $\sim F_1 b_1$', which are tautologous in standard systems, are taken to hold simply because they are such patterns. In such cases, '(f) [(x)(fx v $\sim$fx) $\supset$ (fb_1 v $\sim$fb_1)]' would hold without recourse to '(f) [((x) (fx v $\sim$fx) & Eb_1) $\supset$ (fb_1 v $\sim$fb_1)]'. Consequently, the difference between contexts like 'Eb_1 v $\sim$Eb_1' and '$F_1 b_1$ v $\sim F_1 b_1$', on the basis of which I tried to distinguish predicates like 'F_1' and 'E' disappears. However, even in such "systems," a corresponding difference emerges. If (I) replaces (II), the corresponding rule for existential generalization will be

(I') $$\frac{\psi a \ \& \ Ea}{(\exists x) \ \psi x.}$$

Then, with 'ψ' taken to be 'E' we have

$$\frac{Ea \ \& \ Ea}{(\exists x) \ Ex}$$

and, hence,

$$\frac{Ea}{(\exists x) Ex.}$$

This means that for 'E' (and "compounds" of it) alone, among nontautologous predicates, (I') *reduces* to

$$\frac{\psi a}{(\exists x) \ \psi x,}$$

the "standard" form of the generalization rule. 'E' is thus *the* nontautologous predicate that is not restricted by (I'). One can respond that this merely reflects that 'E' is unique, in that it is used to limit the application of the instantiation and generalization rules. The point, however, is that picking out 'E' for such a role involves providing grounds for not classifying it as a predicate "among" predicates. After all, we specify what a predicate is, as we specify what a name is, in terms of *both* the *formation* and the *inference* rules. That was the point of the above discussion of definite descriptions.

We have been considering two alternative views. On one, sentences like '$F_1 b_1 \vee \sim F_1 b_1$' would be tautologous, irrespective of whether 'b_1' named or not; on the other, such a sentence would not be so taken. One might speak of truth value gaps, or of the appropriate tautology being '$E b_1 \supset (F_1 b_1 \vee \sim F_1 b_1)$', or of an extended sense of "tautology," whereby a sentence pattern would be tautologous if there was no possibility of it being false. We, thus, allow for a tautology to be either true or have a value gap for every possibility. To take a disjunction like '$F_1 b_1 \vee \sim F_1 b_1$' to be a tautology is to recognize that where we have a universally quantified logical truth like '$(x)(F_1 x \vee \sim F_1 x)$', the instances of it, in the sense in which '$F_1 b_1 \vee \sim F_1 b_1$' is an instance of it, are also logical truths or tautologies. We might, then, take contexts bound by the universal quantifier, such as '$F_1 x \vee \sim F_1 x$', as being *analytic contexts* when the universally quantified sentence is logically true. By (D$_1$), 'Ex' is such an analytic context. Yet, no instantiation of it will be logically true. Thus, 'Ex' will differ from all nonanalytic contexts in that the universal quantification of 'Ex' is a logical truth; but, it will differ from all other analytic contexts in that no instance of it is logically true, whereas all instances of other analytic contexts are. On the other hand, if one does not treat sentences like '$F_1 b_1 \vee \sim F_1 b_1$' as tautologous, then we not only return to the fundamental difference between 'E' and other predicates that we noted earlier, namely that '$E b_1 \vee \sim E b_1$' will be tautologous if 'E' is to carry the sense of 'exists', but one pays the price of introducing truth value gaps or some similar device for the introduction of names like 'b_1'.

If 'E' is introduced as a primitive predicate, rather than in terms of the open sentence '$(\exists y)(y = x)$', then one difference between 'E' and predicates like 'F_1' disappears. But, new problems arise. Consider

(VI) $(x)(Ex \equiv (\exists y)(y = x))$.

If 'E' is defined by (D_1), then (VI) is a consequence of the definition, in an unproblematic sense of consequence. If 'E' is primitive and one wishes to hold (VI) to be true, or even to be a theorem, what justification is there? One could justify it by assuming '(x)Ex'. But, the same problem arises about '(x)Ex' as about (VI), with 'E' as a primitive predicate. One seems forced to appeal to intuitions or stipulations about *existence* and 'E'. Yet, this is hardly a cogent way of resolving the perennial puzzle concerning the property of existence. A proponent of the use of 'E' as a primitive predicate who denies (VI) acknowledges either

> (VII) $(\exists x)[Ex \,\&\, \sim(\exists y)(y = x)]$

or

> (VIII) $(\exists x)[(\exists y)(y = x) \,\&\, \sim Ex]$.

(VII) leads directly to a contradiction, if we assume such a one retains '$(x)(\exists y)(y = x)$'. But, to acknowledge (VIII) is to accept

> (IX) $(\exists x)\sim Ex$.

This means that the existential quantifier no longer involves an "existential" claim. Hence, there is no longer a point in restricting (II) by introducing (I). For, with the standard rules for quantifier conversion and propositional logic, the point of (I) is to prevent

$$\frac{\emptyset b_1}{(\exists x)\emptyset x}$$

where 'b_1' does not refer to anything. In short, as we noted above, (I) goes along with or can be put in terms of the generalization rule (I'). With (IX), both (I) and (I') become pointless. The proponent of 'E' cannot then deny (VI). To neither accept nor deny (VI) avoids the issue. I conclude (VI) must be accepted. But, if 'E' is taken as primitive, (VI) and '(x)Ex' are "intuited" or stipulated. (VI), then, amounts to a stipulated axiom. This reveals the emptiness of taking 'E' as primitive. One might just as well use (D_1) to define 'E'.

There is yet another point. In standard systems, where we do not recognize names that do not name,

> (X) $(x)[(\exists y)(y = x) \equiv x = x]$

238   Existence, Predicates, and Properties

is a theorem. This would suggest, in view of (VI), that we could define 'E' by

(D₂)   Ex = _df. x = x.

But, if we wish to allow for names like 'b_1' that do not name, then we shall have to hold that '$b_1 = b_1$' is false, since, if 'E' is to both transcribe 'exists' and be defined in the schema by (D₂), 'Eb_1' and, hence, '$b_1 = b_1$' will be false. One who does not wish to acknowledge the "possibility" of '$b_1 = b_1$' being false must then reject (D₂). However, there is an interesting feature of the connection between 'Ex' and 'x = x'. In view of (X), and on other grounds as well,

(XI) $\hat{x}(Ex) = \hat{x}(x = x)$

holds. Suppose one now constructs the following argument. Since b_1 does not exist '$b_1 \notin \hat{x}(Ex)$' is true, hence, by (XI), '$b_1 \notin \hat{x}(x = x)$' is also true. Therefore, by

(XII) $x \notin \hat{x}(\emptyset x) \equiv \sim \emptyset x$

we may conclude '$b_1 \neq b_1$'. It would immediately be pointed out that an illicit move was made in going from conditions about classes, in (XI) and (XII), to '$b_1 \neq b_1$', since we are making an implicit universal instantiation which could only be justified with the additional premise 'Eb_1'.

But, this points to another peculiarity of 'E'. For any standard predicate '$\emptyset$' and any zero-level constant 'a', given that '$\sim \emptyset a$' is true, '$a \in \hat{x}(\sim \emptyset x)$' will also be true. This condition, call it C₁, does not hold for the predicate 'E'. I am not claiming that '$b_1 \in \hat{x}(\sim Ex)$' or '$b_1 \in \Lambda$' cannot be allowed since a contradiction ensues. This would be incorrect in that one cannot go from '(x)(x \notin \Lambda)' or (x)(x \notin \hat{x}(\sim Ex))' to '$b_1 \in \Lambda$' or '$b_1 \notin \hat{x}(\sim Ex)$', since the instantiation would require the additional premise 'Eb_1'. There would be nothing surprising in deriving a contradiction from contradictory premises. Similarly, one cannot arrive at '(∃x)(x ∈ Λ)' from '$b_1 \in \Lambda$'. Hence, I am not claiming that something formally paradoxical is involved in the acceptance of '$b_1 \in \Lambda$'. I am merely claiming that the acceptance of '$b_1 \in \Lambda$' as true is problematic in terms of its transcription as "b_1 is a member of the empty class."

Insofar as this is taken to be a problematic consequence, whether it is rejected on such grounds or not, we arrive at a further difference between 'E' and "standard predicates." But, suppose one disagrees and finds nothing problematic in taking '$b_1 \in \Lambda$' to be true. The peculiarity persists in the treatment of the identity context '$b_1 \neq b_1$'. Since '$b_1 \in \Lambda$' is true, so is '$b_1 \in \hat{x}(x \neq x)$'. But, although the latter is true, '$b_1 \neq b_1$' is not taken to be true. Thus, the problematic situation is merely reversed. Instead of 'E' violating C_1, we have '=' conflicting with another condition, C_2: for any standard predicate '$\emptyset$' and any zero-level constant 'a', given that '$a \in \hat{x}(\sim\emptyset x)$' is true so is '$\sim\emptyset a$'. This is not true for '=', given the apparatus that goes along with the introduction of 'E' and names that do not name. Insofar as one is forced to reject either (C_1) or (C_2) or both, one should see the point behind Russell's assertion that both 'Eb_1' and '$\sim Eb_1$' are unacceptable renditions of ascriptions of existence and nonexistence.

(VI) points to yet another peculiar feature of 'E', a feature that borders on the paradoxical. Let 'E' be primitive. Then (VI) will not have

(VI') $Eb_1 \equiv (\exists y)(y = b_1)$

as an instance unless one ignores the restriction imposed by (I). But, this is absurd, since, in view of the double use of 'E' and '$(\exists y)(y = x)$' to transcribe "exists," (VI') ought to hold irrespective of whether 'Eb_1' and '$(\exists y)(y = b_1)$' do. In fact, we may say that we know that every instance of (VI) does hold, irrespective of whether the instantiation is to a naming or a non-naming name. But, we cannot derive the instantiations to the non-naming names without violating (I). The situation is no better with 'E' as defined by (D_1). One way of understanding such definitions is in terms of adding equivalences to the axioms of the schema. In this case, the relevant axiom is (VI). But, then, the same problem arises. Hence, one must make an exception for (VI) with respect to (I) or deny that (D_1) amounts to the use of (VI) as an axiom. The same point applies to the case of any defined predicate. We must deny that defined predicates apply to non-naming names in that the relevant biconditionals are consequences of the "definitional axioms," or deny that definitions may be presented in that form, or exempt such cases from the restriction imposed by (I). Of course, just as one may hold that '$F_1 b_1 \vee \sim F_1 b_1$' is a logical truth in virtue of its "form" irrespective of whether 'b_1' actually names something, one may hold that (VI') also is such on similar grounds. But, such an ad hoc move merely amounts to another way of denying the universal application of the proposed rule (I) to avoid the problematic consequences it brings with it.

Given the differences we have noted about 'E', and the correlated role of '=', one may conclude that to call it a predicate is like calling definite descriptions 'singular constants'. The descriptions have certain grammatical characteristics of such constants, as 'E' has of predicates, but there are crucial logical differences. There is also a historical point worth noting. Constructing a "logic" allowing for names that do not name along the lines we have been considering amounts to no more than applying Russell's calculus for descriptions to the zero-level constants. Recall that

$$E!(\iota x)(\psi x) \supset . (x)\psi x \supset \psi(\iota x)(\phi x)$$

is the crucial "instantiation theorem" regarding descriptions. In this sense, we remove one of the fundamental logical differences between names and descriptions when we introduce names that do not name, with the use of (I) replacing (II). Since the origin of the theory of descriptions was, in part, an attempt to provide a way of speaking "about" nonexistent "objects," there is an ironic note to the use of its patterns to obliterate the fundamental distinction it involved. In short, so-called free logics are no more than problematic applications of Russell's theory of descriptions to all nonlogical zero-level signs.

There is a further connection with the theory of descriptions. Much of the criticism, by Strawson and others, of Russell's theory of descriptions is based on the contextual ambiguity of ordinary language statements of the form "This is a $\emptyset$" and "The $\emptyset$ is a ψ." Part of the credibility of claims that 'Eb_1' and '$\sim Eb_1$' involve obviously legitimate uses of 'exists' as a predicate stems from a similar contextual ambiguity. Consider a domain of three objects: a_1, a_2, a_3. Call the domain a universal domain, D. Let any subset of objects of D be a domain such that subscripts will indicate which domain it is. 'D_{a_1, a_2}' stands for the domain with the objects a_1 and a_2; i.e., for the class, $\hat{x}(x = a_1 \lor x = a_2)$. Given that we have D, we can consider subsets of D that do not contain a_1. In this sense, we can say that a_1 does not *exist in* such a domain. If we consider the sentence 'Ea_1', we can then think of it being true or false depending on which domain we consider. Thus, considering the various subsets of D provides a situation like the variable contexts for ordinary statements of the form 'This is $\emptyset$'. Just as such sentences are true or false depending on the context, so 'Ea_1' is true or false depending on the relevant domain. Russell sought to eliminate the dependence on context. We can do so here by considering existence statements to be relational, so that 'Ea_1' is not a statement but '$E(a_1, D_{a_1, a_2})$' is. Now, existence statements are seen to be trivial in that they are set-theoretical truths or falsehoods. For, to say that a_1 exists in D_{a_1, a_2} is to assert '$a_1 \in \{a_1, a_2\}$'. Eliminating contextual dependence thus eliminates one motive for introducing 'E'. Moreover, the peculiarity of '$b_1 \in \Lambda$' is no longer with us. For, although

$$a_3 \in \Lambda \equiv \sim E(a_3, D_{a_1, a_2})$$

is false, since the left side is false and the right side is true, we clearly do not identify $\hat{x}(x \notin D_{a_1, a_2})$ with *the* null class. But, treating 'E' as a relational predicate and, thus, as a trivial predicate, raises the objection to Russell's claim that goes back to Moore. It seems that we can significantly say, about a_1, that it *need not* have existed. Hence, the statement that it *does exist* should not be trivial. Moreover, an adequate calculus should allow for such nontrivial statements. The objection is easily answered. We can do so by noting a mistake regarding Russell's view. The mistake is in thinking that Russell's view implies that objects which *do exist* are taken to *necessarily exist* since, first, Russell holds that we cannot say, of an existent, either that it exists or that it does not, and, second, that the sentence '$(\exists x)(x = a_1)$', where 'a_1' is a name, is, on Russell's view, a logical truth. The first thing to note is that Russell does not quite say that you cannot say *of* an existent that it exists even though he says: "So the individuals that that there are in the world do not exist, or rather it is nonsense to say that they exist and nonsense to say that they do not exist."[2] For, he goes on to say: "It is not a thing you can say when you have named them, but only when you have described them."[3] He does, therefore, acknowledge that there is *a* way in which one can say *of an object* that it exists, but not by using a purely demonstrative or indicating sign, a label or name, referring to it. The point is clear. By the use of a purely designating sign or name, given that names name, it becomes superfluous to make a positive existential claim and paradoxical to make a negative one.[4] But, a negative existential claim's being paradoxical does not mean it is contradictory. Suppose I indicate an object and claim "This doesn't exist." *Given the conventions governing the use of the demonstrative*, I am, in one clear sense, uttering a false sentence. That such a sentence is false is a consequence of such rules or conventions or, if you will, of the "meaning" of 'this'. In that sense, one may say the claim that "This exists," properly used, is necessary in that it cannot sensibly be taken to be false. This must not be confused with the claim that the object necessarily exists or must exist, or that the claim that it exists is logically true. That the object need not have existed or does not necessarily exist is reflected, on Russell's approach, in two ways: first, the object is not a member of every subset of D and, second, the domain we start from need not have been the one we do in fact start from. To put it another way, *given that an object* exists, it is useless to use a purely indicating sign to say about the indicated object that it exists. Thus, that the object exists is *shown* by the occurrence of the sign indicating it in a schema that is understood to be a so-called ideal or perspicuous language. But, no perspicuous or ideal language is such necessarily. This fact reflects the point that nothing need exist. Thus, we can note that Moore's point is observed by Russell. It is observed in that although a_1's existence is shown by an appropriate interpreted schema, what is thus shown is a matter of fact. Moreover, what is shown by the schema can be stated in a metalanguage for the schema, as I just did. To say existence is not a property or 'E' is not a predicate is to say that in a perspicuous language the predicate does not, or need not, or, perhaps, cannot (unproblematically) occur. The point is that an adequate calculus can *reflect* what Moore wants it to be used *to state*. Since we can reflect what Moore is after, there is no need to explicitly state, in the schema, what Moore wishes to state or what we can easily state, in ordinary language, about the schema. The differences we have considered between 'E' and standard predicates amount to a way of making this point. Given such differences, if *existence* is taken to be a property, it is so in the sense that one member of a group of "equals" is said to be "a bit more equal." Just as the phrase stretches the sense of "equal", the claim about existence stretches the sense of "property."

But, now, one may object to my argument that holding *existence* to be a property is trivialized by treating it as a relational property in that we can do the same for all properties. On the view that properties are functions from objects and worlds onto truth values, we can replace a predicative expression, say '$F_1 x$', by a "relational" expression, say '$F_1(x,w)$', where the latter is read as 'x is F_1 in w', with 'w' as a variable ranging over "worlds." If we then specify "worlds" in terms of the factual conditions obtaining, as one specifies domains in terms of which objects exist or are elements, a sentence such as '$F_1(a_1,w_1)$' will be as trivial as '$E(a_1,D_{a_1,a_2})$'. I agree with the point. But what it points to is not that existence is no less trivial than "normal" properties, but that construing properties as functions of the kind suggested is problematic and trivial. This claim would be reinforced by arguing, first, that in effect one makes use of the notion that a world is a class of facts (including negative or "possible" facts) and, second, that cogently spelling out the notion of a "fact" will involve one in a use of "property" that is different from the use whereby properties are functions from objects and worlds onto truth values. To defend such a claim is not my present concern. Here, I merely note its connection to the questions at issue.

The discussion of Moore and Russell leads to another objection. Wilfrid Sellars has long maintained that a perspicuous ideal language should employ names in different type fonts, in lieu of monadic predicates, and spatial relations among such names, in place of relational predicates.[5] Predicates are, thus, replaced by syntactical characteristics of names. One may now suggest that by so doing we can avoid normal predicates, as I have suggested omitting 'E'. Hence, what goes for 'E' goes for such predicates. The differences I have been stressing between 'E' and normal predicates, in the discussion of Moore and Russell, are thereby eradicated. Just as an object's existence is *shown* by the occurrence of a name for it, an object's having a property is shown by the name for it occurring in a particular form. The objection overlooks something. There would be the fundamental difference between the name *occurring* in a neutral font and the name occurring in a *particular guise*, whereby the latter stands for a property the object purportedly has. The neutral name form merely stands for the object as such. If anything, a perspicuous language of the kind Sellars employs would neatly record the differences we have been considering. Moreover, just as Sellars *does not* employ such a perspicuous schema as an argument against taking properties as *basic* entities,[6] I have not relied on the fact that we can omit 'E' from a perspicuous schema, without loss of expressive power, as a basis for rejecting *existence* as a property. It is, rather, the problematic consequences of including 'E' in a purported perspicuous schema that provide such a basis. Such features do not accompany the use of "normal" predicates. There is a further difference. I shall argue, in Chapter X, that Sellars does not avoid using predicates, whereas we can avoid the use of 'E', since we have '∃' and a way of *expressing* what Moore wants to state. Perhaps, it is all summed up in noting the need to retain quantifiers along with 'E', and the peculiarities of sentences like '$(\exists x)Ex$', '$(x)Ex$', '$(x)[Ex \equiv (\exists y)(y = x)]$', '$\sim(x)Ex$', etc. Nothing comparable is involved for normal predicates and "properties."

There is another, somewhat ironical, thread involved. Strawson's critique of Russell's theory of description hinges on the claim that the use of a description to ascribe a property to an object involves *presupposing* an existential claim rather *than explicitly making* such a claim. Russell's account of names, by contrast, involves his holding that the use of a name to ascribe a property to an object *presupposes*, but does *not make*, an existential claim. Those who would permit the use of non-naming names, with rules like (I) and (I'), in effect, advocate the explicit assertion of the existential claim presupposed by Russell's use of a name. Thus, although Strawson attacks Russell's distinction between descriptions and names by holding that the use of both names and descriptions to make (subject-predicate) assertions with truth values presupposes, but does not assert, an existential claim, the attack by the advocate of non-naming names cancels the basic distinction between names and descriptions in that the use of neither *presupposes* an existential condition. Both critics obscure the fundamental difference between names and descriptions: names are *simple*, *indicating* labels not involving the *use* of any predicate. This difference is reflected by the logical features of a *Principia*-type schema and the interpretation rule requiring that names name. It is not reflected either by a calculus permitting names that do not name, along with a rule like (I), or by one that treats descriptions as referring signs like names.

We might note one final way of indicating the triviality of 'E' as a predicate. One can achieve what those who advocate the use of non-naming names and 'E' wish to achieve by having two syntactically different kinds of zero-level constants. Those of one kind would name; those of the other kind would not. The standard inference procedures would apply only to the former. One could employ 'E', as defined by (D_1), in appropriate true and false sentences, depending on which type of name was used. We could also arbitrarily decide about the use of non-naming names with other predicates: whether such "sentences" were well-formed or not; if well-formed, whether they have truth value gaps or regular truth values, and, if the latter, which value. Thus, one could rule that all atomic sentences containing non-naming names be false.[7] This would cause no problems owing to the restrictions on the inference rules confining the standard inferences to the naming names. Thus, it would not follow that *something* was not F_1 though '$\sim F_1 b_1$' would be true. The arbitrariness and the pointlessness of such a "free logic," as the basis for a calculus that would be, in the traditional sense, a perspicuous or clarified schema, is obvious. Insofar as it is, it reflects on the emptiness of the claim that 'E' is a predicate among predicates.

I have ignored the two-fold question of whether predicates "stand for" properties and, in particular, whether defined predicates stand for properties. These questions, though crucial, are tangential to the issue concerning admission of non-naming names in addition to names that name. It is in terms of the introduction of non-naming names (or the elimination of all names in favor of definite descriptions) that sentences like '$(\exists x)(x = a_1)$' (or their replacements through the use of descriptions) become nontrivial and, hence, that they may be said to state existential conditions. However, the question of the reference of predicates is relevant to a number of issues we have considered, and I shall turn to it. Before doing so, there is one last point I wish to make about non-naming names. The attraction of non-naming names, paradoxically, both rests on and overlooks a simple feature of names.

(A)   'a_1' names a_1

supposedly states a fact: that a sign has been coordinated to an object. Similarly,

(B) $(\exists x)(x = a_1)$

supposedly states a fact: that a certain object exists. Therefore, we can treat neither (A) nor (B) as a "logical" or "linguistic" truth; nor can we treat them as expressing the same fact, since one is *about* a sign and the other is not. But, such comments overlook the fact that the name 'a_1' is *used* in both (A) and (B). Since 'a_1' is used in both sentences, they *show* what they are supposedly used to *state*. One cannot prevent them from doing so, unless one allows for the possibility of non-naming names. Moreover, where names are understood to name, we have the consequence that (A) and (B) not only show what they supposedly state, but also show that what they purportedly state is true. The situation parallels what we noticed earlier about the proper use of 'this' in 'this exists'. Thus, the idea that names, to be names, must name forestalls the significant use of (B) or 'Ea_1' to state that a_1 exists. One committed to the idea that we must be able to significantly state that a_1 exists and to the sharp separation of (B) from both (A) and '$(\exists x)('a_1'$ names x)' is forced to introduce non-naming names, if one retains names at all. An alternative is to give up names altogether and seek to employ only definite descriptions as "singular terms." Then, the nonredundancy of patterns like '$E!(\iota x)(\emptyset x)$' and the *absence* of patterns like " '$(\iota x)(\emptyset x)$' names $(\iota x)(\emptyset x)$" will emphasize the significance of existential claims. In either case, one rescues the significant use of 'exists' with "singular terms" by breaking down the basic difference Russell stressed between names as mere labels and definite descriptions as nonreferring singular terms.

The question of the relation of predicates to properties leads into a contemporary way of dealing with the classical problem of universals. I do not wish to get into that issue in any detail in this book, though there are aspects of it that are relevant to the themes I am concerned with. We can get at those by noting a simple mistake that is common to two opposed contemporary views about predicates and properties. Strawson has sought to provide a basis for distinguishing subject signs from predicate signs in terms of their standing for different sorts of *things*: particulars and properties. His subsequent and required attempt to distinguish the latter two categories fails for precisely the same reason that Carnap's argument for rejecting the claim that predicates can be taken to *stand for*, or *name*, properties fails.

Russell had held that particulars are to be distinguished from properties (relational or nonrelational) in that there is a basic relation, call it exemplification, such that a particular is what may not be exemplified by something (or a pair, triple, etc., of things) but may exemplify something. A property, by contrast, is what may be exemplified. Call this condition (R). Strawson seeks to offer a different asymmetry, which may be put in several ways or, perhaps, he offers a set of closely related asymmetries. One way of characterizing the difference between particulars and properties is to note that

(1) $(x)(\exists f)fx$

is a standard logical theorem, but

(2) $(f)(\exists x)fx$

is not. Alternatively, we may note that

(3) $(x)(\exists f)(\exists g)[fx \ \& \sim gx]$

is a standard theorem, but

(4) $(f)(\exists x)(\exists y)[fx \ \& \sim fy]$

is not. Finally, we may note that

(5) $(f)(\exists g)(x)[fx \equiv \sim gx]$

is a theorem, but

(6) $(x)(\exists y)(f)[fx \equiv \sim fy]$

is not.

Strawson does not put matters as I have in that he expresses the asymmetries in more or less natural language terms.[8] Nevertheless, what it all comes down to is that there is a null and a universal class, that though every particular belongs to some class, no particular belongs to every class, and that properties have contradictories, particulars do not.[9] All these claims, taken in their proper context, are true. However, they do not provide us with an asymmetry or a set of asymmetries that do not presuppose (R). Since (R) *suffices* to make the distinction and is *presupposed* by Strawson's differences, we may consider his asymmetries to reflect (R). To see that this is the case, note that if we raise the types in (1)-(6), what distinguishes particulars from properties now distinguishes second-level properties from first-level properties. In short, the distinguishing characteristics noted in (1)-(6) point to the distinction between that which is attributed and that to which it is attributed. Both what is attributed and the subject of attribution can be properties. It is only when we recognize that there is a *lowest level* or type or if we hold that there are no higher-level properties that we distinguish particulars from properties by (1)-(6).[10] But, why is there a lowest level, or, for that matter, what does it mean to state that there is a lowest type? (R), and (R) alone, provides an answer. Similarly, if we hold that there are no higher-level properties, we must already recognize the distinction between particulars and properties as specified in (R). To claim that there are no higher-level properties is to strengthen (R) to claim that what may be exemplified by something may not, in turn, exemplify anything. But, then, (1)-(6) distinguish particulars from properties in virtue of the asymmetry specified in (R), whether in the weaker or stronger version. One ultimately appeals to the asymmetry of the exemplification relation, as Russell did, to distinguish particulars from properties. Thus, the very use of (1)-(6) for Strawson's purpose already makes use of the asymmetry of the exemplification relation. Strawson's asymmetries

may be taken to distinguish *a* subject level from *a* predicate level—
not particulars from properties. However, he was supposedly distinguishing subjects from predicates on the basis of the difference
between particulars and properties. He, thus, fails or falls back on
(R). Note, further, that the weaker version of (R) suffices to distinguish particulars from properties and that, with (R) acknowledged, (1)-(6) merely record, and do not explicate, the distinction. For, we understand that the 'x's and 'y's are *lowest-level*
variables that may not occur in the predicate place.[11]

The problem with Strawson's analysis is highlighted by one of
his own linguistic devices. He introduces 'ass(i c)', "where 'i' represents particular-specification, 'c' concept-specification and
'ass( )' propositional combination."[12] *Propositional combination*
is understood to be "mutual" or symmetrical. Thus, Strawson
had earlier written, "I speak, in symmetrical style, of the particular individual and the general character or kind being presented as
assigned to each other because asymmetries of direction or fit do
not here concern us."[13] Thus, we may have:

$$\text{ass}(i\ c) \leftrightarrow \text{ass}(c\ i)$$

in contrast to:

i exemplifies c but c does not exemplify i.

This shows that we, supposedly, do not make use of (R) and the
appeal to the assymetry expressed in it. But, do we permit any of

(s_1) ass(i i)
(s_2) ass(c c)
(s_3) ($\exists i$)ass(i i_1)
(s_4) ($\exists c$)ass(c c_1)

to be well formed and true? The question points to an ambiguity
in the notion of *exemplification* being asymmetrical and of *ass* being symmetrical. A standard sense of asymmetrical is that a relation R^2 is asymmetrical if and only if '$(x)(y)(xR^2y \supset \sim yR^2x)$'
holds. With *exemplification* as the "relation" and in the context of
a Russellian-style type theory, this condition holds, *in a sense*.
(Of course, in a *strict sense* it cannot even be stated without modifications of the syntax of the schema.) By contrast, *ass* is sym-

metrical. But, that is not what is relevant for the issue. The sense
in which exemplification is asymmetrical, in that (R) expresses an
asymmetry between particulars and properties, is that particulars
can exemplify but *cannot be exemplified* but properties *can be
exemplified*. And Strawson, in spite of having *ass* be a symmetrical
"relation," makes use of the same *asymmetry* expressed in (R), if
he rules out (s_1) and (s_3). This he has to do to fit with his own
discussion of negation, which we shall touch on later. For to allow
(s_1)—(s_3), aside from the intrinsic absurdity involved, is to allow
for negations of such "sentences." Equally obviously, Strawson
will allow for (s_4), since he allows for "higher principles of grouping, principles which serve to group them [concepts] in ways analogous to the ways in which expressions signifying properties (or
kinds) of particulars serve to group particulars."[14] But, then, he
does make use of (R) in his understanding of 'ass'. Moreover, consider a relational case such as:

(s_5) $ass(i_1 \ i_2 \ R^2)$.

What sense does the purported symmetry of *ass* make here, even
in the *weak* sense involved in the "standard" notion of a symmetrical relation? Clearly, Strawson has packed the asymmetry *expressed* in (R) into his notation, the use of '*c*' and '*i*', and his understanding of 'ass', the rejection of (s_1) and (s_3) and the acceptance of (s_4), to superficially advocate the symmetry of *ass*. It is
not just that the relation has a *sense* in (s_5), as Russell put it, so
that we must distinguish '$i_1 \ R^2 \ i_2$' from '$i_2 \ R^2 \ i_1$', but that we cannot allow 'i_1 and R^2 stand in i_2'.

Carnap purported to show an ambiguity in the "name-relation":
that 'is a name of' is ambiguous.[15] If correct, his argument would
preclude taking predicates to be terms that "stand for" properties.
Rather, predicates would have properties as their *intensions*. Interestingly enough, his argument fails for the same reason that Strawson's analysis fails. Carnap's argument went as follows. Consider
two predicates 'H' and 'B' (read as 'is human' and 'is a biped') and
the true sentence, S_1, '(x) [Hx ⊃ Bx] '. The predicates can be taken
to stand for either properties or classes. For, we cannot infer from
any set of true sentences employing such predicates, in a standard
system of logic, whether properties or classes are the "nominata"

of predicates. To say the predicates stand for classes is merely to adopt one "mode of speech." To hold that classes are the "nominata" is to adopt another. Thus, sentences such as S_1 and 'Hs' can be read as "Anything which has the property H has the property B" and "s has the property H" or as "Anything which belongs to the class of H's belongs to the class of B's" and "s is a member of H." The same will hold for sentences like 'sϵ x̂(Hx)' and 'x̂(Hx) ⊂ x̂(Bx)'. Thus, assuming the standard uses of the connectives and quantifiers, we may choose the interpretation or "semantical analysis." This supposedly shows that the name relation is ambiguous. The obvious solution is to add an axiom of extensionality to the set of true sentences. We would then have:

(a) $(x) [fx \equiv hx] \supset f = h$.

With (a), we apparently cannot take 'H' and 'B' as signs for properties, provided we read '=' as 'identical' and assume we can have coexistensive but different properties. The use of (a) forces us to take predicate signs to stand for classes, not properties. But, this presupposes that we treat '=' as the identity sign. Carnap argues that we may take '=' as a sign for coextensiveness of properties, when it occurs between predicates, as in (a). Thus, with 'F' read as 'featherless biped',

(b) $(x) [Hx \equiv Fx] \supset (H = F)$,

is true, not false. Thus, (b) is true whether we take the predicates to stand for properties or classes, so long as we shift the interpretation of '='. Carnap's ambiguous reading of '=' provides sufficient ground to reject his "argument." But, that aside, his argument still fails. He must restrict the system of logic to the lower functional calculus. If we employ a higher functional calculus, the argument obviously fails. Consider,

(c) $(x) [Hx \equiv Fx] \equiv (^2f) [^2f(H) \equiv {}^2f(F)]$

and

(d) $H = F \equiv (^2f) [^2f(H) \equiv {}^2f(F)]$,

with the superscripts indicating variables and quantifiers of the second level. Both are true when classes are taken as the "nominata" of the predicates 'H' and 'F'. But, if properties are so taken,

(c) is false. Carnap's reading of '=', as in (d), in terms of the co-extensiveness of properties does not affect the point. That only means that (d) is read as (c), and (c) is false, if the predicates stand for properties. This suffices to refute his attack on the name relation. Thus, as in Strawson's case, a consideration of an extended system of logic reveals Carnap's analysis to be inadequate.

Recognizing Carnap's argument to be inadequate does not mean that one can simply take predicates to be signs that stand for properties and predication, as a relation between signs, to stand for Russell's basic asymmetrical relation between particulars and properties. One must distinguish the cases of primitive and defined predicates. Assume we distinguish particulars and properties and take a set of primitive predicates 'F_1', 'F_2', ..., 'F_n' to stand for properties. If we limit the logical apparatus to the lower functional calculus, then we may consider expressions like '$F_1 x \lor F_2 x$' to be predicate expressions and use patterns like '$G_1 x$' to abbreviate them. But, such "predicates" need not be taken to stand for properties. They are classed as predicates in terms of (a) the way they are formed, using primitive predicates (or variables) which, as one says, range over such predicates, and (b) their being taken to function syntactically like the primitive predicates, i.e., '$G_1 a_1$' is a well-formed formula, if we include such defined signs in the schema. These points we noted in our discussion of 'E'. However, if we extend the logical apparatus so that we have a higher functional calculus, such "definitions" are no longer available. We can no longer define predicates where we take predicates to stand for properties without a major syntactical innovation. It is a standard observation to note that 'G_1', as defined above, cannot occur in the subject place of a sentence. A standard way of remedying this is to use an abstraction operator. This amounts to holding that '$^2\emptyset(G_1)$' is elliptical for '$(\exists f)(x)[(fx \equiv (F_1 x \lor F_2 x)) \& \, ^2\emptyset(f)]$' and '$G_1 a_1$' is elliptical for '$(\exists f)(x)[(fx \equiv (F_1 x \lor F_2 x)) \& fa_1]$'. A moment's reflection reveals that 'G_1' is now taken to be a class sign, since one presupposes the uniqueness of the "property" had by all and only those things being either F_1 or F_2. In short, we deal with the class $-\hat{x}(F_1 x) \cup \hat{x}(F_2 x)$. There is no other way, as far as I can see, of defining 'G_1', while having it stand for a property.

One is forced, then, to take expressions like '$F_1 \lor F_2$' as undefined predicates, in that sentences like '$^2\emptyset(F_1 \vee F_2)$' are not abbreviations for other sentences. Yet, we recognize that '$F_1 \vee F_2$' is constructed from primitive predicates and 'v', where the latter sign is not used as *the sign for disjunction* that combines sentences into compound sentences. This means, first, that we do not define predicates, where we take predicates to stand for properties in extended functional calculi, and, second, that to have "complex predicates" we require additional "logical" signs to form such predicates. We would, thus, require the construction of a calculus for properties that would, among other things, specify the connection between 'v' as the standard sign for disjunction and, say, '$^\vee$' as used to form complex predicates. Thus, we would need to provide a basis for sentences like

$$(x)\,[(F_1 x \vee F_2 x) \equiv F_1{}^\vee F_2(x)]$$

as well as specify "identity" conditions so that we have grounds for assigning truth values to sentences like

$$F_1{}^\vee F_2 = F_2{}^\vee F_1.$$

In short, we would have to construct a "logic" of properties.[16] This is not my concern here. Rather, I wish to consider Quine's well-known criterion of ontological commitment and its employment as a justification for not recognizing properties (or classes). Supposedly, such entities are not among the ontological commitments of a schema employing primitive predicates but only the logical apparatus of the lower functional calculus. Or, to put it another way, when predicates are employed only as "general terms," we purportedly do not make ontological commitments by their use. The justification of such a move appeals to the claim that general terms may be "true of" individuals, without such individuals being taken to exemplify properties. This claim, in turn, may be justified in one of two ways. On one gambit, a philosopher appeals to the use of a background language (or schema or framework), so that, for example, one may say that 'F_1' is true of a_1 since a_1 is $\emptyset$, where '$\emptyset$' is the metalinguistic (background) rendition of 'F_1', and so end the matter. On another gambit, one may hold that the truth condition for '$F_1 a_1$' is a relation between the sign 'F_1' and the object a_1. Both gambits can, I believe, be shown to be inadequate, and I shall argue that case elsewhere. There is, however, a third aspect of Quine's discussion (and that of other "nominalists") that has not been fully appreciated owing to the failure to recognize that we cannot define predicates if such defined predicates are to stand for properties. To introduce the apparatus of a higher functional calculus is to allow for expressions like

$$(P_1) \quad (\iota f)(x)(fx \equiv (F_1 x \lor F_2 x)).$$

This is what is behind Quine's concern with the lower functional calculus, and the avoidance, by its use, of "abstract entities." Such an expression, as we noted, will not do for a calculus where the predicates are signs for properties. To take the predicates as property signs forces us to use something like

$$(P_2) \quad (\iota f)(f = F_1{}^\lor F_2)$$

or simply

$$(P_3) \quad F_1{}^\lor F_2,$$

where we have understood rules for the formation of such predicates in that neither (P_2) nor (P_3) can be taken as an abbreviation of (P_1). Thus, '$F_1{}^\lor F_2$' is not a defined sign but formed from the predicates 'F_1' and 'F_2' by the use of a new basic sign '$\lor$'. The latter is distinct from, but "associated with," the *connective* '$\lor$'. Thus, (P_2) is like '$(\iota x)(x = a_1)$', where 'a_1' is a proper name. Just as the definite description '$(\iota x)(x = a_1)$' can only be formed if 'a_1' is a name, so (P_2) is a legitimate symbol only if '$F_1{}^\lor F_2$' is. But, '$F_1{}^\lor F_2$', like 'a_1', is not something that can be contextually eliminated, as it would be if we used (P_1). Recognizing '$F_1{}^\lor F_2$' as an ineliminable, though complex, predicate enables us to make a distinction.

A traditional ontological gambit has involved the claim that only the primitive signs, and not the defined signs, involve us in ontological commitment. Defined predicates would, on such a view, not stand for properties or classes. But, we cannot define predicates, where predicates stand for properties. Thus, if we introduce complex predicates such as '$F_1{}^\lor F_2$', we cannot hold that they do not stand for properties on the grounds that we deal with an eliminable defined sign. There is a parallel feature in the case of sentences. An atomic sentence is a complex sign, yet such sentences may stand for facts, as I have suggested and as I shall argue later in the book. But, we do not pair such sentences with facts, as we pair (or interpret) primitive predicates and names with properties and particulars. Rather, one holds that given any atomic sentence, an appropriate fact is *indicated*: the fact specified in terms of the particulars, properties, and in the case of relations, the "direction" of the relation. Formation rules for sentences reflect how sentences are taken to stand for facts. Insofar as one does not interpret sentences as one interprets primitive signs, one may hold that facts are not taken to *exist* in the sense that particulars and properties are so taken. What one means by this is an explication, in part, of this use of 'exist'. It is based on the distinction between primitive constants and sentences, on the one hand, and between particulars and properties, as opposed to facts, on the other. The same may be said with respect to 'F_1' and '$F_1{}^\vee F_2$'. What we should note is that in the case of the lower functional calculus, there is no need for a sign like '$F_1{}^\vee F_2$', or, better, we could eliminate such a predicate by noting that any sentence employing it is superfluous. We can hold that '$F_1{}^\vee F_2(a_1)$', for example, is true precisely for the reasons and under the conditions that '$F_1 a_1 \vee F_2 a_1$' is. The same will hold for all such compound predicates. It is only when we use such predicates as subject terms that questions may arise. Is '$F_1{}^\& F_2 = \overline{F}_1{}^\vee \overline{F}_2$' true? So long as predicates function only as predicates, we can hold that atomic and negative facts suffice to ground the truth of sentences like '$F_1 a_1$', '$\sim F_1 a_1$', '$F_1 a_1 \vee F_2 a_1$', etc. We need not recognize disjunctive, conjunctive, etc., facts. I shall argue this point in detail later. For the moment, we need only note that to say that we need not recognize such facts is to say that we need not recognize conjunctive, disjunctive, etc., properties.

All this points to a correct feature of Quine's view. Insofar as one may avoid complex properties by use of the lower functional calculus, one does not embrace a certain kind of "Platonism," namely, the claim that *where we have predicate expressions in the sense of open sentences we have corresponding properties*. But, this ignores the question of whether we recognize such abstract entities by using primitive predicates. Thus, we may see one theme behind and supporting Quine's approach, while also noting why that approach to ontological issues is basically inadequate. In a higher functional calculus, we recognize complex predicates for a very simple reason. Take the nonempty set of objects, a, exemplifying two primitive properties, F_1 and F_2, and assume that F_1 and F_2 are the only primitive properties that all members of a exemplify. Then, it will be the case that

$$(x)\,[x \in a \equiv (F_1 x \mathbin{\&} F_2 x)]\,.$$

Assume, also, that

$$(\exists x)(\exists y)(F_1 x \mathbin{\&} F_2 y \mathbin{\&} \sim\! F_2 x \mathbin{\&} \sim\! F_1 y)$$

holds. Is

$$(P_4) \qquad (\exists f)(f \neq F_1 \mathbin{\&} f \neq F_2 \mathbin{\&} (x)[fx \equiv (F_1 x \mathbin{\&} F_2 x)]\,)$$

true? If we limit the predicate variables and quantifiers to the properties indicated by the primitive predicates, (P_4) will be false. If we allow complex properties, either "modeled" on classes and indicated by expressions like '$(\iota f)(x)(fx \equiv (F_1 x \mathbin{\&} F_2))$' or, as considered above, indicated by expressions like '$F_1{}^{\mathrm{v}}F_2$' and '$F_1{}^{\&}F_2$', (P_4) is true. If our predicates are taken to stand for classes, (P_4) is obviously true. Since we characteristically think in terms of such calculi being suitable for interpretation in terms of set-theoretical models, we readily accept (P_4) as true. This is reinforced by our thinking of such calculi as holding for classes with an extensionality axiom and for properties without such an axiom. Since the presence or absence of an extensionality axiom does not affect (P_4), we tend to hold that just as there is a class a, there is *a* corresponding property, and perhaps more than one, that *determines* the class. In effect, we employ a kind of comprehension axiom for properties.

If we do not do that and limit the quantificational apparatus to primitive properties, we might proceed as follows. Let there be a denumerable number of primitive properties and corresponding predicates, 'F_1', 'F_2', 'F_3', ... We can consider our logical apparatus to be compartmentalized, along lines somewhat reminiscent of Russell's ramified theory of types, so that we have quantifiers and variables "ranging over" such properties. (P_4) will then be false, with the quantifiers so understood. Consider a second set of quantifiers and variables ranging over the first domain of properties *and* over *complex* properties, where we have expressions like '$F_1{}^{\mathrm{v}}F_2$' standing for such *complex* properties. (P_4), interpreted in terms of the latter quantifiers, will be true. Call the two schema P and C, recognizing that P is a part of C. C is still not a class calculus. To make it one, we can add an extensionality axiom. To make it *explicitly* not a class calculus, we can add the negation of such an axiom. Working out the details of such a modified schema would provide, in one sense, a "logic" of properties. What I wish to note here is that we can distinguish between talk about the existence of properties in two ways. First, primitive properties can be taken as *elements* in an ontology expressed by C in that such objects *are coordinated* to primitive predicates to provide an interpretation for the latter. Complex predicates do not stand for entities in this sense. Rather, complex predicates are meaningful signs of the system in that they are formed, according to general syntactical rules, from primitive predicates which are so interpreted. One may then suggest that we speak of complex properties as a result of our linguistic apparatus having certain features, i.e., we talk of such properties in virtue of C having certain features. By contrast, primitive predicates require properties in order for such predicates to be legitimate signs of the schema. The former feature may lead some to speak of our "constructing" some properties or classes. It, perhaps, also lies behind the attempt to interpret quantifiers "metalinguistically." As long as we recognize the fundamental difference between C and P and the "entities" involved, there is no need to speak in either way. The problem is caused by a theme implicit in Quine's approach to ontological questions. He, and others, think in terms of existents being the entities we take to ground the truth of existentially quantified sentences. In holding (P_4) to be true in the context of C, we are, thus, led to overlook the differences between the claims that 'F_1' stands for a property and that 'F_1&F_2' stands for a property. The differences are not merely that we *coordinate* the sign 'F_1' to a property and *stipulate* that 'F_1&F_2' *indicates* a complex property. Recall, that in the case of the lower functional calculus, one has no need to speak of an object's having a complex property as being a fact grounding the truth of the sentence. I cannot help wonder if this recognition of the superfluity of complex properties combines with the notion that all properties are, so to speak, in the same "ontological boat" to lead to the conclusion that no properties need be recognized as existents.

The distinction between simple and complex properties points to something else. We can form complex predicates. We do not have complex names. In short, parodies of the logical connectives can be used to form complex predicate expressions of the same syntactical kind as those predicate expressions they contain. To do a similar thing with names would be totally trivial. Suppose we construe '$a_1{}^v b_1$' so that we allow

$$(P_5) \quad F_1(a_1{}^v b_1) \equiv F_1 a_1 \vee F_1 b_1,$$

and let a_1 be the only "ordinary" individual that exemplifies F_1. Since the left side of (P_5) is true, as the right side is, do we have

$$(\exists x)(x \neq a_1 \ \& \ F_1 x)$$

as true? Does the "complex individual" $a_1{}^v b_1$ exemplify F_1? What we recognize in such questions is not only the absurdity of complex names, but the total redundancy of using complex signs at *only one level*. '$F_1{}^v F_2$' is just as pointless a sign in the lower functional calculus. Do we have the fact that a_1 is F_1 *and* the fact that a_1 is F_1 or F_2? But, in the case of complex names two features are missing. We have no extensions, as we do with predicates functioning as predicate terms, to give sense to questions about corresponding complex entities. We also do not have the peculiarity introduced by negation and the question of negative facts. It would appear to be obvious that in *addition* to the fact expressed by the true sentence '$F_1 a_1$' we do not have a disjunctive fact expressed by '$F_1 a_1 \vee F_2 a_1$'. But, it is not at all clear that we do not require a negative fact corresponding to the true sentence '$\sim F_2 a_1$'. Yet, both '$F_1{}^v F_2$' and '$\sim F_1$' are predicate expressions formed from elementary predicates and logical parodies. One cannot, as we shall see, dismiss negative facts as easily as disjunctive facts. This may tempt one to speak of negative properties. This, too, we shall discuss. But can anyone seriously talk about *the* negative individual indicated by '$\sim a_1$'? Our discussion of complex signs thus reflects, in yet another way, the fundamental distinction expressed in (R) between particulars and properties.

Strawson has argued against the coherence of the notion of a *negative individual*.[17] But his arguments are not cogent. What he does, in effect, is contrast:

(d$_1$)   '$\bar{a}$' for '$(\iota x)(\emptyset)(\emptyset x \equiv \sim\emptyset a)$'

with

(d$_2$)   '$\overline{\emptyset}$' for '$(\iota f)(x)(fx \equiv \sim\emptyset x)$'

and observe that 'E!$\bar{a}$' is a contradiction but 'E!$\overline{\emptyset}$' is not. This is unfair to the proponent of *negative individuals*, if such there be. The issue is about the introduction of negative subject terms, as opposed to negative predicate terms. All one need do to introduce the former and avoid the "contradiction" is to introduce '$\bar{a}$' by contextual definition as follows:

(d$_3$)   f$\bar{x}$ = $_{df}$ $\sim$fx.

This, of course, parallels the *introduction* of '$\overline{\emptyset}$' in terms of the pattern

(d$_4$) $\bar{f}$x = $_{df}$ $\sim$fx.

The latter will do, as long as we limit the use of such predicates to predicate place. We need have recourse to (d$_2$) only if we employ predicates as subject terms. This shows two things: First, this "issue" is connected with the earlier discussion of (R) and of Carnap. Second, Strawson does not recognize that he runs into the problem about using predicates to stand for properties while employing them as subject terms. He tells us that we can introduce predicates such as '$\overline{\emptyset}$' and '$\emptyset^v\psi$' by:

$\overline{\emptyset}$x ↔ $\sim$$\emptyset$x

$(\emptyset^v\psi)$x ↔ $(\emptyset x \lor \psi x)$.

But, we can do so only if we confine such predicates to predicate place. Likewise, we could not use (d$_3$) if we did not confine terms for particulars to subject place. Moreover, it will not do to reply that in view of the identical right sides of (d$_3$) and (d$_4$), we have not really introduced terms for negative individuals by the use of (d$_3$). For, Strawson's claim is: "So, in introducing such a term, we have introduced a negative predicate. But there can be no parallel procedure for introducing negative subjects into subject-predicate propositions of our basic class."[18] It should also be obvious that we return to a fundamental question: In what sense do we acknowledge negative properties, as well as conjunctive, disjunctive,

etc., properties, by introducing "defined predicates" as in (d₄)?
Clearly, there is something wrong with explaining the role of predicates in terms of their standing for properties (concepts) while
implicitly holding that we introduce properties by introducing notational devices for rewriting sentences.[19] But, once we distinguish
between primitive and defined predicates, a significant part of
Strawson's discussion evaporates.

One could point out that:

$$(E_1) \quad (f)\,[f\bar{a} \supset (\exists y)fy]$$

cannot be allowed if we recognize '$\bar{a}$' as a subject sign, and, in that
sense, '$\bar{a}$' does not function as 'a' does. By contrast, with predicate
quantification, we can permit:

$$(E_2) \quad (x)\,[\bar{\emptyset}x \supset (\exists f)fx].$$

But, this simply returns us to the difference between '$(f)(\exists x)fx$'
and '$(x)(\exists f)fx$'. This is clearly seen when we replace '$\bar{\emptyset}x$' by its
"definition" in (E_2) and make the corresponding replacement in
(E_1).

The distinction between particulars and properties is, paradoxically enough, the basis for Quine's revival of nominalism. The
paradoxical element is superficially removed by expressing the distinction as a difference between linguistic terms, rather than kinds
of entities. Quine writes:

The distinction between singular and general terms is more vital from a logical
point of view. Thus far it has been drawn only in a very vague way: a term is
singular if it purports to name an object (one and only one); and otherwise
general. Note the key word 'purports'; it separates the question off from such
questions of fact as the existence of Socrates and Cerberus. Whether a word
purports to name one and only one object is a question of language, and is
not contingent on facts of existence.[20]

The phrase 'question of language' is also vague. If Quine means
"question of syntax" and takes *naming* to be a semantic matter,
while *purporting to name* is construed as a syntactical property,
the singular terms of a clarified language would be those having
the relevant syntactical property irrespective of whether or not
they actually named anything. Yet, such a syntactical characterization, whatever it may be, is not sufficient for Quine's purposes,

since the schema must be so interpreted that terms of that kind will be permitted to refer to one and only one thing. Such terms *may refer* to one and only one object. Thus, the notion of "purporting to refer to one and only one entity" would involve both a syntactical characterization and an implicit interpretation rule. Terms of a certain syntactical kind will "purport to name" and be "singular" irrespective of whether they actually refer, and those which do refer will be *names*. Hence, we take *naming* to be a semantical relation obtaining between singular terms and (nonlinguistic) objects.

From the above quotation it is not clear if the general terms of the schema are thought to be terms with a different syntactical characterization that *may* stand in the *same* semantical relation to objects that singular terms do but that *may* stand in *that relation* to more than one object. Alternatively, general terms could be taken not to stand in that relation (*naming*) to anything but be permitted to stand in a different relation to objects. If Quine is making the latter claim, then a syntactical characterization of general terms would be associated with a further semantical relation which would be such that terms *could* stand in it to many objects. This seems to be the intent behind his use of "is true of."

> The general term may indeed "be true of" each of *many* things, *viz.*, each red thing, or each man, but this kind of reference is not called naming; "naming," at least as I shall use the word, is limited to the case where the named object purports to be unique.[21]

But, what does it mean to say that *an object* "purports to be unique"? This can only be a metaphorical way of stating the implicit interpretation rule. A class of signs will be held to be such that member signs will be coordinated with one and only one object. Such signs will be said to purport to name one and only one object and the objects with which they are coordinated will be said to purport to be unique. General terms either will be coordinated to many objects (or be "permitted" to be so coordinated) or will be permitted to stand to many objects in a relation that is not based on being coordinated or assigned to objects.

Recall our domain (D). In addition to the three objects and their assigned names, let 'W' and 'B' be predicates so that, with standard formation rules, 'Wa_1', 'Ba_1', etc. are *wffs*. We may then *assign* the predicates to objects, 'W' to a_2 and a_3, and 'B' to a_1 alone. On the basis of such an assignment, we may then say that 'Wa_2' is a true sentence and 'Ba_3' is a false sentence. In allowing for the formation of 'Ba_3' along with 'Ba_1', we can state what we mean by saying that 'B' does not *purport* to uniquely refer to a_1, even though a_1 is the only object to which 'B' is assigned. This shows that a term is general if it is a predicate in the standard sense, and a term is singular if it is a *syntactical name* or zero-level constant, with the understood semantical rules. (We shall consider definite descriptions shortly.) But, if this is what is meant, we obviously have not *explained* the difference between *names* and *predicates* in terms of the notions of *singular* and *general*. We have merely used the latter pair of terms as synonyms for the former pair.

Instead of assigning the predicates to objects, we may claim that some predicates are "true of" certain objects. Then, if we note that " 'a_1' refers to a_1 " and " 'B' *is true of* a_1 " both hold, we may claim that although the first merely *reflects* the trivial fact that the sign 'a_1' has been coordinated with the object it *stands for*, the second states a nontrivial fact, since *is true of* is not to be identified with *refers to*. One may now hold that a term is singular if it *may* stand to an object in the relation indicated by 'refers to', whereas it is general if it *may not* so stand. General terms *may* stand to objects in the relation *is true of*, but singular terms *may not* stand in that relation at all. Thus, we can apparently explain the difference between subject and predicate terms, by means of the two relations *refers to* and *is true of*. Singular, or subject, terms may stand in the first but not the second relation; general, or predicate, terms may stand in the second but not the first relation. The use of 'may' is crucial, but ambiguous, since a contradictory predicate *may not* stand to any object in the relevant relation, yet it *may* occur in a *wff* as a predicate. A name or definite description *may not* even occur as a predicate in a *wff* and, hence, *may not* stand to any object as predicates stand. We deal with the "stronger" sense that is embodied in the formation rules and not that reflected by logical truths and falsehoods. I earlier avoided considering definite descriptions by speaking of *coordinating* names. A description is also said to "purport" to uniquely refer. Yet, it is not "coordinated" to one and only one object. Consider '$(\iota x)(Bx)$' and the context '$(y)(By \equiv y = x)$'. One may say of such a "predicate" that it *can apply* to only one object, for if it *applies* to anything it will apply to only one thing. But, the "predicate" does *not purport to refer* to one and only one thing. However, '$(\iota x)(Bx)$' *purports to refer* to one and only one thing since '$(\iota x)(Bx)$' is a *subject term* and *not a predicate*. Just as '$(y)(By \equiv y = x)$' purports to *uniquely apply since* if it applies at all it applies to one and only one thing, so '$(\iota x)(Bx)$' *purports to uniquely refer since* if it refers at all it refers to one and only one thing. We may conclude that a description, like '$(\iota x)(Bx)$', and a name, such as 'a_1', are of a *kind*, in that both may be juxtaposed with predicates to form sentences. Yet, there is a difference in the sense in which they may be said to refer. Moreover, to speak of '$(\iota x)(Bx)$' as *singular* since it purports to uniquely refer clearly *presupposes* the basic distinction between subject terms and predicates. It does so in that all one means by asserting that '$(\iota x)(Bx)$' *refers* to one and only one thing is that 'Bx' *applies* to one and only one thing, just as all one means by saying that '$(\iota x)(Bx)$' *purports* to uniquely *refer* is that '$(y)(Bx \equiv y = x)$' purports to uniquely apply. Therefore, we must make implicit use of the predicative sense of 'apply' as well as the distinction between predicates, which *may be said to apply*, and terms like '$(\iota x)(Bx)$', which *may not be said to apply*.

Consider a typical realist's answer to questions about truth and reference. A general term or predicate is *true of* an object if the object *exemplifies* the *property* that the predicate names or refers to. A name cannot be *true of* an object since a name does not stand for a property. The crucial difference between singular terms and predicates is based on the different *sorts of things* the terms *stand for*. That difference, in turn, rests on the asymmetry of the exemplification *relation* or *nexus* or *tie*. A nominalist such as Quine must explain his use of 'is true of' without mentioning properties, or other "abstract" objects. He can attempt to do so in one of two ways. He can hold that *is true of* is a basic relation between signs and objects, or he can hold that *is true of* is to be understood in terms of *satisfaction* and the consequent claim that an object, say a_1, *satisfies a predicate* (or open sentence, or atomic sentence), say

'Bx', if and only if a_1 is B. The first claim is absurd. For, on it, a sentence, say 'Ba_1', will be true *in virtue of* a relation obtaining between a sign and a thing. This "idealistic" absurdity we shall discuss further in Chapter X. For the present we may note that it can be taken to avoid facts, such as *that a_1 is* B, by introducing *relational* facts, such as *that* 'B' *is true of a_1*. The second claim merely avoids the issue by *using the predicate* (or its metalinguistic correlate) in a *predicative way to explain* what it is for a predicate to be true of an object. One thereby uses the familiar *redundancy* of the predicate 'true' to avoid talking about properties (or classes). I shall argue in the next chapter that this alternative also fails. For the present I only wish to argue that *granting*, rather than challenging, the nominalist's response, the explanation offered can be seen to be circular.

On the pattern we are discussing, a general term is one that can *be true of* something. A singular term is one that can *refer to* something. Quine may defend the cogency of the distinction in one of three ways, depending on his construal of *is true of*. First, he may hold that there is nothing to be explained. We simply recognize two *basic relations* between signs and things. These relations neither require nor are capable of further explication. Second, he may hold that singular terms simply differ from general terms in that the former, but not the latter, may *stand for* entities. Third, he may claim that there are two relations involved but one, *is true of*, may be explicated, as indicated above, in terms of the "redundancy" of 'is true'. The second claim is question-begging in that one assumes what is at issue, and the first reply forces the nominalist to do something that the realist does not have to do. The latter recognizes only one basic relation between simple descriptive signs (names and primitive predicates) and objects—*reference* or *naming*. For the realist, such predicates *refer to* attributes as names *refer to* objects. This reveals that in one sense Quine does not offer a *simpler* gambit than the realist. For, Quine acknowledges *two* fundamental relations between signs and things, and the realist recognizes two fundamental kinds of "things," but *only one* connection between signs and things. Yet, the realist must also recognize a relation between the two kinds of entities, particulars and properties. But, even this feature of the realist's view is matched by the nominalist, for the latter does not merely *assign* predicates to particulars. In fact, nominalists do not really take *is true of* to be basic. If they were to so take it, they could not specify the *truth condition* for 'B' being true of a_1 that they characteristically appeal to. Such nominalists generally hold that 'B' is true of a_1 since a_1 is B. Thus, the first reply reduces to the third. If they take *is true of* as a *basic* relation, they must do one of two things. They must either assert that we have two different connections between signs and the objects they are assigned to, and one such *assigned connection* is the ground of truth, or hold that predicates stand in a relation to objects that *accounts for* the truth of atomic sentences *irrespective* of our assignment of predicates to objects. On the second, atomic sentences are held to be true in virtue of some basic relation between predicate signs and objects that obtains irrespective of our assignment of predicates to objects. Such *facts* become the grounds of truth. Some nominalists avoid both alternatives by invoking Tarski's Convention T and holding that a predicate 'B' is true of a particular on *the condition* that the particular is B. Such nominalists *assume* that we may *use* the predicate ascriptively without assigning it to any entity. This, of course, is precisely what is at issue. Hence, to counter the realist's objection and avoid the above absurdities, nominalists must assume what they purport to establish. By recognizing attributes, the realist is not forced to *use* the predicate, in an explanation of its use, in the way nominalists must. The realist holds that 'Ba_1' is true because the object that 'a_1' refers to has the property that 'B' refers to. A nominalist like Quine holds that 'Ba_1' is true *because* 'B' is true of a_1, which is so *since* a_1 is B. He thus *uses* 'B' (or a metalinguistic transcription of it) in his explanation. This reveals, first, that his gambit is no simpler than the realist's and, second, that the explanation he gives assumes what he purports to prove: that general terms may be used without commitment to attributes.[22]

Although singular terms are held to be those terms that *can* refer, they are also taken to be the terms that *can* replace variables or that *can be* generalized from or instantiated to. This feature connects Quine's criterion of ontological commitment with his discussion of singular terms and reference. The use of Quine's conception of ontological commitment presupposes the equivalence of the two ways of characterizing singular terms.[23] It immediately follows that in a scheme employing lower functional logic, the constant predicates of the schema are not taken as *referring to* anything, let alone "abstract" entities. But, clearly, we so take them since we merely assume that only singular terms, i.e., zero-level terms, *may* make ontological commitments. Thus, Quine offers no argument, merely a reiteration of his thesis in different words.

Quine's *criteria* are not intended to preclude his applying his terminology to extended functional calculi, even though it is only in a lower functional calculus that his "distinctions" will separate singular and general terms into mutually exclusive classes. Yet, the application of such terminological distinctions to higher calculi reveals a further fundamental defect in the "argument."

Quine may be taken to suggest that we should have, in a perspicuous *realistic* schema, as in natural languages, *two terms*, instead of *one* predicate.[24] One term will be distinctively singular, but not general, the other will be general. If 'white' is the English transcription of a descriptive constant *predicate* in a schema with predicate quantifiers and variables, and if we acknowledge existential quantification from it, we are using "it" as a singular term. Such use commits "us" to an abstract entity *named* by *the term*. This suggests that we should have another term, transcribed by 'whiteness', that would be a singular term and would *refer to* or *name* that entity. Frege, recall, held that a term could not *function predicatively* and *stand for* an "object," but a term in subject place did not function predicatively and did stand for (or purport to stand for) an object. Thus, 'white' in 'White is a color' stood for an object—a concept correlate—that it did not stand for in 'This is white'. In the latter sentence, it stood for a function or concept. Thus, as we earlier noted, *the term* stands for different "things" in the two cases and, hence, is ambiguous as a term. Following Frege's avoidance of the ambiguity one might employ two terms, as we did in Chapter VI. One term, say 'Wx', would be used as a predicate, and the other, say 'Wx̂', would be used as a subject term. 'Wx' refers to a function (or concept) and 'Wx̂', as an "abstract singular term," refers to a Fregean *concept correlate* or, for present purposes, *abstract entity* — a realist's *universal*. Recall, further, that for Frege the sentence 'a_1 is white' is taken to be "equivalent" to 'a_1 falls under *the* concept white', where the phrase 'the concept white' must be taken to stand for an *object*. Keeping to that pattern, we can transcribe those sentences, respectively, as 'Wa_1' and '$U_2(a_1, W\hat{x})$', with 'U_2' for 'falls under', as in the earlier discussion of Frege. Thus, when, and only when, (the function) Wx maps the object a_1 onto *The True*, (the function) $U_2(x,y)$ maps *the pair of objects a_1 and $W\hat{x}$* onto *The True*. One may also put matters in a distinctively non-Fregean way and hold that the object a_1 is white if and only if it stands in the exemplification relation to the object $W\hat{x}$. The exemplification relation is asymmetrical. Hence, even with $W\hat{x}$ taken to be an object or individual, as a_1 is, there is a fundamental difference between objects like a_1 and objects like $W\hat{x}$. The function $U_2(x,y)$ separates the objects into two distinct kinds that are quite familiar: those objects that *may* and those that *may not* have other objects *fall under* them.

The Fregean pattern is adopted by Quine to characterize the realist. A realist is held to take predicates as singular terms and, consequently, to adopt '$W\hat{x}$' in place of or in addition to 'Wx'. Quine's discussion thus reveals that he identifies *existents* with *individuals*. *Whiteness* is an *existent* in that it is an *individual*, albeit an abstract one. It differs from a_1 in that one is a *concrete individual* and the other is an *abstract object*. Both "names," 'a_1' and '$W\hat{x}$', are zero-level constants in a *Principia*-type schema and both can thus stand as subject terms juxtaposed with first-level predicates. It is as if the nominalist only recognizes the realist's entities if the latter are construed as the nominalist's individuals, according to the nominalist's notion of an *individual*. When we recall that the issue is about the need to recognize entities other than individuals, this alteration of the question is striking and significant. The realist holds that since we require primitive predicates, we recognize universals. Quine holds that we need not recognize universals, since we may use predicates without commitment to referents of such predicates. What we see is that he rejects the realist's criterion of ontological commitment since he insists that we need only recognize *attributes* if they are taken to be *individuals*. But this transforms the issue. The issue is not whether there are *abstract in-*

dividuals in addition to *concrete individuals*. The issue is whether there are *universals* in addition to *individuals*. Quine avoids a commitment to universals by transforming the question. His concern with singular terms, 'whiteness' and 'W$\hat{x}$', is symptomatic of this. We can see the flaw in his transformation of the issue by noting that he runs together the claims that:

> *Only individuals exist*, hence attributes (properties, universals) do not exist.

and

> *Only concrete individuals exist*, hence abstract individuals (universals, classes) do not exist.

Quine then equates an argument for the first claim with an argument for the second by adopting his criterion of ontological commitment. For, he, in effect, holds that the realist must claim that 'a_1 is white' is to be transcribed, in a perspicuous schema, by '$U_2(a_1, W\hat{x})$' and not by 'Wa_1'. By claiming that '$U_2(a_1, W\hat{x})$' is not needed, since 'Wa_1' will do, Quine "establishes" that abstract individuals do not exist and, "therefore," that attributes do not exist.

Frege's concern with identity aids Quine's pattern. Following Frege, Quine emphasizes the role of the law of identity in ontological issues. Just as satisfying the predicate "self-identical" was the criterion for *being an object* for Frege, it is the criterion for *being an entity* for Quine. Since *identity* is generally represented by a predicate, say '=', an argument emerges. If 'Wx' stands for an entity (object), then that entity (object) must be self-identical. (No entity without identity.) If so, to express that by 'Wx = Wx' is problematic since that expression is not a sentence in that it contains a "free variable." Hence, we should use 'W$\hat{x}$ = W$\hat{x}$' and thereby recognize the use of 'W$\hat{x}$' as a *subject term* (singular term) standing for the appropriate entity (object). But, there are two issues here. One is whether we must extend a schema to include the use of '=' between predicates, if we hold that predicates stand for properties. A second issue is whether predicates then "give rise" to corresponding terms that are singular but not general. The former point overlooks the fact that one may hold that ontological claims are made through comments *about* a schema and need not (even cannot sensibly) be made *in* a schema (in terms of $(\exists f)(f = W)$, for example). The second issue may seem to be an idle dispute over terminology. It is more than that since it raises the question of the use of predicates in subject place. Moreover, it reveals that Quine begs the question at issue, for it reflects his belief that terms can refer only if they can occupy subject place. But, he was supposed to *establish that* by appeal to the distinction between singular and general terms. Yet, that distinction is based on the distinction between subject terms and general terms *as* predicates. Thus, Quine assumes that predicate terms do not refer in that they are *only* predicate terms and not subject or singular terms.

A correlate, like $W\hat{x}$, of a general term, like 'W' or 'Wx', reveals another circular argument in the nominalist's pattern. If we add such correlates to a schema[25] with predicate quantification, we may then assert '$(\exists f)(f = W)$' and '$(\exists x)(x = W\hat{x})$' (as well as '$Wa_1 \supset (\exists f)fa_1$') and make a twofold ontological commitment to the "abstract" individual—the attribute. However, once we introduce '$W\hat{x}$', we no longer require predicates like 'W'. To say that a_1 is white we may now assert, in Fregean fashion, that a_1 *stands to* $W\hat{x}$ in a relation—*falling under* or *exemplification*—and, hence, replace 'Wa_1' by '$U_2(a_1, W\hat{x})$'. We may do this for every standard predicate. Thus, the realist, on the nominalist's view, would acknowledge only one *distinctively general predicate* term, the term for the exemplification relation, 'U_2'. In fact, Sellars has claimed that this is what the realist must do. *Ordinary* relations would also be construed as *individuals* so that 'a_1 is to the left of a_2', for example, could be expressed by '$U_2(a_1, a_2, L\hat{x}\hat{y})$', with '$U_2$' understood to be "multigrade," as Quine and Goodman have put it. But, then, what about the exemplification *relation*? If we treat *exemplification* as an *individual*, we encounter a version of Bradley's "paradox." We cannot transform 'a_1 exemplifies whiteness' into '$U_2(a_1, W\hat{x}, U_2\hat{x}\hat{y})$' without introducing a *new general term*, 'U_2', or allowing for the retention of 'U_2' *along with* '$U_2\hat{x}\hat{y}$'. Hence, if we take the realist to hold that there are two *kinds* of individuals, which are signified by "singular terms" but distinguished by the asymmetry of the exemplification relation, Bradley's "paradox" reveals that realism is self-refuting. Exemplification cannot be *solely represented* by a singular term and, hence, cannot be taken as an "individual" or "existent." Realism can only be maintained if we recognize that there are entities that are not *individuals*. It cannot be maintained if we take the realist to hold that there are *abstract* individuals in addition to *concrete* individuals. One may suggest that the realist should claim that we need not recognize *a* relation of exemplification, since we merely use a general term to *express* (but not refer to) such a relation. Such a move will not do, as the realist then adopts the basic move of the nominalist's pattern. The point to note is that realism cannot be cogently stated in terms of the nominalist's notions of *singular* and *general terms*. These concepts, consistently used, force the rejection of realism.

X

Facts and Possibilities

Like properties, facts have long been the target of philosophical attacks. These have ranged from purported paradoxes, like the fallacy we considered earlier, to the profound and genuine problems that Bradley pointed out. The latter we shall consider in the next chapters. Somewhere in between lies the kind of criticism that considers the appeal to facts to be empty and trivial, just as some nominalists see the reference to properties to be empty of explanatory value. The idea is that to say that a fact is the ground of truth for an atomic sentence is not really to say anything. Part of the problem stems from a misconception of philosophical analysis. Acknowledging properties and facts is not like discovering a new particle in subatomic physics. Obviously, one does not "explain," in the sense in which doctors and physicists explain, why something is red or why a sentence is true by saying that it has the property red or that the sentence stands for a fact. This misunderstanding goes with the conviction that the appeal to properties and facts is just a way of stating, in other words, that predicates apply to objects and that sentences are true. That is supposedly why the proponent of facts does not say anything. But, of course, one does not *mean* by "a fact" that which makes a sentence true or grounds the truth of an atomic sentence. Confining our discussion to atomic facts for the time, we can specify what a fact is. It is one or more particulars in an asymmetrical relation (exemplification, say) to a property or relation. Perhaps, such a response is not felt to be satisfactory unless one specifies what is meant by 'particular', 'property', 'relation', and 'exemplification'. This brings us to an aspect of the question that I have acknowledged to be problematic and which we shall consider in due course: Bradley's paradox. It also involves a number of other philosophical problems about concepts like 'particular', 'universal', 'nexus', etc. Some of these we have taken up; others we shall discuss. It is acknowledged that facts cannot be analyzed in the sense in which one takes an analysis to specify a "reduction" of a "complex" to its constituents. But, we shall see that this is not really problematic, though it acknowledges that in one sense we cannot specify what a fact is. A fact contrasts in this sense with a list or a collection of elements. It is not a class of its constituents that can be specified by enumeration, even though the constituents can be enumerated. A fact is a set of constituents in a structural connection. This is not to say that one cannot distinguish the sequence 'aRb' from the sequence 'bRa' by means of classes. Of course one can, along the lines used for taking ordered n-tuples as classes. What one cannot do is take the class to be the fact, because the constituents of the fact are not the members of the class. We can distinguish the fact aRb from the fact bRa by associating the class $\{\{a\}, R, b\}$ with the one and the class $\{a, R, \{b\}\}$ with the other. That is not the point. The unit class of a is not a constituent of either fact: the constituents are the same in both cases. This leads to another objection to facts. What differentiates the fact that aRb from the fact that bRa? No thing differentiates them. The constituents do not individuate in this case. The structure of the fact or "direction" of the relation does. What does this mean? I know what it means, since I know what relations are. Just as I know what it means for black to be darker than gray, since I know what the colors are and what the relation *darker than* is. To know what it is for something to be black is to know, in turn, what it means for an object to have a property. To know what a two-term relation is is to know what it is for one thing to stand in a relation to another thing. This does not mean that one has a philosophical position that helps to explicate the notion of 'predication' or that one is familiar with the "logic of relations." Recall, at this point, our discussion of Moore's use of 'analysis' in Chapter II.

There is another aspect to the question of individuation that is contained in the popular dictum "No entities without identity." This means that one must furnish "identity criteria"when one speaks of a kind of entity. What is the condition of identity for facts? In one sense, we can give a simple answer: an atomic fact, f_1, is identical with an atomic fact, f_2, if "they" consist of the same constituents structured or arranged in the same way. This leads to questions about the identity of the constituents and of the structure. The first question is about particulars and properties. As we deal with atomic sentences, let us assume that we have a set of particulars and properties and our concern is with the facts composed of them. When, then, are the structures the same? In one sense, this is merely another way of asking an admittedly unanswerable question: a question about the nature of the predicative tie. To answer it would be to say what Russell's basic asymmetrical relation is or what an alternative connection would be on a "bundle" theory along Moore's lines in Chapter IV, and to resolve Russell's worries about the "forms" of facts. Since such ties are basic, and facts are not analyzable, one cannot reply, in one sense. However, there is a reply in two other senses. By furnishing a theory along the lines of Russell or of Moore or of Bradley, one provides one kind of answer. By noting that we know what it is for an object to have a property or for two objects to stand in a relation in a quite ordinary and straightforward sense, we answer the question in yet another way. We know such things as we know what it is to be grey or to be black without "analyzing" or being able to "explicate" the terms and without knowing a host of facts of scientific optics. Moreover, we need not let matters stand there. We can specify, along familiar lines, that atomic sentences stand for facts and that two such sentences stand for the same fact when their predicates stand for the same property or relation and when the name of a particular at an arbitrary subject place in one sentence stands for the same particular as the corresponding name in the other. If we deal with a perspicuous schema that permits only one name for each particular and one primitive predicate for each property, we need not even bother specifying such a condition. One may now be dismayed by the use of sentences to specify identity conditions for facts, since we appeal to facts as the basis of truth for sentences. But we do not base the identity or difference of atomic facts on sentences. We specify when sentences refer to the same fact. The difference of facts is understood in terms of difference in either constituents or structure. The answer to the question is simple and trivial, but this reflects on the question, not on the status of facts.

A further aspect of the question is reflected in Wittgenstein's worry about the logical equivalence of 'F_1a' and '$(\exists x)(F_1 x \,\&\, x = a)$'. Do they stand for the same fact? If so, what is its structure? If not, why not? This raises a query about the very idea of an atomic fact since there will be a corresponding existential sentence for every atomic sentence. The problem arises, in part, owing to the failure to make a distinction. A fact grounds the truth of a sentence. It is an entity such that its existence is the ground of truth of the sentence; just as an object is an entity that is the condition for a name being a genuine proper name. But, this does not mean that the fact which makes a sentence true is "referred" to by that sentence. The object a being F_1 suffices to ground the truth of '$(\exists x)F_1 x$'. This does not involve our holding that the existential sentence stands for the fact as the sentence '$F_1 a$' does. Wittgenstein's example is only a more complicated case in that the existential sentence implies the atomic sentence. How does one decide that the existential sentence does not stand for a fact? One has to present an argument. This will involve specifying just what questions are involved in concerns about molecular and quantificational truths stating facts. We shall take up such questions in subsequent chapters. I shall argue that we need not take a sentence like Wittgenstein's existential sentence to *stand for* a fact, though it is true because a certain fact exists. For the present, I am concerned with atomic facts and not with problems that result from the use of molecular or quantified sentences. But, there are traditional questions that appear to present similar problems about atomic facts. A simple one concerns the sentences 'a-left-of-b' and 'b-right-of-a'. Do they stand for one and the same fact or, if not, do we have two existent facts and, if not, which fact grounds the truth of both sentences? I do not think the questions point to problems about identity conditions for facts. One answers such questions in the context of a philosophical position. One does not answer such queries by "finding out" which fact (or facts) is (are) involved as one finds out "who did it" or as one proves that the set of all even primes is the set of all natural numbers between 3 and 1. Rather, one notes that questions of ontological parsimony and of dialectical feasibility are involved, as well as other concerns. Thus, queries about "identity conditions" cover up the nature of the questions and theories about facts and truth. Similar themes are involved in our asserting or denying that complex predicates stand for properties or that definite descriptions are "referring" signs, and, hence, they affect the handling of questions about identity of properties and individuals. To answer such questions in the context of a philosophical position does not mean that one's answers are arbitrary, though it might mean that for some questions it does not matter what answer one gives, since alternatives are equally viable. Recognizing all this, we should recognize that for atomic facts there are no real problems about so-called identity conditions.

There is a specious issue about identity of properties that lends some plausibility to the disdain for facts. One notorious reason for preferring classes to properties is that we supposedly have an identity condition for classes and not for properties, since classes are extensional. But, for a philosopher's concerns about identity and predication, the condition for classes is not satisfactory as a ground for such preference. It presupposes that we take individuals as different without conditions. Otherwise, we obviously cannot hold that '$a = b$' is true on the condition that one belongs to a class if and only if the "other" does. The circle is simple and vicious. That we ordinarily use a variety of criteria to determine questions of identity of individuals is totally irrelevant. What detectives and medical researchers take to be evidence of identity is not a matter of "identity conditions" in terms of our issues, just as a mathematician's starting from a set of elements is irrelevant. What is wanted is either a definition of '=' for individuals or the acknowledgment that one uses a primitive notion of *identity* or *difference*. Clearly, we have done nothing toward resolving philosophical problems by using both

$$x = {}_i y = {}_{df.} (a)(x\epsilon a \equiv y\epsilon a)$$

and

$$a = {}_c \beta = {}_{df.} (x)(x\epsilon a \equiv x\epsilon \beta),$$

with '$=_i$' and '$=_c$' as the identity signs for individuals and classes, respectively. If we acknowledge a basic notion of difference for individuals, we can make use of such a notion with respect to properties. Red is different from triangular and from white. I need not have "criteria" for knowing that, any more than I need criteria to know that my left hand is not my right. This does not mean that there are not problems about the notions of identity and difference in such contexts. Some of those we discussed earlier in connection with Moore and Russell. Just as one may hold that difference is basic and not analyzable for individuals, one may, perhaps must, hold this to be so for properties. Alternatively, one can *offer* a definition or analysis of identity for properties along the lines of the Russell-Leibniz construal of identity of individuals:

$${}^1 f = {}^1 g = {}_{df.} ({}^2 f)({}^2 f({}^1 f) \equiv {}^2 f({}^1 g)).$$

To complain that this does no good because we must then know that some second-level property is identical to or different from some "other" second level property, in order to settle a question about first-level properties, is to confuse two questions. It is one thing to know what 'identical' means and, in that sense, have criteria of identity. It is another thing to know when criteria have been fulfilled. Perhaps, it helps to recall that it is one thing to know what it is to be a logical truth; it is quite another thing to know if a given statement is one.

The above observations do not constitue a denial that there are problems about the identity of properties. One has to do with whether we take complex predicate expressions like 'F$\hat{x}$ & G$\hat{x}$' to stand for properties and, if so, when such expressions stand for the same property. But, such questions do not affect our concerns. Atomic facts contain constituent properties indicated by primitive predicates. In the tradition of the logical atomists, such properties are simples or basic entities. Admittedly, such notions are controversial and there is an extensive literature about them. Such issues are not my concern in this book, although we have touched upon them. But, it is worth observing that the problems about facts supposedly arise even if we start from a set of specified individuals and properties. We are concerned with a question of when atomic sentences stand for the same fact. Putting matters as I have presupposes that we take such sentences to stand for facts, *since* their constituent signs stand for elements of the fact and the arrangement of the signs stands for the arrangement (or ordering or structuring) of the constituents in the fact. This, itself, seems to invite part of the criticism of facts. For, by so putting matters, we hold that the sentence '$F_1 a$' stands for the fact that a is F_1, which appears as uninformative as the proverbial response that 'Mrs. Smith' is the name of Mr. Smith's wife. To be suspicious of facts on such grounds is to confuse philosophical analysis with the teaching of a language. To learn to use the sentence 'It is raining' is to learn to use it in the appropriate circumstances—when the facts warrant it, as we might say. Undoubtedly, it will not help very much if one is told: "Use 'It is raining' when it is raining"; but our concerns are a bit different.

We coordinate the names of the schema to particular objects. Ignoring for the present the controversial nature of the coordination of predicates with properties, assume we do the same for the primitive predicate constants. Clearly, such coordinations will not suffice to "connect" atomic sentences to the "conditions" that ground their truth or falsity. Therefore, we must connect sentences in addition to the coordination of names and predicates. Of course, we cannot connect sentences as we connect names and predicates. To do so would be to treat sentences as names of facts. Sentences could not then be false. This means that we take sentences to stand for "conditions" irrespective of whether they are true or false. That is basically all that is involved in holding that sentences represent "possibilities" or "possible facts" or, as Wittgenstein put it, "situations." This is, undoubtedly, one source of the discomfort about facts. There is another. To speak of connecting sentences to possibilities is then to acknowledge that one does not connect the "two" as one connects names to objects. In the latter case, we connect two "existents": a sign and a thing. The same holds for the connection of primitive predicates to properties and would even hold if we named existent facts. Part of the problem, then, is how we know what we are talking about when we speak of possible facts. This theme I shall return to more than once.

In an earlier discussion of Frege, we noted that a sentence, like a name or a primitive predicate, is a basic expression in two senses: it is not reducible, or cannot be construed as a set of its constituent signs; it is not eliminable. The former feature corresponds to the basic feature of facts. They are objects structured or connected and not sets of constituents. The latter feature indicates a difference between a sentence and an expression like 'Fx̂ & Gx̂', in a schema with the logical apparatus of the lower functional calculus, or an expression like '(ιx)(Fx)'. The two features together reflect that sentences and facts are complexes but are like *simple elements* in that they are not simply sets of elements and, hence, not "reducible" to such elements. Talking of possibilities simply reflects our holding that atomic sentences, as basic sign patterns of the schema, are taken to have "ontological" significance along with names and primitive predicates. This, in turn, is a way of stating that we cannot connect the schema to what it is about, and in terms of which the sentences are true or false, without *connecting* the atomic sentences *as* sentences. It does not suffice to connect the names and predicates to the objects and properties. This should help to remove "possible facts" from the limbo of Disneyland. Perhaps, the ultimate problem about possible facts is simply a result of necessarily having sign patterns that are both *complex* and *basic*.

Speaking of possibilities does enable us to dispel part of the supposed puzzle about facts. One line of argument against facts depends on holding that speaking of facts is empty and circular. The idea is that the philosopher who defends facts holds that atomic facts are the entities that ground the truth of atomic sentences and then holds that the condition for an atomic sentence referring to a fact is that the sentence be true. However, the truth condition for the sentence is taken to be the existence of the fact. It, thus, appears that the appeal to facts is circular. Such an argument oversimplifies matters and fails to establish the circular pattern, for it depends on an ambiguous use of the term 'refer'. One may speak of an atomic sentence referring to a fact in two senses. In one sense, an atomic sentence *refers* to a "possibility," irrespective of the sentence being true or false and, hence, irrespective of whether the fact exists. In another sense, one speaks of a sentence referring to a fact when the fact exists and, hence, the sentence is true. Distinguishing between these two uses of 'refer', we recognize that the circle has disappeared. In the sense in which an atomic sentence is said to stand for a possibility, irrespective of whether the sentence is true or false, an existent fact is *not a condition of reference*. The *existence* of the fact that the sentence stands for *is the condition of truth*. Of course, this brings up the problem of *possible facts*, which we must resolve.

Our speaking of facts and truth conditions naturally leads to recent attempts to avoid the appeal to facts as truth conditons by holding that Tarski's semantic concept of truth and the relation of satisfaction involved suffice to explain 'being true'.

> The semantic concept of truth as developed by Tarski deserves to be called a correspondence theory because of the part played by the concept of satisfaction; for clearly what has been done is that the property of being true has been explained, and nontrivially, in terms of a relation between language and something else.[1]

Suppose we consider a limited domain of two or three objects that exemplify a small number of color and shape properties, and a schema with corresponding names and predicates where we have only atomic sentences. Suppose, further, that we add a truth predicate and satisfy the Tarski-type condition so that, for example,

$$T'W_1 a' \equiv W_1 a$$

holds, where '$W_1 a$' transcribes 'a is white' and 'T' transcribes 'is true'. What this means is that the sentence '$W_1 a$' is true if and only if a is white. With this, one need not argue. But, philosophers have traditionally worried about the connection of sentences, like '$W_1 a$', with a ground of truth, such as the fact that a is white or the coherence of the proposition expressed by the sentence with other propositions. What Davidson offers, if he offers anything at all, is the object a, since a is white. Thus, he takes the English rendition of '$W_1 a$', along with the object, as the ground of truth. This is disguised, somewhat thinly, by speaking of a *satisfying* the appropriate linguistic pattern provided a is white.

There is an obvious question about the adequacy of taking Tarski's Convention-T to provide a sufficient condition for a *theory* of truth. There is a further question about taking such a convention to specify a sufficient condition for the introduction of a truth predicate into a schema. For, it is not at all obvious that the introduction of such a predicate provides a theory or that the presence of an adequate theory requires the introduction of such a predicate. Having no answer to such questions, Davidson makes them disappear behind a cloud of verbal abuse:

> The central merit of Convention T is that it substitutes for an important but murky problem a task whose aim is clear. After the substitution one appreciates better what was wanted in the first place, and gains insight into the aetiology of confusion. The original question is not confused, only vague. It is: what is it for a sentence (or utterance or statement) to be true? Confusion threatens when this question is reformulated as, what makes a sentence true? The real trouble comes when this in turn is taken to suggest that truth must be explained in terms of a relation between a sentence as a whole and some entity, perhaps a fact, or state of affairs. Convention T shows how to ask the original question without inviting these subsequent formulations.[2]

Aside from substituting rhetoric for argumentation, Davidson is unable to do what he suggests—answer the original question in the clarifying light of Convention-T. He cannot provide a general answer to the question: "What is it for an atomic sentence to be true?" Given a specific atomic sentence, such as '$W_1 a$', he can provide the illuminating answer that such a sentence is true if and only if a is white. Tarski, of course, was concerned with the purely technical question imposed by having to satisfy Convention-T in cases other than those involving atomic sentences:

> Even a superficial analysis . . . shows that in general composite sentences are in no way compounds of simple *sentences*. Sentential functions do in fact arise in this way from elementary functions, *i.e.* from inclusions; sentences on the contrary are certain special cases of sentential functions. In view of this fact, no method can be given which would enable us to define the required concept directly by recursive means. The possibility suggests itself, however, of introducing a more general concept which is applicable to any sentential function, can be recursively defined, and, when applied to sentences, leads us directly to the concept of truth. These requirements are met by the notion

of the *satisfaction of a given sentential function by given objects*, and in the present case by given classes of individuals.[3]

Tarski also noted a consequence of the appeal to Convention-T that should give pause to any philosopher, though, understandably, it would not phase one determined to avoid philosophical problems:

> If the language investigated only contained a finite number of sentences fixed from the beginning, and if we could enumerate all these sentences, then the problem of the construction of a correct definition of truth would present no difficulties. For this purpose it would suffice to complete the following scheme: $x \in Tr$ if and only if either $x = x_1$ and p_1, or $x = x_2$ and p_2, . . . or $x = x_n$ and p_n, the symbols 'x_1', 'x_2', . . . , 'x_n' being replaced by structural descriptive names of all the sentences of the language investigated and 'p_1', 'p_2', . . . , 'p_n' by the corresponding translation of these sentences into the metalanguage.[4]

Hence, one can give a "correct definition of truth" or a "theory of truth" by *listing the true sentences*, in such a finite case. The obvious inadequacy and irrelevance of such a "theory" for philosophical problems reveals the absurdity of attempting to replace a philosophical question by one that is not. This becomes even more evident when we recall Davidson's claim that Tarski's semantic concept of truth deserves to be called a "correspondence theory," in that a sentence, 'W_1a', is characterized as true since *a satisfies* 'W_1a'. For, *a* satisfies 'W_1a' since *a* is white. Few philosophical circles have ever been completed so quickly. Just as a list of true sentences suffices, in the case of a language with a finite number of enumerable sentences, it suffices to respond *"because a is white"* to a question about the truth condition for 'W_1a'. There is another interesting feature of Davidson's appeal to Convention-T. In avoiding *relational* facts like the fact that Dolores loves Dagmar, Davidson speaks of ordered "n-tuples" of ordinary objects such as *the pair* Dolores and Dagmar *in that order*. He, thus, appeals to a further kind of entity, *an ordered pair*. Philosophers might question the ontological parsimony and conceptual clarity gained by speaking of an ordered pair that satisfies 'Dolores loved Dagmar', while disdaining to talk of such metaphysical and vague entities as facts.

But, again, we can understand how Davidson comes to make such a move. Logicians and mathematicians deal with n-tuples in a systematic manner. In this sense, much is known about such "things." Thus, the philosophical problems about truth and facts disappear, in part, in favor of the textbook treatment of nonphilosophical aspects of logic and mathematics. It is worth noting how the relational case and the ordering involved suggest a plausibility that is totally absent from the monadic case of 'W_1'. In the latter case, one can only appeal to the object a as the ground of truth of '$W_1 a$'. This is what forces one to justify the truth claim by appealing to a's being white. A related problem arises for those who suggest that the fact that an object, say a, stands in a relation to another object, b, is best represented by a juxtaposition of the signs for a and b, and not by a sentence employing a relational predicate. In the monadic case, they must make a different move. This we shall return to when we discuss Sellars's suggested use of different type fonts, in a perspicuous language, so that different ways of writing a name replace monadic predicates. A nonlinguistic version of the problem arises when some commentators on Wittgenstein's *Tractatus* speak of a fact as a *configuration* of objects without allowing properties as "objects." They then analyze facts like *that a* is white in terms of a configuration of esoteric particulars, in order to avoid introducing properties as consituents of facts. For Davidson, no such philosophical complications arise; he stops, where others begin, with the observation that a is white.

Davidson pretends to find unclear what is asked when a philosopher raises the question "What *makes* a sentence true?" Such purported puzzlement about the term "makes" apes the approach, if not the literary and philosophical style, of the later Wittgenstein. But, the puzzlement about usage is easily dispelled. When a philosopher asks what it is for a sentence like '$W_1 a$' to be true, the question is, what *nonlinguistic entity* is such that its existence grounds or *provides a sufficient condition* for the truth of the sentence. The existence of the object a obviously does not furnish such a ground, since its existence is compatible with the sentence being false. Of course, one could develop a view whereby the existence of the object would be a sufficient condition for the veridical ascription of the predicate 'W_1'. For example, one could hold, along lines discussed in earlier chapters, that objects like a were to be construed as classes or bundles of properties like W_1. One may, then, so understand an object that predicative ascriptions, if veridical, are necessarily so, in some sense of "necessary." The existence of the object a might be taken as a sufficient condition for the truth of 'a exists'. But, it obviously cannot be taken as such a condition for the truth of '$W_1 a$', if we acknowledge that the object a need not have been white. By contrast, the philosopher who introduces facts does provide a satisfactory ground of truth for '$W_1 a$'. Given that the fact exists and that we deal with an appropriate schema, it follows, in the context of such a view, that the sentence is true.

In his 1925-26 lectures, Moore wrote:

There is one fundamental fact, extremely obvious but constantly overlooked, which is such that no answer to this question can be right, unless it is consistent with it. And it is because *only* a correspondence-theory as to what truth is, is consistent with it, that I say some such theory must be right; & because all coherence & pragmatist theories wh. are answers to this question are inconsistent with it, that I say they are certainly wrong.

The fact is this. For all values of p, where p is a prop. in our sense (1) p is true if & only if p; or to put it another way; (2) in order that p should be true, it is both a necessary & sufficient condition that p; or finally (3) p is true both entails & is entailed by p. . . .

E.g. (1) It is true that the sun is larger than the moon if & only if the sun *is* larger than the moon.[5]

Moore thus took Convention-T to state a necessary and sufficient condition for a "theory" of truth to "satisfy." But, this was due to his understanding the condition of p's being true to be that it stated a fact. Thus, he considered the *meaning* of 'is true' in terms of something like;

T'Wa' $\equiv$ If anyone were to believe Wa, he would, so far as he was believing *that* be believing correctly.

To believe correctly was to have a belief that stood in a special relation to a fact—*directly proved by*. This pattern we started with in Chapter I. Moore's interesting twist here is to suggest that Convention-T suffices to rebut coherence theories of truth. He suggests this because on such theories it is not logically possible for

'Wa' to be true unless there is a set of propositions, not including 'Wa', with which 'Wa' coheres, whatever 'coheres' is taken to mean. (I shall not need to discuss, for purposes of this argument, whether *what coheres* are sentences, propositions, facts, conditions, or some of all these *kinds*.) That means that it is not possible to have 'Wa' true unless there are further propositions (and, perhaps, facts). Yet, as Moore understood it, by his early version of Convention-T, 'Wa' is true provided only that a is W, irrespective of any other propositions (or facts). Thus, he took coherence theories to be incompatible with that convention. Moore's argument may be said to assume what is at issue, that some sentences stand for, and are made true by, *atomic facts*. Along this line, one might suggest, as many do, that Convention-T could not possibly do what Moore thinks it does, since such a convention is neutral with respect to competing theories of truth. All the convention requires is that we assign the same truth value to both sides of the biconditionals. But, let us consider the sentence on a coherence theory that would correspond to the sentence "'Wa' *Ref.* Wa & Wa" in our earlier discussion of Frege's attack on correspondence theories. We should have a set of sentences not containing 'Wa', call it '$\{\delta\}$', and a relation of *coherence*, indicated by 'CO'. Then we have

$$(C_1) \quad \text{T'W}a' \equiv \text{'W}a' \text{ CO} \{\delta\}$$

stating that 'Wa' is true if and only if it coheres with the members of $\{\delta\}$. But, such an account, unlike a correspondence theory, does fall victim to Frege's regress argument. For, the right-hand side is true on the condition that *it* coheres with some set of sentences and not on the condition that 'Wa' does. In short, the right-hand side of (C_1) does not state the condition of truth for 'Wa' in the way that the corresponding right-hand side does for the correspondence theorist. This begins an *infinite* chain of truth conditions, since there are no atomic facts to halt it or, as we saw earlier, to ground the truth of an infinite chain of sentences. Moreover, if one seeks to halt the sequence by holding that

$$(C_2) \quad \text{'W}a' \text{ CO} \{\delta\}$$

is true, not in virtue of any new condition, but simply in virtue of the sentence 'Wa' cohering with the set of sentences $\{\delta\}$, one has, paradoxically, abandoned the coherence theory and adopted, for such sentences, the correspondence pattern. For, one is saying that the sentence (C_2) is true on the condition that

'Wa' CO $\{\delta\}$.

Thus, Moore has a point. Convention-T is not so innocent, if we think of it as involving the statement of truth conditions and not merely in terms of "assigning" truth values. A coherence theorist may agree to assign the same truth value to both sides of (C_1). That is not the point. What is the point is that on the theory, the right-hand side cannot state the ground of truth for the relevant sentence without giving rise to a further condition which is not stated. On the correspondence theory, there is no further condition.

The difference can be put in terms of the so-called T-sentence;

$$T\text{'W}a\text{'} \equiv Wa.$$

A correspondence theorist takes the right-hand side to *state* its truth condition. For, to say that a is white is to say that it is a fact that a is white or that a's being white is a fact or, less commonly, that the fact that a is white obtains or exists. This is not, as I shall later argue, to advocate the introduction of 'exists' into the schema as a predicate attaching to sentences. On the coherence theory, one does not take the right-hand side of the T-sentence to state its own truth condition. For, the condition is stated by a different sentence, namely (C_2). This is what Moore is pointing out and finding problematic. An adequate theory of truth must allow some sentences to *state* their *own truth conditions*. The correspondence theory does this; the coherence theory does not. Davidson's approach refuses to recognize that 'Wa' must be *construed* in some way and not *merely repeated*. He, thus, fails to understand a simple point. A correspondence theorist asserts that the fact that a is white obtains if and only if a is white. This is not *merely* to assert that a is white if and only if a is white.

One may hold that we need not appeal to facts, since the relation of satisfaction, holding between the object a and the sentence 'W$_1 a$', or, perhaps, between the object and the "open" sentence

'W_1x', provides a suitable ground or condition of truth. Such a gambit, unlike the mere recital of "provided Dolores loves Dagmar" or "snow is white," does constitute a philosophical move. But, it is grossly inadequate. To see why, ignore the temptation to observe that the biconditional

a satisfies '$W_1 a$' (or '$W_1 x$') $\equiv a$ is white

provides a basis for rejecting talk of *satisfaction* here as empty. (It is obvious, in one sense, that such an appeal to *satisfaction* merely repeats that '$W_1 a$' is true on the ground that a is white and, hence, avoids the question.) Instead, concentrate on the left-hand side of the above biconditional as a statement of the truth condition in that it purportedly offers a satisfactory ground for '$W_1 a$' being true. One then appeals to the fact that the satisfaction *relation* holds between the object a and a *linguistic expression*. Such a "fact" becomes the basis or ground of truth, in lieu of the fact that a is white. This means that the truth ground necessarily involves language. The ground of truth, *not* the *bearer* of truth or what is true, is, therefore, in part linguistic. Such a line not only jars with a fundamental piece of common sense—the way things are is the basis for our statements about them being true—but reveals an implicit idealist theme in the talk of satisfaction and Convention-T. If sentences are the sort of things that are true or false, then we cannot have *truth*, in one obvious sense, without having language and, hence, the originators and users of language. This is one thing. It is not to say that the conditions or the grounds for sentences being true involve language and its users. That there were mountains on earth before sentence tokens, I take to be true. Taken literally, the gambit presently under discussion holds that a relation between the objects that were mountains and certain expressions (whether tokens or types matters not here) constitutes the sufficient condition we were concerned with. This means that the condition or ground of truth—that in virtue of which the claim is true—had to await the advent of language and its users. This is a way of saying that mountains exist and are the sorts of things that they are in virtue of the use of language (or "thought" on the more traditional pattern).

There is an ambiguity in the phrase "truth condition" that lends a specious plausibility to the idealist gambit. Since the object *a* satisfies a certain expression, say 'W_1a', if and only if *a* is white, one can think of the truth condition alternatively as *a*'s being white or as *a*'s satisfying the expression. To offer the latter as a response to my query about a sufficient condition is to accept the idealist's view. To simply repeat that *a* is white is to ignore the question. Perhaps, the shifting back and forth between the two responses that is characteristic of the talk of *satisfaction* reveals a simple error. The error consists of failing to distinguish between the obvious truth that if sentences are the bearers of truth, one must have language for ascriptions of truth and the far from obvious claim that it is a *connection* between language and objects that *constitutes the ground or basis* for sentences being true.

There is another point that is skirted by those who disdain talk of facts or "grounds" of truth by means of the appeal to Convention-T. If asked about the ground of truth of an atomic subject-predicate sentence, such as 'W_1a', one who acknowledges properties and facts can reply:

(T′)   A subject-predicate sentence is true if and only if the the object denoted by the name exemplifies the property denoted by the predicate.

One can, thus, furnish a general condition of truth for atomic subject-predicate sentences (and, correspondingly, for sentences with relational terms). By contrast, Davidson, who appeals only to objects, sequences, and satisfaction, cannot provide a general criterion. He requires a specific sentence, like 'W_1a', so that he can reply to a query *about that sentence*:

'W_1a' is true if and only if W_1a (or *a* is white).

One cannot employ variables so that

a subject-predicate sentence 'Fx' is true if and only if Fx

becomes an alternative to (T′). What he can do is give the T-sentence for each subject-predicate sentence of a schema of a certain kind. This is not to do what (T′) does. That reveals it is one thing to provide a condition for attaching a so-called truth predicate to a subject-predicate sentence and another thing to state what *it is* for a sentence to be true. It will not do to claim that

(T″)   A subject-predicate sentence is true if and only if the object denoted by the name satisfies the sentence (or a corresponding open sentence containing the predicate).

does exactly what (T′) does without mentioning properties and exemplification. For, with (T″) we either embrace the idealistic absurdity I discussed above or do not offer a ground of truth. It is also to go against the basic theme of the gambit employing satisfaction and not to do what (T′) does. The idea behind characterizing satisfaction, in the case of a and '$W_1 a$', involves holding that the object satisfies the sentence *provided* that a is white. This is precisely what cannot be characterized in the general case, for one cannot characterize the condition in general. The point is simply that given a specific sentence like '$W_1 a$', one can state the condition for a satisfying it (or '$W_1 x$'), i.e., the condition for the sentence being true:

$$W_1 a.$$

Without the specific sentence being furnished, one must use the term "satisfies" as in (T″) rather than eliminate it as in the specific case of '$W_1 a$'. It is interesting that Tarski, unlike Davidson, explicitly recognizes the philosophical irrelevance of Convention-T when he rejects, *rather than* replaces, *the* philosophical problem.

I have heard it remarked that the formal definition of truth has nothing to do with "the philosophical problem of truth." However, nobody has ever pointed out to me in an intelligible way just what this problem is. . . .

In general, I do not believe that there is such a thing as "the philosophical problem of truth." I do believe that there are various intelligible and interesting (but not necessarily philosophical) problems concerning the notion of truth, but I also believe that they can be exactly formulated and possibly solved only on the basis of a precise conception of this notion. . . .

In fact, the semantic definition of truth implies nothing regarding the conditions under which a sentence like (1):

(1) *snow is white*

can be asserted. It implies only that, whenever we assert or reject this sentence, we must be ready to assert or reject the correlated sentence (2):

(2) *the sentence "snow is white" is true.*[6]

This clearly reveals that, even to Tarski, the relevance of Convention-T for a philosophical "theory" of truth is, at most, the specifying of a necessary condition for such a theory. A theory must not permit 'p is true' and 'p' to have different truth values for any sentence 'p'. It must, as it were, preserve the redundancy of the phrase 'is true'. The dispute between the advocates of Convention-T and philosophers who speak of facts seems to be a case of the typical tempest in the teapot. One wonders what the fuss is about. Perhaps it all comes down to the notion of a *truth condition*. Davidson gives a truth condition trivially, by stating "that *a* is white." He does not, thereby, state what a truth condition is. There are truth conditions. What are they? Facts? Sentences? Relations between objects and words (and, therefore, facts)? The difference between (T′) and (T″) is that simple. One gives a truth condition. The other does more; *it explicates what its proponent takes a truth condition to be*. One who uses Convention-T as a shield to ward off the philosophical problem of truth offers no such explication. However, one who adopts the "idealistic" reading of (T″) does offer an explication, but an inadequate one.

There is an ironic feature in the use of the idealistic pattern to defend the avoidance of facts. It is not merely that Moore and Russell long ago stressed the role of facts in their combined attack upon idealism. Rather, there is a sign of a "murky" metaphysical theme in the talk of the satisfaction of predicates by objects as an alternative to talk about facts. In rejecting facts through the "reformulation" of the classical question, so that a significant innovation in logic is used to illicitly bypass philosophical problems, philosophers who adopt the idealistic defense of what they do find themselves in strange company. The pattern they employ has been articulated in detail by Jean-Paul Sartre. Seeking to argue for a universal moral responsibility, as well as for "freedom" upon which it is based, Sartre, in a well-known passage, claims that we are responsible even for our "births" and that, in a sense, we "choose" to be born.[7] Ethical issues aside, the point is that we "make" things the way they are by construing them as we do in terms of our conceptual scheme. A hurricane is such because we classify *it* or think of *it* as a hurricane, as destructive, as terrifying, etc., in terms of our needs, values, and so forth. If one were to observe that there are the atoms whirling, aside from any notion of a hurricane, the response is obvious. In talk of atoms, motion, causation, etc., we also apply our scheme of classification. Atoms are what they are because we have the concepts we have. But, this is not idealism, for there is ultimately *something that* we classify and characterize. We could not classify if there were not that which is classified. What is it? To specify *it* under a concept would be to take it as classified or informed or made. Hence, it is mere *Being*.[8] The ultimate source of such characterizing and, hence, the opposite of *Being*, is consciousness or *Nothing*. The overall similarity of pattern is striking. For the defender of the idealistic reading of (T″), there is no fact that *a* is W$_1$. There is the relation between a predicate and an object. The object is there. We, as it were, contribute the predicate. But, if one pushes the gambit, one ends up with Sartre, just as Aristotle, in a related way, was ultimately led to prime matter. Suppose we ask what the objects are that predicates are true of? Clearly, for any expression like 'a chair', 'a mountain', etc., we can "separate" off the predicate that is satisfied by "something." That is, if it is *a chair* or *this chair* that is used to respond to the question, then there is "something," in turn, that satisfies 'is a chair', and so on. To put it another way, what is there, independently of our use of predicates, can only be an object as *unclassified*: perhaps a *Great Bare Particular*. Sartre's *Being* is precisely that. Thus, he is not an idealist, and the defense of satisfaction that I have called "idealistic" must be understood to be so in a qualified way. Just as Sartre is a realist, so is the defender of *satisfaction*. It is the object *as* a mountain that we make. By holding that the truth condition for its being a mountain is a relation between the object and the predicate 'is a mountain', *we do not make the object qua object*. Thus, such a one is no more or less of an idealist than is Sartre.

The irony is compounded in the case of a philosopher like Davidson and the fallacy of "The Great Fact." For, there is clearly a sense in which the modified idealism, implicit in the defense of (T″) I have been discussing, ends, like Sartre with *Being*, Bradley with *The Real*, and Frege with *The True*, in some *One*. The defender of atomic facts does not have to encompass *The Great Fact*, but his "idealistic" opponent finds *Being*.

There is one further theme that could lead one to believe that the appeal to facts is problematic. If we appeal to entities like facts, one might hold that we ought to be able to speak about them in a perspicuous schema. After all, Tarski showed us how to introduce a truth predicate into such a schema without facing familiar paradoxes. Since the existence of a fact is a truth condition, we should be able to state that. But, if we take something like

(1) Ex(W*a*)

to state that the fact that *a* is W exists, there is an obvious problem, or, rather, group of problems. One has to do with the use of the sentence as a subject term; we shall take up that question in other, related contexts in later chapters. Aside from that, (1) will obviously not do since a Fregean question immediately arises about the truth condition for (1). We can either say that *a* is W or assert

(2) Ex(Ex(W*a*)).

The first answer shows (1) to be pointless; the second answer shows (1) to be indefensible. This situation may be an underlying reason for taking the appeal to facts to be inadequate as a theory of truth. Just note the similarity of (1) to "T'W*a*'" which is supposedly explicated by "T'W*a*' ≡ W*a*". The latter does not involve a regress or circle. But, equally, it offers no philosophical explication of the concept of "truth." If we wish to use "T'W*a*' ≡ W*a*" as a basis for, or a reflection of, a philosophical position, we should replace it by

(3) T'W*a*' ≡ ['W*a*' *Ref.* W*a* & W*a*] .

The philosophical explication would consist of specifying the role of " 'W*a*' *Ref.* W*a*" in the theory and its application to the traditional problems about "thought," "reference," and "belief." This is the context in which one will talk about propositions, possible facts, etc. But, as we noted earlier, with (3) we do not "eliminate" the expression "'W*a*'", as we can with "T'W*a*' ≡ W*a*." If one then thinks of (3) as specifying truth conditions for "T'W*a*'", one could, following Frege, require the specification of such conditions for "'W*a*' *Ref.* W*a*". But, what one does in this case is provide the philosophical account I just spoke about, and not a formal procedure along Tarskian lines. One who is preoccupied with the latter type of task always comes back to something like "*a* is white," without any explication of the concept of a truth condition.

The point is that asserting (1) is not the way to state a view that appeals to facts. It is as fruitless as seeking to show the recognition of *exemplification* by introducing a relational predicate for such a notion. Theories about exemplification and facts are presented by pointing to certain features of a purported perspicuous schema and by commenting about such features and the classical issues in the background schema or language. We might remember that we coordinate names, like '*a*', and predicates, like 'W', to objects and properties, respectively. As I argued in an earlier chapter, it would be futile to add "'*a*' refers to *a*" and "'W' refers to W" to our schema *to replace* such a coordination or interpretation. Such sentences, at best, reflect that a coordination was made; they cannot establish it. Likewise, "'W*a*' *Ref.* W*a*" may reflect the fact that a philosopher, who employs such a pattern, takes atomic sentences to stand for possible facts and to be true when certain facts exist. It is not used to make such claims, just as the sentence 'W*a*' is not *used* to state that it stands for a possibility or a fact. It merely states that *a* is W.

All this returns us to the puzzles about possibilities, which go along with the way I have spoken of facts. In holding that possibilities must be recognized, I am making an ontological claim. This requires that I attempt to specify and clarify just what I take to be involved in such ontological claims. A philosopher who claims that universals exist does not ask us to recognize a special and unique kind of entity which philosophers, and only philosophers, introduce or recognize. Rather, the claim is that an ordinary sort of "thing," like a color, must be understood in certain ways and not in other ways. We deal not with entities that only philosophers recognize, but with ordinary things that only philosophers speak about in certain ways. The same thing goes for "particulars" or "individuals" or "physical objects." A philosopher might say that there are no particulars, since the ordinary things we all recognize as individuals or objects, as opposed to properties, are taken to be classes of properties. This is not to deny that in our ordinary context there are things like chairs and tables and sensations. It is to hold that, for a number of reasons specified and defended in a far from ordinary context, we construe or consider or speak of such things as classes of other things like colors, shapes, etc., just as when a philosopher says that particulars exist, it is clear that he is not simply repeating the obviously trivial truth that there are chairs, tables, sensations, etc. The philosopher is holding that in the context of certain philosophical questions one must think of such objects, and the facts about them, in certain ways and not others. Such questions as are relevant are those relating to the classical philosophical puzzles. Similarly, to acknowledge facts and possibilities, is to do something of the same sort that one does when one advocates the acknowledgment of particulars or universals. It is to hold that our ordinary talk about something being the case, or of it being a fact, or of a statement being true, or of something being possible is to be reflected in certain ways in a philosophical scheme and not in other ways. In short, in the ordinary context, we seem to recognize that there are objects, properties, truths, facts, possibilities, and much more. The question is how such ordinary "things" and talk are to be reflected in a philosopher's proposed ontological analysis. To claim that there are facts is to claim that no account of truth will do that does not ultimately appeal to the *ground* or *condition* "provided Dagmar loves Dolores," that such conditions cannot be adequately reconstructed or eliminated, and that a philosopher must *explicate* the notion of a truth condition. A philosopher cannot merely repeat that 'Dagmar loves Dolores' is true provided Dagmar loves Dolores. Facts, like properties and objects, are quite ordinary objects of experience. We readily acknowledge seeing an object, *the color* of it, and *that it has* that color rather than some other color. We also distinguish the object from its color and both from the fact. If one doubts this, just recall the way one speaks of the colors, the shapes, and the colored areas of a Mondrian as well as of the *arrangements* of such "things."

Possibilities, however, seem to differ radically from objects, properties, and facts. Unlike the latter, they are not confronted by normal people having normal experiences. It appears that the acknowledgment of possibilities cannot be construed as being a way of reflecting, in an ontological analysis, something that we ordinarily experience. 'Possible fact' does not appear to stand to 'possibility' as 'universal' does to 'property', where the first of each pair of terms is a term of the philosopher's vocabulary, and the second is a term of the ordinary context. By talking of possible facts, we appear to introduce a special *kind of thing* and not just a special way of talking about something quite ordinary. The same sort of problem appears to arise when one speaks of negative facts. This is not surprising, since some philosophers hold that there is only a verbal difference involved. Yet, although philosophers as diverse as Russell and Sartre have insisted that negative facts must be recognized (and Sartre appears to hold that one may be said to see that some thing is *not* white, as one sees that another thing is white), possibilities were obviously not acceptable to Moore and Russell. "Negative" entities are one thing; nonexistents are another. Possibilities are problematic in that we do not coordinate atomic sentences with such "entities" as we coordinate names and primitive predicates to particulars and properties. Rather, one *holds* that a complex sign, an atomic sentence, stands for such an entity in order to account for *how* sentences are *about* facts. It is as if entities are *postulated* for metaphysical purposes—to respond to certain problems. Since a philosopher introduces such entities for such purposes, the questions that lead to doing so become suspect. In a way, this likens the treatment of sentences as standing for possibilities to the claims that defined predicates stand for properties or that classes exist through comprehension rules. If one could hold negative facts to be on a par with atomic facts, as presented in experience, such existent facts may serve as a basis for resolving the issues without appealing to possibilities, as nonexistents. To say that an atomic fact is merely possible is to say that a negative fact exists. To put it another way, as Russell virtually did, an atomic sentence and its negation are taken, as a pair, to refer to a fact. The fact being negative makes one true; its being positive makes the other true. Again, we end with two fundamental categories, but there are two apparent differences, for *both negative and positive facts are existents* and *both are claimed to be objects of experience*, in that we supposedly experience cases of both kinds. For, we purportedly see that something is not white just as we see that something is white. One may then argue that the philosopher's talk of facts, negation, and possibility is on a par with our categorizing things as universals and particulars, as a special or extraordinary way of talking about very ordinary things. Moreover, it is relevant to recall the supposed inability to explicate the *existent-possible* dichotomy with respect to facts. Given that to speak of *negative* and *positive* facts is an alternative way of handling the problems involved, we can readily understand why such an explication cannot be offered. It would amount to explicating the concepts of *exemplification* and *negation*. That the former cannot be done, and why, we have discussed in detail at several points. To do the latter would amount to (a) defining *negation* and (b) showing how negative facts may be avoided. That one can neither avoid a basic concept of negation nor avoid negative facts is a theme Russell adhered to long ago. It is a theme I shall reiterate later, when we shall consider a solution to the problem posed by "possibilities." For the present, we may recall an observation of Russell's.

There is implanted in the human breast an almost unquenchable desire to find some way of avoiding the admission that negative facts are as ultimate as those that are positive. The 'infinite negative' has been endlessly abused and interpreted. Usually it is said that, when we deny something, we are really asserting something else which is incompatible with what we deny. If we say 'roses are not blue', we mean 'roses are white or red or yellow'. But such a view will not bear a moment's scrutiny. It is only plausible when the positive quality by which our denial is supposed to be replaced is incapable of existing together with the quality denied. 'The table is square' may be denied by 'the table is round', but not by 'the table is wooden'. The only reason we can deny 'the table is square' by 'the table is round' is that what is round is *not* square. And this has to be a *fact*, though just as negative as the fact that this table is not square. Thus it is plain that incompatibility cannot exist without negative facts.[9]

But, though he acknowledged negative facts, Russell found it problematic to claim acquaintance with such entities. In fact, just as he and others found claims of acquaintance with bare particulars to be unfounded, Russell held it to be obvious that we were not acquainted with negative facts. "There is no way of visualizing 'A-not-to-the-left-of-B'. When we attempt it, we find ourselves visualizing 'A-to-the-right-of-B' or something of the sort. This is one strong reason for the reluctance to admit negative facts."[10] Yet, Russell did see that there was a problem for one, like himself, who held to a principle of acquaintance, which required him to hold that all primitive terms of an ideal schema refer to *aspects of experience*. For, one can raise a question about the logical terms that we take as primitive. Thus, if one excludes the logical terms from such a requirement, one must provide a reason for doing so in the form of an account of how such terms function in judgments "about" what is or is not the case. It is worth recalling that this question about "logical" terms was involved in Moore's dispute with the idealists, in Bradley's worries about judgment, and in Frege's account of meaning. It is especially pointed to recall that Frege recognized *The False* as an *object* and that idealists can be taken to claim that the existential quantifier must range only over objects of experience to be meaningfully used. With respect to a criterion for meaningful terms, Russell held that: "Every proposition which we can understand must be composed wholly of constituents with which we are acquainted."[11] Here, we must understand that the "constituents" he speaks of are constituents of his propositions$_R$, in the sense of Chapter VII, or, as we have been using the term, of *facts*. On the other hand, the proposition we "can understand" is a proposition$_V$. The question involved is really twofold. One aspect is about the existence of negative, universal, and existential facts, if we confine our concern about logical terms to negation and the quantifiers. The other aspect concerns the question of acquaintance with the *correspondents* of those logical terms. For Russell, this latter question was one of understanding how the logical notions functioned in judgment or belief.

Sellars has recently raised the problem by criticizing Russell for not realizing a damaging consequence of his use of definite descriptions.[12] Russell, along the lines we discussed in connection with Moore's attack on idealism, held that we can use definite descriptions to "denote" material objects. We could not *refer* to *them* by logically proper names, since we are not *acquainted* with (do not directly apprehend) such objects. Sellars finds this problematic for Russell, since expansions of sentences with such definite descriptions will contain the universal quantifier ranging over all material objects. Hence, every material object would be a constituent of such a proposition (fact). Consequently, Russell would have to claim acquaintance with all material objects, if he is to adhere to the above quoted view about propositions we can understand.

If correct, Sellars's criticism would be a serious one. But, Sellars has presupposed two things. First, he assumes that if there are universal facts, Russell would hold them to have one or more constituents in virtue of which they are universal facts and, second, that the constituents in virtue of which they are such facts will be all the objects in the range of the quantifier. However, although Russell does hold to the existence of negative, existential, and universal facts in the lectures on logical atomism, he does not hold to either of Sellars's implicit assumptions. He is quite explicit about the case of negative facts in "On Propositions":

It must not be supposed that the negative fact contains a constituent corresponding to the word 'not'. It contains no more constituents than a positive fact of the correlative positive form. The difference between the two forms is ultimate and irreducible. We will call this characteristic of a form its *quality*. Thus facts, and forms of facts, have two opposite qualities, positive and negative.

. . . The subject of negative facts might be argued at great length, but as I wish to reach the proper topic of my paper, I will say no more about it, and will merely observe that a not dissimilar set of considerations shows the necessity of admitting *general* facts, i.e., facts about all or some of a collection.[13]

Notice that Russell, in the last sentence, speaks of general facts being "about" all or some of a collection. This is *not* to be taken as the claim that such facts *contain* all or some members of the collection *as constituents*. In the 1918 lectures, Russell is again quite explicit: "I do not profess to know what the right analysis of general facts is. It is an exceedingly difficult question, and one which I should very much like to see studied."[14] Moreover, there is a logical consideration that weighs very strongly against Sellars's assumptions. Russell's well-known argument for universal facts is:

> It is perfectly clear, I think, that when you have enumerated all the atomic facts in the world, it is a further fact about the world that those are all the atomic facts there are about the world, and that is just as much an objective fact about the world as any of them are. It is clear, I think, that you must admit general facts as distinct from and over and above particular facts. The same thing applies to 'All men are mortal'. When you have taken all the particular men that there are, and found each one of them severally to be mortal, it is definitely a new fact that all men are mortal; how new a fact, appears from what I said a moment ago, that it could not be inferred from the mortality of the several men that there are in the world.[15]

Suppose each material object was a constituent of a fact Sellars is discussing. There would still have to be some further *aspect* of the fact to ensure that such constituents were actually *all* objects of that kind. In short, Sellars's construal *could be* correct if one took a universal fact as a conjunction of atomic facts and acknowledged conjunctive facts. But, Russell explicitly rejects this way of construing universal facts. According to Russell, there is some other aspect, he knows not what, that makes a fact universal. Moreover, it might well be that such an aspect would not merely be a necessary condition for a fact being universal. It might be a sufficient condition as well. Thus, the presence of such an aspect would mean that the universal fact did not contain all material objects as constituents. One could then be acquainted with that aspect without being *acquainted* with all material objects in order to "understand" the proposition. Furthermore, given Russell's "logical Platonism"[16] in the years before his Logical Atomism, it is possible that Russell would still hold that such logical aspects were not constituents of facts but "entities" nevertheless. In any case, Sellars cites a passage from *The Problems of Philosophy* written when Russell clearly is a logical Platonist. Thus, his criticism fails.

Russell's talking of propositions the way he does helps muddle matters. He is thinking in terms of so-called image propositions depicting facts. Thus, an image proposition "about" a white square object being over a green rectangle could consist of an image that *was* white and square in the appropriate spatial relation to another image that was green and rectangular. The fact having the images as constituents *is the proposition* about the fact having the represented objects as constituents. Talk of acquaintance here means that the image proposition being understandable presupposes that the constituent objects, properties, and relations of the *represented* fact are known by acquaintance. Word propositions are then associated with image propositions or, in effect, replace them. Thus, names, such as '*a*' and '*b*', will replace the image that is white and square and the image that is green and rectangular, and a predicate, 'O', will replace the spatial relation the images stand in. We can then have as a verbal image the visual pattern

$$(V_p) \quad aOb,$$

which, like the more colorful visual image, stands for the fact that the original objects stand in a specific spatial relation. We understand *the token* (V_p), if we are acquainted with those objects and the spatial relation. The question that concerns Russell, and which is basic for us, is one regarding the treatment of patterns like

$$\sim aOb$$

and

$$(x)(\sim xOb),$$

assuming we allow for such patterns on their customary "understanding." Given Russell's *Principle of Acquaintance*, one question is about the introduction of the *logical signs* in conformity with it. Another question relates to the analysis of the *logical facts*, if I may so call them, that Russell acknowledges: existential, universal, and negative facts.

Sellars's argument presupposes, without any basis, a solution that would treat logical terms as Russell treats names and predicates—as standing for constituents of facts. Moreover, he further, and without basis, specifies what the constituents are in the case of a universal fact. Thus, his criticism fails on two counts. Yet, we can understand how Sellars is led to think of Russell's analysis in the way he does when we recognize a basic feature of Sellars's own analysis of such issues. Considering that will also reveal a crucial common thread that connects Sellars's views on logical concepts, abstract entities, and the analysis of thought. It will also reveal that the same glaring defect is at the very basis of all three analyses.

Sellars uses the same approach to eliminate the problem about negation that he has used to defend nominalism and to deny a basic intentional or referential connection between thought and language, on the one hand, and what the latter intend or refer to, on the other. He introduces the device of dot quotes so that we may form "metalinguistic sortals" that apply across languages and, hence, classify different terms that play the same linguistic role in different languages. Thus, whereas we might say:

(w₁)   'white' designates white

but

(w₂)   'white' does not designate blanc,

we could have

(w₃)   ˙white˙ designates white and blanc.

However, to avoid the "Platonistic" flavor of (w₃), Sellars takes

(w₄)   The 'white' and the 'blanc' are ˙white˙s

to more perspicuously express what (w₃) does. (w₄), in turn, is elliptical for:

(w₅)   (x) [(x is a 'white' or x is a 'blanc') ⊃ x is a ˙white˙] ,

which brings out the predicative role of the metalinguistic sortals. He then proceeds to apply the pattern to: (a) The claim that predicates stand for properties; (b) The claim that there is an intentional or referential connection between signs and things, as in " 'a' stands for a"; (c) The problem about the connection between negations of atomic sentences and facts.

Sellars holds that we construe 'white is a property' as 'the ˙white˙ is a predicate' and, in this vein, treat 'a exemplifies whiteness' as 'the ˙white˙ is true of a'. The latter sentence holds if

˙a is white˙ is true,

which Sellars explicates as

    $^\bullet a$ is white$^\bullet$s are semantically assertible.

It is this last move that Sellars sees as differentiating his view from the triviality of Davidson's and Quine's appeal to 'is true of'.[17] Thus, in place of:

    'W_1' is true of $a \equiv$ '$W_1 a$' is true $\equiv a$ is white,

Sellars uses:

    'W_1' is true of $a \equiv$ $^\bullet W_1 a^\bullet$s are true $\equiv$ $^\bullet W_1 a^\bullet$s are semantically assertible.

In so doing, he makes two claims: first, that the problem of abstract entities is reduced to the problem of truth; and, second, that the problem of truth is reduced, in turn, to the explication of 'semantically assertible'. This notion, hereafter 'S-assertible', is relative to a "conceptual structure" and, hence, the unqualified sense of 'true' that *we* use is to be understood in terms of *our* conceptual structure. So, something is true when it is S-assertible in our conceptual structure. This structure (or framework or background schema) links up with extralinguistic reality in that "singular first-level matter-of-factual statements" have the job of "picturing." For them to play such a role depends on referring expressions being correlated with nonlinguistic objects. Such correlations are to be understood in terms of the "natural laws" governing the production of tokens of such sign patterns under appropriate conditions, the connections of tokens in accordance with "intralinguistic uniformities," and the production of further behavior consequent upon the occurrence of such tokens. Sellars's talk of correlations and laws brings to mind the sorts of things discussed in Charles Morris's *Signs, Language, and Behavior* and Russell's discussion of signs in *An Inquiry into Meaning and Truth*. In virtue of the lawful connections between tokens and objects, singular matter-of-factual propositions, as pictures, can be more or less adequate or correct. In its way, what Sellars says is true enough. If I assert a token of 'a is W_1', then for it to be a (more or less) correct picture (or element of a more or less correct picture of the world), the *production* of the token of 'a' (response) will be connected in the *natural order* with the object (partial stimulus). The token will also have numerous connections (via its type) with other linguistic patterns, through the "logical appratus" for example. It will also have effects, including causal connections with dispositions to behavior. The problem of abstract entities, or universals, is connected with all this insofar as bringing such matters into the discussion enables Sellars to specify just what the ground of truth is for 'W$_1$a' without recourse to the realist's universals. But all Sellars tells us, quite anticlimactically, is that the singular matter-of-factual statement 'W$_1$a' is a correct picture when tokens of that kind are correlated with *the appropriate object that is white:*

'f*a*'s (in L) correctly picture O as ∅
must be carefully distinguished from
'f*a*'s (in L) stand for that ∅O, and that ∅O is true.

The former tells us that (in L) utterances consisting of an 'f' concatenated with an '*a*' are correlated with O, which is ∅, in accordance with the semantic uniformities which correlate utterances of lower-case letters of the alphabet with objects such as O, and which correlate utterances of lower-case letters of the alphabet which are concatenated with an 'f' with objects which are ∅.[18]

In spite of Sellars's introduction of the device of dot quotes and his emphasis on "metalinguistic sortals," he thus ends up doing precisely what Davidson and Quine do when they take predicates to be "true of" particulars and not to refer to properties that particulars exemplify. Like Quine, Sellars holds that the realist must use *abstract singular terms*. This provides the appearance of another argument. As Sellars sees it, the realist's (w$_1$) is more perspicuously put as:

(w$_1$') 'white' designates whiteness.

But, as (w$_5$) or '(x)[x is a 'white' ⊃ x is a •white•]' states what is required, one may avoid such singular abstract names as 'whiteness' and, hence, avoid realism. Avoiding realism, the nominalist has supposedly linked the singular matter-of-factual statements with "extralinguistic reality" with a minimal ontological commitment. But, focusing attention on the use of abstract singular terms obscures matters. The problem of abstract entities or universals is a question of *to what*, if anything, primitive predicates *need be linked* so that Sellars's singular matter-of-factual statements (first-level atomic sentences) may be about and true of "extralinguistic reality." When we realize this, we also realize that the use of dot quotes and the transposition of (w_1), where both " 'white' " and 'white' function as subject terms for the relational predicate 'designates', into a statement with " 'white' " and '•white•' as *metalinguistic predicates*, does not disguise the fact that Sellars ultimately makes the same move made by those who employ Tarski's Convention-T to avoid facts and properties. For, he ultimately tells us that '$W_1 a$' is a correct picture of extralinguistic reality since the object that 'a' is correlated with is a white object. Thus, the move to "semantically assertible" merely postpones the inevitable appeal to the *two-fold* condition for '$W_1 a$' being a correct picture: (1) the name 'a' is correlated with an object O, and (2) '$W_1 a$'s are correlated with an object O that *is* white. Sellars thus *uses* the predicate 'white' in a predicative ascription, which is what gives rise to the problem of universals. He must, then, like Quine, simply beg the question about the ontological significance of such uses. There is, however, a difference between Sellars's gambit and that of someone like Davidson. Sellars can state what a truth condition is, in his own terms. A truth condition for an atomic sentence is an *object's being something*. In our example, it is the object *a being white*. For, the sentence '$W_1 a$' correctly pictures *a as white*. But, for Sellars, this does not involve the recognition of any entity besides the object *a*.

Sellars coordinates his critique of realism with a critique of a basic intentional relation. Consider:

'a' stands for *a*.

To Sellars this is a way of stating:

'a's are •a•s,

which is to say that

(x)(x is an 'a' ⊃ x is an •a•).

And this is to say that the tokens of 'a' in a language function according to the linguistic role for which "•a•" stands. The specification of such a role involves the characterization of the causal and logical context of the production and use of tokens of '*a*'. But, we cannot specify such conditions in terms of such tokens *referring to* anything. This means that Sellars cannot explicate the sense of 'reference' involved in our discussion of the stipulatory acts of Chapter III. When I label an object by

Let '*a*' stand for . . .,

I neither predict nor prescribe future natural connections between tokens of '*a*' and the object labeled. I do correlate *the sign* with an object and thereby take it to refer to the object. This does not mean that every future occurrence of such a token will be so used. Even if each token were so used, that would obviously not explain what it *means to use the token to refer.* Moreover, sometimes one may refer to an object by a pure demonstrative, 'this' or 'that', without any correlation being stipulated in a distinguishable thought. One may do the same with names. Consider an object with the property F. Without baptizing the object by the name '*a*', you may say to yourself that *a* is F knowing *that* you are referring and to *what* you are referring. Such simple facts of thought and reference suffice to reject Sellars's appeal to the causal context and dispositions to utter sentences. Sellars's appeal to "momentary" dispositions that are to be identified (in the scientific millenium) with micro states does not help. At most, we would be offered the traditional correlation that the materialist seeks to transform into an identity. This aspect of the issue we touched on in an earlier discussion of Moore in Chapter III, and we shall return to it in later chapters. If the most one can claim is that dispositions to behave and micro states are factually correlated with thoughts, then one can obviously not *explain* what it *means* to use a token referentially by appealing to such dispositions and states.

Another pattern of Sellars's will also not help, since it will not do to treat cases of reference, even explicit stipulations of a "baptismal" sort, along the lines of either rules for games or moral prescriptions. Consider a rule of chess about the moves of the pawn. Given the rule, we may say that a certain move obeyed the rule, under appropriate circumstances. Given a semantical "rule" of the form 'Let _ _ _ stand for (refer to) . . .', we may also speak of the use of a token to refer to the object in question as obeying the rule. But, it will do so if and only if it is an appropriate token that *is used to refer to* the appropriate object. Yet, one cannot appeal to the rule to explain what it means to refer to the object on a given occasion. Rather, one can only understand what it is to obey the rule in terms of using a token to refer to the appropriate object. Thus, Sellars can explicate neither the *use* of 'refers to' nor what is *meant* by saying that a given token refers to a given object.

Sellars employs the same pattern in the case of logical terms that he uses in the rejection of abstract entities and reference.[19] In fact, the case of logical terms supposedly provides a *reductio* of both realism and the construal of 'stands for' as a relational predicate indicating a basic relation between a sign and an entity. The argument goes as follows. If one takes " 'white' stands for the color white" to indicate a correlation between a sign and an entity, then one should also take " 'not' stands for not" in the same way. But, the latter is clearly absurd. Hence, so is the former. In the case of 'not', we clearly connect a sign with another sign. Thus, " 'not' stands for not" should be seen to be like " '∼' stands for not," which explicitly shows that we correlate a sign of one language with a sign of another language. More perspicuously yet, we should use

'∼' and 'not' are (translations) terms with the same role (roughly).

But, then, we can have a term, '•not•', for that role irrespective of a particular schema. Thus, we can use

'not's in English are •not•s.

Actually, the latter is not so puzzling, given the use of English as the background or metalanguage being employed in the discussion.

We can readily understand how Sellars's pattern guides his argument, but that is not to say that there is any force to the latter. Of course, we would not claim that 'not' stands for some nonlinguistic entity on the basis of sentences like:

'∼' stands for not
'inte' in Swedish stands for not
'not' stands for negation.

We can also recognize that the second of these sentences is a way of stating a correlation between terms of different languages. But, all this should not be confused with a philosophically relevant argument that refutes philosophical claims regarding logic and ontology. No realist bases his case on the truth of "'W_1' stands for white" anymore than he naively overlooks the fact that one can state that "'W_1' is transcribed by 'white'" or "'vit' means 'white'." Rather, the realist tries to argue that one must take primitive predicates to stand for universal properties to account for and analyze truths such as 'a is white and b is white'. Analogous problems arise about logical terms. Sellars no more disposes of the issue about negation and negative facts than he disposes of abstract entities and *reference*. Supposedly, just as the replacement of (w_1) by '(x)(x is a 'white' ⊃ x is a •white•)' disposes of the need for acknowledging the property white, that replacement also shows that *designates* (or *stands for* or *refers*) is a "pseudo-relation." But, to show *that*, one must claim that specifying what it *means* to be a •white•, i.e., to have a certain "role," does not require taking such a term to signify the color and this, of course, is circular. We also saw that this is not an issue limited to the problem of abstract entities, for the same issue arises for proper names. But, since it is clearly *possible* for an occurrence of a token of a sign pattern to occur in a thought and *refer or not, irrespective of the causal context and the micro state of the person*, Sellars's attempt to buttress his cases against abstract entities and intentional relations by linking the purported "pseudo" entities and "pseudo" relations fails. As so often happens in such matters, the linking of two issues "cuts" both ways.

Sellars's transposition of his "neo-Fregean" account of belief into his version of a behavioral account of thought brings into stark relief his attempt to avoid the recognition of an intentional relation. As one would expect, Fregean propositions become linguistic roles, and beliefs become dispositions to utter tokens of an appropriate kind. Consequently, the questions about substitution and quantification in belief contexts become questions about the replacement of and quantification from *tokens* in such contexts. Jones's belief that −fa, which we discussed in Chapter VIII, is characterized in terms of Jones being disposed to utter a token that is an `•fa•`.[20] This, in turn, can be construed in terms of Jones being disposed to utter an "•f• concatenated with an •a•." Then, to make the obvious point, we cannot replace the "•a•" by '(ιi)(i = •a•)' or by "•(ιi)(i = a)•" or by "•(ιi)(i = •a•)•". Likewise, we can generalize to:

> There is some role such that Jones is disposed to utter a token that is an •f• concatenated with a token characterized by that role.

However, we cannot get:

> Jones is disposed to utter a token that is an •(∃x)• concatenated with an •f• concatenated with an •x•.

In short, the problems are handled by taking belief contexts to involve quoted expressions rather than references to Fregean entities. What is, then, clearly problematic is the *connection* between Sellars's linguistic roles, and tokens, and what they are used to *state*. Sellars can only answer that:

(1)   The •a• is *correlated* with a, and

(2)   The •fa• is *correlated* with a which is f.

'Correlated', recall, here means that tokens that are •a•s are *connected* with a, which is f, in the *natural order* in accordance with the *semantic uniformities*. Thus, to say that Jones believes that −fa is to hold that he is disposed to utter appropriate tokens under appropriate circumstances. This clearly will not do as an analysis of what it is to believe that a is f, even though it may well be true that one has such a belief if and only if one is so disposed. This is the same problem we noted earlier in the discussion of "W" and "not", and which arose for Russell's version of the behavioristic account. We shall return to the question in Chapter XIII.

There is a minor point worth noting in connection with recent attempts to dismiss facts and correspondence theories of truth. Some philosophers have suggested that one can eliminate talk about "meaning" in terms of speaking about truth conditions. Thus,

> s knows the meaning of 'p'

is supposedly analyzable in terms of

> s knows that ['p' is true if and only if Ø] ,

where 'p' is a definite sentence and 'Ø' is a "metalinguistic" statement *of* the condition for 'p'. Given that the traditional appeal to facts and possibilities trivially involves

> s knows the meaning of 'p' if and only if s knows that 'p' *stands for or means* p,

where the relevant sentence is an atomic sentence, the *new* gambit is new only in that it attempts to avoid "s knows that 'p' *means* p" in favor of "s knows that ['p' is true if and only if Ø] ." This obviously reflects the difference between acknowledging and avoiding facts and possibilities. Thus, the *new* appeal to truth conditions, to avoid "meaning," is merely *the adoption of the picture or reference theory of meaning*, of the logical atomists, *coupled with the denial that there are facts as truth conditions*. Hence, if the rejection of facts is not plausible, along Davidson's lines, the account of meaning in terms of "truth" is pointless.

Russell's
Theory of Judgment
and Sellars's
Critique of It

In *The Problems of Philosophy* of 1912, Russell proposed to construe a sentence like

(S₁)   Othello believes that Desdemona loves Cassio

as expressing a four-term relation, say Bel^4, holding among Othello, Desdemona, Cassio, and *loves* as *terms*. Thus,

(S₂) Bel^4 (Othello, Desdemona, loves, Cassio)

would more perspicuously exhibit the form of the *fact* stated by
(S₁). He advocated such a view because he held that to take (S₁)
to express a two-term relation between Othello and a proposition
(that Desdemona loves Cassio) or other complex (Desdemona's
love for Cassio) would be to introduce entities corresponding to
false sentences. This would be unacceptable since it would mean
that we "would require that there should be objective falsehoods,
which subsist independently of any minds; and this . . . is a theory
to be avoided if possible."[1] In the fourth essay of the lectures of
"The Philosophy of Logical Atomism" of 1918, Russell again took
up the question of the logical form of (S₁), or, rather, of the fact
corresponding to it. He still rejected the view that would analyze
(S₁) in terms of a relation between Othello and a proposition.

The awkwardness of that is that obviously propositions are nothing. Therefore that cannot be the true account of the matter.

To suppose that in the actual world of nature there is a whole set of false

309

propositions going about is to my mind monstrous. . . . I think a false proposition must, wherever it occurs, be subject to analyses, be taken to pieces, pulled to bits, and shown to be simply separate pieces of one fact in which the false proposition has been analysed away.[2]

His point was that I cannot take 'I believe p' as expressing either a relation between myself and a fact or as a relation between myself and a proposition. The reason is that we must have the same analysis, irrespective of whether the belief is true or false. Hence, since when the belief is false there is no fact, the belief cannot be analyzed in terms of a relation between a person and a fact. Since false propositions do not exist, one cannot analyze a belief in terms of a relation to such a proposition. Thus, the fact that there are false beliefs rules out the analysis in terms of either facts or propositions. Russell concludes:

The logical form is just the same whether you believe a false or a true proposition. Therefore in all cases you are not to regard belief as a two-term relation between yourself and a proposition, and you have to analyze up the proposition and treat your belief differently. Therefore the belief does not really contain a proposition as a constituent but only contains the constituents of the proposition as constituents.[3]

But, what is the structure of such a belief-fact? By this time, Russell is no longer satisfied with the account of 1912. The point of dissatisfaction is the occurrence of two verbs in the account that makes use of (S_2), or, to put it another way, that account employs a verb as a *term* while retaining its function as a verb.

You have this odd state of affairs that the verb 'loves' occurs as relating Desdemona to Cassio whereas in fact it does not do so, but yet it does occur as a verb, it does occur in the sort of way that a verb should do. I mean that when A believes that B loves C, you have to have a verb in the place where 'loves' occurs. You cannot put a substantive in its place. Therefore it is clear that the subordinate verb (i.e., the verb other than believing) is functioning as a verb, and seems to be relating two terms, but as a matter of fact does not when a judgment happens to be false. This is what constitutes the puzzle about the nature of belief.[4]

With this, Russell leaves us with a problem. We must recognize that we have two verbs. This is not only problematic in itself but apparently forces us to recognize what obviously does not exist, which is not acceptable. One year later he returned to the problem in his essay "On Propositions: What They Are and How They Mean." In this essay, he used his acknowledgment of negative facts, which he had already accepted in the lectures on logical atomism. Given a set of constituents:

(C) {Desdemona, loves, Cassio},

he held that there is a fact of one of two correlated forms:

(S₃) Desdemona loves Cassio

(S₄) Not-Desdemona loves Cassio.

As we noted in the previous chapter, Russell holds that negation is not a constituent of a fact but a "quality" of it: facts are of a negative or positive character. But, such a way of putting matters invites an obvious question. Is a fact, as a subject of such a quality, to be recognized as an entity? If so, do we not then have a three-fold dichotomy: *something*, the fact, indicated by the atomic sentence irrespective of the latter's truth value *and* that *something as qualified*, which is then the ground of truth of one sentence and of the falsehood of the other sentence of the pair? Depending on which quality, positive or negative, the fact has, the atomic sentence of the pair will be true or false. But, then, is this not merely a way of acknowledging *possibilities* that *are* either *actual* (positive facts) or *mere possibilities* (negative facts)? If not, what force is there in the use of the term 'quality' as it applies to a characteristic of facts? But, there is no point in disputing whether or not Russell's discussion reveals an implicit acknowledgment of possibilities. He holds that to a set of appropriate constituents we have correlated either a positive or a negative fact. One may suggest, therefore, that we need not talk of possibilities. Alternatively, one may observe that we speak of *a pair* of facts, one positive and one negative, for *each* such *set* of constituents. Yet, of the pair, only one such fact will exist. I see no difference in such talk from talk of a possibility that is actual or not, but, be that as it may, Russell proceeds to his analysis of (S₁).

The structure of his view may be put in the following way. In the simplest case there occurs a fact composed of images (or of sensations and images) such that the image-fact represents the fact that Desdemona loves Cassio. The latter "fact" is now called the *objective* of the belief, and the former fact is classified as the content. In addition, there is a feeling of a particular kind that is related to the content and in virtue of which the occurrence of that content is a belief, rather than a doubt. In short, the view suggested in Chapter III is basically modeled on Russell's account. But, what Russell does not account for is the distinction between the belief as a particular fact and the belief as a *kind*, of which that particular fact is an instance. Nor does he apparently recognize that in holding such a view he is explicitly forced to recognize the *objective* when it does not exist. For, to account for the belief being of the kind it is will require that he hold that it is so either in that it is related to an objective or in that it has a character shared with all particular beliefs of the same content. Thus, he will be forced to propositions, in a Fregean sense, or propositional characters, in Bergmann's sense, or nonexistent facts, in Moore's sense, or possibilities. In his way, Russell makes the same mistake Moore did. Whereas Moore avoided the embarrassment of speaking of what "obviously does not exist" by uncritically speaking of "nonexistent facts," Russell apparently believes he avoids the problem by the acceptance of negative facts. The distinction between positive and negative facts does not help here, even though it might be taken to suffice for the account of the truth or falsehood of (S_3). For, given the occurrence of the belief content, as a fact that *represents* another fact, it is clear that the content represents in virtue of its connection to something else—the fact it represents. If the content is false, the existence of a negative fact will not account for that connection unless one explains that the content is *connected with a pair of facts*. But, this, I have suggested, acknowledges possibilities in other words.

We can put the problem quite simply. Let there be two image facts, or contents in Russell's sense, that are instances of what we would say are the *same* belief. Being instances of the same belief, they share a characteristic, say $\emptyset$. The question that arises is, "In virtue of what, on Russell's view, are both facts instances of $\emptyset$?" That is, what is the analysis of the assertion that both facts are $\emptyset$'s? The only answer Russell can give is that both represent the same pair of facts, one positive and one negative, which make the belief true or false, depending on which one of the pair exists. This acknowledges possibilities. Russell, however, does not give this or any answer. Like Moore, he glides over the problem. However, Russell returned to the problem in *An Inquiry into Meaning and Truth*. There he acknowledged that particular beliefs, or instances of a belief, intend what they do in virtue of a common property.

> There is one important respect in which the above theory is still incomplete; it has not decided what two states must have in common in order to be instances of the same belief. When verbal habits are sufficiently developed, we may say that two states are instances of the same belief if they can be expressed by the same sentence. Perhaps the only definition is causal: two states are instances of the same belief when they cause the same behavior. (This will, in those who possess language, include the behavior that consists in uttering a certain sentence.)[5]

Taken one way, Russell's characterization of $\emptyset$ says nothing in that the problem is to characterize or specify when two particular states may be expressed by the same sentence. Taken in another way, he specifies $\emptyset$ in terms of behavioral responses. In simplest terms, a mental state, m, is taken to be a $\emptyset$-state if a person having m does r under conditions s. Russell's speaking of a causal "definition" can also be taken in two ways. He could be offering the following definition of "person p is in a $\emptyset$-state":

> p is in a $\emptyset$-state = $_{df}$ p does r in s, or if p is in condition s, then p does r.

This would construe a mental state as a "disposition" of a person to behave in a certain manner under certain circumstances. Alternatively, Russell could mean to characterize $\emptyset$ causally and not to define '$\emptyset$-state', just as one might characterize or identify a color in terms of its being the color of a certain object without thereby "defining" a color predicate. In this vein, he might take $\emptyset$ to be a state that a person is in if and only if the person does r under s, but he does not hold that to say that p is in $\emptyset$ is to say that if p is in s, then p does r. Thus, he does not take *being in $\emptyset$* to be a *disposition* to do r under s. Rather, being in $\emptyset$ is to be in a mental state that is *the cause* of doing r under s. In effect, this is to specify $\emptyset$ by means of a definite description as *the* mental state which causes p to do r under s. Such a way of specifying $\emptyset$ poses two problems.

First, one must presuppose that there is a unique state that is *the* cause of behavior *r* under conditions *s*. Second, one offers neither a significant causal connection or law nor a satisfactory solution to the philosophical problem involved. To propose a significant causal connection would be to offer the "law":

(L)   (p)(p is in $\emptyset \supset$ (p is in $s \supset$ p does r)).

But if $\emptyset$ is specified as Russell specifies it, that law becomes

(L′)   (p) [(p is in *the* state M which is such that for any q, q
          is in that state $\equiv$ ((q is in s) $\supset$ (q does r))) $\supset$
          (p is in $s \supset$ p does r)] .

(L′), however, trivializes (L) in the sense that given that an individual, say p_1, fulfills the *left side* of (L′), it *logically follows* that p_1 fulfills the right side. We, thus, have neither a law nor an explanation of the behavior of p_1. Moreover, unless one thinks in terms of causal connections being the necessary connections of the rationalist tradition, it is clear that the mental state *m*, of p_1, need not have the causal consequences it does have while being one and the same state. Thus, aside from the triviality of using (L′), Russell's "causal account" of $\emptyset$ will not do as a purported *analysis* of the fact that *m* is a $\emptyset$-state, for to give such an analysis is to give, on the account in question, purported necessary and sufficient conditions for the existence of what is analyzed and to deny the possibility of having either the analysans or the analysandum without the "other." Thus, if one takes a fact that *a* is F to be a particular, *a*, exemplifying a universal property, F, then, given that we have *a* exemplifying F, we have the fact and vice versa. That account cannot acknowledge, given the proposed analysis, that one can have the fact that *a* is F without having the proposed analysis. Of course, one can insist that we cannot have *m* as the kind of thought it is without having the causal context both *for and of* it. But, this involves the proposed analysis in two paradoxical consequences. First, the causal analysis must turn the notion of "causal account" into a problematic concept by holding that causal connections are "analytic." Second, the account does not jibe with the preanalytic notion that the statements of the causal consequences of having thoughts of certain kinds are significant factual claims. These problems are reflected in Russell's problematic use of (L') in place of (L). One problem with Russell's causal account is that one cannot have such an account involve a cogent philosophical claim while allowing for nonanalytic causal claims. The same kind of problem besets the view that takes the property of being in a Ø-state *to be* a disposition to behave, but we shall take up that view later. Russell does not, then, resolve his problems with the analysis of (S_1) even as late as the *Inquiry*. In fact, by looking to a causal account, he, in effect, abandons the philosophical problem.

In "On Propositions," Russell had yet another problem: how to account for beliefs involving negation:

Othello believes that Desdemona does not love Iago.

With beliefs of the form *that a is not R to b*, Russell's account faces the classical puzzle we noted in the last chapter. He must account for the occurrence of the negative "content" while adhering to his views about meaning and acquaintance. Russell could have held that one is acquainted with the "quality" of a negative fact and thereby provided a basis for the occurrence of negation in the content of a belief. But, this would not fit with his denial that we can have an image of a negative fact. What he did was deny that negation belongs to the content of basic image propositions. In the case of such propositions, negation enters as a "feeling" *directed* to the content and not as part of the content. Thus, negation is to be understood in terms of *disbelief* of what is expressed by the content. He, thus, came to deny an earlier claim he had made in a criticism of Meinong:

Admitting, as it seems we must, that negation can only be derived through propositions, there is an important distinction to be made, without which confusions will become almost unavoidable. To deny a proposition is not the same as to affirm its denial. The case of an assumption will itself make this clear. Given any proposition p, there is an associated proposition not-p. Either of these may, as Meinong points out, be merely supposed or assumed. But when we deny p, we are not concerned with a mere assumption, and there is nothing to be done with p that is logically equivalent to assuming not-p. And direct inspection, I think, will show that the state of mind in which we reject a proposition is not the same as that in which we accept its

negation. . . . It would seem there are two states of mind which both have p
for their object, one affirming and the other denying; and two other states of
mind, having not-p for their object, one affirming and the other denying.[6]

But, now, under pressure to account for the "meaning" of 'not'
in 'not-p', Russell appeals to the view he earlier rejected. In a word
proposition, there can be, he claims, two kinds of contents:
those that contain negation signs and those that do not. It is with
his basic image propositions that he must find a way to introduce
negation in conformity with his views about acquaintance. What he
claims is that we know what the negation sign means by (1) knowing what a feeling of disbelief is and (2) holding that there are two
qualities of facts so that a fact with one quality makes a disbelieved image proposition a true belief. Note that what is true is not
the "propositional content" in the case of such an image proposition. Rather, it is the content *plus* the feeling of disbelief that is
the true belief. This raises a problem that Russell had been impressed by in his earlier discussion of Meinong, but that he apparently overlooks in his later discussion. When Russell introduces
word propositions, he can still speak of a feeling of belief and a
content as well as of a feeling of disbelief and a content. We then
have a negation sign that can be "part of" the content of a word
proposition. Hence, we can consider the contents in two cases to
be:

(C_1)   Desdemona loves Iago

(C_2)   Not-Desdemona loves Iago,

with (C_1) being accompanied by a feeling of disbelief while (C_2) is
the *object* of a feeling of belief. We then have two *particular* beliefs (or states of belief) that are *combinations* of *contents* and appropriate *feelings*. Both beliefs, as such combinations, are true (let
us imagine). Are such particular facts, as combinations of content
and feeling, instances of the *same* belief or not? Russell has no answer, for there are two conflicting themes. On the one hand, the
contents are different; on the other, the difference of content has
been originally accounted for in terms of the difference in feeling
—in the case of the basic image propositions in terms of which
word propositions are "given" meaning. Since the *feeling* of dis-

belief *about a content* is what provides a basis in experience for the meaningful use of the negation sign when one believes (C_2), Russell should either hold that negation does not belong to the content or distinguish between the verbal content, containing a negation sign, and what that verbal content expresses or represents. Since he seeks to avoid propositions in a Fregean sense, he does not make the latter distinction explicitly, perhaps thinking that his distinction between image propositions and verbal propositions takes care of the matter. But, it does not. Rather, Russell has introduced a number of problems. Recall that Russell has used negation in another way by talking of the quality of a fact. How is such a negative quality "known" by "acquaintance"? Russell seems to have forgotten about such a "quality" in his focusing on the feeling of disbelief. Talking about the latter does not answer the query about the former. If anything, it leads to a further problem. What is the connection between the quality of negation that some facts "have" and the feeling of disbelief directed to some contents? It would appear that the feelings about contents *represent* the qualities of facts, so that the feeling-pair, belief and disbelief, are taken to be involved in true or false judgments, depending on which member of the quality-pair, positive and negative, characterizes *the fact*. But, then, just as we have recognized contents distinct from feelings, have we not recognized what they represent—facts or possibilities—distinct from their two qualities? Once again, Russell's attempt to avoid talking about what "obviously does not exist" seems frustrated.

There is another problem involved in his way of putting matters. For, he has apparently forced himself into the awkward position of holding that the positive judgment or belief, that is true or false as the case may be, is a combination of the content plus the feeling of assent or belief. Thus, truth and falsity take on a dual function; for contents, like (C_1), are true or false and combinations of content and feeling are true or false. Since (C_1) is false, a combination, which is a fact consisting of a positive feeling of belief directed to (C_1), is false. This dual role of truth and falsity reveals a basic fault in Russell's analysis. In the case of negative verbal contents like (C_2), the negation sign stands for either the

318   Russell's Theory of Judgment

quality of the fact or the feeling of disbelief. If it stands for the latter, one fails to get the right content, if one wishes to express that

Othello believes that not-(Desdemona loves Iago).

This is so, since Othello does not believe that disbelief is directed toward (C_1). If the negation sign in (C_2) stands for the quality in virtue of which some facts are negative facts, Russell still faces his original problem, in spite of all the talk about negation in terms of belief and disbelief. He must, in keeping with his principle of acquaintance, hold that he knows such a quality by acquaintance. But, this he explicitly denies. And, he no longer, as in "The Philosophical Importance of Mathematical Logic" and the unpublished "Theory of Knowledge," appears to directly know subsistent logical objects. Thus, his analysis ultimately fails to meet his "empiricist" criterion of acquaintance. In short, he may hold that he is acquainted with a feeling of disbelief, but he must also hold that such a feeling is connected with the *quality of negation* in order to adequately account for beliefs being true or false in terms of positive or negative facts existing. Such a quality of negation is a basic *element* of his analysis of judgment and of truth. Yet, it is "something" with which he is not acquainted, for Russell, apparently, is no longer acquainted with logical *forms* or *entities*, as Platonic objects. Thus, he faces the problem of the meaningfulness of logical *terms* while adhering to a more restrictive version of a principle of acquaintance. But, about this he wavered (note 14, Chapter X).

Sellars has criticized Russell on another tack.[7] He has long argued against taking predicates to stand for "objects" and sees Russell as being trapped by such an error. Sellars's discussion takes off from Wittgenstein's puzzling but well-known remark:

> 3.1432 We must not say: 'The complex sign "*aRb*" says "*a* stands in the relation *R* to *b*"'; but we must say, '*That* "*a*" stands in a certain relation to "*b*" says that *aRb*'.

Wittgenstein's "insight," as Sellars interprets it, and as Russell had earlier interpreted it, is that the signs '*a*' and '*b*' stand in the relation

> . . . is to the left of the sign '*R*' which is to the left of the sign ____

(or something of that sort) and hence that 'R' does not function as a referring sign as the names '*a*' and '*b*' do. This suggests that we could have a simpler version of the point by using a spatial relation between tokens of the signs '*a*' and '*b*'. Instead of '*a*R*b*', we would have something like '*ᵃb*', and instead of *b*R*a*', we would use '*ᵇa*', and so forth. I think Sellars has misunderstood Wittgenstein's claim. In the *Tractatus*, Wittgenstein is very much of a Fregean. Although names stand for *objects*, predicates and relation terms stand for *functions*. But, in keeping with the extreme picture theory of language, Wittgenstein thinks that what represents a function should itself *be* a function and *not merely be* a sign for a function with a special syntactical characterization. Names for objects *are* themselves objects; function signs *must be* functions. Thus, for Wittgenstein, the sign 'xRy' is not merely a function sign, it *is a function*. Just as one might hold that the function for which the sign stands correlates a pair of objects to facts, say the pair $\{a;b\}$ to the fact *that* aRb, so the function, *that the sign is*, correlates a pair of signs $\{'a'; 'b'\}$ to a sentence, '*a*R*b*'. A statement of Ramsey's from this period is very revealing:

> In this respect there is an important difference between functions of functions and functions of individuals which is worth examining closely. It appears clearly in the fact that the expressions 'function of functions' and 'function of individuals' are not strictly analogous; for, whereas functions are symbols, individuals are objects so that to get an expression analogous to 'function of functions' we should have to say 'function of names of individuals'. On the other hand, there does not seem any simple way of altering 'function of functions' so as to make it analogous to 'function of individuals', and it is just this which causes the trouble. For the range of values of a function of individuals is definitely fixed by the range of individuals, an objective totality which there is no getting away from. But the range of arguments to a function of functions is a range of symbols, all symbols which become propositions by inserting in them the name of an individual.[8]

If my interpretation of Wittgenstein is correct, his nominalistic interpreters get no comfort from the *Tractatus*. Wittgenstein is not denying that there are functions, as Sellars seeks to do; he is merely *depicting them* in a unique way.

Sellars holds that we need not recognize the representational role of predicates. Hence, he suggests:

We can now construe (B) as having the form Believes (Othello: 'Desdemona' $R_{\text{'Loves'}}$ 'Cassio')

where this says that the propositional event occurring in Othello consists of a symbol for Desdemona and a symbol for Cassio with a 'loves' between these two symbols. The word 'loves' no longer appears as a constituent of the propositional event, hence we no longer have to specify that 'loves' symbolizes *loves*, but only that

> A propositional event consisting of a 'Desdemona' and a 'Cassio' with a 'loves' between them signifies that Desdemona loves Cassio.

And on the right side of *this*, 'loves' occurs as a *verb*. Our specific problem about relation words occurring only as relating has disappeared.[9]

What is the point Sellars seeks to make? He believes the problem lies in the use of 'loves' as a substantive term. Hence, if one avoids such a use and uses the term solely as a verb, the problems we have considered in the analysis of (S_1) are solved. We can see what Sellars is getting at if we momentarily ignore our concern with belief sentences and simply consider a pattern like 'aRb', where the signs 'a', 'b', and 'R' belong to a schema that we have not yet interpreted. One may supply a set of coordinating statements or interpretation rules as follows:

(1)   'a' refers to the object a.

(2)   'b' refers to the object β.

(3)   'R' stands for (the relation or relational property) is-to-the-left-of.

By giving such a set of coordinations, one may argue that we recognize the property R, just as we recognize the objects a and b. We recognize all *three entities* as a condition for the use of the signs 'a', 'b', and 'R', in the schema, to formulate sentences *about a* and b which involve 'R'. There are further conditions. We shall also have to employ formation rules such as:

(4)   A pattern consisting of a name followed by a two-termed predicate followed by a name is a sentence which states that the object named by the first name stands in the relation indicated by the predicate to the object named by the second name. ·

or, perhaps, something like:

(5)   A name followed by an 'R' followed by another name
       states that the first named object is-to-the-left-of the
       second named object.

One who seeks to avoid the claim that he has recognized properties and relations may believe he does so by using (5) in place of
(4) and, moreover, observing that by using (5) he need not use
(3). This latter move is important to such a philosopher since, in
(3), one uses the relation term 'is-to-the-left-of' as a substantive or
subject term and not as a predicate applying to a pair of subject
terms. But, to avoid (3) by the use of (5) is merely to avoid the
issue, if not to blatantly beg the question. For, such a philosopher
makes use of the phrase 'is-to-the-left-of' in a *supposedly* noncommittal way to interpret the term 'R'. Yet, the problem stems
from the question of whether a phrase like 'is-to-the-left-of' is
used in a noncommital manner, with respect to the problem of
universals, in statements like 'this object is-to-the-left-of that object'. One attempt to resolve such a question involves considering
a schematic perspicuous schema, about which we can ask which
terms need to be coordinated to objects, properties, relations, etc.,
so that the sentential patterns of the schema will purportedly describe situations obtaining in the domain we talk about. In setting
up the question this way, we take the objects *and* the properties
and relations to be acknowledged in a noncommittal way. That is,
there is a clear and straightforward sense in which there are colors
and spatial relations acknowledged, as well as objects, when we
say that an object has a color or that an object is-to-the-left-of
another object. What one may do is seek to avoid acknowledging
all such things by connecting terms of the schema to only some of
them and, nevertheless, obtaining correlates, in the schema, of
English sentences that *appear* to involve the acknowledgment of
the entities in question. What Sellars does is by-pass the question
by *using*, presumably in an innocent manner, the predicate and
relation terms of a natural language, as in (5), to obtain correlations of natural language sentences in the perspicuous schema. He
consequently avoids the problem of universals, rather than resolves

it, and concludes that he has disposed of our problem about belief contexts, since he feels Russell's problem is embodied in the use of (3) and (4).

With these distinctions and strategies under our belt, let us return to the problem of belief. We are asking how we can give the truth conditions for the belief ascribed to Othello by

(B) Believes (Othello, 'Desdemona', 'loves', 'Cassio').

The initial answer was that the belief is true just in case

(F) Desdemona loves Cassio.

The problem arose, however, that this is correct only if

(M) 'Loves' symbolizes *loves*,

which seems to require that the 'loves' on the right is a substantive expression which stands for a term in a symbolizing relationship. How can the relating relation of (F) be identical with a term of (M)?[10]

According to Sellars, when one uses (3), one is caught by the problem of using a relational term as a substantive. He then proceeds to offer the solution we considered earlier. But, notice just what Sellars's solution amounts to. We have been concerned with how the "content", or the *propositional fact*, expresses or states what it does and with what entities one acknowledges in giving a satisfactory account of that situation. Russell ran into the problem of acknowledging possibilities, as well as negative facts, in his attempted analysis. Sellars, in effect, asks "What is the problem?" The occurrence of a token of 'Desdemona' followed by the occurrence of a token of 'loves' followed by a token of 'Cassio' does not express what it does because

(A)   'Desdemona' stands for Desdemona
(B)   'Cassio' stands for Cassio
(C)   'loves' stands for loves
(D)   'Desdemona loves Cassio' stands for the situation (by a rule like (4)) that Desdemona loves Cassio.

Rather, forgetting all that, and particularly (C) and (D), the "token-fact" expresses what it does without our recognizing relations, facts, or possibilities, because the token fact states that Desdemona loves Cassio! That is all there is to it. The solution is as simple as the recognition that '*a*R*b*' is true, not because *a* stands in the relation is-to-the-left-of to *b*, but because *a* is-to-the-left-of *b*! Sellars, thus, applies his avoidance of the problems of universals and facts to the analysis of belief contexts. If he is considered to be successful in the former cases, we may acknowledge he wins the day in the latter case as well. If, however, one takes him, as I do, to avoid both questions and replace them with others — questions about the causal and behavioral context for our use of predicate expressions and our developing and exhibiting or "manifesting" beliefs — he resolves neither the problem of universals nor those stemming from belief contexts.

It is true that Russell, like Sellars, took the problem of analyzing belief contexts to involve the avoidance of the use of relation terms as substantive terms. For Russell, this did not mean that one sought to escape the recognition of relations. Rather, Russell could not see, in Fregean fashion, how a term could both function as a subject term and retain its role as a relation term. If we free ourselves from such a Fregean attitude, which, recall, involves holding that a predicate like 'red' cannot be a subject term in a sentence like 'Red is a color', one of Russell's problems is recognized as more apparent than real. The real problem in the use of the predicate 'loves', as a term in (S_2), is a different one, but, before dealing with it, a difference between Sellars and Russell is worth emphasizing. Following Frege, Russell held that a predicate could not function as a subject term in a sentence and still play its "predicative" role. For Russell, as for Frege, this meant that any sentence of the form 'F(f)', where 'F' and 'f' were constant predicate expressions of the appropriate types, was problematic. We noted earlier what problems this led to for Frege. Russell sought to resolve the "problem" by rejecting such problematic sentences. He did so by holding that all such sentences could be construed as sentences in which the subject term, here 'f', occurred only as a predicate and where the apparent predicate, here 'F', did not occur at all. Thus, if our example was 'Red is a color', we could construe such a sentence as

$(x)(Red(x) \supset Colored(x))$,

with the use of the *first-level predicate* 'colored' *replacing* the apparent second-level predicate 'color'. The obvious model for such elimination of the apparent second-level descriptive predicate 'color' was the treatment of logical predicates, like 'transitive', in the theory of relations Russell had developed. Recall that one may define 'transitive', as it occurs as a second-level predicate, as follows

$$\text{Trans}(R) =_{df.} (x)(y)(z)[(Rxy \ \& \ Ryz) \supset Rxz].$$

In the defining sentence pattern, no second-level predicate occurs. What Russell thus advocated was the doctrine that there were no primitive descriptive predicates of the higher types in a perspicuous or ideal schema. On some views of ontological commitment, this would mean that he held there were no descriptive properties of the higher types. Thus, he could be taken to advocate the doctrine some refer to as *elementarism*. For philosophers like Sellars and Quine, it is as if the doctrine of elementarism (and Russell's reasons for holding to it) becomes transformed into nominalism. In fact, Ryle literally employed Russell's transcription of sentences using predicates as subject terms into sentences using them only as predicates to argue that we need not recognize properties as Platonic entities.

'Colour involves extension' means what is meant by 'Whatever is coloured is extended'; 'hope deferred maketh the heart sick' means what is meant by 'whoever for a long time hopes for something without getting it becomes sick at heart.'

It is my own view that all statements which seem to be 'about universals' are analysable in the same way, and consequently that general terms are never really the names of subjects of attributes. So 'universals' are not objects in the way in which Mt. Everest is one, and therefore the age-old question what *sort* of objects they are is a bogus question. For general nouns, adjectives, etc., are not proper names, so we cannot speak of 'the objects called "equality," "justice," and "progress." '

Platonic and anti-Platonic assertions, such as that 'equality is, or is not, a real entity,' are, accordingly, alike misleading, and misleading in two ways at once; for they are both quasi-ontological statements and quasi-Platonic ones.[11]

Ryle, thus, quite early, applied the "Fregean pattern" in an explicitly ontological gambit that was to become the heart of Quine's *defense* of nominalism, through the distinction between "singular" and "general" terms and the corresponding claim that terms used in subject place or "quantified over" are the key to ontological commitment. It is also the root of Sellars's gambit. (S_2), of course, violates this view of predicates and properties. Consequently, it leads both Russell and Sellars to reject (S_2) as an adequate explication of (S_1). But, one need not subscribe to the view, restricting predicate terms to predicate places in sentences, to reject (S_2) as involving a problematic use of 'loves' and 'Bel^4'. For, in (S_2) we employ the relation Bel^4 not only to order the *terms* it relates but to order the terms related by the relation *loves*. In the sentence (S_2), the relational predicate 'Bel^4' is so construed that the names 'Desdemona' and 'Cassio' are arranged in the appropriate order in the sentence 'Desdemona loves Cassio'. The relation Bel^4 thus functions quite differently, with respect to the fact that (S_2) supposedly expresses, from the way an ordinary relation, say *loves*, does in the (supposed) fact that Desdemona loves Cassio. In the case of the latter fact, and the corresponding sentence 'Desdemona loves Cassio', we have an understood ordering of which terms in which order fill the gaps in the sentential form '. . . loves . . .'. No single gap is a place holder for a sentence, but neither does any sequence of gaps, when replaced, yield a sentence. This contrasts sharply with the case of the predicate 'Bel^4', where the ordinary language sentential form is '. . . believes that . . . .' and the replacement of the last three places *must* yield a sentence. This shows that although we do treat *loves* as a two-term relation, our construal of Bel^4 as a four-term relation is simply a "verbal" transformation. Such a transformation disguises the fact that we really treat *believes* as a two-term relation, where one linguistic term is a sentence. This point emerges quite clearly when we recognize that we shall introduce either a three-term relation, Bel^3, a five-term relation, Bel^5, and so on, to handle sentences like 'Othello believes that Desdemona is beautiful' and 'Desdemona believes that Othello gave her handkerchief to Iago' or be forced to treat *believes that* as a "term-ambiguous" relation. To believe that we have shown that 'believes that' can be treated like 'loves' in virtue of the use of (S_2) is to be deceived by a mere grammatical manipulation that neither reflects a philosophical analysis nor provides an insight into the issue. I find it no accident that the view in question has recently been resurrected by Quine, who, recall, advocates the replacement of grammatically proper names, 'Pegasus' for example, by introducing defined predicates, 'Pegasizes' in this case, in terms of sentences like

$$x \text{ Pegasizes} =_{df.} x = \text{Pegasus}$$

and then *dispensing* with the name. One who believes that he has dispensed with the "name" in such a manner may well believe that (S_2) is more than a mere rewriting of

(S_5)   Bel(Othello, Desdemona loves Cassio),

where one term is clearly a sentence.

On the basis of a criticism by Wittgenstein, Russell came to realize the inadequacy of (S_2). As Wittgenstein saw it, we make use of the rule that in the sentence form '. . . believes that . . . .' the replacement of the last three places must yield a well-formed sentence and not a nonsensical sequence of words.[12] What this clearly means is that we *explicate* (S_2) in terms of (S_5), rather than explicate (S_1) in terms of (S_2).

There is a further fundamental problem with the view that proposes to explicate (S_1) in terms of (S_2). We can get at it by considering a supposed advantage of that view over a view that involves the acknowledgment or the *introduction* of entities corresponding to the sentential term *in* (S_5), irrespective of whether that sentential term is a true or false sentence. Recall a problem we discussed earlier in connection with sentences like

(S_6)   Scott = Sir Walter.

and

(S_7)   George IV believes that Scott is (identical with) Sir Walter.

On the view which recognizes propositional entities, some feel forced to hold that we must abandon the rule that singular terms may replace other singular terms referring to the same entity in all contexts. The idea is that the propositions expressed by 'Scott is Sir Walter' and 'Scott is Scott' are different and, hence, (S_7) may be true but

(S$_8$)   George IV believes that Scott is Scott

may not be. Russell, recall, not accepting propositional entities in "On Denoting" and holding that names were purely indexical signs, maintained that (S$_8$) did follow from (S$_6$) and (S$_7$). One who advocates the use of (S$_2$) may, along similar lines, hold that the inference is permissible and no problem ensues. Thus, such a view attempts to retain the substitution rule for names in *episte-mic* contexts. Moreover, a corresponding problem regarding existential generalization does not arise on the view employing (S$_2$) but does arise on the view that acknowledges propositional entities and makes use of (S$_5$). For, from (S$_2$) one can unproblematically go to

(S$_9$) $(\exists x)\text{Bel}^4$ (Othello, Desdemona, loves, x).

Whereas, employing (S$_5$), we face the problem of distinguishing between

(S$_{10}$)   Bel(Othello, $(\exists x)$(Desdemona loves x))

and

(S$_{11}$) $(\exists x)$Bel(Othello, Desdemona loves x)

or, as we may render them in more ordinary terms,

(S$_{12}$)   Othello believes that there is someone whom Desdemona loves

and

(S$_{13}$)   There is someone such that Othello believes that Desdemona loves *that* individual.

Alternatively, one may hold that the relational view obscures the distinction. The supposed problems for the propositional view are several. Does (S$_{10}$) follow from (S$_5$)? If it does, what is the content expressed and what logical rules permit the introduction of the quantifier *within* the sentence pattern? If it does not, how does the view account for the apparently obvious truism that if Othello believes that Desdemona loves Cassio, he *must* believe that there is someone Desdemona loves? Does (S$_{11}$) follow from (S$_5$)? If it does, what is the content expressed and how does one reconcile the propositional view with the fact that the sentential term in (S_{11}) is a propositional function and not a proposition? That is, how can one believe what is expressed by an incomplete expression? If it does not, have we not abandoned an elementary rule of logic: existential generalization? We shall return to these issues in the next chapter. Here I am concerned with defects in the relational view that advocates the use of (S_2). The criticism of the propositional view reveals the problem for the relational view. For, although a proponent of the relational view may hold that there is no problem with regard to the existential generalization from (S_2), he must account for the obvious difference between (S_{12}) and (S_{13}). Although (S_9) may be taken to transcribe (S_{13}), one must offer a transcription of (S_{12}).

The attempt to transcribe (S_{12}) and distinguish it from (S_9) has involved a device we are familiar with from other contexts. One introduces a predicate, in this case '$(\exists x)(\hat{y}$ loves $x)$', which functions as a term in a sentence like

(S_{14}) Bel^3 (Othello, $(\exists x)(\hat{y}$ loves $x)$, Desdemona)

and which is held to be "true of" Desdemona. In short, as I would put it, the predicate stands for a "relational property" of Desdemona, and (S_{14}) and (S_9) thus become the respective transcriptions of (S_{12}) and (S_{13}) on the relational view. For one, like Quine, who is not disposed to speak of relational properties, or attributes at all, in such contexts the device of *semantic ascent* is readily at hand.

But there is a way of dodging the intensions which merits serious consideration. Instead of speaking of intensions we can speak of sentences, naming these by quotation. Instead of:

w believes that . . .

we may say:

w believes-true '. . .'.

Instead of:

w believes y(. . . y . . .) of x

we may say:

w believes '. . . y . . .' satisfied by x.

The words 'believes satisfied by' here, like 'believes of' before, would be viewed as an irreducibly triadic predicate.[13]

Here, I do not wish to reiterate the line of argument expressed in connection with similar applications of semantic levitation in our consideration of the views of Davidson and Sellars. There is a further point to be made, irrespective of whether one talks of relational properties or simply uses words about words by talking of relational predicates. But, since the point is more simply and obviously made in terms of properties and relations, I shall first put it in such a way. The relational view is forced to use '$(\exists x)(\hat{y}$ loves $x)$' as a monadic predicate term. Thus, it uses that predicate in a way that we need not do in nonintentional contexts. To say that the property *beautiful* is had by Desdemona or that Desdemona has the property of *being beautiful* is to say that Desdemona is beautiful. Similarly, to say that $(\exists x)(\hat{y}$ loves $x)$ is a relational property that Desdemona has is to say that there is someone Desdemona loves: $(\exists x)(\text{Desdemona loves } x)$. But, to make such a transcription in (S_{14}) is to transform (S_{14}) into (S_{10}) and return to the propositional view. Such a transformation cannot be permitted on the relational view. Thus, one either recognizes properties corresponding to relational predicates like '$(\exists x)(\hat{y}$ loves $x)$', *in addition to relations like loves*, or merely makes use of the notational difference, between such a one-term predicate and the two-term relation predicate, to hold that (S_{14}) is different from (S_{10}). The point comes out explicitly if we consider the relational property of *loving Cassio*. We could then write:

(S_{15}) $\text{Bel}^3(\text{Othello}, \hat{y} \text{ loves Cassio, Desdemona})$

to transcribe (S_1). But, it is clear that (S_{15}) is merely another way of writing (S_2). Actually, it is no more than a rewriting of (S_5). All one need do to see that is to replace the "variable" by the name. That aside, to reinforce the present point, consider the suggestion that '$\text{EX}(a,W)$' is a philosophically insightful or perspicuous way of writing 'Wa', with 'EX' for 'has', or 'exemplifies', or 'falls under'. Aside from the obvious connection with Bradley's puzzle, we would not find the suggestion illuminating. Similarly (S_{15}) is hardly a perspicuous way of rendering (S_2) and, consequently, we are not forced to acknowledge a monadic property indicated by '$\hat{y}$ loves Cassio' in addition to the relation indicated by 'loves'. This is obviously so if one believes that to say that Desdemona has the property is to say that she stands in the relation to Cassio. But, *there is no corresponding elimination procedure for the predicate* '($\exists$x)($\hat{y}$ loves x)' *in* (S_{14}). Thus, using (S_{14}) forces the recognition of the monadic relational property *loving someone*, in addition to the relation of loving. The relational view thus pays a two-fold ontological price in that it recognizes an indefinite number of belief relations of logically different kinds (three-term, four-term, etc.) and acknowledges relational properties in addition to relations. Alternatively, we may take such ontological excesses to reveal that the view is based on a notational, rather than a substantive, difference from the propositional view.

Perhaps, the absurdity inherent in the relational view can best be seen by putting matters slightly differently. Take the predicate '$\hat{x}$ loves Cassio' and the two sentences

(S_2) Bel^4 (Othello, Desdemona, loves, Cassio)

and

(S_{15}) Bel^3 (Othello, $\hat{x}$ loves Cassio, Desdemona).

It is clear that on the relational view, one must hold that they are logically equivalent. For, if not, such a one acknowledges that the situation one sentence describes could hold, but the situation the other describes need not hold. Yet, this is clearly absurd on the relational view, for it would amount to claiming that we could have Desdemona exemplifying *$\hat{x}$ loves Cassio* while not standing in the relation of loving to Cassio, or vice versa. But, by what inference rule would one derive one sentence from the other? If we consider the sentence form

$\hat{x}$ loves Cassio (Desdemona)

to be a subject-predicate sentence, we would recognize that as just another way of writing

Desdemona loves Cassio,

much as if we had introduced a defined predicate 'L^c' by

$L^c(x) =_{df.}$ x loves Cassio

and then observed that 'L^c(Desdemona)' was elliptical for 'Desdemona loves Cassio'. But, to apply this pattern to the case of (S_2) and (S_{15}) is to acknowledge that they are both ways of writing

(S_5)   Bel(Othello, Desdemona loves Cassio).

That is the first point. The second point is that in the case of the predicate, $(\exists x)(\hat{y}$ loves x)' and the sentence (S_{14}), there is no further corresponding sentence that plays the role (S_2) plays in relation to (S_{15}) and which shows '$\hat{x}$ loves Cassio' to be dispensable with (S_{15}).

The same problem occurs in the terms of those who practice semantic escape. Thus,

(S_{14a}) Bel^{3a}(Othello, '$(\exists x)(\hat{y}$ loves x)', Desdemona)

is either elliptical for

(S_{10a}) Bel^a(Othello, '$(\exists x)$(Desdemona loves x)'),

or one denies that

'∅' is true of a

is interchangeable with

'∅a' is true

in

w believes that . . . .

Niceties aside, this means that either one recognizes that the relational view, in its semantically ascended form, amounts to the propositional view, in its "loftier" version, or one holds to a correlate of the earlier recognition of relational properties by holding that to claim that '$(\exists x)(\hat{y}$ loves x)' is true of Desdemona is not to claim that '$(\exists x)$(Desdemona loves x)' is true.[14] Since the relational view in its ascensional form appears to deal with words and sentences, there appear to be no problems either about relational properties in addition to relations or about using a disguised version of the propositional view. For, of course, we distinguish monadic predicates from two-term predicates and do not hesitate to acknowledge (S_{10a}) as acceptable. Once again, we come to the whole issue behind the use of semantic ascent and the device of quoted expressions. What is interesting here is that it serves to cover, though not very well, a crucial defect of the relational view. There are some further questions and arguments regarding the general approach that is involved in the attempts of Sellars, Quine, and Davidson to avoid ontological commitments by using semantical devices. I shall take up these by continuing the discussion of Sellars's critique of Russell. Before proceeding with that, there is a connection of the particular theme we have just considered to an earlier issue that is worth noting and briefly pursuing.

The connection may not have escaped the reader. It is an apparent inconsistency in different themes I have presented. In earlier chapters of the book, I considered a way of construing and responding to *the* problem of individuation by acknowledging relational properties, in addition to relations. In a subsequent discussion of properties, I indicated a sense in which predicate abstracts like 'F$\hat{x}$ & G$\hat{x}$' may be said to indicate properties in addition to the properties referred to by the constituent primitive predicates. One may then extend that discussion to the case of abstracts like '($\exists$x)($\hat{y}$ loves x)' and hold that such an abstract indicates a relational property in addition to the relation indicated by the two-term predicate 'loves'. Moreover, the discussion in Chapter V could be taken to suggest that we may indicate the relational property of *loving someone* by a primitive predicate. This would fit with the discussion of properties in Chapter IX, since we noted that, properly construed, the device of forming complex predicates like 'F$\hat{x}$&G$\hat{x}$' involves our holding that

$$(y) [(F\hat{x}\ \&\ G\hat{x})y \equiv (Fy\ \&\ Gy)]$$

is not true "by definition." The same would then hold for

$$(z) [((\exists x)(\hat{y}\ \text{loves}\ x))z \equiv (\exists x)(z\ \text{loves}\ x)].$$

Yet, in the present discussion, I have criticized the relational view for being forced into acknowledging a relational property in addition to a "corresponding" relation. It, thus, appears that I accept such "properties" for my purposes and deny them, as problematic, to the proponent of the relational view. There are several things to be said. One is that, aside from any question about the recognition of relational properties, the proponent of the relational view does not appear to recognize the need to acknowledge such properties. One reason for this is the presentation of that view in the dress of "semantic ascent." Another thing to note is that, in the case of the relational analysis of belief, the problem arises owing to the forced use of the relational predicate as a subject term and, hence, as a term that *cannot be eliminated* in the context of its proposed use. By contrast, the appeal to such predicates in the context of the problem of individuation did not involve their use as subject terms in the *transcription* of ordinary statements such as '*b* is to the left of something'. The appeal to such predicates, as opposed to their corresponding relation terms, was in the context of presenting a philosophical position and a *list* of constituent entities of a particular object. I take this difference to be significant, though, admittedly, it does not resolve the question. Moreover, I did point out that such an appeal to relational properties forces the adoption of a doctrine of "internal relations," which has traditionally been a problem for a "bundle" theory. All this is quite different from advocating a relational analysis of *belief* without recognizing the *ontological commitments* involved. A third point to note is that I did not appeal, finally, to relational properties to resolve the question of individuation. Rather, I sought to show that the purported problem was more apparent than real. There, nevertheless, remain the problems we noted about "complex" properties in terms of Chapters IV, V, and IX. I do not propose to try and resolve those in this book, though we shall deal with another aspect of the issue in a later chapter when we return to questions about the ontological significance of logical signs and logical truths. Nevertheless, there are two points to note in connection with my criticism of the relational view. First, irrespective of the problems about "complex" properties, the relational view cannot present an analysis of belief contexts by appealing to *basic* entities alone. Second, even though a philosopher ultimately appeals to certain entities to resolve a problem, it is significant to note whether or not a different problem *need* involve an appeal to such entities. The relational view must appeal to relational properties; the propositional analysis need not. Weighing alternative philosophical positions involves noting such differences. In any case, Russell's analysis faces the other problems we noted before discussing Sellars's gambit. I conclude that Russell fails but his attempt is highly suggestive. Modified to meet the criticisms offered here, it will provide, along with features of Moore's analysis, the basis for a viable analysis.

Since Sellars's position derives from Russell's and Bergmann's is derivative from Moore's, it should be no surprise that the analysis proposed will be reminiscent of aspects of their attempted solutions. Although suggestive, Sellars's view ultimately fails owing to his pervasive nominalism, which leads him to obtain too simple a solution at too cheap an ontological price. As we noticed, the heart of his strategy is to focus the problem on the avoidance of the use of predicates as subject terms and, hence, to employ (5) in place of (4) and (3).

Sellars has objected to criticism of his views on predicates and properties, along the lines of that presented above and in Chapter X, by claiming that the coordination of a predicate to a property is not unproblematic, as I take it to be.[15] He holds that our talk about color properties and spatial relations is problematic and invites further analysis. Of course, in one sense, he is quite correct. There is, after all, the host of problems that constitute *the* problem of universals: Are we to recognize, as a response to such problems, the *existence* of universals (properties and relations) in an ontology that provides a basis for resolving the classical disputes? When I held that there is an unproblematic way in which we recognize colors and spatial relations, I was not claiming that we had thereby answered the classical questions along Platonistic lines. Rather, we may construe the classical questions as queries about a purported perspicuous schema, whereby we either coordinate the terms of the schema to "things" that we recognize in our ordinary context—particulars, colors, shapes, spatial relations, facts, etc.— or show how we can use the patterns of the schema as transcriptions of ordinary language sentences without such coordinations. What Sellars does is avoid the coordination by simply taking the patterns of the schema to transcribe ordinary language sentences. This makes pointless the construal of the classical questions in terms of the coordination of terms of the schema to "things" we recognize in unproblematic contexts. One may then respond that my construal is equally pointless, since it forces the recognition of particulars, properties, relations, and facts. But, that response is overly simple and inadequate for a number of reasons. I have left it open as to whether primitive predicates of the schema need be coordinated to properties, classes, quality instances, or even the same particulars to which the names are coordinated. For that matter, it is even an open question whether the names need be coordinated to particulars. Attempts to treat particulars as classes of properties might well involve attempts to avoid doing that. Different arguments will be required to refute alternative gambits. It is also left open whether primitive predicates are, in fact, needed. I believe that attempts to avoid them can be refuted, but that is not the point. Such gambits are not ruled out by fiat. Moreover, at the very least we can recognize that Sellars "plays the game" by different rules when he employs ordinary language statements in a way I find question begging. Taking the questions the way I have involves an attempt to explicate and resolve the classical problems by use of purported perspicuous schemata. Sellars employs such a schema to reflect the way in which he has resolved the questions. He explicates the questions by taking them to be problems about the complexities of the causal network surrounding our uttering, and being disposed to utter, tokens of predicate terms. Although he may answer some questions about predicate terms by doing that, he does not answer or resolve the classical issues: he does away with them. Thus, we may readily acknowledge Sellars's point regarding the problematic feature of accepting properties. The question is how to resolve it. It is not that I uncritically accept such entities or that he uncritically rejects them. Rather, there is a difference in the way we construe the problem of universals. Thus, it is not very surprising that we end up with different answers. We may, perhaps, agree about two things. First, there is *a* or a *series* of historical questions about which way of construing the classical problems jibes better with the traditional dialectical disputes. Second, I shall readily agree that one need not accept properties, either in my sense of accepting properties or in Sellars's terms, if one construes the issue as he does. Not in my sense, because the relevant question is not even asked; not in his sense, because of the way the question is transformed.

There is a further feature of Sellars's discussion that relates to a number of themes we have considered. He takes the acknowledgment of properties as entities to involve and fall to Bradley's paradox. The idea is that if we accept the property F as an entity, we acknowledge that *a* exemplifies F and, hence, that *a* and F are related by exemplification. This being so, we must acknowledge that exemplification is a further entity and that we consequently introduce an infinite series of such relations.

In the tradition of Ramsey, Sellars rejects the solution to Bradley's paradox implicit in Russell and explicitly adopted by Bergmann, Johnson, Wisdom, and Strawson. All of the latter hold that the answer to Bradley's paradox is to be found in the recognition of a special *tie* or *nexus* of exemplification. Holding that such a tie, unlike an ordinary relation, requires no further tie or relation to connect it to what it in turn connects, Bradley's problem is rejected. A tie, as opposed to a relation, is just what does not require a further tie in order to connect or relate things or entities—i.e., individuals, properties, relations. Such a tie is represented in a perspicuous schema by the juxtaposition of terms, the type distinction, and implicitly by the rules and context for the use of the language. It is not represented by another sign. Thus, it is tempting to think of such a tie as "logical" or a matter of "form," rather than as descriptive or a matter of content. Exemplification is, in other words, a logical relation. Yet, the solution to Bradley's puzzle depends on recognizing that such a tie "exists." This leads Sellars, like Ramsey, to dismiss the "solution." No doubt Bradley would have held that to talk of ties, as opposed to relations, as Johnson, Strawson, and Bergmann have, or constituents as opposed to components of facts, as Wisdom did, or of a fundamental asymmetrical relation, as Moore and Russell did, is merely to assert that the problem does not exist. More recently, Bergmann once again felt the pinch of Bradley's regress and the inadequacy of his solution. Consequently, he complicated his view by holding that a fact like *a*'s being F must be analyzed in terms of a particular, a universal property, a fundamental tie of exemplification, *and* a *circumstance* that the tie binds the universal to the particular. When 'F*a*' is true, the fact is *actual*. If the sentence 'F*a*' is false, the fact is *potential*. This clearly attempts to get at Bradley's paradox by making the fact, under another name, a proper part of itself.

To see what is wrong with Bergmann's gambit, as well as with the other "solutions" mentioned earlier, we should first note that the paradox is looked at in the following way. The fact that *a* is F cannot be the class whose members are *a* and F, for, first, there is such a class if there are the entities *a* and F, irrespective of whether *a* is F, and, second, there must be a connection between *a* and F that constitutes the fact. A class does not furnish such a connection holding between its members. Moreover, if one adds a connecting tie—say EX—this does not help, since the fact cannot be the class whose members are *a*, F, and EX for exactly the same reasons as it cannot be the class whose members are *a* and F. One may then be tempted to stipulate that EX solves the problem by saying that the fact is *a* and F tied by EX or, like Bergmann, to introduce a new entity, the circumstance, which allows one to say that the fact is the class composed of *a*, F, EX, and the circumstance that *a* is tied by EX to F.[16] On either "solution," one looks at the problem as a challenge to list the constituents of a fact in a way that avoids the regress. So doing, one must conclude that the list

(L$_1$)   *a*, F, EX

does not do either because one is forced to add the condition that EX connects *a* to F or because one is forced to alter the list to include a further element which, in effect, says the same thing. Thus, we could have

(L$_2$)   *a*, F, EX, the circumstance that *a* is F

replacing (L$_1$). (L$_2$) is a peculiar kind of list, since, unlike (L$_1$), it not only lists the constituents of the fact, but, in so doing, manages to tell us which constituents are connected and how. Instead of (L$_1$) or (L$_2$), we might consider

(L$_3$)   EX(*a*, F)

as a solution to the same problem. In (L$_3$), one makes explicit use of the ordering of the signs in lieu of either a statement of the condition accompanying (L$_1$) or the introduction of the additional circumstance of (L$_2$). Bradley, of course, would point to the necessity of the ordering in (L$_3$) and of the use of "is" in the phrase "the circumstance that *a* is F" as reflecting his claim that there is a problem and, hence, that the use of (L$_2$) or (L$_3$) provides no more of a solution than (L$_1$) does. But, there is a difference in *why* they fail. (L$_1$) omits the *structure* of the fact. (L$_2$) and (L$_3$) sneak it in. If we recognize that the problem *arises only* as a challenge to analyze a fact solely in terms of its *constituent* elements, a simple and straightforward solution is forthcoming. We need merely acknowledge that such an analysis cannot be given. Obviously not, since the fact is the constituent elements *structured* or *connected* in a certain way. This is why Bergmann must introduce, as a further element of the fact, the *fact* that the elements are *connected* or *structured*. What he does is mistakenly introduce the structure of the fact as a constituent. He stops the regress, but only because he makes the fact a constituent of itself. This avoids one paradox by embracing another. Alternatively, *that the elements are in a certain structure* may be declared to be something that *is not an element*. It cannot be taken as an entity in one's analysis of a fact. This is what is involved in the claim that ties need no further tie. But, both gambits are simply indirect ways of acknowledging that facts are not *reducible* to their elements and hence *not analyzed*. Recall that in the *Tractatus*, Wittgenstein spoke of the world decomposing or being reduced to its constituent atomic facts. What he meant was that the world was not an additional entity constituted by the atomic facts in a relation or connection. By contrast, a fact is something in addition to its constituents, since it is the constituents connected or structured or related. Thus, a fact does not reduce or decompose into its constituents in the way that the world, as Wittgenstein spoke of it, dissolves or is reduced to its constituent atomic facts. Another way one may put it is that the world is *merely a class* of atomic facts, since the members of a class are not connected or structured in a certain way to form or constitute the class. There is a feature of Russell's analysis of definite descriptions that bears on the issue. On such an analysis, definite descriptions are eliminable from a perspicuous language by contextual definitions. Such signs may then be taken to be reducible, in context, to other signs, since expressions involving them are replaceable by expressions involving only the other signs. If one philosophizes in the tradition of Russell and Wittgenstein, one may speak of the things supposedly referred to by definite descriptions being *reduced* to the things mentioned in the defining expressions or, simply, being *eliminated* (or *dissolved*) by *analysis* from one's ontology. By contrast, one remains committed to those entities that are referred to by primitive terms such as names—these latter signs not having been eliminated from a language in the way in which all definite descriptions are eliminable or reducible. Sentences *are not* eliminable from a language in the way in which definite descriptions and defined signs generally are. Hence, some facts are not eliminable from an ontology or reducible to other entities. Facts must, therefore, be recognized as existents in addition to constituents of facts. Consider also how some philosophers have thought of reducing certain things to others—physical objects to phenomenal ones, for example. A physical object is construed in terms of a number of phenomenal things standing to each other in various spatial, temporal, and other relations. On such a view, one claims that physical objects have been eliminated or reduced to phenomenal things *and, if he is cautious, facts* involving such phenomenal objects. But, physical objects are no longer recognized in such an ontology unless one now takes them to be (classes of) facts with phenomenal constituents. Whether one then holds that there are no physical objects (ultimately) or that physical objects are classes of facts with phenomenal constituents makes no difference for our purposes here. For, again, one cannot eliminate facts in such a manner. When one says that a fact *is* a set of constituents in a certain structure (or relation or connection), one is not reducing the fact to such constituents or the set of such constituents or to the set of the constituents including the connecting tie.

We may then take the point of Bradley's paradox to be that facts cannot be reduced to their elements and, hence, are not analyzable. They are not analyzable in two senses. First, a primitive (hence unanalyzable) connection or tie is introduced to bind the other constituents; second, even with such a tie, a fact is not reducible to the constituents including the tie, but must be taken as an *arrangement* of the constituents. Such a point, however, does not involve a paradox or regress. What it does is show that a fact is

an "irreducible" entity (albeit complex) in an ontology recognizing particulars, properties (or functions), and relations and that its
structure is not an entity. The point can be emphasized by contrasting the case of facts with yet another issue. Suppose one acknowledges atomic facts that are indicated by true sentences like
'Fa' and 'Sa'. Is there also a conjunctive fact indicated by 'Fa &
Sa'? As I shall argue later, one may say no, since the atomic facts
suffice to ground the truth of the conjunctive sentence. Thus, one
need recognize neither such complex facts nor that '&' so used
stands for a relation among facts. By contrast, the constituents of
an atomic fact, taken as entities, do not suffice to account for the
truth of a sentence like 'Fa' (nor even for what is asserted when
the sentence is false). To put it somewhat paradoxically, conjunctive facts *reduce* to constituent atomic facts. Facts do not reduce
to their constituent particulars, properties, relations, and nexus.
But, the claim that ties need no further tie and the introduction
of circumstances are merely roundabout and unclear ways of acknowledging that since facts are structured, they are basic, though
complex, entities.[17]

Although there is a point to Bradley's argument, there is no
paradox involved. The solution I have indicated is, of course, one
of the cardinal points of the *Tractatus*, though Wittgenstein does
not explicitly discuss Bradley. There is another relevant, but relatively minor and "Frege-like," aspect of Bradley's argument.

Given the fact expressed by 'Fa', Bradley may be taken to argue
that we must recognize another fact expressed by '$R_1(F,a)$', and
so on ad infinitum. In short, any fact is held to generate an infinite
number of facts; and we create a puzzle analogous to Aristotle's
that knowing any truth, like a's being F, involves knowing an infinite number of truths, since we must know that it is true that a
is F, and so on ad infinitum. But, both make the same mistake; for
the most one can argue is that if 'Fa' is true, then so is a sentence
of the form '$R_1(F,a)$' (or "'Fa' is true"), and so on. The point is
that one and the same fact makes the whole series true, in both
cases, just as the fact indicated by 'Fa' makes that sentence, as
well as the disjunction 'Fa v Ga' and the conjunction 'Fa & Fa',
true. Since the disjunction is a logical consequence of 'Fa', the
fact grounding the latter also suffices to ground the former. Like-

wise, if 'R_1 (F,a)' does follow from 'Fa', and 'R_1' must be so construed that it does to even talk about a "paradox" (just as "true"
must be so construed that "'Fa' is true" follows from 'Fa'), then
the fact grounding the truth of 'Fa' suffices to ground the truth of
'R_1 (F,a)'. Hence, one need not recognize an infinite number of
facts. We need recognize, at most, only the possibility of there being an infinite number of true sentences. But, this only creates a
paradox if one holds that *understanding* the sentence 'Fa' involves
understanding a further sentence, and so on. Thus, assuming first,
that 'R_1 (F,a)' is not simply defined to be an alternative expression for 'Fa', second, that one cannot *comprehend* 'Fa' unless one
comprehends an infinite number of relations or sentences, and,
third, that it is impossible to grasp an infinite number of such relations or sentences leads to the conclusion that 'Fa' and, hence,
exemplification is incomprehensible. This weak feature of Bradley's argument is relatively uninteresting, and the grounds for rejecting it are rather obvious.

We may conclude, I believe, that Bradley's paradox is not a
paradox: it is merely the insistence that given the fact that a is F
(and a kind of comprehension rule to the effect that when there is
a fact of a certain structure, there is fact of a more complex structure, i.e., if there is a fact consisting of a particular and a property
in a two-term exemplification relation, there is a fact containing a
particular, a property, and a two-term exemplification relation *in*
a three-term exemplification relation, and so on), we may infer
that there are an infinite number of facts involving a and F. Such a
multiplicity of facts may provide embarrassment, but they do not
necessarily yield a paradox. However, as we noted above, *with additional problematic assumptions* one can produce puzzling consequences. But, Sellars is wrong, I believe, in holding that we cannot
prevent the generation of facts from beginning by insisting that exemplification is not a relation among relations. One feature of the
Bradleyian regress is the insistence that facts cannot be analyzed,
in a certain sense of analysis. To hold that ties need not be tied, in
turn, admittedly does nothing to alter that situation. Thus, a major point of Bradley's argument is not blunted. However, the present theme is another matter. The point here is whether exemplification or, to put it somewhat differently, the structure of the fact

is another constituent of the fact. One may reasonably say no and, moreover, provide an argument for doing so.

Every complex entity is a set of constituents in a structure. It is, thus, paradoxical to take the structure as another constituent of *that* entity. This is the feature of Bradley's problem that we have concentrated on. I think Bradley thought he was presenting the paradox *that the structure must be taken as a constituent* of the fact of which it was the structure. The idea was that in saying the fact is a particular exemplifying a property we are *analyzing the* fact we start from: that *a* is F. Hence, we produce the need for a further exemplification relation, since we must carry the analysis of the fact one step further, by analyzing the *new* fact that *a* and F stand in the exemplification relation, and so on without end. The paradox was then two-fold: first, the exemplification relation introduced *to structure* the fact failed to do so, since it was really just another constituent of *that* fact; second, no analysis was ever forthcoming since the process continued indefinitely. But, the most one may claim is that there is *another*, more complex, fact. However, no argument is offered for the need to recognize such a fact, except that we must take the two-term exemplification relation between *a* and F as a *term* or *constituent* of some fact. And the only reason that Sellars appears to offer for that is that if we do not do so, we recognize that we need not accept a relation like *loves* as a *term* or *constituent* of a fact. We can treat such a relation as the structure in which the related objects stand. Hence, we need neither take such a relation as an entity (term, constituent) nor appeal to exemplification at all. One can offer arguments against Sellars's construal of relations without exemplification by pointing to the "double role" relations then take on. Consider the two (purported) facts expressed by

> Desdemona loves Cassio
> Desdemona hates Iago.

We may observe that there is a similarity in structure as well as a difference in relation. If one treats relations along Sellars's line, one gives each relation a double function. Thus, *loves* and *hates* supply *two features* to the facts in question. If one thinks along more Russellian lines, as in "On the Relations of Universals and Particulars," such relations contribute the differentiating feature to the facts and the *connection* of exemplification provides the *structural* feature. (This means we recognize that exemplification *ties* and *ties in an order* or *structure*. This is why taking exemplification as a constituent of a fact does not help to analyze a *fact into* constituents.) We may observe here how neatly that distinction is reflected in a standard *Principia*-type symbolism, where we have relational predicates *in* sentences while recognizing that sentences have *a* structure. Of course, that is why Sellars looks to a different type of perspicuous schema. But he cannot escape the difference. For even where we represent our two facts by, say,

Desdemona

Cassio

and

Desdemona Iago,

there are the differences in the patterns *in addition* to a crucial *similarity*: the names in both are *ordered in a spatial juxtaposition to each other*. This simple fact rebuts his pattern. Moreover, Sellars's type of view ultimately fails, and fails dramatically, for another reason: there are monadic properties. One cannot hold that the property F is the structure of the object *a*, which it characterizes, unless one suggests that *the object being* F is to be understood in terms of other objects, perhaps micro-objects with respect to *a*, in a relation or configuration. This involves a move radically different from the corresponding move from

Desdemona loves Cassio

to

Desdemona

Cassio,

which suffices to make it suspect. It also fails on other grounds.

It obviously will not do for phenomenal objects. Of course, one can seek to avoid such attributions of properties to phenomenal objects by eliminating such objects and adopting a behaviorist or physicalist philosophy of "mind." Yet, even for physical objects, it is a factual claim that a macro-object having a property F correlates with a set of micro-objects being in a state S. To speak of reduction or analysis of the one in terms of the other does not add anything; it merely stipulates a use of 'reduction' and of 'analysis'. Moreover, there is something paradoxical about eliminating the ordinary material object to avoid attributing properties to it. The problem about monadic properties thus connects materialism with "micro-reductionism." In an equally dramatic vein, Nelson Goodman seeks to avoid properties by holding that we attribute predicates, ultimately, not on the basis of properties of objects but in terms of the ways *we* have of classifying objects.[18] He, thus, seeks to avoid properties by embracing a form of idealism that he relabels (perhaps "reclassifies" would be better) "relativism." It is curious to what lengths philosophers will go to avoid acknowledging properties of objects. Moreover, clearly such philosophers will have to deny that the micro-objects have monadic properties. No doubt the way in which one may take characteristics like velocity, mass, and position to be relational and the latest terminology of physicists will provide some illusory semblance of success in such a venture. One is reminded of the attempts some years ago to base human freedom on indeterminacy in quantum physics and more recent suggestions that the relativity or factual nature of logic can also be supported by appeals to quantum mechanics.

Such matters aside, we may recognize one of Bradley's points to imply that it is futile to take the structure of a complex as a constituent among constituents. Sellars appears to take Bradley's point to imply that if we take properties and relations to be objects and terms, we must take the fact's structure, in the form of the exemplification relation, to be a constituent. Bradley obviously thought so as well. Both then make the correct point that adding exemplification as a constituent of the fact does not *suffice* for the analysis of the fact. Sellars proceeds to draw further, incorrect, conclusions. One is that exemplification, not sufficing, is not necessary, and, hence, that ordinary properties and relations may structure the fact. I am suggesting that this *seems* to be plausible only in the case of relations where one *may* take the relation in a two-fold manner: to order or structure the fact so that it is a two-term relational fact pairing the objects in a definite order *and* to supply some *content* so that it is a case of *loving* and not of *hating*, say. But, even if we do not question the running of these two aspects together, the monadic case clearly provides a refuting example. There is no plausible way to take a property of an object as a *structure* of *that* object. The very notion of structure involves us in talk of more than one object or constituent. This is why one may then seek to eliminate, in some manner, the object we start with. But, this would involve a final irony on Sellars's pattern. A coherent pattern would require him to hold that the monadic case is like the relational case. (This is reminiscent of Russell's thinking of monadic properties as "one-term" relations.) But, in the relational case one takes a relation, say *loving*, as the structure in which two objects stand and thus does not acknowledge that the objects *and loving* are, in turn, in a structural pattern. By contrast, in the monadic case one would hold that *a* and F are *not* in a structural pattern, since F *is* the structure, not of *a*, but of further objects that constitute *a*. In the one case, one gets rid of the relation in favor of the objects and the structure: in the other, one gets rid of *all three things*—the original object, the monadic property, and the exemplification tie. Paradoxically, to attempt to apply the relational pattern to the monadic case involves admitting that it cannot be applied. Thus, in the monadic case, one may simply retreat to the argument that we considered in Chapter X: all that need be said in the monadic case is that *a* is F, or, to put it "perspicuously," all that need be done is to write '*a*' in appropriate type font.

Sellars's advocacy of the use of type fonts in writing names of objects, in place of predicates, to perspicuously reveal that predicates do not stand for properties has always appeared to be an artificial device. I suspect one reason is the stark contrast with the relational case where one uses a relation among names, rather than a relational predicate, to express that the objects named are related in a certain way. This grammatical point is a reflection of what I have been discussing. Moreover, Sellars's use of such fonts embodies a final irony worth noting. For his pattern to make sense, we must have a neutral form or font of the name. Otherwise, one would be stating that the named object had some monadic property in using the name in a relational pattern to express that the named object stood in some relation. It is not too far-fetched to observe that by being forced to recognize such a neutral form, Sellars has given eloquent "pictorial" representation to the bare-particular gambit. For, the name as occurring in a monadic "sentence" merely differs in type font from the name as an indicator of the object. On the view which recognizes properties and facts and, hence, predicates and "normal" sentences, there is a categorial difference between a name, as an indicator of an object, and a sentence. Names and monadic sentences are logically of a kind for Sellars. Sellars, of course, would look at it the other way. By using the same name form in different sentences, one may be thought to be indicating the object irrespective of its "form" or properties and, hence, as a bare particular. He would have a point, although he does the same sort of thing by using the same neutral form in different "relational sentences." It is the point I discussed much earlier, when I held that the concept of a bare particular, in part, stems from and reflects our use of names as mere labels. Here, I am merely illustrating another facet of the discussion of "bare" particulars. When one deals with such an ambiguous notion, one must be content with pointing to different ways in which such a phrase may be taken. Such concepts are, as it were, to be *explicated* and not *used*. Speaking of "the structure of a fact" may create puzzlement in that it seems to force one to either recognize a further entity or identify *the structure* with *the fact*. The former move is pointless; the latter is paradoxical. But, to speak of a fact having a structure is not to refer to some*thing particular to* that fact any more than one "refers to" *the love of Desdemona for Cassio*. To say that a fact has a structure is to insist that (a) facts are complexes, (b) complexes are not classes of constituents, and (c) *is-a-constituent-of* is a basic relation and is not *is-a-member-of*. Different kinds of facts have different forms. Yet, a form is neither a constituent nor a property of a fact (or possibility). In the relational case, there is also the direction of the relation. This can be represented by '$a\emptyset b$' without altering the point that facts are not analyzable, since the fact $a\mathrm{R}b$ is not the class $\{a, b, \mathrm{R}, a\emptyset b\}$.

XII

The Structure
of Thought: Part I

In *The Analysis of Mind*, Russell abandoned mental acts on much the same grounds he was to use to decisively "exorcise" bare particulars in *An Inquiry into Meaning and Truth*. Both kinds of things conflicted with his principle of acquaintance and, hence, were not to be acknowledged by one with empiricist scruples.

> The first criticism I have to make is that the *act* seems unnecessary and fictitious. The occurrence of the content of a thought constitutes the occurrence of the thought. Empirically, I cannot discover anything corresponding to the supposed act; and theoretically I cannot see that it is indispensable. We say: "*I* think so-and-so," and this word "I" suggests that thinking is the act of a person. Meinong's "act" is the ghost of the subject, or what once was the full-blooded soul. It is supposed that thoughts cannot just come and go, but need a person to think them.[1]

The reference to the occurrence of the content of a thought constituting the occurrence of thought shows that what Russell is rejecting is the existence of acts in the sense in which Bergmann and Moore acknowledged such things: as particulars which are related to something else, a proposition or propositional character, which supplies their "content." He is not rejecting acts as I have been construing them, as facts. As we saw, the view he proposed in "On Propositions," and which he elaborates in *The Analysis of Mind*, is very similar to that suggested in Chapter III. In this chapter, I shall develop that view. But, before turning to the main themes, I shall discuss some structural connections between Russell's rejection of acts and bare particulars, on the one hand, and a philosopher like Bergmann's acceptance of both, on the other.

Bergmann attempted an analysis of intentional contexts and mental acts along Moore's lines, while writing within a framework influenced by the development of logical positivism.[2] Moore's elaboration of his view is neither as clear nor as explicit as is Bergmann's. This is why I adopted much from Bergmann's manner of presentation of his own views in my explication of Moore. This, as well as the closeness of Bergmann to Moore, will become apparent as we proceed. According to Bergmann, statements with intentional verbs (believes, remembers, is aware of, etc.) require for their analysis the introduction of the following entities: propositional characters, represented in a perspicuous language by sentences in quotes (later changed to "corners"); particulars that exemplify such propositional characters; and generic properties that are also exemplified by such particulars. The generic properties provide the ground for distinguishing different kinds of mental states, such as being aware, being in doubt, believing, etc., and the propositional characters provide a basis for a mental state having a specific content or intention. Besides such entities, Bergmann also introduces a unique *logical* relation designated by the sign 'M' and read as "means." This relation is stipulated to be such that sentences like

(B$_1$) $\ulcorner$Desdemona loves Cassio$\urcorner$ M Desdemona loves Cassio

can be formulated. That is, where '. . .' is replaced by a sentence, the result of such replacement for both occurrences of the dots in

(B$_2$) $\ulcorner$. . .$\urcorner$ M . . .

yields a well-formed sentence. The relation M is called *logical* for two reasons. First, the schema (B$_2$) is taken to result in a true sentence when the same sentence replaces both occurrences of the dots and otherwise in a false one. Well-formed sentences resulting from replacement of the dots in (B$_2$) can then be seen to be true or false by inspection of the resulting sign pattern. This is analogous to speaking of tautologies as logical truths in virtue of the nonvacuous occurrence of the logical signs, since 'M' and the quoting device occur nonvacuously in a similar way. Compare

(B$_3$)   p v ~p

and

(B₄)   ⌐p⌐ M p.

(B₃), as a tautologous form, yields another such form or sentence if both occurrences of 'p' are replaced by the same variable or sentence, while holding the 'v' and '∼' constant. The same is true for (B₄) with the quotes and 'M' playing the role of 'v' and '∼'. Thus, one may think of 'M' and the quoting device as functioning like logical constants. Moreover, the truth of (B₄), like that of (B₃), can then be said to be a matter of form, or linguistic rules, or *logic*, rather than a matter of fact. The sentence (B₁) seems to be true for somewhat the same reasons that 'This is red v ∼This is red' is true and to be quite different from a sentence like 'This is red'.

There is a second point behind calling 'M' a logical sign. Consider the conjunction sign as a two-term relational sign with sentences as the linguistic terms. Thus, we might write '&(R*ab*, R*bc*)' by analogy with 'R*ab*', where 'R' stands for a relation and '*a*', '*b*', and '*c*' are names. One of the main themes of Wittgenstein's *Tractatus* is the claim that the logical connectives do not stand for relations or, indeed, for anything at all:

> 4.0312   The possibility of propositions is based on the principle that objects have signs as their representatives.
>
>   My fundamental idea is that the 'logical constants' are not representatives; that there can be no representatives of the *logic* of facts.

What he had in mind was the two-fold point that I have reiterated a number of times in previous chapters: true atomic sentences correspond to facts and such facts are complex entities, consisting of constituent elements but not reducible to such elements. Facts are not mere classes of elements. The world, by contrast, is merely a class of facts and, hence, is *determined* by such facts, as a fact is not determined by its elements:

> 1.11   The world is determined by the facts, and by their being *all* the facts.
>
> 1.2   The world divides into facts.

By contrast, if '&(R*ab*, R*bc*)' is true, there is no one fact corresponding to that sentence. It is true since there are facts corresponding to the atomic sentences. Hence, one might take the true conjunction to correspond to the class of those atomic facts or hold that a "conjunctive fact" divides, like the world, into those facts. The only constituents involved would be the constituents of the atomic facts. '&', not corresponding to a constituent or a connection among constituents, does not stand for a genuine relation. *Conjunction* is not included in an ontological assay of the universe. There are no logical objects, properties, or relations as constituent entities of the world. To call '&' a sign for a "logical relation" is to take conjunction as a *pseudorelation* — a nonexistent. In his early writing, Bergmann followed Wittgenstein in this denial of ontological significance to "logical relations." Since 'M' is a logical sign, it does not stand for a relational universal.

Like Russell, Bergmann rejected the classical view which analyzed the fact that someone believes that *Rab* in terms of a mental act (or subject) standing in a relation to the proposition that *Rab*. In our discussion of Frege, we noted that a serious problem arises for a philosopher who acknowledges propositions as entities and who also accepts facts as the conditions for such propositions being true or false. The proposition, recall, furnishes the basis for a mental state having the content it does, even in a case of false belief, where a fact does not exist. Accepting both propositions and facts forces one to hold that the proposition stands in a relation to the fact that "makes" it true, if it is true. But, this, as we noted earlier, turns one in a problematic circle. For, one must face the question of *what* the proposition is related to when it is false. Why is it that the nonexistence of a specific fact makes a specific proposition false? Propositions were supposed to deal with the problem of false belief, but introducing them forces us to raise another question of the same kind. One attempt to answer this is to introduce possibilities in addition to propositions. One need not share Russell's aversion to the "nonexistent" to find such an answer pointless. Frege's *thoughts* conveniently referred to *The True* and *The False*. When Moore was confronted with the issue, he spoke both substantively and poetically of "nonexistent" facts. Bergmann's first attempt at a solution depended on taking M as a logical relation. To see what is involved, let 'm_1' be a name of a particular mental act and let 'B' refer to a generic characteristic exemplified by m_1. Since m_1 exemplifies B, we have a mental act or state that is one of *believing*. Further, let '$\lceil Ra \rceil$' abbreviate '$\lceil a$ is red$\rceil$', and recall that a sentence within corners functions as a predicate. Let such a predicate refer to a propositional character that is also exemplified by m_1. In short, the expressions to the left of the sign 'M' in (B$_2$) become predicates when sentences replace the dots. Such predicates refer to the propositional characters that determine the content or intention of the act. Since m_1 exemplifies the *property* $\lceil Ra \rceil$ (which is referred to by the *predicate* '$\lceil Ra \rceil$') *and* the *generic property* B, we have a *belief that a is red*. Thus,

(B$_5$) $Bm_1 \,\&\, \lceil Ra \rceil m_1$

provides the analysis of the specific act of belief we are discussing. It also gives us the general pattern for analyzing an intentional context,

(B$_6$) $Fx \,\&\, \lceil p \rceil x$,

where 'F' may be replaced by any generic character of mental states, 'p' by any sentence expressing the content or intention, and 'x' by the name of an individual mental state. Suppose, now, that the sentence 'Ra' is false. How is it that the propositional character it stands for can *express* or *mean* a specific fact without being connected to a possible fact or nonexistent fact? The answer is that 'M' is a logical sign and

(B$_7$) $\lceil Ra \rceil$ M Ra

a logical truth. Since 'M' is a logical sign and (B$_7$) a logical truth, there is no need to take M as a relation between two *terms* (entities), for logical relations do not connect terms. Just as '&' does not stand for a relation between facts in 'Rab & Rbc', 'M' does not stand for a relation between a propositional character, on the one hand, and a fact, possible fact, or nonexistent fact, on the other. Thus, (B$_7$) is true, but not in virtue of the propositional character $\lceil Ra \rceil$ standing in the relation M to the fact (actual, possible, or nonexistent) Ra. To claim this is to deny any version of the classical relational account that gives ontological status to possible or nonexistent facts. In (B$_7$) only the expression to the left

of 'M' stands for anything. It is a predicate standing for a propositional character (property) of mental states. (B_7) is true in virtue
of its "form" and not because anything stands in a relation to
something else. The problem is "solved" by turning an ontological
question into a logical one within the context of a view that denies
ontological significance or import to logical relations. Even with
M, like exemplification, as a logical relation Bergmann's propositional characters are *simple* universals. Yet, they apparently have a
structure, since they are indicated by *sentences* in corner quotes.
To be simple, whatever else it implies for the tradition of the logical atomists, involves being without structure. Thus, we have a
clash. An apparent remedy is easily hit on. To see the remedy, we
must slightly correct the simplified treatment I presented when
taking (B_5) as the analysis of a belief that a is red. (B_5) should be
a conjunction of three clauses as follows:

$$(B_{5'}) \quad Bm_1 \ \& \ \ulcorner Ra \urcorner \ m_1 \ \& \ \ulcorner Ra \urcorner \ M \ Ra.$$

The last conjunct, being a "logical truth," means that ($B_{5'}$), in a
standard sense, is *logically equivalent* to (B_5). ($B_{5'}$) presents Bergmann's analysis of the belief in question. With 'F_1' as a primitive
first-level predicate, one could replace ($B_{5'}$) by

$$(B_{5''}) \quad Bm_1 \ \& \ F_1 m_1 \ \& \ F_1 \ M \ Ra.$$

The simple propositional character would not, then, be represented by a sign that had a structure but by a simple predicate sign.
However, once one stresses the simplicity of the propositional characters, the plausibility of the claim that sentences like (B_7) are logical truths becomes suspect. Compare the final conjuncts of ($B_{5'}$)
and ($B_{5''}$). There is, at least, some initial plausibility in the claim
that '$\ulcorner Ra \urcorner$ M Ra' is a logical truth; but 'F_1 M Ra'? On either alternative, it is problematic to speak of propositional characters as
simple properties. The problem shows itself on the first alternative
in the use of a structured sign for a simple entity. It emerges on
the second alternative in the specious claim that there is a *logical*
connection between a simple property and a fact or possible fact.
Moreover, one may well wonder if there is really any difference
between either alternative and the more traditional view that recognizes independent propositions; for, such propositions play the

logical role they do, namely, allowing for beliefs to be true or false, in virtue of being explicitly taken to be complex entities like facts. That is, they are constituted by a structural relation holding among constituents. Bergmann's propositions are purportedly simple. Yet, they perform their role of giving content to a belief only in virtue of being logically connected to a complex entity that is an actual or possible fact. Thus, an obvious question arises about whether '⌐Ra⌐ M Ra' (or 'F$_1$ M Ra') holds when no mental state is exemplifying the propositional character. Since it is a logical truth and not a matter of fact, it would appear that such a statement holds irrespective of whether any mental state exemplifies or ever has exemplified the relevant propositional character (⌐Ra⌐ or F$_1$). Of course, a sentence like 'Ra v ~Ra' holds irrespective of whether anything exemplifies R; but, by the truth table and rules for disjunction, one of the disjuncts must be true. M is not a truth function but a relational tie. By the rules and context governing it, a propositional character must be connected by M to a fact (actual or possible) in order that '⌐Ra⌐ M Ra' be true. Hence, even if no mental state exemplifies it, the propositional character is related to a fact. This gives propositional characters the same sort of Platonic existence that is characteristic of the traditional propositions, and such a move is something Bergmann sought to avoid. Although he set out to develop an account of intentional contexts that would require neither Platonic propositions nor possibilities, he is forced, in the end, to accept both.

Bergmann's analysis is essentially a variation of Moore's in *Some Main Problems of Philosophy*, with *M* playing the role of *Ref.* in our discussion of Moore. Yet Moore, in his way, saw what Bergmann did not. Once possible facts (or nonexistent facts) are admitted, propositions are no longer required for the role in which Bergmann (and Moore at places) uses them. Thus, Moore took mental acts to have a generic characteristic, but their content was determined by *the act* standing in a unique relation to a fact (nonexistent or existent). To put it another way, once possible facts enter the ontology, the propositional characters of Bergmann's analysis can be indicated by *defined* predicates. Thus, 'F$_1$' or '⌐Ra⌐' can be defined along lines we considered in Chapter III:

$(D_1) F_1 = df. (\iota f) fM Ra.$

All one need recall to see the adequacy of the definition is that on Bergmann's view only one propositional character stands in the relation M to the "fact" indicated by the sentence 'Ra'. What this shows is that there is only a verbal difference between Moore's rejection of propositions, by having "beliefs" stand in a special relation to facts, and Bergmann's insistence that some particulars exemplify propositional characters, which stand in a special relation to facts. For the rest, we can note that although Moore did not speak of the special relation as logical, he was struck by the fact that one indicates a belief *and* the fact it is related to by the same sentence. One need only look back at (B_1) to see the import of this.

On Bergmann's pattern, we have bare particulars that by exemplifying propositional characters and generic properties *are* mental acts. In one sense, the mental acts are the particulars with their properties, as a red square patch is a bare particular exemplifying redness and squareness. The bare particular is, thus, that which grounds the individuality of the act, just as another such particular does the same for the red patch. Given such a way of looking at the problem of individuation and, hence, of particulars, Bergmann must locate the content of the act in a propositional character of it or, more directly in Moore's fashion, in a proposition that such a particular is directly apprehending. The particular, on the more explicitly Moorean pattern, would still exemplify a generic character. The problem of individuation thus forces Bergmann to treat acts in the way Russell finds problematic. Alternatively, Russell will find the solution to the problem of individuation in terms of properties and relational properties. The ordinary particular will become a bundle of its characteristics. In a similar way, the act will become identified with the content of the belief. In the one case, by dropping the bare particular, one is left with the properties of the ordinary object. In the other case, what remains is the content and the generic "feeling." But, then, what distinguishes two numerically different thoughts with the same content? The *content* must be individuated, so that we have two particular thoughts or *occurrences* of belief, and yet *it* must be universal or what is common to the two. The particular thoughts or beliefs thus become much like the quality instances of the early papers of Moore and Russell. In a way, that is what Russell's *thoughts* become. For, the solution is found by taking the particular token occurrences, whether of nonverbal images or of (visual or auditory) verbal tokens, *to be* the individual or particular thoughts, while supplying the content by their being tokens of the same type. Hence, different tokens may have the same *interpretation* or *meaning*. Thus, Russell not only avoids acts, in Bergmann's sense, and their bare constituents, but he also seeks to avoid the classical propositions, which we saw Bergmann ends up with in the guise of simple properties. Bergmann has claimed that one cannot really recognize universal properties without acknowledging bare particulars that exemplify them. I do not think he is right, but, that aside, here we see that he accepts the classical act and gets the classical proposition along with it.

We noted a number of problems in the last chapter that Russell did not resolve, on the pattern he proposed. Yet, they are resolvable. To do so, it will be helpful to continue to make use of Bergmann's linguistic devices for a time. Consider a set of individual constants 'm_1', 'm_2', etc., to stand for particular acts, which we shall take to be particulars in the sense in which a red patch or a chair is a particular. That is, we shall ignore the question of whether we take the particular to be "bare," in Bergmann's sense, or to be the mental act, as complex, in his sense. Since we are developing a view along Russell's lines, this will cause neither confusion nor problems. To emphasize the difference with Bergmann, I shall use, hereafter, the predicate 'Bel' for the generic character that all acts which are beliefs, rather than doubts or disbeliefs for example, have, but I shall retain Bergmann's device of placing a sentence inside corner quotes to form a predicate. Such predicates will stand for a property of those mental states which, as Russell speaks, have the content expressed by the sentence. Thus, if Othello believes or has the thought that Desdemona loves Cassio, there is an act, m_1 say, that has a certain content and also exemplifies Bel. Let 'H' stand for a relation between a person and one of his mental states. Then,

(1)   ⌜Desdemona loves Cassio⌝ (m_1) & Bel(m_1)

and

(2)   H(Othello, m_1)

respectively state that m_1 is a particular belief or thought that Desdemona loves Cassio and that m_1 is a belief or thought of Othello's. If (1) and (2) hold, it is certainly true to claim that Othello believes that Desdemona loves Cassio. This latter claim may be expressed by:

(3)   ($\exists$x) [⌜Desdemona loves Cassio⌝(x) & Bel(x) & H(Othello,x)] ,

which is a straightforward case of existential generalization from the conjunction of (1) and (2). In the terms we have been using, (3) states that there is a mental state of Othello's which is a state of belief that Desdemona loves Cassio. We have, thus, provided for one kind of existential generalization in intentional contexts without any problem. We can also resolve some other problems.

On Bergmann's analysis, the use of the corner predicates involves acknowledging that the propositional characters the predicates stand for mean or intend the state of affairs expressed by the sentence from which the predicates are formed.[3] The *link* is the basic intentional *tie* or relation referred to by the quite unique predicate 'M'. Recall that 'M' is unique for Bergmann in that it connects other predicates with sentences, and it is "logical" in that such resulting sentences are, as Bergmann sees it, logical truths or falsehoods. Thus, every sentence of the form

⌜. . .⌝ M . . .

is a logical truth, where the dots are replaced by the same sentence to the right and left of the predicate 'M'. If we then take an instance of that pattern

(4)   ⌜Desdemona loves Cassio⌝ M Desdemona loves Cassio,

we may unproblematically infer

(5)   ($\exists$x) [⌜Desdemona loves Cassio⌝ M Desdemona loves x]

as a simple case of existential generalization. Thus, the structure of Bergmann's pattern provides an obvious and trivial solution to another question about existential generalization in the case of intentional contexts. In the case we considered earlier, we quantified from or "over" mental acts; here, we quantify with respect to an "intended" object. Moreover, the pattern preserves an obvious difference in the scope of the quantifier in such contexts. For, on the pattern, we could not infer

(6) ⌜Desdemona loves Cassio⌝ M (∃x)(Desdemona loves x)

from (4) by existential generalization. (6) is false on Bergmann's pattern, since the propositional character does not mean or intend what is expressed by the sentence '(∃x)(Desdemona loves x)'. There are, furthermore, a number of other cases regarding existential generalization from a context like (4) that are easily distinguishable on the present pattern and for which the pattern provides an answer to questions concerning the validity of inference. Thus, we can note that none of

(∃x)⌜(Desdemona loves x)⌝ M Desdemona loves Cassio,

(∃x)⌜(x loves Cassio)⌝ M Desdemona loves Cassio,

⌜(∃x)(Desdemona loves x)⌝ M Desdemona loves Cassio,

⌜(∃x)(x loves Desdemona)⌝ M Desdemona loves Cassio

are legitimate inferences from (4). In fact, none of the four are true sentences and the first two are not even well-formed sentences. The latter two are well formed, but false, by Bergmann's rule regarding contexts with 'M'. The former pair are not well formed, in that the corner quotes do not surround a sentence in either case. Thus, neither '⌜Desdemona loves x⌝' nor '⌜x loves Desdemona⌝' is a well-formed propositional predicate, as neither is formed from a sentence, and, hence, *neither* indicates a propositional character. Both of the latter pair are false for precisely the same reason that we noted in the case of (6); the predicate expression to the left of 'M' does not stand for a propositional character that means or intends the state of affairs that is indicated by the sentence to the right of 'M'. This contrasts with (5), which states that the propositonal *character* ⌜Desdemona loves Cassio⌝ *means* a state of affairs that consists of Desdemona loving someone. That is clearly true, in the context of a schema where all names are indeed names. This does not, of course, require that we hold that the state of affairs *exists* and, hence, that the sentence 'Desdemona loves Cassio' is true. What is involved is the question of possible facts, to which we shall return.

Just as questions concerning the zero-level quantifiers are resolvable, so are queries involving quantification with predicate variables. Thus,

$$(\exists f) [\ulcorner \text{Desdemona loves Cassio}\urcorner \text{ M (Desdemona f Cassio)}]$$

is a consequence of (4), but

$$\ulcorner \text{Desdemona loves Cassio}\urcorner \text{ M } (\exists f) [\text{Desdemona f Cassio}]$$

and

$$\ulcorner (\exists f)(\text{Desdemona f Cassio})\urcorner \text{ M Desdemona loves Cassio}$$

are not consequences and, in fact, are false. As in the similar case of quantification over individual variables,

$$(\exists f) \ulcorner \text{Desdemona f Cassio}\urcorner \text{ M Desdemona loves Cassio}$$

is not a well-formed sentential pattern.

Finally, with respect to contexts like (4) and the question of existential generalization, a pattern like

$$(\exists x) [\ulcorner \text{Desdemona loves x}\urcorner \text{ M Desdemona loves x}]$$

would not be a consequence of (4) but would be an ill-formed pattern. It would be ill-formed, like the previous cases, since '$\ulcorner$Desdemona loves x$\urcorner$' is not a propositional predicate, or any kind of predicate on Bergmann's view. Does this mean that we cannot have *thoughts* to the effect that *Desdemona loves x*? Obviously, it depends on what one means by a *thought*. Surely, mental events can occur that we would describe in terms of the sequence of signs 'Desdemona', 'loves', and 'x'. One can acknowledge such occurrences without holding that such *thoughts* mean or intend anything. In one sense, then, they are taken as thoughts and, in another sense, they are not so classified. As we shall see, such *events* cause no problem for the view we are developing.

There are further questions regarding existential generalization.

To get at them, let us return to (3) and raise a question about the derivation of

(7) $(\exists x) [\ulcorner (\exists y)(\text{Desdemona loves y}) \urcorner (x) \ \& \ \text{Bel } (x)$
$\& \ \text{H}(\text{Othello, x})]$

from (3). (7) states that Othello has a thought or belief state with the content that there is someone whom Desdemona loves. To acknowledge the inference of (7) from (3) would be to hold that *because* one kind of mental act occurs in a person's "mental life" an act of another kind also occurs. Clearly, the occurrence of the one mental state does not logically imply that the other occurs as well. The prohibition of existential generalization *within* the corner quotes preserves this feature. It might be that *in fact* when a state of the one kind occurs, a state of the other kind also occurs. This would have the status of something like a law about mental states. One could then derive (7) from (3) *and* a suitable additional premise expressing such a universal generalization. But, that does not affect the question of existential generalization from (3) to (7).

If we recall the different senses of 'belief' we distinguished in Chapter VIII, then by taking 'Bel' to function ambiguously in (3) and (7) we can acknowledge that (7) is a consequence of (3). Thus, if we hold that where an individual has a belief state of kind $\ulcorner p \urcorner$, and where 'p' implies 'q' then the individual *believes* that q, we can acknowledge that, in this sense, (7) is a consequence of (3). So long as we recognize that we are employing different senses of *belief*, there is no problem. In fact, we may employ different senses of the term 'belief' in more than one way in such matters. Suppose we restrict ourselves to one *basic* sense of belief along the lines of Chapter VIII. We may then distinguish three cases: (a) Othello has a belief state expressed by 'q'; (b) Othello has a belief state expressed by 'p' but neither has a belief state expressed by 'q' nor by "'p' implies 'q'"; (c) Othello has a belief state expressed by 'p' and by "'p' implies 'q'" but not one expressed by 'q'. This may lead us to distinguish three different senses in which Othello may be said to believe *that* q. However, he will have a belief in the *basic* sense only in the first case. But, in the case of believing an implication, one may hold that we deal with another "basic" sense of belief. To believe an implication is not necessarily to have a mental state with something like "'p' implies 'q'" as its text. Rather, in such a case we deal with attitudes, dispositions, knowledge and so forth with respect to a variety of notions and linguistic devices. Believing *that* 'p' implies 'q' is, thus, basic in the sense that one is not said to have that belief because one has a mental state of belief with respect to some proposition which *implies that* 'p' implies 'q'. Yet, it is not basic in the sense that one has a mental state that is expressed by "'p' implies 'q'." We may, thus, arrive at a large number of senses of 'believe' that are relevant to the question regarding the inference to propositions *like* (7), with suitable predicates in place of 'Bel'. Understanding that there are such complications suffices for our purposes without our having to probe into them. However, an aspect of the problem will occupy us when we consider the question of dispositional analyses of belief.

As we noted in Chapter VIII, a variant of our talk of different senses of belief arises in connection with the replacement of different names on the basis of true identity statements. Thus, we can, as suggested earlier, resolve the corresponding puzzles that arise in the case of George IV and Scott. To transform that problem into our present terminology, consider:

$(\exists x) [\ulcorner Scott = Sir\ Walter \urcorner (x)\ \&\ Bel\ (x)\ \&\ H(George\ IV,x)]$

$(\exists x) [\ulcorner Scott = the\ author\ of\ Waverley \urcorner (x)\ \&\ Bel(x)\ \&$
$H(George\ IV,x)]$

$(\exists x) [\ulcorner Scott = Scott \urcorner (x)\ \&\ Bel(x)\ \&\ H(George\ IV,x)]$.

Given the distinctions we have made and the pattern we are using, we can easily specify the statements that are logically connected and why. Shifting the sense of 'Bel' in the above sentences will be required to have any one of them be a consequence of any other. For, taking it in the basic sense we have been using it, it will not be the case that if there is a mental state, characterized by any one of the above propositional characters, there is, on Bergmann's pattern, a mental state characterized by one of the others. Thus, allowing the replacement of names on the basis of true identities, in such contexts, does not rest upon whether one knows or believes the identity to hold, if we restrict ourselves to the original sense of 'Bel'. Even if I believe or know that the requisite identity holds, it does not follow from my having a mental state exemplifying one propositional character that I have a mental state exemplifying another propositional character. Yet, all this raises a problem for the use of Bergmann's pattern. Consider, for simplicity, the true sentence;

Scott wrote *Waverley*.

On Bergmann's pattern we have

(8) ⌜Scott wrote *Waverley*⌝ M Scott wrote *Waverley*.

May we not, then, infer from (8) and 'Scott = Sir Walter' that

(9) ⌜Scott wrote *Waverley*⌝ M Sir Walter wrote *Waverley*

holds? For here, unlike the three existential sentences we just discussed, the replacement occurs outside the corner quotes. But, if we allow for such a replacement, then we easily arrive at

(10) ⌜Sir Walter wrote *Waverley*⌝ M Scott wrote *Waverley*.

With (8) and (10), we have *two* propositional characters that *mean* or *intend one* and the same fact. On Bergmann's pattern, this would imply that the two propositional characters are one and not two. Yet, on his pattern, wherever we have typographically different sentences within the corner quotes, they stand for different propositional characters.

For Bergmann, there is no problem on the surface, since he rejects (9) and (10) as false and would refuse to allow (9) as an inference from (8) and the relevant identity statement (or (10) as an inference from the appropriate sentence like (8)). His doing so testifies to the "evolutionary" character of his position that we traced earlier. Since he added the recognition of possible facts to an already developed theory, there are points, not surprisingly, at which the "new" entities do not quite fit into the already developed account. By rejecting (9), Bergmann contradicts the theme that propositional characters mean possible states of affairs or facts, since statements of the form '⌜...⌝ M ...' *introduce* and provide the interpretation for propositional predicates. They do so by connecting the predicate, and its correlated property, with a possible fact. To save his theory and yet justify the rejection of (9) as false, and as not being a consequence of (8) and the identity claim, he must do one of two things. He may hold that the sentences to the right of the sign 'M' in (8) and in (9) stand for different possible facts, or he may ban different names for the same thing from his perspicuous language. The first alternative is paradoxical, and the latter has an air of the dogmatic and ad hoc. Some years ago, in an article I jointly authored with Bergmann, we proposed that in a strong sense of 'identical', the statement 'A is identical with B' is false even though 'A' and 'B' were two names of the same thing.[4] This was dictated by the restraints of his analysis which lead to precisely the problem we are considering now. The idea regarding the strong sense of identical is worth going into here, since we shall consider some points about *concepts* that are related to it.

If one takes the Russell-Leibniz notion of identity, whereby we hold

$$\ldots a \ldots \equiv \ldots \beta \ldots \equiv a = \beta,$$

with the dotted patterns indicating *any* context, and allow such contexts to include intentional ones like '$\ulcorner p \urcorner$ M p', the idea is easily seen. By the rules for 'M' contexts, with (9) false and (8) true, we have a context

$\ulcorner$Scott wrote *Waverley*$\urcorner$ M . . . wrote *Waverley*

which holds with 'Scott' replacing the dots and fails for the replacement by 'Sir Walter'. Thus, 'Scott = Sir Walter' is false in that "strong" sense of 'identical', even though they are two names for one thing. This is, of course, puzzling. In its way, it may be taken to manifest a form of idealism, in that we held that by thinking about something in different *terms* we dealt with *two* things and not one. Alternatively, one can look at our claim more charitably as merely reflecting the consequences of the rule for 'M' contexts. For, we did acknowledge that in the world "without mind," where we restrict the contexts to extensional ones, such an identity held. It may even be taken to reflect a point about '='. We were talking about identity sentences holding, as we used one sense of 'identical', so that a sentence of the form '. . . is identical with ____' would be true only if one and the same sign pattern replaced the dots and the dashes. We were not talking about the sentence being true if the signs referred to one and the same thing. That way of talking goes along with the notion, which I take to be cogent but shall not argue in this book, that identity is not a *relation* in which a thing stands to itself. In short, an identity sentence is not true because a thing is identical with itself but, rather, because two signs stand for one thing, or the thing for which one sign stands has a certain property ('Scott is the author of *Waverley*'), or, in the most trivial case, that we understand that tokens of the same type stand for one and the same object when they occur on either side of an identity sign. Be all that as it may, the point here is that the same problematic rule about contexts involving 'M' that led to a puzzling claim about identity results in the present problem.

To merely ban the duplication of names is not only ad hoc, but it prevents us from noting some interesting features of the situation. One may hold that by the very notion of an "ideal language" such a schema would not need, and hence not have, more than one name for one thing. There is much to be said for such a claim. But, we must always recall that the purpose of using schematic perspicuous languages is as a tool for the formulation and explication of philosophical puzzles. Insofar as preconceived notions regarding such schemata interfere with their use as tools for resolving a puzzle, they are not to be taken as catechism. The point here is that there is clearly something wrong with an analysis of intentional contexts that gets into trouble in a very basic way if one merely allows an object to have two names. To save the theory by appealing to the idea of an ideal language only prevents us from seeing how the problem may be resolved by modifying the account.

An alternative would be to abandon Bergmann's conception of 'M' contexts and allow for the replacement that yields (9) and, hence, recognizes (9) as true. We, thus, allow for the standard replacements in contexts to the *right of* 'M', though not within the corner quotes to the left. After all, this is to do no more than allow for the same sort of thing that other philosophers traditionally do when they allow for the inference from the appropriate identity and

'Scott' refers to (or names) Scott

to

'Scott' refers to (or names) Sir Walter,

but deny the inference to

'Sir Walter' refers to (or names) Scott.

But, there is an immediate and important consequence of allowing such replacements in 'M' contexts. We must now recognize that different propositional characters may mean or intend the same fact. This introduces a major crack into Bergmann's theoretical edifice. The characters, or propositions if one prefers, would differ since the sentences used to construct the predicates referring to them differ. But, as they intend the same fact, they then, paradoxically, *mean* the same *thing*. Put this way, the problem with Bergmann's view becomes glaring. Given that he has recognized possibilities, he would have to hold an atomic sentence, say 'aRb', stands for a possibility. He would also have to recognize that 'aRb' and '$a = c$' yields 'cRb'. Talk of intentional contexts aside, either 'aRb' and 'cRb' stand for the same possibility or not. If not, there is something radically wrong with his notions of "fact" and "possible fact." If they do, the restriction on the replacement in '$\ulcorner aRb \urcorner$ M aRb', while holding that such a sentence expresses an intentional tie between a propositional character and the *fact* it means, is a glaringly inadequate move.

There are further problems for Bergmann's analysis. If we permit, as I have argued we must, the substitution that allows for the inference to (9) from (8) and 'Scott = Sir Walter', we *in effect* allow for substitution *within* the corner quotes for *such* sentences. For, we have, *in effect*, already gone from (8) to (10) in a "roundabout" way. Recall that on Bergmann's pattern we can form a propositional predicate for any sentence by enclosing the sentence in corner quotes. Thus, take any atomic sentence 'Fa' and an identity sentence '$a = b$'. By Bergmann's rules, we have

$\ulcorner Fa \urcorner$ M Fa.

We may then arrive at

$\ulcorner Fa \urcorner$ M Fb

by replacement to the right of M. By the rules for 'M' we also have

$\ulcorner Fb \urcorner$ M Fb

and may arrive at

⌜F*b*⌝ M F*a*.

Thus, given the identity, we can derive both '⌜F*a*⌝ M F*b*' and '⌜F*b*⌝ M F*a*'. This, in effect, is to permit the substitution within the corner quotes, even though one does not literally make that move in any one step.

The point can be put another way. As we saw in the discussion of Bergmann's pattern, there is only one propositional character intending or meaning a specific possibility, and thus for any given possibility, p, we can characterize the relevant propositional character as '(ιf)fMp'. Since both ⌜F*a*⌝ and ⌜F*b*⌝ intend the same possibility, "they" are the same. Thus, we are led, or forced, to conclude that replacement to the right of 'M' involves allowing replacement to the left of 'M' as well. Just as we have only one possible fact, irrespective of how many names we have for a particular constituent of it, there is, on Bergmann's view, only one "proposition" corresponding to it. This, again, is another consequence of Bergmann's late recognition of possible facts, which he interjected into a pattern from another tradition. The device of the propositional predicates stems from a pattern where difference of sign indicates difference of "thought" or content along the lines of a Fregean assignment of different senses to different names of the same thing. It is, in its way, the recognition of the classical propositional entities where we may have several propositions *picking out* or intending the same fact. The use of possible facts to provide the content or intention of thoughts stems from a pattern that dispenses with propositions, as we saw in the earlier discussion of Bergmann and Moore. Bergmann blends the two and, consequently, by introducing possibilities after acknowledging the classical propositions, he ends in the problems we have considered. These can be covered by stipulations that refuse to allow schemata with two names for one thing as "ideal" languages. An alternative "solution" would be to hold that 'F*a*' and 'F*b*' do not indicate the same possibility. This would amount to the same problematic "creation" of entities to correspond to linguistic patterns that marks the pattern that appeals to senses and Fregean propositions. It would suggest one has reintroduced propositions, in yet another way, *renamed* as facts. The obvious problems about such *ad hoc* entities would return us to Russell's arguments against Frege and should remind us of Moore's early identification of facts and propositions, with the grounding of truth by an *internal* arrangement of the constituents of the proposition.

Bergmann's view is indeed in trouble. But, the problem suggests another modification. Since sentences of the form '$\ulcorner p \urcorner$ M p' state a relation between a propositional character and a possibility or possible fact, we may consider permitting those replacements in such patterns, based on true identities, which preserve true statements of relationship between a propositional character and a possibility. It does not matter whether such replacements occur to the right or the left of the sign 'M'. But, to resolve the problems we have been led into, we must also recognize that more than one propositional character can intend or mean a specific possibility. Hence, although 'Fa' and 'Fb' stand for the same possibility, '$\ulcorner Fa \urcorner$' and '$\ulcorner Fb \urcorner$' do not stand for the same propositional character. How, then, are we to understand such propositional characters? Let me get into that matter by recalling some questions and problems we mentioned in the previous chapter.

Recall the propositions

   (S_{12})   Othello believes that there is someone whom
                  Desdemona loves

and

   (S_{13})   There is someone such that Othello believes that
                  Desdemona loves that individual

from our discussion in the previous chapter and the problems concerning their perspicuous transcription, as well as their relation to 'Othello believes that Desdemona loves Cassio' on the "propositional" view. On the present pattern, we have resolved questions about the connection between (S_{12}) and (S_1), as well as those regarding their transcriptions. But, what about (S_{13})? On Bergmann's pattern, one might, as a first try, suggest something like

   (11)   ($\exists$y)($\exists$x)[$\ulcorner$Desdemona loves Cassio$\urcorner$(x) &
            H(Othello, x) & Bel(x) & $\ulcorner$Desdemona loves
            Cassio$\urcorner$ M Desdemona loves y] .

This is, on Bergmann's pattern, an existential generalization from something logically equivalent to (3):

(12) $(\exists x)$ [⌜Desdemona loves Cassio⌝ (x) & Bel(x) &
         H(Othello, x) & ⌜Desdemona loves Cassio⌝
         M Desdemona loves Cassio] ,

since the last conjunct of (12) is, on Bergmann's view, a logical truth. But, there is a peculiarity. For, although we would normally think that if Othello believed that Desdemona loved Cassio then (S_{13}), properly construed, would be true, we would not think that from (S_{13}) it followed that it was Cassio whom Othello believed Desdemona to love. Normally, an existential generalization does not imply the "ungeneralized" proposition it may be inferred from. But, from (11) we do know that it is Cassio that Othello is suspicious of, and, hence, (11) cannot be a satisfactory rendition of (S_{13}). Paradoxically, on Bergmann's view, (12) follows from (11) (and the logical truth '⌜Desdemona loves Cassio⌝ M Desdemona loves Cassio'), just as (11) follows from (12). We may even put it more dramatically. Given the logical truth '⌜Desdemona loves Cassio⌝ M Desdemona loves Cassio', it follows that (3) holds if and only if (11) does. Thus, (3) is logically equivalent to (11)!

A second attempt might be the use of

(13) $(\exists y)(\exists x)(\exists f)$ [(f M Desdemona loves Cassio) &
         fx & Bel(x) & H(Othello, x) & ⌜Desdemona loves
         Cassio⌝ M Desdemona loves y] .

But, since there is only one property that stands in M to the possibility that Desdemona loves Cassio, (13) fails for the same reason that (11) does. We must find a way of specifying that Desdemona is believed to love someone without specifying too much, whom it is that she is believed to love. To this end, one might suggest:

(14) $(\exists f)(\exists x)(\exists p)$ [fx & Bel(x) & f M p &
         H(Othello, x) & p $\equiv$ $(\exists y)$(Desdemona loves y)] .

But, (14) holds if Othello has a belief state expressed by '$(\exists y)$ (Desdemona loves y)' and, hence, does not provide the distinction we want between (S_{12}) and (S_{13}). Formulating an expression without mentioning Cassio by name would naturally lead us to consider:

(15) $(\exists y)(\exists f)(\exists x)[fx \ \& \ Bel(x) \ \& \ H(Othello, x) \ \&$
        $f \ M \ Desdemona \ loves \ y]$.

This does plausibly render (S_{13}), but it points to another facet of a problem we have already noticed. (15) is the result of existential generalization from

(16) $(\exists x)[\ulcorner Desdemona \ loves \ Cassio \urcorner (x) \ \& \ Bel(x) \ \&$
        $H(Othello, x) \ \& \ \ulcorner Desdemona \ loves \ Cassio \urcorner$
        $M \ Desdemona \ loves \ Cassio]$,

which, recall, is logically equivalent to (3), since the last conjunct of (16) is a logical truth for Bergmann. (3) would transcribe 'Othello believes that Desdemona loves Cassio'. If we now generalize from (16) to

(17) $(\exists f)(\exists x)[fx \ \& \ Bel(x) \ \& \ H(Othello, x) \ \&$
        $f \ M \ Desdemona \ loves \ Cassio]$,

a question arises as to what (17) could be taken to express. And, for the same reasons we rejected earlier attempts to transcribe (S_{13}), we must conclude that (17) transcribes the same claim as (3) does: that Othello believes that Desdemona loves Cassio. Thus, the uniqueness of the propositional character intending a possible fact implies that there are alternative renditions of ordinary belief statements. In a way, all this is reminiscent of Wittgenstein's being puzzled about the logical equivalence of an atomic sentence like 'Fa' and the existential claim '$(\exists x)(Fx \ \& \ x = a)$'. Except here, the equivalence derives from the rules about intentional contexts and not those regarding identity and quantification. One must not think, however, that all this means that Bergmann's view faces the familiar problem that has received considerable discussion from the time of Russell's early observations in "On Denoting" to Quine's and Sellars's recent discussion of "opaque" and "transparent" contexts. We might normally think in terms of Othello's believing that Desdemona loves Cassio by *means* of a thought that involves those terms or by means of a thought, in other terms, that is, nevertheless, about the same fact. One might then suggest that (17) being equivalent to (3) shows that Bergmann cannot distinguish the two cases. For, (3) would be true when and only when the thought was expressed by means of the sentence 'Desdemona loves Cassio', whereas (17) would be true even if the thought was expressed in other terms. This would be a misunderstanding of Bergmann's view. In both cases, on his view, the thoughts would be instances of the propositional character ⌜Desdemona loves Cassio⌝. The mental state, being the kind it is, does not really depend on the terms used. The distinction between the two cases would be specified in terms of further relations between the thoughts, as particulars, and the particular occurrences of the verbal tokens, as sounds, images, etc. The case does not differ from the traditional use of the term "proposition," whereby the same proposition is held to be expressed by different sentences in different languages (or the same language). This shows how close Bergmann's propositional characters are to the Fregean propositions. In short, Bergmann's schema, as we have considered it, would not reflect the difference, but the difference would be easily arrived at. It would not, however, be of any interest, as he sees it, for the explication of intentional contexts. We can, thus, note two things. First, a connection with and perhaps a motive for the avoidance of different names for the same object. Second, a basis for holding that Bergmann's propositional characters are, in spite of their being properties, propositional entities of the Fregean variety. This is why his M relation is as mysterious as the R of Frege and why there is a problem about M-sentences being logical truths.

There is a further connection of this discussion of "propositions" with some issues we have considered. Having the traditional propositional entities to account for the content of a thought, irrespective of the language or medium *in which the thought is expressed*, what is to distinguish two thoughts with the same content? As I see it, one has three choices. He may hold that the particular thought is the actual occurrence of the linguistic tokens (auditory or visual images and sensations, or, perhaps, "inner speech"). Or he may introduce *particulars* — mental acts — to exemplify or be related to (recall Moore's DA) the propositions. Or, finally, he may have recourse to talk about behavior, physiology, and the causal context in the fashion of Sellars. A philosopher who has resolved the problem of individuation in terms of bare particulars and who takes the actual verbal occurrences to be irrelevant to the thought's being what it is (in the sense of content) is easily led to the second alternative. Thus, we have the acts Russell held to be "ghosts," the propositions he took to be problematic, and the intentional relation M he saw as mysterious. Here, we are developing a view akin to Russell's, which means taking the first alternative and showing how the propositional predicates become unproblematic. In the course of doing that, we shall also see some further reasons for rejecting the third alternative.

Having rejected Bergmann's refusal to allow different propositional characters to intend one and the same possibility, we can take (17) to reflect the claim that Othello has *a* belief that Desdemona loves Cassio without thereby claiming that the mental state exemplifies the character ⌜Desdemona loves Cassio⌝. This corresponds to the claim some philosophers make when they say the belief is *about* Desdemona and Cassio, even though it is not expressed by means of the terms 'Desdemona' and 'Cassio'. (3), by contrast, would reflect the way in which the belief *about* Desdemona and Cassio is expressed. Finally, (15) captures the sense of (S_{13}). So taking (S_{13}), we resolve the question of whether

(S_{11}) $(\exists x)$ Bel(Othello, Desdemona loves x)

is a consequence of

(S_5) Bel(Othello, Desdemona loves Cassio).

Since (S_5) is taken as (3) and as (3) is equivalent to (15), (S_{11}) is a consequence of (S_5). For, (S_{11}) is taken as (15). (S_5) has been revealed to be ambiguous in that it may be taken, in one sense, as (3) and in another sense as (17). Taking it as (17) makes it clear that (S_{11}) is a consequence of (S_5) by existential generalization, since (S_{11}) is transcribed by (15), which is an existential generalization of (17). Taking (S_5) in terms of (3), we still get (S_{11}), as (15), by existential generalization. For, (3) is logically equivalent, on the pattern, to (16), and (16) yields (17) by two applications of existential generalization. We have also answered the question about *what* proposition Othello believes when (S_{11}) is true. He believes some proposition that intends or means the fact that Desdemona loves Cassio, without having to specify which proposition. That is, (S_{11}) is true, on our pattern, when there is a belief state that exemplifies a propositional character that intends the possibility that Desdemona loves Cassio. (S_{11}), taken as (15), involves an *existential reference* to a propositional character, if I may so put it.

Our analysis may be taken to uncover yet another ambiguity of such contexts. Just as one may take (S_5) to be ambiguous in the sense that we may render it as either (3) or as (17), one may take (S_{11}) to be ambiguous in that there is a sense in which it, too, may be rendered as (17). For, in (17) we are claiming that Othello has a belief that will be "made" true if Desdemona loves Cassio but without claiming anything else about the propositional character of the belief state. This naturally leads us to ask a question about the use of a definite description of Cassio in such contexts. Such a question, in turn, connects this discussion with some themes from Chapter VIII.

Let '$(\iota x)(Gx)$' be a definite description such that 'Cassio = (ιx) (Gx)' is true. The first point to note is in connection with the sentences

   (18)   Desdemona loves Cassio

and

   (19)   Desdemona loves $(\iota x)(Gx)$,

where we assume that (18) is an atomic sentence, or would correspond to such a sentence of a perspicuous schema. (18) stands for a possible fact. The existence of that fact is the condition for the truth of (18). It is also the condition for the truth of (19), *given that the identity is true*. The identity statement is equivalent to

   $G(Cassio) \& (y)(Gy \supset y = Cassio)$.

Assume, to keep things as simple as possible, that '$G(Cassio)$' is an atomic sentence. A sufficient condition for the truth of (19) is expressed by the conjunction:

   Desdemona loves Cassio & $G(Cassio)$ & $(y)(Gy \supset y = Cassio)$.

We can think of other conditions that could have been sufficient for the truth of (19). The situation is merely a more elaborate version of the point that although '$G(Cassio)$' implies '$(\exists x)G(x)$', the implication does not work in reverse. I shall argue in a later chapter that we need not recognize either conjunctive and existential facts or possibilities corresponding to sentences like (19) and '($\exists$x)G(x)'. In that vein, (19) does not stand for a possible fact. Properly construed (19) amounts to

(20)   ($\exists$x) [Gx & (y)(Gy $\supset$ y = x) & Desdemona loves x] .

As such an existential conjunction, it does not stand for a possible fact, though it may be true owing to the existence of the facts for which other sentences stand. This I merely assert here. the argument will occur later. So understanding matters means that

(21) $\ulcorner$Desdemona loves (ιx)(Gx)$\urcorner$ M Desdemona loves (ιx)(Gx)

does not express a relationship between a propositional character and a possible fact, since the expression to the right of 'M' does not stand for a possible fact. We can then recognize why one could hold that '(ιx)(Gx)' cannot replace 'Cassio' to the right of the 'M' in

$\ulcorner$Desdemona loves Cassio$\urcorner$ M Desdemona loves Cassio

to yield

$\ulcorner$Desdemona loves Cassio$\urcorner$ M [(ιx)(Gx)] . Desdemona loves (ιx)(Gx).

We can deny that such a replacement is legitimate without running into the embarrassment that ensues with the forbidding of different names for the same object to replace each other in such contexts. This reflects a basic idea of Russell's, regarding definite descriptions and reference, that we discussed in Chapter VIII. Unfortunately, it has not been digested by a number of his critics, as well as by those who would use his theory to propound purported paradoxes involving reference and "singular terms." The signs '(ιx)(Gx)' and 'Cassio' do not *refer* to the same object or individual, since the former does not *stand for* any object irrespective of whether or not there is one and only one thing which is G. Yet, we can allow for

[(ιx)(Gx)] . $\ulcorner$Desdemona loves Cassio$\urcorner$ M Desdemona loves (ιx)(Gx)

since that is merely elliptical for

(∃x) [Gx & (y)(Gy ⊃ y = x) & ⌜Desdemona loves Cassio⌝
M Desdemona loves x] ,

which will be true when the identity is true. This is simply a consequence of our being able to allow for existential generalization from (4) to (5). This corresponds to the points noted in our earlier discussion of Russell's attempt to distinguish names from descriptions, in terms of their function in sentences like 'George IV wished to know if Scott is the author of *Waverley*'. A distinction Russell made then frequently is reiterated in the aptly phrased distinction between transparent and opaque contexts. It should be obvious that we do not allow

⌜Desdemona loves Cassio⌝ = ⌜Desdemona loves (ιx)(Gx)⌝

as a consequence, anymore than we allow the identity 'Cassio = Cassius' to yield ⌜Desdemona loves Cassio⌝ = ⌜Desdemona loves Cassius⌝.

The use of descriptions in belief contexts poses a number of intermixed problems. Some have to do with replacement on the basis of true identities. These we have just resolved. Others have to do with questions of truth conditions for existential statements and the providing of content for the occurrence of quantifiers and other logical signs in the texts of beliefs. In that we do not link existential sentences to possible facts or situations, how do they connect with the conditions that make them true or false? This matter we have yet to take up. Still other questions arise in connection with the equivalence of sentences with definite descriptions to existential expansions "of them." These latter we have also resolved, if we take the present discussion in the context of our earlier consideration of descriptions in Chapter VIII. In addition, we have easily resolved the topical puzzles about "quantifying into" and "out of" belief contexts, without ending up with problems that Quine faces, on the basis of his proposals, or those that arise on Sellars's and David Kaplan's neo-Fregean gambit. This requires some explanation and defense.

I think it is readily apparent how we can handle Quine's cases of striving to find lions, wishing for sloops, denouncing Catiline, and the adventures of Ortcutt. What is interesting is how a case that is problematic for him turns out. To facilitate quotation and discussion, it will be best to adopt the examples he uses. Hence, we shall leave Russell's Shakespearean realm of tragedy for Quine's more prosaic fable of Ralph and Ortcutt. The prologue is simple. On two occasions, Ralph sees Ortcutt. Once, he believes the man he sees to be a spy. The second time, not recognizing the man he sees as the man he saw, he believes the man he sees not to be a spy. On Quine's version of the relational view, the two belief situations are expressed as:

(Q_{15}) Ralph believes z(z is a spy) of Ortcutt.

and

(Q_{22}) Ralph believes z(z is not a spy) of Ortcutt.

And Quine concludes:

> Thus (15) and (22) both count as true. This is not, however, to charge Ralph with contradictory beliefs. Such a charge might reasonably be read into:
>
> (23)   Ralph believes z(z is a spy. z is not a spy) of Ortcutt,
>
> but this merely goes to show that it is undesirable to look upon (15) and (22) as implying (23).[5]

What is puzzling about Quine's conclusion is that there is a sense in which Ralph does have contradictory beliefs, but, by adopting the relational view for the rendition of some statements of belief, Quine handles belief in such a way that we cannot say *what* it is *that is believed* in the one case that contradicts *what* is believed in the second case. Yet, he is also correct in holding that Ralph does not have contradictory beliefs; for in some sense, he does not. The point is to clarify that sense as well as the sense in which he does. The pattern we have developed provides a ready answer, in fact it enables us to make some further relevant distinctions.

In our terms, we construe (Q_{15}) to state that there is a belief state which Ralph has and which has a propositional character that intends the possibility that Ortcutt is a spy, while taking (Q_{22}) to state that there is a belief state that intends that Ortcutt is not a spy. We may then recognize senses in which *there are* as well as senses in which there are not contradictory beliefs. Ralph has contradictory beliefs in that the intended situations are contradictory. He does not have contradictory beliefs in the sense that the construals of (Q_{15}) and (Q_{22}) do not involve the use of propositional characters which are construed from contradictory sentences (we make use of a quantified predicate variable in each case). This reflects what we might ordinarily express by saying that he has contradictory beliefs without knowing that he does, since he does not believe the requisite identity. There is another point. Since we express his having a belief in terms of an existential claim about a particular belief that Ralph has, we can note that to hold that

$(Q_{15'})$ $\quad$ ~Ralph believes z(z is a spy) of Ortcutt,

is naturally rendered as the claim that every belief state of Ralph's is not a state that has a propositional character intending that Ortcutt is a spy. This is not equivalent to (Q_{22}), nor does it follow from (Q_{22}). This might be taken as a further sense in which Ralph does not have contradictory beliefs. And, finally, as Quine notes in his own terms, it is not the case that there is a belief state of Ralph's that has a contradictory sentence as the basis for the propositional character it exemplifies. But, there is one awkward feature of Quine's account. Let us change the situation to a case where Ralph is aware that it is the same man on both occasions, but where Ralph never obliges us with *a* belief state that exemplifies a contradictory propositional character. For Quine, (Q_{15}) and (Q_{22}) would still describe the two situations and Ralph would still not have contradictory beliefs. This clearly will not do.

Kaplan's criticism of Quine will not do either. He holds that

For in the same sense in which (Q_{22}) and (Q_{15}) do not express an inconsistency on Ralph's part, neither should (Q_{15}) and $(Q_{15'})$ express an inconsistency on ours. Indeed it seems natural to claim that $(Q_{15'})$ is a consequence of (Q_{22}). But the temptation to look upon (Q_{15}) and $(Q_{15'})$ as contradictory is extremely difficult to resist.[6]

But, it is not at all "in the same sense" that we may hold that (Q_{15}) and $(Q_{15'})$ do not express an inconsistency. As we just construed them, they clearly do. What Kaplan apparently has in mind is that if one can truly say of Ralph that he has the belief that Ort-cutt is not a spy, then $(Q_{15'})$ is true. His next sentence bears that out. But, this appears to confuse the sense in which Ralph may be said not to have *a* belief, when no belief he has is a belief of that kind, with the sense in which he does not have the belief if he has a belief in the negation of the relevant claim. I say "appears to confuse" because Kaplan proceeds to make a very similar distinction in his own terms. Before getting to that, we might note more precisely why his claim that "in the same sense" (Q_{15}) and $(Q_{15'})$ should not express an inconsistency is mistaken. (Q_{15}) could be rendered as

(E_1) $(\exists f)(f = \hat{x}$ is a spy & Bel(Ralph, f, Ortcutt))

and $(Q_{15'})$ would be

(E_2) $(\exists f)(f = \hat{x}$ is a spy & $\sim$Bel(Ralph, f, Ortcutt))$,

assuming Quine would not shirk from the use of the quantifier. He should not, since he is using predicate abstracts in subject place and has temporarily acknowledged "intensions" as "creatures of darkness" that will be left behind when he eventually semantically "ascends." Recognizing such "creatures of darkness," however temporary the association is, one would recognize a suitable com-prehension condition for "attributes." Thus, given the predicate 'x is a spy', we have '$(\exists f)(f = \hat{x}$ is a spy$)$' as a "theorem" of the schema employed. Hence, (E_1) and (E_2) are contradictories. Or, if one balks, the point may be simply put in terms of

$(\exists f)(f = \hat{x}$ is a spy$)$ & (E_1) & (E_2)

being a contradiction.

We may also render (Q_{22}) as

(E_3) $(\exists f)(f = \hat{x}$ is not a spy & Bel(Ralph, f, Ortcutt))$.

We then clearly see that $(Q_{15'})$ is not a consequence of (Q_{22}). One line of Kaplan's criticism thus misses the mark.

Kaplan mixes the question of (Q_{15}) and $(Q_{15'})$ being contradic-tories with another question. This latter deals with the supposed in-ability of Quine's formulation to distinguish two cases that depend on the characterization of beliefs in terms of the signs used to "ex-press" their content. In a way, this criticism is beside the point, since, first, Quine has acknowledged that distinctions can be made, but he finds them to be problematic, and, second, it is not clear that Quine's semantically ascended view cannot embody those distinctions along Sellars's lines, for he does retain beliefs *in sentences*. On the first point, Quine notes: "Belief$_1$ was belief so construed that a proposition might be believed when an object was specified in it in one way, and yet not believed when the same object was specified in another way."[7] Where Kaplan is correct is that in accepting "intensional" entities like propositions and "attributes," Quine has not "gone all the way" and acknowledged "senses" of individuals and quantification over senses, concepts, and propositions. Moreover, Quine has not clearly specified the relation between belief sentences, taken "intensionally," and semantically "ascended" versions; nor has he clearly stated how he construes the latter. We need not bother with Kaplan's notion of a "vivid name" and its reflection of a mixing of questions about causal conditions, behavioral responses, introspective ruminations, Fregean entities, and philosophical problems about "reference." What he is claiming is that if we "break-up" the Fregean propositions into typical Fregean constituents and quantify over these, as in (F) of Chapter VIII, we can distinguish cases that Quine does not distinguish on his analysis. A relevant case would be where we distinguish the claim:

(I)   There is a proposition and a constituent sense that denotes Ortcutt and the proposition contains the concept *is a spy* predicated of the sense, and it is not the case that Ralph believes that proposition.

from the claim:

(II)   For any proposition that contains the concept *is a spy* predicated of a sense that denotes Ortcutt, it is not the case that Ralph believes that proposition.

This presents a distinction that involves a simpler case than Kaplan's, since I do not bother with talking about terms in Ralph's vocabulary that express the sense in question. The point is that certain distinctions necessitate construing the proposition or sentence as a complex with constituents. But, now, if one takes the gambit to literally involve us with propositions, senses, and concepts, Kaplan has not presented us with an account that renders such entities unproblematic or, for that matter, with any detailed account at all. Were he to work one out, it would likely amount to a variant of Sellars's or Bergmann's. The heart of the latter analysis, recall, is the employment of specific sentence patterns in the account of belief, through the use of 'M' and sentences to the right of that sign in patterns like '⌜. . .⌝ M . . .'. If Kaplan's account involves believing sentences, rather than propositions, he has not made clear what this could mean, or even whether it would significantly differ in structure from the first alternative. Perhaps, it would involve something like Sellars's modification of Russell's pattern. Quine has also suggested such a view, and I take it he has something in mind similar to Sellars's approach.[8] Along such lines, it is hard to imagine that one who speaks of believing sentences will not eventually treat sentences as composed of words and, consequently, acknowledge patterns like "there is a word and there is a sentence such that the word is a part of the sentence . . ." as well as distinguish between believing different "sentences" with words for the "same thing." This, as we noted earlier, is what Sellars does.

There is an obvious problem with Kaplan's analysis that recalls an earlier discussion of Sellars. It is indicated by my use of (I) and (II) above. Suppose we take the corners to turn sentences into names of propositions as, on Bergmann's view, one turns them into names of propositional characters. How do we then transcribe the mixture of symbols and English

$$(\exists a) \, \text{Bel}(\text{Ralph}, ⌜a \text{ is a spy}⌝)$$

into an English sentence? We cannot say that there is a *sense* such that Ralph believes that . . . What we must say is something on the order of the following. There is a proposition and there is a sense that is a constituent of it, and the concept *is a spy* is a constituent of the proposition, and the form of the proposition is such that the concept *is a spy* is predicated of the sense and Ralph believes the proposition. I shall readily agree that my use of the phrase "English sentence" above requires a bit of charity on the reader's part. But, what is clear is that we "quantify over" a variety of entities as well as employ notions like *constituent* and *form*. We also make use of a predicative connection within the proposition and of a referential connection between senses and objects. Kaplan's understanding of his "convention" covers up all this. Once we have unpacked it, as it were, it becomes clear that Kaplan has not quantified into corner contexts without radically complicating the notion of a corner context that we started with. Consider the case of forming a name of a sign, say 'Desdemona', by putting standard quotes around it, as I just did, and then considering

$$(\exists x)(\text{'Desdemonx'})$$

to be an existential quantification over letters and read as "There is a letter such that placed for the 'x' in 'Desdemonx' the *latter becomes* a name." Clearly, we are no longer merely using the quoting device according to the original convention, for we are not rejecting " 'Desdemonx' " as gibberish nor treating it as a name of the pattern within the quotes. To perspicuously render what Kaplan attempts would bring us back to (F) of Chapter VIII and, hence, to features characteristic of Bergmann's analysis or of Sellars's.

XIII

The Structure
of Thought: Part II

Our pattern permits the derivation of

(B₁′)   ⌜Desdemona loves Cassius⌝ M Desdemona loves Cassio.

Hence, we considered permitting the substitution of *names* within the corner quotes in *such* cases, i.e., in contexts like '⌜...⌝ M ...'. The question then arises about substitution within the corner quotes in all contexts. An obvious problematic case is provided by identities like:

⌜Desdemona loves Cassio⌝ = ⌜Desdemona loves Cassio⌝

and true denials of an identity such as;

⌜Desdemona loves Cassio⌝ ≠ ⌜Desdemona loves Cassius⌝;

since, although they are true, to permit the substitution of names on the basis of 'Cassio = Cassius' would yield the falsehoods:

⌜Desdemona loves Cassio⌝ = ⌜Desdemona loves Cassius⌝

and

⌜Desdemona loves Cassio⌝ ≠ ⌜Desdemona loves Cassio⌝.

One might take this to be a justification of Bergmann's approach, or at least a reason behind it, as well as a problem for the view we are developing. But, there is no reason to allow for replacements within the corner quotes. Moreover, the problem does not really arise. We have been employing the propositional predicates for the sake of developing a pattern. One who is familiar with the type of view involved will suspect that the names do not really occur inside the predicate expressions, when we have adequately specified how we construe the latter. As we have been developing the view, it is clear that what we want is to have (B_1') be a consequence of our analysis and the identity 'Cassio = Cassius', but we also want to hold that

$$(\exists x)[\ulcorner \text{Desdemona loves Cassio} \urcorner (x) \ \& \ \text{Bel}(x) \ \& \ \text{H(Othello,}x)]$$

and the identity statement do not imply

$$(\exists x)[\ulcorner \text{Desdemona loves Cassius} \urcorner (x) \ \& \ \text{Bel}(x) \ \& \ \text{H(Othello,}x)] ,$$

since the propositional characters indicated by the *different* propositional predicates are different, even though they both intend one and the same fact. To work this out is to explain the construal of the propositional properties on the view being developed.

We can begin by considering two particular mental states occurring at different times, but both of which *consist* of the auditory sensations one gets if one pronounces aloud, but to oneself, the sentence 'Desdemona loves Cassio'. Call these two states 'm_1' and 'm_2'. Let 'm_3' and 'm_4' refer to two other particular mental states occurring at different times but both consisting of phenomena one experiences when he "says to himself," but does not audibly pronounce, the same sentence. We have four distinct states in that there are four different acts occurring at different times, but m_1 and m_2 have a property, call it 'F_1', which neither m_3 nor m_4 has. They have this property in virtue of consisting of auditory sensations and of being tokens of types interpreted in a certain way. Similarly, m_3 and m_4 have a corresponding property, call it 'F_2', which neither m_1 nor m_2 has. F_1 is a property had by all auditory patterns that are like m_1 and m_2 in a way analogous to the way in which different tokens of a linguistic type are like each other. F_2 is a similar kind of property applying to mental states composed of phenomena like those contained in m_3 and m_4. Compare, for example, F_1 and F_2 to properties characterizing, respectively, all tokens of the *sentence* 'Desdemona loves Cassio' written in black ink and all tokens written in red ink. Both F_1 and F_2 *intend* or *mean* the fact or possibility that Desdemona loves Cassio, just as we might consider the type-in-black as a sentence and the type-in-red as a sentence, both of which would mean or stand for the same "thing." Suppose, further, that all four states are beliefs and hence characterized by Bel. In one sense, both F_1 and F_2 may be taken as the same propositional character, just as the type-in-black and the type-in-red may be taken as the same sentence type. In another sense, they are different characters or properties, just as the sentence types are different, if we bring in the color of type in addition to the properties of shape and arrangement. They are the same in that they *mean* the same fact. In that sense, *two* propositional characters are the same₁ if they mean the same possibility. They are different in *that they are two properties* and not one. Since F_1 is the same₁ as F_2, m_1, m_2, m_3, and m_4 are individual states of belief that involve *the same belief*. Since F_1 is not identical with F_2, one may also say that m_1 and m_3 are not literally cases of the *same* belief, though m_1 and m_2 are. Let us say that m_1 and m_3 involve the same₁ belief, but not the same₂ belief.

Consider next two states, m_5 and m_6, such that m_5 is like m_1 except that it contains an auditory sensation of the word 'Cassius' (taken as another name for Cassio) instead of the word 'Cassio', and m_6 is like m_3, except for containing an "inner pronouncement" of the word 'Cassius'. In view of these features, let m_5 and m_6 be said to have, respectively, the properties F_3 and F_4. Since 'F₃M Desdemona loves Cassio' and 'F₄M Desdemona loves Cassio' are both true, F_3 is the same₁ as F_4, just as F_1 is the same₁ as F_3. But, F_1 is not *identical with* F_3, as F_3 is not identical with F_4. Thus, m_5 and m_6 involve the same₁ belief as each other and m_1, m_2, etc., but they do not involve the same₂ belief. Yet, there is a sense in which m_1, m_2, m_3, and m_4 are instances of the *same* belief in a way in which none of them is an instance of the *same* belief as m_5 or m_6. None of the first four states contain tokens of the name 'Cassio'. In virtue of this, let m_1, m_2, m_3, and m_4 be instances of the same₃ belief, and m_5 and m_6 be the same₃ as each other, i.e., instances of the same₃ belief, but neither is the same₃ as any of the preceding states. The introduction of 'same₃' raises some problems and provides an occasion for some clarifications.

Consider two schemata employing the "same" indexed letters except that one makes use of capital letters and the other employs lower case letters as zero-level constants. Let each individual constant of the one schema be said to be *correlated to* its obvious "partner" in the other schema. Consider the names and predicates of the first schema to be coordinated to, or interpreted into, certain individuals and properties. Let it be understood that such an interpretation also interprets the correlates in the second schema. Suppose, further, that we allow different constants in the first schema to be interpreted onto the same objects. Let 'a_1' and 'a_2' be two such constants corresponding to the same object. Consider the two sentence types '$F_1^1(a_1)$' and '$F_1^1(a_2)$' of the first schema and '$F_1^1(A_1)$' of the second schema. In one sense, we have three types; yet, in another sense, '$F_1^1(a_1)$' and '$F_1^1(A_1)$' are the same in a way in which neither is the same as '$F_1^1(a_2)$'. Even if we say all three "say the same thing," this does not reflect what is involved. For, through the correlation of 'a_1' with 'A_1' and of 'F_1^1' with itself, the interpretation of one sentence type provides an interpretation of the other, whereas '$F_1^1(a_2)$' says the "same thing" in virtue of a further act of interpretation or interpretation rule. Thus, we can consider tokens of the types '$F_1^1(a_1)$' and '$F_1^1(A_1)$' to be tokens of the *same* type in a sense, without considering tokens of '$F_1^1(a_2)$' to be tokens of *that* type, even though tokens of all *three* types stand for or state the same fact. This is not to deny that in another sense tokens of '$F_1^1(a_1)$' and of '$F_1^1(A_1)$'. are tokens of different geometrical patterns and, hence, of different types. In an analogous way, m_1, m_2, m_3, and m_4 are instances of the *same* belief over and above their exemplifying propositional characters, which *mean* the same state of affairs. In that case, the correlation between auditory sensations and inner pronouncements of the *same* verbal patterns replaces the correlation between the signs 'a_1' and 'A_1' and, hence, of the relevant sentence patterns. Thus, one can hold F_1 and F_2 to be the same$_3$ without claiming that they are identical or collapsing the sense of 'same$_3$' with that of 'same$_1$'. This brings out something our earlier example of red and black type glossed over. This third sense of '*same*', whereby F_1 and F_2 are the *same*$_3$, enables us to resolve a puzzle. For, one objection to distinguishing the belief-type that Desdemona loves Cassio from the belief-type that Desdemona loves Cassius, as we did earlier, would be that we would be forced to distinguish *the belief* that Desdemona loves Cassio from *itself*, since F_1 is a different propositional character from F_2. m_1 and m_3 are instances of the *same* belief not only in that the same fact is intended, as in the case of m_4 and m_5, but in that F_1 and F_2 are the same$_3$. The auditory sensations and inner pronouncements involved in m_1 and m_3 are correlated in the way that 'a_1' and 'A_1' are correlated. They are not "connected" as the result of two independent coordinations of signs and things, as are 'a_1' and 'a_2' and as are the components of m_1 and m_5. Thus, we have yet another sense of 'belief', whereby sentences, related as are '$F_1^1(a_1)$' and '$F_1^1(A_1)$', may be said to express the same belief. Mental acts, exemplifying the appropriate propositional characters formed from the sentences with 'a_1' and 'A_1', would be instances of the same belief in a way that instances of characters formed from sentences with 'a_1' and 'a_2' would not be. In short, when Samuel Clemens was baptized, tokens of a written sign pattern (many such patterns, of course) of auditory patterns, etc., were purportedly involved or 'covered." The tokens of the name 'Mark Twain' involve another ceremony or set of circumstances. As I have been using 'same$_3$', we may hold that *two* propositional characters are the same$_3$ if they are *interpretation correlates* in the sense in which '$F_1^1(a_1)$' and '$F_1^1(A_1)$' (or F_1 and F_2) are such correlates. One may feel that the notion of an *interpretation correlate* has not been made precise enough, for I have not specified "criteria" for such correlations. Nor have I dealt with the question of criteria for deciding when tokens are instances of the same pattern. Moreover, many questions can be raised about what is involved in a baptismal ceremony that is relevant for a name being *attached* to its designation and for *its* subsequent use to refer to that designatum. Some of these questions are not relevant for our concerns, interesting though they may be for those who are interested in the detailed workings of natural languages. Others are relevant, and we shall deal with them shortly. One point of employing simplified schemata is to enable us to separate questions of a philosophical or logical kind from questions that are more properly the concern of linguists, sociologists, psychologists, anthropologists, and so forth. Here, I ignore irrelevant questions about when two tokens are tokens of a type and about the complexities involved in the correlation of written and spoken signs (in natural languages) by considering a simple schema to avoid the first and a stipulated pairing to avoid the second. Nothing is lost by so doing. The justification of doing so lies in the consequent clarifications we get of the various strands of the classical puzzles. The fundamental philosophical problems involved are precisely those that can be retained by considering such a simplified schema. We shall soon return to this theme in our consideration of dispositional states and causal analyses. For my present purposes, I believe I have been as specific as one need be about the notion of an interpretation correlate. However, there is a philosophical point that may motivate the request for further explication of that notion.

Recall the earlier criticism of Bergmann's view that propositional predicates are formed from *sentences yet* refer to simple *properties*. Or, to put the matter linguistically, the predicates referring to the propositional characters are formed from sentences by use of the corner quotes. Yet such predicates are taken as undefined or primitive terms. I suggested that one feature of Bergmann's view responsible for such an objection would be eliminated if we defined propositional predicates along the lines of the pattern

$$\ulcorner p \urcorner =_{df.} (\iota f) f \, M \, p.$$

But, this would force one to hold that F_1, F_2, F_3, and F_4 were the "same," since "all four" intend the same possibility. As I have considered the issue here, four different predicates are *linked* to the same possibility but *refer* to different properties. What properties? Consider F_1 and F_2. Any mental state exemplifying F_1 consists of a series of auditory sensations—the sound *of* 'Desdemona', *of* 'loves', *of* 'Cassio' occurring in that order in more or less immediate succession. Such a sequence constitutes a fact composed of three particulars in a temporal relation. We may continue to refer to such facts by terms like 'm_1', etc., and introduce, along the lines of Chapter V, a relational predicate for a notion like "contains," say 'Con', so that we may consider a sentence like '$F_1(m_1)$' to be elliptical for or defined by

(I) $(\exists x)(\exists y)(\exists z) [Con(m_1,x) \, \& \, Con(m_1,y) \, \& \, Con(m_1,z) \, \& \, \emptyset_1(x) \, \& \, \emptyset_2(y) \, \& \, \emptyset_3(z) \, \& \, R_1(x,y,z)]$

where the 'Ø's' are used to specify that something is an auditory token of 'Desdemona', etc., and 'R_1' stands for a relational property ordering the three tokens. By contrast, the sentence, '$F_2(m_3)$' would be elliptical for

(II) $(\exists x)(\exists y)(\exists z)[\text{Con}(m_3,x) \,\&\, \text{Con}(m_3,y) \,\&\,$
$\text{Con}(m_3,z) \,\&\, \emptyset_1(x) \,\&\, \emptyset_2(y) \,\&\, \emptyset_3(z) \,\&\, R_2(x,y,z)]$

where the '$\emptyset$'s' are used to specify that something is an inner pronouncement of 'Desdemona', etc. In short, something that is a $\emptyset_1$ is a correlate of something that is a $\emptyset_1$, just as tokens of 'a_1' and tokens of 'A_1' were correlates. R_2 may be taken as a correlate of R_1 or as the same temporal and ordering relation. Particular mental states like m_1 and m_3 are, thus, facts, much as Wittgenstein spoke of propositions being facts in the *Tractatus*.

> 5.542.   It is clear, however, that 'A believes that p', 'A has the thought that p', and 'A says p' are of the form ' "p" says p': and this does not involve a correlation of a fact with an object, but rather the correlation of facts by means of the correlation of their objects.

What Wittgenstein means is, I think, clear enough in spite of the variety of interpretations the passage has engendered. What, after all, is the *form* of

"p" says p

in Wittgenstein's terms? It expresses the connection between a sentence and a fact, and, recall, much has been made of the notion that sentences are facts. Thus, it expresses the claim that there are two facts capable of correlation in the manner Wittgenstein speaks of throughout the *Tractatus*:

> 2.141   A picture is a fact.
> 2.1   We picture facts to ourselves.
> 2.21   A picture agrees with reality or fails to agree; it is correct or incorrect, true or false.

With this, we are familiar. To say "A thinks that p" is of this form is to say nothing more than that when A thinks that p we have a fact, which is the thought, that correlates to a *situation* or possible state of affairs in exactly the same way that a sentence does. The thought is a fact as a sentence token is a fact. In this sense, thoughts are sentence tokens. Of course, they need not be auditory or visual tokens of any natural language. Recall Russell's image propositions, which he writes about in the period of the *Tractatus*. Wittgenstein's thoughts could be such image patterns. There is only the remark "I don't know *what* the constituents of a thought are . . ." in the 1919 letter to Russell to suggest that they are some sort of mysterious "thought elements." Nor is the point about not having a coordination between a fact and an object, but, rather, a coordination of facts by means of a coordination of their objects, puzzling. He is not, as Sellars misleadingly holds, reiterating Sellars's interpretation of the passage about *a*R*b*:

> Wittgenstein's elaboration, "Here we have no coordination of a fact and an object, but a coordination of facts by means of a coordination of their objects", simply enriches the account by relating it to his thesis that one says that *a*R*b* by placing an '*a*' in a counter part relation to a '*b*'.[1]

The main point Wittgenstein is asserting is quite clear, given the context of the statement in the *Tractatus* and his later "discussion" of the self in that book. Just before this passage, he writes:

> 5.541   At first sight it looks as if it were also possible for one proposition to occur in another in a different way.
>
> Particularly with certain forms of proposition in psychology, such as 'A believes that p is the case' and 'A has the thought p', *etc.*
>
> For if these are considered superficially, it looks as if the proposition p stood in some kind of relation to an object A.
>
> (And in modern theory of knowledge [Russell, Moore, *etc.*] these propositions have actually been construed in this way.)

And he immediately follows 5.542 with an explication of that statement:

> 5.5421   This shows too that there is no such thing as the soul—the subject, *etc.*—as it is conceived in the superficial psychology of the present day. Indeed a composite soul would no longer be a soul.

The theme, in short, is that the self or "soul" does not belong to the world. There is no object that is a self. A sentence like 'A thinks that p' seems to express a connection between a self, A, and a proposition or fact, p. That it does not is Wittgenstein's claim. Since there are no selves, we cannot treat such expressions of thought, belief, etc., as relations between selves and something else—facts, propositions, words, things, etc. Recall that Russell's "relational view" in "Knowledge by Acquaintance and Knowledge by Description" and in *The Problems of Philosophy* involved a self as a *term* in a "belief fact." Thus, the relational view that Russell proposed is unacceptable. In fact, Wittgenstein immediately follows 5.5421 with the cryptic criticism of Russell's view that I alluded to and expanded upon in an earlier chapter:

> 5.422   The correct explanation of the form of the proposition, 'A makes the judgment p', must show that it is impossible for a judgment to be a piece of nonsense. (Russell's theory does not satisfy this requirement.)

The point is that if one requires that a belief or judgment not be "a piece of nonsense," such as,

Bel^4 (Othello, Desdemona, Iago, Cassio)

or

Bel^4 (Othello, Desdemona, Cassio, loves)

or

Bel^4 (Othello, Desdemona, loves, loves)

and so forth, then one introduces a rule to the effect that the last three terms form a meaningful sentence. This reveals that the relational analysis amounts to a mere *rewriting* of the propositional view and is not a substantive alternative. This point seems to be what Wittgenstein expressed in the June 1913 letter to Russell; 'aRb v $\sim aRb$' could only "directly follow" if 'aRb' is a sentence.

Russell, too, came to reject his earlier view and denied both the act, as a "ghost" of the self, and the self as an object, by construing the latter along Humean lines as a *bundle* of thoughts, sensations, images, etc. This fits with his rejection of particulars, in the sense of bare particulars, and his consequent attempt to construe objects as bundles or collections of properties, which he misleadingly insisted on calling 'particulars'.[2]

Not acknowledging selves does not mean, for Russell or Wittgenstein, that one does not acknowledge thoughts. What, then, are thoughts? Facts of the kind we have spoken of are familiar from our discussion of Russell and Moore. The point about the "correlation of their objects" is also easily understood. It is simply a reiteration of the familiar *Tractarian* point that a sentence is connected with a situation or possibility by the coordination of the elements of a sentence with the elements of a situation or possibility: the interpretation of the signs of the schema. The names in the sentence are the objects of the sentential fact taken as the occurrence of tokens of the name type; their correlates are the objects in the fact the sentence expresses or stands for. A thought is a mental occurrence, a fact that is a token of a sentence pattern. Thus, Wittgenstein's view and Russell's view in "On Propositions" and *The Analysis of Mind* are variations on a theme. We can, then, understand the two cryptic remarks that occur earlier in the *Tractatus*:

3.5   A propositional sign, applied and thought out, is a thought.

4.   A thought is a proposition with a sense.

It is helpful to recall how Wittgenstein uses 'sense' in such contexts:

4.031   In a proposition a situation is, as it were, constructed by way of experiment.
Instead of, 'This proposition has such and such a sense', we can simply say, 'This proposition represents such and such a situation'.

But, one may now raise a problem about the interpretation of the notorious and puzzling 3.1432 that was involved in my earlier criticism of Sellars. For, 5.542 seems, as Sellars interprets it, to assert that thoughts, and sentences, are correlated with situations by "means of the correlation of their objects." Hence, there would be no correlation of predicates with relations or monadic functions, as I suggested, since the latter are admittedly not objects. How, then, do I square my interpretation with 5.542?

We must always keep in mind in dealing with the *Tractatus* that the "picture" metaphor of language and thought is dominant. As Wittgenstein says at one point in the book, the essence of a proposition, and hence of a thought, is to be found in hieroglyphic script:

4.016   In order to understand the essential nature of a proposition, we should consider hieroglyphic script, which depicts the facts that it describes.

And alphabetic script developed out of it without losing what was essential to depiction.

And just before he had written:

4.011   At first sight a proposition—one set out on the printed page, for example—does not seem to be a picture of the reality with which it is concerned. But no more does musical notation at first sight seem to be a picture of music, nor our phonetic notation (the alphabet) to be a picture of our speech.

And yet these sign-languages prove to be pictures, even in the ordinary sense, of what they represent.

4.012   It is obvious that a proposition of the form 'aRb' strikes us as a picture. In this case the sign is obviously a likeness of what is signified.

What these passages make clear, I think, is that aside from any question of whether propositions contain predicates and relational terms in Wittgenstein's perspicuous schema, the relationship among the names in a proposition ('aRb' or 'a_b') represents a relationship among the objects in the fact. After all, the occurrence of a note *after* another in a score represents the playing of the one *after* the other in the performance. This is made perfectly clear by:

2.15   The fact that the elements of a picture are related to one another in a determinate way represents that things are related to one another in the same way.

Let us call this connection of its elements the structure of the picture, and let us call the possibility of this structure the pictorial form of the picture.[3]

The point is not only that the elements of a picture represent but that the structure of the elements in the picture represents the structure of the objects depicted, even if the structure is the *same*. Thus, the painted mouth being *below* the painted nose (in a portrait properly hung) represents the fact that the subject's mouth is *below* his nose (when the subject is in a "normal" upright position). One may take the relation in the picture and in the depicted fact to be literally the same, *being below*, but it is understood that the relation as occurring in the picture *represents* the same relation as occurring in what is depicted. But, there are radical differences between the correlation of objects and the correlation of structures or relationships that are probably responsible for the varied interpretations. First, in the case of a literal picture, the relationship can be understood to be literally the same, in some cases, and, hence, the correlation is understood rather than made. Or, perhaps better, understanding that the painted mouth and nose represent a mouth and nose, we naturally take the relationship among the painted patches the way we do. Second, we can correlate objects to objects independently of the structure of the fact they are constituents of, but we cannot correlate the structures independently of the objects. An illustration will make the point. Suppose two objects are such that one is above the other, i.e., we have *the* fact that one object is above the other. Suppose, further, that we have the uninterpreted sentential pattern 'aRb' and that we intend to interpret the pattern in terms of that fact. There is an obvious and simple asymmetry to note between the objects, on the one hand, and the structure, on the other. Every fact can have at most one structure (*and* "relation") but any number of objects. Thus, if we start with a fact and the sentential pattern 'aRb' and correlate the names to objects, there is no room for choice with respect to the function sign 'xRy'. Remember, we are dealing with a definite fact, and every fact has only one structure. By contrast, if we start by correlating the function sign to the structure of the fact, we may still correlate the names to the objects in two ways. Of course, one way will yield a true sentence and the other a false sentence, but it is a basic thesis of the tradition of logical atomism that the "meaning" or "sense" of a sentence is one matter and the truth value is another. The question of interpretation has to do with meaning and sense alone. In fact, one could put it cryptically: we do not have to bother interpreting the function sign, since there is only one function sign in a sentence and one structure in a corresponding fact. Thus, if we think in terms of starting from facts and sentential patterns, two stark contrasts emerge: (I) we do not have any choice in interpretation or correlation of function signs and structures of facts, and (II) function signs and structures of facts thus contrast sharply with the respective objects they arrange or order. However, this is not to deny that we acknowledge *both* structures, or relations, holding among the objects of facts *and* the corresponding function signs, as functions, holding among names. The point helps us understand why Wittgenstein says the sorts of things he does. Part of the problem stems from the fact that the proponents of alternative interpretations of Wittgenstein, those who take relations and properties to be objects and those who deny that they are objects and, hence, that they are acknowledged at all, share a misconception. They both think in terms of a list of signs and a list of entities and a correlation between elements of such lists. The picture is misleading, for purposes of grasping how Wittgenstein is thinking, though it is, I believe, ultimately adequate for understanding what is implicit in the view of the *Tractatus*. What is misleading about it is that as we study Wittgenstein's statements and examples, it is clear that he is thinking in terms of a comparison between a picture and what it depicts. Thus, he is comparing the sentence *as a whole* with a fact. The correlation of the *function* or structure of the sentence with that of the fact is thus determined, or, to put it as I did above, one need not make such a correlation. Putting it yet differently, *it shows itself*. Understanding matters so, it should be clear that my earlier interpretation fits, rather than jars, with Wittgenstein's talk about propositions as pictures. In turn, this helps connect the view being presented here with that of the *Tractatus*, as well as with Russell's analysis of "On Propositions." We may now return to the further development of our analysis.

The mental states m_1 and m_3, as well as the properties F_1 and F_2, are correlates, since their constituent particulars, the properties they exemplify, and the patterns they form are correlated. Just as we simplified matters by considering only one correlate for 'a_1', i.e., 'A_1', in our earlier example, let us assume we have to deal with only auditory patterns and inner pronouncements. We can, then, consider a propositional predicate like '⌜Desdemona loves Cassio⌝' to be defined as a disjunctive predicate in terms of 'F_1' and 'F_2'. This would clearly show that it is specious to consider "things" that exemplify properties like F_1, and F_2, and ⌜Desdemona loves Cassio⌝ to be *simples*; just as it is specious, in view of (I) and (II), to take the predicate '⌐Desdemona loves Cassio⌐' to be a *primitive* predicate referring to a *simple* property. One problem associated with Bergmann's view thus disappears. A second problem is also avoided. Bergmann problematically holds sentences of the form '⌐p⌐ M p' to be logical truths. We can see what is justified in his claim. Such sentences are merely reflections of our interpretation rules for patterns (and their tokens) of the kind that exemplify the property ⌐p⌐. Resulting from such a stipulation or interpretation, M-sentences may be held to be "logical" or "linguistic" truths. But, there are two other aspects that must not be overlooked. We have held that propositional patterns *stand for* possibilities. This claim is hardly a linguistic or logical truth. It involves a problematic philosophical assertion. Bergmann packed both claims into the declaration that sentences like '⌐p⌐ M p' were logically true, since 'M' stood for an intentional relation. As treated here, the use of 'M' merely indicates that we have stipulated an interpretation for certain patterns. It involves no mystery. Nor is there anything mysterious about a propositional character like ⌐Desdemona loves Cassio⌐ holding of different kinds of states, in view of the notion of a correlation. *Propositions, as intentional entities, are no longer required.* A state like m_1 does not "intend" what it does in virtue of a peculiar thing called a proposition. It intends what it does since it contains tokens whose types have been interpreted the way they have. We have had, of course, to speak of possibilities. But, this, I have argued, we must do in any case, to deal with the questions of how sentences are about the world and true or false of it. Moreover, we shall see, in the next chapter, that possibilities can be made quite "palatable" to a philosopher with a "vivid sense of reality." Once we speak of facts and possibilities, propositions, as philosophers like Bergmann employ them, are not needed. Thus, the problem of the connection between propositions and facts disappears. It was this question that made Bergmann's claim that (B_1) is a logical truth suspect, since, as we noted, part of what is involved in his view is the claim that a propositional character (proposition) and a possibility stand in the relation M. The view presented here recovers, I believe, what is sound in Bergmann's claim that statements like (B_1) are logical truths and in Moore's earlier point that we use the same sentence to stand for both a fact and a belief. But, the present view also recovers what is sound in the objections raised to Bergmann's view, since it is obviously not analytic to claim that possible facts correspond to certain sentences. All we need do, to do justice to both lines of thought, is explicitly separate the claim that atomic sentences, and mental states whose content is expressed by such sentences, correspond to possible facts from the point that all mental states and sentences with that content are correlates composed of correlated constituents. In so doing, I have treated mental states as composites, like sentences, which are composed of tokens that are correlates of the linguistic tokens in sentences like 'Desdemona loves Cassio'. It is obvious that we can introduce a further predicate, say 'LF', parallel to the definitions of 'F_1' and 'F_2' in (I) and (II), where such a predicate would stand for a property that would characterize, not individual mental states, but written sentence tokens. Such a defined predicate could then be added as a further disjunct in a modified definition of the relevant propositional predicate. What is involved is merely the recognition that mental states of belief are propositional, not in that they are related to special entities called propositions or exemplify propositional characters, but in that they are literally sentence tokens. If one insists, at this point, that we still recognize "propositional entities" in that we have predicates like 'F_1', 'F_2', etc., he has missed the two-fold point that not only are such predicates defined, but they function no differently than a predicate applying to all tokens of a name. To say that there are propositions, on the present schema, is to say that there are *interpreted sentence types*.

We are now in a position to resolve some problems regarding the notion of a "concept." Moore, as we saw, thought of such concepts more or less as universals or properties. Thus, *the concept red* was *the universal property red* or *redness* and not something that was *the concept of red* and, hence, distinct from the property. Frege appears to transform talk about properties of objects into the vocabulary of concepts that objects fall under. As we also saw, there is a basis for distinguishing concepts from properties in Frege's system. But, generally, there has been a tendency on the part of philosophers to identify universal properties with concepts. This goes along with the pattern whereby one speaks of particulars being experienced or sensed and concepts or properties being intuited or being objects of thought or cognition. No doubt, this is one basic theme behind the traditional idea that properties or universals are *abstract* objects. Abstract objects are grasped in thought, the mind being that which has the power of abstraction. Concrete, or particular objects, are grasped by sense. Sensation, being a bodily function rather than a "mental" one, is more suited to the "experiencing" of particulars located in space, as is the sensory apparatus. Even Platonism incorporated such themes. The properties of particular objects were, after all, particular instantiations of the universal concept or form, which the mind grasped or "remembered." In Frege, we find a basis for the distinction between the *universal* property and the concept of it: the concept and the concept correlate, as I considered the latter in an earlier discussion. This distinction was, in its way, incorporated in the pattern Bergmann and I had proposed in "Concepts." But, on that pattern, concepts, like the concept *of* red, were construed as propositional characters. Having abandoned such entities in the traditional sense, which is basically Bergmann's sense, to be replaced by characteristics along the lines of linguistic types, I wish to apply that pattern to the notion of a concept. Consider the property red, or, to be prosaic, think of it. What takes place? There is a thought, which is a mental state. Call it 'm_r'. What makes m_r a thought of the property red? Suppose m_r consisted of an occurrence of a token of the "inner" sound of 'red'. In one sense, what occurred was a fact: a token of a kind. But, in that sense, tokens of 'Desdemona loves Cassio' are facts composed of facts. That sense of fact we may ignore. For, by it, all occurrences are facts, since one does not find any particular that does not have or exemplify a property. Or, perhaps a better way of putting it would be to acknowledge that if we note that sense in which m_r is a fact, then we have an unproblematic sense in which thoughts are facts and all thought is "propositional" in form. The point, though, is that we can think *of* red without thinking anything about red: that it is a color or that it exists or that it is self-identical, and so forth. m_r will share a property with all other thoughts of red, just as m_1 is an instance of F_1 along with other thoughts of "the same kind." Call such a property 'R_1'. Just as we may say

396 The Structure of Thought: Part II

that 'red' refers to or means red, we may say that R_1 refers to or "intends" or *means* red. It is *a* concept of red, just as F_1 is *a* thought (though not a *particular* mental state) that Desdemona loves Cassio. We can speak of *the* concept of red if we recall the various senses of "same" that are applicable in such matters. By contrast with the propositional characters of thought we have considered to this point, R_1 is not a propositional character. Yet, it characterizes thoughts or mental states that are thoughts. Thus, not all thought is propositional. Yet, we can note two "reasons" for holding that it is. It makes no sense to say that we believe *that* red, or even *in* red. Thus, though one may speak of a thought here, one cannot speak of a belief. The idea that thought is just a connection with a content, but that belief or disbelief is the adoption of an attitude toward the content, must surely be partly responsible for the claim that contents are propositional. What may also be partly responsible is the melding of the notion of a concept with that of a property. One who recognizes properties, and is more at home in the empiricist tradition than the Platonic, generally holds that we only experience properties as exemplified or instanced. Experience, if I may so put it, is factual. We neither perceive properties unexemplified nor particulars without properties. It is very easy to transform the pattern to the realm of thought. Yet, it is not easy to hold that when one thinks of a property, one thinks of some particular having it. Hence, one is held to think something about it: that it exists, or what have you. Nothing but dogma preserves the pattern. Thus, we may recognize thoughts, like m_r, with properties like R_1, which are concepts *of* properties like red. Individual concepts pose another problem. In a sense, one has an individual concept when one thinks *of* an object in terms of a definite description, rather than by means of a proper name or mere label. Part, if not all, of the turmoil over bare particulars has to do with the claim that one must think of individuals in terms of properties or descriptions. Some philosophers, less inclined to deal with the traditional problems in the traditional terminology, now dispute about whether names are disguised descriptions or whether, when one *really* or *legitimately* uses a name, one has "in mind" a "back-up" description or can produce such a description in response to the appropriate questions. Thus, there is an issue of whether a thought can be of an individual if it is a "token" of a name in the sense in which m_r is a token of R_1. As we noted in Chapter VII, one may raise the same issue about concepts of properties and derive yet another sense in which one may claim that thought is propositional. To have a thought of the property red would involve thinking of it in terms of a definite description rather than a name or, at least, being able to provide such a description. It is interesting that the question that has historically been raised regarding particulars does not generally get raised about properties. No doubt, the theme that properties, as concepts, are abstract objects that one "grasps" in thought is partly responsible. Another thread would naturally be the common theme in classical philosophers, such as Descartes and Berkeley, that properties, as qualities, are the content of experience as opposed to the assumed substratum. If we recall Descartes' example of the piece of wax, it appears sensible to think in terms of the qualities and *that* which is left *and which has* the qualities. One, thus, arrives at the "notion" of a substratum or bare particular. But, it would seem absurd to take a quality, say red, and seek to distinguish its content from some unknown aspect in virtue of which it is a quality or which is connected in some way to the content to "form" the quality red. Properties are naturally not "bare." This sort of theme is one thing behind Russell's rejection of particulars, and his construal of objects as bundles of qualities. It is also involved in the similar pattern that Berkeley and Bradley have promulgated and which, in its way, has become characteristic of traditional idealism. (Though Bradley rejected "bare universals" in favor of universals with an "aspect of particularity.")

The point behind it all seems to be that in the case of particulars, if we have a thought, m_p, that is a token of the kind $\emptyset$, and we then ask "In virtue of what is m_p about the object O_1?", one has a natural reply if $\emptyset$ is in the form of a definite description or a "conjunction" of predicates. The answer would be that O_1 has the properties specified by the predicates or is the object satisfying the unique condition of the description. If $\emptyset$ specifies a type for a name, no such answer is forthcoming. All one can say is that the name refers to O_1. In the case of properties, it is as if the question is missed, since, having a predicate, one has a property it refers to.

But, this clearly does not indicate a real difference with the case of thoughts of particulars. In fact, it points to a problem. For, can we not raise the very same question in turn with respect to the signs in the definite description or the predicates in the group of predicates composing Ø? That is, what seems to be behind the problem of how a thought of an object can involve a mere label is a question regarding how a given token of a label, occurring as a thought, means or intends the object of that thought. The appeal to descriptions and predicates, as well as the general failure to raise the question regarding properties, is an attempt to answer the question by presupposing that there is no corresponding problem in the case of predicates and properties. In fact, as I have raised the question, it generally is not raised. One reason for this is that it tends to be confused with another question I shall consider shortly. Another reason is that one might think the query is answered either by holding that the type has been interpreted to "mean" the corresponding object or property or by taking a more "sophisticated" line and noting that the type stands for the object or property in some language L. Hence, all we need do is relativize our references by talk of "refers to O_1 in L" and so forth. But, none of these "answers" even touch the question which, in its way, is at the heart of the problem of intentionality. We can best get at it, and the related question I mentioned, by returning to the case of propositional characters that reflect sentential forms, for the question arises there as well. Solving it for that case, we can readily apply the point to the case of concept-characters for thoughts of individual objects and properties. Before doing so, let us momentarily recall that subject to resolving the issue at hand, we have noted two things about concepts. They are construed as characteristics of thoughts along the lines of properties like F_1, F_2, and our construal of ⌜Desdemona loves Cassio⌝ as a disjunctive property. We, thus, have concepts of individuals and concepts of properties. The thoughts that exemplify such concept-characters are, in one perfectly clear sense, not propositional in form, by contrast with thoughts like m_1. Concepts of properties are not identified with properties anymore than the propositional character ⌜Desdemona loves Cassio⌝ is identified with the possible fact *that* Desdemona loves Cassio. In the case of individual objects or particulars, we may distinguish those concept-characters that apply to tokens of names from those that apply to tokens of definite descriptions. This gives us yet another distinction in the case of "individual concepts." Needless to say, a corresponding distinction can be made for the case of concepts of properties. The distinction between descriptions and names enables us to make a point regarding Frege's "mysterious" relation between a sense and a denotation, since our concepts play a role similar to that of his senses. Where the concepts are name types, the relation is simply that of stipulated reference. Where the concepts are description types, the relation is two-fold. The predicate of the description stands for a property, in the sense of stipulated reference for primitive predicates, and that property is exemplified by the object. Thus, the mysterious D^* of Frege disappears on our treatment in terms of stipulated reference and exemplification. I shall now turn to our basic problem.

Taking the mental state m_1 as a token of the kind it is, one may still ask why it intends what it does, since the notion of "intending" is ambiguous. In one sense, a mental state that is a token of a certain kind *intends* a situation (possible fact), since the type of the token has been interpreted in a specified way. But, consider a case where such a mental token occurs without the person believing, doubting, etc. It simply runs through one's mind so that *the mental state*, which is the instance of the pattern, does not intend the situation that *the type* represents or stands for. What is the difference between such a state and an intentional state? Having generic properties such that states, as tokens, are said to be of a certain kind in that they are instances of such properties (or connected in some way to such instances) takes care of one aspect of the problem. For a state to intend in one sense, $intend_1$, is for it to be a token of an interpreted type. For a state to intend in a second sense, $intend_2$, is not only to be such a token but to exemplify a generic characteristic of acts such as believing, doubting, remembering, etc. This, of course, is one crucial difference between a thought, as both a sentence token and a fact, and a token of a sentence that occurs in a book. But, a problem remains. Suppose we have interpreted certain geometric patterns (auditory patterns, etc.) in two ways, so that, for example, *the name* 'Desdemona' is the name of two people. How does one determine which situation is represented by an occurrence of a token of $\ulcorner$Desdemona loves Cassio$\urcorner$, even where the token, which is a mental state, exemplifies an appropriate generic property of acts? For Bergmann, *this* problem does not *seem* to arise, since he considers philosophical problems in terms of an ideal language that does not involve such ambiguities. Nevertheless, the problem still does arise. For, the question is about why a particular token on a particular occasion refers to the object coordinated with the type. This problem is not removed by restricting the interpretation of the types. But, we may start by considering the case where we have allowed for the ambiguous interpretation of the "name." One can, then, suggest that we deal with tokens of *different* types, in that two tokens of *the same geometric pattern* are *not* tokens of *the same sentence* type, since, the sentence type is a pattern with a specific interpretation. To speak somewhat paradoxically, *the name* 'Desdemona' would not be involved, since we have two names, not one, in that we have one name being the sign pattern *with* one interpretation, and the other name is the same sign pattern with a different interpretation. Although this distinction solves some related problems, it does not solve our problem. We must now specify why one token is a token of one sentence type and the other token is of the other type. To appeal to an additional content *in*, or accompanying, the act invites an obvious infinite regress. It will not help to appeal to causal conditions, dispositions, or contextual circumstances. Such factors are relevant to someone else inferring what my mental states are or my resolving problems about past states of my own. They do not solve the present problem, in that it is clearly *possible* to satisfy such conditions and yet not have the appropriate state, or not satisfy them and have it. The case is analogous to attempting to "analyze" someone's being in pain in terms of overt behavior, dispositions to behave, physiology, environment, etc. Insofar as we admit the logical possibility of having the behavior, physiology, etc., without the phenomenal state, and vice versa, such an *analysis* is inadequate. We are dealing with a third sense of 'intend' (intend$_3$). We have an intention$_1$, since we have a token, and we have an intention$_2$, since we have a generic property characterizing the token, say Bel. But, we are now trying to determine why the token *intends* the situation it does in fact intend. In one sense, there is no answer. It is not in virtue of anything that the occurrence of such a pattern is a token of the type representing one situation rather than another. There is no account to be given in the sense that one can point to a feature or constituent of the mental state that provides the answer. Rather, one has to point to a feature of thought. As we noted earlier, Sartre has held that all acts, though directed to their objects and in that sense "aware of" such objects or contents, are also self-awarenesses, in a basically different sense of "awareness." He is, I think, mistaken phenomenologically and ad hoc logically, but his pattern is, once again, suggestive. Acts of thought not only intend situations in that they are intentions$_1$ and intentions$_2$, but they are awarenesses of which situations they do intend, and, hence, in having the act *one* is aware of which situation is intended. It is this feature that makes them intentions in the third sense of 'intend'. Such a "solution" invites the contemptuous response that nothing is said, since what is said is that acts intend what they do *because* they intend what they do. But, that is not correct for a number of reasons. Acts intend what they do in the first two senses of 'intend' *because of* interpretations of types and generic properties they have. They do not intend what they do in the third sense *because of* anything. This simply means that in specifying the structure of the situations corresponding to belief sentences of the kind we have considered there is no element of such situations that grounds the fact that a token refers to what it does. To speak of a "conglomeration of images, names, and partial descriptions which Ralph employs to bring x before his mind" is to resort to an antiquated "thought as image" psychology as well as a problematic use of 'name'. It is also to confuse two quite different questions. There is one question regarding the causal conditions for the occurrence of the belief states we have considered. Answering such a question may involve talk of images or even of "bringing things before one's mind," whatever that might mean. In a similar way, one may talk about conditions, including physiological ones, for a subject being in pain. But, just as such *correlated* conditions do not provide a *description* or analysis of *the situation* that obtains when one is in pain, they do not provide an analysis of what takes place when we refer to something. The second question involved is a question about the structure of the situation that does obtain when I refer to someone. What is the analysis of the situation that obtains when such reference takes place, or, to put it another way, what is the fact corresponding to the sentence 'Othello believes that Desdemona loves Cassio'? To claim that the two questions are distinct is not to deny either that there may be causal accounts for the occurrence of such mental events or that such causal explanations will involve physiological and environmental factors. It no more does so than the denial that phenomenal entities or states, say a pain or the state of being in pain, are "analyzable" or "reducible" to behavioral, physiological, and environmental things and states involves the denial that the occurrence of such phenomenal entities is causally explainable in terms of such physical factors. All that is claimed is that such considerations do not suffice to cogently *analyze* statements of the kind we have considered. Thus, the italicized uses of 'because' are to be understood as indicating the connection between an *analysans* and an *analysandum* and not a *causal* connection. I was, then, merely claiming that one sense of 'intend' (or 'refer'), whereby we say a thought token *intends* or *refers* to what it does is not analyzable. There is an interesting feature of the relation between causal accounts and accounts or analyses of the "nature" of thought. On the one side, we find those like Sartre, who, in one way or another, convince themselves that thought involves the feature I have discussed in terms of 'intend$_3$' and illicitly conclude that such a feature is irreconcilable with causal explanation. Denying causality in such matters, Sartre proclaims "freedom." On the other side, we have those who seek to specify the intentional nature of beliefs by recourse to the physiological, behavioral (including dispositions to utter linguistic tokens), and environmental factors. Determined to insist on the causal efficacy of the physiological processes and behavior conditioning, they end up by denying not only the existence of intentionality but of mental entities and processes. Neither side seems able to render unto the other its due. What this may show is that in spite of the homage it has received, Hume's lesson about causality and necessity is too difficult to digest. For, insofar as one treats causality in terms of "constant correlations," rather than in terms of "necessary connections," and insofar as we distinguish causal accounts from analyses, why should we not have our intentional states along with causal explanations of them?

Distinguishing the causal account from the question of the structure of the relevant fact enables us to safely ignore the criticism that all that has been said is that acts intend what they intend. That criticism is based on a natural, but mistaken, tendency to treat the queries about why a token refers to what it does and what it "means" to refer as requests for a causal account that explains, in one obvious and legitimate sense of 'explain', the fact that a token referring to someone occurs. Consider someone asking "Why is Jones in pain?" A normal response would not be "There is a pain, a phenomenal entity, which Jones has." In *ordinary circumstances*, to *account* for Jones being in pain in terms of such a claim would be pointless and irrelevant. What is wanted in such circumstances is either a causal explanation for Jones being in pain (having a pain) or a specification of the evidence for believing that Jones is in pain. Yet, to speak of phenomenal entities is at the heart of the antiphysicalist's *account* in the *context of a philosophical dispute* about mental entities. The same distinction is relevant for the present issue. We can, then, understand the temptation to appeal to causal accounts or elaborations of the ordinary circumstances of cases of reference. It results from the construal of our question as either a request for specifying what conditions are causally connected with the use of a token to refer to someone or a request for specifying how one knows that someone uses a token in such a way. But, to so take matters is to overlook the problems we have been concerned with and to fail to recognize a distinctive feature of thought and reference. One may easily convince oneself of this. Think of someone or something. You know that you refer and to whom or what you refer. But, now ask yourself what you mean by saying that you refer, why the thought is about whomever or whatever it is in fact about, and how you know that you refer and to what you refer? The questions point to three distinct claims involved in the discussion. First, reference is not analyzable by appeal to causal circumstances or what we normally take to be evidence that I refer to someone on a given occasion, even though such considerations obviously suffice to resolve nonphilosophical problems regarding cases of reference. Second, the intentional feature of a thought, whereby a token on that occasion does refer to someone, is neither analyzable nor represented by an element of the situation that obtains. If I may so put it, only the referring token need occur as an element of the act of thought, and not the fact that the token stands for what it does. Third, I sometimes know what I refer to without there being any further account of that fact to be given and, hence, anything more to be said. If one sums all this up by saying that all that has been said is that thoughts intend what they do because they intend what they do, the slogan makes a point but not a critical one.

Causal accounts of intentionality are linked with so-called dispositional accounts of thought. On the analogy with a property like *solubility*, being taken as dispositional in that one holds that objects are soluble if they dissolve *when* placed in water, one holds that *thinking-that-p* can be treated as a disposition to behavior B under conditions C. Thus, to say that I am thinking-that-p at time t is to say that at t I have the disposition θ, where we understand 'θ' in terms of

$$\theta x =_{df} Cx \Rightarrow Bx,$$

with the use of the '⇒' in place of '⊃' to recognize the traditional problem of counterfactuals. That problem will not be our concern here, since the notion is that it is no more problematic for 'θ' than for 'soluble'. But, there are serious problems with the dispositional account. Consider a case of pain and "associated" behavior that reveals that a subject is in pain. We normally take the pain to be the, or a, cause of the behavior or take the behavior to be a "symptom" of the pain or of someone being in pain. To say of the subject, s, that he is in pain is thus to account for or "explain" his behavior; it is not to state, in other words, that he behaves the way he is in fact behaving. In a similar fashion, we take my exhibiting behavior of kind B under C to be explained by my having a thought. The statement that a subject who is thinking-that-p will do B under C is taken to be a significant factual claim. It is not taken to be a short-hand way of expressing the trivial claim that a subject who will do B under C will do B under C. To avoid the triviality, the proponent of the dispositional account asserts that an "analysis" is being offered. But, that is not the point. The analysis is such that upon it a significant statement becomes trivial. This points up a difference between the case of thinking-that-p and "soluble." To speak of a piece of sugar being soluble is to hold that the object is of a kind, sugar, and "sugar is soluble."[4] In short, there is a law involved, however implicitly or explicitly we put it. One may wonder what the corresponding law is in the case of θ, and consequently, what the "kind" is that correlates with the disposition. Clearly, the relevant characteristic is the property of thinking-that-p. This would be the "law" that would *account for s* having θ, i.e., any subject that thinks-that-p does B under C. But, to recognize such a "law" is to give up the dispositional analysis! One may, then, look for another characteristic to lawfully connect with θ. Two obvious candidates are (1) antecedent conditions that would causally explain *s* thinking-that-p and (2) supposed correlates at *t*, physiological perhaps, of *s* thinking-that-p at *t*. Call these C_1 and C_2, respectively. Then

（a） $(x)(C_1 x \supset \theta_x)$

（b） $(x)(C_2 x \equiv \theta_x)$

will both be nontrivial "laws". But, (a) and (b) do not really help, for the proponent of the dispositional analysis must still take *thinking-that*-p to be stipulated to be θ and, hence, still trivialize the claim that if *s* thinks-that-p, then *s* does B under C. He must also hold that it is impossible to think-that-p without doing B under C, and vice versa, just as the classical behaviorist held that it is "absurd" to claim that *s* could exhibit *all* the behavior *associated with* pain without being in pain, or be in pain without exhibiting *any* of the relevant *symptoms*. Note that the assumption of the dispositional account allows for a causal account of intentionality in terms of (a) and (b). Hence, one who holds the causal account I considered earlier to be inadequate should balk at a dispositional account. But, this is not to say that a causal account would not be forthcoming in that I denied the possibility of laws like (a) and (b) or "laws" linking mental states with behavioral states such as

（c） $(x)[C_1 x \supset (\exists y)(H(x,y) \,\&\, \ulcorner p \urcorner\, y)]$

or

（d） $(x)[(\exists y)(H(x,y) \,\&\, \ulcorner p \urcorner\, y) \equiv \theta x]$.

All that was denied was that (c) or (d) yield an analysis of s *thinks-that-p*. This is no more surprising than the claim that even if we have laws correlating physiological with macro-behavioral states, we cannot take the statements about the physiological states to constitute an *analysis* of the macro-behavioral statements in that the former *explicate* the latter.

There is also a problem with talk about "laws" connecting phenomenal states with behavioral states or with physiological states. They are more in the realm of the philosopher's imagination than in the domain of the psychologist's or physiologist's field of research. This is why one has heard of that fanciful invention "the auto-cerebrescope," which will enable one to both feel a pain and observe the corresponding physiological state. The problem is simple. It is that the private data of the phenomenal realm are not the sorts of things one deals with in the "intersubjective" realm of science. What the psychologist observes is the behavior of the subject, not the pain. Even if one puts matters in terms of observing that the-subject-is-in-pain so that the relevant characteristic becomes being-*in*-pain, a characteristic of an observable subject, rather than the property of being-*a*-pain, a property of a "private" phenomenal entity, matters do not change. For, the property of being-in-pain will be, as the psychologist uses it, a behavioral property, specified in terms of behavior and physiology.[5] Thus, to speak of "laws" in such contexts is irrelevant to our concerns in a very basic way. When properly specified, the laws are not laws that correlate physiological and phenomenal states. We can, of course, speculate about there being correlations between phenomenal and physiological or behavioral states. But, such speculations are more for the purpose of proposing philosophical positions rather than projections of future scientific discoveries. Of course, the behavioral scientist and the physiologist operate in a common-sense context, where one assumes that pain-behavior indicates pain and verbal responses go along with mental states. Yet, these notions do not belong in either the theories or laws proposed. In the common-sense context in which the scientist operates, they function as a set of unquestioned assumptions, whereby we take for granted that behavior of a certain sort expresses or indicates pain or that certain processes produce pain in a subject. It is granted that such common-sense assumptions are not questioned in other than philosophical disputes. The simple point is that they cannot, then, be a basis for advancing a philosophical position regarding mental states. The situation is no different from that regarding our common-sense knowledge of other minds. That is one thing. It is quite another thing to *base* a philosophy of mind on such "knowledge." What is an acceptable basis for our common-sense approach to people and situations is one thing. What is an adequate basis for a philosophical resolution of the classical puzzles about mind and *the mental* is quite another thing. It is blatantly question begging to use the one to resolve the other, or, at least, it returns us to the sort of approach we witnessed in the case of Malcolm's dismissal of the phenomenalist on the basis of "correct" usage and our ordinary conceptual scheme.

Our analysis of intentional contexts enables us to understand a misleading feature that appears to support the dispositional-behavioral analysis. As we speak or write, we engage in mental activity, just as we do when thinking or speaking to ourselves. What, then, are the mental states in such cases of "public" speaking? Convinced that such activities reflect or express mental states, some philosophers declare that such inner states must accompany or precede the "outer" behavior. Others, convinced that there are no inner states, in addition to the outer states, in such cases, stipulate that the obvious cases where we have inner states are to be construed in terms of dispositions to manifest outer states. Once again, each extreme distorts the apparent facts for the sake of some sort of conceptual coherence. How, then, are we to construe cases of public "expression of thought"? Note, first, that the very phrase "expression of thought" lends itself to the view that the public speaking or writing expresses some other "state" or "thought." But, how literally need we take such an expression? The proponent of the view that there is an inner thought may leap to the conclusion that there is some sort of vague isomorphism between an inner episode and the written or spoken sentence, thus inviting an opponent to press for a description of such a ghostly occurrence. Ironically, he might then feel forced to find it in the physiological apparatus and, thus, turn a defense of the mental into a form of materialism. Clearly, there is something besides the sentence *as* a pattern of sounds or blobs of ink, but "it" need not be a mysterious state that is isomorphic to the overt behavior that produces the sounds or script. Of course, there is also an "inner" physiological state, but that is not a mental state, though it may correlate in similar ways to an "inner" thought and a "public expression." What, then, is there in such cases of speaking and writing? The written or spoken marks are instances of interpreted propositional characters; thus, they, like inner thoughts, may be intentions in the first sense of that term. But, even then, let us distinguish between such tokens as written or spoken, i.e., as the kind of product that they are as opposed to the physical objects that they are. There is the old puzzle about the monkeys typing Shakespearean sonnets or the wind forming "sentences" in the sand. Given that what is formed is a token of an interpreted pattern, we may say, in that sense, it *expresses* or states something. Given that it is not a product of a certain process, being written by a person who comprehends the language, it is not, in another sense, an expressive token. There is nothing really worth arguing about. But, there is a more important theme. In *producing* such a product, a person intends, in the second and third senses, exactly as he does in the case of inner episodes of thought. There are acts of inner thought, of inner speech, of outer speech, of writing (gesturing, too, if you will) that are all intentional acts, though the constituents of some of the acts (which, recall, are facts) are mental and those of other acts are physical. The inner thought that Desdemona loves Cassio is, thus, contrasted with the spoken declaration. But, both may be intentions in the second and third senses. Does this mean that "physical actions" can intend objects and possible situations? Yes and no. There is a difference between my writing and the wind "writing" in the sand. My writing of a token of the name 'Scott' differs in a way that enables one to say that the token of *the name* is not merely the blob of ink or the mark in the sand. It is a blob of ink *as formed in a certain way and context* that *is the name*, just as much as it is the blob of ink *in a certain geometrical shape* that is the typographical token. Alternatively, it is the inner image of that typographical shape that is the token in the case of an "inner thought." As formed in a certain way, the typographical (sentential) ink patterns are tokens of thoughts, just as inner patterns of images are such tokens. We may have sentences composed of images and sentences composed of blobs of ink or marks in the sand. So long as we recognize the filling out that the phrase "composed of" requires, we can say that in a similar way thoughts may be composed of images or of externally written patterns. We may, then, ignore the absurd temptations to throw out the inner thoughts in favor of dispositions to "external thoughts" or postulate a "hidden" or "unconscious" inner thought for every external one. I may truly think out loud or *in* writing, just as I may think to myself. I *may* just as truly have mental states with no present or future *macro-physical manifestation*, dispositional or overt. Again, this does not deny the *possibility* of correlations involving mental states and macro- or micro- "behavior." It does not reflect on the general belief that every mental episode has a physiological correlate, for example. (In fact, establishing "common" physiological correlates for "inner" thoughts and intentional physical states would neatly fit with what has been said.)

Bergmann's propositional characters and acts ground the connection between a thought and its content and, hence, between a *name* and "its" referent. This is done in Fregean fashion, since the act exemplifies a property that stands in M to a (possible or actual) fact. Thus, exemplification and M connect the thought to its intention. On Frege's pattern a sentence expresses a proposition that stands in D* to a truth value. Replace Frege's truth values by the facts of a correspondence theory and the formal similarity is even more striking. Following Russell, I have tried to suggest a way of retaining non-ghostlike acts and linking them to states of affairs. The link between a token and an intention is provided by a basic intentional relation, which requires no further "ground." But, a problem remains in connection with the use of tokens as labels for objects and properties that are not directly apprehended when the token occurs.

Suppose one holds that when a token of a name or primitive predicate occurs, in the absence of the object or property, there is no basis for saying that we intend the object or property. In such cases there is only the occurrence of the tokens as tokens of types that have a "role" in the complex network of past conditioning, behavior, etc. So long as we recognize that tokens *are* intentions of objects and properties, in situations where such objects and properties are directly apprehended, nothing fundamental is altered, as far as the arguments of this book are concerned. What is affected is the claim that objects and properties are thought of when not apprehended. Observe a white spot and assert "This is white." That you know what object you refer to (and that you refer to it) is not open to question. That you also know what property you refer to (and that you refer to it) is likewise not debatable. The claim that the property is a property referred to on other occasions by the predicate is supposedly implicit in the use of the predicate. This purportedly involves memory and, hence, is problematic in a way in which the references to the presented property and object are not. Assume that this is so. It does not mean, as some think it does mean, that the assertion that the object is white becomes transformed into an assertion that the object has a property that it has. One still indicates an object and a property and asserts that a connection obtains between them. Suppose one had named the object 'Walter'. Later, no longer presented with the object, one judges that Walter was (or is) white. Assume that it is not viable to hold that one can be said to *know*, as one does in the case of the presented object, that the token of 'Walter' refers to the object and the token of 'white' refers to the color. There is merely the occurrence of arranged tokens which are events that belong to the "natural order," as Sellars says. Clearly, there need not be occurrences of tokens of descriptions for which the name is elliptical—not even the description " 'the object called 'Walter'." There are neither Fregean senses, nor nonlinguistic descriptions, nor other species of ethereal entities to be found in such a case. Even if there are images, they do not help, as the same question arises about the intentional role of images. And, if there is a token of a description, with or without an image ("the object resembling the image"), the problem occurs in connection with the token of the predicate in the description. One may insist that the case of properties is different; that one can intend properties not presently apprehended, but not particulars. The traditional notion that we *conceive* properties but only conceive of a particular in terms of properties thus enters the discussion. As I indicated earlier, I cannot see any basis for distinguishing properties from particulars in such matters. Thus, one either acknowledges that particulars that are not presented can be intended or denies that properties, not presently apprehended, are intended. Taking one side, one holds that we have the occurrence of tokens, images, etc. in the causal order but not as intentional tokens. Taking the other side, one holds that we intend both particulars and properties in cases where neither are apprehended. One may be misled by a specious reason for the first alternative. If I claim to intend a particular not presently apprehended, I claim that there is such an object. But, there is obviously *a sense* in which I cannot *know* that there is such an object, since I cannot know that it continues to exist, as I know that a presented object does exist. By contrast, I can know that a property, once apprehended, does not cease to exist, though I cannot know, owing to the contingencies of memory, that I intend what I intended on previous occasions. But, this difference, if such a difference exists, does not provide a ground for holding that one may intend nonpresented properties but not nonpresented objects. All it does is show that one reason for holding that one does not intend a nonpresented particular may not be applicable in the case of properties.

The key point to the puzzle is memory. I can remember an object once presented, just as I can remember a property. I cannot remember an object or property that was never presented. To intend a nonpresented object or property is to remember it. This does not mean that one cannot be mistaken, since memory is fallible. But, all this means is that one cannot be certain that one is intending an object or property in cases of thinking about nonpresented items. In the case of an object or property that was never presented, one cannot remember it at all, irrespective of any question about its existence or knowledge of its existence. This can be overlooked, since one theme involved in distinguishing between particulars and properties is that properties can be recognized but particulars can not be recognized, except insofar as one identifies them in terms of properties. But, the question of recognition of a presented object or property is not to be confused with the question of remembering such items. Yet, when do I remember, hence intend, an object or property, given the occurrence of a token?

There are no criteria in one sense. In another sense, one can make use, in principle, of the "causal network" within which such kinds of occurrences take place. What one must not do is confuse such uses of *empirical correlations* with *philosophical analyses*.[6]

There is another issue we must resolve. On the view presented, we still recognize generic properties like Bel. If one takes such characteristics to be properties of acts, we are faced with a fundamental extension of logic in that we allow for properties of facts. Unlike '$F_2(m_3)$', which is merely elliptical for (II), something like 'Bel(m_3)' would require an extension of our syntax. One might suggest taking such generic characteristics to be properties of particulars, rather than facts, that *accompany* the appropriate facts. But, to state that such a particular, which exemplifies Bel, is related to m_3 is to use m_3 as a term in a relational fact and, hence, to avoid monadic properties of such facts only to run into relational properties of the same logical kind.[7] Russell skipped by the issue with his talk of "feelings" of belief and disbelief. I can see no way of not recognizing such "complex" facts and, hence, violating a basic tenet of Logical Atomism: the idea that facts do not contain other facts as constituents. But, there is a qualification. One need not think of the problem in terms of stating that the generic character is connected to m_3. Suppose it to be the case that one does not have different mental states at the same time. One could hold that a particular occurs, simultaneously with m_3, that exemplifies Bel. That m_3 expresses what is believed is shown by the occurrence of that particular along with the constituent particulars of m_3. It, so to speak, overlaps the sequence of particulars that are constituents of m_3. To state that such a particular is directed to m_3 is to state that it has such temporal relations to the constituents of m_3. We need not state that it is related to m_3, using a subject term for the latter. But, aside from the assumption that is necessary, nothing is really gained by claiming that the *connection* is shown rather than stated. We just seek to avoid recognizing that we have taken facts as terms of relations. Moreover, we have, in effect, already done so in holding that m_3 *contains* specific particulars in relation. We might just as well treat m_3 as a new kind of subject term or, alternatively, employ the device of the '$<>$' brackets from a previous chapter. Doing so, we allow for the formation of a complex term to stand for a complex entity, a fact. It is important to realize that a term like 'm_3' or one like '$<p>$' does not stand for a possibility, as an atomic sentence does. Like genuine *names* of particulars, such signs stand for existents, albeit, facts. Consequently, we cannot introduce a name like 'm_n' or, better, a sign like '$<p>$' for every sentence 'p'. In that sense, the '$<>$' brackets are quite different from Bergmann's corner quotes. We also recognize that sentences within the '$<>$' brackets are not functioning as mere sentences but as true sentences. This brings up a question about the two-fold use of sentences—as sentences and as constituents of terms referring to facts—which we shall return to in another context.

In Chapter III we noted a problem about the complexity of facts which are acts of thought. Are they conjunctive facts, since it is the occurrence of tokens of types in relations to each other that constitute such facts? Since it is *the tokens* that refer, and not the facts that such tokens are tokens of their respective types, I do not see any need to construe thoughts as conjunctive facts. But, no problem arises if we take them to be such, for they will not be *conjunctions* in the problematic sense in which some philosophers speak of conjunctive facts. Let '$<p_1>$', '$<p_2>$', and '$<p_3>$' stand for the three relevant facts which obtain when we have a token of 'W', a token of 'a', and the first juxtaposed with the second. The relevant thought is a complex of $<p_1>$, $<p_2>$, and $<p_3>$. We can refer to it by '$<p_1, p_2, p_3>$', or '$<<p_1>, <p_2>, <p_3>>$', or '$<p_1> \& <p_2> \& <p_3>$'. Yet, in the last expression, the sign '&' does not occur as a sign for the truth-functional connective, and terms like '$<p_1>$' are not sentences, but names. Thus, if we recognize facts named by '$<p_1, p_2, p_3>$', for example, we do not take them to be the grounds of truth for, or the "referents" of, conjunctive sentences like '$p_1 \& p_2 \& p_3$'. As we shall see, the latter kind of complex fact is neither necessary nor unproblematic.

Logic, Fact and Belief

Russell argued that negative facts exist.[1] The argument was quite clear, but the implicit criteria used never became explicitly recognized or stated. If they had, I believe that he would have been less hesitant about rejecting disjunctive facts (and, by implication, other molecular facts) and that he would not have accepted universal and existential facts in the way he did.[2] We have already considered one line of argument for negative facts in the arguments for possible facts. I have claimed that, for certain issues, the appeal to negative and positive facts does not significantly differ from the appeal to possible and actual facts. The basic point is that two kinds of facts are required to "account for" how sentences are *about* the world and true or false *of it*. We shall now consider another argument pattern that leads us to conclude, with Russell, that there are negative facts. We shall then consider the connection with possibilities and the question of belief with "logical content," i.e., beliefs expressed by sentences with logical signs.

We start with the notion that an atomic fact grounds the truth of an atomic sentence. Such facts, as truth conditions, are sufficient conditions for the truth of atomic sentences. Consider a domain of two objects; one black, one white, and both square. Call the first '*b*', the second '*a*', and let the predicates 'B', 'W', 'S' have the obvious interpretation. We, then, have atomic facts corresponding to the sentences:

414

(L$_1$)   Bb, Wa, Sb, Sa.

In virtue of such facts, the sentences on (L$_1$) are true. So are the molecular sentences that are conjunctions or disjunctions of the members of (L$_1$):

(L$_2$)   Bb & Wa, Bb v Wa, Bb & Sb, etc.

Are there, then, conjunctive and disjunctive facts corresponding to the sentences on the list (L$_2$)? The answer is "No." The facts that are the sufficient conditions for the truth of the members of (L$_1$) suffice as conditions or grounds for the truth of the members of (L$_2$). Given that there are facts corresponding to the atomic sentences, the conjunctions and disjunctions are true. The point is a simple one that is, as it were, reflected in the two logical rules of conjunction and addition, 'p, q $\vdash$ p & q' and 'p $\vdash$ p v q'.

It is also true, in our domain, that the sentences on

(L$_3$)   ~Wb, ~Ba

are true. Do the atomic sentences on (L$_1$) stand for facts that suffice to ground the truth of the sentences on (L$_3$)? If our criterion is in terms of logical implication, as we just used it to avoid the acknowledgment of conjunctive and disjunctive facts, the answer must be "No." Neither 'Bb $\vdash$ ~Wb' nor 'Wa $\vdash$ ~Ba' are valid patterns. The truth tables for '&' and 'v' enable us to hold that the sentences of (L$_2$) are true, given the facts making the sentences of (L$_1$) true. Such truth tables do not suffice to warrant our holding that '~Wb' and '~Ba' are true. Of course, we could say that since 'Wb' and 'Ba' stand for facts that are "nonexistent," those sentences are false and, hence, their negations are true. But, we now appeal to the category of "nonexistent" facts, and, in so doing, follow Moore in adopting the dichotomy "existent-nonexistent" in place of "positive-negative." Clearly, the two "pairs" play the same role. It is just that by using the word 'nonexistent', we do not appear to acknowledge any *thing*, since, obviously, one does not recognize what one takes to be "nonexistent" to exist. The point is emphasized if we consider the list (L$_1$). In dealing with the atomic sentences we speak only of what is *on* the list. If we speak of '~Wb' being true, as revealed by the *absence* of 'Wa' from the list, we make use of the notions of "being on" and "being absent from." By contrast, if we take (L_1) and (L_3) to form an extended list, we need employ only the idea that facts are *shown* by sentences "on" the extended list.

The failure to articulate criteria for acknowledging facts may lead a philosopher to mix questions about negative facts with corresponding questions about "other molecular" facts. Another theme may be involved. We cannot define all logical connectives in a perspicuous schema. We can, however, construe conjunction in terms of negation and disjunction or disjunction in terms of negation and conjunction. This can lead one to think of the connectives as being on a par in that the *meaning* of 'not' cannot be expressed without some primitive connective and, given negation, we still cannot express conjunction and disjunction. Moreover, we can use either conjunction or disjunction, with negation, to express the other. One may conclude that it is arbitrary to acknowledge either conjunctive or disjunctive facts without the other kind and, since we must acknowledge one category, we, therefore, must acknowledge both categories. Thinking along such lines confuses two questions. One question has to do with facts as grounds of truth. The other has to do with the definition of signs. They are naturally linked, since there is a tradition whereby only primitive signs are taken to involve ontological commitments. But, we can, and must, separate the two themes. To say that conjunctive and disjunctive facts are not needed is not to claim that 'Wa & Bb' can be *expressed* solely in terms of atomic sentences and negation. The ontological question is not a question about the definition of logical signs. We can understand how a philosopher may come to think that it is, in view of the traditional links between "ontological reduction" and "eliminative definitions" and between *reference* and *meaning*. A familiar theme, recall, is that Russell removed the need to recognize "nonexistent entities" by "referring to them" by definite descriptions, which are contextually defined signs and, hence, meaningful and eliminable. Moreover, to have a thought with the text expressed by a conjunctive sentence is clearly not the "same" as having one or more thoughts with atomic texts. This, too, is irrelevant. The issue, to repeat, is about what facts

suffice as truth conditions for conjunctive, disjunctive, and negative sentences.[3]

Another confusion may be responsible for the antagonism to
negative facts. When there is a fact that makes 'Wa' true, '~Wa' is
false. One may, then, think that the appeal to negative facts is the
same sort of thing as the introduction of a *false* fact that makes
'~Wa' false. Since one introduces negative facts, why not false
facts as well? The supposed analogy is inept. Negative facts are introduced *as grounds of truth*. Such truth conditions suffice as
grounds for holding that sentences like '~Wa' are false. This is reflected by "Wb ⊢ '~Wb' is false," which is a valid pattern with
appropriate linguistic devices, or, more simply, by 'p ⊢ ~~p'.
Both are analogous to patterns like 'p, q ⊢ p & q'. With Russell,
we may reject entities that *only ground* the falsehood of sentences.

One may seek to find a basis for avoiding negative facts in synthetic a priori connections of incompatibility. In effect, one attempts to assimilate the case of '~Wb' being true to that of '~Wa'
being false. Russell argued that such a line fails. On it, one can
hold that the fact indicated by 'Bb' grounds the truth of '~Wb',
since W is *incompatible* with B. But, this introduces *the fact* that
W is incompatible with B as part of the truth condition for '~Wb'.
This seems to be merely another way of introducing negative facts.
Alternatively, one can hold that the generality '(x)(Bx ⊃ ~Wx)', together with 'Bb', suffices to ground the truth of '~Wb'. Aside
from problems about the status of the generalization, the question
is begged in that it is a generalization and, hence, would indicate
a fact of a further kind. In addition, the generality contains a negation sign. Finally, one may appeal to a direct inference from
'Bb' to '~Wb', without using an additional premise stating an incompatibility or generality. Thus, one holds that '~Wb' may be
inferred from 'Bb', just as " '~Wa' is false" may be inferred from
'Wa'. But, the justification for such an inference, as well as the
very notion of *inference* in such cases, has never been clearly and
unproblematically stated. Moreover, the *inference* from 'Bb' to
'~Wb' will correspond to the *necessary truth* that W is incompati-

ble with B or that all B's are not W's, just as the inference from
'p & q' to 'p' corresponds to the tautology '(p & q) ⊢ p'. Thus, as
in the previous two cases, the question about negative facts will be
begged. This indicates that there is only a verbal difference between the third alternative and either one of the other two.

One can seek to ignore the need to connect the fact expressed
by 'B*b*' with the truth of '~W*b*' by a declaration of an implication
holding in "virtue of the meaning" of the terms involved. Such a
claim is made by Richard Gale:

> It is claimed that even in cases in which there is a positive ground for an ob-
> ject's lacking Ø, a proposition reporting this positive ground logically entails
> that it lacks Ø only if we add as a premiss the negative proposition that this
> positive ground is logically incompatible with Ø. Therefore, it is not true that
> a singular negation is entailed by a positive proposition *alone*. It cannot be de-
> duced that my pen is not red from the single premiss that it is blue but only
> from this premiss in conjunction with the additional proposition that being
> blue is incompatible with being red.
>
> To me this objection is no more plausible than saying that the proposition
> that Else is a cow entails that she is an animal only if we assume as an addi-
> tional premiss that every cow is an animal, or saying that a set of premises p
> entails a proposition q only if we assume as an extra premiss that p entails q.
> There is nothing enthymemic about the argument "My pen is blue, therefore
> it is not red" or "Elsie is a cow, therefore she is an animal." In both cases the
> conclusion follows from the single premiss in virtue of the meaning of the
> terms which compose it.[4]

Let us ignore the obvious points that a predicate like 'cow' may
be taken as defined in terms of the more generic character term
'animal', so that 'x is a cow' is elliptical for 'x is an animal and
. . . x . . .', and that 'p, p ⊃ q ⊢ q' is a formally valid argument pattern without use of the *suppressed premise* 'p, p ⊃ q ⊢ q'. Although there may be no relevant differences to Professor Gale,
there are quite crucial differences that a cogent analysis must take
cognizance of. But, those aside, consider the claim that '~W*b*' follows from 'B*b*' by the "meaning" of the terms. The classical problem has always been to do more than use the term 'meaning' in
such a statement. It has been to give an explication of that use. As
we noted in an earlier case, the appeal to the "meaning" merely reveals that one cannot carry the analysis further. In this case, it

merely amounts to a way of acknowledging the reason for the introduction of negative facts without accepting such entities. Nothing is accomplished. In short, what Professor Gale does is to restate the problem as a purported solution of it. There is another point. What Gale does amounts to the use of the term 'meaning' to cover an appeal to a *synthetic* a priori connection. This is why it becomes crucial to distinguish the case of Elsie from that of Gale's pen. If one probes such matters, a question arises about the ground of such connections. Of course, Gale could be using 'meaning' here as a kind of report of common usage. But, in that sense, nothing is said that contributes to the philosophical problems involved.

The point to keep in mind is that Gale cannot eliminate negative facts by appealing to the criteria we employed in the rejection of conjunctive and disjunctive facts. Whether one, then, says that we have eliminated negative facts by appealing to an unexplicated use of 'means' and 'follows from' or whether one acknowledges such entities because of the *need to make such* an appeal in order to "eliminate" them is merely a matter of using different terms to describe the same situation. The philosophical task is to note the crucial differences that lead to the traditional ontological assertions.[5]

Acknowledging negative facts poses a problem. An atomic fact is a complex of a particular and a property in a relation of exemplification. A negative fact would, then, seem to be either a complex containing a property, a particular, a tie of exemplification, *and* something else—the negative constituent—or a complex of a property and a particular in a different kind of relational tie, say negative exemplification. But, the first alternative, as it stands, will not do. For, one would have exemplification as a tie between a particular and a property in a positive fact *and* as a tie between a particular, a property, and the negative element in a negative fact. Thus, we either have a tie playing a double role or are forced to acknowledge an additional tie besides exemplification. Whether one takes this further tie to connect the negative element to the complex composed of the particular, the property, and exemplification or takes it as a three-term relation between the negative element, the property, and the particular makes little difference. On either alternative, one recognizes a negative element as well as a second nexus or tie. Thus, it is simpler to recognize two forms of exemplification, without introducing a negative element. Moreover, such a move would put negation on a par with exemplification, as a matter of "form," rather than taking '∼' as a label of a *constituent* of facts. A question arises regarding the role of negation in molecular sentences like '∼∼p', '∼(p & q)', and '∼(x) [Fx ⊃ Gx]'. Such uses may be regarded as alternative formulations for statements where negations occur only in front of atomic forms. Hence, no problem arises for accounts of negation, either in terms of a negative nexus or in terms of negative properties. Yet, questions remain about the ontological status of the logical truths and rules used in such transformations. This raises the traditional question of "logic and ontology." We may also note that on the basis of our earlier discussions of the concept of a particular, and the distinction between a particular white patch and another sense of "particular," whereby the patch contains a particular substratum or ground of individuation, complications arise regarding negation. Since one acknowledging bare particulars would hold that such entities stand in the exemplification nexus to the properties, and thereby constitute the ordinary particular, one could take such a substratum to be what stands in the relation of negative exemplification to a property. If one holds that an ordinary particular, like the patch, is to be analyzed only in terms of a set of qualities in a relation, then the tie of negative exemplification could be taken to hold between the complex particular (the patch) and a simple property it does not have, i.e., which is not a constituent of it. There would, then, be a fundamental asymmetry, on such a view, between the analysis of '*a* is white' and '*a* is not black'. In the former case, the predicate would be taken to indicate a property joined with other properties by a tie or nexus to constitute the object. In the latter case, the nexus of negative exemplification would connect the property to the complex particular composed of properties. One holding to bare particulars could also adopt a structurally similar move by holding that negative exemplification is properly construed as a connection between the *complex* "ordinary" particular and the property in question. A similar distinction could be used in the treatment of monadic, as opposed to relational, predication.[6]

The two sentences 'Wb' and '~Wb', then, reflect the two possibilities that b is connected to the property W either by exemplification or by negative exemplification. That the sentences are contradictories reflects the impossibility of a particular standing in both ties to one and the same property. This way of putting things points to a further difference between the case of 'Wb' and '~Wb', on the one hand, and that of 'Bb' and 'Wb', on the other. For, it would seem that if one held to a synthetic a priori necessity or incompatibility between B and W, this would be reflected in the claim that a particular cannot simultaneously stand in the exemplification nexus to two properties that are incompatible, rather than not being able to stand in two relations to one property. But, this difference disappears, if we accept a third alternative account of negative facts. One may hold that there is neither a negative element nor a negative nexus and seek to account for negative facts by means of negative properties. Thus, a negative fact would be analyzed in terms of a particular standing in the exemplification tie to a negative property. On this view, both synthetic a priori incompatibilities and logical incompatibilities would involve a particular not (possibly) standing in the exemplification tie to two (or more) properties. Yet, one could hold that the sense of "possibly" would still be different in the cases of synthetic a priori and logical impossibility, but this difference would be reflected by the distinction between properties and negative properties, rather than by that between exemplification and negative exemplification. For, incompatible properties, like B and W, are not related as are a property and its negative correlate, say B and ~B. This assumes '~B' is not taken as a "simple" sign referring to a "simple" property, but that the former is defined in terms of '~' and 'B' and the latter is taken as a complex property having B as a constituent, in some sense. If the negative properties are taken as simple, one abandons the explication of *logical necessity* along the lines propounded by Wittgenstein in the *Tractatus*. For, one will have to base logical truths on necessary relations between *simple properties*. This treats logical truths in the way some philosophers have spoken of synthetic a priori truths. Thus, analyzing negative facts in terms of either complex negative properties or negative exemplification preserves a distinction between logical incompatibility and synthetic a priori incompatibility. This difference may go along with another. One who adheres to synthetic a priori necessities recognizes *an additional kind of fact*. Thus, the incompatibility of B and W would be reflected by the addition of something like 'I(W,B)' to the list (L₁), where 'I' stands for a primitive notion of incompatibility.

Negative properties pose a basic problem. If we think in terms of a lower functional calculus, either we define the predicate '$\overline{F}$' in terms of '~Fx' or we take it as primitive. The latter move not only abandons a standard explication of logical necessity but forces one to abandon a principle of acquaintance for primitive predicates. Whatever is held about experiencing negative facts, once one knows what the primitive "positive" predicates mean, he cannot sensibly hold that a predicate like '$\overline{F}$' is coordinated to an experienced property and also functions like a "negative predicate." To treat the predicate and the corresponding negative property as "complex" or "constructed" with respect to the "simple" property F is to admit that some facts have complex properties as constituents. This acknowledges *two kinds* of facts, in a sense of 'kind' that one may take to be more radical than that which the recognition of positive and negative facts, in terms of different ties, involves. Moreover, he faces the problem of specifying just what a complex property such as $\overline{F}$ is composed of. One is left with a mysterious constituent and, consequently, like a previous gambit we rejected, requires a new "nexus" to *form a property* like $\overline{F}$.

In this discussion and earlier in the book, I have referred to possible facts as an alternative to the introduction of negative facts or as an additional category that might be involved in the discussion of negation. It is to that issue and the related question of "logical" or "necessary" facts that we shall now turn.

Suppose we begin with the array of positive and negative facts represented by the list

(L₄)   Wa, Bb, Sa, Sb, ~Wb, ~Ba,

and the account of negation in terms of a tie of negative exemplification. We must still recognize two things that suggest the notion of possibilities: that for each atomic sentence either a positive or negative fact *must* obtain and that both cannot obtain. There is a further point that emerged in our consideration of Russell: each atomic sentence stands for a fact, irrespective of whether that fact exists. If one thinks that these features are accommodated, in Russell's fashion, by holding that a pair of sentences, one positive and the other negative, are held to stand for a fact *that* will, then, be either positive or negative, one might ponder the need to appeal to a positive sentence, negative sentence, *and a pair of sentences.* In any case, that answer *might* serve only as long as we were concerned to show that at least two fundamental categories of facts were required to deal with the issues we discussed. It will not serve when we probe a little deeper into the issues and raise questions about the structure of positive and negative facts. They are complex existents of different kinds. As I have considered the matter thus far, the difference is purportedly based on a different structural relation or tie that connects the constituents. This prevents our holding that a pair of sentences is coordinated (or stipulated to correspond to), *a fact* that is then positive or negative. To speak of a pair of sentences corresponding to *a* fact in such a manner is to use 'a fact', 'positive', and 'negative' to state what one might express by holding that the pair of sentences is taken to stand for a possibility that is then actual (existent, positive) or *not* (merely possible, nonexistent, negative). The difference between the two sets of terms amounts to our apparently ascribing the two *modes* of *possibility* and *actuality* to one and the same entity, while holding that it cannot be an instance of both. Thus, one speaks of a fact as one speaks of a particular that exemplifies either a property or its negation. It is one and the same thing that has the one property and *would* have the other. By contrast, in speaking of positive and negative facts one suggests that there is nothing corresponding to the particular: we deal with two complexes that differ in that their respective exemplification relations are different. Hence, nothing supposedly corresponds to the entity that is an instance of one of the two modes. Russell may be taken to have blurred matters by speaking of positive and negative facts. For, by talking of them in terms of *qualities*, he spoke as we have construed possible and actual. If he had not, he might have ended with positive and negative facts which were then either actual or possible or, as he and Moore seemed to prefer, one of which was nonexistent. But, we need not compound the verbal quandry. All one does is acknowledge that an atomic sentence stands for something, a fact, irrespective of the sentence being true or false. The truth of the sentence would be based on the fact being of one kind or mode; its falsity and the truth of the corresponding negation are based on the fact being taken to be of the other kind or mode. What is recognized is that there are *facts that are in one of two modes*, or are of one of two kinds. Such is the ontological ground for atomic sentences being about a domain or "having meaning," for the use of the negation sign with atomic sentences, and for atomic sentences and negations of atomic sentences being true or false. We, thus, need not introduce two kinds of exemplification in addition to the "modes."

A version of what I just called the "verbal quandry" arises in contexts like Russell's discussion of judgment and belief. Let '~Wa' be the text of a belief state. I have accounted for belief states expressed by atomic sentences having the content they have in terms of the sentence type standing for a possibility. Are we, then, forced to compound matters by recognizing positive and negative possibilities as well as facts? For, what does account for the content of a belief state with '~Wa' as its text? Russell, recall, sought to avoid such an appeal to negations by suggesting that the logical signs are to be construed *metalinguistically*. To believe that a is not W is to hold that a is W is false. This need not involve the gambit that Russell had very early rejected, but which he later, along with Bradley, appeared to hold: that we understand negation in terms of a psychological act of rejecting or disbelieving a content. For, as we noted in an earlier discussion of Russell, he employed two fundamental uses of negation: (a) *the feeling of disbelief* that was the basis for the meaning of the negation sign in verbal propositions; (b) *the negative quality* of some facts. Russell construed the first in a manner we might reasonably call "metalinguistic." He seems to have taken this to resolve any questions about the second. Thus, he overlooked the problems leading us to talk about possibilities, as well as the need to connect his two uses of "negation." We might, then, wonder about the possibility of treating Russell's *quality* of negation "metalinguistically." To deal with that question, it will be helpful if we consider some aspects of Bradley's views.

Bradley was bothered by negation as he was bothered by the notion of a bare particular. He could not see any part of the "content" of a thought being an *idea* of a bare substratum or a *concept* of negation.[7] We noted how he replaced subject-predicate contents with existential judgments in the former case. In the latter case, he tried a two-fold gambit. One theme corresponds to the attempt to define negation in terms of incompatibility. The other amounts to the claim that just as a complex concept was ascribable to *The Real*, or reality as a whole, and, in his terms, was "accepted" by *The Real*, it could be denied of *The Real*, which, in turn, could be considered *to reject* the concept. Just as we could be said to *ascribe* or *deny* that a content applied to the world, the latter could be said to accept or reject the content. Simply put, the predicative tie between a subject and predicate is replaced by a connection between the predicative content and *The Real*, with a judgment now thought of as the ascription or the denial of the content to *The Real*. The latter is not, then, part of the content or thought. Consequently, we can consider negation in terms of our *denial* of contents as belonging to *The Real*. Bradley, thus, makes use of two basic psychological acts, ascribing and denying, and two connections between contents and *The Real*. The latter two correspond to exemplification and negative exemplification. The former distinction, between ascribing and denying, grounds the difference between a thought with the content 'W*a*', in our terms, and one with the content '~W*a*'.

Frege, we noted earlier, embraces the same pattern. Only, instead of having two connections or talking of two kinds of facts, Frege has two distinct entities, *The True* and *The False*, and one connection that obtains between propositions and such entities—*reference* (the R of Chapter VI or the D* of Chapter VII). A proposition, then, stands in that one relation to one of two entities. Bradley has *one* basic entity, *The Real*, and *two* connections between thoughts (propositions) and such an entity. Structurally, the gambits thus reveal a basic similarity to each other and to Russell's recognition of two kinds of facts. But, Frege's pattern, so construed, raises a fundamental problem that we touched on in Chapters VI and VII. The condition for the truth of a proposition, on the Fregean pattern, may be taken to be the obtaining of the relation R (or D* of Chapter VII) between the proposition and *The True*. (Recall the form of the expression (A) of Chapter VI, 'R(p,T)'.) If we so take Frege's pattern, we run into the same problem about propositions that we noted in the case of singular terms and senses. The proposition must be taken to speak about itself, on the assumption that a proposition "states" its truth condition. On the appeal to facts, we take a proposition to stand for a fact and state that it has one quality rather than another. We cannot take the proposition to state that it represents the fact or stands for a specific fact, which, then, exists or not. But, on Frege's pattern, the condition of truth appears to be the fact that the proposition stands in R to *The True*. Thus, to state its truth condition, it must refer to itself, if we take the truth condition to be the standing of the proposition in R to *The True*. This points to a feature of Russell's view.

I spoke, above, of Russell thinking in terms of a "metalinguistic" treatment of negation. We must distinguish the role of *negation with facts as truth conditions and "its" role in thought as part of the content* or "feeling."[8] In the former case, the attempt to treat negation metalinguistically would be to hold that '~W*a*' is to be construed in terms of " 'W*a*' is false." But, this clearly and simply amounts to an alternative way of stating that the possibility that 'W*a*' stands for is in one *mode*, rather than another. This is precisely the way we treated negation in taking the distinction between negative and positive facts to reflect the two modes "in which," so to speak, the possibility could exist. This enables one to forgo holding that two kinds of facts, positive and negative, could, then, be either actual or possible. One may suspect that another problem some find with the notion of a possible fact is that it supposedly involves us with the four-fold categories of positive, negative, actual, and possible. It does not, if we carefully separate the different strands of the issue. Thus, the attempted metalinguistic rendering of negation amounts to another formulation of the theme that the negation sign reflects the modes of facts. It does not enable us to avoid such "qualities." But, it does enable us to remove some of the peculiarity of talking about "nonexistent" entities. By recognizing possible facts, as we do, we are not acknowledging a strange new category of facts. Two comparisons will help. Aristotle spoke of prime matter and of forms. He held that such *categories* were involved in the "analysis" of *objects* and *predication*. He did not hold that there were "chunks" of prime matter in addition to chairs, tables, etc. In a similar way, *there are* facts that are of *one* or *the other* "quality," to use Russell's terminology, *positive* or *negative*. A possible fact corresponds to Aristotle's prime matter; it exists *as* positive or negative. Recognizing possible facts only means that we take atomic sentences to stand for facts independently of which quality such facts have. One may, thus, say that only existent facts are acknowledged as entities. Contrasting this way of talking about possibilities with the way some talk about possible worlds helps make the point. A world is a set of facts. A possible world is a set with at least one constituent being a possible fact. The *actual* world is taken to be one set among a domain of sets, each of which is an *entity* on the pattern. This differs from the way I have talked of possibilities in two crucial ways. First, it recognizes a possible fact as an element of such sets in a way that I do not. Take '*Wa*' as false. As I construe it, the entity involved is the *existent* negative fact that makes '~*Wa*' true. As others construe it, the element of the possible world is the *possibility* that makes '*Wa*' true *in* some alternative worlds. Second, there are no possible worlds, as I construe matters, since there are no facts of the requisite kind to be elements of such sets. This point will be expanded upon shortly.

There is the second aspect of the "metalinguistic" construal of negation: the rendering of the concept of negation as it occurs in thought in metalinguistic terms. The idea is that we apply negation to a propositional content, just as we apply the concepts true or false. To believe '~*Wa*' is to believe something about or "react" to the proposition expressed by '*Wa*'. Bradley, in denying that negation could be a part of the content of a thought, spoke of the act of denying. Frege acknowledged negation as a concept or function and distinguished the rejection of a proposition from the assertion of its negation. Russell, by contrast, tried to explain what it is for a thought to have a negative content by holding that we ascribe falsehood to the positive content. Thus, negative judgments are to be understood as having sentences as their proper subjects. This is what leads to the idea that the logical connectives are "metalinguistic." Hence, the text of the belief that *a* is not W is "'W*a*' is false." The latter, in turn, is to be understood in terms of the *feeling* of disbelief. Simply to object that the thought *that p is false* is a different kind of thought than the thought *that not-p* is not cogent. Given the earlier distinctions of the various senses of 'same', we can note that in some senses they are and in some they are not different. They are the "same" in that both correspond to the same truth condition: they are both true when the fact for which 'p' stands is negative. If Russell's gambit purports to reflect this point, he is correct. However, he is wrong, as we noted earlier, in not seeing that the pattern of philosophical analysis embedded in the philosophy of Logical Atomism is forced to recognize the three-fold dichotomy with respect to facts. What Russell is apparently trying to do is to suggest that negation is to be understood in terms of 'false', which is to be understood in terms of *disbelief* or *rejection*.

But, now a classic problem arises. Is the text of the relevant belief *that* p *is merely possible* (or *that* 'p' stands for a negative fact)? And, in the corresponding positive case, is the content *that* p *is actual* (or *that* 'p' corresponds to a positive fact)? On our pattern, 'p' stands for a possibility, but a token of 'p' occurring as a thought or belief is not a token of 'p is a possibility' nor is it one of 'p is an existent fact'. We noted in an earlier chapter that considering such a way of rendering truth conditions, so that we say that a sentence stands for an existent fact, would not do and was, perhaps, one reason why some philosophers reject facts. Here, we do not deal with quite the same question. We are concerned with why a belief or thought expresses what it does, not with what a sentence stands for. Since a belief content is a sentence token, these questions are easily mixed. But, the occurrence of a thought is not just the occurrence of a content anymore than the occurrence of a token of a name, *in thought*, that refers to an object on that occasion, is just a matter of the occurrence of a token whose type has been interpreted. The crucial point here, as earlier, is that there is nothing more to appeal to. We, apparently, have a corollary of Bradley's paradox and Frege and Russell's concern with the assertion stroke. In believing that *a* is W, one believes a fact to exist, but it is hopeless to express that by adding to the content of the belief. No part of the content can express that without futility or paradox. Thus, we seem to have a version of the "problem" that arises when one tries to express exemplification by a relational predicate or show that a sign refers to a specific object on a certain occasion by the addition of another token of some sort. In none of the cases will the introduction of a new constituent help express the assertive or referential feature of thought, as it does not help to express the predicative tie. In a way, Bradley's point is correct in all three cases. Thus, he held that in judgment we *ascribe* a content, and neither the *ascriptive* character of predication nor the *assertive* character of the judgment is represented in the content. In their own ways, Frege, Russell, and Wittgenstein noted the puzzle.[9] There is the assertive feature to be recognized and accommodated, but it cannot be represented. However, it need not be, for Russell did solve the problem by his appeal to a feeling of belief. Before seeing why, we should observe that the Fregean gambit is left with an unsolvable version of the problem if it is taken to use (A), however implicitly, as the pattern for expressing the truth condition of an atomic sentence. As we have construed them, atomic sentences express their truth conditions by stating what facts must exist for the sentences to be true. Frege's *propositions* (as entities expressed by sentences) do not *state* or *express* or *indicate* any such thing, if the condition of their truth is that they refer to *The True*. What makes the Fregean proposition true is the obtaining of the *condition stated by* (A). If we explicitly use that pattern, different facts are coordinated to different propositions. With such facts, as truth conditions, a puzzle about facts and existence arises for this version of the Fregean pattern, since using (A) is tantamount to claiming that a proposition states, about itself, that it is true. This is a corollary of a problem we noted earlier. The Fregean proposition, to use my terms, refers to a fact of which it is a part. It is a variant of the problem Russell raised about Fregean senses; only we now see it to occur in connection with Fregean "thoughts."

One might object to Russell's attempt to capture the "assertive" feature of belief states by appealing to "feelings" of belief and disbelief, as generic characteristics, in that what is believed or disbelieved is *that a possibility is in a particular mode*, being merely possible or actual. One does not believe or disbelieve the content simply as that stands for a possible situation which may or may not obtain. The feeling of disbelief, in short, is disbelief that a possible fact exists. This, one may argue, cannot be represented; it simply is part of the "structure of thought." We understand that that is how we take contents, but in analyzing the structure of an "intentional fact," we do not *represent* that feature. There is a point here, but not a problem. Although it is true that we cannot represent such a feature by an addition to the content, it is "carried" by the relational predicate 'Bel'. That a state exemplifies such a character indicates the way we take the patterns expressing that there is a belief with a certain content. What the objector might have in mind is something like the following. If we represent, in a perspicuous schema, the assertive feature along our "Russellian" lines, we would use something like

(R′)   Bel $<m_1>$ & $\ulcorner Wa \urcorner <m_1>$

(where the sign '$\langle m_1 \rangle$' reminds us that 'm_1' is shorthand for a complicated sentence describing relationships among "inner" tokens) to state that the mental state is a belief, and hence that what is believed is that *a* is W. The objection would, then, be that in using a sentential pattern we run into the problem reminiscent of the Bradley paradox. For, being a sentential pattern it stands for a possibility. Hence, one may ask when 'Bel$\langle m_1 \rangle$' is true. It is true, if the fact $\langle m_1 \rangle$ has the generic characteristic Bel. Although it is true that no *element* of (R′) shows that m_1 is *a belief* that a possibility is actual, the fact that *it* is a *belief* with the content it has *shows* that aspect. Suppose, then, one wants to *express* that a mental state is a belief that 'Wa' expresses a possibility? There is no problem, though there are several different senses in which it could be taken. One way will have to do with the introduction of a term for the modality, and the intention will be that a *sentence* expresses a possibility—hence, one will not intend the possible fact that *a* is W but, rather, that a certain sentence expresses a possibility. This raises no problem for the present pattern.

As we have recognized the modalities to be reflected by the negation sign and the rules for the latter, we can take the truths of propositional logic to express relationships among the modalities. In this sense, there is a point to the old idea that the laws of logic are laws like excluded middle and noncontradiction. All tautologies are, in a way, on a par, as one commonly reads in introductory texts. In another sense, they are not. The sense in which they are not is that some may be taken to be rather direct expressions of the use of 'F' and 'T' in the truth tables: we put either a 'T' or an 'F' on a line—never both, but at least one. One may express that such relationships hold by talking of the modalities and necessary facts or "the world's form." The point is that the modalities of facts supply an ontological ground for logic. To adopt a "logic" whereby such conditions do not hold is to abandon the use of the connectives of the calculus to reflect the modes of facts. Hence, in a simple sense, the connectives then have a different meaning. In this sense, we cannot deny the "laws of logic." To speak of 'p v ~p' possibly being false is to use 'v' or '~' or 'possibly' in some different sense. To say this is not to say that we stipulate that 'p v ~p' is always to be counted as true and, hence, hold that logic is a matter of convention. In a celebrated paper, Nagel held such a view.[10] He correctly observed that we would reject any purported case of 'p & ~p', and he concluded that this showed that there is no need to recognize an ontological ground for logical terms or logical truths. The matter reflects our decision, which is not "arbitrary," to reject any contradictory proposition. Nagel, I believe, makes a simple error. We do not stipulate that the law of contradiction holds. Nor do we "justify" such a "convention" as instrumental in our achieving a coherent system of physics. Our particular use of '~' and '&' reflects that we acknowledge the law to hold. This does not mean that we *can* take *negation* in some other sense. We could, of course, use the pattern '~p' in some other way. That is obviously trivial and irrelevant. That the sense of '~' changes if we employ a three-valued schema does not mean that we *stipulate* the "meaning" of *negation* and the acceptance of the standard logical truths. The "concept of negation" does not change. What might change is merely that the sign '∼' would no longer stand for *it*.[11]

I earlier argued that we need not recognize conjunctive and disjunctive facts to ground the truth of conjunctive and disjunctive sentences. The point can be reinforced by noting that we *cannot* unproblematically bring in conjunctive or "compound" facts as "correlates" of conjunctive sentences.

The point is simple and a corollary of our talk about possibilities. If we acknowledge conjunctive facts, we acknowledge conjunction as some sort of relation that takes facts as its terms. Let 'K' be a sign for such a relation, and let 'p' and 'q' be two atomic sentences. Assume the sentence

(c)   pKq

to state that the fact p stands in the relation K to the fact q. But suppose 'p' is false. It does not, then, stand for an existent positive fact but for a *mere* possibility or a possibility without a quality or the fact with the "wrong" quality. (c) cannot, then, state that a relation obtains among atomic facts. To put it simply, one cannot have sentences function as they normally do, standing for possibilities that may be positive or negative in quality and, hence, *possibly being true or false*, and also treat conjunction as a relation. We can see the point in some detail by noting a connection with Russell's theory of descriptions and "nondesignating" subject terms.

Behind Russell's theory is a simple pattern that we have repeated several times. A subject-predicate sentence is used to ascribe a predicate to a subject, and a relational sentence like 'aR_1b' is used to assert that the two objects named stand in the relation. If they do so stand, the sentence is true; if they do not so stand, it is false. The sentence in question being true or false thus presupposes a condition, the names '*a*' and '*b*' must actually stand for objects. If they do not, then obviously we *neither* have *the* objects *standing nor failing to stand* in the relation. When a "subject" term does not stand for anything in a *properly clarified language*, it is treated as a contextually defined sign. This means that a sentence pattern like '$\emptyset(\iota x)(\emptyset x)$' is only an *apparent* subject-predicate sentence.

The point is that the "subject" term need not stand for an object in order to be used in an *apparent* subject-predicate sentence, for such a sentence will be treated as an existential claim. Thus, the truth or falsity of such a sentence does not presuppose that what the sign stands for has or does not have a certain property, since it does not presuppose that the sign stands for anything at all. But, the crucial point is that the sentence '$\emptyset(\iota x)(\emptyset x)$' is only *apparently* a subject-predicate sentence. This treatment of subject terms that do not stand for anything allows one to retain (a) the view that a genuine subject-predicate sentence is true if the object which the subject term stands for has the property that is indicated by the predicate term and is false if *it* does not have the property, and (b) the *use* of apparent subject terms that do not stand for anything. It also enables us to retain the fundamental connections between the notions of truth, falsity, and negation expressed by our holding that subject-predicate sentences are either true or false, if a sentence is true (false) its negation is false (true), and that a subject-predicate sentence is true or false according to whether or not something has or does not have a certain property. Treating '$\emptyset(\iota x)(\emptyset x)$', '$[(\iota x)(\emptyset x)] . \sim \emptyset(\iota x)(\emptyset x)$', and '$\sim [(\iota x)(\emptyset x)] . \emptyset(\iota x)(\emptyset x)$' along Russell's lines, such sentences are not true or false in virtue of something's having or lacking a property, but in virtue of there being or not being something of a certain kind. The grounds of the truth or falsity of such sentences are *not* facts *like those* that involve some specified object having a property or lacking it or something's standing or not standing in a relation to something else. Consider, for example, the sentence pattern '$(\iota x)(xR_1 c)R_2 b$' and assume that no object stands in the relation R_1 to c. Thus '$(\iota x)(xR_1 c)R_2 b$' is false, as is the sentence '$aR_1 c$'. But, in the latter case, we can say that the sentence is false, since the object that the sign 'a' stands for does not stand in the relation R_1 to the object for which the sign 'c' stands. We cannot say this about '$(\iota x)(xR_1 c)R_2 b$', though we can say it is false and why. That we cannot speak about '$(\iota x)(xR_1 c)R_2 b$' as we do about '$aR_1 c$' is crucial. To see the connection of all this to the issue of whether facts may be constituents of further facts and whether sentences may function as terms in further sentences, consider a sentential pattern like '$(bR_2 c)K(aR_1 b)$'. If it is to purport to state a relational fact, then, like the sentence '$aR_1 b$', it is used to state that one "thing," in this case a fact, stands in the relation K to another "thing," in this case another fact. Consider, next, the sentence pattern '$(bR_2 c)K(aR_1 c)$'. Let '$bR_2 c$' and '$aR_1 b$' be true, and, hence, correspond to facts, and '$aR_1 c$' be false and not so correspond. Thus, '$(bR_2 c)K(aR_1 c)$' could not be said to be either true or false depending on whether the fact $bR_2 c$ stood in the relation K to *the fact $aR_1 c$*. The latter does not exist. Hence, *it* cannot be said to stand or fail to stand in the relation K to $bR_2 c$ in the same sense in which $aR_1 b$ might be said to so stand or fail to. The same sort of question that arises in the case of subject terms that do not stand for anything arises in the case of sentences that do not indicate facts, when such sentences are employed as subject terms.

One might suggest that sentences asserting that relations hold among facts can be formed only if such facts exist. This means that the terms 'a', 'R_1', and 'c' can be used to form the sentence '$aR_1 c$', when that sentence does not indicate a fact, and that the sentence can, so to speak, be used only *as a sentence* and not as a term in a further relational sentence. But, this clearly involves using the notion of a sentence in two ways. A sentence, as opposed to a name or a "label," is a sign sequence that can be used to say "something," i.e., as a sentence, whether or not there is a fact that makes it true. By contrast, the name or label is precisely that kind of sign that must stand for some existent, to be used as a name or label. To allow some sentences, but not others, as terms of further relational sentences is to turn some sentences into names: to use them in a role that is not that of sentences. Of course, one could introduce names for facts, either by introducing a set of signs 'F_1', 'F_2', etc., or as we did earlier, 'm_1', 'm_2', etc., for that purpose or by introducing a device like the '$<>$' brackets to form names from sentences. In the former case, we would not have signs which had constituents that were themselves signs of the schema, and, hence, not "show" that we were naming "complexes." None of these points affect our referring to mental states, as facts, either by the use of the '$<>$' brackets or by names like 'm_1'. For, we admittedly do not use *such* signs *as sentences*. But, this move is not open to one who thinks of *conjunction* as a relation among facts. He must use 'K' as a connector of sentences, not of names. Because of this, one cannot imitate Russell's handling of definite descriptions and hold that sentences like '$(bR_2 c)K(aR_1 c)$' are really elliptical for more complex expressions involving quantification over variables taking facts as values. This will not do in the way in which Russell's theory suffices for the problems regarding names that do not name and descriptive phrases that do not "denote." As a false sentence, '$bR_2 c$' would not be construable in terms of some expression analogous to a definite description, but, as a purported term in a sentence of the form '$(bR_2 c)K(aR_1 c)$', it would be so taken. This amounts to the double use of designating sentences, as sentences and as names, which the proponent of K as a relation cannot employ.

One may seek to avoid taking a conjunctive fact to have atomic facts as constituents by suggesting that K relates the terms — b, R_1, c, a, R_2 — just as Russell once suggested that *belief* be construed as a relation holding among Othello, Desdemona, loves, and Cassio, to recall an earlier example. But, exactly the same problem arises in the present case, since

$$K(R_1, R_2, a, b, c)$$

would have to be so "understood" that '$bR_2 c$' and '$aR_1 b$' are the relevant "sentential terms." This, as in Russell's case, reveals the "analysis" to be merely a verbal transformation. It helps, however, to reveal yet another problem for the relational account of belief. Let Othello believe that

Desdemona loves Cassio and not Iago.

On Russell's early account, we would have either one fact expressed by

Bel(Othello, Desdemona, loves, Cassio, not, Iago)

or two facts. The first alternative presents a further complication for the "arrangement" of the constituents. The second alternative forces him to hold that there are two belief states when one believes *a* conjunction. Neither gambit will do. Such "conjunctive" beliefs present no problem for the present alternative. We need not recognize conjunctive facts. Consequently, we must explain how we take

⌜p & q⌝ M p & q.

This reduces to assigning a meaning to '&'. The conjunction sign is, as Russell once took it, a "metalinguistic" sign. Its meaning is to be understood in terms of the relevant possibilities being taken as positive or negative. That possibilities are one or the other is not itself a further fact. The truth condition for 'p & q' is, in short, not a fact. We give '&' an interpretation in terms of a truth table, not by assigning a conjunction to a further kind of fact. The link between conjunctions and "the world" is already supplied by the link between atomic sentences and facts. The same may be said about the other connectives.

The recognition of facts, on a pattern of analysis that is in the tradition of Logical Atomism, forces one to acknowledge possibilities and their qualities. The problem is, then, to do justice to the dialectical issues that give rise to an ontology without offending that "vivid sense of reality" Russell appealed to. Russell, Moore, and Wittgenstein all failed to do the former, and Bergmann failed to do the latter. From our consideration of the reasons for the inadequacies of their gambits, modifications of their analyses emerged that, I have suggested, ought not to offend one of Russellian sensibilities. This means that the present analysis purports to be compatible with Russell's principle of acquaintance. By contrast with those who take possibilities to be existents, in some shadowy sense, who speak of possible worlds, in ways reminiscent of science fiction, and who talk of possible objects, as if such *things* generically differ from existent things, I have spoken of possibilities by analogy with Aristotle's prime matter and Bergmann's bare particulars. There are only existent facts and not possible facts. Yet, existent facts are possibilities that are either positive or negative. This means that I take the way that I have considered possibilities to be fundamentally different from the way others construe possible facts. That point requires elaboration.

I have recognized existent facts (or, since there are no non-existent facts, simply, facts) as involving two aspects: the possibility (or subject) and the quality (or mode) such a subject has. In the sense that any (existent) fact is composite in that manner, we have recognized possibilities. But, in such form, possibilities should be palatable, since they are, in one sense of the term, "constituents" of presented, existent facts. We are not speaking about possibilities that are actualized and possibilities that exist as mere possibilities. Rather, we deal with possibilities that exist as positive and possibilities that exist as negative. Both kinds of existents are, as facts, "objects" of experience. The difference between possibilities and possible facts can be emphasized by returning, once again, to a small domain of two objects, a and b, and two properties, W and B, where 'Wa' and 'Bb' hold. Thus,

(L$_1'$)   Wa, Bb, $\sim$Wb, $\sim$Ba

characterizes what some would call the "actual" world. Supposedly,

(L$_2'$)   Wb, Ba, $\sim$Wa, $\sim$Bb

characterizes a "possible" world. On the present view, recall, "worlds" are, in Wittgenstein's fashion, classes of facts and, hence, not existents in an ontological assay. That point aside, classes have members. The members of the class that is the actual world are existent facts. Those of the possible world are supposedly possible facts. Such a supposition is based on a misleading picture that derives from Wittgenstein's talk of possibilities in the *Tractatus* and Carnap's subsequent talk of state descriptions. One thinks of a list of facts, say,

(L$_3'$)   Wa, Bb,

giving a description of one world, while another list,

(L$_4'$)   Wb, Ba,

gives a characterization of a possible world containing "possible facts." It is as if we have a set with the sentences on (L$_3'$) and (L$_4'$) representing members of such a set, where the members are of one of two kinds. Paradoxically, one then takes a possibility as a kind of fact. It is not paradoxical to treat (L$_1'$) as a list of (actual) facts. Each fact is a complex in two senses. First, it has constituents in that it contains a particular and a property in a structural relation. Second, we distinguish what an *atomic* sentence represents from the existence of what is represented as a positive or negative fact. Thus, 'Wb' and '~Wb' are taken, as a pair, to stand for a fact, irrespective of whether that fact is the ground of truth of the one or of the other. The fact is either positive or negative, but, whichever quality it has, we recognize its quality as distinct from what is qualified. The latter is not a possible existent any more than, on a substratum view, the substratum, which is possibly W or not —W, is a possible existent. This is quite different from taking possible facts, as entities, that may, then, be actual (existent) or merely possible (nonexistent). The absurdity of the latter gambit is shown by the fact that the members of (L$_2$') do not stand for anything, if they are taken to stand for positive and negative facts. Hence, the set or world whose members are listed on (L$_2$') is empty. Possible worlds are not only nonexistent in that they are sets but in that a possible world is either an empty set or, innocuously, a mere subset of the set of actual facts. Thus, the very notion of a possible world is empty.

Since possibilities have been acknowledged on the present gambit, we may recognize a list

(L$_5$')   Wa, Bb, Wb, Ba,

of such for our miniature domain. But, neither such a list, nor any part of it, characterizes a possible world. For, the part of the list that consists of 'Wb' and 'Ba' is not the list (L$_4$'). The latter is a list of purported nonexistent facts. To give a nonempty set of "possibilities" that will constitute a possible world would be to take the list (L$_4$') as a list of "possibilities" in a different sense of 'possible' than (L$_5$') involves. We would have to take the *entities* (facts) of a possible world, listed by (L$_4$'), as possibilities that are *merely possible*, as opposed to actual. One, thus, recognizes possibilities in two senses: there are possibilities, indicated by atomic sentences, that, then, exist as merely possible or actual. It is the need to recognize possibilities, as subjects, existing as mere possibilities (a subject in a mode) that reduces the view to absurdity and makes talk of possible facts paradoxical, as well as tongue twisting.

To so construe possibilities, and one who speaks of possible facts in possible worlds must do so, is to acknowledge negative facts. These, too, will exist as mere possibilities or as actual facts. One, thus, accepts existent negative possibilities. And this is not a result of verbal gymnastics. To acknowledge a mode as applying to "something" is to accept that something as existing in that mode. Moreover, by recognizing the mode of possibility, in addition to the possibilities that are subjects in that mode, one invites the Bradley problem in the form of embedded possibilities. I say 'invites', rather than involves, since there is a line of defense. We may see both by noting a further contrast between the two approaches. I have argued that one viably grounds the recognition that *a* is W, but could have been not-W and B, by accepting facts and an analysis of their role in terms of possibilities, a positive quality, and a negative quality. To attempt to generate a Bradleyian regress by seeking to attribute such qualities to positive and negative facts, in turn, fails. It fails for two reasons. First, it makes no sense to hold that a positive fact could have been negative, or vice versa. Second, we have not recognized modes of possibility and actuality. Thus, one cannot ask if such modes could apply when they, in fact, do not. Here, we see a point behind the adoption of Russell's terms 'positive' and 'negative'. For much of the discussion of the complex of issues involved, one may, as we did, interchange the pairs 'positive-negative' and 'possible-actual'. This does not lead to problems so long as we recognize the three-fold pattern involved: possibilities with one or the other quality. But, the appeal to the qualities, positive and negative, rather than the modes, possible and actual, is ultimately and fundamentally different. It does not involve the recognition of subject possibilities *existing* in the mode of possibility and, hence, being *nonexistents*. But, if one speaks of a possibility having a quality, must one not recognize a *tie* between the subject and the quality? It really makes no difference. The fundamental point was made when we saw that in the case of a fact, one must acknowledge a structure, whether or not one speaks of a tie as a constituent of the fact. Thus, one can avoid taking the tie to be a constituent by recognizing that the structure of the fact (a) connects the constituents and (b) connects them in a certain way. In the monadic case, the particular is not only connected to the property, but they are connected in that the particular exemplifies the property, and not vice versa. In the case of a dyadic relation, the constituents are connected and connected in that the relation is exemplified in a *direction*. The crucial point, to meet the Bradleyian problem, is the recognition of structure and the realization that it cannot be a constituent. Bergmann failed to solve the puzzle because he took the structure to be a constituent.[12] Sellars may be taken to have seen that acknowledging exemplification does not, by itself, solve any problem. He, then, taking the relational case as his model, seeks to eliminate relations, along with exemplification, and simply retain the structure among particulars. Sellars fails, as we saw, on two counts. He must give the structure yet another role by taking it to supply the content provided by the descriptive relation, and he cannot handle the case of monadic properties.

If we recognize a tie or if we merely hold that the (subject) possibility and a quality constitute a structured entity, the Bradleyian march is halted. We need not recognize further modes to assign to such existent facts. That the positive fact, which grounds the truth of 'Wa', need not have existed, since the possibility could have been negative rather than positive, is grounded in our recognition of possibilities, the two qualities, and our holding that a possibility always exists as qualified by one of them. We have no need to speak, in any other way, of possibility and actuality. The alternative way of speaking about possibilities mixes two senses of 'fact'. A fact, say $fact_1$, is a composite of a possibility, in my sense, and a quality, positive or negative. A fact, say $fact_2$, is a composite of a $fact_1$ and a mode, possible or actual. *A possibility* as a "subject" of a $fact_1$ must be kept separate from *possibility* as a mode "in" a $fact_2$. One who speaks of possible worlds speaks of $facts_2$, which contain the mode of possibility, *as possible facts*. Once we make the appropriate distinctions, we see that we need not recognize either such entities or the modes involved. To attempt to raise the Bradleyian problem about the view I have advocated is to argue that if we recognize facts in the sense of $fact_1$, and their constituent possibilities, we must recognize facts in the sense of $fact_2$. But, we can now see that there is no force to the line of argument. It is parallel to the weak version of the Bradleyian argument which *merely insists* that there must be a fact with $n + 1$ terms for every fact with n terms. On the alternative view, the modes of possibility and actuality are acknowledged (whether implicitly or explicitly) and, in effect, facts of two kinds, $facts_1$ and $facts_2$. Such a view thus allows for a question about the application of the modes to facts$_2$, taken as "subjects," even though they are composites of facts$_1$ and modes. The point is even more forceful when we recognize that the view acknowledges, as I have put matters, that some facts, facts$_1$, are involved in others, facts$_2$, by combining with a mode. This provides an opening for the Bradleyan question. Yet, the proponent of such a view may observe that he is not forced to admit such a regress in view of the fact that he takes the modes to apply to facts$_1$ to form facts$_2$. This does not obligate one to take the modes to apply to facts$_2$ to form further, more complex, combinations. But, blocking the Bradleyan regress in this way is not as cogent as on the alternative defended above. On that analysis, the Bradleyan regress is blocked from the outset, since we recognize neither the mode of possibility nor the two kinds of *possible* facts. By so doing, we have accommodated the bipolar feature of propositions in an ontological assay which remains as faithful to Russell's vivid sense of reality as Logical Atomism can.[13]

I have been concerned with an ontological question. What grounds the connection between language and thought and the facts that they are about? There is another question that Pears, in his discussion of the issue, rightly separates from it.[14] How do sentences get meaning for us? Here, there are really two philosophical questions aside from the questions about the learning process that psychologists and linguists are concerned with. One has to do with linking the constituent terms to experience. The other is a question about how a sentence can be understood, since it is more than the set of its terms. We have dealt with some aspects of the first question at different places in the book. Other facets of the question would involve examining the viability of a principle of acquaintance and entering the disputes about the "given" and the analysis of perception. We have also touched on some of the latter, but they are not within the scope of the book. The second question we have implicitly dealt with. Properly understood, it should be seen to be an unfortunate hangover from the reductionist tendencies in the empiricist tradition that lead to the rejection of relations. It is sufficiently answered by noting that we do recognize, on the basis of experience, relations and, in particular, exemplification. For the rest, it is a request to do what cannot be reasonably asked, to analyze what is not analyzable. Pursued, it leads to Bradley's regress*es* and talk of Fregean functions as unsaturated constituents of propositions.

Possibilities provide a satisfactory basis for treating thoughts as token facts. That has been a recurrent theme. It can be seen, from a slightly different perspective, by considering a defect in Strawson's well-known attack on Russell's views on meaning and reference. Since that critique leads to the reintroduction of Fregean senses and propositions, in the guise of "assertions," it bears on a number of issues we have discussed. Consider, once again, a small domain of two objects, a white square and a black circle. Consider also, the sign sequence 'W*a*', where we coordinate the sign '*a*' to the square and the sign 'W' to the color white. Suppose we also coordinate the name to the circle and the predicate to the color black. With the appropriate grammatical rules, we may, then, use the sign sequence 'W*a*' to assert either that the square is white or that the circle is black. Doing so, we make two different assertions with the "same sentence." Both are true. But, we could make a false assertion if we took '*a*' to refer to the square and the predicate to stand for the color black. Hence, what is true or false cannot be the sentence. Thus, we must recognize assertions as the subjects for our ascriptions of truth and falsehood. So runs one of Strawson's main arguments for assertions and against the view that sentences are true or false. It is obviously a version of a traditional argument for propositions. The view differs from the traditional appeal to propositions, since it does not take assertions to be the meanings of sentences. Assertions are merely what we ascribe truth and falsity to. Yet, the argument is inadequate. The mistake is marked by the substitution of 'sentence' for 'sign sequence'. It is indeed true that the sign sequence 'W*a*', as a set of tokens on paper or as a type, is neither true nor false. But, neither is it, as such, a sentence. It is a sentence upon interpretation. The sign sequence may be given many interpretations. Thus, it may be used to utter or assert different sentences. On one interpretation, we have one sentence. On another interpretation, we have another sentence. But, a sentence, unlike an assertion, is merely a string of *interpreted* tokens (or types of such). To say the marks are interpreted is to note that they have been coordinated, not that there is something called an *assertion* or an *interpretation* to which I ascribe truth or falsehood. What is true or false is a sentence. A sentence, however, is not merely a string of marks or tokens or types. We assert sentences. But we need not recognize "assertions," as Strawson does, even though, as we commonly speak, we make assertions. Recognizing that interpreted strings of marks are sentences, we also recognize that there is a sense in which two strings of tokens, of different geometrical patterns, can be tokens of the same sentence type. They have the same interpretation and, hence, may be used to assert the same thing. The same holds for thoughts as facts. How, then, is a sentence or a thought, as a fact, interpreted without recognizing Strawson's assertions or Frege's propositions? We *do not coordinate* the sentence to an object (a fact or a possibility). An atomic sentence is interpreted in that we have *a rule* for all atomic sentences, as *we have coordination rules* for each primitive predicate and name. In virtue of that rule, we are committed to facts of both a positive and a negative kind. Thus, the rule also provides for the interpretation of the negation sign. Keep in mind that we have observed atomic facts—that an object is white. And we do distinguish between the object, the color, and the fact that the one has the other. That we do so is no more problematic than our distinguishing the color from the shape of the object. Suppose we then wish to coordinate 'W*a*' to the fact we observe. Having distinguished the various "things," the fact, the color, and the object, we do not simply coordinate 'W*a*' to the fact, as we coordinate '*a*' to the object. For, in coordinating the sentence, we coordinate '~W*a*' as well. This is summed up in the claims that the coordination is made by a general rule about atomic sentences and that 'W*a*' stands for a possibility that is either positive or negative. Moreover, on any occasion of the occurrence of a token of a thought, as a sentence token, there are the unanalyzable features of the intentional situation. The constituent tokens *represent* what they do, and their arrangement *represents* what it does. Consequently, the fact (thought) represents what it does. This simple, unavoidable, and unanalyzable feature of thought suffices for the refutation of all schemes of materialism and of purported causal "explications" of the nature of thought and the mental.

Difference, Existence, and Universality

As I noted in an earlier chapter, we need not recognize existential facts like '$(\exists x)Wx$'. Given that 'Wa' is true, the fact it indicates suffices to ground the truth of '$(\exists x)Wx$'. Just as the rule for conjunction shows we need not recognize conjunctive facts, the rule of existential generalization does the same for facts like '$(\exists x)Wx$'. But, as Russell observed, we do not have

$$\frac{Wa_1 \,\&\, Wa_2 \,\&\, \ldots \,\&\, Wa_n}{(x)Wx}$$

as a valid argument form. He thought we must recognize the universal fact that $a_1, a_2, \ldots, a_n$ were *all the objects*. With such a claim as a *further* premise, we can deduce '$(x)Wx$' from the appropriate conjunction of atomic sentences. But, we have acknowledged *a* universal fact. Yet, for any finite domain, we need recognize only *one* such universal fact. We may reflect this by an appropriate sentence like

$$(x)(x = a_1 \lor x = a_2 \lor \ldots \lor x = a_n),$$

or by "understanding" that the names correlate to all members of the domain or "world." This calls attention to our having implicitly acknowledged *an* existential fact as well, in that we take all names to name and to name different objects, in an appropriate kind of perspicuous schema. Hence, we can recognize a further "fact" expressed by:

$(\exists x_1)(\exists x_2) \ldots (\exists x_n)(x_1 = a_1 \,\&\, x_2 = a_2 \,\&\, \ldots \,\&\, x_n = a_n \,\&\, a_1 \neq a_2 \,\&\, \ldots \,\&\, a_{n-1} \neq a_n)$.

In short, we are claiming that there are a specific number of objects by means of three notions: *existence, difference,* and *universality*. We might then hold that there is such *a* fact about each finite domain and express it by

(D) $U(a_1, a_2, \ldots, a_n)$.

(D) is so understood that

(D$_1$) $a_1 \neq a_2, a_2 \neq a_3, \ldots, a_{n-1} \neq a_n$
(D$_2$) $(\exists x)(x = a_1) \,\&\, (\exists x)(x = a_2) \,\&\, \ldots \,\&\, (\exists x)(x = a_n)$
(D$_3$) $(x)(x = a_1 \,\vee\, x = a_2 \,\vee\, \ldots \,\vee\, x = a_n)$

are all consequences of it. (D$_1$), (D$_2$), and (D$_3$) make explicit the factual claims regarding *universality, existence,* and *difference* for the domain or world. We can, then, take such *notions* to correlate to *a relation* (or three such relations) that obtains among the members of the domain and for which 'U', in (D), stands or which is reflected by (D$_1$), (D$_2$), and (D$_3$). Moreover, following themes in Moore, Russell, and Bergmann, we can claim that such notions have an experiential basis. One perceives that a_1 is not a_2 and that both exist or "are something." Hence, *numerical difference* and *existence*, although not ordinary properties or relations, do not "violate" the motivation behind a principle of acquaintance. [Speaking in this manner does return us to a basic feature of Moore's disagreement with the idealists, which was a theme we encountered at the very beginning of the book: taking existence to be an empirical concept and extending its application to the nonexperiential.] Similarly, as Bergmann has argued, one may take the notion of universality to connect with experience. Draw two black crosses enclosed by a circle. One sees that *there are two* crosses in the circle and that *every* cross in the circle is black. With such a basis, in experience, for construing *difference* and the *quantifiers*, we can take the generalization-instantiation rules and statements like '$a_1 \neq a_2$' and '$(\exists x)(x = a_1)$' to reflect the "fact" (D) and not to stand for possible facts. Just as the rules for conjunction provide a basis for thoughts with conjunctive texts, so the generalization-instantiation rules and (D) provide a ground for the other "logical" texts.

One may suggest, in Fregean fashion, that the zero-level quantifiers be taken as properties (or functions) of the second level. Hence, '(x)Wx' would be expressed by something like '^{2}U(W)', and '^{2}U(W,S)' would render '(x)(Wx $\supset$ Sx)'. General facts would, then, be "atomic facts" of higher order. Aside from other difficulties such a proposal may involve, it does not capture the use of the quantifier in (D$_3$). Of course, one could introduce a relational property of the first order, as in (D), to render (D$_3$). But, then, we acknowledge distinct "quantifier relations" at different levels. Yet, *both range over* the same individuals. This complication is in addition to one, similar to the use of different *belief* relations on the "relational" analysis, that is already involved in the use of '^{2}U' in both monadic patterns like '^{2}U(W)' and relational patterns like '^{2}U(W,S)'.

Geach has argued that we must hold that a_1 *is a different $\emptyset$ from* a_2 and never simply that a_1 is different from a_2.[1] He is clearly wrong. But, that aside, the underlying motive may well be the rendering of the quantifiers as second-level properties à la Frege. For, his argument would apparently remove the obstacle to the Fregean pattern. What rebuts Geach, as well as the Fregean pattern, is the simple fact that Moore and Russell made a cornerstone of the early attack on idealism: the existence of numerical difference as a simple, unanalyzable concept. It is worth recalling that, after Russell adopted what has come to be known as the Russell-Leibniz analysis of identity, Wittgenstein insisted on the unanalyzability of numerical difference in his criticism of Russell's analysis.

I have spoken of finite domains. An infinite domain, if such a notion is sensible, need not affect the pattern of the analysis. One would be required to acknowledge facts corresponding to general sentences like '(x)Wx' and '(x)(Wx $\supset$ Sx)', in addition to modifying (D), only if one held that such sentences required a ground of truth as atomic sentences do. But, one might deny that such general sentences are "true" in the sense in which atomic sentences are and, hence, deny that there are universal facts, other than the domain fact. There is a reason for doing so that connects the present discussion with issues about "laws," "conventionalism," "verification," and so forth. These questions are related to the issues of this book in that one, if not *the*, relevant ontological issue concerning the ground of truth for "laws" is the question of universal facts. If one does not acknowledge universal facts corresponding to statements of natural laws, one does not take the relevant statements of the laws to be true in the sense in which statements of fact are true. As Wittgenstein put it in the *Tractatus*:

6.37   There is no compulsion making one thing happen because another has happened. The only necessity that exists is *logical* necessity.

This means that "the world" does not contain facts that correspond to and ground the truth of lawful generalizations any more than it contains disjunctive facts corresponding to and grounding the truth of disjunctive sentences. Wittgenstein's theme is a crucial one for Logical Atomism. Suppose laws were true in virtue of general facts. Then, there would be, in virtue of *the* fact corresponding to a law, a connection between atomic facts as well as connections between the general fact and atomic facts. Such connections would provide a basis for holding that, in a quite specific sense, there were factual necessities and, hence, a form of determinism would be implied. Logical Atomism is incompatible with such connections among facts and the existence of such *necessities*. This requires some further comments on the notion of "necessity." Before turning to that, we might note that Wittgenstein's rejection of laws as depicting facts is clear:

6.363   The procedure of induction consists in accepting as true the *simplest* law that can be reconciled with our experiences.

6.3631 This procedure, however, has no logical justification but only a psychological one. It is clear that there are no grounds for believing that the simplest eventuality will in fact be realized.

6.36311 It is an hypothesis that the sun will rise tomorrow: and this means that we do not *know* whether it will rise.

6.371   The whole modern conception of the world is founded on the illusion that the so-called laws of nature are the explanations of natural phenomena.

One cannot argue that he is merely claiming that we can never know what the laws, depicting facts, are and is not denying that there are such facts. This would run counter to 6.37 and miss the point that he is explicating, partially, the notion of a *law* in the above passages, just as Hume explicated the notion of *necessary connection* in terms of a "customary connection in the thought or imagination between one object and its usual attendant; and this sentiment is the original of that idea we seek for."[2]

The denial of general facts points to a distinction between a stronger and a weaker form of a Humean-style analysis of causality. If there are no general facts "depicted" by statements of law, then in one simple and clear sense, there are no causal necessities, necessary connections, dispositional properties, or "dispositional facts." I say "simple and clear" since we easily specify what the relative sense of 'necessity' is: to say that there are such necessities is simply to say that there are general facts corresponding to statements of law. One who holds that there are such general facts may, in turn, hold that *they* are (or are not) *necessary* facts. This involves a further sense of 'necessary'. This latter claim may be challenged by a Humean type attack on the concept of *necessity* involved and the grounds for making such a claim. There is not a corresponding problem about the *concept of necessity* involved in the claim that *there are factual necessities, since there are general facts* of a certain form. The stronger version of a Humean position, which is involved in Logical Atomism, is the denial that there are such facts. There is an argument for such a view that is independent of the traditional Humean attack on the concept of necessity. In a finite domain, there is no need to appeal to general facts to ground the truth of general statements. Hence, the stronger form of the Humean view is "supported" by Occam's razor.[3] Moreover, it is awkward for the (weaker version of the) non-Humean position to depend on the assumption that the domain is infinite. However, aside from such questions about laws and necessity, a question remains about *truths* like '(x)Wx' in an infinite domain.[4]

A critic may feel that I have too quickly turned away from a problem by speaking of our knowing the meaning of '&' in terms of the truth table for it and of the quantifiers in terms of the generalization-instantiation rules, the existential and universal facts reflected in (D), and the experiential basis for notions of *existence*, *difference*, and *generality*. The point can be seen, however, if we keep distinct the two basic questions in both cases: the question of the ontological ground of statements and the question of the content of beliefs (as well as keep both questions distinct from irrelevant questions about the learning process). We first recognized, in the case of atomic sentences, the need to appeal to facts and possibilities. In dealing with negation, we were led to see the threefold dichotomy involved in the notions of *fact* and *possible fact*. We did not need to appeal to *anything* further in order to ground the truth of conjunctions or to link conjunctive belief contents with what language is about. In short, we did not have to recognize any additional ontological implications in our use of conjunctive sentences in the way that we did have to recognize facts and their "qualities" in our use of atomic sentences. In the case of the quantifiers, we did have to recognize, first, additional "facts," and, second, *correlates* of '($\exists$x)', '(x)', and '$\neq$'. The latter were spoken of as "relations" or "concepts" reflected in (D), (D_1), (D_2), and (D_3). They may also be taken, in view of our understanding of (D), to be the basis of the generalization-instantiation rules. All this accounts for the truth conditions of the relevant statements, for the linking of belief contents with the appropriate texts to their respective truth conditions or "intentions," and for the use of the appropriate logical rules. Thus, we have acknowledged the ontological price for the use of such notions without, as far as I can see, begging any question or avoiding any relevant issue.[5]

In speaking of *existence* as I have, we have returned to the early dispute between Moore and the idealists. Given that a concept of existence is based on experience, can it be cogently extended to the nonexperiential? In an earlier chapter, I argued, following Russell, that the use of labels is so understood that statements like '*a* exists' or 'this exists' are redundant. *Existence*, so to speak, is carried by the use of labels just as *difference* may be expressed by a limitation on the use of names and predicates. By a principle of acquaintance, one limits one's labels to stand for objects of experience and experienced properties. *Existence*, then, could be taken to belong only to objects and properties of experience, *if* one confusedly mixes such points with the assertion that an existential claim is limited to objects of experience. Given the introduction of a quantifier, the sentence

(D$_4$) $(\exists x)(x \neq a_1 \ \& \ x \neq a_2 \ \& \ \ldots \ \& \ x \neq a_n)$

is well formed. Hence, by using it, we can express something we could not express, if we took (D) by itself and did not "separate off" the notion of existence, as in (D$_2$). That (D$_4$) is well formed may be taken to express one theme in Moore's argument. But, nothing follows from (D$_4$) regarding there being an unexperienced object unless we understand that any experienced object *would be* an a_i. This amounts to introducing a primitive predicate, say 'P', transcribed as 'being an object of experience' and holding that

(D$_5$) $(\exists x)\sim Px$

is also well formed. This has nothing to do with issues of whether (D$_4$) and (D$_5$) are false or *even logically false*! To get to (D$_5$) we have had to hold that we have the concepts of *existing* and of *being an object of experience* as *simple* and *separable*. Moreover, there is no problem about my use of the terms 'simple' and 'separable'. I have treated existence as if Moore's early discussion is correct. The issue about 'P', as about 'exists', reduces to the kind of question where argument ends, and where Moore appeals to what amounts to a direct apprehension of a simple (experienced) property of *being experienced* (as well as of *existence*). We, thus, end with what some would call a *phenomenological* question. But, there is, perhaps, some consolation for the idealist in that Moore must, first, make the same kind of claim about both *exists* and P, and, second, the claim that *being an object of experience* is itself experienced has the air of a forced and paradoxical move.

An obvious objection can now be made. In recognizing (D$_4$) as well formed, have we not recognized existential possibilities in a sense of 'possible' rejected in the previous chapter? To put it another way, must we not recognize that different domains, i.e., worlds, are *possible* in the sense of being a domain with a different number of (set of) objects? How does one deal with that sense of 'possible'? One answer would be the claim that we have a negative fact for each such possibility. Hence, there is no difference with respect to the handling of 'possible'. The difference is in the recognition of negative existential facts. Such existential facts are characterized in terms of the notions of existence, difference, and generality, and, hence, are not problematic. They would be problematic if we took (D) to express a basic relation holding among the objects $a_1, a_2, \ldots, a_n$ of the domain—the relation U. Then, we would have to express one such negative fact by

$$(\exists x) [U(a_1, a_2, \ldots, a_n) \,\&\, x \neq a_1 \,\&\, x \neq a_2 \,\&\, \ldots \,\&\, x \neq a_n \,\&$$
$$(z)(z = a_1 \lor z = a_2 \lor \ldots \lor z = x)].$$

This would show that 'U' does not stand for a basic domain relation, since we cannot state the possibility that obtains among objects of a larger domain by the use of 'U' without the quantifiers and '≠'. We could introduce a series of relations like U to "possibly" hold, or take 'U', as Quine takes 'believes . . . of', to be variant in the number of its terms. But, this clearly introduces a problem in that we have a series of basic relations that are not exemplified but for which we know the truth conditions. To say that there is one relation that is "multigrade" merely hides the problem. In Quine's case, the cover-up is provided by the belief predicate really being two-term, where the second term is a sentence. In our case, the point to note would be the implicit use of variants of (D_1), (D_2), and (D_3) to characterize any domain. Or, to put it simply, irrespective of how many objects there are in a finite domain it is characterized by an existential and a universal clause, as in sentences like

$$(D_6) \quad (\exists x)(\exists y) [x \neq y \,\&\, (z)(z = x \lor z = y)],$$

which contain '=' and '≠'. We can, then, recognize patterns like (D_6), involving existence, generality, and difference to indicate possibilities that are negative facts. We can, but we need not. Recall that the recognition of a *kind* or *category* of facts stems from our need to ground the truth of a sentence. But (D), understood in terms of (D_1), (D_2), and (D_3), grounds the truth of the negation of every alternative sentence characterizing a domain. Hence, given this simple arithmetical "fact," we need not recognize facts corresponding to such sentences.

However, this claim leads to a further problem. Ontological positions usually stumble over one or all of (a) the problem of "falsity" and nonexistence; (b) the problem of intentionality; (c) arithmetic. We have been concerned with (a) and (b). I believe the logistic pattern of analysis for (c) is essentially correct, and I have given some reasons elsewhere.[6] Here, I am concerned with a problem for such a pattern. If one follows Russell, he requires, through an axiom of infinity, what would be an infinite domain fact. This, he must assume. Thus, there are two problems. The appeal to a fact and the making of an assumption. An alternative is to introduce numbers as properties. One must accept complex properties on such a move. This we have discussed in Chapters IV, V, and IX. One who accepts the negative existential facts that we just saw are not required could make use of the infinite number of such facts, and the domain predicates, as a basis for a Russell-Frege-type analysis of arithmetic. But, such facts are not needed for the analyses involved in (a) and (b). Hence, on either alternative we analyze arithmetic along the lines of the logistic thesis at the cost of introducing entities. This conflicts with one motive for such an analysis, taken as a philosophical or ontological analysis of elementary arithmetic.

Treating *existence*, *universality*, and *difference* as I have recalls Moore's appeal to the simplicity and unanalyzability of crucial concepts: *exists*, *direct apprehension*, *numerical difference*, *good*. His early views forced him to acknowledge a direct and, in effect, intuitive *grasp* of conceptual *entities* represented by the *words* 'exists', etc. This matched Russell's "Platonism" of the period before "The Philosophy of Logical Atomism." Yet, the arguments to establish the simplicity and unanalyzability of such concepts increasingly involved the exploration of the common usage of the words for such concepts. Thus, one may understand the evolution of a quite natural move to his placing the emphasis on the usage of words as opposed to the intuition of *ideas*. This had the two-fold attraction of avoiding an explicit and seemingly problematic appeal to immediate "intuition" or "experience" of concepts, while converting an implicit method into an explicit and defensible procedure. It was also in the spirit of the period, for appeals to *intuition* and *experience* in such matters are not only philosophically questionable but *unverifiable* and *private*. Ordinary usage, by contrast, is open to public exploration and furnishes a context for posing *resolvable* questions. Thus, Moore's early appeals to the simplicity and unanalyzability of concepts naturally led to his increased concern with the analysis of the complexity of linguistic usage. For many, influenced by him, the very method of analysis came to replace the entities it was earlier taken to reveal, and language, rather than ontology, came to be the focus of philosophical concern.

Notes

Notes

Chapter I

1. G. E. Moore, *Some Main Problems of Philosophy*, hereafter *SMP* (George Allen & Unwin, London, 1953), Chapter III.

2. On this matter, see the appendix Moore added to *SMP*, pp. 374-78 as well as pp. 34-35. It is worth noting that the same ambiguity is present in Russell's early discussions of "sense data"; see B. Russell, *The Problems of Philosophy* (Oxford University Press, London, 1956), pp. 11-16. The ambiguity is connected with Russell's claim that only particulars are sensed and that *a sense datum* is *a datum of sensation*; see his "Sensation and Imagination," *The Monist*, 25, 1915, pp. 28-44, and "Definitions and Methodological Principles in Theory of Knowledge," *The Monist*, 24, 1914, pp. 582-93. In the latter article, Russell virtually notes the ambiguity, p. 585. The question is discussed in detail in my article "Moore's Ontology and Non-Natural Properties," *Review of Metaphysics*, 15, 1962, pp. 365-95, reprinted in a revised version in *Studies in the Philosophy of G. E. Moore*, hereafter *SGEM*, ed. by E. D. Klemke (Quadrangle, Chicago, 1969), pp. 95-127. The issues are further debated in: John M. Nelson, "Mr. Hochberg on Moore: Some Corrections," *SGEM*, pp. 128-40, and my "Some Reflections on Mr. Nelson's Corrections," *SGEM*, pp. 141-54. For related discussions of "quality instances," see D. Brownstein,

Aspects of the Problem of Universals (University of Kansas Press, Lawrence, 1973); Ivar Segelberg, *Begrippet Egenskap* (Svenska Tryckeriaktiebolaget, Stockholm, 1947); G. Bergmann, "The Ontology of Edmund Husserl," *Methodos*, 12, 1960, pp. 359-92, reprinted in G. Bergmann, *Logic and Reality* (University of Wisconsin Press, Madison, 1964), pp. 193-224; E. B. Allaire, "Existence, Independence, and Universals," *The Philosophical Review*, 69, 1960, pp. 485-96; R. Grossmann, "Sensory Intuition and the Dogma of Localization," *Inquiry*, 5, 1962, pp. 238-51. The latter two articles are reprinted in *Essays in Ontology*, E. B. Allaire et al. (Martinus Nijhoff, The Hague, 1963).

3. On the role of such a principle and a *principle of acquaintance* in ontological analysis, see my articles "On Being and Being Presented," *Philosophy of Science*, 32, 2, 1965; "Ontology and Acquaintance," *Philosophical Studies*, 17, June, 1966, pp. 49-55; "Elementarism, Independence, and Ontology," *Philosophical Studies*, 1961, 12, pp. 36-43, reprinted in *Essays in Ontology*; "Metaphysical Explanation," *Metaphilosophy*, 1, No. 2, April, 1970, pp. 139-65.

4. There is a problem involved in this claim that I shall take up in Chapter III.

5. On the pattern of his indirect realism in *SMP*, no material object "can" be an object of direct apprehension. This is not to say that he holds that his *analysis* consists of a set of necessary truths. He writes in *SMP*, p. 131:

> There follows, I think, from the two last that all material objects have the important property that none of them are ever directly apprehended by us: since nothing that exists is ever directly apprehended by us except sense-data, and our minds and acts of consciousness.

The problems about the existence of propositions are also implicit in this passage.

6. Moore "defines" a material object "as something which (1) does occupy space; (2) is *not* a sense-datum of any kind whatever and (3) is not a mind, nor an act of consciousness," *SMP*, p. 131. From this, as we saw in note 5, he concludes that they are not directly apprehended. It is the latter "property" of material objects that is crucial to the attack on idealists and phenomenalists. For some later comments by Moore on material objects and direct apprehension, see his replies to Bouwsma and Mace in *The Philosophy of G. E. Moore*, hereafter *PGEM*, ed. by P. A. Schilpp (Northwestern University, Evanston, 1942), pp. 629-45.

7. B. Russell, *Introduction to Mathematical Philosophy* (George Allen & Unwin, London, 1953), pp. 60-62, and *The Problems of Philosophy*, Chapter V. Russell's talk of acquaintance with "logical objects" in his unpublished manuscript "Theory of Knowledge" of 1913, in the Russell archives, is also relevant. There is an ambiguity in the notions of *experience* and *direct apprehension* that affects the use of a principle of acquaintance and complicates the preceding discussion. Russell and Moore write as if one directly apprehends Platonic concepts or universals. Thus, one may speak of the direct apprehension of a concept without an instance of the concept being an object of experience or being directly apprehended. In the preceding discussion I have used the notion of *apprehension* in a way that would imply that one could only hold a *simple concept* to be directly apprehended if one directly apprehended an instance of it. In this context, other phrases Moore sometimes uses, 'directly perceives' in "The Nature and Reality of Objects of Perception," *Proceedings of the Aristotelian Society*, 1905-1906, and 'directly sees' in *Commonplacebook*, 1919-1953, ed. by C. Lewy (George Allen & Unwin, London, 1962), pp. 322-23, are more suggestive than 'directly apprehends'. We shall return to this issue in Chapter III.

8. G. E. Moore, "Some Judgments of Perception," *Proceedings of the Aristotelian Society*, 1918-1919, reprinted in *Philosophical Studies*, hereafter *PS* (Humanities Press, New York, 1951), pp. 248-49.

9. *SMP*, p. 71.

10. *SMP*, pp. 32-35, 113-17.

11. *SMP*, pp. 34, 105.

12. *SMP*, pp. 34-35, 116, 137.

13. *SMP*, pp. 146-47.

14. *Some Judgments of Perception*, pp. 233-34. Taken one way, Moore's analysis relies on a hopelessly circular use of definite descriptions. He, in effect, specifies (one could say 'defines') the predicate 'R' in terms of 'the relation which a material object stands in to the sensa which are such that the material object stands in *that* relation to them'. Moreover, he *identifies* O as *the material* object that stands in R to a_1, while taking R to be *the* relation that O stands in to a_1. In a way, this merely points to the need to provide an *explication* of 'R'. Taken another way, Moore is claiming to know that, given the datum a_1, there is *a* relation and *one* material object such that the object stands in the relation to a_1. This does not attempt to specify the relation. But, as we shall soon see, it is inadequate for his purpose.

15. *SMP*, p. 125.

16. *SMP*, p. 125.

Chapter II

1. G. E. Moore, "The Refutation of Idealism," *Mind*, 12, 1903, reprinted in *PS*, pp. 1-30.

2. *Ibid.*, pp. 29-30. In reading Moore's argument in "The Refutation," one should keep in mind Moore's occasional fusing of *the property* (blue), *the sense datum* (blue patch), and *the quality instance* (the blue of the patch) that we noted in Chapter I. Moore's views are complicated by the fact that he also holds that we do perceive *universal* color properties in sensation, but such properties are specific *shades* of color and not colors like white and blue, *Commonplace Book*, pp. 18-19, 50-55, 58-62, 74, 326-27.

3. Moore does not overlook the point; he ignores it in developing his argument. He briefly touches on the question at the opening of his paper and tells us his argument is designed to

at least refute Mr. Taylor's Idealism, if it refutes anything at all: for I *shall* undertake to show that what makes a thing real cannot possibly be its presence as an inseparable aspect of a sentient experience. (*Ibid.*, p. 8)

I mention the point merely for its bearing on the assumption Moore makes that the relation of awareness is the same no matter what the "object" is.

4. J. P. Sartre, *The Transcendence of the Ego*, (The Noonday Press, New York, 1971), trans. by F. Williams and R. Kirkpatrick, pp. 40-45. Sartre follows a familiar phenomenological pattern and asserts that acts must *intend* "transcendent" objects. Hence, idealism is refuted. This is, as it is intended to be, a twist on the idealist's argument that Moore seeks to refute. This can lead to a misguided argument against Moore, since one can now ask if Moore's argument shows that there can be an act without an object. It does not. Acts are objects that stand in DA to some other object. If something did not

so stand to an object, it would not be an act. What one has to ask is whether what *is* an act *need be* that kind of thing. This is another question, and it is one we shall return to in the next chapter.

5. That is, he begs the question in respect to his argument that purportedly establishes realism and, in that sense, refutes idealism. This is not to say that he has begged the question with respect to the line of argument that depends upon the distinction between an act, an object, and the relation DA that holds between them. This aspect of Moore's argument has misled W. T. Stace in his "The Refutation of Realism," *Mind*, 43, 1934. Stace purports to refute realism by claiming that the realists cannot prove that material objects do, in fact, exist unexperienced. In one sense, neither Moore nor Russell tried to prove that. As Russell put it: "In one sense it must be admitted that we can never *prove* the existence of things other than ourselves and our experiences." (*The Problems of Philosophy*, p. 22) Moore, however, does purport to prove that some unexperienced objects exist, i.e., *acts*, since the denial of such an existential claim leads, as he see it, to an infinite regress. Even in "A Defence of Common Sense," Moore did not purport to prove that material objects existed, though he did claim to know with certainty that they did exist. G. E. Moore, "A Defence of Common Sense," in *Contemporary British Philosophy* (2nd series), ed. J. H. Muirhead (George Allen & Unwin, London, 1925), re-reprinted in *Philosophical Papers*, hereafter *PP* (George Allen & Unwin, London, 1959), p. 42.

6. See the preface to *PS* and his reply to Ducasse in *PGEM*. But, he continued to maintain that to say of a "directly seen" object *such as* the "side of a page" that "I shall cease to see it" is not to say that "if I close my eyes, it will cease to exist," *Commonplace Book*, pp. 194-95.

7. G. E. Moore, "The Status of Sense Data," *Proceedings of the Aristotelian Society*, 1913-1914, reprinted in *PS*, p. 182. Also see *SMP*, p. 129.

8. *PGEM*, p. 653.

9. *PGEM*, p. 658.

10. *PGEM*, p. 658.

11. *PGEM*, pp. 658-60.

12. *SMP*, p. 2.

13. "A Defence of Common Sense," pp. 36-37.

14. N. Malcolm, "Defending Common Sense," *The Philosophical Review*, 58, 1949, reprinted in *SGEM*, pp. 200-19.

15. *SMP*, p. 135.

16. Malcolm, "Defending Common Sense," p. 202. For a classic and elegant presentation of the sort of analysis Malcolm attempts, see O. K. Bouwsma's "Moore's Theory of Sense-Data," *PGEM*, pp. 203-21. It is worth noting that Bouwsma's well-known contrast between sounds, odors, and tastes, on the one hand, and "sights," on the other, is briefly discussed by Russell in *The Problems of Philosophy*, p. 24.

17. *SMP*, p. 205. Moore does not mean to explain "analysis" in terms of the definition of a term. See *PGEM*, pp. 664-65.

18. Moore is uncomfortable and ambivalent about the "existence" of propositions. Thus, he writes in the preface, written in 1953, to *SMP* (lectures from 1910-1911):

> The second point . . . concerns the relation between what I say about *propositions* in Chapter III and what I say about them in Chapter XIV, pp. 265-6, and again in XVII, p. 309. In III, p. 56, I say "There certainly are in the Universe such things as propositions", whereas in XIV (p. 265) I say that I am recommending a view about the *analysis* of belief which may be expressed by saying "There simply are

no such things as propositions", and in XVII (p. 309) I say "I don't now believe that there are such things as propositions at all". Now this looks as if, when I wrote XIV and XVII, I had abandoned the very view which in III I had decided to be certainly true; and certainly I had, *if* in III I had been using the expression 'There are such things as propositions' in the same sense in which I was using it in XIV and XVII. But I now feel doubtful whether in III I had been using that expression merely in that sense. I think it is possible that in III I was using it, partly at least, in such a sense that the truth of what it expresses would follow from the mere fact that such expressions as 'I believe the *proposition* that the sun is larger than the moon' are perfectly correct ways of expressing something which is often true—as they certainly are. (*SMP*, p. xii)

Thus, in 1953, he suggests that his use of 'proposition' in Chapter III was an "innocent" use of the term, much as Strawson might suggest that his use of 'assertion' is ontologically innocent. I think Moore was wrong about his early use, and I suspect he changed his view as the lectures developed. The example he cites, about the sun being larger than the moon, is used in his 1925-26 lectures on *Propositions and Truth* (G. E. Moore, *Lectures on Philosophy*, ed. by C. Lewy (George Allen and Unwin, London, 1966, p. 143). It is clear, from his discussion of *propositions* in those lectures, that he is concerned with the same problems of Chapter III of *SMP*, and he speaks of propositions being expressed by sentences and being related to facts. (On this question, one should also see the *Commonplace Book*, pp. 359-62, and the 1927 paper "Facts and Propositions," *Proceedings of the Aristotelian Society*, Supplementary Vol. 7, 1927, reprinted in *PP*. This paper appears to be based, in part, on the earlier lectures.) The main point, however, is that the analysis of belief early in *SMP* requires propositions as entities. We shall return to this point in Chapter III.

19. The long passage from the preface of *SMP* cited in note 18 continues:

whereas in XIV and XVII I was using 'There are such things as propositions' in a way which is perhaps more doubtfully correct, namely in such a way that it would not express a truth unless such expressions as 'I believe the proposition that the sun is larger than the moon' can be correctly *analyzed* in a certain way— which is a very different usage.

The point I suggested in the previous note was that this latter use was the use in Chapter III of *SMP*.

20. Moore obviously recognized this kind of point and even seemed to agree with it. See his reply to Wisdom in *PGEM*, pp. 669-70.

21. On Moore's use of 'part' with respect to 'part of a physical object', see "Some Judgments of Perception," *Proceedings of the Aristotelian Society*, 1918-1919, reprinted in *PS*, pp. 238-47.

22. The use of 'redundant' is intended to forestall any unnecessary quibbles about '$\emptyset(\iota x)(\emptyset x)$' being analytic since '$\emptyset(\iota x)(\emptyset x) \equiv E!\ (\iota x)(\emptyset x)$' is a theorem. On such a point, see my articles: "St. Anselm's Ontological Argument and Russell's Theory of Descriptions," *The New Scholasticism*, 33, 1959, pp. 319-30; "Things and Descriptions," *American Philosophical Quarterly*, 3, 1966, pp. 1-9; "Strawson, Russell, and The King of France" in *Essays on Bertrand Russell*, ed. by E. D. Klemke (University of Illinois Press, Urbana, 1970). For a related discussion, see D. F. Pears, *Bertrand Russell and the British Tradition in Philosophy* (Collins, London, 1967), pp. 80-81.

23. For comments by Moore on his notion of *analysis*, see *PGEM*, pp. 660-67. They reveal the relevance of his concern with the *identity* of concepts and of *necessary* con-

nections among them. For some commentaries on Moore's "method" of analysis, see E. D. Klemke, *The Epistemology of G. E. Moore* (Northwestern University Press, Evanston, 1969); A. R. White, *G. E. Moore: A Critical Exposition* (Basil Blackwell, Oxford, 1958); and a number of essays in *G. E. Moore: Essays in Retrospect*, ed. by A. Ambrose and M. Lazerowitz (George Allen and Unwin, London, 1970).

Chapter III

1. *SMP*, pp. 255-56, 263-69.

2. *SMP*, pp. 257-58.

3. *SMP*, pp. 267-68.

4. *SMP*, p. 269.

5. *SMP*, p. 278.

6. *SMP*, p. 279.

7. The need to specify "the relation" raises a problem similar to that discussed in Chapter I. As in that discussion, I ignore the complication involved in the claim of uniqueness.

8. One might object that my use of '$\langle L(I_2, I_1)\rangle$' oversimplifies matters since *the* relevant *facts* are (1) *that* I_2 is a token of 'W' *and* (2) *that* I_1 is a token of 'a_1,' *and* (3) *that* I_2 is to the left of I_1 *and* (4) *that* such a pattern is an instance of the interpreted type $[Wa_1]$. (4) raises a crucial issue that we shall return to at several points. The remaining question amounts to the suggestion that the appropriate sentence is really

$$[Wa_1] (I_2, I_1)$$

with '$[Wa_1]$' taken as a defined relational predicate specifying the conditions in (1), (2), and (3). This means that we deal with a fact of the form

$$\langle p_1 \& p_2 \& p_3\rangle \text{ or, perhaps, } \langle\langle p_1\rangle \& \langle p_2\rangle \& \langle p_3\rangle\rangle$$

in place of $\langle L(I_2, I_1)\rangle$. Hence, we acknowledge the introduction of conjunctive facts and the treatment of '&' as a relation that connects facts into compound facts. The issue recalls a familiar criticism, going back to Russell, that Wittgenstein's claim about the isomorphism between thoughts (sentences) and the facts they represent is mistaken since a token of the sentence 'Wa_1,' taken *as a fact*, is more complex than the fact that a_1 *is* W. The former is, at least, a conjunctive fact along the lines of (1), (2), and (3), while the latter is atomic. I shall return to this issue at the end of Chapter XIII and in the discussion of conjunction in Chapter XIV.

9. The propositional character $[Wa_1]$ is obviously being taken differently in such contexts, where one directly experiences the fact that a_1 is W. It is not being taken as a complex property applying to an act containing constituents that *refer* to a_1 and W. This points to Bergmann's claim that such propositional characters are *simple*. Adopting this gambit, one would then treat such characters along Bergmann's lines and not implicitly treat, as I have, the predicate '$[Wa_1]$' as a defined predicate. We shall return to this question and such definitions in Chapter XIII.

10. The difference between directly apprehending the fact that a_1 is W and having a thought that a_1 is W follows Russell's way of distinguishing between acquaintance and belief, as in *The Problems of Philosophy*, Chapter XII.

11. The symbolism I have used in presenting Moore's views owes much to Bergmann's writings on intentionality. See, in particular, his essays "Intentionality," *Archivio di Filosofia*, Rome: Bocca, 1955, pp. 177-216, reprinted in G. Bergmann, *Meaning and Existence* (University of Wisconsin Press, Madison, 1960); "Acts," *Revista de Filosofia*,

51, 1960, pp. 3-51, reprinted in *Logic and Reality* (University of Wisconsin Press, Madison, 1964); and his book *Realism* (University of Wisconsin Press, Madison, 1967).

Chapter IV

1. For a detailed analysis of Moore's early view, see my article "Moore's Ontology and Non-Natural Properties," in *SGEM*.

2. G. E. Moore, "The Nature of Judgment," *Mind*, 30, 1899, p. 183.

3. *Ibid.*, pp. 179-80. The explicit reason Moore gives for rejecting a correspondence theory of truth is that it would make simple concepts true or false, whereas truth and falsity can only sensibly belong to "complexes." Yet, his pattern also gives him a simple basis for rejecting a coherence pattern, as well as Bradley's road to absolute idealism. N. Rescher has claimed that Bradley is prepared to grant the merits of "the correspondence approach to the intrinsic nature of truth: 'Truth to be true must be true of something, and this something itself is not truth. This obvious view I endorse.' Rather, the aim of the coherence theory is—or should be—to afford a *test* or criterion of truth." [*The Coherence Theory of Truth* (Oxford University Press, Oxford, 1973), pp. 23-24.] Though it is obviously risky to claim to understand what Bradley means, I do not think that Rescher has grasped the import of Bradley's idealistic monism. The above quotation from "On Some Aspects of Truth," in *Essays on Truth and Reality* (Clarendon Press, Oxford, 1950), p. 325, continues, "endorse, but to ascertain its proper meaning is not easy. And it commonly is misinterpreted so as not to be tenable." Bradley proceeds to reiterate a prevalent theme in his philosophy—that *truth* and *reality* are, *ultimately*, one and the same. The separation of truth from reality is only due to our abstracting, hence distorting, judgments—to the nature of thought. It is not only that we are forced to accept coherence as a criterion of truth, but, ultimately, the coherent system of truths is reality. Truth, as it were, disappears in *fulfilling itself*. We speak of truths only in that we lack reality, as a whole. Thus, truth is spoken of as "ideal" rather than "real." This is another of Bradley's "paradoxes." For there to be "real" or "perfect" truth *it* must become other than what *it is*—reality. So long as we take truths to be distinct from reality, however, *they are not*, paradoxically, truths. They are merely reflections of our limited, hence distorted, judgments. Aside from the fanciful language, the position is clear. Reality, for Bradley, is the totality of coherent judgments and experiences.

> The division of reality from knowledge and of knowledge from truth must in any form be abandoned. And the only way of exit from the maze is to accept the remaining alternative. Our one hope lies in taking courage to embrace the result that reality is not outside truth. The identity of truth knowledge and reality, whatever difficulty that may bring, must be taken as necessary and fundamental. Or at least we have been driven to choose between this and nothing.
>
> Any such conclusion, I know, will on many sides be rejected as monstrous. The last thing to which truth pretends, I shall hear, is actually to be, or even bodily to possess, the real. But though this question, I know, might well be argued at length, the issue in my judgment can be raised and can be settled briefly. Truth, it is contended, is not to be the same as reality. Well, if so, I presume that there is a difference between them. And this difference, I understand, is not to be contained in the truth. But, if this is so, then clearly to my mind the truth must so far be defective. How, I ask, is the truth about reality to be less or more than reality without so far ceasing to be the truth? . . .
>
> And, if we are to advance, we must accept once and for all the identification

of truth with reality. I do not say that we are to conclude that there is to be in no sense any difference between them. But we must, without raising doubts and without looking backwards, follow the guidance of our new principle. We must, that is, accept the claim of truth not to be judged from the outside. We must unhesitatingly assert that truth, if it were satisfied itself, and if for itself it were perfect, would be itself in the fullest sense the enitre and absolute Universe. ("On Truth and Copying," *Essays on Truth and Reality*, pp. 112-14).

In this vein he wrote in *Appearance and Reality* (Macmillan, New York, 1897), pp. 172-73:

But if truth and fact are to be one, then in some such way thought must reach its consummation. But in that consummation thought has certainly been so transformed, that to go on calling it thought seems indefensible.

I have tried to show first that, in the proper sense of thought, thought and fact are not the same. I have urged, in the second place, that, if their identity is worked out, thought ends in a reality which swallow's up its character. I will ask next whether thought's advocates can find a barrier to their client's happy suicide.

And, as if to forestall interpretations such as Rescher's, he had written in "On Truth and Copying": "And thus, if we are asked for the relation of truth to reality, we must reply that in the end there is no relation, since in the end there are no separate terms," (p. 117). This is followed by, "But from a lower point of view it may be convenient to speak of truth as corresponding with reality and as even reproducing facts. . . . But, as we have seen, such a way of speaking is not permissible in the end" (pp. 118-20).

4. G. E. Moore, "Identity," *Proceedings of the Aristotelian Society*, 1, 1900-1901. My discussion of Moore's views in this paper is based on my article, "Moore and Russell on Particulars, Relations, and Identity," in *SGEM*. In reading what follows one should keep in mind that Bradley also objected to what he called "bare universals" and "bare relations." This is connected with the notion of a "concrete universal" and his claim that a universal idea is a particular "event in my mind" with an "aspect of particularity" which my awareness of it "as universal negates" ("A Discussion of Some Problems in Connexion with Mr. Russell's Doctrine," in *Essays on Truth and Reality*, pp. 296-97). For my purposes here, the simplification of Bradley's view does no harm.

5. *Ibid.*, p. 108. At one place, p. 116, Moore speaks as if 'numerical difference' is *defined* in terms of difference in a relation or a property. But, he is concerned with the numerical difference between a universal and an instance of it, since they do not differ conceptually.

6. *Ibid.*, pp. 108-9. Moore uses 'predicate' for 'concept' and 'property'.

7. *Ibid.*, p. 109.

8. It is possible that Moore mixes the notions of *class* and *class-concept*, for he writes: "A class-concept, on the other hand, on does imply at least one *member* conceptually different from it. . . . It is, moreover, always also a universal, but may have no particulars." (*Ibid.*, p. 117) The notion of a class-concept is undoubtedly that in B. Russell, *The Principles of Mathematics* (George Allen and Unwin, London, 1956), pp. 19-20, 67, hereafter *The Principles*.

9. *Ibid.*, pp. 109-10.

10. On this point, see my "Properties, Abstracts, and the Axiom of Infinity," *Journal of Philosophical Logic*, 6, 1977, pp. 193-207.

11. This is so for any finite domain of objects. An infinite domain, of white spots in a row, for example, may preclude the use of a property like R^1. But, to speak of infinite domains in such cases is problematic. Max Black's well-known example of the symmetri-

cal universe of two spheres presents no problem. That is not a case of two objects sharing all relational properties, but, rather, of the conditions of description being so confined that any description that *can be formulated* will fit both objects or neither. M. Black, "The Identity of Indiscernibles," *Mind*, 61, 242, reprinted in M. J. Loux, *Universals and Particulars: Readings in Ontology* (Doubleday, New York, 1970), pp. 204-16.

Chapter V

1. "Identity," p. 127.

2. B. Russell, "On the Relations of Universals and Particulars," *Proceedings of the Aristotelian Society*, 1911-1912, reprinted in R. C. Marsh (ed.), *Logic and Knowledge: Essays 1901-1950*, hereafter *LK* (George Allen and Unwin, London, 1956), p. 110.

3. *Ibid.*, p. 113.

4. *Ibid.*, p. 118.

5. *Ibid.*, p. 120.

6. *Ibid*, p. 117.

7. One may construe the object either as a complex universal, with a "constituent" spatial property, or as a universal of a higher type, which is exemplified by all the "ordinary" qualities of the object including an individuating spatial property. The latter resembles what Russell later did in *An Inquiry into Meaning and Truth*. Such universals would violate Russell's present implicit assumption that a universal is what *can be* at two places or, at least, *be* common to *two objects*.

8. "On the Relations of Universals and Particulars," p. 111.

9. For a detailed discussion of this point, see my "Strawson, Russell, and the King of France," in *Essays on Bertrand Russell*.

10. These comments do not apply to the question of the Russell-Frege "reduction" of elementary arithmetic to logic. We do not start from "objects" and "facts" containing them in such a case. Rather, the question is how to cogently "introduce" arithmetical notions. On this point, see my "Russell's Reduction of Arithmetic to Logic," in *Essays on Bertrand Russell* and "Peano, Russell, and Logicism," *Analysis*, 16, 1956, pp. 118-20.

11. There is an extensive recent literature on the problem of individuation and the notion of a "bare particular." Besides the writings of Gustav Bergmann, see E. B. Allaire, "Bare Particulars," in *Essays in Ontology*; R. Grossmann, *Reflections on Frege's Philosophy* (Northwestern University Press, Evanston, 1969) and *Ontological Reduction* (Indiana University Press, Bloomington, 1973); F. Wilson, "The Role of a Principle of Acquaintance in Ontology," *The Modern Schoolman*, 47, 1, 1969, pp. 37-56; *Universals and Particulars: Readings in Ontology*, ed. by M. J. Loux (Doubleday & Co., New York, 1970); P. K. Butchvarov, *Resemblance and Identity* (Indiana University Press, Bloomington, 1966); H. N. Castañeda, "Individuation and Non-Identity: A New Look," *American Philosophical Quarterly*, 12, 2, April 1975, pp. 131-140; M. J. Loux, "Recent Work in Ontology," *American Philosophical Quarterly*, 9, 2, April 1972, pp. 119-38; and my articles "Universals, Particulars, and Predication," *Review of Metaphysics*, 19, 1965, "Things and Qualities," in *Metaphysics and Explanation*, ed. Merrill and Capitan, (University of Pittsburgh Press, Pittsburgh, 1966), and "Things and Descriptions," *American Philosophical Quarterly*, 3, 1, January, 1966, pp. 1-9, reprinted in *Essays on Bertrand Russell*.

12. Recently, there has been much fuss about the *referential*, as opposed to the *attributive*, use of definite descriptions. One may cut through the tedious ordinary language examples by means of a simple thought experiment. Imagine that you *name* your

next child "The King of France in 1905." If this is not permitted in the United States, it surely is in England. Imagine next that you assert "The King of France in 1905 is my child." Now imagine that a friend who knows your child's "name" points out that you have made a false (or incorrect or inappropriate) claim since your child is not a king. As Malcolm uses 'correct', recall Chapter II, your friend is, of course, correct. Imagine that he also acknowledges that you have made a true claim, as obviously you have. Then, ask yourself if the *token*, of the *phrase* 'the King of France in 1905', which you uttered or wrote is a token of a definite description. Whatever answer you give, ask yourself "why?" Then, imagine giving the opposite answer and your reasons for so doing. Finally, ask yourself if by naming your child as you did you had refuted Russell. The point is that a "logically proper" definite description contains a predicate *used predicatively*. That an expression begins with the definite article does not mean that all of its tokens are used as instances of such "logically proper" descriptions. Russell was careless in suggesting that in ordinary usage one could determine the "logical form" from the "grammatical form" in the case of descriptive phrases ("On Denoting," in *LK*, p. 41). However, as he explicitly distinguished between a *sign as a name* and the use of a token of the sign as a name or as a description, he was undoubtedly aware of the same distinction in the case of *a* description and a token of such a phrase *used* as a name. See the quotation from the essays on Logical Atomism cited on p. 199.

13. So Russell once argued in *My Philosophical Development* (Simon and Schuster, New York, 1959), p. 115.

Chapter VI

1. In "Frege on Concepts as Functions: a Fundamental Ambiguity," *Theoria*, 37, 1971, pp. 21-32.

2. Some claim that he does. H. Jackson cites passages from (then) unpublished manuscripts to support the claim; see his "Frege on Sense-Functions," *Analysis*, 23, 1962-1963, pp. 84-87. But, at most the passages show that Frege sometimes speaks as if the sense of a function sign is a function. This is also apparent from the familiar published material. The question is whether Frege clearly distinguished f_1 and f_2 from each other and from the incomplete constituent of propositions. It is clear that he did not when we recall his well-known definition of a *concept* as a function that takes truth values for its values; see G. Frege, *The Basic Laws of Arithmetic*, trans. by M. Furth (University of California Press, Berkeley, 1967), p. 36.

3. G. Frege, "Negation," in *Translations from the Philosophical Writings of Gottlob Frege*, ed. by P. Geach and M. Black (Basil Blackwell, Oxford, 1970), pp. 131-32.

4. We shall shortly discuss Frege's critique of correspondence theories of truth.

5. In the present context, we may forget the *three* entities, f_1, f_2, and the incomplete constituent of propositions, and merely think of the predicate 'F_1' (or, as earlier, '$F_1 x$') standing for *the* function (or concept). The expression "concept correlate" is, I believe, due to Rulon Wells.

6. Frege would, and Fregeans will, object to my way of putting matters. But it helps to bring out a point about U_2.

7. M. Dummett, *Frege: Philosophy of Language* (Harper & Row, New York, 1973), pp. 212-20. Some will recognize this as a variation on a theme of Carnap's.

8. G. Frege, *The Foundations of Arithmetic*, trans. by J. L. Austin (Northwestern University Press, Evanston, 1968), p. 85e.

9. Philosophers pay interesting prices to avoid the recognition of properties and the use of predicates as subject terms. Thus, Frege must recognize that some propositions are composed of constituents, no one of which is saturated or complete. The incomplete signs 'x is green' and '(x)[x is $\emptyset$ v ~x is $\emptyset$]' illustrate such a case. To avoid recognizing concepts as objects, Frege may be taken to acknowledge categorially different *ways* in which *concepts* enter into propositional combinations. This amounts to having different kinds of exemplification. Moreover, this is in addition to the unique role of U_2 and its correlation with exemplification on the pattern of the logical atomists. For a discussion of some related themes, see my "Mapping, Meaning, and Metaphysics," *Midwest Studies in Philosophy*, 2, 1977, "Nominalism, Platonism, and 'Being true of'," *Nous*, 2, 1968, and "Nominalism, General Terms, and Predication," *The Monist*, July 1978.

10. We may ignore the distinction between a "course-of-values" and an extension.

11. G. Frege, "The Thought: A Logical Inquiry," trans. by A. M. and M. Quinton, *Mind*, 65, 1956, pp. 289-311, reprinted in *Essays on Frege*, ed. by E. D. Klemke (University of Illinois Press, Urbana, 1968), p. 510.

12. Dummett makes such a claim, as well as others, on behalf of Frege's attack on the correspondence theory. See his *Frege*, Chapter 13, especially pp. 444-52, 463-64. Since I believe all of his arguments are disposed of, either by the present discussion of Frege or by other elaborations of the "correspondence" account presented in this book, I do not specifically discuss his defense of Frege. In the manuscript "The Nature of Truth," June 1905, in the Russell archives, Russell argued, along Fregean lines, that the correspondence theory of truth was circular and involved a regress. He objected to the theory's need to appeal to "objective falsehoods" in "On the Nature of Truth," *Proceedings of the Aristotelian Society*, 7, 1906-7, pp. 45-47. Bradley also offered a version of the "Fregean paradox" in "On Truth and Copying," p. 110.

13. In addition to the functions f_1 and f_2 that we earlier connected with the predicate 'F_1x' (or 'F_1'), Dummett "emends" Frege's view to include *the sense* of the predicate 'F_1x' as an *object*. But, such an object will not do as a constituent of Fregean propositions expressed by sentences with 'F_1x'. For, as an object, it is complete or saturated. Thus, on his emendation one ends up with four *entities* associated with predicates. (Dummett, *Frege*, p. 294.) Dummett also appears to hold that we need not generate an infinite series of senses in "oblique" contexts, since the sense of an expression, in such a context, can *coincide* with its referent. But, since he holds that the sense of a predicate expression is an object, he cannot give a uniform account of Frege's view. He must take the predicate term to denote the *function* that maps senses onto propositions. But this is not the sense of the predicate, on his reading. This also shows that he mixes the sense-function with the incomplete constituent of the proposition. The sense-function is a constituent of its propositional "value" for an *argument* which is a *sense*. Also, although senses of singular terms denote themselves, in oblique contexts, senses of predicates do not. But, his pattern is quite ad hoc. For, the sense of the predicate does not enter as a constituent into propositions expressed by the relevant sentence (or referred to by it in oblique contexts). It is, as it were, suspended in the realm of sense. Moreover, in the case of the expression 'the sense of the predicate . . .', either that expression will express yet a new sense, denoting the "standard" sense, or the standard sense will be denoted as well as expressed. In the latter case, the standard sense will denote itself. Thus, we have either four entities associated with a predicate, in *addition* to the incomplete constituent of a proposition which Dummett mistakenly identifies with the sense function, or the sense of the predicate can denote any one of *three* entities. (*Ibid.*, pp. 268-69)

14. *Ibid.*, p. 373.

Chapter VII

1. B. Russell, "On Denoting," *Mind*, 1905, reprinted in *LK*, pp. 48-51.

2. In my article "Russell's Attack on Frege's Theory of Meaning," *Philosophica*, 18, 1976, pp. 9-34.

3. "On Denoting," p. 41.

4. *The Principles*, p. 53.

5. *Ibid.*, p. 54.

6. *Ibid.*, p. 502.

7. However, there is a striking similarity between Russell's views about the difference of the role of *the concept human* in the two propositions expressed by the sentences 'Socrates is human' and 'Socrates has humanity', and Frege's distinction between *the* incomplete concept and the concept correlate. *Ibid.*, p. 42, pp. 45-46. Russell held, in *The Principles*, that it was the same concept that functioned both as the subject of an attribution and as the "property" attributed. He criticized Frege for denying this, *Ibid.*, p. 510. In the case of the proposition expressed by 'Socrates has humanity' a relation connected the concept human with Socrates, while in the case of the other proposition the concept is not connected by a further relation. Thus, very early, Russell took "predication" in two ways. This bears on his concern with Bradley's paradox and his later pattern in "Logical Atomism" (see note 10, Chapter IX). His treatment of 'Socrates is human' is thus very close to Frege's avoidance of a connecting tie.

8. *Ibid.*, pp. 43-47.

9. "On Denoting," p. 46.

10. *Ibid.*, p. 46.

11. *Ibid.*, p. 42.

12. G. Frege, "On Sense and Reference," in *Translations from the Philosophical Writings of Gottlob Frege*, p. 58.

13. *Ibid.*, p. 59.

14. Dummett purports to rebut Russell's point by holding that the expression "displays" the sense or, borrowing from the *Tractatus*, "we *say* what the referent of a word is, and, thereby *show* what its sense is" (Dummett, *Frege*, p. 227). This is either no answer or a shift from an ontological question to a point about our ordinary use of terms and our understanding of their "semantic roles." It is no answer, since, like Byron, we must "wish he would explain his explanation."

15. F. H. Bradley, *The Principles of Logic*, vol. 1 (Oxford University Press, 1958), pp. 10-13, 27, 33-35, 61.

16. But, even if we take him to be talking about denoting complexes in the sense of denoting concepts, rather than in the sense of *denoting phrases*, his point can be made. See "Russell's Attack on Frege's Theory of Meaning," pp. 22-23.

17. *The Principles*, p. 502. The passage shows that the introduction of meanings like m**, which denote other meanings, already bothered him.

18. This claim is anticipated in *The Principles*:

Moreover, if Frege's view were correct on this point, we should have to hold that in an asserted proposition, it is the meaning, not the indication, that is asserted, for otherwise all asserted propositions would assert the very same thing, namely the true. (p. 504)

19. Dummett holds that for Frege "a fact is simply a true thought." (Dummett, *Frege*, p. 369) But, this solves nothing. It merely turns a proposition into its own truth condition. To give some content to the claim, one would have to take true propositions

to differ "internally" from false propositions, as the early Moore did, or hold that true propositions are so *because* they *stand in a relation* to *The True*, and false ones *do not*. Thus, we are back to the Fregean facts of Chapter VI. Dummett further holds that Russell "at one time, held the same about propositions and facts." (p. 369) If he is referring to *The Principles*, the claim is misleading. For, recall, there are propositions$_R$ that are not propositions$_F$. It is just that in the case of verbal propositions with proper names there are not propositions$_F$. If he is referring to Russell's views of 1905-7, what he says is also misleading, since Russell held that there were *facts* and *fictions* (objective falsehoods). Thus, though facts *were* true propositions, *there were also fictions*. Moreover, neither *facts* nor *fictions* were existents. Hence, Russell believed, as did Moore, that there were *entities* that were not existents.

20. I ignore the complication that '*being uniquely* G' is not a *primitive* predicate. This brings in the question of logical concepts and our understanding of them.

21. For a consideration of some other questions about the use of descriptions to "interpret" names, see my "Strawson, Russell, and the King of France," in *Essays on Bertrand Russell*.

22. Moore speaks of sense data "representing" a physical surface in the *Lectures on Philosophy*, ed. by C. Lewy (George Allen & Unwin, London, 1966), p. 100. As the problem of the "self" is not gone into in this book, I speak of a *datum* (or an image or a token) *intending* as well as of a person *intending*. But, this is not to say that my speaking of a *token intending* is meant to be explicated in terms of a person using a token to intend. If one holds to a "bundle" view of the self, along the lines of Hume and Russell, one would take the occurrence of such tokens to involve the basic sense of 'intend'.

23. The claim that reference can be made to an object that one once was acquainted with but which is not presently presented, in the sense in which what one now "sees" is presented, is like Russell's early claim that such an object is *immediately before the mind*. This follows Pears's interpretation of Russell as holding that one is acquainted (presently) with past objects, in D. F. Pears, "Russell's Theories of Memory," in *Questions in the Philsoophy of Mind* (Barnes and Noble, New York, 1975), p. 225. This use of 'acquaintance' is problematic, but that need not concern us since the problem is the one raised in terms of the present discussion. One may object on the grounds that (a) no argument has been given and (b) no real distinction has been made between such cases of reference (or acquaintance) and that of Bismarck. This overlooks the role of memory. In referring to an object of previous acquaintance we remember it by intending it. We *cannot* remember Bismarck. In short, there is a kind of memory that is not propositional (remembering that . . .) but which functions on some occasions when tokens occur. I shall return to this claim at the end of Chapter XIII. But, even assuming that (a) and (b) are correct, the proper conclusion is that we can only refer to presented objects in the sense of objects we directly apprehend and not merely objects *before the mind*. This, as we noted, places a basic limitation on thought when we apply the pattern to tokens intending properties.

Chapter VIII

1. B. Russell, "On Denoting," in *LK*, p. 47.
2. L. Linsky, *Referring* (Routledge & Kegan Paul, London, 1967), pp. 67-69.
3. "The Philosophy of Logical Atomism," in *LK*, p. 245. Russell here claims that true identity statements employing names, and not truncated descriptions, are *tautological*.

4. At one place, Russell suggests that to say that Scott is Sir Walter is simply to say that one person is called or referred to by two names, *ibid.*, p. 244. But, see note 3 above. One should note that, as Russell uses 'name' here, to use '*a*' and '*b*' as names is to *know* that *a* is *b*, if they name the same thing. We shall return to this theme later. It should also be noted that to speak of 'this' and 'that' as pure demonstratives is not to deny that in cases of communication, they are context dependent and sometimes ambiguous.

5. "On Denoting," pp. 51-52. Here, 'proposition' is clearly used as 'proposition$_V$'. It would be foolish to deny Russell's tendency to speak of *propositions* in a confused way, just as he, in puzzling fashion, speaks of Socrates as an "incomplete symbol" in "The Philosophy of Logical Atomism," p. 253. But one can recover the point involved: Socrates is a class, hence a nonexistent, and, thus, what represents Socrates in a perspicuous schema is an incomplete symbol. To put it paradoxically, in the case of Socrates there is only the symbol and not the man, and even the symbol, being an incomplete symbol, is not really a constituent of any perspicuous sentence. Part of the problem stems from Russell's notion that a sentence is a class of similar patterns in one language, while a proposition is, on the one hand, common to several such classes and, on the other, is a union class of such classes. See his later discussion in "Logical Positivism" in *LK*, pp. 380-81. Another part of the problem is his taking propositions, in one sense, to contain the *same constituents* as the facts they correspond to ("The Philosophy of Logical Atomism," p. 248). This is a result of his early account of belief, whereby the content of a belief was explained in terms of a relation between the believer and the constituents of the fact that would obtain if the belief were true. What is believed or asserted, one naturally says, is a proposition. The proposition is thus identified with the *complex* which *is* a fact if the belief is true, and a *fiction* if the belief is false.

6. Linsky's version appears in Linsky, *Referring*, p. 72.

7. "On Denoting," p. 52.

8. Such a sense of 'believe' makes states of belief differ just as sentences differ when they contain different signs or a different arrangement of the same signs. We shall consider the details of such a notion in Chapters XII and XIII.

9. "On Denoting," p. 52.

10. One can quickly see this by the use of a system employing an existential instantiation rule and recalling the universal quantification in the expansion.

11. See J. Hintikka, *Knowledge and Belief* (Cornell University Press, Ithaca, 1962); the symposium *The Logic of Knowledge and Belief*, papers by R. Chisholm, H. N. Castañeda, R. Sleigh, and J. Hintikka, in *Nous*, 1, 1, March, 1967; D. Føllesdal, "Knowledge, Identity, and Existence," *Theoria*, 33, 1967, pp. 1-27.

12. "On Denoting," p. 52.

13. Linsky, *Referring*, p. 69.

14. *Ibid.*, p. 69.

15. *Ibid.*, p. 69.

16. C. E. Cassin, "Russell's Distinction between the Primary and Secondary Occurrence of Definite Descriptions," in *Essays on Bertrand Russell*, ed., by E. D. Klemke (Univ. of Illinois Press, Urbana, 1970), p. 275.

17. There is a minor problem regarding the *Principia* conventions that is irrelevant here. See my "Descriptions, Scope, and Identity," *Analysis*, 18, 1958, pp. 20-22. Reprinted in *Essays on Bertrand Russell*.

18. D. Davidson, "True to the Facts," *Journal of Philosophy*, 66, 21, pp. 752-53.

19. The proof of such equivalence involves only (a) elementary moves of proposition-

al logic, (b) extracting and inserting the sentence 's' out of and into the scope of quantifiers according to the standard rules governing vacuous quantification, and (c) standard equivalences for the expansions of the descriptions.

20. W. V. Quine, "Reply to Professor Marcus," in *The Ways of Paradox* (Random House, New York, 1966), p. 182.

21. Dagfinn Føllesdal has made a similar point in "Quantification into Causal Contexts," *Boston Studies in the Philosophy of Science*, Vol. II (Humanities Press, New York, 1965), pp. 263-274. What is ultimately involved is simply the fundamental difference between names as labels and descriptions as contextually defined signs. See my "On Pegasizing," *Philosophy and Phenomenological Research*, 17, 1957, pp. 551-54; "The Ontological Operator," *Philosophy of Science*, 23, 3, 1956, pp. 250-59; and "Professor Quine, Pegasus, and Dr. Cartwright," *Philosophy of Science*, 24, 1957, pp. 191-203.

22. W. V. Quine, "Reply to Sellars," in *Words and Objections*, ed. by D. Davidson and J. Hintikka (Reidel, Dordrecht, 1969), p. 338.

23. W. Sellars, "Some Problems About Belief," in *Words and Objections*, p. 193.

24. *Ibid.*, p. 200. I follow Sellars's omission of the indication of opacity or transparency.

25. D. Kaplan, "Quantifying in," in *Words and Objections*, pp. 206-42.

26. W. Sellars, "Reply to Quine," in *Essays in Philosophy and Its History* (Reidel, Dordrecht, 1974), pp. 148-71.

27. "Some Problems about Belief," pp. 199-200.

28. W. Sellars, *Science and Metaphysics* (Routledge & Kegan Paul, London, 1968), p. 84.

29. To attempt to remedy the situation by using *logical equivalence* rather than *material equivalence* is to return to Carnap's *Meaning and Necessity* and a previous era.

30. "Reply to Quine," p. 153. Hereafter, I omit superscripts for 'B'.

Chapter IX

1. One need not be concerned that I am presupposing that predicates refer to properties. It will become clear that such an issue is irrelevant, and I shall return to the point at the end of the chapter. For a number of references to systems with a predicate like 'E', see G. E. Hughes and M. J. Cresswell, *An Introduction to Modal Logic* (Methuen and Co., London, 1972), p. 179; also see W. Salmon and G. Nakhnikian, " 'Exists' as a Predicate," *Philosophical Review*, 66, 1957, and Bergmann's discussion in *Logic and Reality*, pp. 77-78.

2. B. Russell, "The Philosophy of Logical Atomism," in *LK*, p. 252.

3. *Ibid.*, p. 252.

4. D. F. Pears makes this point, which he acknowledges to "follow up" ideas of Moore, in his paper, "Is Existence a Predicate?" reprinted in *Philosophical Logic*, ed. by P. F. Strawson (Oxford University Press, London, 1967), pp. 97-102. Pears notes that MacBeth's "nonexistent" dagger does not affect the point, as Russell had also observed in "The Philosophy of Logical Atomism," in *LK*, pp. 257-58.

5. W. Sellars, "Naming and Saying," in *Science, Perception and Reality* (Routledge and Kegan Paul, London and New York, 1963), pp. 225-46.

6. Some critics have misunderstood Sellars on this point. See my "Mapping, Meaning, and Metaphysics" and W. Sellars "Hochberg on Mapping, Meaning and Metaphysics" in *Midwest Studies in Philosophy*, vol. 2, 1977.

7. W. V. Quine long ago casually suggested such a "free" logic. On this point, see

W. V. Quine, *From a Logical Point of View* (Harvard University Press, Cambridge, 1953), pp. 166-67, and my papers, "On Pegasizing," *Philosophy and Phenomenological Research*, 17, 1957, pp. 551-54, and "Professor Quine, Pegasus, and Dr. Cartwright," *Philosophy of Science*, 24, 1957, pp. 191-203.

8. He used a number of such asymmetries in lectures he gave at Ohio State University in 1967. In "The Asymmetry of Subjects and Predicates," *Logico-Linguistic Papers* (Methuen & Co., London, 1971) and in a recent book, he focuses on concepts being "logically competitive" and particulars not.

> Consider on the one hand a set of concepts belonging to a given range and, on the other, the entire field of particulars which come within that range. Then, for any concept of the range . . . no particular which exemplifies it can at the same time exemplify its competitors. But we can form no symmetrically competitive range of particulars. Indeed we cannot find a single particular such that there is any other single particular which competes with it for concepts. *Subject and Predicate in Logic and Grammar* (Methuen & Co., London, 1974), p. 18.

It is easy to see that his *competitive concepts* form a special case of (5) and (6). All we need do is take the range as a concept and its negation.

9. Taking account of contraries does not really add anything, as we shall see in a moment.

10. This is why bringing contraries into the discussion does not add anything. Strawson criticizes Russell's attempt to explain the distinction between subject-terms and predicate-terms by means of the notions of *individual, universal,* and *atomic proposition.* He gives no reference to a particular work of Russell's, but he appears to be referring to a work before "The Philosophy of Logical Atomism," as he speaks of *individuals* being constituents of propositions, which are expressed by sentences, on Russell's view. (For example, see "Mathematical Logic as Based on the Theory of Types," *American Journal of Mathematics*, 30, 1908, in *LK*, p. 76.) That usage does not fit with Russell's use of the term 'proposition' in the later work. Strawson complains that Russell does not give an independent account of the nature of the extra-linguistic items. But, Russell has given the account, in (R), in a number of places. It is found in "Mathematical Logic," p. 76; "On the Relations of Universals and Particulars," in *LK*, pp. 109, 123; *The Problems of Philosophy*, p. 93; *The Principles*, p. 54; and, in the altered and somewhat Fregean form that the asymmetry takes in "The Philosophy of Logical Atomism," *LK*, p. 205. In the unpublished "Theory of Knowledge," Chapter VII, he holds that predicates are terms that have the relation of predication to other terms. Moreover, it is clear that Strawson believes that he will explain what Russell has failed to explain (*ibid.*, p. 5). I am arguing that Russell's principle (R) is "presupposed," not explained, by Strawson's analysis. Russell, under the pressure of Bradley's argument, gradually abandoned (R) for a somewhat "Fregean" pattern, clearly and explicitly in the case of relations, less explicitly in the case of attributes. On this matter, see "Logical Atomism" in *LK*, pp. 334-38 and note 7, Chapter VII. He also came to think that his views on types and the paradoxes were relevant in that one could not take a property or relation as a term of a relation in the sense in which particulars were such terms. In this vein he also held that names and predicates did not refer to objects and properties in the same sense.

11. I do not discuss a second asymmetry Strawson cites as "asymmetry between particulars and general characters of particulars in respect of the possession of sufficient and/or necessary conditions" ("The Asymmetry of Subjects and Predicates," p. 103). This does not alter matters. On the one hand, it is obvious that if we have incompatible

characters, we have necessary and sufficient conditions. On the other hand, we can add a few additional pairs of formulas, such as:

(7) $(\exists f)(\exists g)(x) [f \neq g \& (fx \supset gx)]$

(8) $(\exists x)(\exists y)(f) [x \neq y \& (fx \supset fy)]$.

In an empty domain both are false; in any *normal* domain, (7) holds but (8) does not. Such formulas lead to problems about identity of characters that Strawson, as far as I can tell, ignores. We shall discuss these shortly.

12. *Subject and Predicate*, p. 25.

13. "The Asymmetry of Subjects and Predicates," p. 101.

14. P. F. Strawson, "Singular Terms and Predication," *Journal of Philosophy*, 58, 15, pp. 393-412, reprinted in *Logico-Linguistic Papers*, p. 74.

15. R. Carnap, *Meaning and Necessity* (University of Chicago Press, Chicago, 1947), pp. 100-6.

16. For some suggestions about such a theory of properties and its connection with problems involved in Russell's reconstruction of elementary arithmetic, see my "Properties, Abstracts, and the Axiom of Infinity," *Journal of Philosophical Logic*, 6, 1977. Gustav Bergmann has made the crucial point about the inability to eliminate "defined" predicates in nonextensional languages in "Contextual Definitions in Nonextensional Languages," *The Journal of Symbolic Logic*, 13, 3, 1948, p. 140.

17. *Subject and Predicate*, p. 28.

18. *Subject and Predicate*, p. 24. I am not claiming that one, simply and straightforwardly, can match the use of logical "parodies" with predicates in the case of subject signs, or that it can be done at all in a "reasonable" way. All that I have claimed is that Strawson's argument against negative subject terms will not do.

19. This, ironically, almost amounts to a mirror image of Quine's denial that predicates stand for properties since predicates, not being referring terms, do not refer. They are not referring terms, as we shall see, because there is a basic difference between predicating and referring.

20. W. V. Quine, *Methods of Logic* (Routledge & Kegan Paul, London, 1952), p. 205.

21. *Ibid.*, p. 205.

22. Quine later appears to take the grammatical distinction between subject and predicate terms and the asymmetry of the predication relation as basic features. If we take the relevant ontological question to be one about what such features reflect, Quine's answer appeals to *is true of* and the *use* of the relevant predicate in the purported explanation, see *Word & Object* (MIT Press, Cambridge, 1960), p. 96.

23. In fact Quine sometimes explicates the one, as well as his use of 'purports', in terms of the other. "In terms of logical structure, what it means to say that the singular term "purports to name one and only one object" is just this: *The singular term belongs in positions of the kind in which it would also be coherent to use variables 'x', 'y', etc.*," *Methods of Logic*, p. 205.

24. W. V. Quine, "Identity, Ostension, and Hypostasis," in *From a Logical Point of View*, second edition (Harvard University Press, Cambridge, 1964), p. 76, and "Reification of Universals," in *From a Logical Point of View*, pp. 113-14.

25. Nino Cocchiarella has examined features of calculi that include such "nominalized" predicates. See his "Whither Russell's Paradox of Predication?" in *Logic and Ontology*, edited by M. K. Munitz (New York University Press, New York, 1973), pp. 133-58; "Properties as Individuals in Formal Ontology," *Nous*, 6, 1972, pp. 165-87;

"Fregean Semantics for a Realist Ontology," *Notre Dame Journal of Formal Logic*, 15, 1974, pp. 552-68.

Chapter X

1. D. Davidson, "True to the Facts," *The Journal of Philosophy*, 66, 21, 1969, pp. 757-58.
2. D. Davidson, "In Defense of Convention T," *Truth, Syntax, and Modality*, ed. H. Leblanc (North-Holland, Amsterdam, 1973), p. 80.
3. A. Tarski, "The Concept of Truth in Formalized Languages," *Logic, Semantics, Metamathematics* (Clarendon Press, Oxford, 1956), p. 189.
4. *Ibid.*, p. 188.
5. G. E. Moore, *Lectures on Philosophy*, ed. by C. Lewy (George Allen and Unwin, London, 1966), p. 143.
6. A. Tarski, "The Semantic Conception of Truth," *Philosophy and Phenomenological Research*, 4, 1944, reprinted in *Semantics and the Philosophy of Language*, ed. by L. Linsky (University of Illinois Press, Urbana, 1972), p. 33.
7. J. P. Sartre, *Being and Nothingness*, trans. by H. Barnes (Philosophical Library, New York, 1956), pp. 487-89, 553-56.
8. *Ibid.*, pp. xlv-lxvii, pp. 180-90.
9. B. Russell, "On Propositions: What They Are and How They Mean," in *Proceedings of the Aristotelian Society*, supplement to Vol. II, 1919, reprinted in *LK*, pp. 287-88.
10. *Ibid.*, p. 317.
11. B. Russell, *The Problems of Philosophy*, p. 58.
12. W. Sellars, "Ontology and the Philosophy of Mind in Russell," in *Bertrand Russell's Philosophy*, ed. by G. Nakhnikian (Barnes and Noble, London, 1974), pp. 57-100.
13. "On Propositions," pp. 287, 289.
14. "The Philosophy of Logical Atomism," *LK*, p. 237. One should keep in mind that not too many years earlier Russell explicitly held that "general" statements did not express or assert facts (or propositions as he also called facts, and that such entities, where asserted at all, were acknowledged even when the assertion was false); "Les Paradoxes de la Logique," *Revue de Metaphysique et de Morale*, September, 1906, pp. 642-43. In the case of a general statement, one asserted "ambiguously" or "indeterminately" *any* one or *some* one of the appropriate set of propositions. Propositions *were not affirmed* by statements containing "apparent variables" (*Ibid.*, pp. 643, 649). An English version of the paper is published under the title, "On 'Insolubilia' and Their Solution by Symbolic Logic," in *Essays in Analysis*, ed. by D. Lackey (George Braziller, New York, 1973). One should also recall the treatment of the quantifiers in *Principia*; 'We may similarly assert a proposition of the form "(x). $\emptyset x$," meaning "all propositions of the assemblage indicated by $\emptyset x$ are true," ' A. N. Whitehead and B. Russell, *Principia Mathematica* (Cambridge University Press, Cambridge, 1950), second edition, vol. 1, p. xx. In *My Philosophical Development*, Russell wrote:

> I have maintained a principle, which still seems to me completely valid, to the effect that, if we can understand what a sentence means, it must be composed entirely of words denoting things with which we are acquainted or definable in terms of such words. It is perhaps necessary to place some limitation upon this principle as regards logical words—e.g., *or, not, some, all.* (p. 169)

15. "The Philosophy of Logical Atomism," *LK*, p. 23.

16. On this matter, see the 1911 lecture "The Philosophical Importance of Mathematical Logic," *The Monist*, 22, 4, 1913; Chapters IX and X of *The Problems*; and the unpublished manuscript "Theory of Knowledge" of 1913.

17. W. Sellars, "Hochberg on Mapping, Meaning, and Metaphysics," in *Midwest Studies in Philosophy*, vol. 2, 1977. For a recent attack on the correspondence theory of truth, see E. B. Allaire, "Truth," *Metaphilosophy*, 6, 1975, pp. 261-75.

18. W. Sellars, *Science and Metaphysics* (Humanities Press, New York, 1968), p. 136.

19. *Science and Metaphysics*, pp. 77-84.

20. W. Sellars, "Reply to Quine," pp. 166-70. Sellars would deny (and has denied) that he is a "logical behaviorist" who rejects mental episodes. But, this has to do with his talking about "theoretical" explanations of behavior and the "theoretical entities" involved. Thus, *sensa* are postulated and, in a sense, *physical* constituents of neural states, "Science, Sense Impressions, and Sensa," *Review of Metaphysics*, 24, 3, 1971, pp. 391-447.

Chapter XI

1. Bertrand Russell, *The Problems of Philosophy* (Oxford University Press, London, 1956), p. 125.

2. Bertrand Russell, "The Philosophy of Logical Atomism," in *Logic and Knowledge*, ed. by R. C. Marsh (George Allen and Unwin, London, 1956), pp. 223-24.

3. *Ibid.*, p. 224.

4. *Ibid.*, p. 225.

5. Bertrand Russell, *An Inquiry into Meaning and Truth* (Penguin Books, Baltimore, 1969), p. 184.

6. Bertrand Russell, "Meinong's Theory of Complexes and Assumptions," in *Mind*, 13 (April, July, October), 1904, reprinted in *Essays in Analysis*, ed. by Douglas Lackey (George Braziller, New York, 1973), p. 41. Russell's "new" theory of "On Propositions," is also a return to a previous pattern he had sketched in the third section of "On the Nature of Truth" of 1907 — the section that was dropped when the essay was reprinted in *Philosophical Essays*. In the original essay, he held that beliefs consisted of "several interrelated ideas" which would be true if the "objects of the ideas" stood "in the corresponding relation" (p. 46). Pears, in his lucid account of the development of Russell's theories of judgment in *Bertrand Russell*, pp. 197-238, speaks of Russell's "new theory" without noting its earlier appearance. Russell refers ("On the Nature of Truth," p. 46) to his essay "Les Paradoxes de la logique," *Revue de Metaphysique et de Morale*, September, 1906, as showing that a version of "the liar paradox" can be avoided by this way of construing belief. The point is that "all" does not correspond to a constituent of a fact, see note 14, Chapter X. It is also clear why Russell abandoned the earlier view. In "Knowledge by Acquaintance and Knowledge by Description" he sets forth a relational theory of judgment not only to avoid "objective falsehoods" but to avoid a Bradleyian regress over the *connection* between an "idea" and its "object." This latter worry does not get expressed in the shortened version of the essay published as a chapter in *The Problems of Philosophy*.

7. W. Sellars, "Ontology and the Philosophy of Mind in Russell," in *Bertrand Russell's Philosophy*, ed. by G. Nakhnikian (Barnes and Noble, London, 1974), pp. 57-100.

8. F. P. Ramsey, *The Foundations of Mathematics* (Littlefield, Adams, & Co., New Jersey, 1960), p. 36. On this point, 4.126 is crucial and 4.24 and 5.5261 are suggestive.

One should also consult the entries in the *Notebooks* for October 8, 1914, April 3, 1915, and May 31, 1915, L. Wittgenstein, *Notebooks: 1914-1916*, ed. by G. H. von Wright and G. E. M. Anscombe (Harper and Row, New York, 1969). The letter of January 1913 to Russell is also relevant. It is printed in *Notebooks*, pp. 120-21. There is also a highly significant remark in *Principia Mathematica*: "Given an atomic proposition $R_n(x_1, x_2, \ldots x_n)$, we shall call any of the x's a "constituent" of the proposition, and R_n a "component" of the proposition" (*Principia Mathematica*, p. xx). The statement is accompanied by the footnote, "This terminology is taken from Wittgenstein." J. Wisdom used the terms 'constituent' and 'component' in this sense in "Logical Constructions I," in *Mind*, April, 1931, reprinted in *Logical Constructions* (Random House, New York, 1969), p. 55.

Russell had also written in *My Philosophical Development*, p. 113:

> Wittgenstein held that the same is true of the linguistic assertions of a fact. He said, for example, that, if you use the symbol '*aRb*' to represent the fact that *a* has the relation R to *b*, your symbol is able to do so because it establishes a relation between '*a*' and '*b*' which represents the relation between *a* and *b*.

For an illuminating discussion of *the issue* and its relation to Wittgenstein's 1929 paper "Remarks on Logical Form," see E. B. Allaire, "The Tractatus: Nominalistic or Realistic?" in *Essays in Ontology*.

9. Sellars, "Ontology and the Philosophy of Mind," p. 84.

10. *Ibid.*, p. 83.

11. G. Ryle, "Systematically Misleading Expressions," in *Proceedings of the Aristotelian Society*, 1931-1932, reprinted in *20th Century Philosophy: The Analytic Tradition*, ed. by M. Weitz (The Free Press, New York, 1963), p. 191.

12. See "Notes on Logic" in *Notebooks*, p. 97, the letter to Russell of June, 1913, and *Tractatus* 5.5422.

13. W. V. Quine, "Quantifiers and Propositional Attitudes," in *Reference and Modality*, ed. by L. Linsky (Oxford University Press, London, 1971), p. 109.

14. One might raise a complication for the argument by holding that sentences like "'a' names a" state facts, but my point will still hold. Some aspects of such issues I have discussed in Chapters VI and IX.

15. W. Sellars, "Hochberg on Mapping, Meaning, and Metaphysics," pp. 221, 223.

16. One familiar with Bergmann's views will object that I have not accurately presented his analysis. The objection would be well taken, but the simplification I have allowed myself does not affect the point. Bergmann holds that atomic facts have a form and an ordering (if the facts are relational). A circumstance is spoken of as the *internal relation* that holds between a fact and its form and that does not require a tie or nexus to hold. It is also spoken of as consisting of a fact and its form. The order of a relational fact is *grounded* by a similar sort of "entity" or "internal relation." Bergmann, thus, introduces several "entities" and seeks to escape Bradley's regress by holding that some complexes do not require a nexus or tie. See his presidential address to the Western Division of the American Philosophical Association, "Diversity," in *Proceedings of the APA*, 1967-68, 16, p. 33. In holding that the forms of facts are entities, he invokes a theme strikingly similar to one of Russell's.

17. Wisdom made this point as follows:

> Bradley's argument . . . has brought out the fact that we cannot analyze what is meant by saying of one thing that it is united or tied to another. We can only point to cases of one thing's being united to another. We may express this by say-

ing that the conception of unitedness is ultimate. I cannot *tell* you what is meant by saying of one thing that it is united to another. I can only point to what is meant.

It is a mistake to express this by saying that there is "in every fact something which eludes analysis". For (1) unitedness is not *in* a fact. (2) We are not hunting its analysis, therefore it doesn't elude us. (*Logical Constructions*, p. 54).

The last sentence heralds things to come.

18. N. Goodman, "Predicates without Properties," in *Midwest Studies in Philosophy*, vol. 2, 1977.

Chapter XII

1. B. Russell, *The Analysis of Mind* (George Allen & Unwin, London, 1971), pp. 17-18.

2. Bergmann's views are presented in a number of essays in his essay collections *Meaning and Existence* and *Logic and Reality* as well as in his book *Realism*.

3. For a consideration of the use of "corner predicates" to stand for properties of states of affairs, see my article "Phenomena, Value, and Objectivity," *Philosophical Quarterly*, 8, 32, 1958, p. 12.

4. G. Bergmann and H. Hochberg, "Concepts," *Philosophical Studies*, 8, 1957, pp. 19-27.

5. W. V. Quine, "Quantifiers and Propositional Attitudes," *Journal of Philosophy*, 53, 1956, reprinted in *Reference and Modality*, ed. by L. Linsky (Oxford University Press, London, 1971), p. 106.

6. D. Kaplan, "Quantifying In," in *Words and Objections: Essays on the Work of W. V. Quine*, ed. by D. Davidson and J. Hintikka (D. Reidel, Dordrecht, 1969), p. 234. The quoted passage has been slightly altered to conform with our numbering. In his reply to Kaplan (*Words and Objections*, pp. 337-38), Quine links Kaplan's discussion with a difficulty raised by Sleigh (R. Sleigh, "On Quantifying into Epistemic Contexts," *Nous*, 1, 1967, pp. 23-31) and Kripke:

> Lately, however, Sleigh raised a difficulty that bears on the point. Jones, like all of us, believes there are spies, though, unlike Ralph, he has nobody in particular under suspicion. Also, he believes, not unreasonably, that no two births are quite simultaneous. Consequently, he believes the youngest spy is a spy. Then, if the inference from (1) to (2) [*This would amount to the inference of* (S_{15}) *from* (S_1) in Chapter XI, *added to quote.*] was right, Jones believes of the youngest spy that he is a spy. But then, by existential generalization from this transparent construction, we can infer after all that there is someone whom Jones believes to be a spy. Kripke pointed out to me that this paradox of Sleigh's can be resolved by ceasing to recognize the form of inference that led from (1) to (2).

What is puzzling is all the *puzzling about* and *solving of* the puzzle Russell noted and resolved, in exactly the same way, in "On Denoting," pp. 52-53. With descriptions, it is, so to speak, a problem of scope; with names, it becomes a question about existential generalization.

7. "Quantifiers and Propositional Attitudes," p. 104.

8. *Ibid.*, pp. 109-11. Quine uses a most incredible argument to defend semantic ascension. He writes:

However, if anyone does approve of speaking of belief of a proposition at all and of speaking of a proposition in turn as meant by a sentence, then certainly he cannot object to our semantical reformulation 'w believes-true S' on any special grounds of obscurity; for, 'w believes-true S' is explicitly definable in *his* terms as 'w believes the proposition meant by S'. (*Ibid.*, p. 109)

He thus, apparently, forgets that if he defines 'w believes-true S' in such a way, *he* accepts propositions, in order to make semantic ascension acceptable to one who approves of propositions, and *he*, consequently, does not make use of semantic ascent. After all, if he gives a "definition," he is merely talking about a proposition in two typographically different ways.

Chapter XIII

1. W. Sellars, "Ontology and the Philosophy of Mind in Russell," p. 96.

2. See Russell's reply to Morris Weitz in *The Philosophy of Bertrand Russell*, ed. P. A. Schilpp (Northwestern University Press, Evanston, 1944), p. 685. What Russell had in mind is based on the principle (R) of Chapter IX. A shade of color, on his bundle theory, would not be represented by a term occurring in predicate place, but such a term would occur in subject place, i.e., 'Red is a color'. Thus, he spoke of a color as a particular that "may occupy a *dis*continuous portion of space-time."

3. The structure is the *obtaining* of a relation among objects. Speaking of facts, Wittgenstein deals with a relation obtaining. This does not mean that he denies that there are relations by speaking of the structure. If anything, he would be denying that there are structures as logical objects, in Russell's sense. Wittgenstein, in Fregean fashion (as well as in the fashion Russell adopted in "Logical Atomism" and in "The Philosophy of Logical Atomism"), takes a function or relation sign to exhibit the "structure"—as 'xRy' shows that the relation is to hold between some x and some y (in that order). In the present discussion, I shall follow Wittgenstein's use of structure for the obtaining of the relation. Hence, I shall speak of *structure* where I might also use 'relation' and of a function sign correlating to the structure of a fact. What is involved, once again, is that the Fregean pattern involves a jumbling of the relation, exemplification, and the structure of the fact since they are all "packed into" the *function*. What Wittgenstein and Frege thus (seek to) avoid is taking exemplification and logical structure as entities. Thus, Wittgenstein speaks of form in terms of "possibilities" and "essences," as in 2.033.

4. See my "Dispositional Properties," *Philosophy of Science*, 34, 1967, pp. 184-204, and F. Wilson, "Dispositions: Defined or Reduced?" *Australasian Journal of Philosophy*, 47, 2, 1969, pp. 184-204.

5. For some related points, see my articles "Physicalism, Behaviorism, and Phenomena," *Philosophy of Science*, 26, 1959, pp. 93-103; "Intervening Variables, Hypothetical Constructs, and Metaphysics," in *Current Issues in the Philosophy of Science* (Holt, Rinehart and Winston, New York, 1961), pp. 448-60; "Of Mind and Myth," *Methodos*, 11, 1959, reprinted in *Essays in Ontology*, pp. 166-87; and "Phenomena, Value, and Objectivity," p. 18.

6. If one allows for intentional reference to objects and properties that are not presently *apprehended*, in the sense of *directly perceived*, along the lines I have suggested, then one acknowledges that memory is involved in such cases. If one then speaks of "acts" of memory in these cases, we have (a) acts that are particulars rather than facts, and (b) acts that are constituents of other acts. The token acts, however, may be con-

strued as facts in that they are tokens of types (with characters). This we touched on earlier in another context, and I shall return to the question at the end of the present chapter.

7. The same kind of problem arises in the analysis of value statements, see "Phenomena, Value, and Objectivity."

Chapter XIV

1. In "The Philosophy of Logical Atomism" and in "On Propositions," in *LK*, pp. 211, 287.

2. *Ibid.*, pp. 236-37.

3. I argued against the need for *complex* facts in "Negation and Generality," *Nous*, 3, 1969, pp. 325-43. R. Grossmann has used similar arguments to argue against *complex* properties in his paper "Russell's Paradox and Complex Properties," *Nous*, 6, 1972, pp. 53-64. But, Grossmann, in effect, merely rules out questions that we discussed in Chapter IX. D. Brownstein raises some interesting questions about negative exemplification in his paper "Negative Exemplification," *American Philosophical Quarterly*, 10, 1, January, 1973, pp. 43-50.

4. R. Gale, *Negation and Non-Being* (Blackwell, Oxford, 1976), p. 41.

5. For another mistaken *solution*, see J. F. Rosenberg, "Russell on Negative Facts," *Nous*, 6, 1972, pp. 27-40. For an interesting attempt to avoid negative facts within the framework of a correspondence account of truth see D. M. Armstrong, *Belief Truth and Knowledge* (Cambridge University Press, London, 1973), pp. 131-32.

6. See my "Universals, Particulars, and Predication."

7. *The Principles of Logic*, pp. 114-17. Also see F. H. Bradley, *Appearance and Reality* (Macmillan, New York, 1897), Chapter XV. For a relatively simple and clear account of the pattern of "absolute idealism," see B. Bosanquet, *The Essentials of Logic* (Macmillan, London, 1948).

8. The difference is not clearly seen by Rosenberg in his critique of Russell, "Russell on Negative Facts," pp. 30-31.

9. Wittgenstein writes:

4.022. A proposition *shows* its sense.
        A proposition *shows* how things stand *if* it is true. And it *says that* they do so stand.

This passage helps to call attention to the fact that there are two aspects to what I have called the "assertive character" of judgments. One aspect is reflected in the recognition that both a positive and a negative sentence *stand for* one and the same possibility, and they *state* that it is of one quality (mode) or the other. The other aspect is the one we are presently discussing. It concerns the generic property of the mental state or act. A belief (act) that *a* is W shows that a person intends that the possibility is in the positive mode, a disbelief that it is in the negative mode. Thus, the mental states as exemplifying generic characteristics like *belief* and *disbelief* and as the subjects of such characteristics may be taken to be true or false. In the latter sense, they are taken as tokens of types which are beliefs that are true or false.

10. E. Nagel, "Logic without Ontology," in *Naturalism and the Human Spirit*, ed. Y. H. Krikorian (Columbia University Press, New York, 1944). Nagel is, in pragmatic fashion, holding that the justification of a system of logic lies in its utility for the furthering and systematizing of "inquiry." Thus, although conventional, logic is not a matter of arbitrary whim.

11. Dummett has recently argued with Putnam along such lines, see *Frege*, pp. 603-7. For another dispute, see my "Professor Storer on Empiricism," *Philosophical Studies*, 5, 2, 1954; D. Kauf, "A Comment on Hochberg's Reply to Storer," *Philosophical Studies*, 5, 4, 1954; T. Storer, "The Notion of 'Tautology'," *Philosophical Studies*, 5, 5, 1954; and my " 'Possible' and Logical Absolutism," *Philosophical Studies*, 6, 5, 1955.

12. Russell recognized the "logical forms" of propositions that "subsist" in a "world of universals" in "The Philosophical Importance of Mathematical Logic" *The Monist*, 22, 4, 1913, pp. 485-87, 492. In "On the Nature of Truth and Falsehood," p. 158, he spoke of the "sense" of a relation, and in the unpublished manuscript "Theory of Knowledge," Chapter VII, he also speaks of the "sense" and "direction" of a relation. But, though he here speaks of logical forms as "objects," he denies that they are further constituents of propositions to avoid a Bradley-type regress. For a discussion of the manuscript, see D. Pears, "The Relation between Wittgenstein's Picture Theory of Propositions and Russell's Theories of Judgment," *Philosophical Review*, April, 1977, pp. 177-96. Pears agrees with K. Blackwell and E. Eames that the first six chapters, missing in the manuscript, were published as articles in *The Monist* between January 1914 and April 1915 ("Russell's Unpublished Book on Theory of Knowledge," *The Journal of the Bertrand Russell Archives*, 19, 1975, pp. 6-7). But, Pears does not note that the view about the existence of and experience of such logical entities is quite clearly stated in "The Philosophical Importance of Mathematical Logic." It is worth noting that this article was given as a lecture in 1911 and originally published in French in 1912. Thus, the paper antedates, by quite some time, the letter from Russell to Ottoline Morell mentioning Wittgenstein's criticism. In his article, Pears insightfully suggests that Wittgenstein's rejection of the form of a fact as a further constituent of the fact led to his holding that forms are "possibilities inherent in the constituents of states of affairs" (*Ibid.*, p. 187). On the question of possibilities as such "natures" or "essences" of objects, see my "Facts, Possibilities, and Essences in the *Tractatus*," in *Essays on Wittgenstein*, ed. by E. D. Klemke (University of Illinois Press, Urbana, 1971), pp. 508-33, especially pp. 527-33. The impact of Wittgenstein's criticism on Russell is unclear. Though Russell abandoned the relational account of belief in 1919, he still spoke of *forms* of facts, see, p. 297.

13. We noted that Russell raised a regress argument against the correspondence theory in a 1905 manuscript. The argument does not occur in papers on *truth* published in 1906-1907.

14. D. Pears, *Bertrand Russell*, pp. 205-11.

Chapter XV

1. P. T. Geach, *Reference and Generality* (Cornell University Press, Ithaca, 1962), p. 39.

2. D. Hume, *An Enquiry Concerning Human Understanding*, Section VII, Part II.

3. There is an old puzzle for those interested in the problems of induction and confirmation that stems from the logical equivalence of (1) '(x)(Wx ⊃ Sx)' and (2) '(x)(∼Sx ⊃ ∼Wx)'. Whether confirming instances of the one are also such for the other is not my concern here. What is relevant to note is that if there are facts corresponding to (1) and (2), and if logically equivalent sentences correspond to the same fact (if they correspond to any fact), then (1) and (2) stand for the same fact. However, either what is "evidence" for the existence of the one fact is evidence for the existence of "the other" or "confirming" a generalization has nothing to do with establishing the existence of a fact, but merely with the acceptance of sentences. Either alternative is awkward for a proponent of general facts.

4. It is relevant to recall Ramsey's claim that our "inability to write propositions of infinite length" is "logically a mere accident," *The Foundations of Mathematics*, p. 41.

5. The ontological price is a non-Platonic variant of the logical realism Russell advocated, in one form or another, between 1903 and 1918 and that Moore less clearly espoused in "The Nature of Judgment."

6. See my "Russell's Reduction of Arithmetic to Logic," in *Essays on Bertrand Russell*, "Properties, Abstracts, and the Axiom of Infinity," and "Arithmetic and Propositional Form in Wittgenstein's *Tractatus*," in *Essays on Wittgenstein*.

Indexes

Name Index

Subject Index